CAMBRIDGE CLASSICAL TEXTS
AND COMMENTARIES

65

CICERO: *DIVINATIO IN Q. CAECILIVM*

CICERO
DIVINATIO IN Q. CAECILIVM

EDITED WITH
INTRODUCTION AND COMMENTARY
BY

C. B. WATSON
University of Oklahoma

CAMBRIDGE
UNIVERSITY PRESS

CAMBRIDGE
UNIVERSITY PRESS

Shaftesbury Road, Cambridge CB2 8EA, United Kingdom

One Liberty Plaza, 20th Floor, New York, NY 10006, USA

477 Williamstown Road, Port Melbourne, VIC 3207, Australia

314–321, 3rd Floor, Plot 3, Splendor Forum, Jasola District Centre, New Delhi – 110025, India

103 Penang Road, #05–06/07, Visioncrest Commercial, Singapore 238467

Cambridge University Press is part of Cambridge University Press & Assessment, a department of the University of Cambridge.

We share the University's mission to contribute to society through the pursuit of education, learning and research at the highest international levels of excellence.

www.cambridge.org
Information on this title: www.cambridge.org/9781108844079

DOI: 10.1017/9781108933292

First published 2025

Printed in the United Kingdom by CPI Group Ltd, Croydon CR0 4YY

A catalogue record for this publication is available from the British Library

Library of Congress Cataloging-in-Publication Data
NAMES: Cicero, Marcus Tullius, author. | Watson, Charles B. (Charles Benjamin), 1981– editor.
TITLE: Divinatio in q. caecilium / Cicero ; edited with introduction and commentary by C.B. Watson, University of Oklahoma.
Other titles: Divinatio in Caecilium
DESCRIPTION: Cambridge ; New York, NY : Cambridge University Press, 2024. | SERIES: Cambridge classical texts and commentaries | Includes bibliographical references and index.
IDENTIFIERS: LCCN 2023041840 | ISBN 9781108844079 (hardback) | ISBN 9781108928007 (paperback) | ISBN 9781108933292 (ebook)
SUBJECTS: LCSH: Speeches, addresses, etc., Latin. | Verres, Gaius, active 1st century B.C. | Cicero, Marcus Tullius. Divinatio in Caecilium. | LCGFT: Speeches. | Literary criticism.
CLASSIFICATION: LCC PA6282 .A4 2024 | DDC 875/.01–dc23/eng/20231204
LC record available at https://lccn.loc.gov/2023041840

ISBN 978-1-108-84407-9 Hardback

CONTENTS

FIGURES

PREFACE

The *Diuinatio in Caecilium* is usually circulated in modern editions along with the voluminous speeches against Gaius Verres. Cicero's colourful caricatures of Rome's poster child for maladministration and his depictions of provincial government often dominate the reader's view; the *Diuinatio* itself is often skipped over. Yet it is a speech unlike any other from Antiquity. It is our sole surviving example of the Roman legal procedure of *diuinatio*, in which potential prosecutors made their claims to indict the accused, and in no other speech does Cicero call such attention to his rhetorical methods of persuasion or seem so self-consciously literary in his publication. He delights in the generic ambiguity of the *diuinatio*. And in the hands of such a master of persuasion, we should avoid the common pitfall of assuming this speech to be representative of its kind.

This new commentary and critical edition aims to return the *Diuinatio* to the scholarly main, to question the assumptions that have been made about legal procedure and representation as drawn from the speech, and to present a more complete assessment of the challenges confronted and strategies deployed by the young orator. A new text and critical edition have been prepared in light of recent manuscript discoveries and rely on a full collation of the major witnesses to the tradition.

This volume began in part as a doctoral dissertation at the University of Oxford but has been expanded and extensively developed in the intervening years. The culmination of this long-term project owes thanks to many individuals and institutions. I owe especial thanks to Tobias Reinhardt, who supervised the dissertation with unwavering support and taught me to always ask more of our text, to Kathleen Coleman, who first stoked my interest in the Verrines as an undergraduate at Harvard, to Michael Reeve, who shared his unpublished work on the manuscript tradition with me, and to Stephen Oakley, who along with Professor Reeve read and commented on multiple drafts of the book. They have all been exacting yet patient teachers and advisors. Along the way, I have also benefited from discussions with Bob Kaster, Stephen Heyworth, T. P. Wiseman, Kyle Harper, Christopher Craig, Tony Corbeill, Luca Grillo, and Alex Sens. Further gratitude is due to Oriel College, Oxford, the Department of the Classics at Harvard University, The Clarendon Fund, Lawrence University, The University of Oklahoma, and the many libraries that have supported this research. Michael Sharp and the editors at Cambridge University Press have been extraordinary throughout. Especial thanks are due to Bethany Johnson and Anna Oxbury, who guided the project through the last stages of publication. All involved have immeasurably improved the final book and have my enduring gratitude. What errors remain are my own. Of course, none of this would have been possible without the support of my loving family to whom this book is dedicated.

PREVIOUS EDITIONS AND COMMENTARIES

Following the system established by Berry in his *Pro Sulla*, only select editions, commentaries and translations of the *Diuinatio in Caecilium* published after 1800 are listed here. For works earlier than 1800, one may consult J. C. Orelli and J. G. Baiter (1836) *Onomasticon Tullianum* I 197–215, 238–252, 257, 275–276 and W. Engelmann (1847) 287–290, 293–295, 299. 'E', 'C' or 'A', and 'T' denote 'edition (or reprinted text)', 'commentary' or 'annotations' (the latter for those with limited notes), and 'translation'.

C. G. Schütz	Leipzig 1815	E
J. C. Orelli	Zurich 1826	E
C. T. Zumpt[2]	Berlin 1831	E
J. Sluiter	Leiden 1832	C
R. Klotz	Leipzig 1838	E C
R. Klotz	Leipzig 1852	E
C. A. Jordan (Orelli)	Zurich 1854	E
C. L. Kayser	Leipzig 1861	E
G. Long	London 1862	E C
W. E. Heitland and H. Cowie	Cambridge 1876	E C
F. Richter – A. Eberhard	Leipzig 1884	E C
K. Hachtmann	Gotha 1891	E C
C. F. W. Müller (Teubner)	Leipzig 1891	E
E. Thomas	Paris 1892	E C
J. Schmalz	Leipzig 1895	C
H. Nohl	Leipzig 1897	E C
K. Halm – G. Laubmann	Berlin 1900	E C
J. R. King[2]	Oxford 1912	E C
F. Ramorino	Bologna 1915	E A
W. Peterson (Oxford Classical Texts)[2]	Oxford 1917	E

A. Klotz (Teubner)	Leipzig 1923	E
L. H. G. Greenwood (Loeb)	London 1928	E T
P. Fabbri	Naples 1931	E C
H. de la Ville de Mirmont (Budé)	Paris 1938	E T
P. Michel	Paris 1938	T
S. Broccia	Rome 1955	E A
G. Calisti	Milan 1957	E C
G. Morabito	Milan 1966	E T A
G. Bellardi	Turin 1978	E T
G. Krüger (Reclam)[2]	Stuttgart 1983	E T
A. Biscardi, et al. (Corpus Iuris Romani Publici)	Milan 1984	E
R. Salinas	Mexico City 1987	T A
M. Rodríguez-Pantoja and J. M. Miguel Requejo Prieto (Biblioteca Clásica Gredos 139)	Madrid 1990	T A
N. Marinone and L. Fiocchi (Biblioteca Universale Rizzoli)[2]	Milan 1994	E T A
M. Fuhrmann (Tusculum)	Zurich 1995	E T A

ABBREVIATIONS

Berger	Berger, A. (1953), *Encyclopedic Dictionary of Roman Law*, *TAPS* 43.2 (Philadelphia, PA).
B.N.F.	Bibliothèque nationale de France.
CAH	Various authors. (1984–2005), *The Cambridge Ancient History* (Cambridge).
CIL	Various editors. (1873–) *Corpus Inscriptionum Latinarum* (Berlin).
Ernout–Meillet	Ernout, A. and A. Meillet (1959), *Dictionnaire étmyologique de la langue latine* (Paris).
Forcellini	Forcellini, E. (1831–1835), *Totius Latinitatis Lexicon.* Leipzig. 4 volumes.
GLK	Keil, H. (1857–1880), *Grammatici Latini* (Leipzig). 7 volumes.
Greenidge	Greenidge, A. H. J. (1901), *The Legal Procedure of Cicero's Time* (Oxford).
Hellegouarc'h	Hellegouarc'h, J. (1963), *Le vocabulaire latin des relations et des partis politiques sous la République* (Paris).
Heumann–Seckel	Heumann, H. and E. Seckel. (1907), *Heumanns Handlexicon zu den Quellen des römishen Rechts*^{9} (Jena).
Hofmann	Hofmann, J. B. (1985), *La lingua d'uso latina*^{3}. Trans. Ricotilli (Bologna).
H-Sz.	Hofmann, J. B. and A. Szantyr (1965), *Lateinishe Syntax und Stilistik* (Munich).
K-St.	Kühner, R. and C. Stegmann (1912–1914), *Ausführliche Grammatik der lateinischen Sprache*^{2}, 2 volumes. (Hannover).

Laurand	Laurand, L. (1907), *Études sur le style des discours de Cicéron* (Paris).
Lausberg	Lausberg, H. (1998), *Handbook of Literary Rhetoric: A Foundation for Literary Study* (Leiden). trans. Bliss, Jansen, and Orton.
LGRR	Gruen, E. (1974), *The Last Generation of the Roman Republic* (Berkeley, CA).
LSJ	Liddell, H. G., R. Scott., H. Stuart Jones, and R. McKenzie, eds. (1968), *A Greek–English Lexicon* (Oxford).
Merguet	Merguet, P. A. H. (1877–1897), *(Lexikon zu den Schriften Ciceros) Lexikon zu den Reden.* (Jena).
MRR	Broughton, T. R. S. (1951–1986), *Magistrates of the Roman Republic* (New York & Atlanta). 3 volumes.
Neue-Wagener	Neue, F. and Wagener, C. (1892–1905), *Formenlehre der lateinischen Sprache*[3] (Berlin).
N-P	Cancik, H. and H. Schneider, eds. (1996–2004), *Der neue Pauly: Enzyklopädie der Antike* (Leipzig).
OLD	Glare, P. G. W., ed. (1982), *Oxford Latin Dictionary* (Oxford).
OLS	Pinkster, H. (2015), *The Oxford Latin Syntax,* 2 volumes. (Oxford).
Parzinger	Parzinger, P. (1911–1912), *Beiträge zur Kenntnis der Entwicklung des Ciceronischen Stils*[2] (Landshut). 2 volumes.
RE	Wissowa, G. et al. (1893–1980), *Paulys Real-Encyclopädie der classichen Altertumswissenschaft* (Stuttgart and Munich).
RLM	Halm, C. (1863), *Rhetores Latini Minores* (Leipzig).
Schmalz	Schmalz, J. (1905–1907), *Antibarbarus der lateinischen Sprache* (Basel). 2 volumes.
Seyffert	Seyffert, M. (1878), *Scholae Latinae: Beiträge zu einer methodischen Praxis der*

	lateinischen Stil- und Compositionsübungen. (Leipzig). Volume 1[4].
	———. (1872), *Scholae Latinae: Beiträge zu einer methodischen Praxis der lateinischen Stil- und Compositionsübungen.* (Leipzig). Volume 2[3].
Stangl	Stangl, T. (1912), *Ciceronis Orationum Scholiastae* (Leipzig).
Staats.	Mommsen, Th. (1887–1888), *Römisches Staatsrecht* (Leipzig).
Straf.	———. (1899), *Römisches Strafrecht* (Leipzig).
Statutes	Crawford, M. H. (1996), *Roman Statutes* (London). 2 volumes.
Sutherland	Sutherland, J. G. (1891), *Statues and Statutory Construction* (Chicago).
TLL	*Thesaurus Linguae Latinae* (Leipzig 1900–)
TLRR	Alexander, M. C. (1990), *Trials in the Late Roman Republic: 149BC to 50BC* (Toronto).

References to ancient works will follow the abbreviation system of the *OLD* and LSJ. Citations from Latin and Greek texts are normally from the editions listed in the Packard Humanities Index and the *Thesaurus Linguae Graecae*, respectively. For other citations, including epigraphic sources, the editor will be indicated.

INTRODUCTION

I. THE SETTING

With the benefit of hindsight and knowledge of Gaius Verres' premature flight into exile, it would be tempting to assume that Cicero knew an easy target when he saw one. Yet, at the outset of the year 70,[1] when charges for extortion were being prepared, Verres was no mere pushover. He had ascended the political ladder to the second highest position on the *cursus honorum* – a post that only two out of every five new senators had hopes of attaining – and all this from a family only newly senatorial.[2] On his way up, he had proven to be an adroit and savvy politician. He started out as an adherent of the Cinnan faction, but while serving as a *proquaestor* under Cn. Papirius Carbo in 83, he deserted his superior officer to fall in league with Sulla. The dictator rewarded him handsomely for his defection. He also made close connections among the other leading figures of the regime, including Q. Catulus, L. Lucullus, three members of the Metellan clan,[3] and the renowned orator, Q. Hortensius Hortalus. He continued to ascend the ranks as a legate for Dolabella, whom he subsequently helped convict for extortion, and was later elected *praetor urbanus* for 74. After his term as *praetor*, he served as the *propraetor* of Sicily for the years 73–71. A slave revolt in southern Italy required other leading senators to be dispatched to quell the uprising, and as a result, Verres saw his tenure in Sicily prorogued for an additional two years beyond

[1] All dates are BCE unless referring to 'centuries' or otherwise noted.

[2] Mitchell (1986) 5.

[3] Quintus, Marcus, and Lucius. In the year 70, Quintus was elected consul, Marcus was to become the praetor in charge of the *quaestio de repetundis*, and Lucius was assigned as the governor of Sicily.

the original term.[4] He eventually left office on the first day of the year 70 to return to Rome.

Meanwhile, Cicero was still a relatively young *nouus homo* on the rise. His path of ascendancy was through advocacy. He had first spoken in the Roman courts in 81 and gained a favourable reputation for his skills when he defended Sextus Roscius in 80 on criminal charges of patricide. He would further hone his skills of persuasion with additional education under the Stoic philosopher Diodotus, the Epicurean Phaedrus, the famous rhetorician Molon of Rhodes, and additional teachers of rhetoric in Asia Minor.[5] He put this training to work and spoke, with mixed success, as an advocate in a number of venues – before a tribune, the senate, and a provincial governor, as well as in both criminal and civil courts.[6] During this time in the spotlight, he gained entry into the senate when he was elected to the office of quaestor for the year 75. Although he would later express dismay at how little reward he would reap for the conscientious dispatch of his duties, he served out his year in the western Sicilian city of Lilybaeum. In the intervening years, as he converted his oratorical success into political capital, he looked forward to canvassing for the next office on the Roman political ladder. He was eligible to campaign for the aedileship at the age of 36 – in the year 70.

The broader political landscape of that year had its share of intrigue. Legislative changes were afoot. The Sullan reforms that made the courts the purview solely of the senate and substantially reduced the power of the tribunate faced revision. In 75 the ability of former tribunes to seek higher office had been restored, and in the year 71, Pompey had promised to 'give thought' to the issue of renewing the full powers of the office. There were also discussions of redistributing jury duty to include non-senatorial members. The two consuls of the year 70 were Cn. Pompeius Magnus and M. Licinius Crassus, and the time seemed right to amend further some of the late dictator's

4 See Introduction, §III.

5 Fantham (1996) 31; see §39 *Athenis* n.

6 *Pro Quinctio* was his first recorded civil trial. For a full list of his known appearances as an advocate, see Powell and Paterson (2004) 417–422.

measures. In fact, during that year, the veto power of the tribunate and office of the censor would be reinstituted, and the *lex Aurelia* would assign senators, *equites*, and *tribuni aerarii* to serve on juries in equal measure.[7]

Of course, at the beginning of the year, these changes had not yet been enacted. And this was also the time that Verres' term as governor of Sicily drew to a close. Divested of *imperium*, he was no longer protected from prosecution. When it became clear that a Sicilian delegation would have him arraigned on charges of extortion, Hortensius came to his defence. The situation must have looked enticing to Cicero: a senator of praetorian rank would be defended by the man who was then Rome's leading orator. Political and legislative developments were waiting to be exploited. Higher office beckoned. In front of this backdrop, Cicero came before the Extortion Court to bring charges against Verres. But he was not alone. Before the trial could go forward, he would need to make his case to be the lead prosecutor against another would-be accuser – Verres' own quaestor, Q. Caecilius Niger.

II. THE OPPONENT: QUINTUS CAECILIUS NIGER

Little definitive can be said about the life of Cicero's opponent and Verres' former quaestor, Quintus Caecilius Niger. Our best source is Cicero's speech against him, but an opponent's characterization merits obvious caution.[8] Other information primarily comes from the scholiast, pseudo-Asconius,[9] and a brief reference in Plutarch's *Life of Cicero*. From these, one can only come to tentative conclusions about Caecilius' origins and career, but even these shine a brighter light on his bid to prosecute Verres and Cicero's challenges in facing him.

In his opening summary of the speech, the scholiast introduces his reader to Cicero's rival; [Asc.] 98 (187 Stangl):

7 *LGRR* 23–37; Vasaly (2009).

8 Lintott (2008) 85–86.

9 [Asc.] 98, 112, 114, 121 (185, 195, 197, 202 Stangl). On pseudo-Asconius, see Introduction §VI, 'Other Sources'.

> *His ita constitutis extitit Q. Caecilius Niger, domo Siculus,* [*et*] *quaestor Verris et eiusdem, ut ipse dicebat, inimicus, qui se potius accusatorem contenderet* [*se*] *constitui oportere, has afferens causas: unam, quod ab eo laesus et ob hoc iure illi sit inimicus, quare praeuaricator esse non possit; alteram, quod, cum quaestor ei tum fuerit, etiam sine inquisitione crimina nouerit Verris; tertiam, quod Siculus pro Siculis agat.*

While discussing the merits of his claim to prosecute the former governor of Sicily, the scholiast twice remarks that Caecilius was himself Sicilian. Yet it is unclear whether the scholiast had other ancient evidence to hand about Caecilius or was simply deducing information from the speech itself.[10] Three passages from the *Diuinatio* do suggest that Caecilius, at the very least, had some familial or economic connection to the island. As he reviews Caecilius' rhetorical education, Cicero disparagingly remarks: '*si litteras Graecas Athenis non Lilybaei, Latinas Romae non in Sicilia didicisses* ...' (§39). An extended period of education on the island would suggest that Caecilius had spent part of his earlier life there, but Cicero has cast Caecilius in the role of an ὀψιμαθής ('late-learner'), so perhaps Cicero is simply suggesting that Caecilius has only recently taken up the study of oratory during his magistracy in Sicily – especially since Cicero makes a pointed reference to Lilybaeum, the seat of Caecilius' quaestorship.[11] Two other comments are more illuminating. At one point, Cicero refers to 'the other Sicilians' (§53 *Sed ceteri Siculi ultorem suarum iniuriarum inuenerunt*)[12] and, at another, says

[10] The ablative of respect with the ethnic (*domo Siculus*) may suggest that he was not a member of the ethnic group of Sicilians but simply an inhabitant of the island. Sherwin-White (1939) 307n remarks: 'Nothing in Cic. *Diu. in Caec.* 4 and 20 suggests that Q. Caecilius was more than a resident of Sicily by economic connection (cf. [Asc.] 98 *domo Sicilia*) [sic]) or remote servile origin (Plut. *Cic.* 7.6).' On the origins of the Sicilian people from Italian residents on the Tiber, see Plin. *Nat.* 3.56, and also 3.71.

[11] If Caecilius had been a Sicilian, it would explain why Cicero adopted this line of invective. Since C. was professing to represent Sicilian clients, exploiting ethnic stereotypes to ostracize his opponent would have been ill advised, but using education as a differentiator would have allowed Cicero to denigrate Caecilius' provincial origins without sullying the culture of his 'clients'.

[12] [Asc.] 121 (202 Stangl) *Saepe in Caecilium utitur hoc conuicio, ut illum non Romanum, sed Siculum dicat.*

of his opponent *te adhuc a nullis nisi ab Siculis potuisse cognosci* (§28).[13]

The only reference outside of Cicero and the scholiast is an anecdote told by Plutarch in his biography of Cicero; *Cic.* 7:

> ὅμως δὲ πολλὰ χαρίεντα διαμνημονεύεται καὶ περὶ ἐκείνην αὐτοῦ τὴν δίκην. βέρρην γὰρ οἱ Ῥωμαῖοι τὸν ἐκτετμημένον χοῖρον καλοῦσιν. ὡς οὖν ἀπελευθερικὸς ἄνθρωπος ἔνοχος τῷ ἰουδαΐζειν ὄνομα Κεκίλιος ἐβούλετο παρωσάμενος τοὺς Σικελιώτας κατηγορεῖν τοῦ Βέρρου, "τί Ἰουδαίῳ πρὸς χοῖρον;"

Although nothing in the speech or the scholiast would lead us to believe that Caecilius was a freedman or Jewish, some have suggested that Plutarch had reliable sources for his biography, for example Tiro.[14] In defence of the quip, one might note that there was a sizable slave population from the East in Sicily during the great slave revolt of 130, and while not a freedman himself, Caecilius could have been a freeborn descendant of a Jewish slave.[15] However, Plutarch's suggestion is unsubstantiated. One might easily counter that the pun on Verres' name was well known and suppose that Plutarch was only mining for a joke.[16]

Whatever his ancestral status or ethnic origins were, the preponderance of the evidence still leads one to believe that Caecilius had a close association with the island, either through descent or domicile. Moreover, this is not prosopographical speculation for its own sake. A relationship with Sicily would have given Caecilius a strategic advantage in the *diuinatio* and recourse to an *argumentum a persona*, since, as the scholiast noted, *Siculus*

[13] At which point the scholiast adds '*Quia aut Siculus ipse est aut quia nisi quaestor in Sicilia nihil aliud fuit Caecilius, in quo nosceretur "quid hominis" esset*'; [Asc.] 112 (195 Stangl). As the scholiast notes, this could just refer to time in political office. Even Cicero lamented that news of his accomplishments during his quaestorship never reached Rome; see *Planc.* 64–65 and Plut. *Cic.* 6.

[14] Pelling (1979) 89.

[15] For anti-Semitism in Cicero, see Bernard (2000). His *nomen* may suggest that he was one of the residents of Sicily granted citizenship by the Metelli. For an example of citizenship granted by Metellus, see *Ver.* II.2.20. His *cognomen*, Niger, offers no help. It was commonly used to distinguish between individuals with the same *praenomen* and *nomen*; see Cameron (1998).

[16] See §57 *aliquo Circaeo poculo factus est Verres* n.

pro Siculis agat. The fact that Cicero so ambiguously alludes to Caecilius' origins may be another point in its favour.

At some juncture, Caecilius made his way to Rome to canvass for the quaestorship, where he would attain the magistracy that placed him in Verres' administration. If he was in fact Sicilian, his political success is even more remarkable, since senators of provincial origin, although more numerous in later generations, were few at this time.[17] Upon election to the quaestorship, he was assigned to Sicily for his term in office. Quaestors were typically appointed by lot (*sortitio*),[18] but if he had a prior connection with Sicily, this may have been grounds for an appointment *extra sortem ex senatus consulto* – a procedure not infrequent at the time.[19] Such arrangements, however, would normally be made at the request of the governor, and if this had been the case with Caecilius, Cicero would have mentioned it in his speech to strengthen his insinuations of *praeuaricatio* against his rival.[20] Therefore it remains a possibility that Caecilius' appointment was from his own request or simply through the luck of the draw.

The date of Caecilius' quaestorship has also been a matter of debate. Verres served as *propraetor* from 73 to 71, and evidence from the Verrines makes it clear that four quaestors served in Sicily during his administration. In §§55–58, Cicero narrates an episode in which Caecilius convenes a court in Lilybaeum in connection with a dispute over slaves requisitioned by a legate of M. Antonius Creticus. Creticus had been dispatched to combat piracy in the region, and though his *imperium* held until 71, his activities in Sicily seem to have been limited to 74 and 73 before going east to Greece and Crete. This suggests that Caecilius was the quaestor stationed at Lilybaeum at the beginning of Verres'

17 For other provincial senators, see Wiseman (1971) 19–23.

18 Schol. Bob. on Cic. *in Clod. et Cur.* (332 Stangl). On the procedure, see introduction to §§59–65.

19 On the procedure of appointment *extra sortem*, see Thompson (1962b) and Pina Polo and Díaz Fernández (2019) 69–78.

20 In any event, if we were to accept this *extra sortem* reconstruction, we must understand Cicero's statements at §46 (*sortis religionem*) and §61 (*coniunctionem sortis*) to be common parlance for the obligation between the governor and his staff upon assignment – whether or not it was actually done strictly by lot. See the introduction to §§59–65.

governorship in 73, and that his counterpart in Syracuse must have been Marcus Postumius.[21] It also seems clear that Caecilius ended his tenure in Sicily before his commander. Verres appointed Caecilius' *scriba*, Potamo, to his staff upon Caecilius' departure.[22]

Caecilius' whereabouts in 72 are more difficult to ascertain. Marinone has convincingly argued from *Ver.* II.5.83–135 that M. Postumius only served one year as quaestor in Syracuse and was replaced by Titus Vettius, which may also imply that Caecilius was only in his post for one year.[23] The slave revolt of Spartacus interrupted the regular change of administration in Sicily and accounts for Verres' prorogation in 72. Before the spread of the revolt, however, Quintus Arrius, who had been a praetor in 73, was originally allocated Sicily as a propraetorian province for 72.[24] The senate probably appointed new quaestors in anticipation that Arrius would take over as governor. At some undetermined date, Arrius was diverted from taking up his place in Sicily and dispatched to combat the slave revolt under the consul, L. Gellius Publicola. Fierce fighting in 72 made it clear that Verres would have to continue to serve in Sicily in 71 before a new governor was assigned.[25] Consequently, there are grounds for believing that Arrius' allotted quaestors, Vettius and Caesetius, took up their posts under Verres in Syracuse and Lilybaeum, respectively. If this is the case, then Caecilius served as quaestor in Lilybaeum and his counterpart, Marcus Postumius, in Syracuse

[21] *Ver.* II.2.44.

[22] §29.

[23] Marinone (1965). For the sole mention of Vettius, see *Ver.* II.5.114.

[24] *Ver.* II.4.43.

[25] See *Ver.* II.2.37; Marinone (1965) 219. Quintus Arrius probably continued to fight the slave revolt in 71 under Crassus. See B. A. Marshall (1975b) 221–231. *Ver.* II.2.37, 4.42; Liv. *Per.* 96; [Asc.] 97, 101 (185, 188 Stangl); Schol. Gronov. 324 Stangl. Marinone (1965) 237: 'Invece per il 71 fu senz' altro prorogato l'*imperium* a Verre e non si procedette ad alcuna nuova nomina per il governo della Sicilia. Sembra molto plausibile inferire che anche i due questori siano rimasti al loro posto a fianco del governatore, in considerazione degli stretti rapporti di collaborazione che si reputava dovessero istaurarsi fra il questore e il suo superiore.' *Contra* [Asc.] 207 (260 Stangl) *apparet, cum triennio Siciliam tenuerit unus Verres, quaestores tamen per annos singulos huic esse mutatos.* Broughton, on the strength of the article by Marinone, corrects the entry for 73–71 in *MRR Suppl.*

only for the year 73,[26] while the quaestors allocated to Arrius, Publius Caesetius[27] and Titus Vettius,[28] remained in their post for the years 72–71.[29]

Caecilius' political career may have stopped here. Owing to Sullan legislative reform, his election to the quaestorship gave him automatic life-membership in the senate. There may have been a tribune in 68 named 'Q. Caecilius', but neither the date nor the identity of this tribune is certain.[30] If Caecilius failed to ascend the political ladder any further, it was certainly not out of the ordinary for the time. Of the senators in the post-Sullan senate, over 100 would not have ascended above the rank of quaestor.[31] Caecilius' attempted prosecution of Verres, in addition to righting whatever wrongs he alleged, may also have had the enticement of re-energizing his political career. Having served so recently as quaestor, he was probably ineligible to canvass in the upcoming election for aedile, but a victory in a high-profile criminal case could certainly help to place him in the spotlight.

Despite Cicero's unsympathetic depiction of him as a struggling neophyte, Caecilius would have had some experience in the courts. Provincial governors would routinely tour their provinces to conduct hearings and issue legal decisions. With limited time and a large geographic area, governors frequently delegated these judicial responsibilities to members of their staff – the quaestor was an obvious choice when he was not busy with financial matters. The post in Lilybaeum came with particularly heavy judicial responsibility, and he would have been able to

26 *Ver.* II.2.44.

27 *Ver.* II.4.146, 5.63.

28 *Ver.* II.3.168, 5.114.

29 This reckoning also establishes a *terminus ante quem* for Caecilius' date of birth; see §70 *ea iam aetate* n.

30 The name is preserved in *CIL* I².2.744 as CAECILI and may have been on the *lex Antonia de Termessibus*. The dates of both these inscriptions are controversial. See *Statutes* 331–340 for a bibliography on the *lex Antonia*; also Syme (1963) 57–58. It is tempting to think that the tribune Q. Caecilius in 68 was Q. Caecilius Metellus Celer; *Man.* 58; *MRR* 3.37.

31 Hawthorn (1962); Syme (1963) 60: 'Numbering 600 in its membership, the Senate after Sulla embraces a mass of more or less reputable nonentities. The bottom 200 at any time evade record and defy recognition.'

exercise nigh-praetorian authority.[32] 'It was only in Sicily, where the second quaestor at Lilybaeum was opportunely situated for the western circuits of the island, that quaestorian jurisdiction was the constant factor in the government of the province.'[33]

We hear nothing of his previous experience as an advocate. The Q. Caecilius mentioned in connection with the prosecution of P. Gabinius (§64) would not have been Cicero's present opponent – much more would have been made of the incident if he were; the name Q. Caecilius was certainly common enough.[34] Cicero's comments strongly insinuate that Caecilius had never led a criminal prosecution, though the emphasis on *causae publicae* does leave the possibility that Caecilius had appeared in civil cases (*causae priuatae*), where many orators presumably spent most of their time.[35]

Even so, after his departure from office, Caecilius may have begun discussing his intent to prosecute Verres. Cicero's insinuations of *praeuaricatio* in the *Diuinatio in Caecilium* are groundless and unsustained.[36] In the trial speeches against Verres, Cicero outlines all the wily machinations of the defence to delay or subvert the course of justice, but Caecilius is implicated in none of them. Caecilius' connection with Sicily and detailed information about Verres' administration would have been to his advantage. He could claim for himself every justification that Cicero did: a history of public service and personal connections on the island as well as a duty to his country to eliminate corruption and defend Rome's reputation abroad. Moreover, as Cicero would

[32] On the various powers of the quaestor, see A. J. Marshall (1966) 237. On the governor's sole *imperium*, see *Prou. Cons.* 3.5; *Q.Fr.* 1.1.3.10; cf. Balsdon (1962) 138. On the delegation of authority, see *Q.Fr.* 1.1.7.20; *Flac.* 49. *Straf.* 247 quotes *Diu. in Caec.* 56, *Ver.* II.2.44, and Suet. *Iul.* 7.1 as attestations for the regular judicial employment of quaestors. The extent of employment of delegates was a matter for the individual governor's decision.

[33] Greenidge 130.

[34] Chief among those who have incorrectly assumed that our Caecilius here and that of the trial of Gabinius are the same: *TLRR* 174 and bibliography; B. A. Marshall (1977a). Not so Shackleton Bailey (1976) 8, 14.

[35] §26: *in mentem tibi non uenit quid negoti sit causam publicam sustinere … ?*

[36] From §36 onward, Cicero would have us believe that Caecilius is more inept than dishonest.

later admit, Caecilius also had justifiable personal motives for prosecuting his former commander.[37]

Caecilius was not the straw man that Cicero makes him out to be and that readers of the *Diuinatio* have long assumed. He had the traditionally acceptable means and motives to mount a sincere and thorough prosecution. So, when Cicero entered his own bid to prosecute Verres, if he was going to avoid the impression of shameless political ambition, he would need to find another, innovative way to distinguish himself from his worthy opponent.

III. PRE-TRIAL LEGAL PROCEDURE IN THE SULLAN *QUAESTIO DE REPETUNDIS*

In Roman criminal law, a statute would establish a court to try a particular offence, such as extortion or embezzlement, and also dictate the procedure to be employed. The first law on extortion,[38] the *lex Calpurnia de repetundis*, had been passed in 149 during the tribunate of L. Calpurnius Piso.[39] This enactment offered foreign litigants standardized access to a civil procedure (*actio sacramento*) initiated by the *praetor peregrinus*. These cases were made through Roman *patroni* and were conducted before a tribunal under the system of *legis actiones*.[40] A true criminal procedure was introduced by the *lex Acilia* of 123 or 122.[41] According to its provisions, a jury sat in judgement of the accused, and if the defendant was found guilty, a penalty of twice the amount of the misappropriated funds was imposed.

[37] *Ver.* II.1.15.

[38] A *lex de repetundis* is literally a 'recovery' law, i.e. a mechanism for recovering extorted property.

[39] For a detailed history, see Balsdon (1938); Lintott (1981); Venturini (1979). A shorter survey is available in Lintott (2004) 68–74. For references to this original *lex*, see *Ver.* II.3.195, 4.56; *Off.* 2.75; *Brut.* 106; *CIL* I² 583. l.74 (81).

[40] On legal *patroni*, see §64 *quod eum sibi Achaei patronum adoptarant* n.

[41] Sometimes called a *lex Sempronia*. It is unclear whether the law was introduced by or at the behest of C. Gracchus. For ancient sources, see *Ver.* I.51, II.1.26; [Asc.] 149, 165 (221, 231 Stangl). This law is generally agreed to be the one preserved on the Tabula Bembina; see §18 *nam* n.

The law was again altered in 106 and 101 by Servilius Caepio and Servilius Glaucia, respectively.[42] It was most likely Caepio's revision that introduced the process of *diuinatio*, wherein multiple prosecutors might come forward with a single lead prosecutor chosen in a pre-trial hearing. Why this innovation proved necessary or compelling is uncertain. Since extortion offences tended to affect more than one group or individual and since Romans had laws safeguarding a defendant against double jeopardy,[43] *diuinationes* may have evolved as a pragmatic measure to compel multiple litigants to combine their allegations into a kind of class-action prosecution. Additionally, there may have been more competition to secure a lead prosecutorial role if trials offered attractive rewards or social ascendancy.[44] At any rate, prosecution by non-Romans seems to have abated *de facto*.[45]

These versions of the extortion law also made other procedural modifications. Caepio's revision assigned a proportion of senators to the jury, and Glaucia's version required a *comperendinatio* (mandatory recess). Under the latter provision, both the prosecution and the defence would be compelled to speak and present witnesses twice. This change seems to have been motivated by frequent instances of juries declaring that they were unable to decide without hearing further arguments.[46] Glaucia's revision also first attests to the period of *inquisitio* for evidence-gathering; would-be prosecutors no longer needed to have gathered evidence before making their indictment.

Some 20 years later, around the year 81, Sulla overhauled the judicial system, including the extortion law, and this overhaul may have introduced a more homogeneous procedure

42 On the *lex Seruilia Caepionis*, see *Inv.* 1.92; *Clu.* 140; *Brut.* 161, 164; *De orat.* 1.225–230, 2.199–200, 223; Obsequens 41. On the *lex Seruilia Glauciae*, see *Ver.* II.1.26, *Scaur.* 2, *Brut.* 224, *Rab. Post.* 8–9, [Asc.] 164 (230 Stangl), [Asc.] 21C.

43 See Alexander (1982).

44 On *praemia*, see Alexander (1985).

45 Lintott (2004) 72; §64 *quod eum sibi Achaei patronum adoptarant* n.

46 The jurors would vote *non liquet*, and the presiding *iudex* would call for an *ampliatio* (or a restatement of the case) until the jury could reach a decision.

throughout the criminal system.[47] The most important of his amendments dictated that juries would be exclusively composed of senators.[48] This law, the *lex Cornelia de repetundis*, seemingly maintained other procedural aspects from previous extortion models and was the statute in effect in 70, when Caecilius and Cicero sought Verres' indictment. Unfortunately, the text of this law, which would also have detailed procedure, has been lost. A reconstruction relies on assuming the continuity of some aspects of the mutilated text of the *lex de repetundis* found on the Tabula Bembina (probably the *lex Acilia*) and procedural indications from this and other Ciceronian speeches and letters.

The recovery court at this time followed pre-trial procedures that were common to most criminal litigation. A potential accuser initiated a criminal prosecution by making an official request (*postulatio*) before the magistrate presiding over the recovery court.[49] At this time he would swear an oath (*iuramentum calumniae*) that his actions were *bona fide*, and this statement was later followed by a written declaration.[50] Next, the names of the accuser and the accused would be publicly posted in the Forum,[51] and in the interim, other potential litigants could come forward.[52] If someone

[47] *Rab. Post.* 8–9; for generic Roman criminal procedure of the period, see Greenidge.

[48] *Ver.* I.37. See Introduction §I for the *lex Aurelia* that would be passed in 70 to alter jury composition.

[49] According to the *lex Acilia*, the Roman judicial year closed for new prosecutions on 1 September. The measure is largely pragmatic as this would seem to ensure that no hearing beginning under one magistrate would have to be transferred to another in the next year: *is eum unde petet in ious ed[ucito ad pr(aetorem), quoius ex h(ace) l(ege) in eum annum quaestio erit, ante k(alendas) Sept(embres), quae eo anno erunt, nomenque eius deferto; —]* (1.6); see *Statutes* 85.

[50] *Statutes* 67, 87: *lex repet.* l.19: *sei deiurauerit calumniae causa non po[stulare, is iudex nomen recipito* ('If he shall have sworn that he is not demanding (a trial) by way of a false charge, [that judge (the president of the court) is to allow the prosecution ...]').

[51] The minimum duration of this posting is uncertain, although some period of time must have been required; cf. *Fam.* 8.6.3, where Dolabella's wife leaves him between the *postulatio* and the *delatio* of his trial.

[52] The number of initial claimants was not limited to two. Several would-be prosecutors came forward to indict Gabinius; *Q. Fr.* 3.2.1 *postridie autem eius diei qui erat tum futurus cum haec scribebam ante lucem, apud Catonem erat diuinatio in Gabinium futura inter Memmium et Ti. Neronem et C. L. Antonios M. f. putabamus*

else did present himself as another prosecutor and none of the rivals stood down,[53] a preliminary trial (*diuinatio*) would be convened to select a lead prosecutor.

Some procedural aspects of the *diuinatio* itself are vague. After the Sullan reforms, jury selection for the *quaestiones perpetuae* and for the pre-trial *diuinatio* followed a standard procedure whereby available senators were listed on an *album iudicum*, which was subsequently divided into groups (decuries) intended to represent senators of all ranks. These decuries were assigned at random to a particular case – and from the group, a jury was chosen by lot. The praetor would empanel a jury specifically for the *diuinatio* apart from the one that would hear the primary trial but drawn from the same *decuria*.[54] Although the number of jurors for the *diuinatio* is unclear, one would scarcely think that it would reach beyond the 30–50 jurors empanelled for the main trial.[55] There is no indication of a right to refuse a set number of jurors (*reiectio*).

Even though a *diuinatio* related to a particular trial, there were practical and equitable reasons for empanelling a new jury before the trial proper. There may have been a significant period of time between the selection of a prosecutor and the trial itself; for example, C. asked for a period of 110 days to collect

fore ut Memmio daretur, etsi erat Neronis mira contentio. Presumably the phrase *apud Catonem* simply means that he empanelled the jurors and not that he alone was making the decision. Cf. Fortun. *Rhet.* 1.21 *Quae est diuinatio? cum de idoneo accusatore quaestio est, id est cum duo uel plures accusationem sibi uindicant.*

53 Caecilius could have conceded to C. without a *diuinatio*; see *Fam.* 8.8.3.

54 For the assignment of senators to a particular *decuria*, see Lintott (2004) 74; Greenidge 437–449. A juror's participation in the *diuinatio*, however, did not preclude him from being selected for the trial of the main charge – in fact, Cicero tells us that some of the jurors at this *diuinatio* were jurors at the trial of Verres; *Ver.* II.1.15 *quo in numero e uobis complures fuerunt.* See, for example, C. Claudius Marcellus, §13; *Ver.* II.4.90. For a prosopographical study of the jurors at the extortion trial of Verres, see McDermott (1977a).

55 Prior to the *lex Aurelia* in 70, these would all have been senators under the *lex Cornelia de repetundis.* The senate, which had doubled in size under the Sullan constitution, had approximately 600 members, but not all were available to serve on juries since their magisterial responsibilities required their absence from Rome. For example, in the year 61, only 415 senators were available; Greenidge 437; *Att.* 1.14.5. On the number of judges in a particular trial, see McDermott (1977a) and Millar (1998) 4, 13; the former suggests over 40, the latter 32.

evidence and interview witnesses in Sicily before Verres' trial. In the intervening period, some of those who had been eligible may have been called away on other administrative duties. The jury was also recomposed for fairness and equity since the *diuinatio* gave an extended opportunity for potential prosecutors to present their allegations against the defendant. Facing the same jury would have posed a disadvantage to the defendant since his accusers would essentially have had more speaking time with no recourse to rebuttal. The presiding magistrate, however, would have remained the same unless the term of his magistracy had concluded or he designated another *iudex quaestionis* in his place.[56]

Trials were often convened under a portico or basilica, but also possibly in the open air. The *diuinatio* would presumably convene in the part of the Forum typically used by the recovery court, which is thought to be somewhere near the Temple of Castor and Pollux.[57]

Other procedural details come from the scholiast in his etymological description of *diuinatio*; [Asc.] 99 (186 Stangl):

> *'Diuinatio' dicitur haec oratio, quia non de facto quaeritur hic coniectura, set de futuro, quae est diuinatio uter debeat accusare. Alii ideo putant diuinationem dici, quod iniurati iudices in hac causa sedeant et, quod uelint, praesentire de utroque possint; alii, quod res agatur sine testibus et sine tabulis, et his remotis argumenta sola sequantur iudices et quasi diuinent.*

Unlike jurors at a traditional hearing, the jurors were not sworn in and would not hear witnesses – only the potential

[56] For a more complete description, see Greenidge 456–504.

[57] *Ver.* II.1.154 *Te putet quisquam, cum ab Italia freto diiunctus esses, sociis temperasse, qui aedem Castoris testem tuorum furtorum esse uolueris? quam populus Romanus cotidie, iudices etiam tum cum de te sententiam ferent, uidebunt*; *Ver.* II.5.186 *uosque, omnium rerum forensium, consiliorum maximorum, legum iudiciorumque arbitri et testes celeberrimo in loco populi Romani locati, Castor et Pollux, quorum e templo quaestum iste sibi et praedam improbissimam comparauit.* There is no conclusive evidence, however, that particular criminal courts always convened in the same location. On the uncertainty of the location of the courts, see Lintott (2004) 63; Bablitz (2007); Vasaly (2009) 113 n. 39. Regarding the possible location of various courts in the Forum, see Millar (1998) 40.

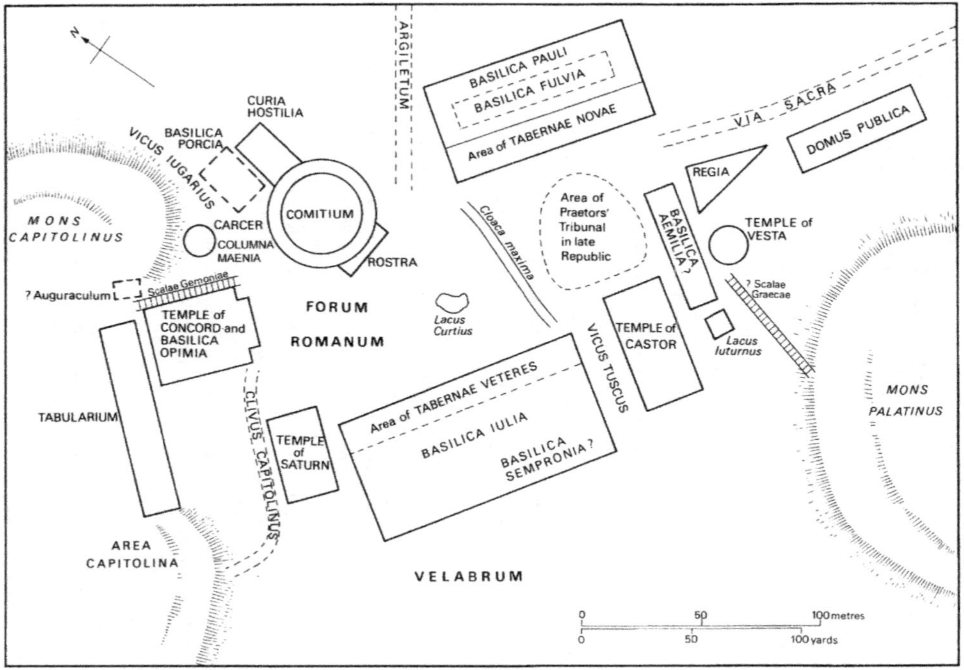

Figure 1: Forum with location of the Extortion Court
(adapted from *CAH* IX, figure 2).

prosecutors.[58] When the claimants spoke, it is possible that the first of the potential prosecutors to make a *postulatio* would have been offered the more advantageous position of speaking last.[59] The claimants would typically emphasize their sincerity and their reasons for wanting to bring the charge, presumably indicating the nature of the offence.[60] After they made their respective cases, the jury would select one to take the prosecution forward. The mechanism by which the jury would deliver this verdict is unclear. Though Cicero refers to the *diuinatio* jurors using wax ballots, the usual method of obliterating an A or C on either side of a wax tablet could not apply.[61] After the verdict, the *diuinatio* jury or the presiding magistrate may also have assigned assistant prosecutors (*subscriptores*).[62]

Once a prosecutor was chosen (in the case of a *diuinatio*) or within some designated period of time after the *postulatio*, a more detailed stipulation of the charge was presented to the chief magistrate at the *nominis* or *criminis delatio*. At this hearing, the defendant was usually required to be present unless he pleaded the *beneficium* of being *rei publicae causa absens*.[63] The

[58] Cf. Gel. 2.4.1–6 *Cum de constituendo accusatore quaeritur iudiciumque super ea re redditur, cuinam potissimum ex duobus pluribusue accusatio subscriptioue in reum permittatur, ea res atque iudicum cognitio diuinatio appellatur. Id uocabulum quam ob causam ita factum sit quaeri solet. Gauius Bassus in tertio librorum quos de origine uocabulorum composuit 'diuinatio' inquit 'iudicium appellatur, quoniam diuinet quodammodo iudex oportet, quam sententiam sese ferre par sit.' Nimis quidem est in uerbis Gaui Bassi ratio inperfecta uel magis inops et ieiuna. Sed uidetur tamen significare uelle idcirco dici diuinationem, quod in aliis quidem causis iudex ea <quae> didicit quaeque argumentis uel testibus demonstrata sunt sequi solet, in hac autem re, cum eligendus accusator est, parua admodum et exilia sunt quibus moueri iudex possit, et propterea, quinam magis ad accusandum idoneus sit quasi diuinandum est. Hoc Bassus. Sed alii quidam diuinationem esse appellatam putant quoniam, cum accusator et reus duae res quasi cognatae coniunctaeque sint neque utra sine altera constare possit, in hoc tamen genere causae reus quidem iam est, sed accusator nondum est, et idcirco quod adhuc usque deest et latet diuinatione supplendum est, quisnam sit accusator futurus.*

[59] This is the conjecture of Stroh (1975) 181–182.

[60] Quint. *Inst.* 7.4.33. See introduction to the *partitio* (§10).

[61] See §24 *ceratam … tabellam* n.

[62] On *subscriptores*, see the introduction to §§47–51. On Caecilius' request, see *Ver.* II.1.15.

[63] Greenidge 461, who also conjectures repercussions for absence; Val. Max. 3.7.9.

prosecutor would then pose a series of questions to the accused (*interrogatio*) and so establish a *prima facie* case for the magistrate. If the president of the court accepted the case, he drafted an *inscriptio* that stated the exact charge. This document was signed by the prosecutor and *subscriptores*, if there were any.

> The importance of this inscription was that it definitely fixed the charge. From this point it was only the offence taken cognizance of by the particular *quaestio*, before which the case was heard, that could be considered, and no other offence proved in the course of the trial could influence the verdict or draw down the penalty (*Inu.* 2.59). Where a law establishing a court took cognizance of a group of offences, the inscription narrowed down the issue to some particular clauses of the enactment ... But it might even happen that a single offence, such as extortion, might rest on a great many separate counts (Quint. *Inst.* 3.10.1), and it is probable that the particular counts which were to be proved had, in quite general terms, to be specified separately in the indictment.[64]

The charge was then formally admitted (*nominis receptio*) and publicly posted (*subscriptio*).[65] In anticipation of the trial, both sides would prepare their cases and collect evidence. Taking into account the *inquisitio*, the accused was assigned a day to appear before the full court and answer to the charges. That time finally came for Verres on the afternoon of 5 August 70.[66]

Efforts to bring Verres to trial began early in the judicial year. In accordance with the procedural rules, the initial *postulatio* was made before the president of the recovery court, Manius Acilius Glabrio, in January 70. Verres had only recently been divested of public office and hence became a *priuatus*, subject to prosecution; in fact, he might yet have to return from his province. There are several indications that Caecilius made the initial request to prosecute and that Cicero only filed afterwards. First, if

[64] Greenidge 466.

[65] Heitland and Cowie (1876) 52–53.

[66] Cicero had only asked for 110 days to collect evidence. On the delay in coming to trial, see Introduction §V.

the *diuinatio* assigned speaking positions in analogy with forensic practice as argued above, the final speech would be offered to the first to file – as he would be the 'defendant' of the initial claim; this advantage went to Caecilius. Second, at the start of his speech, Cicero describes how the Sicilians have approached him to manage their case and his response: *dicebam habere eos actorem Q. Caecilium.* This phrasing intimates that Caecilius had already initiated the prosecution when Cicero made his *postulatio.* Finally, there is the *argumentum ex silentio* – if Cicero had requested the prosecution first, it stands to reason that he would have pointed this out to the jury. It would lend sincerity to his case and add weight to his allegations of *praeuaricatio* against Caecilius. Rather it would have been Cicero's later bid, not Caecilius', that aroused suspicion. The *diuinatio* should scarcely have lasted longer than a day and must have concluded sometime before early February.[67]

Timeline of Verres' Trial[68]

Event	Date	Source
Verres becomes a *priuatus*	1 January 70	
Postulatio by Caecilius	circa 10 January	
Postulatio by Cicero	circa 10 January	
Diuinatio	circa 20 January–early February	
Nominis delatio		
Tempus inquirendi / inquisitio	circa 20 January–20 April	*Ver.* I.6; II.1.16; 2.99
Preliminary investigations (Rome)	circa 20 January–mid February	*Ver.* II.1.50, 60

[67] During this month in fact, the senate's schedule was dominated by the reception of foreign embassies. *Fam.* 1.4.1; *Q. Fr.* 2.12.3; Lintott (2008) 86: 'By a later *lex Gabinia* the senate's agenda in February was confined to hearing embassies until these had all been sent home.'

[68] For these dates and a bibliography, see Marinone (1997) 65–66, though in following Cowles, he lists the *nominis delatio* as coming before the *diuinatio.* This is inconsistent with criminal procedure, as is made clear by *Diu. Caec.* 62, 64; *Fam.* 8.8.3; Lintott (2004) 72; Greenidge 459.

Event	Date	Source
Travel from Rome to Messina	mid February–early intercalary month	
Investigations in Sicily	early intercalary month–early April	*Ver.* II.2.11, 64, 99
In Agrigentum	end of the intercalary month	*Scaur.* 25
Speaks in Syracusa and Henna[69]	March	*Ver.* II.4.137–139 (Syracusa) *Ver.* II.4.110 (Henna)
Travels from Messina to Rome	early April–mid April	
Report to Praetor after 110-day inquest	circa 20 April	*Ver.* II.1.17
Trial delayed by prosecution of the governor of Achaia	end of April–mid July	*Ver.* I.6; II.1.30
Jury formation for Verres' Trial	14–26 July	*Ver.* II.1.17
Elections for the year 69 (C. elected aedile)[70]	27–31 July	*Diu. Caec.* 70, 72; *Ver.* I.17, 26, 36–37; II.1.19; 5.36, 173; *Brut.* 319; *Pis.* 2; *Off.* 2.59; Plut. *Cic.* 8.1[71]
Actio prima	5 August	*Ver.* I.31; II.1.19
Examination of witnesses for the prosecution	6–13 August	*Ver.* II.1.19–20

69 J. Crawford (1984) 8–9.

70 C. never indicates whether he was a plebeian or curule aedile. The balance of the evidence, however, suggests the former; see Taylor (1939).

71 [Asc.] 185 = 22 Stangl states that C. had already been elected by the time of the *diuinatio;* [Aur. *Vict.] Vir.* Ill. 81.3: ([*M. Tullius Cicero*] *Aedilis Gaium Verrem repetundarum damnauit)* suggests that he had already been elected by the *Actio Prima.*

Event	Date	Source
Comperendinatio	mid August	*Ver.* II.4.33–34
Verres goes into voluntary exile	circa 10–15 September	*Ver.* II.1.20, 156; 5.44
Conviction and *litis aestimatio*	circa 20 September	*Ver.* II.1.156
Publication of the *actiones in Verrem* (including *Diu. Caec.*)[72]	end of September–October	

IV. STRUCTURE AND GENRE

> … *de [Verre] non praeiudicium, sed plane iudicium iam factum putatur.*
>
> There is a general notion that this is not really a pre-trial hearing about the charges [against Verres] but that this is, in fact, the trial itself.
>
> (*Diu. Caec.* 12)

No other *diuinatio* speeches have come down to us from antiquity.[73] Yet for the casual reader of Cicero's forensic speeches, the *Diuinatio* has an unmistakable familiarity.[74] The speech may be subdivided, for the sake of discussion, into the following sections:

Exordium §§1–9
- *Anticipatio*: The Imagined Spectator (§1)
- *Narratio*: Personal Obligations (§§2–5)
- *Exordium*, continued: Civic Responsibilities (§§6–9)

Confirmatio §§10–51
- *Partitio*: How to Choose a Prosecutor (§10)
- *Confirmatio* I: The Candidate Most Desirable to the Victims (§§11–22)
- *Digressio*: *Lex de pecuniis repetundis* (§§17–19)

[72] See Introduction §V.

[73] Others had certainly been circulated in Cicero's day; see Suet. *Iul.* 55.2.

[74] For the basic structure of Ciceronian speeches and traditional parts of speech, see Berry (1996) 42–44.

Confirmatio I, continued: *Caecili Siculi plane nolunt*
Confirmatio II: The Candidate Least Desirable to the Accused (§§22–26)
Digressio: On the Ideal Prosecutor (§§27–47)
Confirmatio III: *Subscriptores* (§§47–51)

Reprehensio §§52–71
Reprehensio I: *Iniuria non facta* (§§52–58)
Reprehensio II: *Quaestor eius qui accusatur* (§§59–65)
Digressio: *Consuetudo maiorum* (§§66–71)
Conclusio §§71–73

This apparent familiarity, however, is deceptive. In forming any speech, the appropriate structure and elements were largely determined by genre and then adapted to suit the particular occasion, but a *diuinatio* resists easy generic categorization. Although it is argued in a forensic context before a jury, a *diuinatio* is more akin to a deliberative speech inasmuch as there is no completed *factum* that exists or any legal issue that must be resolved, but rather a *faciendum* – a matter of what must be done in the future.[75] This open-ended and ambiguous genre gave the speaker scope for flexibility and creativity in structuring his speech. Instead, Cicero assessed the challenges he faced in bidding against Caecilius to lead the prosecution and let the disadvantages of the situation dictate his form.

Prosecution could be a disreputable business, and only attempted under very narrow conditions, the most acceptable being personal enmity and injury at the hands of the accused. As a consequence, a potential prosecutor should traditionally identify closely with the aggrieved party (and ideally be a member of it). In this regard, Caecilius was an ideal candidate.[76] Cicero,

[75] 'The speech in the *diuinatio* has a quality that is essentially deliberative (symbouleutic) rather than judicial (dicanic). [Die Rede in der *diuinatio* hat vorwiegend symbuleutischen, nicht eigentlich dikanischen Charakter.]' Stroh (1975) 175–176.

[76] C. would even later admit that his grievances against Verres were justified. *Ver.* II.1.15 *Quod meum factum lectissimi uiri atque ornatissimi ... ita probauerunt ut ei qui istius quaestor fuisset, et ab isto laesus inimicitias iustas persequeretur, non modo deferendi nominis, sed ne subscribendi quidem, cum id postularet, facerent potestatem.* On acceptable justifications for prosecution, see *Off.* 2.50. Personal injury and enmity were chief among them.

meanwhile, had all the trappings of a blatant political opportunist. He had no connection with Verres, but just so happened to be canvassing for the aedileship at the time. So, when he stood to make his case, Cicero was confronting a sceptical and perhaps even hostile audience.[77] He met this difficulty in part by structuring the *Diuinatio in Caecilium* as a λόγος δικανικός.[78] Speech elements such as a *narratio*, a *reprehensio*, and other forensic conventions allowed him to craft a speech that was, at least initially, an exercise in self-defence.[79]

Speech units common to forensic oratory are apparent from the very outset.[80] After a short *anticipatio*, the *Diu. Caec.* contains a *narratio* explaining the events that established Cicero's relationship with Sicily and that lead him to prosecute Verres (§§2–5). What may seem at first glance like an innocuous story betrays its deceptive quality upon closer scrutiny – the primary rhetorical purpose of a *narratio* is, after all, a biased presentation.

> Although it seems from the outset that this narrative could not possibly concern any disputed past event, upon closer inspection that turns out to be the case. The events which led to the *nominis postulatio* of Caecilius and Cicero seem to be a matter of dispute, even though Cicero does not openly address them as such. The incorporation of a *narratio* is ideal [for this indirect approach]. … Because of its 'non-probative' and 'illogical' quality, it presents the opportunity [for the speaker] to suggest backgrounds and contexts that do not in fact exist and that are not explicitly discussed at all.[81]

[77] Cf. *Rosc. Am.* 83 *nam si mihi liberet accusare, accusarem alios potius ex quibus possem crescere; quod certum est non facere dum utrumuis licebit. is enim mihi uidetur amplissimus qui sua uirtute in altiorem locum peruenit, non qui ascendit per alterius incommodum et calamitatem.*

[78] Stroh (1975) 175–176.

[79] For each section discussed, a fuller analysis is given in the commentary *ad loc.*

[80] In the organization and execution of a deliberative speech, the orator could use partitions specifically designed for a deliberative speech, or he could hold to the same rhetorical precepts as those for judicial speeches; cf. *Rhet. Her.* 3.7.

[81] Stroh (1975) 185. [Während es uns nämlich anfangs so schien, als könne es in diesem Verfahren nicht um einen umstrittenen Tatbestand der Vergangenheit gehen, hat sich mittlerweile gezeigt, daß dies wahrscheinlich doch der Fall ist. Die Ereignisse, die zur *nominis postulatio* des Caecilius und Cicero geführt haben, scheinen in der Tat kontrovers zu sein, wobei jedoch diese

As Stroh goes on to note, a critical reader of the *narratio* will notice that Cicero is intentionally vague about timing and sequence.[82] With even a touch of scepticism, one could conclude that the Sicilian delegations sent to pursue Verres' conviction did not come to Cicero specifically and that Caecilius, perhaps with the backing of a delegation, had already taken up the charge. This biased and nuanced presentation by Cicero, however, allows him to create the impression of an initial reluctance that succumbs to his sense of altruism and duty. The misleading *narratio* immediately allows Cicero to sidestep the issue of his candidacy and explain why he has come forward despite no personal relationship with the accused.

An extensive *reprehensio* (§§52–71) along with a sustained invective against his rival claimant may also have been unexpected. According to other ancient references to *diuinationes*,[83] a potential litigant would explain that he has the *maior causa* and that he would bring more rigour and sincerity to the accusation than anyone else. It must therefore have been common for the accuser to indicate the nature and severity of his personal injuries and losses. While the occasional insinuation of *praeuaricatio* may have been a common trope, the potential prosecutor would primarily make a *prima facie* case against the defendant. Since it stands to reason that the person who had suffered the greater injury would be given the lead role by the jury, those with lesser complaints may have been assigned to the suit as assistant prosecutors or been rejected altogether.[84] Though he does offer some broad summaries of Verres' extensive depredations, Cicero's most sustained indictment is against Caecilius himself. *Ad hominem* attacks implicate Caecilius in Verres' embezzlement schemes (§§30–33), denigrate his education and accomplishments (§§37–46), and depict him as a corrupt magistrate subverting the course of jus-

Kontroverse von Cicero nicht offen ausgetragen wird. Hierfür bietet sich nun die Form der *narratio* geradezu an .... In unserem Fall kommt hinzu, daß gerade die *narratio* durch ihren nicht beweisenden, ‚unlogischen' Charakter die Möglichkeit gibt, Hintergründe und Zusammenhänge zu suggerieren, die nicht existieren und die offen auch gar nicht genannt werden.]

[82] See introduction to §§2–5.

[83] See introduction to §10.

[84] On *subscriptores*, see the introduction to §§47–51.

tice for personal gain (§§55–58). The overall effect is not simply to vilify and defame his opponent but to turn Caecilius into a version of Verres himself. Having come to the Extortion Court with reasonable motives and valid allegations, Caecilius has himself become the target of a prosecution. It is only by maligning his rival that Cicero can make his supposed representative advocacy and generic claims of national interest seem compelling.

There are further similarities to forensic speeches that continue beyond the structure of the *Diuinatio*. In §13, Cicero momentarily suggests that he is going to call upon witnesses for testimony – something entirely out of place in a *diuinatio*.[85] The function of witness testimony, however, is given to the Sicilians, who offer an assessment of Caecilius' character (e.g. §§21–22). Cicero also indulges in a display of juristic skill through statutory interpretation (§§17–18) and review of judicial precedent (§§63–65). This imposition of forensic structure and argument comes to play other important roles in Cicero's inventive re-imagining of the *diuinatio* as a rhetorical contest.

Quintilian noted that Cicero used an unconventional *partitio* (§10) in the *Diuinatio*.[86] Rather than the traditional concerns about which party had the *maior causa*, the two points, Cicero claims, that must be considered are (1) *quem maxime uelint actorem esse ii quibus factae esse dicantur iniuriae* (2) *et quem minime uelit is qui eas iniurias fecisse arguatur*. The *confirmatio* that follows on these points is rather hollow and repetitive, but it does usher in an extended discussion of rhetorical training and oratorical ability (§§27–47). It is upon the basis of these qualities, Cicero implicitly argues, that the Sicilians have chosen Cicero to be their champion. The jury, he explains, should choose a lead prosecutor on the same merits. From this point on, the *diuinatio* becomes, for the most part, a rhetorical ἀγών.[87] What better way for Cicero to showcase his forensic rhetoric at an unconventional occasion than by forming the *diuinatio* into a forensic speech that did 'not seem like a pre-trial hearing but the trial itself'?

85 Cicero exploits the semantic range of the word *testes*; see n. *ad loc.*

86 See introduction to §10 and n. *ad loc.* with citation from Quintilian.

87 Diction and *comparationes* between Cicero and Caecilius contribute to the overall agonistic representation. Cicero repeatedly refers to the *diuinatio* as a *certamen* or a *contentio*.

As for the damning question of Cicero's sincerity, in a short *digressio* before the *conclusio*, Cicero will finally address his candidacy (§70). In a sense, the first 69 sections of the *Diuinatio* function as a lengthy *insinuatio* that surreptitiously wins over the jury.[88] Only after he has fundamentally changed the perception of his motives and the character of the *diuinatio* proceeding does Cicero assure the jury that his political ambitions, far from an indication of opportunism, are in fact the greatest assurance of the energy and sincerity that he will bring to Verres' prosecution. When the votes were taken, the jury must have been convinced. Caecilius was not even allowed to assume an assistant's role. Cicero, meanwhile, received the role of prosecutor and an opportunity to set his star on the rise.

V. PUBLICATION

> *Oratiunculas autem et quas postulas et pluris etiam mittam, quoniam quidem ea quae nos scribimus adulescentulorum studiis excitati te etiam delectant.*
>
> As for those humble speeches that you've asked for, I'm going to send them to you along with several others, too; I see that what I've been motivated to write for the education of youths offers you some enjoyment as well.
>
> (*Fam.* 2.1.3)[89]

Though he won the day, it may not have been a foregone conclusion that Cicero would publish his *diuinatio* speech.[90] As a young advocate, Cicero published a fairly high percentage –

[88] On *insinuatio*, see the introduction to §§1–9.

[89] For more on this statement, see Dyck (2008) 10.

[90] The relationship between the published version of the text and the speech Cicero originally delivered is a debate that extends back to Antiquity. This commentary takes the approach of Quintilian and Stroh in treating our published edition as though it were the one delivered despite any corrections that may have been made. Quint. *Inst.* 12.10.54: *An Demosthenes male sic egisset ut scripsit, aut Cicero? Aut eos praestantissimos oratores alia re quam scriptis cognoscimus? Melius egerunt igitur an peius? Nam si peius, sic potius oportuit dici ut scripserunt, si melius, sic potius oportuit scribi ut dixerunt. Quid ergo? semper sic aget orator ut scribet? Si licebit, semper. Sed erunt quae impediant breuitate tempora a iudice data: multum ex eo quod potuit dici recidetur, editio habebit omnia.* See Powell and Paterson (2004) 52–57 and the approach throughout Stroh (1975). Furthermore, if Cicero knew that he was going to be the first speaker, he could have prepared the content of his speech in far more detail before delivery.

around 70 per cent – of his speeches, including unsuccessful ones,[91] but the frequency with which *diuinationes* were published, even among those orators who routinely circulated their work, is unknown. Given the traditionally straightforward and procedural nature of these speeches at a preliminary hearing,[92] they may not have been considered worthy of wider distribution, especially when a successful set of prosecutorial speeches was available.

Cicero's motives for publishing his speeches were manifold. His path to political ascendancy was through oratorical skill rather than military might, and circulated speeches were undoubtedly used to boost his political profile.[93] Publication would also have allowed him not only to draw attention to his forensic success and leave a lasting literary monument for the clients he supported, but also to correct unauthorized publications[94] and provide models for his contemporaries at the bar and for students of rhetoric. Since it is obvious that political considerations and ambitions weighed heavily in Cicero's decision to prosecute Verres, it has frequently been argued that these same motives prompted the publication of the *Diuinatio in Caecilium*. Yet this inevitably leads to a question of timing.[95]

If Cicero had looked for a short-term benefit for the forthcoming aedilician elections from the prosecution itself, this hope was thwarted. After the *diuinatio*, he had requested a 110-day *inquisitio* to collect evidence and to prepare his case,[96] but in the interim another prosecution *de repetundis* had been filed against the governor of Achaia and had been allotted a 108-day *inquisitio*.[97] This permitted the second trial to take precedence on the

[91] See the illustrative graph in Melchior (2008) 285. *Pro Vareno* (of unknown date but sometime between 80 and 70) was unsuccessful, but any publication could have increased his visibility. See J. Crawford (1994) 7–18.

[92] See Introduction §III.

[93] Stroh (1975) 50–52.

[94] This was perhaps the case with *Pro Milone*; see Powell and Paterson (2004) 55 n. 205.

[95] The timing of publication has long sparked debate. See Frazel (2004) for a full bibliography.

[96] Cicero's cousin, Lucius, accompanied him to Sicily to collect evidence, as shown by *Ver.* II.4.145, but it is unclear if he was a *subscriptor*.

[97] *Ver.* I.6, 9; *Ver.* II.1.30; [Asc.] 128–129, 165–166 (207, 232 Stangl); Schol. Gronov. B 331 Stangl. *TLRR* 181 must be read with caution. Alexander incor-

judicial docket and delayed Verres' trial by an additional three months until 5 August – after the election.[98] Publication of the *Diuinatio*, some contend, could have garnered Cicero some of the social and political capital that he would have lost as a result of the delay. And as a matter of typical practice, the pre-consular Cicero was known to publish speeches one at a time.[99] After the *inquisitio*, Cicero would have had around four months in Rome before the aedilician elections to circulate the speech. As the outcome of the trial would be unknown until after the election, success or failure in his prosecution of Verres would be irrelevant, if he published for short-term gains.[100] That could explain why he even bothered to publish a pre-trial speech in the first place.

But the four months leading up to the elections would not have been idle time. Cicero was juggling trial preparation and canvassing to the extent that editing and circulating the *Diuinatio* would have been logistically difficult, if not improbable.[101] Then there are considerations beyond the pragmatic:

> [Though] victories of any kind – in the field or in the Forum – plainly helped candidates at Rome, the main trial, that of Verres, was still hanging in the balance. Circulating the *Diuinatio* by itself, therefore, would involve a gamble: how helpful to Cicero's name would that speech be, if Verres were acquitted? [This suggests that] Cicero released the *Diuinatio* after the successful outcome of the trial as a part of the complete corpus; a bare *diuinatio* to a (potentially) unsuccessful trial would be bathetic.[102]

Since Verres' voluntary exile around the *comperendinatio* could not have been anticipated, Cicero would have prepared much

rectly assigns Q. Caecilius Niger (relying upon §64; see n. *ad loc.*) to trial 174. The bibliography of this disputed trial listed with cases 174, 181, and 182 is more helpful. See also McGushin on Sal. *Hist.* 4.55M.

98 *Ver.* II.1.30. Cicero claimed that this was a cunning tactic by Verres to delay the trial, but there is nothing to substantiate this allegation.

99 Later he would publish them in batches. The grammarians refer to the four Catilinarians, published in 60, as *Inuectiuae*, and *Marc.*, *Lig.*, and *Deiot.* as *Caesarianae*. See Rouse and Reeve (1983) 55.

100 Settle (1962) 94.

101 *Ver.* I.24–26, if we can trust a Cicero prone to exaggeration.

102 Frazel (2004) 134.

of his prosecution in advance, including the material for the *actio secunda*. Therefore, at the successful conclusion of the trial, Cicero could have issued the *Diuinatio* along with both *actiones* in short order.[103]

The literary and pedagogical function of the *Diuinatio* as a written text also argues strongly for delaying its publication until the rest of the prosecution was ready for circulation. It seems as though Cicero himself conceived of the *Diuinatio* as integral to the Verrine corpus.[104] Although he is not consistent in his terminology when referring to the Verrines,[105] he refers to the speeches *In Verrem* as being *in Accusationis septem libris* – a grouping which notably includes the *Diuinatio*.[106]

As a literary production, the *Diuinatio in Caecilium* functions as a preface to the published orations against Verres. On a basic level, there is a correlation of argument. In it, Cicero summarizes many of the topics and allegations to be discussed in the *actiones in Verrem*. For example, the contemporary discussion over jury composition and the restoration of the censorial office that dominates much of the *actio prima* is mentioned in §8, and preoccupation with the public opinion of the Roman senate is pervasive.[107] Cicero also prompts his reader to anticipate many of the major subjects of the *actio secunda*: a survey of Verres' entire political career in addition to his Sicilian praetorship (§38), the embezzlement of public funds and misadministration of the grain tithe (§§30–33), theft of sacred art (§3), and the mistreatment of Roman citizens and miscarriages of justice (§57). This content is also set in its environmental and forensic context. In expectation of the trial, Cicero imagines the din of the Forum, the throngs of onlookers, and the eagerness of the victims seeking redress (§§41–42). Nor does he fail to describe the rhe-

[103] Frazel (2004).

[104] This does, however, strongly suggest a delay in publication until both *actiones* were ready for circulation.

[105] Cf. *Orat.* 167, where C. refers to *Ver.* II.2.4 as *in quarto accusationis*, and the interpretation of this passage in Settle (1962) 108.

[106] *Orat.* 103 *quod igitur in Accusationis septem libris non reperitur genus, quod in Habiti, quod in Cornelii, quod in plurimis nostris defensionibus?* His prosecution of Verres was *the* prosecution.

[107] For more on these issues, see *ad loc.*

torical manoeuvres, arguments, *actio*, and eloquence that one should expect from Verres' advocate.

This connection with the trial proper also goes beyond the description of the context and content of *In Verrem*. In the *Diuinatio*, Cicero even explains *how* he will build his argument and respond to the defence. As he lectures Caecilius on the qualifications of a suitable prosecutor, Cicero has embedded a rhetorical handbook within the speech (§§27–47). The discussion of rhetorical argumentation is so extensive that a few examples here will suffice to give an adequate picture.[108] Caecilius is instructed that an orator must carefully arrange his extensive material to make its presentation comprehensible to the audience (*dispositio*, §38); that a prosecutor should not only include a survey of the defendant's crimes but give a full account of his prior deeds which make the allegations more plausible (*uita ante acta*); that these accounts should be described in such vivid detail that the audience can see them with their own eyes (*enargeia*,[109] §27); that he must be capable of responding to rhetorical trickery (*complexio*, §45); that, when appropriate, the orator should also stir his audience's emotions to grief or anger (*amplificatio*, §§38–39, 46); and that all of this must be delivered from memory with robust stamina, fitting gestures, and a strong voice (*actio*, §§36, 37, 39).

But Cicero's audience does not have to wait for the speeches against Verres to see these qualities exhibited in full. Like a good teacher (but a formidable opponent), Cicero goes on to demonstrate all these qualities for (and against) Caecilius. Among others, he deploys his own *complexiones*,[110] vilifies Caecilius, arouses the audience's resentment and pity, and draws attention to his own performance and delivery. It is this meta-rhetorical quality of the speech that provides an aspect of what Kennedy called *letteraturizzazione*.[111]

[108] See §§27–47 nn. for a fuller discussion of these and other rhetorical issues.

[109] For the terms *descriptio* and *enargeia*, see notes *ad loc.* The relationship between oratory and the plastic arts and the metaphorical description of the former in terms of the latter were already discussed in Antiquity and the medieval period.

[110] See, for example, §§31, 58.

[111] The term was promulgated by Kennedy and applied specifically to the Verrines by Enos (1988) 73–78. Tempest (2007a) provides two salient quotations: 'We

In fact, throughout this central episode, education is such a leading theme[112] that the speech calls attention to the use of published oratory as a pedagogical tool. While the audience and the reader have been able to eavesdrop on his lesson in rhetoric, Caecilius, as the 'pupil', also serves as an apotreptic *exemplum*. Cicero tells his reader that Caecilius has come to court, accompanied by his primary school teacher, with a textbook and a copy of some speeches to mine for one-liners (§§47, 52).[113] The reader of Cicero's text, with scroll in hand, could not help but feel a sense of self-awareness.[114] The *Diuinatio in Caecilium* essentially dictates its own interpretation and employment. For the reader (and the student), there is an emphasis on the creative process, which bridges the gap between the theory and actualization of persuasive speech. If one thinks of the *Verrines* as an extension of Cicero's rhetorical works, the *Diuinatio* is that link between the classroom and the courtroom – rhetorical theory discussed and demonstrated.

To emphasize the pedagogical purpose of the speech is not to downplay the persuasive aspects of Cicero revealing his art. The *Diuinatio in Caecilium* functions both as a persuasive speech in a self-proclaimed rhetorical contest[115] and as a key to under-

may well have in the *In Verrem* one of the prototypes illustrating George Kennedy's notion of *letteraturizzazione* – that is, the shift of rhetoric from its primary function of immediate, oral persuasion to rhetoric in a secondary function, the use of rhetorical techniques for effective literary expression ... With the *In Verrem*, however, we have an instance of the phenomenon of *letteraturizzazione* occurring within one piece of discourse. Such an occurrence reveals an increasing specialization – and separation – of oral and written genres' (74); 'Cicero's *In Verrem* has two dimensions which warrant its preservation: initial orations which offered paradigms of effective legal argument and later orations which provided eloquent models of forensic rhetoric composed in a literate mode' (77).

[112] See §39 in particular. For Roman rhetorical education and a discussion of social reproduction germane to the *Diu. Caec.*, see Corbeill (2007).

[113] For Caecilius as a late-learner (ὀψιμαθής), see §27 *quoniam hoc primum tempus* n.

[114] The Verrines found their way into the education curriculum quickly; see Introduction §VI.

[115] So Andersen (1996) 82: '*Delectatio* and *uoluptas* are conducive to persuasion. They consist in enjoying the speech as such, and in appreciating the art of the speaker. Of particular interest in our context is the fact that Cicero admits that, when the audience have been won over, they are no longer intent on watching or catching the orator, but are now on his side, and wish him

standing Cicero's methods of persuasion and appreciating the accomplishments of the entire Verrine corpus.

VI. THE MANUSCRIPTS AND TEXTUAL TRADITION

The Verrines along with the *Catilinarians* continued to be used as educational texts, particularly for teaching Latin to Greek speakers in the eastern part of the Later Roman Empire. Traces of the Verrines are preserved on papyri from only a century after Cicero wrote them,[116] and a small portion of the *Diuinatio in Caecilium* has been found on a papyrus fragment of the fifth century, P. Ryl. III 477 (*Π*). Otherwise, the manuscript tradition of the *Diuinatio* is entirely medieval. In 1828, J. N. Madvig demonstrated that the medieval tradition of the Verrines divides into two families – one French, the other Italian.[117] The French family,[118] generally thought to be the more accurate of the two, displays a common ancestry with shared errors, chief among them the lack of significant portions of the *actio secunda*. The Italian family preserves the portions of the text lost to the French but is unified by errors of its own. R. H. Rouse and M. D. Reeve further analysed the transmission,[119] and recently Reeve continued this investigation deeper into the medieval tradition and supplemented the catalogue of manuscripts drawn up by Lopez and Piacente in 1973.[120] There are over 90 medieval manuscripts of the Verrines now known.

The French family (γ) all descend from a common ancestor, Parisinus 7775 (*S*, xii), in which the *Diuinatio* is no longer extant.

success; "overcome with admiration for the vigour of his oratory, they do not seek points to criticize" (*Orat.* 210).'

116 The Giessen papyrus (*P. Iand.*), for example, contains part of *Ver.* II.2.4 written in older Roman cursive and dates to the first half of the first century CE. For another from the *actio secunda*, see Gallazzi (1984). For a full list of ancient papyri of Cicero's works with illustrations and discussion, see Seider (1979) and Scappaticcio (forthcoming).

117 Madvig (1828) 7–10. *Est autem codicum in libris Verrinis duplex familia, altera, quam Gallicam dicere possimus, quia praecipui eius generis libri in Gallia reperti sunt, altera, quam Italicam siue uulgarem; harum familiarum codices perpetuo discreti sunt.*

118 Also referred to elsewhere as the northern European family.

119 Rouse and Reeve (1983) 68–73.

120 López and Piacente (1973) and Reeve (2016).

The Italian family can be subdivided into two branches. For the *Diuinatio*, the first branch is solely composed of the oldest complete witness, Parisinus 7776 (*P*), now dated to the eleventh century; the second branch of this family includes many of the so-called *deteriores* (δ), which have been selectively employed and sporadically reported by editors of the Verrines, including Jordan, Klotz, and Peterson. In his exploration of the Italian t radition, Reeve identified that the bulk of the text in this branch of extant *deteriores* comes from Mutinensis Est. Lat. 328 (*M*), whose readings will be fully reported in the critical apparatus.

Papyrus Fragment (*Π*)

Manchester, The John Rylands Library, *P.Ryl.* III 477 is a fifth-century papyrus bifolium fragment written in half uncial by the first hand and later emended, glossed, and annotated, both in Latin and Greek, by several others. It contains a very fragmentary text of §§33–37 and §§44–46 with approximately 30–35 characters per line and 21 lines per folium. The first scribe, A, writing in an ink now reddish-brown, left a gap of four or five spaces when there was a considerable pause in sense; for example between *reperiare* and *quid* in §35 and between *exercitatio* and *intelligo*, between §35 and §36. Whenever A started a new section according to his own system, he began a new line and wrote a larger initial letter that protruded into the margin. Another scribe, B, wrote scholia mostly in Greek with the occasional Latin note. The bulk of the Latin scholia were written later by a third scribe, C, who also made some corrections to the text. Another scribe, D, wrote a few Greek glosses, and a fifth, E, wrote *scopuloso* on the top left corner of 1v. The papyrus was purchased in 1920 and is of unknown provenance, though one may infer Egypt, Oxyrhynchus or Faiyum.[121] In 1938, C. H. Roberts produced a printed edition of the text and scholia with notes.[122] In his overview of the scholia, he writes that:

[121] See Seider (1972) 118–119 with bibliography. Both he and Roberts (see below) incorrectly state in their narrative that the papyrus starts at §35. When Roberts presents his edition of the text, however, he lists the correct section numbers in the margin.

[122] Roberts (1938) 72–77. Other editions are those of Calderini (1945) 32–38 and Cavenaile (1958) 75–78 (entry number 23).

> the Greek annotations, with the exception of the first half of the long note on *indicium* [§34], and perhaps one or two other notes on the same page, consist of translations or adaptations of the Latin text, less elementary and unintelligent than such notes in Latin papyri often are; the Latin notes, and a few Greek exceptions …, in manner and occasionally in substance resemble those of Pseudo-Asconius, which are dated to the fourth or fifth century. The scholium on *indicium* … suggests that it and Pseudo-Asconius may have had a common source, while that on *petitiones* [§44] suggests that the writer was acquainted either with Servius or with a source of Servius.[123]

At §44 it preserves a reading otherwise unattested in the textual tradition: *mod[o di] sserendum | modo altercandum modo o[mni] ratione | pugnandum certandumq[ue s] it*; see n. *ad loc.* This may suggest that the French and Italian families shared an archetype.[124] The digital reproduction of the manuscript is not sufficient to allow for a new collation of *Π*. The readings reported in the apparatus have been collated from Roberts' edition.

The French Family (γ)

The earliest manuscripts of the French family, which may have contained all of the Verrines, no longer have the text of the *Diu. Caec.* and now only preserve portions of the *actio secunda.*[125] Among them are the early ninth-century manuscripts, British Library Add. 47678 + Geneva Lat. 169 (***C***)[126] and Paris Lat. 7774A (***R***). All manuscripts in this family that still have the *Diuinatio* descend from a mid-twelfth-century copy of *R*, Paris Lat. 7775

[123] Roberts (1938) 73. These annotations have also been studied by McNamee (2007) 473–478 and Scappaticcio (2015) 476–482.

[124] See however Housman's dictum at n. 148.

[125] Rouse and Reeve (1983) 61, 68–69.

[126] The foliation suggests that *C* once contained all of the Verrines, though now it contains only parts of *Ver.* II.2 and 4, and it may have come from the textual tradition that passed through the Carolingian court. The speeches that it contains are transmitted in the same order as those listed in a court catalogue; see Rouse and Reeve (1983) 61.

(*S*), though *S* has now lost its text of the *Diuinatio.*[127] During the first half of the thirteenth century, *S* belonged to the library of Richard de Fournival, chancellor of Amiens, until his death in 1260, whereupon it passed to Gerard of Abbeville and later to the Sorbonne, where it was entered into the catalogue in 1338 as *Tulius ad Cecilium oratorem ....*[128] *S* now preserves only *Ver.* II.1.90–111 in addition to II.4 and II.5, but its descendants provide the earlier part of the Verrines through *Ver.* II.1.90, including the *Diuinatio.*[129] In addition to other errors which group them into a family, all descendants of *S* are unified in missing §§65–66 *dubitare quisquam potest ... fortunas defendere* – an error arising from *saut du même au même* at some earlier point in the transmission, or perhaps in *S* itself. There are at least 16 descendants, and collation with the surviving portions of *S* reveals that many of these are independent of the rest.[130]

From the extant sections of *S*, it is also clear that it underwent rounds of correction, both by the original scribe[131] and by a later

[127] Peterson (1907) argued that *S* is a sibling of *R*. Klotz (1923) viii–xii set out in his edition the argument that *S* is firmly a descendant (perhaps even a direct one) of *R*; Reeve (2016) 22 concurs. For example, at *Ver.* II.4.2 the scribe of *S* originally wrote *etiam amplius* before marking *amplius* for deletion and writing *planius* above the line. The error likely arose from the scribe of *R* splitting *planius* across two lines (*etiampla|nius*). For the other members of the French family, which do not descend from *S* and do not include the *Diuinatio*, see Reeve (2016) 31–32.

[128] Rouse (1974) 255, 259.

[129] Reeve (2016) 26.

[130] See Reeve (2016) 23–25. The 16 descendants of *S* are B.N.F. Lat. 7823, B.N.F. Lat. 7822, B.N.F. Lat. 7786, Wolfenbüttel Extrav. 265.2, Wolfenbüttel Weissenburg 41, Leiden Periz. F 12, B.L. Harl. 4105, B.L. Harl. 4852, Oxford Bodl. D'Orville 10, B.N.F. Lat. 7777, B.N.F. Lat. 16226, B.N.F. Lat. 16674, Stuttgart Donaueschingen 12, Vat. Lat. 1751, Escorial R.I.2, and Frauenfeld Kantonsbibliotek Y 227. The first eight were used by Peterson in his Oxford edition.

[131] There may have been more than one original hand in *S*. In my collations, I noted that the first hand of *E*, and occasionally *N* and *H*, displayed a persistent error in which *nihil* was written as *in hoc* (§§8, 36, 43, 47, 71) – an error likely to arise with the abbreviations *nih'* and *in h'*. In the extant portions of *S*, however, *nihil* is written out in full (e.g. *Ver.* II.4.5, 8, 9, 10, 11, 17 and so on), and at these places, *E* carries the correct reading *nihil*. An abbreviation for *iudices* used throughout *S* gave subsequent scribes difficulty, often resulting in *inde*, *modo*, or *uide*. These obvious errors have not been reported in the apparatus.

hand that also supplied the end of *Ver.* II.4.151 *cala*] *mitosus dies ... recuperarant*, which was missing from *R*. Where the corrector found the missing text and the source of the other corrections are unknown.[132] Most of the variants in the surviving parts of *S* are supralineal, and corrections or deletion marks are more common than obliteration or erasure. Though what remains of *S* suggests that there were not many corrections, copyists had to either choose a reading or find a way of incorporating the variants into their own text.

Since *S* has so many independent descendants, this edition relies on full collation of six descendants that display less corruption or contamination from the Italian family than the others.[133] Further collation of manuscripts within the French family is unlikely to yield readings of any authority. However, one symptom of this selectivity, combined with the corrections in *S*, is that readings which may appear to be peculiar to one manuscript or another may originally have stood in *S*. A majority consensus among these MSS with the Italian family usually leaves little doubt as to the oldest recoverable reading, which is not reported in the apparatus.

E

El Escorial, Real Biblioteca del Monasterio de San Lorenzo R.I.2 is among the more notable descendants of *S* as it was written upon the 1351 request of Clement VI, pope at Avignon 1342–1352. It was later moved from the papal library at Avignon to Peñíscola and then sold to Alfonso of Aragon in 1424.[134] The text is written in a fine Gothic textualis hand on 265 folia of vellum in two columns of 45 lines with generally 23–28 characters

[132] Some could simply have come from the scribe checking his work against *R* while others must come from elsewhere. The omission of §1 *consili* makes it unlikely that *S* was corrected from an Italian source, because collation is usually attentive at the beginning.

[133] The corrections in B.N.F. Lat. 7786 are less obvious than those in *E*. Wolfenbüttel Extrav. 265.2 and B.N.F. Lat. 7822 are contaminated from the Italian tradition, while the other descendants of *S* are more corrupt than those collated for this edition.

[134] Reeve (2011) 397–398.

per line (excluding spaces). Accompanied by illumination and decoration throughout, it also includes the Philippics and Catilinarians, along with several philosophical works by Cicero and the epitome of Vegetius wrongly attributed to Cicero;[135] the *Diu. Caec.* is found on 200v–206v. The rubricator has titled the speech above an illuminated capital with: *M. Tullii Necronis* (sic) *in C. Verrem | Liber Primus incipit*, and *In V(er)rem* is written at the top of each side of the folia. A later hand corrected *E* up to *Ver.* II.1.26 both with marginalia and through careful erasure in the original text that is not always apparent at first blush from a digital reproduction. These corrections come from the later Italian tradition of *deteriores* discussed below; for example §9 *boni* for *idonei*, §32 *Verris* for *uere*, §37 *causas* for *causam*. When the original reading is difficult to discern, it can often be recovered from *E*'s descendant, Frauenfeld Y 227 (*t*).

t

Frauenfeld, Kantonsbibliothek Y 227, written on 214 folia in a single column of around 40 lines and approximately 60 characters per line (excluding spaces), contains the Philippics as well as the Verrines with the *Diu. Caec.* on 92r–98v. A second hand has written on the upper right-hand corner *Marci Tullii Ci(ceronis) i(n) G. Verre(m) Lib(er) P(rim)us i(n)cip(i)t.* *t* is a descendant of *E*, but likely through an intermediary. The scribe of *E*, in keeping an orderly and justified column of text, would occasionally end a line with a stroke or an abortive start to the word on the next line and then mark it out for deletion; for example §47 *atque ọ | officio tuo.* In §59 *E* has *q | quid*, without a deletion mark, and *t* repeats the error with *q quid.* But as Reeve noted, at §§4 and 7 respectively, the scribe of *E* wrote out *michi* and *tempore* in full, but *t* corrupts them to *in* and *turpe*, again the sort of error often due to misreading an abbreviation.[136] *t* introduces a host

[135] Rouse and Reeve (1983) 69; Rouse and Rouse (1978) 363.

[136] Reeve (2016) 28. Likewise, *t* misreports the supralineal gloss incorporated into *E* in §1. *horum tem|pore qui sunt* in *E* has become *horum ipsorum ipse qui sunt* in *t*. Though written over two lines, *tempore* should have given the scribe

of errors, but in my collations I note only a few places in which *E* has an error not in *t* or at least where *t* agrees with the French family against *E*, but all can be accounted for by conjecture or fortunate accident.[137] Given the fact that *t* is derived from an extant manuscript, it is of limited utility and only reported when it was used to recover the original text of *E*.

D

Paris, Bibliothèque nationale de France, Lat. 7823 was written by Nicholas de Clamanges in the early fifteenth century. The 196 folia are laid out in a single column of 26 lines with approximately 35–45 characters per line (excluding spaces); the *Diu. Caec.* occupies 1r–14v. The top and bottom margins of the first folio have been cut, but on the facing page, a hand close in time to the first has written *Qu(a)e secuntur hic h(abe)nt(ur) s*[*c*] *ilicet* | *Quidam Libri Tullii. scilicet Orationes* | *quaedam Tullii Ciceronis Inuectiu(a)e d(i)c(t)ae* | *Verrin(a)e. Prima ad C(a)ecilium oratorem.* | *Incipiens 'Si quis uestrum' et secunda inci*|*pit 'quod erat optandum* … etc. *D* belonged to Claude Dupuy and under his name the contents are re-listed and begin with *Ciceronis Diuinatio in C. Verrem* | *Actionis primae in Verrem prooemium, quae uulgo inscribitur Verrina II* … and so forth. The Gothic cursive hand allows the reader to distinguish between letter forms that would have been more ambiguous in its textualis siblings. In places where *S* is extant, collations of *D* show it to be the most accurate of its descendants.[138] The scribe seems to have been able to make better sense of what he saw in *S*, makes fewer mistakes with abbreviations, and notes variants and transpositions in places where the other descendants of *S* only show disagreement. The longer one spends with *D*, the more one has the impression that it is a more sophisticated manuscript than it appears to be. It may then be a conflation of

of *t* no trouble if working from *E* directly, and the error must have arisen in *t*'s exemplar.

[137] §4 tantaeque *E* : tantae *t et cett.*; §42 futura *E* : factura *t*; §49 iam haec *E* : iam hoc *t et cett.*; §56 recognoscit *E* : cognoscit *t et cett.*; §63 pitioni *E* : pithoni *t*.

[138] See Reeve's collation (2016) 28–29.

S and one of its descendants or two independent descendants of *S*. After *D*'s relocation to Saint-Victor, it may have become the source of Harley 4852 (Peterson's *Z*) and Paris Lat. 7777.[139]

G

Wolfenbüttel, Herzog August Bibliothek, Weissenburg 41[140] is a three-part mid-fifteenth-century manuscript written on watermarked paper that contains the portions of the Verrines from the French family as well as a miscellaneous assortment of other texts from authors such as Roger Bacon and Marco Polo. The first of the three parts consists solely of the Verrines (1r–50r) with the *Diuinatio* on 1r–5v. This portion of the manuscript is written in Gothic cursive in a single column ruled for 45 lines with approximately 70–80 characters per line. The beginning of each speech is only indicated by a decorated initial capital, though the rubricator has given the title at the top of 1r as *Verrin(a)e Marci Tullii Ciceronis*. The text of *G* is more corrupt than those of *D*, *E*, and *N*, but also transmits many of the readings only otherwise found in *D*.

N

Paris, Bibliothèque nationale de France, Lat. 16226[141] contains other Ciceronian speeches with *Diu. Caec.* on 137r–144v. It is written on parchment in two columns ruled for 36 lines with 25–30 characters per line (excluding spaces). Above the initial illuminated capital, the rubricator has written *M. T. Cic(er)onis In C. Verrem Lib(er)|P(ri)mus Incipit feliciter*. *N* makes several telling omissions or near omissions. In §11 after *Siciliam*, the scribe started to write *causa iudicium* and so must have gone back to the beginning of the same line (approximately 55 letters); at §50,

[139] Reeve (2016) 25.

[140] Peterson used this manuscript in his Oxford Classical Texts edition and called it G_2. For a full description and a listing of contents, see Butzmann (1964) 161–165.

[141] Reeve (1992) xv–xvi used it for his edition of *Pro Quinctio*; he called it *G* and dated it to the end of the fourteenth century.

there was another near miss in which he first wrote *loco casu … incidi*, skipping over the line that had *aut … sed* (approximately 60 characters); the omissions at §32 *uere defendere … Manci-* and §60 *sine scelere … de iniuria* correspond to 60–70 characters. *N* occasionally reports both the original readings of *S* and corrections made to it, for example *futura uel factura* for *futura* at §42, the gloss on *quicum* in §44, and *intrat uel mittit* for *intrat* at §56.

H

Paris, Bibliothèque nationale de France, Lat. 16674 was commissioned for the Sorbonne by Andreolo Arisi, imperial secretary to Gian Galeazzo Visconti and Milanese ambassador to Paris in the late fourteenth (and perhaps early fifteenth) century.[142] The manuscript, written on vellum in Gothic cursive, contains the French text of the Verrines with the *Diuinatio* occupying 1r–11r. Each page is ruled for 32 lines with approximately 40 characters per line. No title announces the speech except for an illuminated capital, but at the bottom of 11r, the rubricator has written the *explicit* common to *E* and *N*: *M. Tullii de accusatione liber prim(us) explicit. Incipit secundus ….* The only corrections in *H* are those in the first hand, presumably from the scribe checking his work. *H* may be a sibling of *N*; their common errors are:

> §2 cum] eum §5 me] mens vel meus §10 iudices] inde §27 mea] in alia §30 quid] quidem §45 quid] qui §48 eum] ipsum; si] sic; graecis] graeis; §49 moratorum] meator §50 aliquis] aliqui §55 incommodo] me commodo §56 possessionem] possionem §57 redit] rodit §63 neque Gn] ne sine; iudicum] iudicium

All the MSS in the French family are united in the following omissions:

[142] See the note on 117v: *Hunc librum Verrinarum Tullii dedit facundus uir Andreas de Arisiis, natione Lombardus, ambassiator et secretarius domini ducis Mediolanensis Collegio de Sorbona ut poneretur in magna libraria*; Delisle (1874) 143. In addition to his diplomatic duties, Arisi was a man of letters and corresponded with contemporary humanists. Among them was Coluccio Salutati, who in July 1396 wrote to Jean de Montreuil and repeated the rumour that Arisi had found a complete copy of Quintilian *Inst.* For more on his life, see Martini (1962) 198.

§1 consili; §4 post me quaestorem; §8 uim grauitatemque requirit iudiciorum (also P1); §11 a uobis; §14 aut; §15 id; §19 fuit; -que; §21 se; §22 ut; §23 enim inquit; is; §25 et ita… mutandam (also P1); §26 ego; §27 aliquod; §37 res; §42 cum; §44 me; §47 is; §48 iudicium; §52 tu; §54 esse (also O); §65–66 dubitare quisquam… fortunas defendere; §70 -que; §72 habet

The Italian Family

P

Paris, Bibliothèque nationale de France, Lat. 7776, which also contains the rest of the Verrines, is the oldest complete manuscript of the *Diuinatio.* It is written in a regular and easily legible Caroline minuscule on 174 folia of parchment with usually 30 lines per side in a single column with approximately 60–70 characters per line, not including spaces.[143] Although it was originally dated to the thirteenth century, Chatelain and other palaeographers have assigned it to the eleventh, with probable origins in northern Italy.[144] Already in the early thirteenth century, *P* was in Siena, and the coat of arms for Celso Cittadini of Siena, to whom it belonged in the sixteenth century, decorates the bottom margin of the first folio; some marginalia are in his hand.[145] The *Diu. Caec.* occupies 1r–9r and begins simply with *M. Tulli Ciceronis In C. Verrem Lib(er) I.* Before starting the *actio prima,* it finishes with *M. Tulli Cice|ronis de accusatore liber I exp(licit) incip(it) lib(er) II.* There are corrections made in *P* that have been inserted during the process of copying and by later hands, but most of these are supralineal and do not obscure the original reading. *P* preserves some valuable readings (e.g. §45 *facessieris, §49 moratorum*), but in several instances the initial scribe omitted words at the end of a line (e.g. §2 *esse,* §3 *sua,* §11 *esse,* §23 *ut,* §24 *tabellam* between recto and verso, §32 *te* before a supralineal correction). The later

[143] A helpful list of passages restored by P^2 is found in Clark (1918) 252–255 within a full discussion of what was then known of the MS tradition of the Verrines; *ibid.* 212–265.

[144] Chatelain (1884–1900) plate XXXI.

[145] Di Franco Lilli (1970) 82–83 with plate XVII; Reeve (2016) 33.

corrections all seem to originate from another branch within the Italian family; see below on the *deteriores.* Some editors have failed to give this witness its due. Zumpt and Thomas, however, did, and it was the latter who assigned the symbol *p* in his edition of the Verrines; Klotz appropriately adopted the capital letter, which I have retained. In addition to *P*, Klotz and Peterson used members of the Italian family produced in the fifteenth century, among them Florence Laur. 48.29 (Peterson's *q*) and British Library, Harley 2687 (Peterson's *r*), written in Florence or Rome in the second half of the fifteenth century.[146] Reeve has conclusively demonstrated, however, that *r* derives solely from *q* and that *q* is a direct copy of *P*.[147] *P* has a later relative, Paris Lat. 4588A (Peterson's *k*; Zumpt's *Paris. A*), which does not contain the *Diuinatio.*

The *Deteriores* (δ)

The *deteriores* constitute a 'closely knit sub-family', and they have recently been shown to be independent of *P* and the source of corrections in *E*, while a less corrupt ancestor of the extant sub-families supplied the second-hand corrections in *P*.[148] Most

[146] Peterson derives *r* from *q* – and he argues elsewhere that *q* was derived from *P*, but this is not reflected in his printed text. See Peterson (1907) 190–191.

[147] Reeve (2016) 33–34.

[148] There are two notable genuine readings in *M* that are absent from both *P* and the French family, but these omissions can easily be attributed to coincidence in corruption. P^{a} and γ both omit the phrase *uim grauitatemque requirit iudiciorum* in §8 and *et ita [tamen] mutandam* in §25. There should be no doubt that the phrases are genuine. The omission at §8 is an especially destructive one, in that it sprawls over two sentences; the supplement could not plausibly be attributed to a medieval (or even humanist) conjecture, since it heals the two sentences in a way that both fits the sense perfectly and comprises a doublet – joining *uim* and *grauitatem* – of which C. was especially fond. Furthermore, the Gronovian scholiast includes a comment for the lemma *grauitatem req. iud.* (326.11 Stangl *grauitatem req. iud. id est ut equites iudicandi potestatem recipiant.* See 'Other Sources' below on the scholiasts of the *Diuinatio.*) Since the sentence at §25 remains grammatically sound even with the omission of *et ita … mutandam,* a later scribe would not have thought the passage deficient, so the phrase should not arise in *M* from correction, and there are Ciceronian parallels for this repetitive construction; see n. *ad loc.* Reeve (2016) 49 noticed that at *Ver.* II.2.228 only *M* has the whole phrase *etiamne frumentum pro empto gratis dare? etiamne in cellam cum cupiant gratis dare ultro pecuniam addere?* The French family is represented here only by Conventi Soppressi 79, a composite

of the text in the *deteriores* descends from Mutinensis Est. Lat. 328 (*M*). To understand more fully the relationship among its descendants, this edition will also consider six direct or partial descendants of *M*. A direct copy of *M*, Strozzi 44 (*F*), which introduced its own errors, is the ancestor of three branches of manuscripts. The first is represented here by an early descendant, Vadiana 314 (*v*). The second is a composite manuscript, Conventi Soppressi 79 (*O*), which has some errors of *F* and *v*, but not all of them, and whose Italian text of the *Diuinatio* shows contamination from a French source. The third branch, composed of a loose family (ς) of four manuscripts – Ambrosiana B 121 sup. (*a*), Laurenziana Plutei 48.27 (*l*), Bologna Universitaria 2232 (*b*), and Riccardiana 499 (*r*) – indicates its descent from *MF* with some shared errors and appears to be a conflation of *O* (or a relative) and the parent of *v*. Except for *M*, the other witnesses will be treated as *fontes coniecturarum*, and only readings of interest will be cited in the critical apparatus. When *M* is cited in a negative entry, the printed text gives the reading of *P*γ.

M

Modena, Biblioteca Estense Universitaria, Lat. 328 (α.F.8.6) is laid out on paper in 121 folia of double columns, usually 40 lines each with 25–30 characters per line (excluding spaces).

manuscript that includes readings from both the Italian and French families; see the introduction to *O* below. He also noticed the omission from §8, and also came to the conclusion that *P* and *S* omitted the phrase independently of one another: '[*P*]² restores *uim ... iudiciorum*, missing by *saut du même au même* from the descendants of *S* as well as from [*P*]¹; but M may not have been alone in preserving it, because the omission in *S* need not have occurred in any ancestor of *S*.' *Contra* Peterson (1907) 167.

These types of errors are not uncommon in general terms and probably arose independently here from *saut du même au même*. The general principle is succinctly stated by Housman (1927) xx in the introduction to his edition of Lucan: 'When two or more manuscripts agree in an omission which can be thus explained [by palaeography], it does not necessarily follow that the omission is derived from any common source of those manuscripts: the palaeographical cause is universally operative, and manuscripts not akin to one another may be independently affected by it.' Furthermore, if δ had in fact access to an 'extrastemmatic' source, the collations should also have uncovered verbal corruptions.

It contains the whole of the Verrines in Gothic cursive with the *Diu. Caec.* on 1r–7r, which is entitled by the rubricator as *Marci Tulii Cicero(n)is Inuectiuarum contra Gaium Verrem liber incip(i)t.* The top margin of 1r includes the *ex libris* of a Venetian family: *Hic liber est Marci Antonii Basadona q. Pauli.*[149] Reeve, following De Robertis, dates *M* to c.1400 and identifies the hand as one that would be at home 'among younger Florentine contemporaries of Salutati'.[150] Other hands have added some lexical and rhetorical notes and a few corrections. *M* is the parent of Strozzi 44 (*F*; see below) and ultimately the source for most of the *deteriores.*

F

Florence, Biblioteca Medicea Laurenziana, Strozzi 44 is a complete manuscript of the Verrines written on paper by several hands in double columns of around 40 lines of 25–30 characters each (excluding spaces), except for the scribe who copied *Ver.* II.2.186–3.114 in a single column. The *Diu. Caec.*, on 1r–7r, begins *M.T. Ciceronis in C. Verrem or(ati)o p(ri)ma incipit.* This copy belonged to Leonardo Bruni, who complained about the corrections made by a second hand; he writes on 104v: *Hic liber cum ab initio recte scriptus fuisset postea corruptus est ab homine qui cum uellet eum corrigere corrupit. Quare priorem litteram accepta, correctiones reiice.*[151] *F* must therefore have been written no later than the early fifteenth century since Bruni appears to refer to *F* in a letter to Niccola de' Medici on 7 October 1407.[152] Each quire of *F* shows a change of hand. Reeve noticed that blank spaces at the ends of quires show that it was copied from separate quires of the exemplar, and from this he securely determined that its parent was *M*, which has these quires without blank spaces. *F* incorporates some, but not all, of the corrections made to the

[149] For supposition on the owner, see Reeve (2016) 55.

[150] Reeve (2016) 56 n. 90, citing the assessment of T. De Robertis.

[151] Reeve (2016) 51.

[152] *Mitto tibi orationes Ciceronis in Verrem recte quidem scriptas sed ut uidebis male emendatas; qui enim corrigere uoluit eas plane corrupit. Quamobrem tuae diligentiae erit non quae postea mutata sunt sed quae prius erant transcribi iubere.* See further Reeve (2016) 51 n. 78.

original state of *M*. *F* introduced the following errors into its descendants:

§11 Verres] Verrem; §12 Caecili] Q. Caecili; §27 quoniam] q(uonia)m etiam F^1 *ut uid.* : *del.* F^2 : *om.* $O^1 v^1 \varsigma$: *corr.* $F^3 O^2 v^2$; §32 uere] Verre $F^1 v \varsigma$

The First Family of Deteriores

v

St. Gallen, Kantonsbibliothek Vadiana 314 contain the Verrines on 136 folia written on parchment in a single column of 32 lines with 55–60 characters each (excluding spaces). The *Diu. Caec.* on 1r–7v begins with *M. Tullii Ciceronis pro Siculis in C. Verrem incipit Actio Prima ad iudices* and concludes, *Explicit actio prima incipit secunda.* It is an early descendant of *F* and must come from a date before 1417.[153] The descendants of *v* constitute a distinct family of *deteriores*. Among them are manuscripts such as Montecassino 340 and Vatican Lat. 8509, which corrupt the reading of §9 *idonei*, which is in *v*, to *boni*.[154] A member of this subfamily must therefore have been used by the corrector of *E* (see above).

O

Florence, Biblioteca Medicea Laurenziana, Conventi Soppressi 79 is a composite codex that contains the complete text of the Verrines on folia 5–64 with the *Diu. Caec.* occupying two non-consecutive folia, 52 and 63. Other works in the codex include the spurious Sallustian invective against Cicero and the response followed by the Catilinarians, *pro Marcello*, *pro Ligario*, and *pro Rege Deiotaro*. The manuscript begins with a good report of the second and third speeches of the *actio secunda* from the northern European tradition (see above) followed by a second 'ungainly' hand

[153] In §4, a second hand obliterated the last letter of *adduci* in *F*. The later descendants of *F* have *adductum*, including Reims 1110, the earliest dated manuscript, from 1417; see Reeve (2016) 62, 65. *v* has the first-hand reading and so must descend from the state of *F* before 1417.

[154] See the discussion on the descendants of *F* at Reeve (2016) 58–69.

that supplied the remaining speeches of the Verrines including the *Diu. Caec.* from the Italian tradition.[155] The cramped and highly abbreviated script of this speech is written on paper in a single column of about 62 lines with c. 90 characters per line (excluding spaces), and the manuscript has been described as one 'to wish on one's worst enemy'.[156] *O* was rebound at some point, and that presumably accounts for the separation of the *Diu. Caec.* within the codex. There is no *incipit* or *explicit* in the original hand, and so an eighteenth-century hand (probably Lagomarsini) has written: *In Q. C(a)ecilium Oratio de accusatore in C. Verrem constituendo quae Diuinatio dicitur* on the top margin of folio 52r.[157] The text ends at the bottom of 52v, and resumes at 63r with §38 *quae nefarie.* Several hands have made corrections both within the body of the text and in the margins, though some of the latter have been lost during the process of rebinding and on the badly worn edge of folio 52. One hand simply blotted out the text at times, while another used deletion marks that still expose the original reading. It was collated by Lagomarsini in 1739, and it is cited by Zumpt in his 1831 edition and by other editors as *Lag.* 42, but not always accurately; for example, from the very opening sentence in §1, Jordan reports *descendere* when it reads *descend(er)im.*

In stemmatic terms, it resists easy categorization. It will sometimes share readings of the French family and/or *P* against the other *deteriores*, for example

> §8 et γPO] atque *M*; §9 sese γPO] se *M*; §10 diutius γPO^{1}] *om. M exp.* O^{2}; §22 sint γPO] sunt *M* ; §39 expromere γPO^{1}] exponere *M*; §44 suo me $D^{ac}O^{1}$] me suo *cett.*; §50 est γPO] *om. M*; §54 esse *PM*] *om.* γO; sibi illa] illa sibi *O*; §55 quaedam est γPO] est quaedam. *M*; §56 intrat EDO^{2sl}] mittit *uel* mittat *cett.*; §60 in illius uita nullum *EO*] nullum

[155] On the origins of the French text in Conv. Soppr. 79, see Reeve (1982–1983).
[156] Reeve (2016) 85.
[157] The hand matches his collation notes in Ricc. 499 (our MS r, elsewhere referred to as Lag. 5) as well as the indication on 5r that this manuscript was collated by Lagomarsini in November 1739. At the bottom of 52v he noted that the speech stopped midway through and that the reader should *uide post 11 pag(inas)* and then at the top of 63r: *Sequitur medietas Diuinationis in C(a) ecilium qu(a)e suo loco desiderabatur.* The scribe that originally wrote the second and third Verrine did provide the simple title on 5r of *liber Verrinarum.*

nullius illius uita *N*: nullum illius in uita *cett.* ; §61 publici γ*PO*] publicam *M*

If *O* were an independent descendant of δ, there should be a few places where *O* agrees with *P* against *M* and/or the French family. Further evidence that *O* is contaminated from a French source comes in §56, where *O* has the correct reading, *in possessionem … intrat*, only otherwise attested in descendants of *S*. In places where *S* had variants, *O* does not agree entirely with any extant descendant that has been collated for this edition. It therefore stands to reason that *O* or an ancestor was contaminated from an unknown descendant of *S*.

Yet in many other places, *O* behaves like a descendant of *F*,[158] and it shares errors with *v* and another sub-family of *deteriores* (ς; see below). This suggests that an early descendant of *F* was a common ancestor of *O*, *v*, and ς. The shared errors of *Ov*ς are:

§16 mallent… mallent (*also* F^2); §31 tua ista] ista tua (*also* $D^{ac}N$); §35 in eius modi] in huius modi; §51 isto] illo; §62 fere umquam] umquam fere; §64 adoptarant] adoptauerant; §65 auctorem idoneum causae; §67 ac relata] atque relata

At some point, however, *O* was corrected against an early descendant of *M*. In §24 of *O* both *diutius* and *metus* were marked out for deletion.[159] Although *diutius* is completely missing from the *deteriores*, all except M^1 have *metus* since M^2 supplied the correction before *F* was written. Therefore, the corrector of *O* that marked out *metus* must have been collating it against an early descendant of *M* and not *M* itself.

The Second Family of Deteriores (ς)

Another group of *deteriores* has errors that gather them into a second family. The relationship among them and to the other MSS in the *deteriores* is not straightforward. On the one hand, the MSS of this family behave like a descendant of *F* and include errors of

158 Especially in *Ver.* II.4–5; see Reeve (2016) 85.
159 For this error and other related MSS, see Reeve (2016) 84–85.

F absent from *M*.[160] On the other, there must be contamination from an outside source,[161] since they contain some of the errors of *MF* but not all of them. Further contamination within their tradition prevents the relationship among them from being firmly established and defies stemmatic analysis. Although they often take sides in pairs, their alliances are ever changing.[162] The agreement of this group is indicated with the siglum ς. In no MS of ς are there any correct readings unattributable to lucky slip or conjecture that are not also in either *v* or *O*.

a

Milan, Biblioteca Ambrosiana B 121 sup. contains 119 folia, some on parchment with others on paper. The *Diu. Caec.* is written in multiple hands on parchment 1r–6r in a single column of 45 lines with generally 60–65 characters each (excluding spaces), and it has been titled *M. T. C. Verrem Lib(e)r P(rim)us de constituendo accusatore felicit(e)r incipit.* The illumination is absent for the initial 'S', and the ends of quires are left blank, which suggests that the quires of the exemplar were copied simultaneously. The hand varies throughout from Gothic (the hand of the *Diu. Caec.*) to humanistic minuscule.[163]

l

Florence, Biblioteca Medicea Laurenziana, Plutei 48.27 has 131 vellum folia ruled for 35 lines with approximately 60 characters per line (excluding spaces). It contains the whole of the Verrines written in a fine humanist hand once thought to be Poggio Bracciolini's[164] with the *Diu. Caec.* on 1r–7v, signalled by *M.T. Ciceronis*

160 Reeve (2016) 81–82.

161 For a possible source of contamination, see *O*, above.

162 For example, in §7 *a* and *r* have *exterisque* where *l* and *b* have *ceterisque*, yet at §12, *l* and *r* omit *esse* when *a* and *b* do not.

163 Jordan and Wool (1984) 119.

164 See Reeve (2016) 57; de la Mare (1992) 141, 151. At first, de la Mare thought it might have been written by Poggio himself, but later she expressed some doubt. Reeve also remains sceptical of the attribution to Poggio since *l* has a significant number of errors that would be surprising if Poggio had written it.

in Verrem de constituendo accusatore liber primus incipit. The codex once belonged to Cosimo de' Medici, whose *ex libris* is written unostentatiously before the explicit of *Ver.* II.4 on f. 107r; it is listed in a 1418 inventory and may have been written as many as 10 to 15 years earlier.[165]

b

Bologna, Biblioteca Universitaria, 2232 is written on parchment in 118 folia with double columns ruled for 50 lines of around 28–32 characters (excluding spaces). It contains the Verrines and the *De diuinatione* in Gothic textualis; the *Diu. Caec.* on 1r–5v has a miniature of Cicero within the illuminated capital, over which the rubricator has written *Marci Tullii Cyceronis in C. Verrem Liber Primus de constituendo accusatore feliciter incipit rubrica.* The scribe identifies himself and the date on 94r: *qui me finiebat Iohannes de Polonia nomen habebat. Anno domini MCCCCXIX, die ultima mensis augusti.*[166]

r

Florence, Biblioteca Riccardiana, 499 was written on parchment in 165 folia ruled for 31 lines of around 55 characters each (excluding spaces). It contains the Verrines with the *Diu. Caec.* on 1r–9v, starting with the heading *M. Tullii Ciceronis Accusationum Liber Primus incipit.* Written in a fine humanist hand throughout, it identifies itself at the end as *Liber Poggii secretarii Papae* on 165v. Ullman thought it to be the work of Poggio himself and dated it to late 1425 or early 1426,[167] while de la Mare assigns it to his *Gallicus librarius* about a year later; whoever wrote it meets the standard of accuracy that the famed humanist would demand.[168] Other editors have reported this manuscript elsewhere as *Lag.* 5.

[165] de la Mare (1977) 94–95.
[166] Frati (1909) 12.
[167] Ullman (1960) 37–40.
[168] de la Mare (1973) 70, 82, 84.

The *editio princeps* (Rome 1471), assembled by Giovanni Andrea Bussi, is a descendant of *r*.

*

All these manuscripts have been collated in full for this edition. For most of them (*EtNHMOvabl*), I was able to acquire excellent full-colour reproductions from the original, while for others (*DGPFr*) I had recourse to a digitized microfilm. The condition of *O*, as described above, is such that I decided to verify my collation by autopsy, at which point I also took the opportunity to examine *F* and *r* in places. For *O* it was possible to discern that some hands were much later and to confirm that some marginalia are hopelessly lost. For the others, autopsy revealed the second-hand corrections and erasures far better than the greyscale microfilm scan.

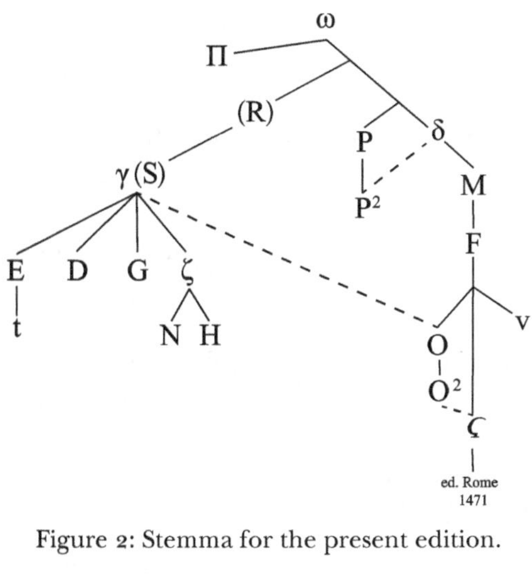

Figure 2: Stemma for the present edition.

Remarks

MSS in parentheses have been mutilated and no longer include the text of the *Diuinatio*, though they include other portions of the Verrines. Contamination among *a*, *b*, *l*, and *r* is so rife that no precise relationship can be depicted; they are represented by the collective siglum ς.

Other Sources

Two sets of scholia exist for the *Diuinatio in Caecilium.* In the summer of 1416, Poggio Bracciolini and Bartolomeo da Montepulciano found a ninth-century copy of Asconius' commentaries in the monastic library at St Gall.[169] Only five of them have proven to be the genuine product of the first-century commentator. In 1828, Madvig convincingly argued that the rest come from a fifth-century grammarian. The scholia on the *Diu. Caec.* and the next three *Verrine* orations are among the latter and are now simply attributed to the nameless pseudo-Asconius ([Asc.] throughout). The author may have drawn upon ancient commentaries.[170] The similarity of his note on §34 *indicium* and the marginalia of the fifth-century papyrus fragment (see *Π* above) is striking, and he is our only evidence for some *diuinatio* procedures, earlier trials, and some alternative readings.

The textual variants represented in his lemmata are of interest, but also warrant a word of caution. The original manuscript (s. ix *ut uid.*) that Poggio and Bartolomeo found languishing in the untidy library at St Gall has been lost.[171] The copy made by Poggio and the descendants of Bartolomeo's manuscript, some contaminated, remain the most direct link.[172] Poggio and other humanists may have made corrections and conjectures as they worked from their exemplar. Stangl's apparatus is not always easy to decipher, so in places that have some bearing, I have

[169] Reynolds and Wilson (1991) 136–140; Zetzel (2018) 259.

[170] Schmiedeberg (1905) 30–35 suggests that the commentary was a compilation of scholia.

[171] Lemmata in several sections of the speech are out of order; e.g. *cuius ego causa laboro* (§23) immediately precedes *te ipsum ulciscantur* (§22), which is in turn followed by *a pueris nobilibus* (§24), etc. The first few lines of Stangl's apparatus, p. 192, note the transpositions.

[172] See Reeve on Asconius in Reynolds (1983) 24–25 and Welsh (2017) for a discussion of the textual tradition. Welsh has argued that the manuscript completed by Sozomeno of Pistoia on 23 July 1417 (Forteguerriana, A. 37) was copied from Bartolomeo and not a direct copy of the one in St Gall as was long thought to be the case.

checked the reading in three MSS: Madrid B.N. 8514, Florence Laur. Plut. 54.5, and Paris Lat. 7833.[173]

Meanwhile, the Scholia Gronoviana also present a short commentary on the *Diu. Caec.* completed by Scholiast B, who was inferior to Scholiast A and drew largely, though not entirely, from pseudo-Asconius.[174] From Stangl's reckoning, he could be dated no earlier than 600 CE. Stangl remarks of Scholiast B, 'He was clearly a man living in a barbaric age that had lost touch with the basic essentials of Roman speech.'[175] He continues:

> His antiquarian comments, and even more so, his historical ones – devoid as they are of full names, clear facts, definite locations, and exact dates unless they are provided in the speech itself – are of no value. Moreover, what is left [to do] for the explanation of individual passages is so much, but at the same time so little, that an engaged reader reaches the end of his journey tired and confused without having been given any 'refreshment' or enlightenment.[176]

Other quotations from the *Diu. Caec.* are given in Quintilian, Gellius, and other Latin rhetoricians such as Victorinus and Grillius. For these sources, I refer to the editions (and apparatus) of:

K. Barwick, ed. (1964) *Flavii Sosipatri Charisii Artis Grammaticae Libri V.*

S. Brandt, ed. (1897) *L. Caeli Firmiani Lactanti Opera Omnia.*

[173] Madrid B.N. 8514 is Poggio's copy; the commentary on the *Diuinatio* is found on 43v–49r. The others are thought to be descendants of Bartolomeo's now lost copy.

[174] Stangl (1884).

[175] Stangl (1884) 15. [Der Mann lebte eben in einer Barbarei, der die Elemente römischer Rede abhanden gekommen waren.] On his style and merit (both lacking), see *ibid.* 15–20.

[176] Stangl (1884) 15. [Die antiquarischen Anmerkungen, noch mehr aber die historischen, welche volle Namen, klare Thatsachen, sichere Oertlichkeiten, bestimmte Daten, soweit sie in der einschlägigen Rede selbst nicht wiederholt ausgesprochen sind, gar nicht kennen, entbehren jeglichen Wertes. Was nach all dem noch erübrigt für die sachliche Erklärung der einzelnen Stellen, ist recht viel; dabei aber zugleich so herzlich wenig, dass der kluge Leser am Ende seiner Bahn nur müde und verwirrt ankommt, ohne jede, aber auch jede Erfrischung und Aufklärung.]

K. Halm, ed. (1863) *Rhetores Latini Minores.* [*RLM*]
A. Holder, ed. (1894) *Scholia Antiqua in Q. Horatium Flaccum.* Volume 1.
L. Holford-Strevens, ed. (2020) *Auli Gelli Noctes Atticae.* Volumes 1–2.
A. Ippolito, ed. (2006) *Marius Victorinus Explanationes in Ciceronis Rhetoricam.*
R. Jakobi, ed. (2002) *Grillius Commentum in Ciceronis Rhetorica.*
H. Keil, ed. (1822–1894) *Grammatici Latini.* Volumes 1–7. [*GLK*]
W. Lindsay, ed. (1903) *Nonii Marcelli de Conpendiosa Doctrina Libros XX.* Volumes 1–3.
(1911) *Isidori Hispalensis Episcopi Etymologiarum siue Originum Libri XX.* Volumes 1–2.
O. Seeck, ed. (1883) *Q. Aurelii Symmachi Quae Supersunt.*
T. Stangl, ed. (1912) *Ciceronis Orationum Scholiastae.*
G. Thilo, ed. (1881) *Seruii Grammatici Qui Feruntur in Vergilii Carmina Commentarii.* Volumes 1–2.
P. Wessner, ed. (1902) *Aeli Donati Quod Fertur Commentum Terenti.* Volumes 1–3.
J. Willis, ed. (1983) *Martianus Capella.*
M. Winterbottom, ed. (1970) *M. Fabi Quintiliani Institutionis Oratoriae Libri Duodecim.* Volumes 1–2.

Of the modern editions of the *Diuinatio*, Peterson's *Oxford Classical Text* is somewhat misleading. As will be noted throughout, he did not always report the incorrect readings and omissions of the French family, and his apparatus has created an undue prejudice against the MSS of the Italian family. Even so, many of his conjectures are good, and further analysis has confirmed his faith in *D.* Thomas' apparatus is lean but highlights the most important variants and is moreover generally reliable. Zumpt did not note every major variant but when editorial intervention beckoned, he explained his choices thoroughly. Jordan followed in his wake, and his edition gives the most complete apparatus, though, one might argue, to a fault.

The Presentation of the Text

In an attempt to keep the apparatus lean while still giving a rather full report of meaningful variants within the French tradition and readings of *P* and *M*, the apparatus is negative wherever clarity allows. The reader may infer *ex silentio* the readings of *γ*, *P*, and *M*. Readings from the remaining MSS are only cited as conjectures.

Other compendia have been employed. If a manuscript has been corrected, I have attempted to distinguish a correction in the first hand from one in a second or third. A first-hand correction is noted with superscript *pc* (*post correctionem*), with the original reading marked with *ac* (*ante correctionem*). When other hands have come into play, numerical superscripts have been used, such as P^1 for the original text and P^2 for second-hand corrections. Supralineal and marginal corrections are further indicated by abbreviations, *sl* and *mg* respectively.

Variations in spelling are not usually recorded in the apparatus. Cicero himself would probably have varied spellings, so for the sake of clarity and ease of reference, the spelling has been standardized. As for *hic* and *is*, which are frequently confused in medieval manuscripts, especially when they are in the dative or ablative plural,[177] context and convention have been the guide.[178]

Arabic numerals in the left margin indicate the traditional sections (§§1–73) originally devised by Alexander Scot in his 1588–1589 edition of Cicero. These are the most common method of reference to the works of Cicero in modern scholarship, and the ones used in this volume throughout. The longer chapters, introduced by Janus Gruter in his 1618 edition of Cicero, are demarcated by Roman numerals (I–XXII) in the same margin.[179]

The Title of the Speech

None of the ancient sources refer to our speech by the title now in common use. Cicero only makes one oblique reference to the speech; see *Orator* 103 *quod igitur in Accusationis septem libris*

[177] See Ziegel (1897).
[178] K-St. 1.619–621.
[179] For the history of these methods of numeration, see Glucker (1984).

non reperitur genus, quod in Habiti, quod in Cornelii, quod in plurimis nostris defensionibus? The convention in most manuscripts of authority – and a convention often confounding for librarians and scholars – is to refer to the speech against Caecilius simply as the first speech *in Verrem.*[180] Some members of the *deteriores* give a title that includes the phrase *de accusatore constituendo,* following references in Gellius[181] and Quintilian[182] rather than any ancient title. At the end of the speech, many MSS have nothing, though the *explicit* in *P* refers to *de accusatore,* while *E* and *N* label the preceding speech as *de accusatione.*

Though I have fallen back on tradition in accepting the modern title *Diuinatio in Caecilium,* the appellation is somewhat misleading. As will be shown throughout the commentary, a *diuinatio* would normally be directed at presenting one's grievances against the accused rather than levelling such a sustained attack against the other would-be accuser(s).[183] The overtly combative nature of this speech is untypical of the genre, and if other *diuinationes* were published by other orators, they would undoubtedly have formed part of the corpus of the speeches in the accusation proper. That readers have so quickly labelled this speech as one *against Caecilius* rather than *against Verres* speaks more to Cicero's unique approach to securing his post as lead prosecutor than to any ancient convention.[184]

[180] See the apparatus on the title page. Other catalogues confuse it with *De diuinatione.*

[181] Gel. 4.9.7 *in oratione de accusatore constituendo*; 13.25.9 *in libro … qui de constituendo accusatore est.*

[182] Quint. *Inst.* 7.4.33 *de accusatore constituendo, quae iudicia diuinationes uocantur*; 11.1.20 *contra Q. Caecilium de accusatore in Verrem constituendo*; 9.2.17 *contra Q. Caecilium.*

[183] See Introduction §IV.

[184] Horsfall (1981) 104 may oversimplify the issue: 'Daly [(1943)] is right to suppose that [an oration] had no formal title at the moment of delivery; but one existed, ready to hand, in the name of the motion or of the individual attacked or supported, and the ancient historians of oratory had no problems of nomenclature.'

TEXT

SIGLA CODICUM

FAMILIA GALLICA

E	Escorialensis R.I.2, s. xiv
t	Thurgovianus Y 227, s. xv
D	Parisinus 7823, s. xv ineuntis
G	Guelferbytanus Weissenburgensis 41, s. xv
N	Parisinus 16226, s. xiv/xv
H	Parisinus 16674, s. xiv/xv

FAMILIA ITALICA

P	Parisinus 7776, s. xi
M	Mutinensis Lat. 328, c. 1400
F	Laurentianus Strozzianus 44, c. 1405
v	Sangallensis Vadianus 314, c. 1415
O	Laurentianus Conv. Sopp. 79, s. xiv/xv
a	Ambrosianus B 121 sup., s. xv ineuntis
l	Laurentianus Plut. 48.27, c. 1410–1418
b	Bononiensis 2232, anni 1419
r	Florentinus Riccardianus 499, c. 1425–1427

COMPENDIA

ω	Fons codicum
γ	Consensus codicum EtDGNH
ς	Consensus codicum albr

FONTES CETERI

Π	Mancuniensis P.Ryl. III 477, s. v (continens §§33–37, 44–46)
Ps-Asc.	Pseudo-Asconius; recensuit Th. Stangl
Schol. Gron.	Scholia Gronoviana B; recensuit Th. Stangl

M. Tulli Ciceronis
DIVINATIO IN Q. CAECILIVM

I 1 Si quis uestrum, iudices, aut eorum qui adsunt, forte miratur me, qui tot annos in causis iudiciisque publicis ita sim uersatus ut defenderim multos, laeserim neminem, subito nunc mutata uoluntate ad accusandum descendere, is, si mei consili causam rationemque cognouerit, una et id quod facio probabit et in hac causa profecto neminem praeponendum mihi esse actorem putabit.

2 Cum quaestor in Sicilia fuissem, iudices, itaque ex ea prouincia decessissem ut Siculis omnibus iucundam diuturnamque memoriam quaesturae nominisque mei relinquerem, factum est uti cum summum in ueteribus patronis multis, tum non nullum etiam in me praesidium suis fortunis constitutum esse arbitrarentur. Quare nunc populati atque uexati cuncti ad me publice saepe uenerunt, ut suarum fortunarum omnium causam

M. Tullii Necronis (*sic*) in C. Verrem liber primus *E* : Marci Tullii Ciceronis in G. Verrem *t*^{2mg}: Orationes quaedam Tullii Ciceronis Inuectiuae dictae Verrinae. Prima aduersum Caecilium oratorem *D*^{g} *in tabula*: *deerat uel periit tit. in D* : M. T. Ciceronis In C. Verrem Liber Primus *N* : M. Tulli Ciceronis In C. Verrem Liber I *P* : Marci Tulii Ciceronis Inuectiuarum contra Gaium Verrem liber *M* : *om. tH*

1 1–6 *Priscianus 18.92, 102 (GLK 3.249.2–5, 254.4–255.2)* 1 *Diomedes (GLK 1.468.8–9)* 1–2 *Priscianus Inst. 18.87 (GLK 3.246.6–7) Pompeius (GLK 5.133.18–19) et Isidorus Etym. 2.21.27* 1–4 *Quintilianus Inst. 4.1.49* Cicero dicit scire se mirari quosdam quod is qui per tot annos defenderit multos, laeserit neminem, ad accusandum Verrem descenderit. *cf. Inst. 9.2.17. cf. Victor RLM 422.29–30* 2 *Grillius 1.4 (Jakobi 31.44)* 2–3 *Victorinus 1.1 (Ippolito 9.42–43) Ps-Asconius 99–100 (Stangl 186.19–22)* Hoc toto capite soloecismi species continetur, nisi addas ‘et’ aut ‘idem’, ut sit: ‘et nunc subito mutata uoluntate ad accusandum descenderim’, quare multi non ‘descenderim’ 4–5 legunt, sed ‘descendere’. 4–5 *Grillius 1.2 (Jakobi 17.27)* 5 *Probus De cath. (GLK 4.42.30) et Sacerdos (GLK 6.495.13–14)* causamque cognovit 6–7 *Diomedes (GLK 1.470.5)* **2** 1–2 *Grillius 1.22 (Jakobi 94.16).* 1–6 *Martianus Capella 503 (Willis 172.24–173.3)*

1 1 qui adsunt *DNHGPM Ps-Asc. 100 (Stangl 186.23)* : qui horum tempore qui sunt adsunt *E*^{1} miratur *F*^{2}*υς Prisc.* : mirantur ω *Isid.* 2 sim ita *P* 3 defenderim *M Prisc.* : defenderem γ*P* 4 descendere *M*^{2}*F*^{2}*ab* : descenderim γ*PM*^{1}*Ovlr* consili *om.* γ 6 in hanc causam *PM* mihi esse praeponendum *M* **2** 2 discessissem γ 4 tum] tamen *M* 6 quare *DGH* : quod *EN* : qui *PM*^{2} *in ras.* 7 fortunarum suarum *D*^{ac}*G*

defensionemque susciperem. Me saepe esse pollicitum saepe ostendisse dicebant, si quod tempus accidisset quo tempore aliquid a me requirerent, commodis eorum me non defuturum.
3 Venisse tempus aiebant non iam ut commoda sua sed ut uitam salutemque totius prouinciae defenderem; sese iam ne deos quidem in suis urbibus ad quos confugerent habere, quod eorum simulacra sanctissima C. Verres ex delubris religiosissimis sustulisset; quas res luxuries in flagitiis, crudelitas in suppliciis, auaritia in rapinis, superbia in contumeliis efficere potuisset, eas omnes sese hoc uno praetore per triennium pertulisse; rogare et orare ne illos supplices aspernarer quos me incolumi nemini supplices esse oporteret.

II 4 Tuli grauiter et acerbe, iudices, in eum me locum adduci ut aut eos homines spes falleret qui opem a me atque auxilium petissent, aut ego, qui me ad defendendos homines ab ineunte adulescentia dedissem, tempore atque officio coactus ad accusandum traducerer. Dicebam habere eos actorem Q. Caecilium, qui praesertim quaestor in eadem prouincia post me quaestorem fuisset. Quo ego adiumento sperabam hanc a me posse molestiam demoueri, id mihi erat aduersarium maxime; nam illi multo mihi hoc facilius remisissent si istum non nossent,
5 aut si iste apud eos quaestor non fuisset. Adductus sum, iudices, officio, fide, misericordia, multorum bonorum exemplo, uetere consuetudine institutoque maiorum, ut onus hoc laboris atque offici non ex meo sed ex meorum necessariorum tempore mihi suscipiendum putarem.

3 3–4 *Servius A. 1.447 (Thilo 1.146.9–10)* 2–5 *Lactantius Div. Inst. 2.4.31* 5–6 *Grillius 1.22 (Jakobi 96.53–57)* 7–8 *Donatus Ter. Ad. 472* *Nonius Marcellus 4 s.u. ora re et rogare (360.37M, 572L ; 383.3M, 611L)* **4** 1 *Nonius Marcellus 4 s.u. tollere (407.21M, 655L)* 3–5 *Arusianus Messius (GLK 7.513.24–26)* 5–6 *Quintilianus Inst. 9.2.59.*

2 8 esse *om. P* saepe[2] *om. M* 10 non me $D^{ac}G$ **3** 1 sua *et* ut *om. P* 3 in suis urbibus *om. Servius* 3 quod deorum *Peterson* : quo deorum *B. L. Harl. 2687* 8 illis P^1 : eos *Non. Marc* 9 isse γ (esse *G*) **4** 3–4 ab ineunte *om. Arus. Mess.* 5 habere eos *PM Quint.* : eos habere γ 6 quaestor *om. G* eadem *PM* : sua γ : Sicilia *Müller* : illa *Eberhard* post me quaestorem *om.* γ 8 molestiam posse *M* demoueri *PM* : di- γ id] idem id γ **5** 2 uetere *Ps-Asc. 102 (Stangl 188.16)* : ueteri ω 3 consuetudine <more> institutoque *Schol. Gron. (Stangl 325.5)* hoc] huius *DGO* 4 non <tamen> ex meo *Ps-Asc. 102 (Stangl 188.18)*

Quo in negotio tamen illa me res, iudices, consolatur, quod haec quae uidetur esse accusatio mea non potius accusatio quam defensio est existimanda. Defendo enim multos mortales, multas ciuitates, prouinciam Siciliam totam; quam ob rem, si mihi unus est accusandus, prope modum manere in instituto meo uideor et non omnino a defendendis hominibus subleuandis-
6 que discedere. Quodsi hanc causam tam idoneam, tam illustrem, tam grauem non haberem, si aut hoc a me Siculi non petissent aut mihi cum Siculis causa tantae necessitudinis non intercederet, et hoc quod facio me rei publicae causa facere profiterer, ut homo singulari cupiditate, audacia, scelere praeditus, cuius furta atque flagitia non in Sicilia solum sed in Achaia, Asia, Cilicia, Pamphylia, Romae denique ante oculos omnium maxima turpissimaque nossemus, me agente in iudicium uocaretur, quis tandem esset qui meum factum aut consilium posset
III 7 reprehendere? Quid est, pro deum hominumque fidem, in quo ego rei publicae plus hoc tempore prodesse possim? Quid est quod aut populo Romano gratius esse debeat, aut sociis exterisque nationibus optatius esse possit, aut saluti fortunisque omnium magis accommodatum sit? Populatae, uexatae, funditus euersae prouinciae, socii stipendiariique populi Romani afflicti,
8 miseri, iam non salutis spem sed solacium exiti quaerunt. Qui iudicia manere apud ordinem senatorium uolunt queruntur accusatores se idoneos non habere. Qui accusare possunt iudiciorum seueritatem desiderant. Populus Romanus interea, tametsi multis incommodis difficultatibusque affectus est, tamen nihil aeque in re publica atque illam ueterem iudiciorum uim et

5 7–8 *Victorinus 1.28 (Ippolito 133.223–224)* **6** 1–2 *Grillius 1.20 (Jakobi 87.25–28)* **7** 5–6 *Pompeius (GLK 7.233.8–9)* **8** 1–2 *Nonius Marcellus 4 s.u. manere (349.22M, 553L)* 1–4 *[Rufinianus] Schem. Dian. 45 (RLM 76.24–27)*

5 6 me] meus *uel* mens *NH* : *om. G* 7 haec] res γ mea] alia γ non tam haec *Victor.* 9 Siciliam *secl. Klotz* si] quia γ accusandum *NE^1 ut uid.* 11 uideor] uideo me γ **6** 1 idoneam] honestam *Grill.* 2 aut hoc] autem *Grill.* me *om. M* 3 aut *om. M* **7** 5 uexataeque *ENHG D^1* **8** 1 solacium exitii *D^{pc}* : exitii solacium *PM Schol. Gron. (Stangl 325.34)* : solac. *uel* consolac. exitu γ 3 possint *Schol. Gron. (Stangl 326.5)* 4 tametsi] tamquam si *E* 5 tamen] tantum *E^{1}tN et fortasse H* nihil] in hoc *E^{1}tNHG* 6 aeque] atque *E^{1}tNHG et fortasse D^1 in ras.*

grauitatem requirit. Iudiciorum desiderio tribunicia potestas
efflagitata est, iudiciorum leuitate ordo quoque alius ad res
iudicandas postulatur, iudicum culpa atque dedecore etiam
censorium nomen, quod asperius antea populo uideri solebat,
9 id nunc poscitur, id iam populare et plausibile factum est. In hac
libidine hominum nocentissimorum, in populi Romani quotid-
iana querimonia, iudiciorum infamia, totius ordinis offensione,
cum hoc unum his tot incommodis remedium esse arbitrarer,
ut homines idonei atque integri causam rei publicae legumque
susciperent, fateor me salutis omnium causa ad eam partem
accessisse rei publicae subleuandae quae maxime laboraret.

10 Nunc quoniam quibus rebus adductus ad causam accesserim
demonstraui, dicendum necessario est de contentione nostra, ut
in constituendo accusatore quid sequi possitis habeatis. Ego sic
intelligo, iudices, cum de pecuniis repetundis nomen cuiuspiam
deferatur, si certamen inter aliquos sit cui potissimum delatio
detur, haec duo in primis spectari oportere: quem maxime uelint
actorem esse ii quibus factae esse dicantur iniuriae et quem
IV 11 minime uelit is qui eas iniurias fecisse arguatur. In hac causa,
iudices, tametsi utrumque esse arbitror perspicuum, tamen de
utroque dicam, et de eo prius quod apud uos plurimum debet
ualere, hoc est de uoluntate eorum quibus iniuriae factae sunt;
quorum causa iudicium de pecuniis repetundis est constitutum.

Siciliam prouinciam C. Verres per triennium depopulatus
esse, Siculorum ciuitates uastasse, domos exinanisse, fana spo-
liasse dicitur. Adsunt, queruntur Siculi uniuersi; ad meam
fidem, quam habent spectatam iam et cognitam, confugiunt;

9 7 *Probus De cath. (GLK 4.42.25–26) et Sacerdos (GLK 6.495.9)* **10** 3–8 *Victorinus 1.22 (Ippolito 99.59–61)* Ego sic intellego, cum de pecuniis repetundis quaestio sit, si nomen cuiuspiam deferatur, haec duo in primis spectari oportere, quem maxime actorem uelint ii qui eas iniurias passi sint, et quem minime uelit is qui eas iniurias fecisse arguatur. **11** 6–8 *Gellius 13.25.10*

8 7 uim et grauitatem requirit iudiciorum *scripsi* : uim grauitatemque requirit iud. MP^{2sl} : grauitatem req. iud. *Schol. Gron. (Stangl 326.11)* : itaque $E^{1}t$: *om.* $NHDGP^{1}$: auctoritatem requirit quorum *Shackleton Bailey* 11 et *γPO* : atque *M* **9** 4 his] ius $EDN^{1}HG$ 7 subleuandam *Vrsinus fort. recte* **10** 1 accesserim *om.* P^{1} 7 dicentur M^{1} 8 minime] maxime *γ* uelit is] uelint P^{1} **11** 3 nos *HG* 6 depopulatum M^{ac} 9 et diu cognitam $P^{2}M$

auxilium sibi per me a uobis atque a populi Romani legibus petunt; me defensorem calamitatum suarum, me ultorem iniuriarum, me cognitorem iuris sui, me actorem causae totius esse uol-
12 uerunt. Vtrum, Q. Caecili, hoc dices, me non Siculorum rogatu ad causam accedere? an optimorum fidelissimorumque sociorum uoluntatem apud hos grauem esse non oportere? Si id audebis dicere, quod C. Verres, cui te inimicum esse simulas, maxime existimari uult, Siculos hoc a me non petisse, primum causam inimici tui subleuabis, de quo non praeiudicium sed plane iudicium iam factum putatur, quod ita percrebruit, Siculos omnis
13 actorem suae causae contra illius iniurias quaesisse. Hoc si tu, inimicus eius, factum negabis, quod ipse, cui maxime haec res obstat, negare non audet, uideto ne nimium familiariter inimicitias exercere uideare. Deinde sunt testes uiri clarissimi nostrae ciuitatis, quos omnes a me nominari non est necesse: eos qui adsunt appellabo, quos, si mentirer, testes esse impudentiae meae minime uellem. Scit is qui est in consilio, C. Marcellus, scit is quem adesse uideo, Cn. Lentulus Marcellinus; quorum fide atque praesidio Siculi maxime utuntur, quod omnino Marcellorum
14 nomini tota illa prouincia adiuncta est. Hi sciunt hoc non modo a me petitum esse sed ita saepe et ita uehementer esse petitum ut aut causa mihi suscipienda fuerit aut officium necessitudinis repudiandum. Sed quid ego his testibus utor, quasi res dubia aut obscura sit? Adsunt homines ex tota prouincia nobilissimi, qui praesentes uos orant atque obsecrant, iudices, ut in actore causae suae deligendo uestrum iudicium ab suo iudicio ne discrepet. Omnium ciuitatum totius Siciliae legationes adsunt praeter duas ciuitates; quarum duarum si adessent, duo crimina uel maxima minuerentur quae cum his ciuitatibus C. Verri
15 communicata sunt. At enim cur a me potissimum hoc praesid-

14 10–11 *Probus De cath. (GLK 4.41.1) et Sacerdos (GLK 6.493.14–15)*

11 10 a uobis *om.* γ 12 esse *om. P* **12** 1 Caeli P^1 dices MO^{2sl} : dicis γPO^1 5 hoc *om.* P^1 7 percrebruit *M*: percrebuit *EDP* : percrebunt *G* : pererebunt *NH* omnis] homines *P* **13** 4 uidere P^{ac} 5 omnes] homines E^1tNHG 6 meae *om. M* 7 scit is *et* scit is] scitis *et* scitis γ 9 utuntur ω : nituntur *Manutius* 10 nomini $O^{2sl}v^2$ *fort.* : non est M^1 : nomine *cett.* **14** 3 aut^1 *om.* γ 4 dubia <sit> $ED^2N^{pc}H$: aut obscura sit *om.* N^{acmg} 6 uos] nos *ENH* 7 diligendo $ENGP^1$

ium petiuerunt? Si esset dubium petissent necne, dicerem cur petissent: nunc uero, cum id ita perspicuum sit ut oculis iudicare possitis, nescio cur hoc mihi detrimento esse debeat, si id
16 mihi obiciatur, me potissimum esse delectum. Verum id mihi non sumo, iudices, et hoc non modo in oratione mea non pono sed ne in opinione quidem cuiusquam relinquo, me omnibus patronis esse praepositum. Non ita est; sed unius cuiusque temporis, ualetudinis, facultatis ad agendum ducta ratio est. Mea fuit semper haec in hac re uoluntas et sententia, quemuis ut hoc mallem de iis qui essent idonei suscipere quam me, me ut mallem quam neminem.

V 17 Reliquum est iam ut illud quaeramus, cum hoc constet, Siculos a me petisse, ecquid hanc rem apud uos animosque uestros ualere oporteat, ecquid auctoritatis apud uos in suo iure repetundo socii populi Romani, supplices uestri, habere debeant. De quo quid ego plura commemorem? quasi uero dubium sit quin tota lex de pecuniis repetundis sociorum causa constituta
18 sit; nam ciuibus cum sunt ereptae pecuniae, ciuili fere actione et priuato iure repetuntur. Haec lex socialis est, hoc ius nationum exterarum est, hanc habent arcem, minus aliquanto nunc quidem munitam quam antea, uerum tamen si qua reliqua spes est quae sociorum animos consolari possit, ea tota in hac lege posita est; cuius legis non modo a populo Romano sed etiam ab ultimis nationibus iam pridem seueri custodes requiruntur.

19 Quis igitur est qui neget oportere eorum arbitratu lege agi quorum causa lex sit constituta? Sicilia tota si una uoce loqueretur, hoc diceret: 'Quod auri, quod argenti, quod ornamentorum in meis urbibus, sedibus, delubris fuit, quod in una

19 2–4 *Gellius 13.25.9*

15 2 petierunt *P* nec ne] a me praesidium nec ne *PM* 3 cum *om. P* id *om. γ fort. recte* 5 dilectum *γ* **16** 3 cuiusquam D^2*PM* : cuiusqui E^1*N* : cuiuspiam *G* : cuiusque *H* : D^1 *incert.* 6 haec *om. γP* **17** 2 ecquid *P* : et quid *M* : id quid *γ* 3 ecquid *P* : et quid *γM* apud nos … nostros … apud nos … nostri *EH G (sed* apud uos[2]*)* **18** 2 et *om. Ps-Asc. 106 (Stangl 191.11)* 4 munitam nunc quidem *M* 7 seuere *P* **19** 1 igitur est *PM* : ergo est *γ* : est igitur *vel* est ergo *fort. recte* lege *editio princeps* : legem ω 4 fuit *om. γ*

quaque re beneficio senatus populique Romani iuris habui, id
mihi tu, C. Verres, eripuisti atque abstulisti; quo nomine abs te
sestertium miliens ex lege repeto'. Si uniuersa, ut dixi, prouin-
cia loqui posset, hac uoce uteretur: quoniam id non poterat,
harum rerum actorem quem idoneum esse arbitrata est
20 ipsa delegit. In eius modi re quisquam tam impudens re-
perietur qui ad alienam causam, inuitis iis quorum nego-
VI tium est, accedere aut aspirare audeat? Si tibi, Q. Caecili,
hoc Siculi dicerent: 'Te non nouimus, nescimus qui sis, num-
quam te antea uidimus; sine nos per eum nostras fortunas de-
fendere cuius fides est nobis cognita', nonne id dicerent quod
cuiuis probare deberent? Nunc hoc dicunt, utrumque se nosse;
alterum se cupere defensorem esse fortunarum suarum, alter-
21 um plane nolle. Cur nolint, etiamsi taceant, satis dicunt; uerum
non tacent. Tamen iis inuitissimis te offeres? tamen in aliena
causa loquere? tamen eos defendes qui se ab omnibus deser-
tos potius quam abs te defensos esse malunt? tamen iis oper-
am tuam pollicebere qui te neque uelle sua causa nec, si cu-
pias, posse arbitrantur? Cur eorum spem exiguam reliquarum
fortunarum, quam habent in legis et in iudici seueritate posi-
tam, ui extorquere conaris? cur te interponis inuitissimis iis qui-
bus maxime lex consultum esse uult? cur, de quibus in prouincia
non optime es meritus, eos nunc plane fortunis omnibus conaris

19 5 *Charisius 1 (Barwick 181.14–19)* Senatuis ut fluctuis. 'ita genetiuum' inquit Plinius 'declinabant, ut G. Fannius Cos. contra G. Gracchum "senatuis consulta", senati Sallustius, "senati decretum fit" ut lauri; Cicero quoque [de] diuinatione in Verrem et pro Oppio II "senati"'. 10 *Probus De cath. (GLK 4.42.31) et Sacerdos (GLK 6.495.14)* **20** *Grillius 1.12 (Jakobi 58.37–41)* Nonne uidetur tibi Tullius ab honesto suadere, dum dicit: 'Caecili, non es rogatus ab Siculis. Turpe est accusari a quaestore praetorem?' Item suadet ab utili et necessario, ubi dicit: 'Non debuisti admittere praetorem ad pecuniam frumentarium, quamobrem etiam tibi periculosum est ut accuses'. Agit etiam a possibili, ut dicat infirmos oratores accusare non posse. 2–3 *Arusianus Messius (GLK 7.457.22–23)* 7 *Probus De cath. (GLK 4.42.31) et Sacerdos (6.495.15)* **21** 5–6 *Rufinianus 30 (RLM 45.32–33)*

19 5 populique] populi γ 7 milies (-ens *codd. aliquot*) ex *M Ps-Asc. 106 (Stangl 191.23)* : mille sex γ P^1 *ut uid.* : mille ex P^2 7 si] sed E^1NHG D^1 *incert.* **20** 2 inuitis ... est *om. Arus. Mess.* **21** 1 tacerent *M* : tacent *Ps-Asc. 107 (Stangl 192.3)* 2 offeres $G^{pcsl}O^{pc}$: offers *cett.* 3 defendis γO^1 se *om.* γ 5 polliceberis *E* sua causa γ *Rufin.* : suam causam *PM* 7 in iudici γ*PO* : iudici *M*

euertere? cur iis non modo persequendi iuris sui sed etiam de-
22 plorandae calamitatis adimis potestatem? Nam te actore quem
eorum adfuturum putas, quos intellegis non ut per te alium sed
ut per alium aliquem te ipsum ulciscantur laborare?
VII At enim solum id est, ut me Siculi maxime uelint: alterum
illud, credo, obscurum est, a quo Verres minime se accusari
uelit. Ecquis umquam tam palam de honore tam uehementer
de salute sua contendit quam ille atque illius amici ut ne haec
mihi delatio detur? Sunt multa quae Verres in me esse arbitra-
tur quae scit in te, Caecili, non esse; quae cuius modi in utro-
23 que nostrum sint, paulo post commemorabo; nunc tantum id
dicam quod tacitus tu mihi assentiare, nullam rem in me esse
quam ille contemnat, nullam in te quam pertimescat. Itaque
magnus ille defensor et amicus eius tibi suffragatur, me oppug-
nat; aperte ab iudicibus petit ut tu mihi anteponare, et ait hoc
se honeste sine ulla inuidia ac sine ulla offensione contendere.
'Non enim' inquit 'illud peto quod soleo, cum uehementius
contendi, impetrare: reus ut absoluatur non peto, sed ut potius
ab hoc quam ab illo accusetur, id peto. Da mihi hoc; concede
quod facile est, quod honestum, quod non inuidiosum; quod
cum dederis, sine ullo tuo periculo, sine infamia illud dederis,
24 ut is absoluatur cuius ego causa laboro'. Et ait idem, ut aliquis
metus adiunctus sit ad gratiam, certos esse in consilio quibus
ostendi tabellas uelit; id esse perfacile; non enim singulos
ferre sententias sed uniuersos constituere; ceratam uni cuique
tabellam dari cera legitima, non illa infami ac nefaria. Atque
is non tam propter Verrem laborat quam quod eum minime
res tota delectat; uidet enim, si a pueris nobilibus, quos adhuc

22 6–8 *Donatus Ter. An. 136* **23** 7–8 *Priscianus Inst. 18.253 (GLK 3.335.19–20)* 9–10 *Nonius Marcellus 4 s.u. concedere (269.24M, 412L)* 12 *Probus De cath. (GLK 4.41.21) et Sacerdos (GLK 6.494.2–3) et Arusianus Messius (GLK 7.490.13–14)*

22 1 adimis] annis $E^{ac}H$ *ut uid.* : aduius *N ut uid.* 3 alium aliquem] aliquem *PM* 6 ecquis $DNP^{2}M^{2}$: etquis *EGHF* $P^{1}M^{1}$ *ut uid.* 7 ut ne *PM Donatus*: ne γ 10 sint γ*PO* : sunt *M* **23** 4 eius *om.* P^{1} <Hortensius> suffragatur $P^{2}M$ 5 a iudicibus γ*O* 7 enim inquit *PM Ps-Asc. 107 (Stangl 192.14)* : *om.* γ *Prisc.* 8 ut *om. P* 9 ab hoc potius *PM* 12 is *PM Arus. Mess.* : *om.* γ **24** 1 aliquis] aliqui $D^{2}E^{1}NH$: cui *inuenitur in quisbusdam codicibus Ps-Asc. 108 (Stangl 193.1)* 2 metus *om.* M^{1} 3 perfacili $E^{1}NHD^{2}$ 4 sententiam *Ps-Asc. 108 (Stangl 193.7)* 5 tabellam *om.* P^{1}

elusit, si a quadruplatoribus, quos non sine causa contempsit semper ac pro nihilo putauit, accusandi uoluntas ad uiros fortes spectatosque homines translata sit, sese in iudiciis diutius dominari non posse.

III 25 Huic ego homini iam ante denuntio, si a me causam hanc uos agi uolueritis, rationem illi defendendi totam esse mutandam, et ita mutandam, ut meliore et honestiore condicione quam qua ipse uult uti imitetur homines eos quos ipse uidit amplissimos, L. Crassum et M. Antonium, qui nihil se arbitrabantur ad iudicia causasque amicorum praeter fidem et ingenium afferre oportere. Nihil erit quod me agente arbitretur iudicium sine magno multorum periculo posse corrumpi.

26 Ego in hoc iudicio mihi Siculorum causam receptam, populi Romani susceptam esse arbitror, ut mihi non unus modo improbus opprimendus sit, id quod Siculi petiuerunt, sed omnino omnis improbitas, id quod populus Romanus iam diu flagitat, exstinguenda atque delenda sit: in quo ego quid eniti aut quid efficere possim, malo in aliorum spe relinquere quam in oratione mea ponere.

27 Tu uero, Caecili, quid potes? Quo tempore aut qua in re non modo ceteris specimen aliquod dedisti sed tute tui periculum fecisti? In mentem tibi non uenit quid negoti sit causam publicam sustinere, uitam alterius totam explicare atque eam non modo in animis iudicum sed etiam in oculis

25 3–4 *Ps-Asc. 111 (Stangl 194.19)* meliore condicione sit. Id est meliorem condicionem habeat meliorque sit, quippe qui et possit et debeat honeste agere .... **26** 4–5 *Probus (GLK 4.40.30–41.7)* quod in primis est nostro tempore uitiosum, Tullius ille non dubitauit uerbo monosyllabo finire structuram, ut est ... ‘id quod populus Romanus iam flagitat, extincta atque deleta sint’. hae compositiones demutatae facient nostri temporis structuras sic, ... ex ditrochaeo et bacchio a longa ‘id quod populus Romanus iam diu efflagitat extincta sit atque deleta’. *Cf. Sacerdos (GLK 6.493.15–16).* **27** 2–3 *Incert. Auct. de Attrib. (RLM 306.35) et Donatus Ter. An. 565* 3–4 *Donatus Ter. Eu. 666* 4 *Nonius Marcellus 4 s.u. explicare (299.24M, 465L)*

24 10 sese *γPO* : se *M* 10 diutius *γPO*[1] : *om. M* **25** 3 et ita mutandam *Peterson*: et ita tamen mut. *P*[2]*MFab* : *om. γP*[1]: et ita causam mut. *Olrv* : et ita totam mut. *Richter* 4 uult uti *Peterson* : uult ut *E*[1]*NH* : uult *DG* : esse uult ut *PM* : esse uult *O* **26** 2 non *PM* : non nisi *EHDO*[1] : non modo nisi *N* : non tantum *G* modo *Peterson* : homo *ω* : *om. Ps-Asc. 111 (Stangl 195.3)* 3 omnino omnis *Peterson* : omnino *ω* : omnis *N*[2sl] *Ps-Asc. 111 (Stangl 195.4)* 5 ego *om. γ* **27** 2 specimen ceteris *M* sed] quando *Incert. Auct.* : aut *Donatus* 3 mente *γ* conspectuque omnium exponere, sociorum salutem, commoda prouinciarum, uim legum, grauitatem iudiciorum defendere?

IX Cognosce ex me, quoniam hoc primum tempus discendi nactus es, quam multa esse oporteat in eo qui alterum accuset; ex quibus si unum aliquod in te cognoueris, ego iam tibi ipse istuc quod expetis mea uoluntate concedam.

Primum integritatem atque innocentiam singularem; nihil est enim quod minus ferendum sit quam rationem ab altero
28 uitae reposcere eum qui non possit suae reddere. Hic ego de te plura non dicam: unum illud credo omnes animaduertere, te adhuc a nullis nisi ab Siculis potuisse cognosci; Siculos hoc dicere, cum eidem sint irati cui tu te inimicum esse dicis, sese tamen te actore ad iudicium non adfuturos. Quare negent ex me non audies: hos patere id suspicari quod necesse est. Illi quidem, ut est hominum genus nimis acutum et suspiciosum, non te ex Sicilia litteras in Verrem deportare uelle arbitrantur sed, quod isdem litteris illius praetura et tua quaestura consignata sit, asportare te uelle ex Sicilia litteras suspicantur.

29 Deinde accusatorem firmum uerumque esse oportet. Eum ego si te putem cupere esse, facile intelligo esse non posse. Nec ea dico, quae si dicam tamen infirmare non possis, te, antequam de Sicilia decesseris, in gratiam redisse cum Verre; Potamonem, scribam et familiarem tuum, retentum esse a Verre in prouincia, cum tu decederes; M. Caecilium, fratrem tuum, lectissimum atque ornatissimum adulescentem, non modo non adesse neque tecum tuas iniurias persequi sed esse cum Verre et cum illo familiarissime atque amicissime uiuere. Sunt et haec

27 11 *Probus De cath. (GLK 4.42.32) et Sacerdos (GLK 6.495.15–16)* **29** *Grillius 1.12 (Jakobi 58.37–41); cf. §20.*

27 8 tempus discedi P^{ac} : dicendi tempus GD^{ac} 9 oporteat $F^{pc}O\upsilon\varsigma$: oporteant γPMF^{ac} alterum *om.* $D^{1}G$ 10 aliquod *om.* γ ipse *om.* $P^{1}M$ istud *NHG* 11 mea] in alia $D^{1}NHG$ voluptate *Probus* 12 ignoscentiam $E^{1}D^{1}NH$ 13 ferundum $E^{1}D$ ab altero *om. Ps-Asc. 112 (Stangl 195.14)* **28** 2 animum aduertere *P* 3 te γPO : et *M* ab nullis *PM* ab Siculis $ED^{pc}PO^{1}$: a Siculis $D^{ac}NHGM$ *Ps-Asc. 112 (Stangl 195.15)* 8 arbitratur *ENH* 10 asportare *PM* : has portare γ **29** 1 eum] cum $E^{1}tH$ 4 te antequam de Sicilia decesseris *om.* P^{1} 6 Caecilium $O\varsigma$: C(a)elium γM : Coelium *P* 7 atque ornatissimum *om. Ps-Asc. 112 (Stangl 195.26)* 9 et *om. bis M*

et alia in te falsi accusatoris signa permulta, quibus ego nunc non utor: hoc dico, te, si maxime cupias, tamen uerum accusa-
30 torem esse non posse. Video enim permulta esse crimina quorum tibi societas cum Verre eius modi est, ut ea in accusando
X attingere non audeas. Queritur Sicilia tota C. Verrem ab aratoribus, cum frumentum sibi in cellam imperauisset, et cum esset tritici modius HS II, pro frumento in modios singulos duodenos sestertios exegisse. Magnum crimen, ingens pecunia, furtum impudens, iniuria non ferenda! Ego hoc uno crimine illum
31 condemnem necesse est. Tu, Caecili, quid facies? utrum hoc tantum crimen praetermittes an obicies? Si obicies, idne alteri crimini dabis quod eodem tempore in eadem prouincia tu ipse fecisti? audebis ita accusare alterum ut quominus tute condemnere recusare non possis? Sin praetermittes, qualis erit tua ista accusatio, quae domestici periculi metu certissimi et maximi criminis non modo susceptionem uerum etiam mentionem ipsam pertimescat?

32 Emptum est ex senatus consulto frumentum ab Siculis praetore Verre, pro quo frumento pecunia omnis soluta non est. Graue est hoc crimen in Verrem, graue me agente, te accusante nullum; eras enim tu quaestor, pecuniam publicam tu tractabas, ex qua, etiamsi cuperet praetor, tamen ne qua deductio fieret magna ex parte tua potestas erat. Huius quoque igitur criminis te accusante mentio nulla fiet: silebitur toto iudicio de maximis et notissimis illius furtis et iniuriis. Mihi crede, Caecili, non potest in accusando socios uere defendere is qui cum reo
33 criminum societate coniunctus est. Mancipes a ciuitatibus pro

30 4–6 *Nonius Marcellus 4 s.u. exigere (290.26M, 449L)* 6–7 *[Rufinianus] Schem. Dian. 43 (RLM 76.18–19)* **32** 2 *Nonius Marcellus 4 s.u. soluere (390.29M, 625L)* 9–10 *Iulius Victor (RLM 412.33–34)* non potest uerus accusator esse qui cum reo criminum societate coniungitur.

29 10 nunc non *om.* $D^{ac}G$ 11 si te *M* 12 non esse γ **30** 2 est] sit *Eberhard* 4 sibi *om. Ps-Asc. 113 (Stangl 196.4)* 6 sexstertiis P^{1} 7 uno] *lac.* D^{1} : illo *suppl.* D^{2mg} : ullo illo *G* 8 quidem *NH* **31** 5 condemnere M^{2} : condemnare γPM^{1} non *om. P* si *M* praetermittis γ*P* 6 tua ista $ED^{pc}PM$: ista tua $D^{ac}NHGO\upsilon\varsigma$ 7 susceptionem *Eberhard* : suspectionem $E^{1}t$: suspicionem *NHGPM* : sponsionem *Peterson* : subscriptionem *Madvig* : suspicionem… mentionem *transp. Pluygers* **32** 3 te accusante *bis* $E^{ac}N^{1}H$ 4 eras] eius $E^{1}N$ 7 te *om.* $P^{ac\,sl}$ tota *P* 9 uere defendere … Manci- *om. N* frumento pecuniam exegerunt. Quid? hoc Verre praetore factum est solum? Non, sed etiam quaestore Caecilio. Quid igitur? daturus es huic crimini quod et potuisti prohibere ne fieret et debuisti, an totum id relinques? Ergo id omnino Verres in iudicio suo non audiet quod, cum faciebat, quem ad modum defensurus esset non reperiebat.

XI Atque ego haec quae in medio posita sunt commemoro: sunt
alia magis occulta furta, quae ille, ut istius, credo, animos atque
impetus retardaret, benignissime cum quaestore suo communi-
34 cauit. Haec tu scis ad me esse delata; quae si uelim proferre,
facile omnes intelligent uobis inter uos non modo uoluntatem
fuisse coniunctam sed ne praedam quidem adhuc esse diuisam.
Quapropter si tibi indicium postulas dari quod tecum una fecerit, concedo, si id lege permittitur; sin autem de accusatione dicimus, concedas oportet iis qui nullo suo peccato impediuntur quo minus alterius peccata demonstrare possint.

35 Ac uide quantum interfuturum sit inter meam tuamque accusationem. Ego etiam quae tu sine Verre commisisti Verri crimini daturus sum, quod te non prohibuerit, cum summam ipse haberet potestatem: tu contra ne quae ille quidem fecit obicies, ne qua ex parte coniunctus cum eo reperiare.

Quid? illa, Caecili, contemnendane tibi uidentur esse, sine
quibus causa sustineri, praesertim tanta, nullo modo potest?
aliqua facultas agendi, aliqua dicendi consuetudo, aliqua in
36 foro, iudiciis, legibus aut ratio aut exercitatio? Intelligo quam
scopuloso difficilique in loco uerser; nam cum omnis arrogantia odiosa est, tum illa ingeni atque eloquentiae multo molestissima. Quam ob rem nihil dico de meo ingenio; neque est quod possim dicere, neque si esset dicerem. Aut enim id mihi satis est quod est de me opinionis, quicquid est, aut, si id parum est, ego maius id commemorando facere non possum.

35 2–3 *Nonius Marcellus 4 s.u. committere, dare (248.32M, 375L ; 279.5M, 429L)* **36** 5–6 *Donatus Ter. H. 463*

33 2 exegerunt *NPM* : exigerunt *E¹DHG* 4 crimen *O¹υ¹ς* 10 benignissime cum quaestore suo *ΠγP Ps-Asc. 114 (Stangl 197.4)* : cum quaestore suo benignissime *M* : ben. suo cum quaes. *P²* **34** 1 a me *γ* 4 indicium *Πr² Ps-Asc. 114 (Stangl 197.7)* : indictum *DNHG* : inditium *P* : iudicium *M E ut uid.* dari] fieri *Π* 5 si] sed *γ* 7 demonstrarent *Π ut uid.* **35** 1 at uide *Π D²mg* : deinde *E¹t* tuamque *ΠγP* : atque tuam *M* 6 essene si *Π¹* : esse e sine *Π²* **36** 2 scrupuloso *P²*

II 37 De te, Caecili – iam mehercule hoc extra hanc contentionem certamenque nostrum familiariter tecum loquar – tu ipse quem ad modum existimes uide etiam atque etiam, et tu te collige, et qui sis et quid facere possis considera. Putasne te posse de maximis acerbissimisque rebus, cum causam sociorum fortunasque prouinciae, ius populi Romani, grauitatem iudiciorum legumque susceperis, tot res tam graues, tam uarias uoce, me-
38 moria, consilio, ingenio sustinere? Putasne te posse quae C. Verres in quaestura, quae in legatione, quae in praetura, quae Romae, quae in Italia, quae in Achaia, Asia Pamphyliaque peccarit, ea, quem ad modum locis temporibusque diuisa sint, sic criminibus et oratione distinguere? Putasne te posse, id quod in eius modi reo maxime necessarium est, facere ut, quae ille libidinose, quae nefarie, quae crudeliter fecerit, ea aeque acerba et indigna uideantur esse his qui audient atque illis uisa sunt
39 qui senserunt? Magna sunt ea quae dico, mihi crede; noli haec contemnere. Dicenda, demonstranda, explicanda sunt omnia, causa non solum exponenda sed etiam grauiter copioseque agenda est; perficiendum est, si quid agere aut proficere uis, ut homines te non solum audiant uerum etiam libenter studioseque audiant. In quo si te multum natura adiuuaret, si optimis a pueritia disciplinis atque artibus studuisses et in his elaborasses, si litteras Graecas Athenis non Lilybaei, Latinas Romae non in Sicilia didicisses, tamen esset magnum tantam causam, tam exspectatam, et diligentia consequi et memoria complecti et oratione expromere et uoce ac uiribus sustinere.

40 Fortasse dices: ‘Quid ergo? haec in te sunt omnia?’ Vtinam quidem essent! uerum tamen ut esse possent magno studio mihi

37 1–2 *Rufinianus 10 (RLM 41.9–11)* 8 *Probus De cath. (GLK 4.42.33) et Sacerdos (GLK 6.495.16)* **39** 1–2 *Donatus Ter. Ad. 101* 6–7 *Grillius 1.1 (Jakobi 11. 56–60)* 8–9 *Symmachus Orat. 1–2* (Seeck 318.16–17) **40** *Quintilianus Inst. 11.1.20*

37 1 hoc *om. Rufin. 10* 3 et tu *secl. Eberhard* 4 quis sis γ consideram *NH ut uid.* 6 grauitatemque γ iudiciorum *Shackleton Bailey* : iudici 7 susceperis *M* : susciperes γP^1 : susciperis P^2 : suscipis *Klotz* res *om.* γ : *ante* tot *Klotz* **38** 3 in Italia] Italia *M* 5 te *suppl. Thomas* : *om.* ω quod <uel> *N* **39** 1 haec *PM Donatus* : hoc γO^1 4 proficere γPM^1O *fort. a.c.* : perficere *cett.* 7 laborasses *P* 11 expromere γPO^1 : exponere *M* : exprimere *Halm* ac uiribus γP^2 : hac uiribus P^1 : et uiribus *MG* a pueritia est elaboratum. Quodsi ego haec propter magnitudinem rerum ac difficultatem assequi non potui, qui in omni uita nihil aliud egi, quam longe tu te ab his rebus abesse arbitrare, quas non modo antea numquam cogitasti, sed ne nunc quidem,

XIII 41 cum in eas ingrederis, quae et quantae sint suspicari potes? Ego, qui sicut omnes sciunt in foro iudiciisque ita uerser ut eiusdem aetatis aut nemo aut pauci plures causas defenderint, et qui omne tempus quod liberum mihi ab amicorum negotiis datur in his studiis laboribusque consumam, quo paratior ad usum forensem promptiorque esse possim, tamen ita mihi deos uelim propitios ut, cum illius temporis mihi uenit in mentem quo die citato reo mihi dicendum sit, non solum commoueor animo sed

42 etiam toto corpore perhorresco. Iam nunc mente et cogitatione prospicio quae tum studia hominum, qui concursus futuri sint, quantam exspectationem magnitudo iudici sit allatura, quantam auditorum multitudinem infamia C. Verris concitatura, quantam denique audientiam orationi meae improbitas illius factura sit. Quae cum cogito, iam nunc timeo quidnam pro offensione hominum qui illi inimici infensique sunt et exspectatione om-

43 nium et magnitudine rerum dignum eloqui possim. Tu horum nihil metuis, nihil cogitas, nihil laboras: si quid ex uetere aliqua oratione, 'Iouem ego Optimum Maximum' aut 'Vellem, si fieri potuisset, iudices' aut aliquid eius modi ediscere potueris, praeclare te paratum in iudicium uenturum arbitraris.

41 3–5 *Victorinus 1.4 (Ippolito 32.106).* 6–7 *Donatus Ter. Ad. 681* ita uelim deos mihi propitios, ut cum illius temporis mihi uenit in mentem, *sed H.* 580 ita uelim deos mihi propitios... 9 *Quintilianus Inst. 11.1.44 Probus De cath. (GLK 4.42.33–43.1) et Sacerdos (GLK 6.495.17)* **43** 2–3 *Servius A. 7.259, 11.301 (Thilo 2.146.20–21, 515.9–10)* 3–4 *Victorinus 1.17 (Ippolito 83.123–124)*

41 2 in iudiciisque *PM* 3 defenderint *$O^2F^2r^2$* : defenderent *cett.* 4 tempus quod liberum *Sydow* : tempus quod ω : reliquum tempus quod *Victor.* 6 mihi deos *γP Ps-Asc. 115 (Stangl 198.4)* : deos mihi *M Donatus* 7 temporis mihi *γM Donatus* : mihi temporis *P* : *Priscianus habet* temp. m. *(GLK 3.355.12–3, 369.11–2) et* m. temp. *(188.5–8, 352.17–20) :* diei mihi *Ps-Asc. 115 (Stangl 198.4)* **42** 4 C. Verris infamia *M* 5 factura] futura *E^1HG* : futura uel factura *N* 6 cum *om.* *γ* **43** 2 nihil] in hoc *ter E^1* aliqua uetere *Servius* 4 posset *Victor.*

44 Ac si tibi nemo responsurus esset, tamen ipsam causam, ut ego arbitror, demonstrare non posses: nunc ne illud quidem cogitas, tibi cum homine disertissimo et ad dicendum paratissimo futurum esse certamen, quicum modo disserendum, modo altercandum, modo omni ratione pugnandum certandumque sit. Cuius ego ingenium ita laudo ut non pertimescam, ita probo ut me ab eo delectari facilius quam decipi putem posse.

XIV Numquam ille me opprimet consilio, numquam ullo artificio peruertet, numquam ingenio me suo labefactare atque infirmare conabitur; noui omnes hominis petitiones rationesque dicendi; saepe in isdem saepe in contrariis causis uersati sumus; ita contra me ille dicet, quamuis sit ingeniosus, ut non nullum

45 etiam de suo ingenio iudicium fieri arbitretur. Te uero, Caecili, quem ad modum sit elusurus, quam omni ratione iactaturus, uidere iam uideor; quotiens ille tibi potestatem optionemque facturus sit ut eligas utrum uelis – factum esse necne, uerum esse an falsum – utrum dixeris, id contra te futurum. Qui tibi aestus, qui error, quae tenebrae, di immortales, erunt, homini minime malo! Quid? cum accusationis tuae membra diuidere coeperit et in digitis suis singulas partes causae constituere? quid? cum unum quidque transigere, expedire, absoluere? Ipse profecto metuere incipies ne innocenti periculum facessieris.

46 Quid? cum commiserari, conqueri, et ex illius inuidia deonerare aliquid et in te traicere coeperit, commemorare quaestoris cum praetore necessitudinem constitutam, morem maiorum,

45 7–8 *Sacerdos (GLK 6.460.12–14)* ut Cicero in Verrinis quid? cum accusationis tuae diuidere membra coeperit (non partiri, quia una accusatio est) et in digitis singulas partes constituerit; non diuisiones, quoniam multae res partiendae sunt post accusationem diuisam. 9–10 *Priscianus Inst. 46 (GLK 2.535.19–20)* ipse profecto metuere incipies, ne innocenti periculum facesseris; inuenitur tamen in quibusdam codicibus 'facessieris'.

44 1 nemo tibi M^1 2 ne] nec *P* 4 quicum] cum quo $\Pi^{2sl}D^{sl}$: qui cum quo cum $E^{ac}NH$ 5 modo altercandum Π : *om. cett.* oratione *M* 7 me *om.* γ 8 numquam] numquid *ter* $D^{2mg}NG$: numquid … numquam … numquid E^1 : numquid *H primum tantum* numqui ullo *M* 9 me suo ΠED^2NHPM : suo me D^1GO^1 **45** 7 diuidere membra *Sacerdos* 8 suis *et* causae *om. Sacerdos* 9 quodque *M* 10 facessieris *P* : facesseris $\Pi\gamma M$ **46** 1 deonerare ΠM *Ps-Asc. 117 (Stangl 199.9)* : dehonerare D^1NEGP^2 : dehonorare D^{2sl} HP^1 3 praetore] populo Romano DE^1G constitutam *om.* Π morem $\Pi^2\omega$: more Π^1

sortis religionem? poterisne eius orationis subire inuidiam? Vide modo, etiam atque etiam considera. Mihi enim uidetur periculum fore ne ille non modo uerbis te obruat sed gestu ipso ac motu corporis praestringat aciem ingeni tui, teque ab institu-
47 tis tuis cogitationibusque abducat. Atque huiusce rei iudicium iam continuo uideo futurum. Si enim mihi hodie respondere ad haec quae dico potueris, si ab isto libro, quem tibi magister ludi nescioqui ex alienis orationibus compositum dedit, uerbo uno discesseris, posse te et illi quoque iudicio non deesse et causae atque officio tuo satis facere arbitrabor; sin mecum in hac prolusione nihil fueris, quem te in ipsa pugna cum acerrimo aduersario fore putemus?

XV Esto, ipse nihil est, nihil potest; at uenit paratus cum subscriptoribus exercitatis et disertis. Est tamen hoc aliquid, tametsi non est satis; omnibus enim rebus is qui princeps in agendo est ornatissimus et paratissimus esse debet. Verum tamen L. Appuleium esse uideo proximum subscriptorem, hominem
48 non aetate sed usu forensi atque exercitatione tironem. Deinde, ut opinor, habet Alienum, hunc tamen a subselliis; qui quid in dicendo posset numquam satis attendi, in clamando quidem uideo eum esse bene robustum atque exercitatum. In hoc spes tuae sunt omnes; hic, si tu eris actor constitutus, totum iudicium sustinebit. Ac ne is quidem tantum contendet in

46 4 *Ps-Asconius 117 (Stangl 199.11)* Pateris ne eius orationi subire? Traslatiue dixit ut magno ponderi subire. *Arusianus Messius (GLK 7.507.12)* subeo illi rei … Cic. in diuinatione poteris † eis oratione subire. *sed scripsit Keil in app.* poterisne eius orationi subire *Schol. in Cic. et Nonius, et sic scripserat Arusianus. Nonius Marcellus 4 s.u. subire (404.2M, 649L)* poterisne eius orationi subire? *Servius 9.369 (Thilo 2.343.21)* 'est locutio de Cicerone poterisne eius †oratione subire?' 7 *Grillius 1.9 (Jakobi 50.28–9).* **47** 3–4 *Nonius Marcellus 4 s.u. componere (257.27M, 391L)* 7–8 *Servius 12.106 (Thilo 2.585.26–27)* **48** 2 *Ps-Asconius 118 (Stangl 199.29–200.3)* Habet Alienum. Caecilius scilicet. 'Alienum' autem uolunt intelligi proprium nomen esse, quasi ab Allia, ut Virgilius: 'Quosque secans infaustum interluit Allia nomen'. Alii 'Alienum' non nomen proprium putant esse sed 'alienum' …. 6 *Probus De cath. (GLK 4.43.1) et Sacerdos (GLK 5.495.18)*

46 4 religione *Π* paterisne *Ps-Asc. 117 (Stangl 199.11)* orationi *Ps-Asc. 117 (Stangl 199.11) Non. Marcell. Arus.* **47** 4 nescioquis $D^{2mg}O^{2sl}$ 10 tamen si *γ* : *corr.* N^{2mg} 11 in omnibus *Ps-Asc. 118 (Stangl 199.25)* is *om. γ* **48** 3 possit *M* attendet *P1* 4 eum] ipsum *NHG* 5 omnes sunt $D^{1}G$ 6 iudicium *om. γ* sustinebit] continebit *P* at ne *M*

dicendo quantum potest, sed consulet laudi et existimatio-
ni tuae, et ex eo quod ipse potest in dicendo aliquantum re-
mittet, ut tu tamen aliquid esse uideare. Vt in actoribus Graecis
fieri uidemus, saepe illum qui est secundarum aut tertiarum
partium, cum possit aliquanto clarius dicere quam ipse primar-
um, multum summittere, ut ille princeps quam maxime ex-
cellat, sic faciet Alienus; tibi seruiet, tibi lenocinabitur, minus
49 aliquanto contendet quam potest. Iam hoc considerate, cuius
modi accusatores in tanto iudicio simus habituri, cum et ipse
Alienus ex ea facultate, si quam habet, aliquantum detracturus
sit, et Caecilius tum denique se aliquid futurum putet, si Alienus
minus uehemens fuerit et sibi primas in dicendo partes conces-
serit. Quartum quem sit habiturus non uideo, nisi quem forte
ex illo grege moratorum, qui subscriptionem sibi postularunt
50 cuicumque uos delationem dedissetis: ex quibus alienissimis
hominibus ita paratus uenis ut tibi hospes aliquis sit recipiendus.
Quibus ego non sum tantum honorem habiturus ut ad ea quae
dixerint certo loco aut singillatim uni cuique respondeam: sic
breuiter, quoniam non consulto sed casu in eorum mentionem
XVI incidi, quasi praeteriens satis faciam uniuersis. Tantane uobis in-
opia uideor esse amicorum ut mihi non ex his quos mecum ad-
duxerim sed de populo subscriptor addatur? uobis autem tanta
inopia reorum est ut mihi causam praeripere conemini potius
quam aliquos ad columnam Maeniam uestri ordinis reos reper-

48 9–11 *Porphyrio Epist. 1.18.14 (Holder 349.22–4)* Vel partis mimum tract(are) S(ecundas): Recte; secundarum enim partium actores omnia summisse agunt; Cic(ero): Vt in actoribus Graecis fieri uidemus, saepe illum, qui est secundarum ac terti<ar>um partium et cetera. *Donatus Ter. Ph. 27* **50** 8 *Probus De cath. (GLK 4.43.2) et Sacerdos (GLK 5.495.18–19)*

48 9 tamen] tantum *EN* in *om. P* Graecis] genis *uel sim.* $E^{1}NH$ 10 uidimus $O^{1}\varsigma$ 11 ipse] ille *Ps-Asc. 119 (Stangl 200.22)* **49** 4 Caelius $D^{ac}G$ 5 sibi $D^{2mg}r^{2}v^{2}$: tibi γPM 6 quartum γPO^{1} *Ps-Asc. 119 (Stangl 200.30)* : quarum *M* 7 moratorum P^{1} *Ps-Asc. 119 (Stangl 200.27)* : meatorum *DG* : meato $E^{1}t$: meator *NH* : mercatorum D^{2mg} *ut uid.* : oratorum *cett.* **50** 2 aliqui $E^{1}NHD^{2}$ 6 nobis $E^{1}NH\varsigma$ 8 nobis $E^{1}NH$ 9 rerum $E^{1}D^{ac}G$ est γPO : *om. M* 10 ad columnam *Ps-Asc. 120 (Stangl 201.15)* : a columna ω Maeniam *Ps-Asc. 120 (Stangl 201.15)* : maenia r^{2mg} : memia b^{2mg} : (a)enea *cett.* uestri] nostri $D^{ac}tHG$

51 iatis? 'Custodem' inquit 'Tullio me apponite'. Quid? mihi quam multis custodibus opus erit si te semel ad meas capsas admisero? qui non solum ne quid enunties sed etiam ne quid auferas custodiendus sis. Sed de isto 'custode' toto sic uobis breuissime respondebo, non esse hos talis uiros commissuros ut ad causam tantam a me susceptam, mihi creditam, quisquam subscriptor me inuito aspirare possit; etenim fides mea custodem repudiat, diligentia speculatorem reformidat.

52 Verum ut ad te, Caecili, redeam, quam multa te deficiant uides: quam multa sint in te quae reus nocens in accusatore suo cupiat esse, profecto iam intelligis. Quid ad haec dici potest? non enim quaero quid tu dicturus sis; uideo mihi non te sed hunc librum esse responsurum quem monitor tuus hic tenet; qui si te recte monere uolet, suadebit tibi ut hinc discedas neque mihi uerbum ullum respondeas. Quid enim dices? an id quod dictitas, iniuriam tibi fecisse Verrem? Arbitror; neque enim esset ueri simile, cum omnibus Siculis faceret iniuri-
53 as, te illi unum eximium cui consuleret fuisse. Sed ceteri Siculi ultorem suarum iniuriarum inuenerunt; tu dum tuas iniurias per te, id quod non potes, persequi conaris, id agis ut ceterorum quoque iniuriae sint impunitae atque inultae; et hoc te praeterit, non id solum spectari solere, qui debeat, sed etiam illud, qui possit ulcisci; in quo utrumque sit, eum superiorem esse, in quo alterutrum, in eo non quid is uelit sed quid facere possit
54 quaeri solere. Quodsi ei potissimum censes permitti oportere accusandi potestatem cui maximam C. Verres iniuriam fecerit, utrum tandem censes hos iudices grauius ferre oportere, te ab illo esse laesum, an prouinciam Siciliam esse uexatam ac perditam? Opinor, concedes multo hoc et esse grauius et ab omnibus ferri grauius oportere. Concede igitur ut tibi anteponatur in

51 2–3 *Probus De cath. (GLK 4.41.25), Sacerdos (GLK 5.494.6), et Martianus Capella 522 (Willis 182.6–7)* **52** 4–6 *Nonius Marcellus 4 s.u. tenet (412.2M, 663L)* **53** 2–3 *Donatus Ter. Ad. 163*

51 2 meam capsam *Probus* 5 non esse hos] nunquam *Ps-Asc. 121 (Stangl 202.3)* **52** 1 redeam Caecili *M* 3 haec] hoc γ*O* : *corr.* D^2 *ut uid.* 4 tu *om.* γ 7 respondeat … dictas P^{ac} 9 esset] est *l* **53** 7 alterum *M* **54** 3 hos] nos γ iudices] inde D^2*GNH* : *del. Eberhard* 4 esse *om.* γ*O* 5 concedis *M* et esse] esse *M* 6 fieri γ (*om.* D^1)

accusando prouincia; nam prouincia accusat cum is agit causam quem sibi illa defensorem sui iuris, ultorem iniuriarum, actorem causae totius adoptauit.

VII **55** At eam tibi C. Verres fecit iniuriam quae ceterorum quoque
animos posset alieno incommodo commouere? Minime.
Nam id quoque ad rem pertinere arbitror, qualis iniuria dica-
tur quae causa inimicitiarum proferatur. Cognoscite ex me;
nam iste eam profecto, nisi plane nihil sapit, numquam pro-
feret. Agonis quaedam est Lilybitana, liberta Veneris Erycinae,
quae mulier ante hunc quaestorem copiosa plane et locuples
fuit. Ab hac praefectus Antoni quidam symphoniacos seruos
abducebat per iniuriam, quibus se in classe uti uelle dicebat.
Tum illa, ut mos in Sicilia est omnium Veneriorum et eorum
qui a Venere se liberauerunt, ut praefecto illi religionem Ven-
56 eris nomine obiceret, dixit et se et sua Veneris esse. Vbi hoc
quaestori Caecilio, uiro optimo et homini aequissimo, nun-
tiatum est, uocari ad se Agonidem iubet; iudicium dat statim,
SI PARET EAM SE ET SVA VENERIS ESSE DIXISSE. Iudi-
cant recuperatores id quod necesse erat; neque enim erat cui-
quam dubium quin illa dixisset. Iste in possessionem bonorum
mulieris intrat, ipsam Veneri in seruitutem adiudicat; deinde
bona uendit, pecuniam redigit. Ita dum pauca mancipia Veneris
nomine Agonis ac religione retinere uult, fortunas omnes liber-
tatemque suam istius iniuria perdidit. Lilybaeum Verres uenit
postea; rem cognoscit, factum improbat, cogit quaestorem suum
pecuniam, quam ex Agonidis bonis redegisset, eam mulieri om-
57 nem annumerare et reddere. Est adhuc, id quod uos omnes
ammirari uideo, non Verres sed Q. Mucius. Quid enim facere

55 6 *Victorinus 1.19 (Ippolito 85.21)* **57** 1–2, 6–8 *Rufinianus De figuris 5 (RLM 39.24–28)* Διασυρμός. Haec figura fit, cum rem aliquam aut personam eleuamus, ut apud Tullium: 'Est adhuc, quod admirari uos uideo, non Verres, sed Quintus Mutius'. Et in eodem: 'Sed repente, tanquam epoto Circaeo, factus est Verres: redit ad se atque ad mores suos'.

55 2 possit *P* 6 quaedam est γ*PO* : est quaedam *M Victor.* 10 Venereorum *M* 12 nomine γ*P* : nomenque M^2 : nomen M^1 sua γ : omnia sua *PM* : sua omnia *O* **56** 2 antiquissimo E^1t : nequissimo G^{ac} 4 paret eam M^1P^{pc} : parretheam γ : parret eam P^{ac} : parent eam M^2 7 intrat EDO^{2sl} : mittat D^{sl} : uel mittat G^{ac} : intrat uel mittit *NH* : mittit *PM* 8 ita] illa *Klotz* : ita illa *Pluygers* 9 Agonidis γ 12 Agonidis *del. Halm et Pluygers fort. recte* **57** 1 id *om. Rufin.*

potuit elegantius ad hominum existimationem, aequius ad leuandam mulieris calamitatem, uehementius ad quaestoris libidinem coercendam? Summe haec omnia mihi uidentur esse laudanda. Sed [repente] e uestigio ex homine tamquam aliquo Circaeo poculo factus est Verres; redit ad se atque ad mores suos; nam ex illa pecunia magnam partem ad se uertit, mulieri reddidit quantulum uisum est.

XVIII 58 Hic tu si laesum te a Verre esse dices, patiar et concedam; si iniuriam tibi factam quereris, defendam et negabo; denique de iniuria quae tibi facta sit neminem nostrum grauiorem iudicem esse oportet quam te ipsum, cui facta dicitur. Si tu cum illo postea in gratiam redisti, si domi illius aliquotiens fuisti, si ille apud te postea cenauit, utrum te perfidiosum an praeuaricatorem existimari mauis? Video esse necesse alterutrum, sed ego tecum in eo non pugnabo quo minus utrum uelis eligas.

59 Quodsi ne iniuriae quidem quae tibi ab illo facta sit causa remanet, quid habes quod possis dicere quam ob rem non modo mihi sed cuiquam anteponare? nisi forte illud, quod dicturum te esse audio, quaestorem illius fuisse. Quae causa grauis esset si certares mecum uter nostrum illi amicior esse deberet: in contentione suscipiendarum inimicitiarum ridiculum est putare causam necessitudinis ad inferendum periculum iustam uideri

60 oportere. Etenim si plurimas a tuo praetore iniurias accepisses, tamen eas ferendo maiorem laudem quam ulciscendo mererere; cum uero nullum illius in uita rectius factum sit quam id quod

57 6–8 *Priscianus Inst. 18.301 (GLK 3.373.11)* ex hoc Romani 'e uestigio' dixerunt, uel quod stans aliquis in eodem uestigio facit – unde 'statim' quoque dicitur –, uel quantum tempus in uno est uestigio faciendo, quod est breuissimum. Cicero in I Verrinarum: 'e uestigio, quasi quodam Circaeo poculo, factus est Verres; redit ad se atque ad mores suos'. *Donatus Ter. Ad. 794 et H. 113*

57 3 ad <colligendam> hom. *Eberhard* : ad hom. exist. <conciliandam> *Peterson* 6 repente *seclusi* e uestigio ex homine *om. Rufin.* : e uestigio *habet Schol. Gron. sed secl. Halm* 7 aliquo] epoto *Rufin. sed Halm ad loc. 'uidetur Rufinianus* poculo Circaeo *scripsisse'* circaeo *PM Prisc. et Rufin.* : circe γ : circes *Ps-Asc. 122 (Stangl 202.26)* 8 auertit *Stephanus* : uerrit *Eberhard* **58** 1 esse *om. Ps-Asc. 123 (Stangl 203.5)* dicis P^{1} *Ps-Asc. 123 (Stangl 203.5)* 2 denique $\gamma P O^{1}$: deinde *M* **59** 1 quod si $\gamma P^{2} O^{1}$ *ut uid.* : quid? si $P^{1} M O^{2mg}$ 3 dicturum te] dicturum P^{ac} : te dicturum P^{pcsl} 5 amicitior γM **60** 2 eas] illas *O* merere *EHO* 3 nullum illius in uita] in illius uita nullum *EO* : nullum nullius illius u. *N* tu iniuriam appellas, hi statuent hanc causam, quam ne in alio quidem probarent, in te iustam ad necessitudinem uiolandam uideri? Qui si summam iniuriam ab illo accepisti, tamen, quoniam quaestor eius fuisti, non potes eum sine ulla uituperatione accusare; si uero non ulla tibi facta est iniuria, sine scelere eum accusare non potes. Quare cum incertum sit de iniuria, quemquam horum esse putas qui non malit te sine uituperatione quam cum scelere discedere?

XIX 61 Ac uide quid differat inter meam opinionem ac tuam. Tu, cum omnibus rebus inferior sis, hac una in re te mihi anteferri putas oportere, quod quaestor illius fueris: ego, si superior omnibus rebus esses, hanc unam ob causam te accusatorem repudiari putarem oportere. Sic enim a maioribus nostris accepimus, praetorem quaestori suo parentis loco esse oportere; nullam neque iustiorem neque grauiorem causam necessitudinis posse reperiri quam coniunctionem sortis, quam prouinciae,
62 quam offici, quam publici muneris societatem. Quam ob rem si iure eum posses accusare, tamen, cum is tibi parentis numero fuisset, id pie facere non posses; cum uero neque iniuriam acceperis et praetori tuo periculum crees, fatearis necesse est te illi iniustum impiumque bellum inferre conari. Etenim ista quaestura ad eam rem ualet, ut elaborandum tibi in ratione reddenda sit quam ob rem qui quaestor eius fueris accuses, non ut ob eam ipsam causam postulandum sit ut tibi potissimum accusatio detur. Neque fere umquam uenit in contentionem de
63 accusando qui quaestor fuisset quin repudiaretur. Itaque neque L. Pithioni in C. Seruilium nominis deferendi potestas est data, neque M. Aurelio Scauro in L. Flaccum, neque Cn. Pompeio

61 1 *Nonius Marcellus 4 s.u. differre (284.32M, 439L)*

60 6 -iuriam … 10 uituperatione *om. t* 8 sine scelere … de iniuria *om. N* 9 incertum *γP* : inceptum *M* : iam actum *Kayser* 10 esse horum *PM* **61** 1 at *D*[2mg] et tuam *EH* 4 omnibus *γ* : ceteris *PM* accusatorem *secl. Halm* 8 reperiri posse *P* 9 publici *γPO* : publicam *M* **62** 2 eum possis M : posses eum *γ* 6 ratione *D*[2]*OF*[2]*υς* : oratione *γPMF*[1] 7 qui] eum cui *r*[2mg] : cum cui *Ps-Asc. 123 (Stangl 203.12)* : cui *Halm* eius *om. Ps-Asc. 123 et del. Halm* **63** 2 Pithioni *Badian* : pithoni *DNHG* : pitioni *E* : pythoni *P* : philoni *M Peterson et alii* 3 neque] ne *E*[1]*tDNH* Cn.] Sn *E* : sine *NH* in T. Albucium; quorum nemo propter indignitatem repudiatus est, sed ne libido uiolandae necessitudinis auctoritate iudicum comprobaretur. Atque ille Cn. Pompeius ita cum C. Iulio contendit ut tu mecum; quaestor enim Albuci fuerat, ut tu Verris. Iulius hoc secum auctoritatis ad accusandum afferebat quod, ut hoc tempore nos ab Siculis, sic tum ille ab Sardis rogatus ad causam accesserat.

Semper haec causa plurimum ualuit, semper haec ratio accusandi fuit honestissima, pro sociis, pro salute prouinciae, pro exterarum nationum commodis inimicitias suscipere, ad periculum accedere, operam, studium, laborem interponere.
XX 64 Etenim si probabilis est eorum causa qui iniurias suas persequi uolunt (qua in re dolori suo, non rei publicae commodis seruiunt), quanto illa honestior causa est, quae non solum probabilis uideri sed etiam grata esse debet, nulla priuatim accepta iniuria sociorum atque amicorum populi Romani dolore atque iniuriis commoueri! Nuper cum in P. Gabinium uir fortissimus et innocentissimus L. Piso delationem nominis postularet, et contra Q. Caecilius peteret isque se ueteres inimicitias iam diu susceptas persequi diceret, cum auctoritas et dignitas Pisonis ualebat plurimum, tum illa erat causa iustissima, quod
65 eum sibi Achaei patronum adoptarant. Etenim cum lex ipsa de pecuniis repetundis sociorum atque amicorum populi Romani patrona sit, iniquum est non eum legis iudicique actorem idoneum maxime putari quem actorem causae suae socii defensoremque fortunarum suarum potissimum esse uoluerunt. An quod ad commemorandum est honestius, id ad probandum non multo uideri debet aequius? Vtra igitur est splendidior, utra illustrior commemoratio, 'Accusaui eum cui quaestor fueram, quicum me sors consuetudoque maiorum, quicum me deorum hominumque iudicium coniunxerat' an 'Accusaui rogatu sociorum atque amicorum, delectus sum ab uniuersa prouincia qui eius

64 6 *Probus De cath. (GLK 4.43.3) et Sacerdos (GLK 6.495.19–20)*

63 5 iudicium *E*[1]*D*[1]*NHG* 12 fuit *om. M* **64** 3 causa honestior *M*[1] est *om. M* 6 iniuria *Sacerdos* 9 et γ : ac *PM* 11 adoptarent *D*[1] **65** 1 etenim cum *PM Ps-Asc. 123 (Stangl 203.19)* : et inimicum γ 3 patrona γ*P* : patrata *M* 5 uoluerint *Klotz* 10 coniunxerant γ an *om. P* iura fortunasque defenderem'? Dubitare quisquam potest quin honestius sit eorum causa apud quos quaestor fueris quam eum cuius quaestor fueris accusare?

66 Clarissimi uiri nostrae ciuitatis temporibus optimis hoc sibi amplissimum pulcherrimumque ducebant, ab hospitibus clientibusque suis, ab exteris nationibus quae in amicitiam populi Romani dicionemque essent iniurias propulsare eorumque fortunas defendere. M. Catonem illum sapientem, clarissimum uirum et prudentissimum, cum multis graues inimicitias gessisse accepimus propter Hispanorum, apud quos consul fuerat,
67 iniurias. Nuper Cn. Domitium scimus M. Silano diem dixisse propter unius hominis Aegritomari, paterni amici atque hos-
XXI pitis, iniurias. Neque enim magis animos hominum nocentium res umquam ulla commouit quam haec maiorum consuetudo longo interuallo repetita ac relata, sociorum querimoniae delatae ad hominem non inertissimum, susceptae ab eo qui uidebatur eorum fortunas fide diligentiaque sua posse defen-
68 dere. Hoc timent homines, hoc laborant, hoc institui atque adeo institutum referri ac renouari moleste ferunt; putant fore ut, si paulatim haec consuetudo serpere ac prodire coeperit, per homines honestissimos uirosque fortissimos, non imperitos adulescentulos aut illius modi quadruplatores, leges iudicia-
69 que amministrentur. Cuius consuetudinis atque instituti patres maioresque nostros non paenitebat tum cum P. Lentulus, is qui princeps senatus fuit, accusabat M'. Aquilium subscriptore P. Rutilio Rufo, aut cum P. Africanus, homo uirtute, fortuna, gloria, rebus gestis amplissimus, posteaquam bis consul et censor fuerat, L. Cottam in iudicium uocabat. Iure tum florebat populi Romani nomen, iure auctoritas huius imperi ciuitatisque ma-

65 14 *Probus De cath. (GLK 4.43.4) et Sacerdos (GLK 6.495.20–21)* **66** 1–2 *Nonius Marcellus 4 s.u. ducere (283.21M, 437L)* **67** 6 *Priscianus 18.257 (GLK 3.338.22–23)*

65 13 honestius sit] non est iussit *P*[r] **66** 3 in amicitia ... dicioneque *Eberhard* 5 Dubitare quisquam ... fortunas defendere *om.* γ **67** 1 M. *Hotomannus et Ver. II.2.118* : D. *uel* Decimo ω Silano *P* : Syllano *M* : Scillano γ **68** 2 ferunt *PM* : fertur γ 3 uti si *M* **69** 3 accusauit *Ps-Asc. 124 (Stangl 204.1)* 4 P. *scripsi* : C. ω 6 uocauit *Ps-Asc. 124 (Stangl 204.3)*

iestas grauis habebatur. Nemo mirabatur in Africano illo quod
in me nunc, homine paruis opibus ac facultatibus praedito,
70 simulant sese mirari, cum moleste ferunt: 'Quid sibi iste uult?
accusatoremne se existimari, qui antea defendere consueuerat,
nunc praesertim, ea iam aetate, cum aedilitatem petat?' Ego
uero et aetatis non modo meae sed multo etiam superioris et
honoris amplissimi puto esse et accusare improbos et miseros
calamitososque defendere. Et profecto aut hoc remedium est
aegrotae ac prope desperatae rei publicae iudiciisque corrup-
tis et contaminatis paucorum uitio ac turpitudine, homines ad
legum defensionem iudiciorumque auctoritatem quam hones-
tissimos et integerrimos diligentissimosque accedere; aut, si ne
hoc quidem prodesse poterit, profecto nulla umquam medicina
71 his tot incommodis reperietur. Nulla salus rei publicae maior est
quam eos qui alterum accusant non minus de laude, de honore,
de fama sua quam illos qui accusantur de capite ac fortunis suis
pertimescere. Itaque semper ii diligentissime laboriosissimeque
accusarunt qui se ipsos in discrimen existimationis uenire arbi-
trati sunt.

XXII Quam ob rem hoc statuere, iudices, debetis, Q. Caecilium,
de quo nulla umquam opinio fuerit nullaque in hoc ipso iudicio
exspectatio futura sit, qui neque ut ante collectam famam con-
seruet neque uti reliqui temporis spem confirmet laborat, non
nimis hanc causam seuere, non nimis accurate, non nimis dili-
genter acturum. Habet enim nihil quod in offensione deperdat;
ut turpissime flagitiosissimeque discedat, nihil de suis ueteribus
72 ornamentis requiret. A nobis multos obsides habet populus
Romanus, quos ut incolumis conseruare, tueri, confirmare ac
recuperare possimus, omni ratione erit dimicandum. Habet
honorem quem petimus, habet spem quam propositam nobis
habemus, habet existimationem multo sudore labore uigiliisque
collectam, ut, si in hac causa nostrum officium ac diligentiam

70 4–6 *Nonius Marcellus I s.u. calamitosum (33.27M, 49L)*

69 10 simulant *D^{pc}GPM* : simulabant *ENHD^{ac}* **70** 2 consueuerat *EGM* : consuerat *DNHP* 4 et aetatis *γPO* : aetatis *M* 8 et *γP Ps-Asc. 124 (Stangl 204.5)* : ac *M* contaminatis *M Ps-Asc. 124 (Stangl 204.5)* : incontaminatis *γP* 9 -que *om. γ* **71** 4 -que *om. P* 12 nihil] in hoc *E^{1}* 13 discedet *P^{1}* 14 requiret *P Ps-Asc. 124 (Stangl 204.8)* : requirit *γMO^{2sl}* **72** 1 habet *om. γ* 3 recipere *P* probauerimus, haec quae dixi retinere per populum Romanum incolumia ac salua possimus; si tantulum offensum titubatumque sit, ut ea quae singillatim ac diu collecta sunt uno tempore uniuersa perdamus.

73 Quapropter, iudices, uestrum est deligere quem existimetis facillime posse magnitudinem causae ac iudici sustinere fide, diligentia, consilio, auctoritate. Vos si mihi Q. Caecilium anteposueritis, ego me dignitate superatum non arbitrabor: populus Romanus ne tam honestam, tam seueram diligentemque accusationem neque uobis placuisse neque ordini nostro placere arbitretur, prouidete.

72 9 singillatim *γPO* : singulatim *M* **73** 1 diligere *P*[1]*M* 5 praetoris *N* tam seueram] causam seueram *O*[2mg] 6 nobis *E* nostro *DE*[1]*HPMFb* : uestro *NGtOvlar*

COMMENTARY

EXORDIUM §§1–9

Hellenistic rhetorical handbooks distinguish between two types of *exordia* for rendering the listener *beniuolum, attentum,* and *docilem*: the direct *principium* and the more nuanced *insinuatio*; see *Inu.* 1.20, *Rhet. Her.* 1.6, and Quint. *Inst.* 4.1.5, 42. The type of case would determine the appropriate approach for the speaker to take. Among the types of *causa* that C. outlines at *Inu.* 1.20, one finds, at the extremes, the *genus honestum* (*cui statim sine oratione nostra fauet auditoris animus*) and the *genus admirabile* (*a quo est alienatus animus eorum qui audituri sunt*). In his summary comments on the *Diu. Caec.*, pseudo-Asconius succinctly concludes that C.'s bid to prosecute Verres was a '*genus causae honestum*', and that is certainly how C. wants his audience to conceptualize it; see §§63–65, 73 and [Asc.] 99 (186 Stangl). Though the scholiast was convinced, this characterization reflects neither C.'s situation nor his tactics. So self-evident were the merits of a *causa honesta* that an *exordium* was largely dispensable. The extensive *exordium* of the *Diu. Caec.*, however, epitomizes the *insinuatio,* which 'by dissimulation and circumlocution unobtrusively steals into the mind of the listener' (*Inu.* 1.21). This was the preferred tactic when a speaker was faced with an audience predisposed to hostility and suspicion.

As C. would say later in *De officiis,* a general wariness persisted about the personal motives and political ambitions of prosecutors. For that reason, he advised that prosecutions only be undertaken rarely and either *rei publicae causa … aut ulciscendi gratia … aut patrocini* (*Off.* 2.50). Furthermore, it was of the utmost importance that an orator avoid the impression of selfish ambition; see *Inu.* 1.23, and Quint. *Inst.* 4.1.7 *praecipua in hoc dicentis auctoritas, si omnis in subeundo negotio suspicio sordium aut odiorum aut ambitionis afuerit.* Given C.'s lack of personal grievance with Verres, and in light of his current candidacy for the aedileship, the audience's suspicions would have been aroused. The *exordium* is therefore lengthy and integral to the persuasive argument of the speech as a whole. It is here that C. sets out his motives (*causam rationemque*) for seeking Verres' indictment.

C.'s opening remarks aim to secure the attentiveness of the audience by presenting it with an apparent paradox (*Inu.* 1.23 *incredibilia*): why is a speaker who has spent his forensic career as a defence advocate suddenly turning to prosecution? This initial *anticipatio* (§1) is developed through the perspective of an anonymous onlooker and allows C. to entertain and appreciate a sceptical view of his actions without validating it; see *si quis … miratur* n. By demonstrating a shared scepticism of prosecution, this initial vignette contributes to the cultivation of the audience's goodwill (*beneuolentia*), which is further elicited in the remainder of the *exordium* through C.'s self-depiction as a reluctant prosecutor dutifully responding to his personal responsibilities toward his Sicilian clients (§§2–5) and his civic obligations to the Roman state (§§5–9).

Yet much of this is a clever ruse. The *exordium* distracts the jury from C.'s lack of personal enmity with Verres and his pure self-interest in pursuing a high-profile prosecution. Only after he has developed a concerned and responsive *ethos* for himself and established his oratorical acumen will he come to address the issue of his candidacy and his political ambitions (§70), which, at that point, he will prove to be his greatest asset; see *Inu.* 1.24 and Stroh (1975) 174–187.

Rhetorical precept advised that an *exordium* should avoid an impression of being too polished (see *Inu.* 1.25, *Rhet. Her.* 1.11, and Quint. *Inst.* 4.1.54–60), and C. largely adheres to these guidelines in the *Diu. Caec.* The *anticipatio* and conversational style of the embedded *narratio* (§§2–5) give a relaxed impression. The style does become elevated in §§7–9, and the speech begins with a rather weighty opening period, but such a lengthy *exordium* allows for a shift of registers – especially in a passage in which C. depicts himself deep in internal conflict and overwhelmed by the pleas of the forlorn Sicilians and the problems of the Roman state. Commentators, ancient and modern, have frequently disagreed on the boundaries of the *exordium.* Following [Asc.], many modern commentators divide the speech so that the *exordium* concludes with §9 (… *quae maxime laboraret*). Loutsch (1994) 179–181 separates §§2–9 as a discrete *narratio.* The Schol. Gronov. distinguishes two *exordia,* a second beginning with §5 *quo in negotio*; see further Lausberg §287. Stroh (1975) 175 extracts §§2–5 as an embedded *narratio* but extends the *exordium* to §9. In this commentary, the *narratio* at §§2–5 will be discussed separately but subsumed as a constituent of the *exordium* since it performs an integral part of the introduction's purpose.

For more on *exordia,* see *Rhet. Her.* 5–11, *Inu.* 1.20–26, Quint. *Inst.* 4.1, and *Sul.* 1 with Berry *ad loc.*; see further Lausberg §§263–288. Loutsch (1994) gives an overview and analysis of C.'s *exordia.* For similarities with *Sul.* and *Rab. perd.*, see Stroh (1975) 188–189. For the use of *anticipatio* in an *exordium,* see §1 *si quis … miratur* n. On securing goodwill through the *ethos* of the speaker, see Arist. *Rhet.* 3.14, *Inu.*1.2, and *Rhet Her.* 1.8.

Anticipatio (§1)

The Imagined Spectator

Someone might be surprised to see Cicero bidding for a prosecution when his entire forensic career up to this point has been devoted to defence. Cicero wants to assure this imagined observer that he has a solid reason for taking this case and that as soon as the listener understands it, he will certainly think that Cicero is the ideal candidate to lead the trial against Verres.

Greek Models

Fulvio Orsini, the sixteenth-century Italian humanist, suspected that the opening section of the *Diu. Caec.* was a direct imitation of Aesch. 1.1–2:

οὐδένα πώποτε τῶν πολιτῶν, ὦ ἄνδρες Ἀθηναῖοι, οὔτε γραφὴν γραψάμενος οὔτ' ἐν εὐθύναις λυπήσας, ἀλλ' ὡς ἔγωγε νομίζω μέτριον ἐμαυτὸν πρὸς ἕκαστα τούτων παρεσχηκώς, ὁρῶν δὲ τήν τε πόλιν μεγάλα βλαπτομένην ὑπὸ Τιμάρχου τουτουὶ δημηγοροῦντος παρὰ τοὺς νόμους, καὶ αὐτὸς ἰδίᾳ συκοφαντούμενος (ὃν δὲ τρόπον, προϊόντος ἐπιδείξω τοῦ λόγου), ἕν τι τῶν αἰσχίστων ἡγησάμην εἶναι μὴ βοηθῆσαι τῇ τε πόλει πάσῃ καὶ τοῖς νόμοις καὶ ὑμῖν καὶ ἐμαυτῷ· εἰδὼς δ' αὐτὸν ἔνοχον ὄντα οἷς ὀλίγῳ πρότερον ἠκούσατε ἀναγιγνώσκοντος τοῦ γραμματέως, ἐπήγγειλα αὐτῷ τὴν δοκιμασίαν ταυτηνί.

The orator's reluctance to prosecute and the notion that his legal action is actually a defence of 'the whole city and its laws' certainly bears a striking resemblance to the opening section of the *Diuinatio* (see §§4, 9, respectively). Although Weische (1972) 32–33 has accepted this hypothesis, the scholarly consensus has rightly rejected the idea of direct imitation given the number of other similar *exordia*. Consider, for example, Demosthenes' speech against Timocrates, 24.6, 8:

ἵνα δ' ὑμῶν μηδεὶς θαυμάζῃ τί δή ποτ' ἐγὼ μετρίως, ὥς γ' ἐμαυτὸν πείθω, τὸν ἄλλον χρόνον βεβιωκὼς νῦν ἐν ἀγῶσι καὶ γραφαῖς δημοσίαις ἐξετάζομαι, βούλομαι μικρὰ πρὸς ὑμᾶς εἰπεῖν· ἔσται δὲ ταῦτ' οὐκ ἄπο τοῦ πράγματος ... ἰδὼν δ' ἠδικηκότα κοινῇ πᾶσαν τὴν πόλιν καὶ περὶ τὴν εἴσπραξιν τῶν εἰσφορῶν καὶ περὶ τὴν ποίησιν τῶν πομπείων, καὶ χρήματα πολλὰ τῆς θεοῦ καὶ τῶν ἐπωνύμων καὶ τῆς πόλεως ἔχοντα καὶ οὐκ ἀποδιδόντα, ἦλθον ἐπ' αὐτὸν μετ' Εὐκτήμονος, ἡγούμενος ἁρμόττοντ' εἰληφέναι καιρὸν τοῦ βοηθῆσαί θ' ἅμα τῇ πόλει καὶ τιμωρίαν ὑπὲρ ὧν ἐπεπόνθειν λαβεῖν.

Here too one finds the reluctant litigant and the proposition that his actions serve the interests of the state. Overcoming a disinclination to prosecute in response to the pleas of others (cf. §3) can also be seen in Demosthenes' speech against Meidias, 21.2:

πολλοί μοι προσιόντες, ὦ ἄνδρες δικασταί, καὶ τῶν ἐν τῷ δικαστηρίῳ νῦν ὄντων ὑμῶν καὶ τῶν ἄλλων πολιτῶν ἠξίουν καὶ παρεκελεύοντ' ἐπεξελθεῖν καὶ παραδοῦναι τοῦτον εἰς ὑμᾶς.

Similarities among these passages with the *exordium* of the *Diu. Caec.* do not necessarily indicate that C. had any particular model in mind so much as they point to a common rhetorical tradition. The Greeks took a similarly suspicious view towards prosecution, and so the image of the reluctant prosecutor working in the service of the greater good may have been a familiar trope that C. drew upon for this occasion. Notably, however, in two of the passages, the litigants are careful to place their own personal grievance (αὐτὸς ἰδίᾳ συκοφαντούμενος, and ἡγούμενος ἁρμόττοντ' … τιμωρίαν ὑπὲρ ὧν ἐπεπόνθειν λαβεῖν) within the wider context of harm done to the state. C. has no personal complaint with Verres and must rely solely on extrinsic considerations to justify his prosecutorial bid.

For other expressions of reluctance in the Attic orators, see Lys.12.3, 22.1, Dem. 24.1, 39.1, [58].2, and [59].12. For more on the Greek mindset regarding prosecution, see Christ (1998) 143–159 and Loutsch (1994) 183. For rhetorical similarities with several speeches of Demosthenes, see Pearson (1968) and Navarre (1900) 235–239. For further analysis of the parallel with Dem. 21.2, see Tempest (2010). C.'s only other prosecutorial criminal speech, *In Bursam* of 52, has been lost; see J. Crawford (1984) 230–234. On other similarities with the Attic orators, see §1 *miratur* n.

Persuasion in the Exordium

Narratological analysis provides an insight into C.'s subtle argumentative and psychological technique at the outset of the *Diu. Caec.* The opening *anticipatio* (§1) includes an explicit secondary focalization, signalled by *miratur* and *putabit,* that provides a perspective, not necessarily that of the narratee (i.e. the judges), but of a hypothetical observer (*si quis*). Other words and phrases such as *subito nunc mutata uoluntate,* the criticism inherent in *descendere,* and the sense of obligation from the gerundive *praeponendum,* implicitly convey this imagined observer's thoughts; see nn. *ad loc.* C. also presents his perspective from two different points in time: the present, when the observer is amazed to see C. vying for a prosecution (*miratur*), and the future, once he has understood C.'s rationale (*cognouerit*). In the subsequent narrative (§§2–9), the focalization shifts. C. will give his own perspective by explaining the rationale behind his decision and by claiming that, from a certain point of view, he is continuing his tradition of defence.

C.'s interpretation of his actions and the initial impressions of the imagined observer present competing and seemingly antithetical perspectives. These work on a broader level throughout the *exordium* to form a *complexio* (dilemma). Which is more likely: that Cicero has had a sudden change of heart and stooped to the level of prosecuting, or that he has a legitimate reason for prosecuting Verres consistent with his previous behaviour? This type of dilemma derives its logical force from plausibility and relies on the underlying assumption in the Roman forensic context of 'fixity of character'. In prosecution speeches, for example, *vita ante acta* is used to establish a defendant's guilt by demonstrating that his alleged crime is not a mere aberration from his normal behaviour but consistent with a lifetime filled with wicked deeds and/or anti-social behaviour; see *Inu.* 2.32–33 and Riggsby (2003) 169. C. is appealing to this general principle when he asks his audience to decide the more plausible motive for his decision to prosecute Verres: that despite his professional history as a defence advocate (*qui tot annos* ...), he has suddenly changed his mind and lowered himself to the role of a prosecutor, or that he has made a reluctant – but reasoned – decision and is conducting what should be regarded as a defence (§5 *manere in instituto meo*).

On focalization, see Hornblower (1994) 131–166, Edwards (2004) 317, Fowler (1990), Genette (1980), Bal (1985), Segre (1980), and de Jong (1987). Short introductions to the subject are provided in Laird (1999) and Rood (1998) 11–14, 296–306. On suggestive language, see Neumeister (1964) 186–192. For the importance of plausibility in rhetoric, see Schmitz (2000). For the εἰκός argument in Greek rhetoric, see Arist. *Rhet.* 1402b14–16, and Rapp (2002) *ad* 2.788– 797. For Roman ideas of the fixity of character, see Riggsby (2004). On *complexiones*, see §31 *utrum* ... *an* n.

§1

1.1 Si quis ... miratur C. had a penchant for opening his speeches with a weighty period and especially a conditional sentence; cf. *Caecin.* 1, *Arch* 1, *Red Sen.* 1, *Sest.* 1, *Cael.* 1, *Balb.* 1, *Prou. Cons.* 1, *Rab. Post.* 1, and *Phil* 14.1. This technique allows 'C. to frame the opening in a tendentious, yet seemingly objective, way by presenting not his own perspective but that of an impersonal, hypothetical other: the audience is invited, not to ask whether that perspective is valid or even reasonable (it is not a true condition, that is) but to accept it as the given framework of thought'; see Kaster *ad Sest.* 1. In assuming this hypothetical perspective, C. anticipates a potential objection to his prosecutorial bid; see introduction above.

This passage became a *locus classicus* for the rhetorical technique of *anticipatio* (πρόληψις). Quintilian cites the effectiveness of this device in capturing the judges' attention in an *exordium* (*Inst.* 4.1.49 *Non inutilis etiam est ratio occupandi quae uidentur obstare, ut Cicero dicit scire se mirari quosdam quod is qui per tot annos defenderit multos, laeserit neminem, ad accusandum Verrem descenderit. Deinde ostendit hanc ipsam esse sociorum defensionem: quod schema prolepsis dicitur*) and procuring their goodwill (*Inst.* 9.2.16–17). See also Julius Victor 15 (*RLM* 422) and Isid. *Orig.* 21.27 (*RLM* 520) προκάταληψις *cum id quod nobis obici poterat, ante praesumimus ad diluendum.* See further Lausberg §§854–855.

By the time of Quintilian, *anticipatio* had become so popular in declamatory exercises that it was considered improper to start a speech without one; see Quint. *Inst.* 4.1.49, 11.1.57. For C.'s use of this device, cf. *Rosc. Am.* 5, *Man.* 22, *Clu.* 144; see further Stroh (1975) 188–193 and W. Allen (1954). Surprise was a common theme in *exordia* of the *genus admirabile* (παράδοξος). Cf. *Rosc. Am.* 1: *credo ego uos iudices mirari* with Landgraf *ad loc.*, and [Quint.] *Decl.* 13.1. Also see Isoc. 6.1: Ἴσως τινὲς ὑμῶν θαυμάζουσιν ὅτι, τὸν ἄλλον χρόνον ἐμμεμενηκὼς τοῖς τῆς πόλεως νομίμοις ὡς οὐκ οἶδ' εἴ τις ἄλλος τῶν ἡλικιωτῶν, τοσαύτην πεποίημαι τὴν μεταβολὴν ὥστε, περὶ ὧν ὀκνοῦσιν οἱ πρεσβύτεροι λέγειν, περὶ τούτων νεώτερος ὢν παρελήλυθα συμβουλεύσων.

iudices When speaking before the jury of a criminal court, C. invariably uses the vocative *iudices* at the outset of the speech. In addition to commanding the jury's attention, the initial vocative signalled for C.'s reading audience the original forensic context of the speech. For *contiones* before the people, he begins with *Quirites,* and for speeches before the senate, with *patres conscripti.* On the process for selecting jurors, see Introduction §III.

aut Corrective; 'or at least'. See K-St. 2.2.101.

eorum qui adsunt The *corona populi* that surrounded trials in the Forum was composed of a variety of people: supporters of either the defendant or the plaintiff including, but not limited to, family members, friends, and political supporters. In addition to individuals directly connected with the trial, there would be those who were seeking a spectacle or deeper involvement in the political life of the city; see Tac. *Dial.* 2, 34 and Millar (1998) 224. The orator could interact with this crowd, elicit their response, or interpret the significance of their presence (or absence) for the jury. The crowd, in turn, could respond to the speaker and contribute to the theatrical performance; see *Brut.* 290, Cat. 53, *Ver.* II.1.12 *meminerit se priore actione, clamore populi Romani infesto atque inimico excitatum, confessum esse duces praedonum a se securi non esse percussos,* and 5.143, 158, 163, 165. Though C. anticipates a large crowd at Verres' prosecution (§42), the *diuinatio,* a pre-trial procedure and long before the trial itself, may have drawn fewer people. Even so, there may have been a group of public spectators and those with a vested interest in the outcome of the *diuinatio.* Within the speech itself, C. appeals to a member of the *corona,* Cn. Lentulus Marcellinus (§13), points out his Sicilian supporters and delegations in attendance (§§11, 14), and draws attention to the lack of supporters for Caecilius (§§28–29); see nn. *ad loc.* For more on attendance at public trials, see Polybius 31.29.8 and David (1992) 463–464. *E* incorporated a marginal or supralineal gloss for *qui adsunt.* The correct reading is also confirmed by the lemma of the scholiast.

miratur The reading transmitted by most MSS is the plural *mirantur,* including *O* (*mirāt͠*), which has been misreported elsewhere, starting with Zumpt. The later hands which provide the singular reading, *miratur*, would have been as much concerned about the grammatical inconcinnity as modern editors. Peterson (1904) suggested that *mirantur* was a copying error for *mirabitur*, though he did not print it in his *OCT*. The trope of surprise in a Ciceronian *exordium*, however, is not an unusual one, and the tense is typically present; see examples above. Souter (1905) countered that *quis* might be a variant of the old nominative plural *ques* and postulated that *probabit* and *putabit* should be amended to the plural as well. It seems more likely, however, that there was an error by synesis (*constructio ad sensum*) in the hyparchetype following the plural partitive and subordinate clause (*eorum qui adsunt*). The paradosis is hardly defendable. For another example of this error, cf. Cato fr. 164 Malcovati: *nam unusquisque nostrum, si quis aduorsus rem suam quid fieri arbitrantur, summa ui contra nititur, ne aduorsus eam fiat.* L. Holford-Strevens in his edition of Gel. *NA* 6.3.16, which reports Cato's speech, adopts the later reading *arbitratur*; see further Holford-Strevens (2020) 79–80 and Löfstedt (1956) 1.7.

1.2 tot annos As C. was still relatively young and a junior senator, this statement may not be reminding the jury of an established reputation, but rather succinctly presenting himself and summarizing his experience to date. C. was active at the bar by age 25 in the year 81, when he represented Publius Quinctius in a civil suit, and made his first appearance in a criminal court (*iudicium publicum*) in 80 defending Roscius on the charge of parricide. C. made at least 11 more speeches in the decade before the *Diuinatio*, which have been entirely or significantly lost or were never published: *Pro muliere Arretina, Pro Titinia, Pro Curtio, Pro Vareno, Pro adulescentibus Romanis in Sicilia, Cum quaestor Lilybaeo decederet, Pro Scamandro liberto, Pro Mustio, Pro Tullio* I and II, and *Pro Sthenio.* For more information on these speeches, see J. Crawford (1984) 33–50. For the fragments of the *Pro Vareno* and *Pro Tullio* II, see J. Crawford (1994) 7–18.

The reading transmitted in Quintilian, *per tot annos,* does not adhere to Ciceronian idiom. When *tot annos* is the second term in a relative clause, *per* is not used; cf. *Ver.* II.4.11, *Caec.* 78, *Arch.* 12, *Mil.* 87, *Att.* 4.8a.2, *Fam.* 7.3.1. However, *per* is used commonly after the relative when *annos* is modified by *eos, hosce, omnis*, or *multos*; cf. *Agr.* 2.37, *Ver.* I.35, II.2.182, 5.58, and *Man.* 38.

causis iudiciisque publicis *Iudicia publica* were Roman criminal courts presided over by a praetor, his delegate, or a *iudex quaestionis* with a panel of jurors established by specific laws to decide upon matters of public offence. Not all criminal matters were tried in *iudicia publica*, but by the time of C., Sullan legislation had established *quaestiones perpetuae* to try issues of extortion (*repetundae*), bribery (*ambitus*), treason (*maiestas*), public violence (*uis*), embezzlement (*peculatus*) and serious private crimes concerning murder (*de sicariis et venificis*) and forgery (*de falsis*); see *D.* 48.1.1, Greenidge 415–428, Riggsby (2010) 195–204 and Tellegen-Couperus (1993) 52. The trials in the *iudicia publica* were more politicized and closely watched than the civil matters adjudicated in the *iudicia priuata*; see *Opt. Gen.* 9. Later, C. will draw attention to Caecilius' lack of experience in criminal trials; see §27. *Causa iudiciumque* is a common pair in C. and may be understood together to mean 'legal proceedings'; cf. §§11, 25, 73, and see Victor. 1.1 (*Ippolito* 37–40). The scholiast incorrectly draws a distinction between *causae* and *iudicia* as referring to private and public trials, respectively; see [Asc.] 100 (186 Stangl).

qui … sim uersatus The perfect subjunctive arises from the causal use of *qui* after *miratur me*; see H-Sz. 559–560 and *OLS* 2.539–542.

1.3 defenderim multos, laeserim neminem The asyndeton and parallel word order highlight the juxtaposition of concepts (defence, injury) and quantity (many, none). *Laedo*, which primarily suggests physical injury (*OLD s.u.*), evokes a common metaphor in oratory comparing forensic proceedings to physical combat; see *TLL* VII 2.869.8–13. C. will develop this metaphor further in §§44–46 as he describes a courtroom battle with Hortensius at Verres' trial; see nn. *ad loc.* The concept of personal endangerment inherent in *laedo* is more appropriate to criminal trials (see §27 *periculum fecisti* n.), though C. may also invoke this metaphor as a form of circumlocution to avoid the verb *accuso*, since in his first civil trial Quinctius was, properly speaking, the plaintiff; see Kinsey (1971) 3–6. On the metaphor of forensic oratory as combat, see Landgraf *ad Rosc. Am.* 32; see further Sawer (1965) 83 and Aßfahl (1932) 83–100. For additional discussions of this metaphor in rhetorical treatises, see *De orat.* 1.32 and *Opt. Gen.* 7. See also Tac. *Dial.* 5.5–7, 10.5, 34.2 with Peterson (1893) lxi–lxii, and Quint. *Inst.* 12.9.2 with Austin (1948) 124–125. For this metaphor imported into poetry, see Cat. 65.5, Hor. *Sat.* 2.1.21, and Juv. 7.173. **defenderim** the perfect tense is the reading of *M* and is parallel to the unanimously reported *laeserim* and supported by the paraphrase in Quint. *Inst.* 4.1.49; see *si quis … miratur* n. above. The imperfect would be nonsensical.

subito nunc mutata uoluntate Focalized speech. It is the imagined onlooker (*si quis*) who perceives the celerity, highlighted by the adverb and ablative absolute construction, and C.'s apparent inconsistency; see §1 introduction. In presenting his own perspective and rationale, C. will demonstrate that this is a false impression; cf. §5 *manere in instituto meo uideor*, §16 *mea fuit semper … uoluntas.*

1.4 ad accusandum descendere Something of a double entendre since *descendere* has both physical and pejorative connotations. Since the Forum was in a low-lying area into which one descended, *descendere* in the parlance of public life meant to go down to the *forum* or *campus*, which in a forensic context was equivalent to 'go (down) to court'; see *TLL* V 1.644.68–645.6, and cf. *Orat.* 2.267, Juv. 7.173 *ad pugnam qui descendit* with Mayor *ad loc.* With *ad* the verb also has a pejorative and moral sense, 'to yield or agree to any act, especially one which is unpleasant or disagreeable; to lower oneself'; see *TLL* V 1.649.36–650.29. C. is fond of this phrase; cf. *Ver.* II.3.6, *Clu.* 10, *Mur.* 60, *Sest.* 89, Quint. *Inst.* 4.1.49, and 9.2.17. C. is 'lowering' himself to the level of a prosecutor. On the negative view of prosecution, see §§1–9 introduction. **descendere** Most of the chief MSS read *descenderim*, including *O*, whose reading has been misreported, while the infinitive, *descendere*, is a second-hand correction in *M.* The textual problem, however, was ancient: [Asc.] 100 (186 Stangl) *Hoc toto capite soloecismi species continetur, nisi addas 'et' aut 'idem', ut sit: 'et nunc subito mutata uoluntate ad accusandum descenderim': quare* *multi non 'descenderim' legunt, sed 'descendere'.* The perfect subjunctive may be a *Perseverationsfehler* after *laeserim.*

1.5 causam rationemque C. is especially fond of doublets, and quasi-synonymous pairs are a durable hallmark of Ciceronian style even after he tamed his *iuuenalis redundantia* (see *Orat.* 107–108). Pairs such as these are close synonyms (συνωνυμίαι) but are not completely equivalent. The effect is two-fold: it intensifies the shared core sentiment in the pair, and it expands the meaning of the core sentiment by including the non-overlapping semantic range of the two words. In other instances, the additional term(s) can contribute to the rhythm of the colon; see e.g. §14 *orant atque obsecrant* (molossus and cretic). See further, Quint. *Inst.* 9.3.45 and Lausberg §651. The pairing of *causa* and *ratio* occurs frequently in C., and he sometimes defines one in terms of the other; cf. *Prou.* 39, *Ver.* II.3.7, 30, 4.130, *Caecin.* 40, *Sest.* 87, *De orat.* 3.114, *Part.* 64, and 110 *causam appello rationem efficiendi.* In this instance, while both terms speak to 'motive', *causa* is a broader term that can refer to an internal or external motivation, but *ratio*, from *reor*, implies a reason which is the result of an intrinsic, mental deduction on the part of the actor. Cf. Sacerdos, *Artes Gramm.* (*GLK* 6.446.13) *inter causam autem et rationem hoc est, quod in ratione semper causa est, in causa uero non semper est ratio, et quod in ratione semper consilium continetur, in causa uero non semper.* See further *TLL* III 661.3–16. In §§2–9, C. will explain both the external influences and personal mental calculations that have gone into his decision to come forward as a potential prosecutor; see introductions *ad loc.* For the proleptic argument that the audience must understand C.'s *ratio*, cf. *Sul.* 2 and *Rab. perd.* 1. For C.'s recapitulation of this idea at the conclusion of the speech, see §63 *semper haec causa ... semper haec ratio accusandi* n.

una et id ... probabit, et ... neminem praeponendum mihi esse ... putabit [Asc.] 100 (187 Stangl) *Principalis diuisio huius causae bipartita est, utrum recte Cicero accuset et utrum Caecilio sit anteponendus.* C. establishes his purported motivation in the exordium (§§2–9), while the remainder of the speech is primarily devoted to establishing his superiority to Caecilius according to the selection rubric that C. provides; see §10 introduction. *Probare* has both a legal and a moral meaning – both of which C. may intend; i.e. the juror should not only give an official legal approval of C.'s actions, but he should also deem his actions moral and just; see *OLD s.u.* 1, 3 and *TLL* X 2.1461.63, 1464.3. For the orator's need to have strong moral grounding, see §27 *integritatem … innocentiam singularem* n. The combination of *una et … et …* is uncommon; see *Phil* 1.21 *una et mente et uoce*, but cf. *Phil.* 4.8, 6.2, and 7.22. For other examples, see Liv. 28.44.6, and Suet. *Cal.* 59.

1.6 profecto Used when the speaker wants to make a strong assertion and frequently so in apodoses, and it 'marks the subjectivity of the expressed opinion'; see Schmalz *s.u.*, *OLD s.u.* 2a, and *TLL* X 2.1672.34. See further Landgraf on *Rosc. Am.* 30, Ramsey on *Phil.* 1.12, Austin on *Cael.* 1, and Gotoff on *Marc.* 3.

1.7 actorem In its most generic sense it means 'counsel'; see *OLD s.u.* 4 and *TLL* I 446.61. Though at other places in the speech *actor* will seem to be virtually synonymous with *accusator*, C. intentionally eschews the latter and uses *actor* as a euphemism, since he will soon introduce the conceit of prosecution as defence; see §5 *non potius accusatio quam defensio est existimanda* n. In other instances, the distinction between *actor* and *aduocatus* has true legal implications regarding a litigant's standing at law. C. is also the *actor* in a legal sense inasmuch as he is indicting Verres in his own name and not *in alieno nomine*; see further §64 *quod eum sibi Achaei patronum adoptarant* n. and Ferrary (1998) 22–23. The second family of the *deteriores* (ς) incorporates into the text the gloss *accusatorem* for *actorem.*

Narratio (§§2–5)

Personal Obligations

During his quaestorship in Sicily, Cicero had developed a lasting reputation among the inhabitants. Consequently, when Verres used his three-year praetorship to rob Sicilians of their riches and rights, a number of Sicilian delegations implored Cicero to take up a case against their ex-governor. Although he suggested that they seek the counsel of another former quaestor, Q. Caecilius Niger, the delegates continued to clamour for his aid. Mindful of his former pledge to assist them in a time of need and aware of the countless examples of other exemplary Romans, he acceded to their request. He is reassured by the fact that his actions could be seen, not as the prosecution of one man, but as the defence of an entire nation.

On the unexpected inclusion of a *narratio* within a *diuinatio* speech, see Introduction §III.

A *narratio* is a biased, persuasive statement of the facts that lays the foundation for the following *argumentatio*; see *Part.* 31 *narratio est rerum explicatio et quaedam quasi sedes ac fundamentum constituendae fidei*; see further Lausberg §348. A few ancient theorists, such as the Apollodoreans, thought it an indispensable part of any speech, but most only considered it fundamental to a forensic speech, directed, as they were, at debating past events – and only then if it were not superfluous or disadvantageous to the case (see *Inu.* 1.30, Quint. *Inst.* 4.2.4–8, Berry 44–46; see further Lausberg §337). In a deliberative speech a *narratio* was optional, though relating past events germane to the question under discussion could be helpful; see *De orat.* 2.330. For students of rhetoric that were straight-jacketed into a rigid speech structure, its natural position in any speech was immediately after the *exordium* and before the *partitio* and/or presentation of arguments, though in practice a narrative could be used at any number of points; see Quint. *Inst.* 4.2.24–27. In regard to style, a narrative should be brief, lucid, and plausible; see *Inu.* 1.28, *Rhet. Her.* 1.14, and *Top.* 97; see further Lausberg §295.

The short narrative in the *Diu. Caec.*, in which C. explains how he found himself in the role of a prosecutor despite his reluctance, appears as a kind of *digressio* within the *exordium* itself; see Quint. *Inst.* 4.3.17. It is therefore the second of the types of *narratio, in quo digressio aliqua extra causam aut criminationis aut similitudinis aut delectationis non alienae ab eo negotio, quo de agitur, aut amplificationis causa interponitur* (*Inu.* 1.27). The nuanced facts that he wants to impress upon the jury are that: (1) he has legitimate connections (*causa necessitudinis*) with the inhabitants of Sicily, (2) the Sicilians, now in a dire state after the depredations of Verres, have approached him for assistance, (3) he was hesitant to acquiesce and so advised them to let Caecilius be the prosecutor, (4) Caecilius is unacceptable to the Sicilians, and (5) he has overcome his reluctance by rationalizing that his prosecution is more akin to a defence. The limited scope of the narrative does not speak to C.'s case as a whole but forms the basis for the first part of the *confirmatio* (§§11–16), in which C. argues that he is the speaker *quem maxime uelint actorem esse ii quibus factae esse dicantur iniuriae* (§10).

The simplicity of the narrative belies contentious claims. The *narratio probabilis* (*credibilis*) aims to persuade the audience of 'the reality of biased content' – here of C.'s reluctance to undertake a prosecution and his pure altruism for powerless provincials. As a matter of central importance to narratives of this sort, a speaker should provide the psychological reasons behind an action; see Quint. *Inst.* 4.2.52 *Credibilis autem erit narratio ante omnia si prius consuluerimus nostrum animum ne quid naturae dicamus aduersum, deinde si causas ac rationes factis praeposuerimus, non omnibus sed de quibus quaeritur, si personas conuenientes iis quae facta credi uolemus constituerimus, ut furti reum cupidum, adulterii libidinosum, homicidii temerarium, uel his contraria si defendemus: praeterea loca, tempora, et similia.* See further Lausberg §328. In this instance, the person involved in questionable actions, whose state of mind and character must be further disclosed, is C. himself. In the opening dilemma of the *anticipatio* (§1), C. has already established a pattern of behaviour for himself and a projected persona. In the narrative, he develops this *ethos* further by purporting to disclose his reaction to external influences (the pleas of helpless individuals, moral obligations, and cultural norms) and by revealing his own internal struggle (also presented as a false dilemma; see §4 *tuli grauiter* ...). The occasional need to judge between competing social and personal priorities and senses of self is a commonality that would resonate with any audience and consequently contributes to the plausibility of the narrative. It also performs one of the primary aims of the *exordium* in winning over the judges through the cultivation of a sympathetic *ethos*; see Quint. 3.8.8 *Aristoteles* [*Rhet.* 3.1415b33–38] *quidem, nec sine causa, putat et a nostra et ab eius qui dissentiet persona duci frequenter in consiliis exordium, quasi mutuantibus hoc nobis a iudiciali genere, nonnumquam etiam ut minor res maiorue uideatur.*

The purported sequence of events also needs further consideration. First, C. passes over the four years between his tenure in Sicily and the present trial with such rapidity as to make the time seem negligible (§2). His ties to 'all of Sicily' may not be as strong as he would lead his audience to believe. Second, C. acknowledges that delegations have been sent officially (*publice*) from Sicily, but he never asserts that they were sent to seek him out specifically; see Stroh (1975) 182. C. certainly gives the impression that he was the first to file (*postulatio*) with the praetor to indict Verres, but subtle hints suggest that Caecilius must have come forward first (see §4 *dicebam habere eos actorem Q. Caecilium* n.) and thus make C.'s motives appear even more dubious; see also Introduction §III. The *narratio*, however, presents a seemingly continuous chain of cause-and-effect that leads the audience to believe that C. has truly accepted this case under compulsion.

The narrative ends with an *expositio* (§5) that both summarizes the *narratio* – and almost the entire speech – and prepares the way for the *argumentatio* (*adductus sum …*); see further Lausberg §346. C. eventually comes to the conclusion that this legal action is more truly a defence of his clients and therefore entirely consistent with his established character. This final paradoxical conceit is a clever way of cultivating his audience's attention and resolving the false dilemma of §1; for this device, cf. *Part.* 32 and Quint. *Inst.* 4.2.121. On *narrationes* generally, see *Inu.* 1.27–30, *Part.* 31–32, *Rhet. Her.* 1.12–16, Quint. *Inst.* 4.2.1–132, Arist. *Rhet.* 3.16; see further Lausberg §§289–347.

§2

2.1 cum quaestor in Sicilia fuissem C. was elected unanimously to the quaestorship at the earliest possible age (*in suo anno*) on 5 December 76 and was assigned to Sicily as one of the two quaestors for 75. He was based in the western city of Lilybaeum and served under the propraetor Sextus Peducaeus; see *Ver.* II.2.2.37, 2.3.216; see further *MRR* 1.98, Drumann and Groebe

(1899–1929) 5.266–267. Cf. Plut. *Cic.* 6 Ἀποδειχθεὶς δὲ ταμίας ἐν σιτοδείᾳ καὶ λαχὼν Σικελίαν, ἠνώχλησε τοῖς ἀνθρώποις ἐν ἀρχῇ, σῖτον εἰς Ῥώμην ἀποστέλλειν ἀναγκαζομένοις. ὕστερον δὲ τῆς ἐπιμελείας καὶ δικαιοσύνης καὶ πρᾳότητος αὐτοῦ πεῖραν λαμβάνοντες, ὡς οὐδένα τῶν πώποθ' ἡγεμόνων ἐτίμησαν. See also Finley (1979) 129. This was his first magistracy on the *cursus honorum*, and it entitled him to membership in the senate under Sullan legislation.

Since the quaestor at Lilybaeum was uniquely stationed away from his praetor, he may have exercised greater autonomy and performed more delegated duties. Caecilius would hold this same position in 73; see Introduction §II. For the development of the Roman quaestorship, see the ongoing evaluation of Mommsen in Harris (1976), Prag (2014), and Pina Polo and Díaz Fernández (2019) 143–151. For C.'s known activities while in Sicily, see Fedeli (1980) and Schickel (1966) 11–15. On Sicily under Roman administration, see Finley (1979) 109–147. For a detailed discussion of Roman governance of the province, see Covino (2005).

iudices The vocative is used to grab the jury's attention and signal a shift in argument, specifically here the transition to the *narratio*. In the early part of this speech, C. uses the direct address to frame developments of his argument; e.g. the end of the narrative digression §5 *iudices … iudices*; the beginning of the *partitio* in §10; the outset of the *argumentum* at §11; and the *peroratio* at §§71, 73. Cf. ὦ ἄνδρες Ἀθηναῖοι in Dem. 4.1 with Wooten (2008) *ad loc.* For the observation that direct address indicates a point of development in the argument, see also Hermogenes 267 on ἀπόστασις and Ronnet (1951) 126. Additionally, the vocative helped to combat inattention and convey emotional intensity; see Bers (1997) 201.

itaque The equivalent of *et ita*, which introduces the consecutive clause *ut … relinquerem*; *OLD s.u. ita* 18b.

ex ea prouincia decessissem Technical terminology, particularly in C., meaning to 'retire from office at the expiration of a term'; see *TLL* V 1.121.68–122.1; cf. §29 *decesseris … decederes* and *Planc.* 65. When used with locations, *decedo* can be completed with *de*, *ex*, or the ablative without a preposition; see Schmalz *s.u.* C. seems to prefer *ex* when describing the departure from a province (with the exception of *Font.* 13–14) and *de* in figurative applications. γ's *discessissem* does not have so precise a sense. C. describes his return journey from Sicily, when he thought that his reputation and accomplishments would be the talk of Rome; see *Planc.* 64–65 and Plut. *Cic.* 6.

2.2 Siculis omnibus An exaggerated claim. C. maintains that he had a good reputation throughout the entire island despite the fact that there were two quaestors stationed in Sicily. In dispatching his duties, C.'s interaction with the eastern side of Sicily was surely infrequent. For more on this hyperbole, see §2 *cuncti* n.

2.3 memoriam ... relinquerem For this image, cf. *Sul.* 89, *Brut.* 38, and Tac. *Ann.* 15.68.3.

nominisque mei For *nomen*, 'good name, reputation, or esteem' *OLD s.u.* 12; cf. §69 *populi Romani nomen.* For *memoriam nominis* in C., cf. *Ver.* II.4.69, *Clu.* 32, *Flac.* 60, and *Vatin.* 8. See further *TLL* VIII 671.80.

factum est uti The entire phrase is reminiscent of an older *style adminstratif*; cf. *Ver.* II.1.130, *Agr.* 2.9, and Caes. *BC* 1.31.4. This was a notable aspect of Caesar's prose; see Odelman (1972).

2.4 cum summum ... tum non nullum 'and while they consider their ancient patrons as their defensive stronghold, they also believe me to be an integral part as well'. *OLD s.u. cum* 14a: 'introducing one of two co-existing or co-ordinate circumstances or actions, usually followed by *tum* which indicates the more particular or noteworthy circumstance'. The sense of *cum* has a slightly concessive tone; see H-Sz. 625. The two adjectives *summum* and *non nullum* coordinate to modify *praesidium*, but they are perhaps better translated adverbially; see *OLD s.u. summus* 14. For the contrast of *summum ... non nullum*, cf. *Fam.* 3.8.6, and *Q. fr.* 2.14.5.

in ueteribus patronis multis [Asc.] 100 (187 Stangl) *Siculi ueteres patronos habent: in quibus Marcellos a <M.> Marcello ortos, qui Syracusas uictor seruauit incolumes; Scipiones, quorum auctor P. Scipio Africanus Carthagine excisa Siciliae ornamenta rettulit sua, quibus* *quondam a Poenis uictoribus spoliata erat; Metellos, quorum familia proxime Siculis patrocinium praebuit, cum fuit Lepidus in ea prouincia praetor, instantibus ad accusandum eum Metellis duobus, Celere et Nepote.* Marcus Claudius Marcellus (*RE* 220) became associated with Sicily during the Second Punic War, when, after an extensive campaign, he captured Syracuse in 212. Though he forbade his troops from demolishing the city, he did bring much of its art and statuary to Rome as spoils. For this episode, see Finley (1979) 122, Plu. *Marc.* 21, Liv. 25.40.2, and Rossi (2000). A bronze statue of Verres was erected next to Marcellus' in Syracuse, and the festival games in Marcellus' honour, the *Marcellia*, were supplanted by the *Verria*; see *Ver.* II.2.51–52 and Brunt (1980) 275 n. 19. The patrician family of the Cornelii Scipiones began their relationship with Sicily at the end of the Third Punic War. When Carthage fell in 146, Scipio Aemilianus, in a magnanimous and calculated gesture, invited delegates from Sicily to come to Carthage so that they might reclaim any artwork or spoils stolen by the Carthaginians during their forays into the island; see App. *Lib.* 133, Liv. *Epit.* 51, Diod. 32.25. Cf. C.'s invocation of Scipio Aemilianus at *Ver.* II.4.79–82, and see §69 *P. Africanus* n. Q. Caecilius Metellus Celer and Metellus Nepos prepared charges against M. Lepidus for mismanagement of the province during his term as governor in 80, but this prosecution appears to have been threatened but never realized; see *Ver.* II.3.212, *TLRR* 131, Gruen (1968a) 274–278, and Brunt (1980) 275 n. 19. Though there appears to be no watershed event that established the Metelli as patrons of Sicily, they may have fashioned themselves as such nonetheless; cf. *Ver.* II.2.20 the enfranchisement of a Sicilian by Q. Metellus; L. Caecilius Metellus' defeat of Hasdrubal in 251 outside Panhormus; on Q. Caecilius Metellus Numidicus' term as governor in 114, see Nicols (1981). Several members of the Metelli may have been governor of the province sometime between 167 and 80 – a period for which records are sparse. L. Caecilius Metellus would succeed Verres in Sicily. Both the Scipiones and the Metelli are backing Verres' defence. Brunt (1980) speculates that Hortensius had encouraged the Metelli to support Verres in exchange for financial support in upcoming elections. Three of them stand out as supporters: Quintus, consul designate along with Hortensius; Lucius, Verres' successor as governor of Sicily; and Marcus, who had been allotted the praetorship of the *quaestio repetundarum* in 69. For Q. Caecilius Metellus Creticus, the consul of 69, see van Ooteghem (1967) 220–231. On the tenure of L. Caecilius Metellus as governor of Sicily as related to C.'s prosecution of Verres, see Brennan (2000) 492–493.

For patronage in the Verrines, see Brunt (1980), Prag (2013), and Eilers (2002) 150–158. On legal patronage in particular, see §64 *quod eum sibi Achaei patronum adoptarant* n.

2.5 praesidium 'their defensive bulwark', a common term in the Roman political vocabulary (and particularly in C.) that is borrowed from military terminology. *Constitutum*, with its literal and figurative senses, neatly completes the analogy. *Praesidium* implies an active role on the part of a patron to prevent or forestall any disaster, while *auxilium*, also frequently used in this context, indicates passive support where aid is offered during a time of need; see Hellegouarc'h 172–173. Cf. Verres' defence built upon wealth and bribery, *Ver.* I.8 *quoniam in pecunia tantum praesidium experiatur esse.*

fortunis 'welfare', not in a strictly monetary sense; see *OLD s.u.* 11 and *TLL* VI 1179.81 (*pace* 1180.49).

2.6 quare Here the Italian tradition unanimously reports *qui.* Though the original reading in *M* is now illegible, the spacing would not allow *quare,* and the second hand may simply have been writing over the faint text of the first. In the French tradition, there must have been an abbreviation in *S. G* has *quare,* as does *D,* which, in other parts of the text, shows itself to be more astute in interpreting the abbreviations that caused trouble for the scribes of *E, H,* and *N,* which all report *quod*; see Peterson (1907) 172. The connecting relative, *qui,* though it gives an acceptable sense, is inferior to *quare.* C. is at pains to explain his motivation for prosecuting Verres and needs to establish his advocacy as a logical consequence of the relationship he developed with the province during his quaestorship. *Quare* signposts this connection more clearly; cf. *Ver.* II.2.3 *Quare P. Africanus*

Carthagine deleta Siculorum urbis signis monumentisque pulcherrimis exornauit, *Quinct.* 12, *Ver.* I. 52, and II. 1.32.

populati atque uexati The pleonasm and homeoteleuton make the phrase striking. This verbal pairing is found again at §7, *Ver.* I.45, and II.3.122. Although many authors, including C., generally eschew the use of *atque* before a consonant, he does use it before a consonant when it renders a desirable *clausula* for the colon – as it does here with a cretic and spondee. *Atque* followed by a consonant is more common in C.'s earlier speeches, though it does appear in stereotyped phrases such as this one throughout his career. On this metrical close and on *clausulae* in C., see Nisbet (1995), Hutchinson (1995), and Berry (1996) 49–54. For other examples in this speech alone, cf. §6 *furta atque flagitia*, §8 *culpa atque dedecore*, §13 *fide atque praesidio*, and §26 *exstinguenda atque delenda sit*. By ending a colon here, additional emphasis is placed on *cuncti* by affording it the primary position in the subsequent colon.

cuncti C. constantly exaggerates the solidarity of the Sicilians. Several major cities in Sicily ignored him or flatly refused to assist him in the prosecution. Verres' policies and activities (whether extortionist or not) were not universally detested and may have benefited large subsections of the population from various regions. Chief among them was Syracuse, seat of the second quaestorship and the praetorship. Although wealthy Syracusans seem to have been disproportionately affected by Verres' policies, the lower classes had benefited from the donation of Heraclius' estate to the local athletic facilities; see *Ver.* II.2.35. Whether a sign of gratitude or a show of obsequious flattery, a statue of Verres was erected in Syracuse and entitled σωτήρ; see *Ver.* II.2.154 and 4.136–138. Among the other cities that refused support, Verres exempted Messana, another major eastern city, from providing sailors and soldiers after the city donated a new cargo ship to Rome at its own expense. Perhaps mindful of this benefaction, Messana also rejected C.'s entreaties. Both Messana and Syracuse decreed *laudationes* and celebrated festivals in his name even though these were later rescinded in Syracuse; see *Ver.* II.4.24, 141–144; *Ver.* II.2.154, 4.24, 151; *Ver.* II.4.145,

150–151, respectively. Yet except for a brief mention in §14 (*praeter duas*), C. will consistently portray the Sicilians as acting in one accord. For C.'s inability to garner total support, see Dilke (1980) 43–51. For support of Verres from Sicily during his extortion trial, see Classen (1980). On these honours for Verres, see Wallace-Hadrill (1990b).

ad me publice saepe uenerunt The adverb *publice* indicates that the Sicilians were sent as official representatives of various communities, not as foreigners with private grievances; see *TLL* X 2.2467.3–10 and Schmalz *s.u.* Cf. *Ver.* II.3.105 *De Aetnensibus perpauca dicam; dixerunt enim ipsi priore actione publice. Memoria tenetis Artemidorum Aetnensem, legationis eius principem, publice dicere Apronium uenisse Aetnam cum Veneriis.*

2.7 suarum fortunarum omnium When *suus* and *omnis* modify the same headword but are separated, the adjective in postposition receives additional emphasis. Frequently in C. the emphasis is placed on *suus*; cf. *Ver.* I.12 *Iam uero omnium uitiorum suorum plurima et maxima constituit monimenta et indicia in prouincia Sicilia*, and *Ver.* II.1.139. The stress on *omnium* here is effective and paralleled elsewhere. Cf. *Ver.* II.2.43 *quid interest utrum praetor imperet uique cogat aliquem de suis bonis omnibus decedere an huiuscemodi iudicium det quo iudicio indicta causa fortunis omnibus euerti necesse sit?*, and *Ver.* II.4.62. There must have been a corrected transposition of *suarum fortunarum* in *S*. The scribe of *D* wrote *fortunarum suarum* but marked it with transposition marks, while the scribe of *G* has the same order as *D* but does not indicate a transposition. Though there are other instances, e.g. *Ver.* II.3.129, the consensus ordering is more emphatic.

causam defensionemque In addition to providing emphasis to the shared meaning of the pair, the second term more precisely clarifies the first. C. introduces the conceit of prosecution as defence; cf. §5 with nn. *ad loc.* For this pairing, cf. *Ver.* II.2.151, 156, *Clu.* 102, and *Font.* 12. On these quasi-synonymous pairs, see §1 *causam rationemque* n.

2.8 saepe esse pollicitum C. made a public speech at the end of his quaestorship in Lilybaeum in which he fashioned himself as a patron of Sicily; see [Asc.] 101 (187 Stangl) *in ea oratione quam decedens Lilybaei habuit.* The text of the speech has been lost, and our only attestations are those from [Asc.] and the fourth-century grammarian Arusianus Messius, who cites a small fragment in his *Exempla elocutionum*, on the use of *detrectare*; see *GLK* 7.469–470. See further J. Crawford (1994) 19–22. **saepe ... saepe ... saepe** the anaphora underscores the persistence of the Sicilians and C.'s loyalty.

2.9 si quod tempus accidisset, quo tempore ... The repetition of an antecedent inside a relative clause was a notable characteristic of precise legal and administrative Latin such as *senatus consulta* and edicts (cf. *Fam.* 8.8.7), but the construction is also found in vulgar Latin and in literary Latin until the time of C. Given the narrative context, C. may be imitating the style of everyday Latin but the tone is more likely magisterial and intended to be a pointed reminder by the Sicilians of C.'s sworn obligation. On this construction, see Löfstedt (1956) 81–84, K-St. 2.2.283–284, H-Sz. 563–564, von Albrecht (2003) 100, Oakley *ad* Livy 6.1.11, and Haffter (1934) 77–78. The verb *accido*, as it is used here, often has an ominous sense; cf. *Phil.* 2.17 and *Fam.* 3.10.2, and see *TLL* I 291.55–293.14.

2.10 eorum Rather than *suis*. For *is* in the place of the reflexive, see Lebreton (1901) 126–131. In his early orations, however, C. occasionally uses the reflexive even in subordinate clauses not 'related internally to the main subject'; cf. *Rosc. Am.* 2 and 6. For more on this aspect of his style, see von Albrecht (2003) 99.

§3

3.1 aiebant introduces a series of four clauses in *oratio obliqua* (*uenisse ... habere ... pertulisse ... rogare et orare*). Asyndeton between the subordinate clauses, along with the imperfect tense of the main verb, gives the impression of an overwhelming number of grievances being repeatedly presented to C. These features and the image of the Sicilians as suppliants (see further §17 *supplices uestri* n.) imbue the reported speech with an emotional appeal that would not be out of place in a *peroratio.* In his self-presentation, however, C. depicts himself as being won over not so much by *pathos* as by his own reasoning and evaluation of social norms and imperatives; see §5. A distinction is sometimes noted between the defective *aio* and *dico*; Don. *ad* Ter. *Ph.* 380 *'ais' dicimus de eis, qui uana loquuntur: 'dicere' autem dicimus de eis, qui ualidiora.* That nuance does not seem to apply here or in C. generally; cf. Nonius Marcellus (78M, 98) *ad* Cic. *Fin.* 2.70 *'aiat': quod est dicat.* The scansion of *aio* is not always consistent; here it provides a typical cretic and spondee rhythm: *tēmpŭs aīēbānt*; see further *TLL* I 1453.22–40 and K-St. 1.822.

sed ut As written, the phrase suggests that the Sicilians are no longer interested in their material possessions, and perhaps C. wants to give that impression. For *non iam … sed* used in a similar phrase of heightened emotive appeal, cf. *Sul.* 89 *non iam de uita P. Sullae, iudices, sed de sepultura contenditur*, and *Dom.* 12, *Ver.* I.49, II.4.60, *Cat.* 3.13, *Mil.* 67, and *Phil.* 5.3.

uitam salutemque Beyond financial restitution, the Sicilians' very lives are at stake. *Vita* and *salus* are frequently associated with one another, but while *uita* denotes simple existence, *salus* extends beyond this notion of *uita* and connotes a quality of life that can also be applied to the well-being of a society as a whole; see *OLD s.u. salus* 5. For a similar pairing in C. and other writers, cf. *Ver.* II.3.164, *Cat.* 1.14, *Sest.* 128, *Planc.* 1, *Deiot.* 30, *Phil.* 3.19, Lucr. 4.506, and Luc. 5.685, 7.639. On quasi-synonymous pairs, see §1 *causam rationemque* n.

3.2 totius prouinciae See §2 *cuncti* n.

defenderem The conceit of defence as prosecution is quickly re-enforced; see §2 *causam defensionemque* n.

ne deos quidem Perhaps eliciting *pathos* at the expense of theological accuracy (see *simulacra sanctissima* n. below), this dire depiction of Sicily, bereft of mortal and divine assistance, is a key motif in the construction of C.'s *ethos* as patron and saviour of the Sicilians. For more on the relationship between supplication and shrines, see Naiden (2006) 250–263. Abandonment by the gods is a common literary theme in Greek tragedy, which C.

undoubtedly evokes here; cf. Poseidon's departure from Troy at E. *Tr.* 1–47.

3.3 confugerent The diction underscores the function of the temple and its cult statue as a place of refuge; see *simulacra sanctissima* n. below. The repetition of the verb (§11 *ad meam fidem … confugiunt*) would seem to liken C. to their protective deity in the wake of the sacrileges committed by Verres. Cf. *Ver.* II.5.126 *Quo confugient socii? quem implorabunt? qua spe denique, ut uiuere uelint, tenebuntur, si uos eos deseretis?* For defendants 'fleeing' to judges for protection, see also *Rosc. Am.* 150, *Mur.* 87, *Clu.* 7, *Quinct.* 98, and *Sul.* 88; see further Winterbottom (2003) 224. For an anecdotal story of refuge-seekers (although probably fictitious), see Liv. 30.20.6.

quod eorum Peterson (1903) 198, citing *Ver.* II.4.151 *qui simulacra deorum abstulisset,* proposed *quod deorum* but did not incorporate the conjecture into his *OCT*. The anaphoric *eorum* is fitting since C. has already placed emphasis on the absence of the gods with *ne deos quidem* above.

3.4 simulacra sanctissima The cult image was sacred and central to the proper function of a religious site. The representation of the god(dess) played a civic role: a place under its gaze was an appropriate venue for oaths or other important transactions, and in some Greek festivals, the removal of statuary from a temple represented the destruction of order. As works of art, these statues could be among the items recovered by the Sicilians after a successful prosecution. But in removing them, Verres has not simply stolen fine art but has also committed a sacrilege that disrupts the proper functioning of Sicilian society and potentially arouses the anger of the gods. For a further discussion, see Burkert in Fox (1988) 27–47. In classical Greece, prayers made before a god's statue were considered to be particularly effective; see Corbett (1970) 151. On temple and cult image, see Burkert (1985) 88–92, Scheer (2000), and Bettinetti (2001). For statues in Sicily, see *Ver.* II.4.46. There is an ongoing debate about the extent to which the Sicilians would have distinguished between the cult statue as representation or manifestation of the god(dess); see Burkert (1985) 88–92, Gordon (1979), and Platt (2011).

Although religious practice in Rome would have been markedly different, the Roman audience would not have failed to see the significance of this theft, and in his depictions of Sicilian religion C. does attempt to 'Romanize' or universalize religious practice in Sicily: e.g. *Ver.* II.4.99 *Sacrarium Cereris est apud Catinensis eadem religione qua Romae, qua in ceteris locis, qua prope in toto orbe terrarum.* Throughout the corpus, gods are referred to by their Roman names. On C.'s presentation of Sicilian gods to a Roman audience and his self-representation as a defender of the gods, see von Albrecht (2003) 206–215. For material evidence of Sicilian religion, see Holloway (1991).

This opening image of Verres is that of the temple-robber (ἱερόσυλος): a stock character of rhetorical exercises and a distinguishing occupation of a tyrant; see [Hermog.] 13.14–23. C. will develop this image of Verres throughout his prosecution, particularly in the fourth speech of the *actio secunda*; see *Ver.* II.4.123 *Ac uidete quanto taetrior hic tyrannus Syracusanis fuerit quam quisquam superiorum, quia, cum illi tamen ornarint templa deorum immortalium, hic etiam illorum monumenta atque ornamenta sustulit.* For other references to Verres' impiety and temple-robbery, see §§11, 19; *Ver.* II.1.9, 11, 45, 49–50, 53–54; 3.6, 23; 4.18, 75, 88, 93, 95–110, 122–123, 127–128. On C.'s characterization of Verres in *Ver.* II.4, see also Vasaly (1993) 109–124. This depiction of Verres remained in the collective memory; cf. Juv. 8.106 *sacrilegus Verres.* For a similar image of a rapacious governor, see C.'s depiction of L. Piso at *Prou.* 7.

The alliteration of *sanctissima* provides emphasis. The clausula ends with a double cretic and allows Verres' name to take the emphatic primary position in the subsequent phrase.

C. Verres (*RE* 1; *MRR* 2.633) For a short discussion of Verres' political career and biography, see Introduction §I. Giving an individual two names (here *praenomen* and *nomen*) was conventional in most formal circumstances – especially at the outset of a speech or in the first reference. Speeches delivered in court seem to have been freer from the rules of naming than political speeches. For a discussion of naming conventions in C., see Adams (1978), Dickey (2002) 51–52, and Shackleton Bailey (1988) 3–8. Other advocates and opponents are typically only referred to by a single name after the first instance.

delubris A temple was a refuge in times of distress and common ground that transcended economic and social distinctions: people of all levels of society could enter the temple to offer prayers in view of the statue. Like *fanum*, *delubrum* denotes a temple primarily for religious purposes and a residence for the gods and their images. C. often uses *templum* and *delubrum* synonymously, or sometimes even uses the pair *templa atque delubra*; cf. *Cat.* 3.22, 4.2, 18, *Dom.* 119, 144, and *Sul.* 19 with Berry *ad loc.* On potential distinctions between the two, see [Asc.] 101 (187–188 Stangl) *Sunt qui 'templa' esse dicant singulorum dis attributorum locorum, 'delubra' multarum aedium sub uno tecto a diluuio pluuiae munitarum. Alii delubra dicunt ea templa in quibus sunt labra corporum abluendorum more Dodonaei Iouis aut Apollinis Delphici, in quorum delubris lebetes tripodesque uisuntur. Sunt etiam qui delubra ligna delibrata, id est decorticata, pro simulacris deorum more ueterum posita existiment, sed male*; see also Schol. Gronov. 324 Stangl. There is no consensus, however, on the etymology of the term; see Ernout–Meillet *s.u.* For other possibilities, see Serv. *A.* 2.225, *GLK* 4.202, and Isid. *diff.* 1.407. On *aedes, templum, delubrum* and *fanum*, see H. Jordan (1879).

3.5 quas res ... pertulisse The suggestion of suffering is inherent in the verb; see *TLL* X 1.1359.62–1362.22 and *OLD s.u.* 7a. Asyndeton highlights the number and scope of Verres' outrages.

luxuries ... crudelitas ... auaritia ... superbia Cf. *Ver.* II.2.9 *sed cum perferre non possent luxuriem crudelitatem auaritiam superbiam ... hoc statuerunt ... istius iniurias per uos ulcisci ac persequi. Luxuries* points to a lack of *temperantia* that keeps someone within the bounds of established social norms of behaviour; see *TLL* VII 2.1920.15–28. *Superbia* connotes a disdain and arrogance associated with nobility and royalty in particular; cf. *Phil.* 3.9 *atque ille Tarquinius quem maiores nostri non tulerunt non crudelis, non impius, sed superbus est habitus et dictus.* See further Haffter (1956) and Hellegouarc'h 439–441. The collocation of *luxuries* and *auaritia* is common; cf. *Rosc. Am.* 75 *in urbe luxuries creatur, ex* *luxuria exsistat auaritia necesse est, ex auaritia erumpat audacia, inde omnia scelera ac maleficia gignuntur, Mur.* 20, and *Rhet. Her.* 2.34 *duae res sunt, iudices, quae omnes ad maleficium inpellant, luxuries et auaritia. Crudelitas* and *superbia* are also commonly associated with one another; cf. *Ver.* II.1.122, 5.32, *Rab. Perd.* 13, *Leg.* 1.18, *Mur.* 8, *Phil.* 3.34, *Att.* 13.28.3, Liv. 3.9.9, 3.56.7, 6.14.3, and 8.33.11.

Taken together, these are the common character traits in Ciceronian invective of a tyrannical, monarchical figure; see Dunkle (1967). These qualities offer a striking foil to the plaintive, desperate Sicilians. C. exploits similar polarities elsewhere; cf. the rustic Roscius and the decadent eastern Chrysogonus in *Rosc. Am.* Among those also listed with three of the four qualities are Gabinius, Sulla, and Catiline; see *Prou. Cons.* 11, *Fin.* 3.75, and Sal. *BC* 12, respectively. C. tends to prefer the fifth declension form *luxuries* to that of the first (*luxuria*); see *TLL* VII 2.1919.65–1920.1.

3.7 hoc uno praetore *Praetore* is here used as a shorthand for *pro praetore*; see *TLL* X 2.1063.16. Verres' tenure as *praetor urbanus* lapsed at the end of 74; however, Roman magistrates that served as governors (generally proconsuls or propraetors) retained the *imperium* of their previous office within their designated provinces. **uno** stresses the fact that this power was concentrated in the hands of one man.

per triennium From 73 to 71. Verres was prorogued as propraetor in 72 when his intended successor, Quintus Arrius, was sent to fight against Spartacus and the slave revolt under the consul L. Gellius Publicola. Fierce fighting in 72 made it clear that Verres would have to continue to serve again in 71. See Introduction §II, *Ver.* II.2.37, and Marinone (1965) 219. Arrius most likely continued to fight the slave revolt in 71 under Crassus. See B. A. Marshall and Baker (1975), *Ver.* II.1.34, 102–158, 5.34, *Clu.* 91, and *MRR* 2.102.

rogare et orare ne illos supplices aspernarer [Asc.] 101 (188 Stangl) *Rogare ut hominem, orare ut deos: iam enim quibus id facerent non habebant.* See also Schol. Gronov. 324 Stangl. Verres' mistreatment of suppliants will be the main subject of II.5. For a history of the development of *orare*, see Heerdegen (1881). On duplication, see §1 *causam rationemque* n. On the image of the Sicilians as suppliants, see §17 *supplices uestri* n.

3.8 nemini C. most often uses *supplex* as an appositive and indicates the *supplicandus* as the indirect object of a verb of motion; cf. *Sul.* 18 *Veniebat enim ad me et saepe ueniebat Autronius multis cum lacrimis supplex ut se defenderem.* Otherwise, *supplex* is found with both the genitive and the dative of the person invoked; see Schmalz *s.u.* and K-St. 2.2.316. As here, the latter construction with the dative may place emphasis on the act of supplication itself; cf. *Dom.* 113 and *Sest.* 170. On the dative with *supplicare*, see *OLD s.u.*

§4

4.1 tuli grauiter et acerbe 'I was greatly troubled'. The nigh pleonastic combination of *grauis* and *acerbus* is common in C.; cf. *Ver.* II.1.152 (*grauiter tum et acerbe homines ferebant*), 5.119, and *Mur.* 7. Though both convey a sense of burden and displeasure and are thus defined in terms of one another (*TLL* VI 2302.25), here the scholiast sees the two as representative of external and internal pressures; see [Asc.] 102 (188 Stangl) *grauiter quod accusare nolebam; acerbe quod Siculorum iniuriis affligebar.* One may also detect a nuanced difference in the acute sharpness suggested by *acerbe* and the ponderousness inherent in *grauiter.* C. emphasizes his displeasure to convey to his audience that he, too, considers the act of prosecution a dubious and often sordid business; see §1 introduction. On the importance of describing the psychological state of the protagonist, see §§2–5 introduction. *Ferre acerbe* is almost entirely Ciceronian until late Antiquity; see *TLL* I 371.63–67; cf. *Planc.* 1. For *ferre grauiter*, see *TLL* VI 2305.8–16 and especially 11–15 for the collocation with *acerbe.*

iudices C. is still within the *narratio,* but the vocative signals a pivot in the narrative, which moves from the Sicilians' pleas to C.'s internal state of mind. See also §2 *iudices* n.

in eum ... locum 'into this situation'; *OLD s.u. locus* 22 and *TLL* VII 2.1538.58–77. **me** the quasi-enclitic use of *me* places it within the prepositional phrase.

4.2 aut eos homines ... aut ego Another *complexio*/διλήμματον. C. presents his own internal conflict as a disjunctive statement – a counter-dilemma to the one presented by the imagined observer in §1; see introduction *ad loc.* Either he must ignore the plight of his clients in order to remain a defence advocate or respond to the *officia* associated with his provincial connection and prosecute Verres. For another example of C. justifying his motives using a dilemma, cf. *Sul.* 10 *Hoc totum eius modi est, iudices, ut, si ego sum inconstans ac leuis, nec testimonio fidem tribui conuenerit nec defensioni auctoritatem; sin est in me ratio rei publicae, religio priuati offici, studium retinendae uoluntatis bonorum, nihil minus accusator debet dicere quam a me defendi Sullam, testimonio laesum esse Autronium.* 'Their apparent exhaustive character prevents the jury from forming an ambivalent view of Cicero's actions and motives' (Berry *ad loc*). For more on false dilemma, see Craig (1993) 47–66 and Seager (2011).

The primary positions of *eos homines* and *ego* intensify the contrast between the desire of one man (C.'s supposed aversion to prosecution) and the needs of many (the Sicilians' request for redress). In accepting the prosecution, C. is depicted as a passive agent (*coactus*) in response to broader social and moral pressure. C. here draws upon the notion of *magnitudo animi*/μεγαλοψυχία, whereby one should address the needs of others or the state at the expense of one's life or mere preferences. Panaetius, whose development of Stoic philosophy had an impact on Posidonius and C., had elevated this characteristic to one of the four cardinal virtues. The triumph of civic needs over the desires of the individual is exploited frequently; see also the depiction of Milo in *Pro Milone* and Dyck (1998). For a discussion of this virtue in general, see *De off.* 1.157 with Dyck (1981).

opem ... atque auxilium The plural, *opes*, relates more precisely to monetary wealth, but in the singular, **ops* connotes an abstract sense of power, which is naturally associated with assistance. It is commonly paired with *auxilium*; cf. *Ver.* II.2.9, 4.107, *Rab. Perd.* 5, *Cat.* 3.18, *Dom.* 27, *Planc.* 73, Liv. 30.3.3, 31.25.8, 34.23.3, 44.26.2, and V. Max. 1.8.6. See further Hellegouarc'h 173–174 and *TLL* IX 2.805.19–24. On quasi-synonymous pairs, see §1 *causam rationemque* n.

4.3 qui me ad defendendos homines ... dedissem C. recapitulates his self-characterization from the beginning of the speech (see §1 *defenderim multos, laeserim neminem* n.) and revisits this point again at §§40–41. For the reflexive use of *dare* with *ad*, see *TLL* V 1.1699.15–21.

ab ineunte adulescentia According to Varro frag. 367 *GRF*, one was a *puer* until age 15 and then an *adulescens* until 30. Isid. *Orig.* 11.2.1–8 uses a 14-year system whereby adolescence is from 14 to 28. From a relational rather than numerical formulation, *adulescentia* could also apply to the period in life in which one was under *patria potestas*; see Leigh (2004). In prose, *ineunte* is most frequently used with *aetate*, *adulescentia*, and *pueritia*.

4.4 officio C. introduces a central theme in the opening sections of the speech. His concept of *officium* was the duty which bound him 'to his family, friends and fatherland, of which the last took precedence over all other claims ... Exactly what he was called on to do depended on the circumstances of the time as he saw them'; see Brunt (1986). Here this is construed as the *officia publica* resulting from C.'s *causa necessitudinis* with Sicily; see §6, *Ver.* II.5.183 *Quam ob rem mihi, iudices, optatum illud est, in hoc reo finem accusandi facere, cum et populo Romano satis factum et receptum officium Siculis, necessariis meis, erit persolutum.* The repetition of *officium* throughout this section highlights his professed reason for undertaking a prosecution despite his reluctance and demonstrates his commitment to upholding social norms. The notion of *officium* in the Roman political vocabulary denotes an obligation to come to another's defence and provide for 'the protection of his civic rights [le sauvegarde de ses droits civiques] (*salus*)'; see Hellegouarc'h 157.

4.5 traducerer '... change my usual habits'; see *OLD s.u.* 6. The emphasis on the drastic change in C.'s professional behaviour has been a consistent theme from the outset until answered in §5 *prope modum manere in instituto meo uideor* .... On fixity of character, see the introduction to §1.

dicebam habere eos actorem Q. Caecilium A subtle admission on C.'s part. The diction here suggests that Caecilius was the first to express his intention to prosecute at a *postulatio*; see Introduction §III. C. presents himself as trying to pass on the task to Caecilius to avoid initiating a prosecution – though the whole situation could be a complete fabrication. This tactic allows C. to appear reluctant, to ascribe a negative opinion of Caecilius to the Sicilians, and to disavow any prior enmity with his opponent. In some respects, it is similar to the '*accusator* as *amicus*' tactic which C. uses in other speeches, in which he addresses his opponent in friendly terms and then shows a key way in which his opponent is inept or unqualified: e.g. Sulpicius in *Mur.*, Atratinus in *Cael.*, and Torquatus in *Sul.* The connection between C. and Caecilius here is not as strong as those in the examples above, but C.'s recommendation of Caecilius and the former experience of both as quaestors in Sicily are meant to suggest a shared experience. For the *accusator* as *amicus* tactic, see Craig (1981).

On C.'s naming conventions, see §3 *C. Verres* n. Subsequent references to opposing counsel could typically be by one name only without any suggestion of disrespect; cf. §27 *tu uero, Caecili, quid potes?* For more about Caecilius' life and career, see Introduction §II.

4.6 praesertim Places emphasis on *qui*: '... especially since he had been ...'; see *OLD s.u.* 2a.

quaestor in eadem prouincia Q. Caecilius Niger served under Verres at Lilybaeum in 73; see Introduction §II. It is interesting that C. here mentions this as grounds for suggesting Caecilius, since in the latter part of the *Diuinatio*, Caecilius' quaestorial service under Verres will feature prominently in the *reprehensio* as a reason why he should be rejected; see §§59–65 with introduction *ad loc.* **eadem** (*PM* : sua γ : Sicilia *Müller* : illa *Eberhard*) Peterson (1907) 174 postulates that the French archetype omitted *in eadem prouincia post me quaestorem* from *saut du même au même* and that *in sua prouincia* was 'an obvious addition ... to fill in the sense'. He furthermore disagrees with other editors about the import of the possessive *sua*, taking it to mean 'in the province from which they (the speakers) came' instead of 'in the province of which he (Caecilius) was native'. However, C., at this juncture, wants to present Caecilius as a suitable alternative and therefore stresses that Caecilius had been quaestor in the same province.

post me quaestorem (*PM* : *om.* γ) The phrase should be accepted since it explains *praesertim*; see Peterson (1907) 173–174. For similar wording, cf. §55 *ante hunc quaestorem* and *Ver.* II.1.111 *post te praetorem.*

4.7 adiumento forms a play on words with *aduersarium*; see below. In its more literal sense, the *adiumentum* was C.'s supposedly helpful suggestion of Caecilius as prosecutor, which might have sufficed to fulfil his obligation to his Sicilian clients. On the role of an *adiutor*, see Hellegouarc'h 88–89.

4.8 posse For the present infinitive after a verb of hoping, see K-St. 2.1.689. **posse molestiam** transposed by *M*, doubtless from the reasonable instinct that *posse* would normally stand next to *demoueri.* The trochaic metron rhythm of *demoueri* is often preceded by a cretic, which here is provided by the reading of γ*P.* The hyperbaton of *hanc ... molestiam* conveys a sense of exasperation. *Demoueri* is frequently abbreviated and confused with *dimoueri.* The former retains the proper sense; cf. *De orat.* 2.208 *eisdem his ex locis et in alios odium struere discemus et a nobis ac nostris demouere.* See further *TLL* V 1.511.31, 74–512.4.

aduersarium Double entendre. C.'s suggestion of an alternative prosecutor has actually worked to his detriment – and Caecilius, who should have been an *adiumentum*, has become both the Sicilians' and C.'s *aduersarius. Contrarius* would be the more common word to describe adverse situations, while *aduersarius* applies specifically to an actual opponent; see Menge (1959) §162 and *TLL* I 843.5–70 – although the article has listed our passage with the more literal meaning at I 842.78–79.

4.9 remississent Here with the dative of the beneficiary (*mihi*): 'to release from an obligation'; see *OLD s.u.* 13b.

istum ... iste is commonly used to refer to one's opponent in court; see *TLL* VII 1.503.25–49. The verb *nossent*, however, may focalize this sentence and the general pejorative sense of *iste* (*TLL* VII 1.500.52–59) through the perspective of the Sicilians.

C. foretells the provincials' damning estimation of Caecilius and his involvement in Verres' provincial mismanagement. C. will return to the character assassination of his opponent later in the speech: see §20 *Si tibi, Q. Caecili, hoc Siculi dicerent: 'Te non nouimus …'*.

§5

5.1 adductus sum This summarizing sentence concludes the first half of the introduction and resolves the first counter-dilemma; see §4 *aut eos homines … aut ego* n. With this resolution, one sees a movement of thought and perspective: shifting from the dilemma as perceived by the imagined observer in §1 to that of C.'s perspective in §4 with a neat ring composition for the latter by beginning and ending the section with *adducere*, which also picks up §4 *traducerer*. The audience and the reader have been carefully offered insight into C.'s decision: for many honourable reasons, he has felt compelled to accept the case. Now C. is ready to offer the final thought process and perspective shift in §5: from another point of view, the prosecution of Verres should be more appropriately reckoned a defence of Sicily.

iudices See §2 *iudices* n.

5.2 officio, fide, misericordia See §4 *officio* n. The second term, *fides*, does not imply a patron–client relationship, but comes closest to the idea of 'good faith' between two unequal partners, in which one side has trust/confidence in the other, and the other has the trustworthiness that justifies the trust; *Clu.* 10. See further Morgan (2015) 30–31, 36–122. For *fides* in the Roman political vocabulary, see Hellegouarc'h (1972) 23–62. *Misericordia*, most often translated as 'pity', implies a privileged position for C. and a dependent one for the Sicilians. While eliciting pity in one's jury is an important persuasive technique, the audience is shown how pity has contributed to persuading C. to take up their case. Responding to these 'morally worthy motives' (e.g. conformity to social norms, the *mos maiorum*, and personal obligations) further characterizes C. as a *uir bonus*; see Quint. *Inst.* 4.1.7 and Lausberg §275α. Cf. *Mur.* 78–85, in which C. links the concept of *officium* with *misericordia.* On *misericordia,* see Pétré (1934) and Konstan (2005) for its difference from *clementia.*

multorum bonorum exemplo, uetere consuetudine institutoque maiorum *Exemplum,* 'precedent'. Aligning oneself with the *institutum maiorum* offered some degree of *auctoritas.* Although a prosecution may not appear to be in keeping with his former practice, C. will go to great pains to demonstrate that he is keeping well within the political tradition. C. sows the seeds of a point that he will present in the *reprehensio* (§§66–71), where he specifically mentions legal actions led by M. Cato, Cn. Domitius Ahenobarbus, P. Lentulus, and P. Africanus. Even there, however, he will have to admit that this sort of legal representation is a *consuetudo longo interuallo repetita ac relata* (§67); see nn. *ad loc.* **uetere**: Neue-Wagener 2.85–87 and K-St. 1.359, who both take the 'best manuscript' approach, recommend *uetere.* The Gronovian scholiast has the termination in *-e,* see 325 Stangl and his apparatus. On the ablative termination in *-i* or *-e,* see also Charisius 5 (75.4–12 Barwick).

5.3 onus hoc ... mihi suscipiendum 'I ought to shoulder this particular burden'; see *OLD s.u. onus* 6 and *TLL* IX 2.646.67–69. The phrase is used again to describe accepting a prosecution (*Ver.* II.2.1 *onere suscepto et recepta causa Siciliensi*) and assuming a defence (*Rosc. Am.* 10). **hoc** forms of *hic* are so frequently abbreviated that confusion can easily occur. Peterson followed the reading of *DGO* and some lesser manuscripts of the *deteriores,* which read *huius* – understood with *laboris.* The reading of *hoc* in postposition is attested in the French tradition and in the best manuscripts of the Italian. Marouzeau 1.162: 'Perhaps *hic* also readily assumes the second place when it conveys the sense of "the (person or thing) present, the (person or thing) I am speaking about". [Peut-être aussi *hic* occupe-t-il volontiers la seconde place quand il a le sens de «le ... présent, le ... dont je vous parle»]'; cf. *Agr.* 1.26 *status hic rei publicae, Fam.* 1.7.10, and *Att.* 2.22.1.

5.4 non ex meo sed ex meorum necessariorum tempore 'not as an opportunity for myself but in response to the situation of these men to whom I feel a sense of obligation'. At the time of the speech, C. was also a candidate for the aedileship, and the jury may have suspected that he was undertaking the prosecution for political gain; see §§1–9 introduction. But after this brief reference, any discussion of his candidacy is delayed until the conclusion, where he explains that his political ambitions may not be his motivation, but they will guarantee the sincerity and rigour of his prosecution; see §§71–72. For *tempus* in these two senses, see *OLD s.u.* 9c, 10a. For a full discussion of *necessitudo*, see §59–65 introduction and §6 *causa tantae necessitudinis* n. below.

5.6 negotio 'annoyance, burden or difficult situation' thematically linked to *onus* above; see further §27 *quid negoti* n.

illa ... res 'this very fact'; the antecedent of the following *quod* clause.

consolatur The diction speaks to C.'s self-representation as agitated and aggrieved by the obligation to undertake a prosecution. Both he and his clients are depicted as in need of solace; cf. §18 *quae sociorum animos consolari possit.*

5.7 uidetur C. introduces another shift in perspective with another verb of focalization, though the point of view is not specified. The passive construction without any ethical dative invites C.'s audience to share this point of view as well.

non potius accusatio quam defensio est existimanda A paradoxical aphorism presented as an 'onomasiological' *correctio*, which rejects the first *nomen* assigned to a particular *res* in favour of a second, i.e. 'not x but y'; see further Lausberg §§784–786. C. has initially accepted the definition of his legal action as a prosecution (§4 *ad accusandum traducerer*), but now presents evidence for his conclusion that the trial against Verres should be more accurately defined as a defence. According to C., there is a disjunction between the actual *uerbum* for his legal action (*accusatio*) and the *factum* itself, which is actually a *defensio* of the Sicilian people. His qualitative argument is primarily based on quantitative grounds: *defendo ... multos ... unus est accusandus.* This subtlety demonstrates a method of argumentation based on the *status finitionis.* C. frequently signals such *correctiones* with *uel potius* (cf. *Sest.* 39 *perditorum ciuium uel potius domesticorum hostium,*

Balb. 51, and *Lig.* 23) and *existimandus* (cf. *Dom.* 93, *Phil.* 11.20, and *De orat.* 1.62).

This onomastic argument was well established in Hellenistic rhetorical theory; see *Inu.* 1.10, Hermog. *Stat.* 4.32–38, Quint. 7.3.4, and Lausberg §§104–122. Victor. *ad Inu.* 1.28 (*Ippolito* 133.221) cites our passage as a prime example: *'Primo', inquit, 'quod factum est, quo id nomine appellari conueniat'. Vtique hoc consequitur; res enim prima est, dein nomen. Homo autem necesse est rei nomen imponat; ita Cicero de nomine constituendo disputat in diuinatione; 'non tam', inquit, 'haec accusatio quam defensio est existimanda'.* For an example of such an argument from Attic oratory, cf. Lycurg. 69: οὐ γὰρ τὴν πόλιν ἐξέλιπον, ἀλλὰ τὸν τόπον μετήλλαξαν, πρὸς τὸν ἐπιόντα κίνδυνον καλῶς βουλευσάμενοι. For the prosecution-as-defence argument, cf. also Dem. 21. 6: εἰ γὰρ οἷόν τε τοῦτ' εἰπεῖν, ἐγὼ νῦν φεύγω, εἴπερ ὑβρισθέντα μηδεμιᾶς δίκης τυχεῖν ἐστί τις συμφορά. For further discussion, see Weische (1972) 33. For a fuller discussion (and demonstration) of the variety of stasis theory, including the *status finitionis*, see §§52–58 with introduction *ad loc.*

5.8 defendo The primary position makes a strong assertion (Marouzeau 2.61), and the etymologizing repetition (*deriuatio*, παρηγμένον; see Lausberg §648) of *defensio* and *defendo* underscores C.'s *correctio*; see above n.

multos mortalis, multas ciuitates, prouinciam Siciliam totam ... C.'s onomasiological *correctio* is argued on quantitative rather than qualitative grounds. This assessment promotes a more democratic ideal: the needs of non-citizens take precedence over a former praetor and Roman senator. For more on this topic, see §7 *aut populo Romano* ... n. On Stoic philosophy and the needs of many, see §4 *aut eos homines* ... *aut ego* n. Klotz bracketed *Siciliam* as an unnecessary gloss. Its inclusion has no effect upon the cretic-trochee rhythm and also affords the final member of the tricolon more syllabic weight.

Mortales can stand as a dignified substitute for *homines*. The semantic range, however, is not exactly equivalent; *mortales* is often found in the context of death, as its etymology might imply, and aptly here as C. has been called upon to defend the lives of the Sicilians (*ut uitam ... defenderem*). In comparison to *omnes mortales*, which C. uses 28 times, the alliterative *multi mortales* is altogether rare (only elsewhere in C. at *Clu.* 202 and *Pis.* 77) and used only in emotionally charged passages. The pairing is more common in Sallust and Livy, and so C. may have thought of it as archaic. See Oakley *ad* Liv. 6.16.4.

5.9 si (*PM* : quia γ) Editors who print *quia* argue that the accretion of words expressing causality presents no problem since the preceding *quam ob rem* is backward-linking (anaphoric), while *quia* looks forward to its own clause. While this may be true, it ignores Ciceronian idiom. *Quam ob rem quia* is unparalleled in C., and when *quam ob rem* is interrupted by a subordinate causal clause, the most common subordinator is *quoniam*; cf. *Phil.* 11.16 *Quam ob rem, quoniam Dolabella hesterno die hoste decreto bellum gerendum est, imperator est deligendus.* The commoner Ciceronian construction is *quam ob rem si*; cf. §62 *Quam ob rem si iure posses …*, *Ver.* II.3.193, 4.81, *Cat.* 2.21, *Caec.* 96, *Clu.* 102, *Planc.* 90, *Rab. perd.* 3, *Mil.* 77, *Cael.* 42, and *Font.* 22.

5.10 unus est accusandus Viz. Verres. *Vnus* gains its point in contrast to *multos … multas … totam* above. The focus on one individual is akin to the 'one man who can make a difference' motif, though this is usually presented from a positive, heroic point of view, such as C.'s *ethos* in the Catilinarians; cf. *Cat.* 1.11 with Dyck *ad loc.* 'This theme often appears in Latin literature with the keyword *unus*: *unus homo nobis cunctando restituit rem*, Ennius *Ann.* 363 Skutsch; *unus erit quem tu tolles in caerula caeli | templa*, Ennius *Ann.* 54–55 Skutsch; *tu Maximus ille es | unus qui nobis cunctando restituis rem*, Virgil *Aen.* 6. 845–846; *unus ille uir, ipse consul, rem publicam sustinuit*, Livy 2.43.6'; Batstone (1994) 237 n. 52. Inversely here, Verres is the one man whose condemnation can make all the difference. One may therefore liken him to a φαρμακός, whose expulsion can solve the ills plaguing the state; cf. Curtius, Liv. 7.6.2.

prope modum signals a conceit; 'virtually' or 'from a certain point of view'. See *TLL* X 2.1971.19–27.

manere in instituto meo resolves the first dilemma from the outset of the speech: C. claims that his prosecution is not only justified but also consistent with his previous forensic activity; see §1 *defenderim multos, laeserim neminem* n.

5.11 uideor (*PM*: *uideo me* γ) The Italian reading ends the clausula with a cretic and resolved spondee, while the French reading is inferior in sense and gives an eschewed heroic clausula; see Quint. *Inst.* 9.4.102. The passive construction of the Italian family also offers a superior sense that offers a shared perspective; see *uidetur* n. above.

non omnino a defendendis hominibus subleuandisque discedere 'not to retire altogether from assisting and defending my fellow man'. This nigh pleonastic collocation is found only here in extant Latin literature (though cf. Phaedrus *App. Per.* 6.10–11 *Defendite armis, hostem ferro pellite; | Amicos subleuate; miseris parcite*). In addition to strengthening the shared sentiment, *subleuare* suggests relieving someone from a misfortune already suffered, while *defendere* points to warding off future harm. This paradigm shift that depicts C.'s prosecution as a defence rounds out the first part of the *exordium* (§§1–5) and resolves the tension established in the first dilemma.

Exordium, continued (§§6–9)

Civic Responsibilities

Even if Cicero did not feel such a personal obligation to Sicily, he could offer no greater aid to the Republic at this time of political and social uncertainty than the prosecution of this notorious scoundrel. Indeed, unrest is prompting a reassessment of the senatorial judicial system, a renewed call for a strengthened tribunate, and an appeal for the censorial lustrum. All these point to a nation that is desperate for good men to take up the righteous cause of the Republic. Cicero consequently stands not just to defend his clients but the entire nation of Rome from the wickedness that threatens her institutions.

The final portion of the *exordium* extends the discussion of C.'s motivation to include the national interest (*rei publicae causa*). He goes to great lengths to contextualize Verres' trial (and the *diuinatio*) within three current political issues: the composition of criminal juries, the powers of the tribunate, and the restoration of the censorship (§8; see nn. *ad loc.*). The outcome of the *diuinatio* and Verres' trial, C. claims, could have a direct impact on the call for these curtailments of senatorial authority. This continues C.'s ethical appeal, which allows him to 'submerge the image of potential destroyer of the life of a fellow citizen beneath the more sympathetic persona of defender of the interests of the Roman people' (Vasaly (2009) 118). In addition to cultivating the goodwill of his audience as part of the *exordium*, this contextualization of the trial within the current political climate is also part of C.'s self-fashioning and electioneering; see §§66–71, §§71–73 introductions, and Vasaly (2009). Of course, this claim of supporting the *res publica* does not apply only to C.; Caecilius could have said the same for himself. C. must therefore devote most of the rest of the speech to distinguishing himself from his rival on other ethical and practical grounds.

Although this section remains part of an *exordium*, the style is not uniformly simple. §§6–7 illustrate a high style of oratory. The sections are replete with literary features and high emotional markers such as tricolon (*tam* ... *tam* ... *tam*), alliteration (e.g. *salutis spem sed solacium exiti*), homeoteleuton (e.g. *populatae, uexatae, funditus euersae prouinciae*), invocation (*pro deum hominumque fidem*), rhetorical questions (*quis* ... *esset, quid est, quid est*), and words of exasperation (*tandem*). The whole of §6, furthermore, is a period of huge weight. A rhetorical display such as this would be accompanied by a raised voice and a heightened emotional appeal; see Quint. *Inst.* 12.10.61–62. C. does not remain in this high emotional state for long. He resumes a more moderated style in §8. For, as he himself remarks, if one speaks in nothing but the high style, he is 'scarcely to be regarded as sane'; see *Orat.* 97–99.

§6

6.1 quodsi ... The second part of the *exordium* begins with a contrafactual condition and, like the hypothetical scenario posited at the outset of the speech (see nn. *ad loc.*), introduces a new framework of thought. The audience is invited to consider what C.'s motives could be even if he had not been petitioned by the Sicilians. A false hypothetical can be used to strengthen an argument; see Quint. *Inst.* 5.10.95–99, especially 95–96 *Illud adiciendum uidetur, duci argumenta non a confessis tantum sed etiam a fictione, quod Graeci* καθ'ὑπόθεσιν *uocant, et quidem ex omnibus isdem locis quibus superiora, quia totidem species esse possunt fictae quot uerae. Nam fingere hoc loco est proponere aliquid quod, si uerum sit, aut soluat quaestionem aut adiuuet, deinde id de quo quaeritur facere illi simile.* This thought experiment also performs the function of an *anticipatio* should anyone seek to discredit his professed connection and obligation to his Sicilian clients and allows him to state an additional motive. For the efficacy of contrafactuals in making legal arguments, see further Lausberg §398. Cf. *Caec.* 55. On the use of *quodsi*, see §54 n. C. uses this hypothetical tactic again with the *prosopopoeia* of Sicily; see §19.

hanc causam tam idoneam, tam illustrem, tam grauem non haberem Anaphora and tricolon give a sense of C.'s heightened emotional state. The tricolon (or longer) with *tam* in C. is common – especially in a negative sense; cf. *Cat.* 1.11 *hanc tam taetram, tam horribilem tamque infestam rei publicae pestem*, 3.17, *Man.* 31, 46, and *Dom.* 105, *Phil* 13.21, and *Att.* 8.4.2. On *grauis*, see §12 *grauem* n. The clause ends with a rousing double trochaic clausula preceded, as often, by a cretic. *Illustris*, from its meaning 'bright', marks out something as 'outstanding' or 'famous', but that sense would be out of place here if it did not also connote some sort of moral goodness; cf. §65 *splendidior … illustrior*, and see *TLL* VII 1.396.33.

6.2 si aut … For the anaphora of *si* after *quodsi*, cf. *Rosc. Am.* 153, *Ver.* II.3.228, 4.114, *Balb.* 41, 49, *Mur.* 9, and *Lig.* 16.

6.3 causa tantae necessitudinis *Causa necessitudinis* or *causa amicitiae* was a fixed phrase: 'ties of friendship'; see *OLD s.u. causa* 12 and *TLL* III 688.4–20. This explains the origin of the *officium* that C. feels he owes the Sicilians; see §4 *officio* n. The nature of the bond of *necessitudo* and the obligations that it puts upon those involved will feature as an important discussion later in the speech (§§59–65). While C. mentions it here as a motive for prosecuting Verres, Caecilius' *causa necessitudinis* with Verres, as C. presents it, should disbar him from leading the case; see

§§59–65 introduction. Speaking broadly, in the nexus of words denoting a relationship (*amicitia*), *necessarius*, more than *familiaris*, implies an obligation to act; see Hellegouarc'h 73–74. For the *necessitudo* between Roman magistrates, see §46 *necessitudinem* n.

6.4 et hoc quod facio *Hoc* refers back to the whole notion of undertaking a prosecution; cf. *Ver.* II.2.118 ... *profecto uereri non debeo ne quis hoc quod facio non existimet me summi offici ratione impulsum coactumque suscepisse.* The 'anadeictic' use of *hic* can refer to more than an 'explicitly expressed antecedent' and 'evoke an entire mental construct'; see Kroon (2017) especially 593. On the anaphoric use of demonstrative pronouns, see *OLS* 1.1139–1143.

rei publicae causa Acting 'on behalf of the Republic' could justify any number of actions, and what constituted the state's best interests was obviously liable to a subjective assessment; e.g. C.'s comments on Gabinius' invasion of Egypt at *Pis.* 50 and *Rab. Post.* 20, or the murder of Gracchus at *De orat.* 2.132. Its evocation is ubiquitous in C. and reigns supreme as the loftiest of motives and justifications; see *Off.* 2.50 *Sed hoc quidem* [conducting a prosecution] *non est saepe faciendum nec umquam nisi aut rei publicae causa.* Here it is intended to serve as C.'s irrefutable reason for his bid to prosecute Verres. Later he will have to reconcile this motive with the consideration of which potential litigator has suffered the most harm at the hands of the accused; see §64 *nulla priuatim accepta iniuria* n.

6.5 cupiditate, audacia, scelere praeditus The asyndeton makes the list of Verres' negative traits seem inexhaustible. *Scelus* is perhaps the strongest word of moral outrage for a crime; cf. 60 *sine scelere* n. Its collocation with *cupiditas* and *audacia* highlights their pejorative meanings. An *audax* endangers the established order; see *Sul.* 16 *sceleris libidinis audaciae* with Berry *ad loc.* and Wirszubski (1961). *Praeditus* always occurs in the final positions after its ablative complements and can be used of both positive and negative attributes; cf. *Clu.* 53 *P. Quintilius Varus, homo summa religione et summa auctoritate praeditus* .... The order here has a sequential rationale. Verres' unbridled desires are put into action by his *audacia*, which results in a moral outrage.

For *cupiditas* and *auaritia* as traits of egocentricity, see Schmalz *ad Lael.* 19. In addition to Verres (*Ver.* II.3.152, 5.32), similar traits are ascribed to Piso and Gabinius (*Prou. Cons.* 43 with Grillo *ad loc.*), Capito (*Rosc. Am.* 101), Catiline (*Cat.* 1.31), and M. Antonius (*Phil.* 3.13). Series of three are prevalent throughout this section; see above *hanc causam tam idoneam, tam illustrem, tam grauem non haberem* n.

6.6 furta atque flagitia An alliterative pair, favoured by the younger C., that occurs unmodified 12 times in the *Ver.* and nowhere else in classical Latin literature. This may have been a hallmark of C.'s more flowery style, which he tempered in later years. *Furtum* applies specifically to theft (the primary charge in an extortion trial), while *flagitium* could refer to any number of disgraceful or shameful activities. As C. will go on to explain, Verres' thefts were also accompanied by a host of other unsavoury acts. *Flagitium* is etymologically related to *flagitare,* as it connotes a crime or scandal which leads to public outcry; see Ernout–Meillet *s.u. flagitare.* C. comes close to this expression again at *Vat.* 13 *quid enim te de Hispaniensibus flagitiis tuis sordidissimisque furtis interrogem?* On alliterative pairs, see the compendium in Wölfflin (1933) 225–281, and for this pair, *ibid.* 262. Alliteration was characteristic of early Latin, and ancient rhetoricians recommend using the device sparingly; see *Rhet. Her.* 4.18. C. uses it moderately to place emphasis on a particular point or image. The conjunction between the two words is not always *atque,* but here it allows the clausula to end with a cretic and resolved trochee. On *atque* followed by a consonant, see §2 *populati atque uexati* n.

non in Sicilia solum sed in Achaia, Asia, Cilicia, Pamphylia, Romae Refers to Verres' previous positions in the army and in elected office. He had been in Achaia and Asia 80–79 as legate to Dolabella in Cilicia after the death of the *proquaestor,* C. Publicius Malleolus. Although he held no official post in Asia or Achaia, C. accuses him of theft and extortion during his journeys with Dolabella. Afterwards, he held the position of *praetor urbanus* in 74. For a full discussion and references to the *actiones in Verrem,* see §38 *quae C. Verres in quaestura, quae in legatione, quae* *in praetura, quae Romae, quae in Italia, quae in Achaia, Asia Pamphyliaque peccarit* with nn. *ad loc.* This geographic/official distribution gives a rough estimation of the *partitio* at the outset of the *actio secunda*; cf. *Ver.* II.1.34. Although his conduct in other positions is not strictly germane to the charge of extortion in Sicily, the Roman prosecutor was tacitly required to demonstrate that the defendant's alleged crimes were part of a wicked past replete with illegal or immoral deeds. The mention of Cilicia and Pamphylia may also have conjured up images of the destructive Mithridates VI and the ongoing Third Mithridatic War.

6.7 denique Introducing the culminating item in a list of three or more; see *Cat.* 4.14 with Dyck *ad loc.* As here, it frequently introduces a phrase with *omnis*; see Schmalz *s.u.* Cf. *Mur.* 78 *ego quod facio, iudices, cum amicitiae dignitatisque L. Murenae gratia facio tum me pacis, otii, concordiae, libertatis, salutis, uitae denique omnium nostrum causa facere clamo atque testor*, *Agr.* 1.9, 2.9, *Ver.* II.3.128, and *Clu.* 146.

ante oculos omnium This prefaces C.'s discussion of vivid description and its importance in a successful prosecution. For more on the meta-rhetorical note, see §27 *in oculis conspectuque* n.

maxima turpissimaque Hendiadys, 'vilest actions'; cf. *Ver.* II.2.78. On *turpitudo*, see §70 *paucorum uitio ac turpitudine* n.

6.8 nossemus The transition to the first-person plural is a subtle psychological ploy. Tempest (2007b) 28 identifies this as the 'everyone knows' *topos*. '[It] is used to shame men into agreement with him by working on the assumption that no one would dare admit their ignorance of an allegedly notorious fact.' This also has roots in Attic oratory; cf. Dem. 21.1 Τὴν μὲν ἀσέλγειαν, ὦ ἄνδρες δικασταί, καὶ τὴν ὕβριν, ᾗ πρὸς ἅπαντας ἀεὶ χρῆται Μειδίας, οὐδέν' οὔθ' ὑμῶν οὔτε τῶν ἄλλων πολιτῶν ἀγνοεῖν οἴομαι. For other connections to Attic oratory, see Tempest (2007b).

me agente 'while I am conducting the case'; see §28 *te actore* n. For *ago* meaning to conduct a case or trial, see *OLD s.u.* 44 and *TLL* I 1395.42–1398.7. On the import of *ago* rather than *accuso*, see §1 *actorem* n.

in iudicium uocaretur 'to be summoned to appear in court'; see Berger *s.u. uocare.*

6.9 quis tandem commonly follows *quodsi* (cf. *Pis.* 40, *Mur.* 4, *Orat.* 58, 101) and frequently introduces a verb of censuring such as *reprehendere* (cf. *Clu.* 142, *Arch.* 13, and *Orat.* 141). *Tandem* connotes protest or impatience, as at *Sul.* 21 and *Cat.* 1.1; see Schmalz *s.u. quis tandem.* This imagined person reminds the reader of the imagined observer first proposed at §1 *si quis* .... C. suggests that the obvious crimes of Verres are enough to allow for anyone to prosecute without suspicion of ulterior motive.

factum aut consilium An echo, in sentiment at least, of §1 *is, si mei consili causam rationemque cognouerit, una et id quod facio probabit,* although this time in a more emotional and emphatic passage. C. is fond of pairing these words and clearly thought of them as complementary; cf. *Ver.* II.3.212–3, *Cat.* 4.20, *Sest.* 36, and *Agr.* 2.6. *Factum* indicates the manifest action, C.'s *postulatio* and appearance at the *diuinatio*; *consilium,* his intended course of action. For *consilium* as opposed to *factum,* see *TLL* IV 441.17.

reprehendere Generally, 'to find fault with' (*OLD* 5a), but perhaps here with a meta-rhetorical play on words suggesting a *reprehensio,* viz. how could Caecilius (or the imagined observer from §1) offer a rebuttal? For *reprehensiones/refutationes,* see §§52–58 introduction.

§7

7.1 quid est ... quid est ... A continuation of the *interrogatio* started in §6. The series of rhetorical questions is another method of conveying urgency and agitation, here strengthened further by the anaphora. On rhetorical questions/*interrogatio,* see *Rhet. Her.* 4.22; see further, Lausberg §§767–770, and Quint. *Inst.* 9.2.6–11 with Winterbottom *ad loc.* for additional references.

pro deum hominumque fidem The *obsecratio* adds an element of pathos to the high style already discussed in §6. This particular invocation occurs elsewhere only in C.'s earlier speeches, at *Rosc. Com.* 23, 50, *Ver.* II.3.137, and 4.7. Also unusual is an invocation at the outset of the speech; it was typically reserved for the *peroratio.* C. would vary between *deum* and *deorum*; see *Orat.* 156. The phrase *pro deum atque hominum fidem* is found in Plautus (cf. *Cur.* 694, *Epid.* 580) and Terence (*An.* 246, *Hau.* 61, *Hec.* 198) and sporadically thereafter (Sal. *Cat.* 20.10. Calp. *Decl.* 20, and 34).

7.2 plus … prodesse possim The alliteration adds to the emotive appeal of the passage. Here C. restates the *rei publicae causa*; see §6. C.'s preoccupation with benefiting the Republic may seem like a common ploy in his forensic and political speeches, but at least in later correspondence, this appears to be a genuine sentiment; see *Att.* 7.3.3, 14.13.4. For this verb with a stronger medical nuance, see §70 *prodesse* n.

hoc tempore C. attempts to associate the trial of Verres with various political developments. Chief among them are jury reform, restoration of the tribunate, and the election of censors; see below. C. was a master of invoking the rhetoric of crisis, and judicial reform will become his central political issue in the first hearing against Verres. For a broader overview of these issues, see Introduction §I.

7.3 aut populo Romano … aut sociis exterisque nationibus … aut saluti fortunisque omnium An ascending tricolon which progresses from a Roman centre (the *populus Romanus*) and works outward to include foreign allies and territories and then universal welfare. The stroke is a populist one. In C.'s depiction of properly functioning government, the state benefits when it responds to the desires of its citizens and subjugated peoples. For the pairing of *salus* and *fortunae,* cf. *Ver.* II.2.118, *Rab. Per.* 3, *Fam.* 2.6.3, 6.9.2, and *Att.* 11.3.1. For *salus* as a political ideal, see Winkler (1995) 30–35.

7.5 accommodatum sit concludes the colon with a typical cretic and trochee rhythm, though when C. uses a form of *accommodatus,* he frequently affords it the final position; cf. *Ver.* II.1.63, 3.155, *Clu.* 36, 79, and *Sul.* 17.

populatae, uexatae, funditus euersae prouinciae αὔξησις/*amplificatio* heightened by asyndeton and homeoteleuton; C. suggests that provincial mismanagement extends beyond Verres' in Sicily and is actually a more widespread problem which is leading to general discontent and the loss of natural resources. This, of course, broadens the implications of Verres' trial. The primary appeal here is to a sense of economic loss and mismanagement of resources rather than to pity. For more on the device of *amplificatio*, see Lausberg §259. Although the participle, *populatae*, is formed from a deponent verb, C. prefers the passive meaning; see Schmalz *s.u.* and Neue-Wagener 3.80. For its coupling with *uexatus*, cf. §2 *populati atque uexati* and *Ver.* I.45. The collocation of *funditus* and *euerto* is common in C.; cf. *Ver.* II.3.48, 77, *Phil.* 2.52, *Dom.* 35, and *Fam.* 5.21.4.

7.6 socii stipendiariique populi Romani Rome's allies were vital to the empire's defence and economic stability. *Ciuitates stipendiariae*, as opposed to 'free' states, were liable to pay tribute to Rome. On the nature of federated states, see Sherwin-White (1973) 150–157 and Lintott (1993) 16–21. On the nature of alliances in the Greek East, see Morstein-Marx (1995) 190–197. On *socii*, see §17 *socii populi Romani* n.

7.7 non salutis spem sed solacium exiti quaerunt *Solacium* is often found with the genitive of the misfortune from which one needs relief; see *OLD s.u.* The pairing of *salus* and *exitium* is characteristic of the *pathos* C. tries to elicit in a *peroratio* (cf. *Rosc. Am.* 149; *Mil.* 100) and further emphasizes the emotional appeals made by the Sicilians. **solacium exiti** are transposed in the Italian tradition and the Gronovian scholiast. Provided *exiti* is written with one long final syllable, either order gives a cretic and spondee rhythm. The French order better preserves the alliterative quality, has a more common chiastic structure (see §32 *graue* … *graue* n.), and leaves the most striking element, *exitium*, for the final position.

§8

8.1 qui iudicia manere apud ordinem senatorium uolunt About ten years earlier, Sullan reforms to the *quaestiones perpetuae* had transferred control of the juries from *equites* to members of the senate. As early as 78, shortly after the dictator's death, proposals were being made to reverse the legislative course; see B. A. Marshall and Beness (1987). In 74 the matter came to the fore when the tribune L. Quinctius defended Oppianicus against allegations of poisoning; see further *TLRR* 149. The defendant was convicted but not without widespread suspicions of bribery – so much so that the senate itself ordered a general inquiry into judicial corruption. Quinctius seized upon this apparent miscarriage of justice to bolster his populist political campaign and to stir up agitation for judicial reform and full restoration of the tribunate (see below). Several riots broke out when Quinctius prepared charges against the *iudex*, C. Junius, who had presided at the trial. Popular pressure, however, forced Junius into exile before he could be brought to court. After Quinctius' campaign, there is no evidence of further popular agitation. The issue was again resurrected in 71, when Pompeius, as consul-elect, announced in a public address that he would at least consider judicial reform; see *Ver.* II.1.45 cited below. For the plight of L. Quinctius, see *Clu.* 74, 77, 89–96, 108–113, Quint. *Inst.* 5.13.39, Schol. Gronov. 351 Stangl, *LGRR* 33–34, and Vasaly (2009) 101–102.

As for those who were opposing the measure to reform the courts, no one is named specifically, though there are a host of theories; see Vasaly (2009) and Twyman (1972). If such a cadre of anti-reformists existed, presumably it originally included leading senatorial conservatives like Q. Catulus and Hortensius. In the first action against Verres in August of 70, C. would remark: *Neque hoc Q. Catulum, hominem sapientissimum atque amplissimum, fugit, qui Cn. Pompeio, uiro fortissimo et clarissimo, de tribunicia potestate referente cum esset sententiam rogatus, hoc initio est summa cum auctoritate usus, patres conscriptos iudicia male et flagitiose tueri; quodsi in rebus iudicandis populi Romani existimationi satis facere uoluissent, non tanto opere homines fuisse tribuniciam potestatem desideraturos* (*Ver.* I.44). But the inferences drawn from this representation run the gamut. 'Might [Catulus] not have gone on in his speech, after this bit of Realpolitik analysis – shared not with the public but with his colleagues in the senate – to admit the inevitability of promulgating Pompey's tribuncian law while strongly advising that a higher standard of judicial conduct be demonstrated to the masses in order to prevent further agitation for changes in the juries?'; Vasaly (2009) 105. Others think that the issue was a *fait accompli* by the middle of the year. 'Nothing attests to any political struggle over passage of the measure. Q. Catulus, among others, conceded that there was no point in unnecessarily rousing public antipathy'; *LGRR* 34–35. But it could be said that giving the *equites* a role in juries led to much of the political strife in the 30 years before Sulla's dictatorship. It made life less easy for senatorial governors, so it would not be surprising that the senate wanted to maintain control. In any event, C. draws a sharp distinction between senatorial conservatives and the *populus Romanus* and looks for ways to exploit real or perceived tensions between them; see *populus Romanus interea* n. below.

8.2 accusatores ... idoneos C. will spend a significant portion of §§27–47 discussing the qualities of a 'suitable prosecutor'. In retrospect, this is a slight to Caecilius; see [Asc.] 102 (188 Stangl) *tangit Caecilius.*

8.4 seueritatem A species of *grauitas.* Hellegouarc'h 282 '*Severitas* also commonly applies to judges whose decisions are not influenced either by corruption or by undue leniency; in this instance, *severitas* is the opposite of *clementia.* It is this quality which prompted the selection of senators as jurors in the trial of Sextus Roscius (*Rosc. Am.* 8); it particularly applies to older individuals who assume a strict moral point of view. [Fréquemment encore, il [*seueritas*] se rapporte aux juges dont les décisions ne sont influencées ni par la corruption, ni par une indulgence excessive; dans ce cas également *seueritas* s'oppose à *clementia.* C'est la qualité qui fait choisir les sénateurs membres du jury dans le procès de S. Roscius; elle est propre aux gens âgés supposés plus forts au point de vue moral.]'

populus Romanus interea C. exaggerates the importance of this hearing by exploiting a perceived rift in senatorial and popular interests. In highlighting both senatorial and popular concerns, C. deploys a deft political manoeuvre in which he can position himself as a bridge between the two. If the jury chooses him, they will have a suitable prosecutor and indicate to the people, who are agitating for social change, that they are also seeking a more honest and rigorous judiciary. He will conclude the *Diu.*

Caec. on a similar note; see §73 with nn. *ad loc.* It is typical of him to treat the self-selective and ever-changing crowd at a *contio* as though it were the *populus Romanus* itself; Morstein-Marx (2004) 120–122. Cf. *Phil.* 7.22, *Att.* 7.18.1. This same tendency for portrayed or assumed homogeneity also applies to the Sicilians (*Siculi uniuersi*, etc.). *Interea* can have an adversative force as it does here; cf. *Mur.* 49 and *Sul.* 17, and see *TLL* VII 1.2183.9–23.

8.5 multis incommodis difficultatibusque [Asc.] 102 (189 Stangl) identifies these as injustices suffered under Sulla. In addition to the land seizures and curtailed power of the tribunate, grain shortages were also a problem in the 70s and required constant intervention; see B. A. Marshall and Beness (1987) and Mitchell (1979) 113. C. himself assisted in providing some relief in acquiring a consignment of grain from Sicily during his quaestorship. Campaigns in Spain and against Mithridates also demanded funds and attention. The senate was frequently hard pressed to provide domestic relief; see *LGRR* 35–36. C. may overplay his hand here; it is hard to imagine that judicial reform would loom large in the minds of those with empty stomachs.

8.6 iudiciorum uim et grauitatem requirit is an emendation of a phrase lost from *P* and the French family (γ) by *saut du même au même* in both. The *deteriores* provide the missing words as *uim grauitatemque requirit.* Although this gives the eschewed heroic clausula (*ēmquĕ rĕquīrit*), the doublet is very Ciceronian: cf. *Har.* 2 *uim et grauitatem*, 41 *quanta ui, quanta grauitate*, *Fin.* 5.12, *N. D.* 2.93 *ui et gravitate*, *Brut.* 88, and *Phil.* 9.15 *uim grauitatemque morbi contenderit.* The antiquity of the phrase is confirmed by a lemma in the text of the Gronovian scholiast, *grauitatem req. iud.* Although the scholiast may have intentionally omitted *-que*, C. could easily have written *et* to join the two terms, and this would give the clausula a more desirable trochaic metron rhythm. For similar rhythmical reasons, Shackleton Bailey (1979) 241 suggested *ueterum iudiciorum auctoritatem requirit*, which would provide a more desirable trochaic metron preceded by a cretic; cf. §70 and *Ver.* I.5. On the heroic clausula, see Quint. *Inst.* 9.4.102 and *Orat.* 217, though interpretations of the latter passage vary.

8.7 iudiciorum desiderio ... begins another ascending tricolon. *Desiderium* expresses grief especially for something lost or missing (see *TLL* V 1.697.73). The anaphora of *iudiciorum* lays the responsibility for public unrest squarely at the feet of the senators, who have mismanaged the judicial system. C. again makes the connection between judicial corruption and clamouring for the restoration of the tribunate at *Ver.* I.44: *Neque enim ullam aliam ob causam populus Romanus tribuniciam potestatem tanto studio requisiuit; quam cum poscebat, uerbo illam poscere uidebatur, re uera iudicia poscebat.*

tribunicia potestas The tribunate had a history of being a platform for social reform or sedition. After the uprisings caused by the Gracchi and Sulpicius, Sulla strictly curtailed the powers of the tribunes. In addition to limiting their power of veto, he deprived them of the right to introduce legislation without the prior sanction of the senate (or perhaps even at all; see Millar (1998) 53–54), and an ex-tribune was forbidden from holding any further office; see e.g. Vell. 2.30 *cuius* [*tribuniciae potestatis*] *Sulla imaginem sine re reliquerat.*

Agitation to reform this policy had begun as early as 78; see Sall. *Hist.* 1.77 and [Asc.] 103 (189 Stangl). A survey of those attempts will bring the political landscape of the *Diu. Caec.* into better focus. The year after the tribune Sicinius had unsuccessfully lobbied for reform, a tribune of 75, Q. Opimius, made partial inroads by working together with the consul, C. Aurelius Cotta, to lift the ban on tribunes seeking further office; see *Ver.* II.1.55, *Corn.* in [Asc.] 66.2–4, 78.18–25, Sall. *Hist.* 2.49, and [Asc.] 200 (255 Stangl). Although this removed a restriction, it did very little to restore the powers of the office to the level where they had once been. The next year, L. Quinctius (see *qui ... uolunt* n. above) managed to associate the issue of full restoration of the tribunate with judicial reform in the public consciousness but failed to effect any change; see *Clu.* 77. The following year C. Licinius Macer strongly criticized the nobility for their recalcitrance but to no avail; see Sall. *Hist.* 3.48. The conservative members of the senate expressed their discontent. Catulus and Hortensius had levelled charges against Opimius for exceeding the bounds of his office and condemned him with a ruinous fine. In later years, Catulus was joined in opposition by C. Curio and members of the Luculli. The matter seems to have lain dormant in 72. But when Pompey returned to Rome in 71 from his campaigns in Spain, he began to build up political capital by championing popular causes – one of which was the restoration of tribunician power; see further *LGRR* 23–28.

Instrumental in this legislation was the tribune of 71, M. Lollius Palicanus, with whom Pompey joined forces; see the coin illustrated in Figure 3 and [Asc.] 189, 220 Stangl, *Brut.* 223, Sall. *Hist.* 4.43, and Wiseman (1971) 237–238. Quinctius' manoeuvre to link the tribunate with judicial reform apparently worked, since in 71 Pompey, then consul designate, spoke at a *contio* on both issues; see *Ver.* I.45:

> Ipse denique Cn. Pompeius cum primum contionem ad urbem consul designatus habuit, ubi, id quod maxime exspectari uidebatur, ostendit se tribuniciam potestatem restituturum, factus est in eo strepitus et grata contionis admurmuratio. Idem in eadem contione cum dixisset populatas uexatasque esse prouincias, iudicia autem turpia ac flagitiosa fieri; ei rei se prouidere ac consulere uelle; tum uero non strepitu sed maximo clamore suam populus Romanus significauit uoluntatem.

At the time of the *diuinatio,* change was on the horizon. Shortly afterward, Pompey and Crassus, the consuls of 70, restored the tribunate to its pre-Sullan powers. For more on these

Figure 3: A denarius of 45 BCE minted by the son of Palicanus (RRC 473/1) depicting Libertas and the rostra and the tribunician *subsellium*; discussed in Morstein-Marx (2004) 52–53.

reforms under Pompey, see McDermott (1977b) and B. A. Marshall (1976) 53–54. For a history of the tribunate from 80 to 71, see B. A. Marshall (1987). For this popular clamour as manifested in the *contio*, see *efflagitata* n. below.

8.8 efflagitata Invariably used in C.'s speeches of a demand vehemently placed before a superior official or body; cf. *Ver.* I.1, 63, 92; see *TLL* V 2.187.50. The insistence inherent in the diction (and in the synonyms *postulatur* and *poscitur*) indicates the expression of popular opinion manifest at *contiones*; see *Ver.* I.45 in n. above.

iudiciorum leuitate *Leuitas* contrasts with *grauitas* above (cf. *Fam* 1.7.7) and indicates weakness or inconstancy; see *OLD s.u.* 3 and *TLL* VII 2.1225.10–54. C. notes it as a quality of the popular rabble and Greek assemblies; cf. *Sest.* 141 and *Flac.* 71. A properly functioning judiciary should consistently and predictably respond to and apply the rule of law; see *D.* 1.3.3–6 and *Off.* 3.43. To fail in that regard undermines confidence in the institution as a whole; see Riggsby (1997). Cf. the trial of Oppianicus at *qui ... uolunt* n. above.

ordo quoque alius ad res iudicandas 'an entirely different class of citizens ought to be empanelled on juries'; i.e. the *tribuni aerarii.* See Schol. Gronov. (326 Stangl). Mixed jury composition beyond simply senators and *equites* must already have come up for discussion, though there may have been multiple rival proposals for judicial reform; see further Vasaly (2009) 107 n. 18. *Alius* is only appropriate with three or more; *alter* would be used if there were only two. The *lex Aurelia,* which passed toward the end of 70, would establish juries of one-third senators, one-third *equites,* and one-third from another *ordo,* the *tribuni aerarii.* What distinguished an *eques* from a *tribunus aerarius* is unclear. Some, following the Schol. Bob. *In Clod. et Cur.* fr. 31 (91 Stangl), set a distinct census qualification for *trib. aer.* of HS 300,000; others hold that the property qualification for *equites* and *trib. aer.* was the same but that they 'were elected in some way to an obsolete military office which distinguished them as an *ordo* within the state, while the *equites* of the *lex Aurelia* were those who belonged or had belonged to the eighteen centuries of *equites equo publico* (i.e. those who had been officially designated as *equites*)'; B. A. Marshall (1975a) 139. For the import of these distinctions upon the political make-up of juries, see Henderson (1963) 61–64, who argues that *equites* proper would have had more in common with senatorial interests than the *trib. aer.* For the military office, which may have paid soldiers their wages, see *N-P s.u. tribunus aerarius. Quoque* is quasi-enclitic and generally placed immediately after the word that it is meant to emphasize; see Schmalz *s.u.*

8.9 culpa atque dedecore They apply both to reprehensible and dishonest behaviour and to the resulting shame and discredit; see *TLL* V 1.252.11–12. This is the only collocation of the two terms in classical Latin; see *TLL* IV 1298.58. The moral rectitude associated with *decus* should have been a distinguishing feature of the senate, on which, see Hellegouarc'h 413–415. For *atque* with a consonant, see §2 *populati atque uexati* n.

censorium nomen The censorship had not been filled since 86. Before the Social War, a censor had regularly been elected every five years for an 18-month term. The upheaval caused by the Social War and Sulla's dictatorship had disrupted the regular appointment. And then the office may have been 'superfluous' under Sulla's constitutional reform; see Suolahti (1963) 457. The censorship would indeed be reinstituted in 70 with the election of Cn. Cornelius Lentulus Clodianus and L. Gellius Publicola, consuls of 72. While carrying out the *lustrum*, they removed 64 members of the senate and counted 910,000 citizens; see [Asc.] 150 (222 Stangl). Although there may have been many reasons for expulsion from the senate, known or suspected judicial bribery was one, and among those expelled were the judges from Oppianicus' trial; see *Clu.* 117–135. Although this purge was considered to be severe, Sulla's reforms had doubled the size of the senate from 300 to 600 members with no election of censors in 15 years; see *Ver.* II.1.143 and *MRR* 1.126. The censorship, however, would not endure; although more censors would be appointed, no other set of censors would complete their official duties before the onset of the Principate. On the Roman censorship, in addition to Suolahti (1963), see *N-P s.u. censores*, Leuze

(1926), Wiseman (1969), and Astin (1985a). On the elections in 70, see *Ver.* II.5.15, *Clu.* 120, *Flac.* 45, Suolahti (1963) 458–463, and *LGRR* 44. For C.'s views on the censorship, see *Leg.* 3.7 and Astin (1985b).

8.10 asperius For *asper* in the context of the censorship, see Vell. 1.10.6 *Aspera circa haec tempora censura Fuluii Flacci et Postumii Albini fuit ....*

8.11 populare et plausibile *Plausibilis* is only found in C. here and at *Tusc.* 3.51. It is altogether uncommon and only found elsewhere in Seneca the Younger and Quintilian. The alliterative pair with the preceding *poscitur* may resonate as the contional response; see above *efflagitata* n. Cf. the onomatopoetic word in final position to describe Pompey's *contio* on the restoration of the tribunician powers at *Ver.* I.45: *grata contionis admurmuratio.* If applause is suggested, it was perhaps a new form of public response; see *Att.* 4.1.6 *quo senatus consulto recitato cum (populus) more hoc insulso et nouo plausum meo nomine recitando dedisset, habui contionem.* **et** (*γPO* : atque *M*) C. tends to use *atque* with a consonant for metrical reasons, but here it is not placed at the end of a colon and would provide a premature clausula. For the coupling, cf. Quint. *Inst.* 12.10.47 *magis existimant populare atque plausibile.*

§9

9.1 libidine This final section of the *exordium* shares several points of similarity with C.'s emotional appeal in the *conclusio,* including the concerns and perspective of the Roman people, the reputation of the courts and the senatorial order, the image of the ailing state, and the role of just and able men in restoring the fortunes of the republic; cf. §§70–73. *Libido* is particularly used to describe the wantonness of magistrates and rulers; see *TLL* VII 2.1334.80–1335.64. Cf. *Ver.* II.3.77 *Eandem istius, qui se regem Siculorum esse dicebat, licentiam libidinemque fuisse cognoscite.*

9.2 quotidiana querimonia Perhaps shorthand for *contiones* and the like. For a meeting expressing public discontent described as a *querimonia,* cf. *Ver.* II.3.132. Public meetings could be a daily occurrence; see *contiones cotidianae* in *Brut.* 305–306, *Clu.* 93, 103, *Mil.* 12, *Sest.* 39, 41, [Asc.] 49 C, and Morstein-Marx (2004) 9. The older spelling of *quotidianus* has been used here in this edition to underscore the alliterative quality of the phrase.

9.3 offensione acts in both an active and passive sense: the act that causes the outrage and the effect of the action (e.g. hostility, discontent). *Totius ordinis* therefore may be understood as both a subjective and an objective genitive: 'the outrageous behaviour of the entire senatorial order' or 'the outrage directed toward …'. On this active and passive meaning, see Hellegouarc'h 195.

9.4 remedium See §70 *hoc remedium* n., where C. develops the emotive allegory of the ailing republic.

9.5 idonei atque integri C. will go on to argue that Caecilius is neither suited to the task (*idoneus*) nor of good character (*integer*); cf. §35 along with §27 *integritatem … innocentiam singularem* n. **idonei** The second hand of *E* writes *boni* in the margin, which helps to identify the source of these Italian corrections as a later descendant of *v*; see Introduction §VI and Reeve (2016) 65–69.

9.6 fateor suggests an admission under compulsion. When C. uses the verb of himself, the sense of reticence is often feigned, as it is here. Cf. *Rosc. Am.* 142, and see *TLL* VI 339.27–38. This is perhaps a play on a *concessio* in which the defendant admits part of the accusations against him; cf. §62 *fatearis* n. and *Rosc. Am.* 94, and see Lausberg §856.

ad eam partem accessisse C. eschewed his own active agency in the first half of the *exordium*; he had been compelled by social obligations (§5 *adductus sum …*). Now at the conclusion of the *exordium* C. becomes an active agent in assuming the prosecution.

rei publicae subleuandae The diction recalls the conclusion of the first part of the *exordium* at §5: *uideor … non omnino a defendendis hominibus subleuandisque discedere.* In developing his purported motives, C. has moved beyond the needs of individuals and taken up the cause of the state. The word choice serves both to connect the second half of the *exordium* to the first and to develop C.'s presentation of a *causa anceps* as a *causa honesta*; see introduction to this section. C. most often uses the noun-with-gerundive phrase in the genitive case; see Laughton (1964) 93–94. As transmitted in the MSS, the phrase must mean 'to have taken up the role of relieving the state, which is suffering gravely'. When C. employs *pars* in this sense, however, he uses the plural form; cf. *Quinct.* 8, *Ver.* II.1.65, 3.131, *Font.* 21, *Sul.* 92, *Balb.* 1, and see *TLL* X 1.464.47–81. Orsini therefore offered the conjecture *subleuandam*, hence 'to have come forward to relieve that part of the state which is in the gravest condition'.

9.7 quae maxime laboraret The image of sickness and the 'state as a body' is common in C.; see §70 *hoc remedium* n. Medical terms, or phrases with that valence, awaken latent metaphor: e.g. *incommodis, remedium, salutis*, etc. With *laborare*, cf. *Rosc. Am.* 154 *ex quibus rebus maxime res publica laborat*, and see *TLL* VII 2.806.29–38.

CONFIRMATIO §§10–51

Partitio (§10)

How to Choose a Prosecutor

C. has explained that he feels obliged to prosecute Verres in the interests of both his Sicilian clients and the Roman people. Now he must establish why he should be chosen as the lead prosecutor against any other claimants. When deciding between potential prosecutors, as C. understands the matter, jurors should consider whom the victims would most want to represent them and whom the accused would least want to prosecute him.

A *partitio* should pinpoint the area of disagreement between opposing parties and/or state the topics that the speaker intends to address. This ensures that the objective and the structure of the speech are clear and precise (*Inu.* 31 *Recte habita in causa partitio illustrem et perspicuam totam efficit orationem*). The audience is thereby allowed to focus on the point of contention and follow the argument closely; see *Inu.* 1.18, 31–33, *Rhet. Her.* 1.4, 17. Many of C.'s speeches do not contain a *partitio* proper, and this passage in the *Diuinatio in Caecilium* is certainly not exhaustive nor is it a *partitio* in the strictest sense. It is generally regarded as the beginning of the *confirmatio* since C.'s bipartite division only covers the topics discussed through §26. The two parts of his argument will correspond to the factors upon which the judges should make their decision. The two primary considerations in the choice of a prosecutor, he argues, are (1) who is most desirable to the victims and (2) who is least desirable to the accused.

Though this *diuisio* demonstrates a clarity of organization broadly in line with rhetorical theory, its contentiousness is disguised. The rationale for deciding among potential prosecutors, which C. articulates as though it were commonplace and around which he structures his argument, represents an argumentative position in and of itself. A passage from Quintilian affords a glimpse into the novelty of C.'s approach. In a discussion of issue theory, Quintilian lists particular occasions on which divisions based on 'quality' are most appropriate:

> De accusatore constituendo, quae iudicia diuinationes uocantur: in quo genere Cicero quidem, qui mandantibus sociis Verrem deferebat, hac usus est diuisione: spectandum a quo maxime agi uelint ii quorum de ultione quaeritur, a quo minime uelit is qui accusatur. Frequentissimae tamen hae sunt quaestiones, uter maiores causas habeat, uter plus industriae aut uirium sit allaturus ad accusandum, uter id fide meliore facturus. (Quint. *Inst.* 7.4.33)

No other *diuinationes* are extant for comparison, but Quintilian's comments are enough to show that C.'s approach and stated rationale were unconventional, and this innovation has broader implications for the *Diu. Caec.* as a whole. Positing new *quaestiones* also entails challenging the traditional basis upon which prosecutors are normally chosen. This implies that C.'s argumentative strategy is atypical of the genre. C.'s novel tactic, in addition to piquing the jury's interest, was more expedient than the traditional selection rubric. Marius Victorinus generally noted C.'s ability to devise a *partitio* that was more advantageous to his case than one that the bare facts would suggest, and cites our passage in particular; Victorinus 1.22 (Ippolito 99):

> Aut si partitio de ipsa causa non sumitur, ea membra ponit orator, quae ipse ingenio inuenit et sibi dicenda constituit,

> non ex negotii factis ad causam sumptis sed argumentatione oratoris in causa conlocatis, ut in diuinatione: Ego sic intellego, cum de pecuniis repetundis quaestio sit, si nomen cuiuspiam deferatur, haec duo in primis spectari oportere, quem maxime actorem uelint hi qui eas iniurias passi sint et quem minime uelit is qui eas iniurias fecisse arguatur.

C. will eventually address motive (*causa*), diligence or ability (*industria aut uires*), and sincerity (*fides*) as a matter of course, but he does not allow them to become the organizing principles of his *confirmatio.* Caecilius may have had a greater claim to a just motive through personal enmity, and he might have been able to make a convincing accusation through his intimate knowledge of Verres' praetorship – particularly in the judicial and financial spheres. Though C. does try to cast suspicion on Caecilius' sincerity, the insinuation of *praeuaricatio* is unsubstantiated and without sustained force. C., on the other hand, could have been accused of political opportunism. The jury might believe his eagerness and diligence would wane if the trial did not coincide advantageously with this canvass for the aedileship. At the very least, a juror might find C.'s political manoeuvring distasteful. However, focusing on the interests of the litigants and the accused shifts attention away from C.'s inability to provide a customary justification for leading the prosecution.

Arguing that jurors in the *diuinatio* should – and, in fact, have a nigh legal responsibility to – consider the wishes of the injured party is tantamount to a *de facto* devolution of the selection process into the hands of Roman subjects; on this argument, see §§17–18 introduction. But they, too, must have their own rationale. His clients are also concerned with *fides* and the personal character of the prosecutor (§§4, 11, 20), but he also suggests that a primary consideration for them and for the jury must be the candidate's oratorical ability. However, C. does not signpost this discussion, since doing so could have been off-putting. Instead, he feigns reluctance throughout and then only makes an oblique approach to the excursus on rhetoric and the *comparatio* between himself and Caecilius that will constitute such a large part of the speech (§§27–47).

On *partitiones/diuisiones*, see *Inu.* 1.31–33, *Rhet. Her.* 1.17, Quint. *Inst.* 4.5.1–28, and Lausberg §347. Of the speeches with proper *partitiones*, Berry (1996) 150 lists *Quinct.*, *Rosc. Am.*, *Ver.* I.2, *Man.*, *Clu.*, *Mur.*, and *Phil.* 7 as meeting narrower criteria, but the *partitio* of *Rosc. Am.* is also strategically limited in its scope; see Kinsey (1985). Quintilian marked out the *partitio* at *Mur.* 11 as exemplary. As his career and oratorical skills developed, C. would less frequently include a *partitio* in his speeches. On this shift, see Berry on *Sul.* 11–14.

§10

10.1 nunc quoniam signals a change in focus; cf. *Ver.* II.5.164 and *Cat.* 3.16, and see Seyffert 1§34. C. moves from discussing his personal motives for seeking the prosecution to presenting a rubric by which a lead prosecutor can be chosen from among competing litigants.

adductus This absolute use of the participle is common in C.; cf. *Ver.* II.1.90, 2.153, 5.158, and see *TLL* I 602.69–75 and Merguet *s.u. adduco.* C. echoes his diction from §5 *adductus sum,* though in the intervening discussion he has given himself the additional motivation of service to the state (*rei publicae causa*).

10.2 dicendum necessario est The gerundive expression of obligation with the adverb *necessario* is a pleonastic collocation found primarily in C.'s early writings; e.g. *Ver.* II.2.1 *Multa mihi necessario, iudices, praetermittenda sunt. Sest.* 14 and *De orat.* 1.219 are later exceptions.

de contentione nostra A metonym for 'the issue under discussion' (*TLL* IV 674.76–77 *id ipsum de quo certatur, argumentum*), which can also be applied to a forensic action generally (*TLL* IV 676.35–53). C., however, is also engaging in some meta-rhetorical wordplay as the *contentio* also particularly applies to the use of contrasting phrases in a bipartite *dispositio* (*TLL* IV 676.68–77, and *Rhet. Her.* 4.21 *contentio est, cum ex contrariis rebus oratio conficitur*); cf. the *partitio* at §10 *quem maxime … quem minime …* n.

10.3 in constituendo accusatore 'in your appointment of a prosecutor'. For this use of *constituo*, see *TLL* IV 523.25–37. Other titles for the speech will occasionally refer to the *Diuinatio* as *de accusatore constituendo*; see Introduction §V.

sequi possitis 'you may be able to use as your guide'; *OLD sequor* 10b.

ego sic intellego 'as I understand it myself'. The phrase emphasizes and draws attention to the following statement, as does the following vocative; cf. *Prou. Cons.* 30 *ego uero sic intellego* with Grillo *ad loc.* For the parenthetical absolute use of *intellegere*, see *TLL* VII 1.2101.81–2102.15.

10.4 cum de pecuniis repetundis nomen cuiuspiam deferatur 'when someone is being indicted for extortion', viz. the pre-trial legal procedure of *nominis delatio.* For this legal procedure, see Introduction §III and Greenidge (1901) 459–466. C. may have used *cuiuspiam* here rather than *alicuius* for a cretic and ditrochaic rhythm and for variation with *aliquos* below; cf. *Sul.* 41. *Quispiam* is uncommon in C.'s earlier speeches; see *Rosc. Am.* 56 with Landgraf *ad loc.* For the legal use of *deferre*, see Heumann–Seckel *s.u.* 3 and *TLL* V 1.316.44–318.42.

10.5 certamen Though legal confrontations are frequently described with military metaphors, there is no reason to think that *diuinationes* were typically combative affairs, but it is to C.'s advantage to characterize it as one. This subtle characterization of the *diuinatio* as a 'contest' or 'confrontation' between potential litigants neatly sums up the antithetical nature of the *diuisio* and will allow C. to recast this particular *diuinatio* as an oratorical contest, in which rhetorical skill more than grievance will be used to determine the victor. This notion of a two-way contest also lays the groundwork for the extended *comparationes* of Caecilius' skills and motives with C.'s throughout the rest of the speech. On military vocabulary in the forensic setting, see §1 *defenderim multos, laeserim neminem* n., and on *certamen* in particular, *TLL* III 885.29–887.31. For the collocation of *contentio* and *certamen*, cf. *Ver.* II.2.3, 3.177, *Agr.* 3.1, and *Flac.* 92. For the staging of the *diuinatio* as a rhetorical contest, see Introduction §IV.

inter aliquos The preposition *inter* does not limit itself to two parties, i.e. it can mean both 'between' and 'among'. Though Quintilian describes *diuinationes* between two potential candidates (see *uter* at Quint. *Inst.* 7.4.33 in the introduction above), there could have been three or more; cf. *Q. fr.* 3.2.1 *apud Catonem erat diuinatio in Gabinium futura inter Memmium et Ti. Neronem et C. L. Antonios M. f.*

potissimum Perhaps with the distinction of 'chiefly' rather than 'exclusively'. Additional assistant prosecutors could be appointed to try the case; see introduction to §§47–51. For this use of *potissimum* in deliberations, see *TLL* X 2.354.82–355.20.

delatio 'the right to prosecute', a narrower legal usage here than simply 'accusation'; *OLD s.u.* 2a. Cf. §34 *indicium … dari* n. No distinction is made in the *TLL*. The alliterative pairing offers a common cretic and trochee conclusion to the clausula.

10.6 haec duo C. asks his audience to keep two salient issues in mind and so prepares them for the different parts of the *confirmatio*, §§11–22 and §§23–27. He does not, however, prepare them for the *refutatio* or the long digression on oratorical ability. Rhetorical theory advises against providing too many subjects for discussion as these may give the impression of over-preparation or incur the audience's displeasure from anticipating an exhaustive presentation; see *Rhet. Her.* 1.17 *Eam* (*enumerationem*) *plus quam trium partium numero esse non oportet: nam et periculosum est, ne quando plus minusue dicamus; et suspicionem adfert auditori meditationis et artificii, quae res fidem abrogat orationi*; but contrast Quint. *Inst.* 4.5.3. C. may not have outlined his arguments for the *refutatio* since, as its organizing principle, it will use the more traditional (and disadvantageous) lines of enquiry associated with *diuinationes*; see §§52–65 introduction.

oportere See §19 *oportere* n.

quem maxime … quem minime … The *partitio* is phrased as a *contentio* (ἀντίθετον), in which two *res* are contrasted with one another, with typical syntactic symmetry; see Lausberg §787: 'With all variants of the *antitheton*, the tendency toward equality of the elements (*isocolon*) may be observed; the outward equality itself forms a contrast to the opposition of the conceptual content' and here gives the impression of completeness. The device is also known as ἀντίθεσις, *contrapositum*, and *contrarium*; see Arist. *Rhet.* 3.1409b33, *Part.* 21, Quint. *Inst.* 9.2.100–101, 3.81–86 with Russell *ad loc.*, *Rhet. Her.* 4.21 with Caplan *ad loc.*, and Lausberg §§443.1, 787–807. For other examples in this speech, cf. §§34, 35, and 61.

The two indirect questions constitute the *quaestiones* around which C. will structure his *confirmatio*; *Inu.* 1.10 *Omnis res quae habet in se positam in dictione ac disceptatione aliquam controuersiam aut facti aut nominis aut generis aut actionis continet quaestionem.* These *quaestiones* are precipitated by a first-order issue (*constitutio*; see Lausberg §§80–81) which is left unexpressed here, but it implicitly asks not 'Who has the greater cause?' but even more fundamentally 'By what rationale should a prosecutor be chosen?' See introduction above. **minime** (*PM* : *maxime* γ) the reading of the Italian family ensures that the answer to both questions is the same, viz. C., and *minime* is further confirmed by the phrase in §22, *a quo Verres minime se accusari uelit.* The citation in Victorinus shows signs of interpolation (e.g. *quaestio*) and fails to summarize the situation under which a *diuinatio* was convened.

10.7 ii quibus There is the usual confusion in the MSS between *ii* and *hi.* As C. is attempting to articulate a general principle for choosing a prosecutor, *ii* is more appropriate than the demonstrative *hi*, which cannot stand alone as the antecedent to the relative clause; H-Sz. 180–181. See further Touratier (1980) and Lavency (1998).

iniuriae When C. assesses a potential claim that Caecilius has the *maior causa*, he will demand a more exacting, legalistic definition of *iniuria*, i.e. that which has been done *non iure* (contrary to the law); see §52 *iniuriam* n.

Confirmatio I (§§11–22)

The Candidate Most Desirable to the Victims

Though it is obvious whom the injured most want to conduct their case and whom the accused least wants, Cicero will address both issues. The former is more important since the extortion court was established to represent the rights of non-Roman victims. Verres has laid Sicily waste. The Sicilians have observed Cicero's steadfastness and have come to him for redress. This is a fact that C.'s opponent, Caecilius, cannot deny, and he would be wrong to say that the wishes of the aggrieved party should not carry weight with the judges. C. remains reluctant to accept the case but yields to the Sicilians' request, because he would rather undertake the prosecution himself than see no suitable candidate come forward.

After establishing the most salient factors to consider in the selection of a prosecutor (§10), C. now turns to address what he has deemed the most important consideration, i.e. whom the aggrieved party most wants as prosecutor, though he claims the answer is obvious (*perspicuum*). Even so, if the *confirmatio* should be the central and decisive core of the speech (Lausberg §348), it is surprising that the first argument of the *Diu. Caec.*, except for some forensic flourishes, is resoundingly hollow and circular. It 'ends with the oddly lame concession, "And yet, all that amounts to the single point, that the Sicilians wish to have me most of all"'; Prag (2013) 269; §22 *at enim solum id est, ut me Siculi maxime uelint.* The discussion in §§11–22 is largely a dramatic recapitulation of the *narratio,* which as a matter of course had already established the Sicilians' preference. To bolster this contention, C. will pretend to summon witnesses (§§13–14), insert a digression on the legislative intent of the *lex de repetundis* and its import for selecting a prosecutor (§§17–19; see introduction *ad loc.*), and attack his rival in an impassioned *interrogatio* in which he claims that Caecilius is not their desired candidate (§§20–22; see introduction *ad loc.*). Otherwise, the argument is characterized by unfounded claims and allusive devices such as *praeteritio, occultatio,* and *reticentia.* Its primary function is to shift the locus of attention to C.'s rhetorical acumen and oratorical bravado and away from his lack of *priuatae inimicitiae* with the defendant.

§11

11.1 in hac causa At the end of the *partitio*, C. has purported to provide a rubric for selecting a prosecutor that is applicable in all *diuinatio* proceedings. He here applies this previous *sententia* to the selection of Verres' prosecutor. For a similar statement and application of a gnomic statement, see §§71–72.

11.2 iudices The vocative marks the start of the *confirmatio*; see §2 *iudices* n.

perspicuum Stating the obviousness of one's position is often an indication to the contrary since no argument would be required otherwise. C. is fond of this assertion with *perspicuum* or negations of *dubium* or *obscurum*; cf. §§14–15; *Quinct.* 80; *Rosc. Am.* 18, 41, 98, 105, 108; *Ver.* I.6, II.2.91, 2.165. The phrase acts as a kind of *praeteritio*, i.e. the speaker could pass over the information as self-evident but goes on to discuss the issue at length; see §28 *plura non dicam* n.

tamen de utroque dicam ... The opening statement of the *confirmatio* fulfils most properly the function of the *partitio* as it summarizes the following discussion and indicates the methods of argumentation to be employed. Even so the boundaries between parts of C.'s speeches are generally fluid; cf. the *conclusio* §§71–73. The remainder of §11 is essentially a recapitulation of material already presented in the *narratio*, esp. §3: a summary of Verres' crimes in Sicily and the assertion that the Sicilians prefer C. to conduct their case. C. labours the point.

11.5 iudicium de pecuniis repetundis est constitutum C. foreshadows the supporting argument (*firmamentum*) based on the legislative intent of the *lex de repetundis* in §§17–19. His statutory interpretation will substantiate his assertion that the most important consideration for the *diuinatio* jury is the desire of the victims; see introduction and nn. *ad loc.* For the history of the *quaestio de repetundis*, see Introduction §III.

11.6 Siciliam prouinciam C. Verres ... depopulatus esse ... dicitur C. begins the accusation on the broadest level (the province itself) and then lists individual entities in the province from the civic, domestic, and religious spheres. These correlate with the alleged crimes of Verres and demonstrate his contempt for the norms and rights associated with civic, religious and social institutions.

These accusatives (*prouinciam, ciuitates, domos,* and *fana*) are each the object of their own verb, all of which are essentially synonymous: *depopulatus esse, uastasse, exinanisse,* and *spoliasse.* C.'s tendency to accumulate synonyms in his early speeches for emphasis and exaggeration, which is also heightened by the asyndeton here, was noted by Gellius *NA* 13.25.9–11:

> sicut in libro eiusdem M. Tulli, qui de constituendo accusatore est, una eademque res pluribus uerbis uehementer atque atrociter dicitur: 'Sicilia tota, si una uoce loqueretur, hoc diceret: "quod auri, quod argenti, quod ornamentorum in meis urbibus, sedibus, delubris fuit."' [§19] Nam cum urbes semel totas dixisset, sedes delubraque addidit, quae sunt ipsa quoque in urbibus. Item in eodem libro simili modo: 'Siciliam' inquit 'prouinciam C. Verres per triennium depopulatus esse, Siculorum ciuitates uastasse, domos exinanisse, fana spoliasse dicitur.' Nonne unam et eandem uim in sese habent? Sane. Sed quia cum dignitate orationis et cum graui uerborum copia dicuntur, quamquam eadem fere sint et ex una sententia cooriantur, plura tamen esse existimantur, quoniam et aures et animum saepius feriunt. Ecquid uidetur, cum Siciliam prouinciam dixerit atque insuper etiam ciuitates addiderit, domos etiam et fana, quae infra posuit, conprehendisse? Verba haec item multa atque uaria: 'depopulatus esse, uastasse, exinanisse, spoliasse', nonne unam et eandem uim in sese habent? Sane. Sed quia cum dignitate orationis et cum graui uerborum copia dicuntur, quamquam eadem fere sint et ex una sententia cooriantur, plura tamen esse existimantur, quoniam et aures et animum saepius feriunt.

This method of amplification, *enumeratio,* is common throughout the speech; cf. §§3, 6, and 9. See further Lausberg §§669–674.

Later members of the *deteriores* construed *dicitur* impersonally, with *Verrem* and *depopulatum* in the accusative. *M* has *Verres* in the nominative but wrote *depopulatum* before correction. The reading of *F* is difficult to discern but may originally have been *Verrem.*

11.7 exinanisse 'emptied out' (*TLL* V 2.1503.70–1504.26). C. often pairs *exinanire* with verbs of similar meaning such as *depopulari, exhaurire, spoliare, vastare,* or *vexare.* Cf. *Ver.* II.5.109 *Qui Sthenium Thermitanum, hospitem suum, cuius domum per hospitium exhausit et exinaniuit, Ver.* II.3.119, 122, and *Pis.* 96.

11.8 adsunt, queruntur Siculi uniuersi Asyndeton is frequent after forms of *adesse*; cf. §14, *Ver.* I.3, 75, II.4.80, 5.22, and *Arch.* 8. Though he does not mention any of them by name, the presence of Sicilians at the hearing is construed as a kind of evidence or inartistic proof which vouches for C.'s claim that they prefer him to lead the prosecution. C. is able to interpret their attendance to suit his purpose; cf. his depiction of the troops and throngs of people surrounding the trial of Milo at *Mil.* 2–3. Probably a deictic gesture accompanied this phrase in delivery. On two-part asyndeton, see Berry with *Sul.* 21. **uniuersi** the postposition provides emphasis; cf. *Ver.* II.1.103, 2.112, 167, and see Marouzeau 1.177–179. But C. whitewashes a more nuanced situation. Messana and Syracuse had sent delegations to support Verres, which C. later admits in §14; see §2 *cuncti* n.

ad meam fidem ... confugiunt Cf. *Quinct.* 10 *Cum tot tantisque difficultatibus adfectus atque adflictus in tuam, C. Aquili, fidem, ueritatem, misericordiam P. Quinctius confugerit.* See further §3 *confugerent* n. and §5 *officio, fide, misericordia* n.

11.9 habent spectatam iam et cognitam The two verbs give a sense of physical (*spectatam*) and mental (*cognitam*) perception of C.'s dependability. C. uses a perfect participle with *habeo* most frequently with *cognitum, perspectum, persuasum, exploratum, statutum*; cf. *Ver.* II.5.188, though see, in this speech alone, §21 *habent ... positam*, §72 *propositam nobis habemus.* See further *TLL* VI 2452.65–2454.11. This construction, especially with verbs of perception or the acquisition of knowledge, places particular emphasis on the result of the action. For the development of this resultative use of *habeo* and the perfect passive participle, see Haverling (2016) with bibliography and *OLS* 1.478–480. This periphrasis, which is not uncommon in C. (see Merguet *s.u.* pp. 445–446) and Plautus (see Happ (1967) 103), tends to be used, as here, in passages of higher stylistic register. For *fides spectata*, cf. *Caec.* 104, *Flac.* 102, Sal. *Cat.* 20.2, Ov. *Pont.* 2.7.82, Liv. 35.49.12, Plin. *Ep.* 8.6.13, and Gell. 1.7.1 and 13.31.6. **iam et** (*γP*: *iam et diu M*) C. frequently links two participles with *iam et*; cf. *Ver.* II.5.174; *Cat.* 3.16; *Har. Resp.* 6; *Pis.* 90. *Iam et diu* is found elsewhere only at Suet. *Tib.* 74.1.

11.10 auxilium An important obligation of *fides* to which C. has just referred, on which connection, see Hellegouarc'h 172. Etymologically, it refers to a build-up of military reinforcements, and *defensorem* and *ultorem* may awaken the latent metaphor; Ernout–Meillet *s.u. augeo*; Var. *L.* 5.90.

a uobis atque a populi Romani legibus Syllepsis; see further Lausberg §§692–708. *A uobis* has been omitted in the French tradition, but *atque* shows that two syntactically equivalent phrases are being connected. The conjunction *atque* may also be more common in elevated speech; see Penney (2005).

11.11 me defensorem … me ultorem … me cognitorem … me actorem Anaphora and homeoteleuton contribute to the heightened register of the passage and underscore the different facets of C's representative ethos. He repeats three of these again as the roles of an extortion prosecutor at §54: *Concede igitur ut tibi anteponatur in accusando prouincia; nam prouincia accusat cum is agit causam quem sibi illa defensorem sui iuris, ultorem iniuriarum, actorem causae totius adoptauit.* **defensorem** in its most literal rather than legal sense, 'one who averts or repels', with the genitive of the thing repelled rather than the thing or person protected (as at §20); see *TLL* V 1.310.55–59, and cf. referring obliquely to himself (*Mur.* 3. *defensorque periculi*) and to Milo's slaves (*Mil.* 58 *conseruatores domini, ultores sceleris, defensores necis*). In the first of four terms, C. foregrounds his depiction of Verres' prosecution as a defence of the Sicilians. One important aspect of this characterization may be the notion of representationality, common in defence but uncommon in prosecutions (see §54 *in accusando prouincia* … n.). By portraying himself as a defence advocate, C. also disguises his lack of traditional motives. On the legal meaning of *defensor*, see Berger and Heumann–Seckel *s.u.* In the imperial period, *defensor* would be a term associated with the patrons of colonies; see *Sul.* 61 with Berry. **ultorem** C. thought that the desire for vengeance (*uindicatio*) was an inherent part of the law of nature (see *Inu.* 2.65), and throughout the speech, C. equates the role of the prosecutor with that of a punishing avenger (*ultor*, see also §§53, 54, *ulcisci*; §§22, 53, 60; *persequi* §§29, 53, 64; *punire* inherent in *impunitus* §53). This diction nods to a developing theory of corrective justice in the function of the *quaestio de repetundis.* Although the name of the standing court, *de repetundis*, suggests that restitution and making the plaintiff 'whole' is its primary objective, legislative and procedural developments in the recovery court show a transition from a court focused upon compensation for the plaintiff to one aimed at punishing the guilty party; see Introduction §III. A broader consideration in this shift may have been the appeasement of Roman subjects, who could focus their animosity on an individual rather than rebelling against Roman rule. For example, *ultor* is frequently used to denote vengeance exacted through violence; cf. *Mil.* 35, 58, 80, and *Sest.* 43. Thus the standing courts for extortion and the rule of law provided a non-violent means of redress and contributed to the stability of the Roman state in its interactions with client and allied states. Conversely, therefore, C. hints that, if the Sicilians cannot look to the courts to control rapacious magistrates, a violent uprising in the province may soon be on the horizon. On this theory of development, see Riggsby (1999) 120–129. For other suggestions of latent violence and unrest, see §8 *efflagitata* n. For *uindicatio* in Roman justice, see Lintott (1968) 22–34, and for vengeance generally, see Verdier (1980–1988). After a crime, the duty of revenge normally fell to someone with close ties to the injured party (usually familial), and therefore C.'s use of the term *ultor* in this context subtly strengthens his purported connection to the people of Sicily; cf. his self-description at *Sul.* 85. **cognitorem** is the only purely legal term in the list, but C. could not be a *cognitor* in the traditional sense, i.e. a party's duly authorized representative at a civil trial, since this would imply that the trial was being conducted *in alieno nomine*; see Berger *s.u*, *TLL* III 1488.24–68 with references to the jurists, and *Q. Rosc.* 53 *Quid interest inter eum qui per se litigat et eum qui cognitor est datus? Qui per se litem contestatur, sibi soli petit, alteri nemo potest, nisi qui cognitor est* *factus*. Ferrary (1998) 24: 'The use of this term is not insignificant: Cicero knows well that, if there is an actual judicial situation that approximates the relationship that he has with the Sicilians and that he wants to use as an argument to be chosen by the judges of the *diuinatio* as the accuser, it is the role of *cognitor* and not of *patronus*, that of the representative and not of the judicial assistant. [L'emploi de ce terme n'en est pas moins significatif: Cicerón sait bien que, s'il est une réalité juridique dont il peut rapprocher le lien qui l'unit aux Siciliens, et dont il veut tirer argument pour être choisi comme accusateur par les juges de la *diuinatio*, c'est celle de *cognitor* et non de *patronus*, de représentant et non d'assistant judiciaire.]' C. advances this conceit further in the *prosopopoeia* in §19, which has suggestions of civil procedure; see nn. *ad loc.* [Asc.] 104 (190 Stangl) makes his own distinction: *Qui defendit alterum in iudicio aut patronus dicitur, si orator est; aut aduocatus, si aut ius suggerit aut praesentiam suam commodat amico; aut procurator, si negotium suscipit absentis; aut cognitor, si praesentis causam nouit et sic tuetur ut suam. Ergo 'cognitorem' dicit modo familiarissimum defensorem.* **actorem** see §1 *actorem* n.

calamitatum A favourite word of C. Originally it applied to the devastation of crops and was later extended to other types of loss, misfortune or destruction; see Ernout-Meillet *s.u.* and *TLL* III 118.61–83. It does not necessarily imply any fault on the part of the afflicted; certainly, in the Verrines, the hapless Sicilians are not to blame for Verres' depredations. C. would frequently refer to his exile as a *calamitas* (as opposed to a *turpitudo*); see Nisbet *ad Dom.* 72 and Woodman (1983) 67. See further Robinson (1993). In other instances, it is contrasted with the *salus communis*; see Grillo (2015) at *Prou.* 17 and Classen (1979).

11.12 uoluerunt A pure rather than aoristic perfect that emphasizes the endurance of the action into the present moment rather than completion; *OLS* 1.446–448 and H-Sz. 318–319.

§12

12.1 utrum ... an ... *Complexio.* Craig (1993) 56: 'The dilemma forms part of the strategy, initiated in the *exordium* and announced in the *partitio*, of concentrating upon the Sicilians' wishes rather than upon the motives of the prosecutors.' It serves as a convenient *diuisio* for the next line of argument in which C. forestalls two potential objections: (1) that C. is not undertaking the prosecution at the Sicilians' behest, or (2) that even if they have asked him to be their representative, their wishes should carry no weight with the judges. He will refute both objections in §§13–16 and §§17–19, respectively.

Q. Caecili Apostrophe; the first of many direct addresses to his opponent, and though C. commonly addresses opposing counsel in his forensic speeches, it may have been unexpected in a *diuinatio*; see Introduction §IV.

dices (*MO*^{2sl} : dicis *P*γ *O*1 *ut uid.*) Though the present tense rests on greater manuscript authority and can have multiple implications of time (see *OLS* 1.395–410, esp. 400 n. 39), context and convention suggest that the reading of *M* is correct. A sense of futurity is certainly intended as C. says *si id audebis dicere* ... and *negabis* below. Ciceronian tendency is more difficult to articulate since C. rarely spoke before his opponent. When he uses the present tense *dicis*, however, he tends to be summarizing or extrapolating, sometimes misleadingly, from his opponent's earlier argument or using a historic present; cf. *Rosc. Am.* 44, 52, 76, *Ver.* II.1.80, 84, and *Rosc. Com.* 43 *utrum dicis Luscio et Manilio an et Cluuio non esse credendum? planius atque apertius dicam* .... Proleptic arguments tend to use the future tense *dices*; cf. *Ver.* II.1.84, in which C. uses both forms of the verb. The tense of the verbs in §21 (*offeres*) and §31 (*praetermittes*) presents similar difficulty; see apparatus *ad loc.*

12.2 optimorum fidelissimorumque sociorum The Sicilians are also so described at *Ver.* II.3.24 (*fidelissimos socios optimosque*), as are the Albans and the Gauls at *Phil.* 4.6 and 7.11, respectively. The accumulation of genitive plurals in *-orum* and *-arum* was usually avoided in a formal style as Latin tended to favour words with fewer syllables; see H-Sz. 756. C. may have opted for the homeoteleuton to dilate on the worthiness of his clients.

12.3 uoluntatem A key concept at the outset of the speech. In the *exordium* and following sections, C. attempts to dispel any perception of inconsistency in his own *uoluntas* (*mutata uoluntate*). However, the arguments set out in the *partitio* shift the debate from the *uoluntas* of the would-be prosecutors to the *uoluntas* of the provincials and the defendant.

hos Viz. the judges. The deictic suggests that C. would have made a gesture in their direction.

grauem 'influential, efficacious'; *TLL* VI 2285.51. With *uoluntas*, cf. *Ver.* II.2.98. C. could also argue the opposite sentiment depending on the situation; cf. *Font.* 32 *grauior igitur uobis erit hostium uoluntas quam ciuium?* On *oportere*, see §19 n.

12.4 cui te inimicum esse simulas C.'s first adumbration of accusing Caecilius of *praeuaricatio*, sc. conducting a sham prosecution to assure Verres' acquittal. The accusation of collusion is of the '*aliud atque aliud*' genus of *anticategoria*, i.e. the prosecutor is guilty of another crime himself. C. uses another form of *anticategoria* in *Rosc. Am.* wherein he implies that the plaintiff is the actual perpetrator of the crime in question (*idem crimen*). For *anticategoria*, see Quint. *Inst.* 3.10.4, and see further Lausberg §197. C.'s suggestion is neither substantiated nor sustained throughout the speech; see Introduction §II.

12.5 causam inimici tui The repetition of *inimicus* is derisive; see §13 *hoc si tu, inimicus eius* n.

12.6 praeiudicium ... plane iudicium A play on legal terminology. A *praeiudicium* could be both a negative predisposition (*TLL* X 2.674.84–675.21 and *OLD s.u.* 3; cf. *Inu.* 2.113) and, in a forensic context, a pre-trial hearing (*TLL* X 2.674.18–35, *OLD s.u.* 1&2, and Berger *s.u.*). Likewise, a *iudicium* can indicate a 'considered opinion', and especially when paired with *facere*, 'to pass official judgement upon an accused person'; see *OLD s.u.* 7&9 and 6b, respectively. The surface-level reading states that there is not simply a negative predisposition towards Verres but that the general populace has already formed a resolute opinion about him. The paronomasia, however, introduces a conceit that resurfaces throughout the *Diuinatio*: that the jurors' decision here (a *diuinatio* itself being classified as a *praeiudicium*) is tantamount to the decision in Verres' trial. *Plane* emphasizes the veracity of the *correctio*; cf. *Ver.* II.2.33, 3.181, *Agr.* 2.9, *Pis.* 66, and see *TLL* X 1.2343.25–32 and *OLD s.u.* 2. On a *diuinatio* as a *praeiudicium*, see Greenidge (1901) 459. For paronomasia, see §28 *deportare … asportare* n.

12.7 percrebruit A verb common in the Verrines but found only once in C.'s later speeches at *Mur.* 50. The spelling of the stem varies between *percrebr-* and *percreb-*; see *TLL* X 1.1225.6–13. The latter has generally been considered to be a later spelling introduced by the dissimulation of the second 'r'. The former spelling, found in *M*, is also the spelling found at *Ver.* II. 2.56 in the third- or fourth-century Vatican codex, Reginensis 2077. 'One can wonder, however, if the forms of the "*crebesco* (*-bui*) type", which appear in older texts (e.g. Cat. 64.274, *Phil.* 14.12), do not bear witness to an archaic form (on a stem devoid of the suffix -**ro-*) that is poorly attested because it lost out early on to the later "*crebresco* type" (itself destined to evolve *phonetically* into *creb*(*r*)*esco*). [On peut toutefois se demander si les formes de type *crebesco* (*-bui*) qui apparaissent dans les textes plus anciens (e.g. Cat. 64.274 ; *Phil.* 14.12) ne portent pas témoignage d'une formation archaïque, sur thème dépourvu du suffixe **-ro-*, peu représentée parce que très tôt victorieusement concurrencée par *crebresco* de type plus récent (elle-même destinée à évoluer *phonétiquement* en *creb*(*r*)*esco*).]' Keller (1992) 382–383 (original emphasis). Words with the prefix *per-* tend to be more prevalent in C.'s earlier speeches; see §23 *pertimescat*. The claim (*Siculos omnis actorem … quaesisse*) is vague at best. C. only states that the Sicilians were looking for someone to conduct a prosecution, not that they had him in mind all along.

12.8 actorem Euphemism for *accusator*; see §1 *actorem* n. In this instance the use of *actor* may have other implied nuances. An *actor* was the person who actually filed the charges in his own name and conducted the case. So here the Sicilians are depicted as looking for someone to file the charges rather than bringing the charges themselves at a *postulatio* and then looking for a legal *patronus*. The ability of non-Romans to bring suit under the *lex Cornelia de repetundis* is debated. It would be dangerous to infer from this passage that non-Romans were legally compelled to find a citizen to initiate a prosecution. Other considerations, including expertise and social standing, may have been at play; see §64 *quod eum sibi Achaei patronum adoptarant* n.

illius The absent Verres is mentioned with a third-person deictic; elsewhere C. resorts to a more vivid first- or second-person deictic; see §33 *huic* n.

§13

13.1 hoc si tu, inimicus eius The pronoun *hoc* often precedes *si* when it summarizes a complex or lengthy phrase from the previous sentence to which it is closely connected; e.g. *Ver.* II.1.25, 29; *Phil.* 13.4. The asyndeton is adversative and the hyperbaton between *hoc* and *factum* imparts a sense of emphasis and incredulity: 'But if you, his (supposed) enemy …'. If Caecilius were to deny that the Sicilians are looking for a prosecutor, he would seem to help Verres' case. The repetition of *inimicus* here and in the surrounding phrases (*causam inimici tui* and *inimicitias*) reaches a sarcastic pitch. C. purports to explain the origins of Caecilius' enmity toward Verres in §§55–58; see nn. *ad loc.* Caecilius' true grievances can hardly be discerned. *Factum* indicates 'fact' (viz. *Siculos omnis actorem … quaesisse* and as opposed to fiction); see *OLD s.u.* 3, and cf. *Rep.* 2.4 *ut iam a fabulis ad facta ueniamus.*

13.2 ipse Verres. C. contemptuously avoids his name. On conventions of non-naming, see §23 *magnus ille defensor* … n.

cui maxime haec res obstat Another vague statement that perhaps prepares the way for the second half of the *confirmatio* (*quem minime uelit* …), but the *factum*/*res* here is simply the Sicilians' search for a prosecutor, not their preference for C.

13.3 uideto ne This is the only example of the future imperative of *uideo* in C.'s speeches and is found only five other times elsewhere (*De orat.* 2.71, *Tusc.* 1.29, *Att.* 1.6.1, 13.23.3, *Fam.* 16.1.2). C. had a proclivity to use the future imperative when the command was accompanied by a subordinate clause with a verb in the future tense as it is here (*hoc si tu ... factum negabis*); cf. *Rosc. Am.* 93, 109, 118, *Ver.* II.1.156, 2.81, 3.25, 72, 4.55, 5.19, 135 (*si uoles, haec dicito*), *Caecin.* 61, *passim*, and see further Lebreton 194–200. Though the future imperative is difficult to distinguish in meaning from the present imperative, there seems to be less immediacy and a reference to a future time 'after the communicative situation' in which the command will come into effect; see *OLS* 1.517. This explains its use in early Latin didactic or legal texts; cf. XII Tab. 1, 6–9 (*Statutes* 594) and Cato *Agr.* 107.2 *commoueto, uideto ne aduras.* See further *Statutes* 16–17 with n. *ad loc.*

Redolent as the future imperative is of statute, it may imbue the passage with a magisterial (and slightly patronizing) tone that C. will develop throughout his attack on Caecilius, especially in his extended discussion of oratorical education and performance (§§27–47). On the future imperative, see *Rosc. Am.* 18 *iudicatote* with Landgraf *ad loc.*; further *OLS* 1.517–520 and Vairel-Carron (1975) 221–250.

familiariter *Familiaritas* implies the bonds of *amicitia* and a particularly strong, intimate connection; see Hellegouarc'h 68–71. In political vocabulary, it suggests mutual political support or durable friendship, though in its more pejorative applications, the close connection of an accomplice; cf. Sal. *Cat.* 14.3 *Catilinae proxumi familiaresque.* Under either interpretation, there is a slight to Caecilius. He is either colluding with the defence or (as C. will argue later) has an existing praetorian–quaestorian relationship with Verres which should disqualify him from the prosecution; see §§59–65 introduction.

inimicitias is juxtaposed intentionally with *familiariter* to highlight the incompatibility of intimacy and enmity and thereby to bring Caecilius' motives into suspicion; see §12 *inimicum esse simulas.* Personal enmity was the most socially acceptable reason for conducting a prosecution; see §64 *ueteres inimicitias iam diu susceptas,* and *Off.* 2.50.

13.4 exercere 'to indulge (one's feelings)' in either a positive or negative sense; *TLL* V 2.1373.31–76. Cf. *Ver.* II.5.145 *ista libido crudelitatis exercendae.*

sunt The primary position of *esse* in its colon demonstrates an existential use of the copula: 'In fact, there are even witnesses …'. The predicate receives additional semantic weight from its length (*testes uiri clarissimi nostrae ciuitatis*); see Marouzeau 2.18. Typical of such phrases is the use of emphatic adjectives (e.g. *clarissimi*); see Adams (1994a). Cf. §29 *sunt … signa permulta*; *Ver.* II.1.89 *Sunt Romae legati Milesii, homines nobilissimi ac principes ciuitatis.*

testes *Distinctio*, i.e. wordplay which exploits the semantic range of a word by highlighting the tension between the customary meaning and a more exhaustive one; see Lausberg §§660–662. *Testis* more commonly refers to a witness in a proper legal sense as someone who validates a legal transaction or gives evidence in court; *OLD s.u.* 1, 2. The audience is briefly led to believe that C. will call upon witnesses to testify to the fact that the Sicilians prefer him to be the lead prosecutor against Verres. According to the scholiast, however, witnesses were not called upon at a *diuinatio* proceeding (and this would be an odd request in the first place); [Asc.] 99 *Alii ideo putant diuinationem dici, quod iniurati iudices in hac causa sedeant et, quod uelint, praesentire de utroque possint; alii, quod res agatur sine testibus et sine tabulis, et his remotis argumenta sola sequantur iudices et quasi diuinent.* C., however, soon clarifies his meaning: *quos, si mentirer, testis esse impudentiae meae minime uellem* ('[men] whom, if I were lying, I would scarcely want to witness my brazen effrontery'), i.e. 'an observer'; *OLD testis s.u.* 5. He continues to exploit this semantic tension later: *Sed quid ego his testibus utor … ?* This continued legal word-play colours the *diuinatio* as though it were a trial itself; cf. §12 *praeiudicium … plane iudicium* n.

uiri clarissimi In addressing or pointing out individuals, *uiri* is often used alone, but if modified, the modifier is always positive. *Clarissimus* in its simplest meaning denotes fame or renown; coupled with *uiri*, however, *clarissimi* is a standard form of polite, respectful address for those of senatorial rank and hence apropos of the two men C. names; see Dickey (2002) 316. Among affectionate adjectives in classical Latin, the superlative is generally weaker than the positive; e.g. a scholar or venerated poet is addressed as '*docte*' rather than '*doctissime*'. For the development of this phenomenon, see Dickey (2002) 137–139.

nostrae ciuitatis Viz. Roman rather than Sicilian. In legal battles that pitted non-Romans against the Roman elite, advocates freely exploited perceived cultural divisions and paraded ethnic stereotypes to assert the cultural or class-based supremacy of the Roman defendant; cf. *Flac.* 6–12, 9 *Primum dicam, id quod est commune, Graecos.* While his reference here to *nostra ciuitas* appears to acknowledge this perception, later C. will go to great lengths to decrease the perceived cultural divide between Romans and his Sicilian clients; see §28 *hominum genus* … n. Verres, on the other hand, will be portrayed as the conventional Greek tyrant. On ethnicity in the Roman court, see Vasaly (1993) 191–244.

13.5 quos omnis … nominari non est necesse Rhetorical exaggeration by means of *occultatio*; see §28 *plura non dicam* n. C. leads his audience to believe that there are many others who could bear witness to the Sicilians' preference.

13.6 impudentiae meae *Impudentia* describes a lack of shame and restraint – a willingness to exceed the bounds of propriety to assert one's position. It expresses a similarity with *audacia*, and the pairing is used repeatedly throughout the prosecution to describe Verres, e.g. *Ver.* II.1.142 *omnia aperta, omnia perspicua reperientur; impudentia, amentia, audacia.* C. claims that if he were shown to be lying, then it would not only be an example of reprehensible behaviour, but an impeachment of character as well. In his discussion of an ideal prosecutor, an unassailable character is first and foremost; see §27. On the relationship between *pudor*, *pudicitia*, and *impudentia*, see J.-F. Thomas (2005).

13.7 scit is … scit is C. builds anticipation through syntactic uncertainty, i.e. the listener would probably expect a complement for *scire* either in the form of an object clause or an indirect question ('He knows that …' or 'He knows what …') rather than being used absolutely as it is here and at §41 *omnes sciunt*. This type of repetition is more prevalent in C.'s early style. Later rhetoricians found fault with his anaphora and careful symmetry, which, rather than heightening the expectations of the audience, draws attention to the orator's excessively wrought manipulation of language; see Lausberg §§1072–1073. Cf. *Rosc. Am.* 13 *accusant ei ... accusant ei ... accusant ei*; *causam dicit ... causam dicit ... causam dicit*; *Ver.* II.2.26 *Verres ... Verres ... Verres ... Verres*; *Man.* 30 *testis Sicilia ... testis Africa ... testis Gallia ... testis Hispania ... testis iterum et saepius Italia* ... with Laurand 298–299. Davies (1968) 309–310:

> The weakness of such reiteration lies in the fact that the weight of the emphasis is placed more on the comparatively unimportant introductory words. In later, more mature speeches Cicero tends to confine such sustained clausal *abundantia* to those places, such as the latter part of the *confirmatio* and the *peroratio*, where a special effort is required in the climax of the speech, as, for example, in the long speech attributed to Milo (*Mil.* 72ff.).

Of course, here, calling attention to his use of language may be precisely the point; see §15 *cum id ita perspicuum sit* ... n. The convergence of *t* and *i* produced *scitis* in the French family.

in consilio 'on the jury'; the term *consilium* reflects the original purpose of the panel to act as an advisory body; Greenidge 304. In the Republican period, the import of the *consilium*'s decision varied depending on the jurisdiction. In the provinces, this name was given to an advisory body appointed by the governor, but the governor was not bound to follow the recommendations of his *consilium* in delivering his judgement and could even change the verdict *ex post facto*; cf. *Ver.* II.5.18. In *quaestiones perpetuae*, those who sat *in consilio* were in fact *iudices*, and their opinion seems to have been more legally binding. Although the presiding praetor or *iudex quaestionis* handed down the verdict, sources seem to suggest that he was obliged to find in accordance with the opinion of the jury. Though *Fam.* 8.8.3 attests a presiding magistrate recording a verdict in contradiction to the findings of the jury, this was apparently rare and of dubious legality; see Shackleton

Bailey *ad loc.* Likewise, the decision of the *diuinatio* jury may also have been the final word.

C. Marcellus C. Claudius Marcellus (*RE* 214; *MRR* 2.84) is singled out for both his familial and political connections to Sicily. A descendant of the five-time consul M. Claudius Marcellus (*RE* 220), C. Marcellus had been a praetor in 80 and immediately thereafter served as proconsul in Sicily for 79 (with a possible prorogation into 78); see Brennan (2000) 483–484. C. depicts him as a model administrator (*Ver.* II.2.8), who had to cure some of the ills visited upon the province by his predecessor, M. Aemilius Lepidus, though this may be part of C.'s flattery. In addition to referring to Marcellus' own *clientela* in Sicily (2.110, 4.37, 4.90), C. refers to his scrupulous administration of the grain tithe (3.42, 212), the *Marcellia* festival at Syracuse that honoured both his recent benefactions and those of his ancestors (2.51; see further Rives (1993)), and the equestrian statue of him erected at Tyndaris for his services to the city and province that became the site of one of Verres' outrages (4.86–90). Although the jury for Verres' trial was reconstituted after the *diuinatio*, C. Marcellus is the only juror known for certain to have served on both panels (though there must have been others; see *Ver.* II.1.15). This may explain why C. refers to him so frequently – perhaps to cajole him into voting for a conviction. Verres must not have considered C. Marcellus to be a staunch supporter of C. in this trial since the defence did not reject him as juror, though perhaps he thought the trial would be delayed and a new jury empanelled; see Brunt (1980) 276. An inscription on an honorific statue base from Tauromenium that bears C. Marcellus' name is preserved at *IG* 14.435. On his relationship to Sicily, see also Eilers (2002) 156. For M. Claudius Marcellus' relationship with Sicily and for M. Lepidus' maladministration and threatened prosecution, see §2 *in ueteribus patronis multis.*

quem adesse uideo I.e. in the *corona* of spectators and not on the jury. This is a type of phrase likely to have been inserted during revision and preparation for publication since Marcellinus' presence may have been obvious to the original audience. On speech revision of this sort, see Levene (2003) 117–146.

13.8 Cn. Lentulus Marcellinus Cn. Cornelius Lentulus Marcellinus (*RE* 228, cos. 56, *MRR* 2.103, 148, 183, 190, 197, 207, 214, 3.19) was originally a member of the Marcelli, but his father had been adopted into the patrician Cornelii Lentuli. As was customary in Roman adoption, he assumed an *agnomen* that was derived from his original paternal *cognomen*. C., who sometimes only refers to him only as 'Lentulus', uses his *agnomen*, Marcellinus, here to draw attention to his relationship to M. Claudius Marcellus and his family's patronage of Sicily; cf. [Asc.] 109. C. says at *Ver.* II.2.103 that as a *patronus Siciliae*, Lentulus Marcellinus had spoken before the senate on behalf of the Sicilians who complained about Verres' prosecution of Sthenius of Thermae and later testified to these complaints. And at *Ver.* II.4.53, C. claims that Lentulus Marcellinus dissuaded an aggrieved Sicilian from suing Verres for financial compensation for stolen silver.

Though Lentulus Marcellinus was no longer legally a member of the Marcelli, willingness to represent the Sicilians before the senate speaks to the nature of hereditary patronage established by conquest, which would continue even when an individual was adopted into another family. The exact circumstances surrounding his father's adoption into the Cornelii Lentuli are unknown, but some have suggested that it may have happened in name only and that he was still primarily associated with the Marcelli; see Brunt (1980) 278 and Syme (1963). In any case, those members of the Marcelli that had become Cornelii Lentuli still chose to emphasize their connection to their former clan and to Sicily. For example, a late Republican denarius (RRC 439, c. 50 BCE) by the moneyer Publius Cornelius Lentulus Marcellinus depicts the head of M. Claudius Marcellus along with the name of the moneyer and the triskeles (a traditional emblem of Sicily) on the obverse, and Marcellus' dedication of the *spolia opima* on the reverse; see Hafner (1968). The iconography clearly establishes the association with the general Marcellus, Sicily, and other Marcellini even after adoption into another family. For the connection of the Marcelli to Sicily, see §2 *in ueteribus patronis multis* n.

An interesting character in his own right, Cn. Lentulus Marcellinus would go on to have a successful political career. Among his posts, he served as legate under Pompey in 67 against the pirates and as consul in 56; *Q. Fr.* 2.5.2 *consul est egregius Lentulus non impediente collega, sic, inquam, bonus ut meliorem non uiderim.* He allied himself with C. during the latter's clash with Clodius, and C. would later refer to his speaking abilities in *Brut.* 247: *Cn. autem Lentulus Marcellinus nec umquam indisertus et in consulatu pereloquens uisus est, non tardus sententiis, non inops uerbis, uoce canora, facetus satis.* His wife, Scribonia, would later become the wife of Augustus and mother of Julia; Suet. *Aug.* 62.2.

For more information about the process of adoption after established independence (adrogation) and testamentary adoption, see Gardner (1998) 114–208. For the process of changing names after adoption, see Gardner (1998) 133–136 and Shackleton Bailey (1991) 51–86. For a full study of adoption, see Lindsay (2009). On inherited patronage, see Eilers (2002) 61–83.

fide atque praesidio See §5 *officio, fide, misericordia* n. and §2 *praesidium* n. For *atque* followed by a consonant, see §2 *populati atque uexati* n.

13.9 Siculi maxime utuntur C.'s reference to the Marcelli does not necessarily indicate that they were actively supporting his bid to prosecute Verres. Whether from diminished political power (no Marcellus had held the consulship since 152) or from apathy, the Marcelli seem to have done nothing to prevent Verres' two prorogations. Nor do they seem willing to offer any additional support during Verres' prosecution – only Cn. Lentulus Marcellinus will purportedly offer testimony; see *Cn. Lentulus Marcellinus* n. above. On the apparent weakness or unwillingness of the Marcelli, see Brunt (1980) 276. In calling upon these two men, C. may be exerting some political pressure and encouraging them to be more active in the prosecution of Verres since the Marcelli had a longer-standing relationship to Sicily.

Nituntur was printed in the *editio princeps* of 1471 and has been reproduced by most editors ever since. Its merits are obvious *ad sensum*, and C. uses a similar construction with *praesidio* at *Piso* 19 … *aut praesidio niti uolebam* and once with *fide* at *Sest.* 27 … *quorum fide res publica niti debuit.* A single minim could have been omitted in the hyparchetype and *utuntur* then persisted through its syntactical similarity. Although C. does not use *utor* elsewhere with *fide*, cf. *Ver.* II.4.17 *utitur hac lege qua iudicium est, communi arce sociorum*, 5.60, *Cat.* 3.8 *ut seruorum praesidio uteretur*, and *Att.* 3.1 *per Epirum iter esset faciendum tuo tuorumque praesidio uteremur.* Furthermore, *utor* allows the final vowel of *maxime* to elide and thereby provides a standard cretic and trochee rhythm. *Nitor* does not. For *utor* with *fide*, cf. Nepos *Ep.* 3.4 and Sal. Jug. 111.2.

Marcellorum nomini Careful diction in the choice of *nomini* rather than the more frequently used *generi. Nomen* is technically more correct since, after his adoption into the Cornelii Lentuli, Cn. Lentulus Marcellinus is not technically a member of the *gens*; see *Cn. Lentulus Marcellinus* n. above. The MSS, except for some later hands in the *deteriores*, transmit the impossible ablative, *nomine.*

13.10 adiuncta est The notion of connection (*coniunctio*) was a common way of expressing a relationship with the obligations of *amicitia* and a *patronus–cliens* relationship; see Hellegouarc'h 80–81. To express this relationship, however, C. and other authors of the classical period more commonly use *coniungere* rather than *iungere* and *adiungere*; see further *TLL* I 707.15.

§14

14.1 hi sciunt hoc The syntactic ambiguity of *scit is ... scit is* is resolved; see §13 n. above. C. continues to reiterate the point that some Sicilians have requested that he prosecute Verres. In mentioning his connection to Sicily in the same breath as that of the Marcelli, he rather boldly includes himself *in ueteribus patronis multis* (§2).

14.2 ita saepe et ita uehementer esse petitum The verb is repeated for rhetorical emphasis rather than out of necessity in order to convey the same sense of fatigue and bombardment that he purports to have felt at the incessant pleading of the Sicilian delegations. The passive construction further underscores passivity and reticence – a contention that he has maintained since the outset of the speech; see §2 *ad me publice saepe uenerunt* n. The repetition of *ita* builds expectation for the result clause that follows. Cf. §25 *et ita mutandam.*

14.3 aut ... aut C. recapitulates the self-inflicted *complexio* that he made in the *narratio,* that he must either accept the case or ignore his obligations; §4 *in eum me locum adduci ut aut eos homines spes falleret ... aut ego ... tempore atque officio coactus ad accusandum traducerer.* The first *aut* is omitted in the French tradition, perhaps by *saut du même au même* after *ut.*

causa ... suscipienda 'take up the case'; see *OLD s.u. suscipio* 8b and *TLL* III 694.50–53.

officium necessitudinis repudiandum C. specifies the nature of his obligations: those associated with *necessitudo.* The nature of *necessitudo* and the imperatives that it implies will become a central point of contention in the *Diu. Caec.* On the one hand, C. will present his *necessitudo* with Sicily as one of the primary reasons why he is obliged to take up this case, e.g. §6 *causa tantae necessitudinis.* On the other hand, he will argue that Caecilius' bond of *necessitudo* with Verres, as a result of their joint political service, should bar him from leading the prosecution. The obligations and nature of *necessitudo,* however, are up for debate and offer C. a malleable concept that he can exploit to his benefit; see the full discussion at the introduction to §§59–65. The severity of the breach implied by *repudiare* is clear from its most literal sense, 'to break an engagement with' or 'to divorce'; *OLD s.u.* 1. With abstract concepts, cf. *Pis.* 9 *tu continentiam, tu industriam, tu animum in rem publicam, tu uirtutem, tu innocentiam, tu fidem, tu labores tuos, quod aedilis non sis factus, fractos esse et abiectos et repudiatos putas?*

14.4 quid ego his testibus utor C. renews the common legal definition of *testis* but casually backs away from the suggestion that he will call witnesses. On the *distinctio,* see §13 *testes* n. C. commonly uses the verb *uti* with witnesses; see Merguet *s.u.*

dubia aut obscura For this common pairing in C., cf. *Caec.* 6 *obscuram dubiamque, Clu.* 73 *obscuritate ac dubitatione,* and *Att.* 1.19.7

ita sunt obscurae … ita dubiae. For its employment in legal contexts, cf. *Dig.* 40.5.22.2 *idque senatus consulto demonstratum est, quo senatus consulto comprehensum est, ne dubium et obscurum esset ….* See further §15 *cum id ita perspicuum sit …* n. Since the issue is obvious, C. contends that he has no need of additional proof.

14.5 adsunt homines … nobilissimi See §11 *adsunt, queruntur Siculi uniuersi* n. The hyperbaton and final position of *nobilissimi* afford it greater weight. Among provincials the adjective refers to the aristocratic classes; see *OLD s.u.* 5a and b. The phrase *homines … nobilissimi* recalls *uiri clarissimi* (§13), and in giving as much weight and importance to the presence and pleas of the aristocratic Sicilians as he does to the potential testimony of the aforementioned senators, C. takes a step in closing the perceived cultural separation between Romans and provincials; see §28 *hominum genus …* n. For further discussion of *uir* and *homo*, see Courtney (2002) 189–191. For *nobilis* as applied to Romans, see §24 *a pueris nobilibus* n.

14.6 praesentes 'by their presence'. C. uses present participles only moderately, and here the nigh instrumental meaning shows the influence of the varied uses of the participle in Greek; see H-Sz. 384–385. For this use in C., see Laughton (1964) 25–28.

orant atque obsecrant A pleonastic pair used frequently by C. that connotes official supplication and conveys a sense of urgency and strong exhortation; see Naiden (2006) 66, and cf. *Ver.* II.2.42, 75, 4.40, 5.21. The meaning must be figurative here, since C. is dictating how the presence of the aggrieved party should be interpreted; cf. §11 *adsunt, queruntur Siculi uniuersi* n. For more on supplication, see §17 *supplices uestri* n.

ut … ne discrepet Negative purpose clauses are sometimes introduced by *ut* with *ne* placed more closely to the word or concept being negated; see K-St. 2.2.209 and Parzinger 2.1–4. Cf. *Clu.* 16 *statuit tamen nihil sibi … grauius esse faciendum, quam ut illa matre ne uteretur.*

14.7 uestrum iudicium … suo iudicio A light form of *distinctio*; see §13 *testes* n. The first understanding of *iudicium* here is a 'legal decision', the latter a non-legal 'judgement'; *OLD s.u.* 6, 9.

The repetition creates a word-play in which word-form equivalents underscore the need for semantic equivalence, i.e. the judge's decision and the Sicilians' considered opinion should be the same.

14.8 omnium ciuitatum ... legationes adsunt praeter duas ciuitates Through repeated rhetorical exaggeration, C. attempts to diminish the importance of Messana and Syracuse, two of the most influential regions of Sicily, which refused to support Verres' prosecution; see §2 *cuncti* n. *Legationes* (πρεσβεῖαι) were official embassies dispatched to Rome by the authorizing body in the individual *ciuitates.* Upon their arrival, they were received by a senior magistrate or otherwise referred to the senate. The *legati* (πρεσβευταί / πρέσβεις) themselves were often high-ranking officials in the respective communities; see Plut. *Mor.* 796c–d; cf. *Ver.* II.4.17 *amplissimus... legatus* and II.1.89 *legati Milesii, homines nobilissimi ac principes ciuitatis.* For embassies and diplomatic relations, see Millar (1977) 363–364 and further Eilers (2009). On the reception of foreign diplomatic delegations, see Coudry (2004).

14.9 duo crimina [Asc.] 105 (190–191 Stangl) *Per unam furatus est, Syracusanam; per alteram furta exportauit, hoc est Mamertinam.* See also *Ver.* II.2.183; 4.84, 150–151, where Messana is mentioned as a prime location for Verres' smuggling operations. As shown by *Ver.* II.2.13–14, a delegate from Messana would give testimony on Verres' behalf. It is perhaps for this reason that Messana receives so much attention from C. in the *actio secunda. Ver.* II.4.17 *Tua te altera patria, quem ad modum dicere solebas, Messana circumuenit – tua, inquam, Messana, tuorum adiutrix scelerum, libidinum testis, praedarum ac furtorum receptrix. Adest enim uir amplissimus eius ciuitatis legatus huius iudici causa domo missus, princeps laudationis tuae, qui te publice laudat – ita enim mandatum atque imperatum est.*

For the episode in which the Messanian Heius is coerced into selling valuable statuary to Verres and later instructed to deliver an official eulogy for Verres at his trial, see *Ver.* II.4.4–28; for Messana's various exemptions and special treatment, see *Ver.* II.5.43–58. It was also the site of the flogging and crucifixion of a Roman citizen, Gavius; see *Ver.* II.5.162.

14.10 minueretur C. takes an inconvenient truth and turns it into an asset: if he were also compelled to represent the interests of Syracuse and Messana, he would need to omit several of Verres' crimes to avoid implicating the provincials. Therefore, C.'s case will be even stronger, he contends, since Syracuse and Messana are not joining the suit.

14.11 communicata sunt Perhaps best translated as 'in which Gaius Verres made these cities his accomplices'. For this nuance of the verb, see §33 and *TLL* III 1956.23.

§15

15.1 at enim marks a pivot point that concludes one argument to progress to another related one (cf. §22 *at enim* ...), introduces an ironic twist, or shifts the current line of argument to a different plane. Kroon (1995) 343–344: 'The *at*-clause counts as an objection or a reproach against a prior move .... It is, moreover, also suggested by the combination of *at* with the interactional (agreement-soliciting) particle *enim* .... The *at*-clause conveys someone else's opinion, the deictic orientation of the reporting being however maintained throughout: we are dealing, not with an opposing interlocutor, but with an opposing "embedded voice".' Cf. §47 *at uenit paratus*....

At this juncture, C. shifts from assessment of fact (*quem maxime uelint*) to the question of motivation, i.e. why do the Sicilians prefer C.? He often asks such questions and then gives himself the pleasure of responding; Laurand 241. Yet here no satisfactory answer is forthcoming. The language throughout seems to draw attention to extra-discursive considerations such as *actio*; see *cum id ita perspicuum* ... n. below. For rhetorical questions that simulate a dialogue, see Quint. *Inst.* 9.2.31–32 and *Phil.* 1.20 with Ramsey *ad loc.*

potissimum See §10 *potissimum* n.

praesidium petiuerunt In this alliterative flourish, C. recapitulates an image from the *exordium*; see §2 *praesidium* n. C. prefers the unsyncopated form of *petiuerunt* as part of a cretic and spondee rhythm, which rules out the reading of *P*; cf. *Ver.* II.2.10, 122, 3.183, 5.130.

15.2 si esset dubium … dicerem *Reticentia*; see §21 *uerum non tacent* n. In an odd back-tracking manoeuvre, C. claims that the motives of the Sicilians in preferring him as the lead prosecutor would only need to be discussed if their preference were somehow in doubt, though he has already mentioned his quaestorship in Sicily as one of the factors that motivated the Sicilians to approach him about Verres' prosecution (§2). The *reticentia* obscures the fact that there are essentially no other possible motivating factors outside of his skills as an orator, to which he subtly draws the audience's attention; see *cum id ita perspicuum …* n. below.

necne (γ : a me praesidium necne *PM*) The Italian family is prone to additions of this sort, and even for this discussion the phrase seems overly repetitive. See further Introduction §VI.

15.3 cum id ita perspicuum sit ut oculis iudicare possitis Throughout the first part of the *confirmatio*, C. has presented much of his argument as self-evident (§11 *utrumque … perspicuum*; §14 *quasi res dubia aut obscura*; §15 *si esset dubium*), which should normally obviate any need for argument or discussion. In this final instance, he draws particular attention, not just to the idea of mental perception, but to the notion of physical sight (*oculis*). Combined with the rather empty content of this part of his argument, it suggests that he is focusing on an extrinsic factor, sc. *actio*. His delivery and self-presentation may already have demonstrated his oratorical ability. Foregrounding these considerations in the selection of a prosecutor anticipates the emphasis on rhetorical skill and delivery that will constitute a large portion of the *Diu. Caec.* (§§27–47 with reference to *actio* throughout) and the characterization of the *diuinatio* as a rhetorical contest. **id** may have been omitted from the French tradition by haplography or introduced into the Italian through dittography. When *perspicuum est* is used in the sense of 'it is obvious that …', the expression is completed by an accusative and infinitive construction or an indirect question; cf. *Sul.* 39, *Ver.* II.4.40, *OLD s.u.* 3.

The pronoun *id* could have removed the syntactical ambiguity, but cf. *Ver.* II.2.165 *Iam igitur est ita perspicuum ut negare non possis.* On the phrase *perspicuum est*, see Berry at *Sul.* 39.

15.4 si id mihi obiciatur 'if this should be laid against me as a charge' is an ironic use of legal terminology; see *TLL* IX 2.56.26–51. **mihi obiciatur** has been transposed in *O* and a branch of the *deteriores* (ς). Although that order avoids a normally eschewed heroic clausula (*ōbĭcĭātur*), this is only an internal colon and the rhythm is 'least undesirable when the final word consists of four or five syllables' since such a word would not normally appear at the end of a hexameter line; see Berry at *Sul.* 11 *duae … constituuntur.* The rhythm may accentuate the irony of the statement; cf. *Cael.* 63 *prosiluerunt* with Dyck *ad loc.*

15.5 delectum *Deligere* is often used in a judicial context for 'designating or appointing'; *TLL* V 1.453.31–38. Some MSS give *diligere*, a common copyist's error for *deligere*, though there are many MSS and some editors, such as Halm, that use *dilectum* for the perfect passive participle of *deligere*; see *TLL* V 1.451.80–84. The difference between the two verbs was the subject of adages such as *Rhet. Her.* 4.29 *deligere oportet quem uelis diligere.* For more on this adage, see Otto (1890) 106–107.

§16

16.1 id … hoc Both are cataphoric; viz. *me omnibus patronis esse praepositum.* See *OLS* 1.1145–1146.

mihi non sumo … *Praeteritio*, perhaps to pass over what may have seemed like indecorous self-promotion, in the form of a tricolon *crescens*: *mihi non sumo … in oratione mea non pono … ne in opinione quidem cuiusquam relinquo. Sumo* with a reflexive dative can mean 'to claim', though with a sense of hubris and self-conceit; see *OLD s.u.* 16. The phrase *in oratione mea non pono* has a touch of metaliterary irony; cf. Catul. 70.4 *in uento et rapida scribere oportet aqua.* See also §26 *in oratione mea ponere.* On *praeteritio*, see Lausberg §882.

16.2 iudices See §2 *iudices* n.

16.3 me omnibus patronis esse praepositum Cf. §2 *factum est uti cum summum in ueteribus patronis multis, tum non nullum etiam in me praesidium suis fortunis constitutum esse arbitrarentur* with nn. *ad loc.*

16.4 non ita est A colloquial negation; cf. Pl. *Ps.* 657, Ter. *Ph.* 326, *Clu.* 148, and see Hofmann §46.

temporis, ualetudinis, facultatis ad agendum 'personal circumstance, health, and ability to conduct a prosecution'. C. offers a suspiciously vague reason why he, rather than someone with a more traditional association with Sicily, is undertaking the case against Verres. Yet he will later admit that this kind of legal representation is no longer customary; see §67 *haec maiorum consuetudo longo interuallo repetita ac relata.* The scholiast makes an untenable assertion: [Asc.] 105 (191 Stangl) *Temporis Marcelli iudicantis tunc; ualitudinis Marcellini, quod erat tunc infirmior ualitudine corporis; facultatis alterius Marcelli, iuris magis studiosi quam eloquentiae causis agendis.* **ad agendum** goes with *facultatis* here to avoid colliding genitives. For *agere*, see *TLL* I 1395.42 and *OLD s.u.* 44.

16.5 ducta ratio est An idiomatic expression, 'to take into account', with genitives dependent on *ratio*; see *OLD s.u. duco* 29b and *TLL* V 1.2155.38–2156.23. Cf. *Quinct.* 53 *offici rationem atque existimationis duci conueniret,* and *Rosc. Am.* 128 *Non enim laborat de pecunia, non ullius rationem sui commodi ducit.* The passive construction leaves the agent vague.

mea The asyndeton and initial position of the possessive adjective is adversative with *ne in opinione quidem cuiusquam*; see Marouzeau 1.134.

16.6 haec The *deteriores* alone preserve this reading, omitted in *P* and the French family coincidentally through haplography. For parataxis of the same pronoun in C., cf. §37 *hoc extra hanc*; *Ver.* II.5.117 *Leuia sunt haec in hoc reo*; Parzinger 1.48–51. *Haec* is cataphorically used as demonstrative determiner for the subordinate clause *quemuis ut hoc mallem … suscipere.* Cf. *Phil.* 6.3 *itaque haec sententia, Quirites, sic per triduum ualuit ut, quamquam discessio facta non esset ….* On this use of *hic*, see *OLS* 1.1.1098–1099 and *TLL* VI 2729.81.

uoluntas et sententia From the outset of the *exordium*, C. has set out to explain his motives (§1 *causam rationemque*) and apparent change of mind (*mutata uoluntate*). Here he finally shows that he has been consistent in both respects. See the introduction to §1. For this *iunctura*, of which he was fond, cf. *Ver.* II.3.193, *Caecin.* 50, *Balb.* 35, *Man.* 69, *Fam.* 1.9.18, 6.13.1, and 6.21.2.

quemuis ut ... me ut Hyperbaton. The primary position of *quemuis* and *me* outside of their respective clauses adds emphasis, and taken with the anadiplosis below, *quemuis ... me, me ... neminem* form an artful contrast. On this ordering, cf. *Quinct.* 84; see K-St. 2.2.614–615.

16.7 idonei C. suggests that Caecilius is somehow unsuitable. This will prompt C. to discuss in further detail the qualities appropriate to an *idoneus accusator*; see the introduction to §§27–47.

me, me Anadiplosis/*reduplicatio*; see Lausberg §619. The asyndeton and strong contrast with *quemuis* conveys an adversative sense.

16.8 neminem See §47 *esto, ipse* (Caecilius) *nihil est, nihil potest.*

Digressio (§§17–19)

Lex de pecuniis repetundis sociorum causa constituta est

It is agreed that the Sicilians prefer C. All that remains to be decided is how their decision should affect the jury. The matter hardly needs discussion: as if there were any doubt that the extortion law had been passed for the sake of Rome's allies. Romans have access to a civil procedure for recovery, but Rome's allies must rely solely on the Extortion Court for their redress of wrongs. Who could possibly deny that the trial should proceed according to the wishes of those whom the law was enacted to protect? Since Sicily cannot conduct her own case and speak for herself, she has chosen a suitable prosecutor to speak for her.

Now that C. has established that he is the prosecutor most acceptable to the Sicilians (*cum hoc constet* ...), the *digressio* in §§17–19 constitutes the supporting argument (*Inu.* 1.19 *firmamentum est ... appositissima ad iudicationem*) for C.'s contentious assertion, stated in the *propositio* (§§10–11), that the most important factor for the judges to consider in selecting a lead prosecutor is the opinion of the injured (non-Roman) party. The rationale for this proposition is presented as a legal argument based on an interpretation of the *lex de repetundis*.

Ancient approaches to legal interpretation tended to be focused on civil law and to emphasize either the letter (*scriptum*) of the law or the intent (*uoluntas*) of the lawgiver; see *Inu.* 2.116, Quint 7.6.1 *Scripti et uoluntatis frequentissima inter consultos quaestio est, et pars magna controuersi iuris hinc pendet*, and Arist. *Rhet.* 1374b καὶ τὸ μὴ πρὸς τὸν νόμον ἀλλὰ πρὸς τὸν νομοθέτην, καὶ μὴ πρὸς τὸν λόγον ἀλλὰ πρὸς τὴν διάνοιαν τοῦ νομοθέτου σκοπεῖν. These same interpretative methodologies could also be applied to criminal statute if the situation warranted. Verres was being accused under the *lex Cornelia de repetundis*, but a literal interpretation of the statute would not serve C.'s purposes here. The *lex de repetundis*, in any of its revisions, did not offer guidelines for selecting a primary accuser. Selection criteria in *diuinationes* seem to have developed from custom and precedent (viz. who had the *maior causa*; see introduction to §10). C. therefore bases his position on the *uoluntas legislatoris* and relies on an interpretation through *ratio legis*, i.e. 'the purpose, the motive which inspired the promulgation of a specific law'; see Berger *s.u.* and *Inu.* 2.124 *quare aut ita sententia inducetur, ut unum quiddam uoluisse scriptor demonstretur, aut sic, ut in eiusmodi re et tempore hoc uoluisse doceatur.* C.'s method of legal argumentation in this passage, though ancient jurisprudence did not articulate this principle so precisely, is akin to modern 'purposive' statutory construction that relies on extrinsic evidence: 'background information about circumstances which led to the enactment of a statute, events surrounding enactment, and developments pertinent to subsequent operation'; see Sutherland §48.1.

Rather than consider this particular version of the extortion law, C. considers the entire legislative history of the statute (*tota lex*) and, implicitly, the state of the Roman judicial system at the passage of the *lex Calpurnia* in 149. Because Roman citizens already had a regularized process for seeking the restitution of stolen property through a civil procedure, it then follows, according to C.'s logic, that the criminal statute on extortion had been specifically drafted to give foreigners a standardized mechanism for redress since previous disputes and claims by non-citizens had to be adjudicated through *ad hoc* measures; cf. Liv. 43.2, where the senate used a civil procedure and appointed *recuperatores* in response to delegations from Hispania; see further Santalucia (1998) 103–109 and Venturini (1979). Therefore, if the law was meant to address the concerns and needs of foreigners, then by extension, their preferences for a legal representative should also carry weight with the jurors. Arguments of this type rely on an implicit appeal to *aequitas* – a term that has a wide semantic range but here appeals to an 'internal or immanent fairness'; see Frier (1985) 120. Though these arguments commonly present a dichotomous antagonism between the letter and the intent (cf. *Caec.* 63), C. is not arguing that the letter of the law should not be followed but asserting that a general principle can be adduced that informs the most appropriate selection criteria in *diuinationes*.

What was the probative force of C.'s interpretation of the *lex de repetundis*? Though disputes on points of law were more common in civil cases, *argumenta ex lege* had their place in Roman criminal trials and are a frequent feature in C.'s orations. He exhibits a number of interpretative methodologies; cf. *Inu.* 2.116–154, *Rosc. Am.* 62–72, *Cael.* 1, 70–71 (an example of the *status translationis*; see Lausberg §§131–133), and *Clu.* 143–160. By modern standards, an argument based on 'legislative history is often ambiguous and inconclusive', and courts that offer published decisions are more reluctant to honour these arguments because in doing so they are actually 'indulging in judicial legislation' since their decisions may crystallize a particular interpretation; see Sutherland §48:2. Though rhetorical handbooks suggested that interpretations derived from intent could be opposed on these grounds (*Inu.* 2.133–134), Roman juries may have felt more open to accepting such arguments since, in rendering their judgement, they did not specifically accept or deny the statutory construction offered by the advocate. But 'in many criminal cases the issues would have concerned only facts, motives and character, with little or no requirement for disputes on points of law. In such cases the techniques of persuasion resorted to by advocates would not have required recourse to legal argument'; Harries (2006) 96. But even less so here since, in a *diuinatio*, there are no points of law at issue and the judges were not obliged to abide by any selection criteria.

This legal exposition in the *Diu. Caec.* does not offer a binding interpretation or definitive guidance, but it fulfils two primary functions central to the speech. First, it distracts the jury from C.'s lack of personal grievance with Verres and provides a reason why the traditional rubric (*mos*) for assessing would-be prosecutors should be rejected in favour of a new paradigm that better represents justice and fairness (*aequitas*). Second, the passage contributes to the colouring of the *Diuinatio* as a *logos dikanikos* and demonstrates the juristic skill required of an adroit advocate – an exhibition which will make it obvious (*perspicuum*) why the Sicilians would prefer him to prosecute Verres.

C. will recapitulate this legal argument at §65 and deploy it throughout the *actiones in Verrem*; cf. *Ver.* II.2.15 *Primum, si ita esset, tamen uos in hac quaestione de pecuniis repetundis, quae sociorum causa constituta est lege iudicioque sociali, sociorum querimonias audire oporteret*, 4.17, and 5.126. For the importance to an orator of possessing some legal knowledge, see *De orat.* 166–203 (especially 201–203), Harries (2006) 111–115, and Bona (1980). On the forensic character of the *Diu. Caec.*, see Introduction §IV. On implied effects of purposive statutory construction in modern law, see Sutherland §55.2.

§17

17.1 reliquum est ... ut A common Ciceronian turn of phrase, which suggests a thorough logical progression, used to move to a new line of argument related to the previous one; cf. *Man.* 59 *Reliquum est ut de Q. Catuli auctoritate et sententia dicendum esse uideatur*, and *Cael.* 56 *Reliquum est igitur crimen de ueneno.*

quaeramus C. frequently uses this verb to introduce a rhetorical *quaestio*; cf. *Rosc. Am.* 83 and *Caec.* 32 *nunc rem ipsam ponamus quam illi non negant et eius rei ius actionemque quaeramus.* These *quaestiones*, stated in the indirect questions *ecquid hanc rem ... ualere oporteat* and *ecquid auctoritatis... habere debeant*, are lines of inquiry designed to advance C.'s assertion in §11 *quod apud uos plurimum debet ualere, hoc est de uoluntate eorum quibus iniuriae factae sunt; quorum causa iudicium de pecuniis repetundis est constitutum.*

cum hoc constet In establishing a *quaestio*, the speaker should identify the points of agreement as well as the points of contention; see *Inu.* 1.18–19, and cf. *Caec.* 32 *cum hoc constet* .... At this point in the speech, C. considers his first claim (*Siculos a me petisse*) to have been proven. The *quaestiones* will aim to determine how that fact should influence the jury's decision.

17.2 ecquid ... ecquid Frequently used to introduce indirect questions, and sometimes paired with a partitive genitive, as in the second instance; see Neue-Wagener 2.484, and *TLL* V 2.57.21–66. In MSS, it is often written incorrectly as *et quid.*

apud uos animosque uestros ualere A neatly packaged phrase with a resonant homeoteleuton and alliteration. *Valere* can take a prepositional phrase governed by *apud* to mean 'to have an influence on'; cf. *Ver.* II.2.78 *Fidem cum proposuisses uenalem in prouincia, ualuit apud te plus is qui pecuniam maiorem dedit,* and see *OLD s.u.* 8b and *TLL* II 343.26–46. **uos** The connection between the two minims causes frequent confusion between 'n' and 'v', especially with manuscripts in a Gothic hand; see §73 *nostro* n.

17.3 oporteat See §19 *oportere* n.

auctoritatis *Auctoritas* is the ability to influence others and is found in an etymological nexus with religious vocabulary such as *augere, auctor, augur,* and *augustus*; see Ernout–Meillet *s.u. augere.* It comes under many guises, and as a personal quality, *auctoritas* expresses the type of authority derived not from legally bestowed power (i.e. *imperium*) but from superior social or political standing, and is therefore frequently attributed to the senatorial order; see Balsdon (1960), and see further Hellegouarc'h 313–314 for how it is applied to foreign communities. Here, however, it connotes the weight or valence of a particular line of reasoning; see *TLL* II 1218.8–1219.78.

in suo iure repetundo 'in their plea for the restitution of their rights'. This is a subtle beginning to C.'s legal argument that follows in §18. The phrasing recalls the gerundive expression *de pecuniis repetundis.*

17.4 socii populi Romani *Socius* refers to any ally or confederate state in Rome's sphere of influence, but the status of *socii* was not standardized throughout the empire. When Sicily came under Roman control in the wake of the Second Punic War, Rome did not incorporate the island into her territory through the same system of alliances that she had used on the mainland – a system which provided men for the Roman army. Messana was the only city outside of Italy listed on the *formula togatorum*, a list normally reserved for Italian *socii* that stipulated the communities' obligations to contribute to the Roman military; see *N-P s.u. socii.* For Sicilian *socii*, Rome maintained a tithe tribute system similar to the one established by Hiero II of Syracause since it provided an effective means of collecting much-needed grain; see *Ver.* II.3.14–22 and Rickman (1980) 37–38. These other Sicilian communities would have been included on the *formula sociorum*, 'a list of both individuals and communities entitled to a formal diplomatic reception at Rome'; see Bowman (1990) 336. According to the opening lines of the *lex repetundarum* preserved on the Tabula Bembina, the right to bring a prosecution was given to *quoi socio no]minisue Latini exterarumue nationum*, 'any man from among the allies, either of the Latin name or of foreign nations ...'. On the nature of international relationships defined as *amicitia*, see §66 *in amicitiam* ... n.

supplices uestri C. recalls the quasi-religious language that he introduced in §3 *illos supplices.* The image of the plaintiff or defendant as a suppliant before the court is common in forensic oratory, particularly in perorations; cf. *Sul.* 88–89 and *Cael.* 78–80. In this passage, by redefining the relationship from plaintiff–juror to suppliant–*supplicandus*, the metaphor encourages the jury to view the proceedings in light of the norms typically associated with the act of supplication. By nature, a suppliant assumes a position of humility and implicitly recognizes the authority of the *supplicandus.* This also places a reciprocal moral imperative upon the *supplicandus* to aid the suppliant, and more precisely in this context, to uphold the rights and guarantees afforded to Roman dependants and allies. This characterization lends plausibility to C.'s assertion that the wishes of the aggrieved are of primary concern; see *Inu.* 1.48 *commune est, quod omnes uulgo probarunt et secuti sunt, huiusmodi: ut maioribus natu assurgatur, ut supplicum misereatur.*

In the earlier passages, C. himself was presented as the *supplicandus.* The possessive adjective *uestri,* however, redefines the relationships in the metaphor: the Sicilians have not made their final appeal for vengeance and protection to C., who now only plays the part of intercessor, but to the court of Roman law. Final authority now rests with the jurors – a responsibility emphasized by the preponderance of second-person pronouns (*uos* ... *uestros* ... *uos* ... *uestri*).

17.5 quid ego plura commemorem A favourite expression of C. which introduces a *praeteritio* or, more accurately, a *percursio*; see Seyffert 1§28. Such a dismissive statement has an ironic effect when C. continues to make a reasoned argument for his supposedly self-evident point of view. Cf. §11 *utrumque ... perspicuum,* §14 *quasi res dubia aut obscura,* §15 *si esset dubium,* cum id ... *perspicuum sit,* and §17 *quasi uero dubium.* For *percursio* and *praeteritio,* see Lausberg §§881–885.

dubium There is a hint of irony in *dubium* and the adversative 'as if' (*quasi uero*). In addition to the irony inherent in a *percursio,* there may actually have been a question in the mind of the jurors as to the accuracy of C.'s statement. Hence the need for the forthcoming explanatory phrase, *nam ciuibus ... repetuntur,* see nn. below.

17.6 tota lex ... constituta sit The original *lex de repetundis,* the *lex Calpurnia* of 149, as indicated by *constituta sit* ('to found or establish' a law or legal institution *uel sim.*; see *TLL* IV 515.72), and every subsequent revision of the law (*tota*), e.g. *lex Acilia, leges Seruiliae, lex Cornelia,* etc. C. claims that the reason for drafting the original statue will guide the jurors in this question of whether or not the opinion of the Sicilians should matter; see introduction to §§17–18. Cf. *Cael.* 70, where in discussing the *lex de ui* C. uses the term *lex* when it must encompass two revisions of the law, a *lex Lutatia de ui* of 78 and a later *lex Plautia de ui*; see Hough (1930) and Lintott (1999) 114 *contra* Berry (1996) 14–16: 'Cicero is … strictly speaking inaccurate'. For a discussion of the *lex de repetundis*, see Introduction §III.

§18

18.1 nam indicates that what follows will provide evidence for the previous assertion; see Kroon (1995) 146–147, Barendt (1902) 208, and Pinkster (1972) 173. That C. thinks an explanation is warranted is notable. The passage has been variously interpreted by legal historians and epigraphers studying the fragmentary text of the *lex de repetundis* preserved on the Tabula Bembina. There is no definitive conclusion about which version of the statute is written on the tablets – some equate it with the *lex Acilia*; others, the *lex Seruilia Glauciae* (c. 104–101) on the basis of *Ver.* II.1.26 and the absence of a *comperendinatio* (mandatory adjournment for a second hearing). In addition to its uncertain identity, the opening section of the law, which stipulates those who may prosecute (*quoi nomen deferre liceat*), has been partially lost. The text resumes at the clause expressly allowing the Latin allies and foreign nations 'within the sovereignty, dominion, power or friendship of the Roman people' to prosecute ex-magistrates for extortion: *quoi socio no]minisue Latini exterarumue nationum, quoiue in arbitratu dicione potestate amicitiau[e populi Romanei.* It was Mommsen's contention, based on this passage in the *Diu. Caec.* and supported by Crawford, that Roman citizens were therefore not allowed to bring suit under the criminal law preserved on the Tabula Bembina. Though there are references to Roman citizens in lines 21–22, 76, 81, and 83, they argue that these may refer to citizens acting on behalf of foreign communities. M. H. Crawford (1996) 95 concludes that 'the words of Cicero [in *Diu. Caec.* 17–18] would perhaps have sounded odd, if the very first words of the *lex de pecuniis repetundis* which underlay all later legislation had been *quoi ceiuei* …'. Yet that is precisely why C. has felt obliged to offer an explanation. His interpretation was contentious. C. is not making a distinction between two exclusive legal avenues, one for citizens and another for non-citizens, but between the *number* of legal processes available to foreigners and citizens. Citizens have the benefit of civil and criminal procedures, whereas non-Romans must rely solely on the latter. This position is also supported by Klenze (1825), Rudorff (1861), Venturini (1979) 82–91, Meyer (1980), and Brunt (1988) 526–531. In general on the Tabula Bembina, see *Statutes* 39–112 and Lintott (1992) 88–169. For identification of the text of the Tabula Bembina with the *lex Acilia*, see Sherwin-White (1972); *contra* Mattingly (1969). For a history of the extortion court generally, see Introduction §III.

ciuibus The position of the noun before the introductory *cum* clause adds further emphasis to the distinction between Roman citizens and *socii*; see §17 *socii populi Romani* n.; see Costa (1927) 1.409 'But rather often the term *socii* serves to indicate provincials in general, in contrast to *ciues*, especially in the numerous instances relating to *crimen repetundarum.* [Ma più spesso il nome di *socii* serve a designare i provinciali in generale, in contrapposto ai *ciues*, specialmente nei numerosi luoghi relativi al *crimen repetundarum.*]'

ereptae pecuniae summarizes the prosecutable actions of the *lex de repetundis. Pecuniae* refers not simply to currency but anything of value (i.e. real property, slaves, artwork); *D.* 50.16.178 pr. *'Pecuniae' uerbum non solum numeratam pecuniam complectitur, uerum omnem omnino pecuniam, hoc est omnia corpora: nam corpora quoque pecuniae appellatione contineri nemo est qui ambiget.* See further, *TLL* X 1.934.67. The language of the *lex* on the Tabula Bembina specifies *pecuniae* over a certain amount or property that had been *ablatum* (stolen), *captum* (seized), *coactum* (extorted), *conciliatum* (procured), or *auorsum* (diverted). On *eripere,* see §19 *eripuisti atque abstulisti* n.

ciuili … actione et priuato iure sc. to treat the extortion as a delict and to seek restitution through a civil procedure; see Greenidge 79–296. Roman private law, however, did not apply to foreigners or members of allied states, and this exclusion is emphasized by the initial position of *ciuibus* and *ciuili.* Only in limited circumstances could foreigners use the civil law system: the *praetor* could issue a *fictio,* which assumed an untruth for the fair application of justice – i.e. that the foreigner was actually a citizen and could therefore use the civil system; see Ando (2015) and Berger *s.u. fictio.* Since there was a regularized process for citizens to seek restitution, the *lex de repetundis,* C. argues, must originally have been drafted to provide legal recourse for external states and allies – and as a result, their choice of prosecutor should be of paramount importance. For the specific legal terms and phrases, see Berger *s.u.* and *Statutes* xxiii–xxv. See Damon and Mackay (1995) 50–55 for the use of extraordinary *fictio* for prosecuting non-magistrates.

fere applies to the phrase as a whole, not any particular word, and indicates that an action is frequent but not without exception; see *TLL* VI 500.14. C. makes it clear that, even if Roman citizens did not personally avail themselves of the legal channel offered by the *quaestio de repetundis,* it was nevertheless still available to them. Even within the Verrines, C. makes claims on behalf of Roman citizens; see *Ver.* II.2.16, 119, 176–177, 182, 185, 3.36, 59–63, 93, 97, and 4.42–47. See further Brunt (1988) 526–530. For the debate about those who could prosecute under the *lex Cornelia de repetundis,* see *nam* n. above and §64 *quod eum sibi Achaei patronum adoptarant* n.

18.2 lex socialis C. only twice uses the adjective *socialis* in the sense 'that concerns allies' (*OLD s.u.* 2a); cf., also referring to this statutory construction, *Ver.* II.2.15 *lege iudicioque sociali.* The normal dichotomy between statutes is *ciuilis/priuata* vs. *criminalis/publica,* i.e. litigation over crimes affecting an individual and those affecting the state as a whole. C. presents new contrasting categories: *ciuilis* vs. *socialis,* i.e. laws protecting the rights of citizens and those protecting the rights of *socii.* He emphasizes the restrictive nature of *leges ciuiles,* which only provide means of redress for *ciues* as opposed to those which provide broader protection and include non-Romans. He refers to the entire history of the law; see §17 *tota lex … constituta sit* n.

ius Not exactly synonymous with *lex.* A '*lex*' referred to a particular statute 'passed in the way legally prescribed by the competent legislative organs'; see Berger *s.u.* along with Gell. *N.A.* 10.20.2, and Gaius *Inst.*1.3. '*Ius*', however, is used more broadly to indicate 'the whole of the law, the laws (*iura populi romani*), without regard to the source from which they emanate'; Berger *s.u.* In our passage, *ius* most clearly means 'the right or rights of an individual' or group.

18.3 arcem For this metaphor of the law as *arx*, cf. *Ver.* II.4.17, 5.126, and *Clu.* 156. C. returns to a recurring military metaphor already deployed at §2 *praesidium* and §15 *praesidium petiuerunt* (see nn. *ad loc.*) in which he and the traditional patrons of Sicily are equated to a defensive garrison that protects the Sicilians from exploitation. *Praesidium* had been apropos in those instances since it is etymologically linked to the actual guardians offering protection (i.e. *praeses*). An *arx* typically refers to a structure that requires manning, the final line of defence located on a citadel. Elsewhere this metaphor is applied to Rome itself. Fantham (1972) 124 'The image of Rome as *hac omnium terrarum arce* employs the familiar *arx* symbol (cf. *Balb.* 39; *Fam.* 1.9.8), but significantly, as the *Arx* is to Rome, so Rome is to the world.' See also Aßfahl (1932) *s.u.* Kriegsgeräte, Waffen. C. has slowly shifted the onus of responsibility from himself to the jurors; see §17 *supplices uestri* n.

minus aliquanto ... quam antea The common reading of *P* and *γ*, *nunc quidem munitam*, gives a molossus-cretic rhythm and stands on better authority than the reading of *M*, *munitam nunc quidem*, though it also gives a satisfactory double-cretic clausula.

18.4 munitam adds deeper colour to the military metaphor in *arcem* above. Although often used to describe the building of a fortification, in this instance, it refers to the presence of soldiers within it; see *OLD s.u. munio* 2 and *TLL* VIII 1658.13–42. Cf. *Prou.* 4, *Pis.* 84, *Rep.* 2.11, and *Sul.* 79 with Berry *ad loc.* Though Merguet lists this as another example of *habere* with a participle, the provincials (the subject of *habent*) are conceptually not the party fortifying the *arx*; cf. §11 *habent spectatam iam et cognitam* with n.

quam antea A jab at the purely senatorial juries of the extortion court as constituted by the *lex Cornelia*, which had previously been administered by *equites* under the *lex Acilia*. Before the close of the year, the *lex Aurelia* would reduce senators to only one-third of a jury; see Introduction §I and §8 nn. *ad loc.*

uerum tamen Conjunctions such as *uerum tamen* are characteristic of C.'s early style. Such phrasing is 'redolent of legal or bureaucratic usage … and would gradually give way to briefer and more elegant expressions' in his later style; see von Albrecht (2003) 99–100.

reliqua spes … Cf. *Cat.* 4.8 *eripit etiam spem quae sola hominem in miseriis consolari solet.*

18.6 a populo Romano C.'s general claim that there was a universal outcry for judicial reform is somewhat exaggerated though the topic must at least have been raised. A recent uprising had occurred in 74; see §8 *qui iudicia … uolunt* n.

18.7 seueri custodes The military metaphor continues. Although they may not be empanelled on the jury to judge Verres, the jurors in the *diuinatio* had the opportunity to be guardians of the law by choosing C. as prosecutor. Since C. has depicted the *diuinatio* throughout as tantamount to Verres' actual trial, a vote for C. is by extension a vote for Verres' conviction. *Seuerus* denotes a kind of rigidity that is the expression of strict morality and imperviousness to bribery and corruption; see Hellegouarc'h 281–282. Cf. §8 *iudiciorum seueritatem*, §§21, 71, 73. **seueri** Applying a term of moral rectitude to the *custodes* (γM) is preferable to the adverb *seuere* (*P*), 'drastically' or 'earnestly'.

§19

19.1 quis igitur est … 'A model of argumentation must be capable of clarifying the underlying assumptions and choices made in the decision process so that they can be submitted to critique'; Feteris (2008). The rhetorical question states the assumption upon which C.'s legal interpretation in §§17–18 rests, viz. legal proceedings, where flexible, should be conducted according to the wishes of the implied beneficiary of the law. This was by no means a prevalent concept in Roman legal interpretation but neatly serves C.'s purposes here as it gives some type of legitimate consequence for the Sicilians' preferences. **igitur est** (*PM*: *ergo est* γ) These concluding particles, *ergo* and *igitur*, have been confused both from similarity of meaning and similarity in abbreviation, sc. g° gⁱ. Either reading is possible; cf. *Ver.* II.3.39 *quid igitur est quod ex hac iniquitate novorum edictorum intellegi velim iudices?*, 3.176, *Rosc. Am.* 80, *Luc.* 79, and *Clu.* 148 *quis ergo est Cluentius?* Given the tendency to abbreviation, however, it is possible that *est* and *igitur* could have been transposed. The more common expression is *quis est igitur qui* ... ; cf. *Planc.* 24 *quis est igitur qui neget ordinis eius studium fuisse in honore Planci singulare?* See also *De orat.* 2.225, *Sul.* 52, and *Tusc.* 1.30.

oportere has a moral valence, and this diction indicates that C.'s interpretation of the *lex repetundarum* rests on a moral, rather than strictly literal, reading of the statute; see *TLL* IX 2.737.21–33 and Ernout–Meillet *s.u.* This appeal to social norms, values, and moral imperatives persists in the *Diu. Caec.* C. uses *oportere* in this sense 15 times in this speech alone. *Oportet* is firmly entrenched in legal parlance as a signpost for a juristic inquiry (although one rarely finds the impersonal *oportet* in actual legislation as a substitute for an imperative), and the diction here suggests that C.'s legal interpretation of the *lex repetundarum* is akin to a juristic *responsum* (*TLL* IX 2.737.53–76). Daube (1956) 16–17: 'No doubt *oportet* in legal language at first always meant *e lege* or *more oportet*, "it is proper because of a statute or custom." ... as a rule *e lege* or *more* would not be expressly put: everybody knew that, in the field of law, those were the standards on which any *oportere* rested'; see further Daube (1956) 8–23, Costa (1927) 1.30, and Greenidge 155–156. For the use of *oportere* in a legal interpretation, see Sen. *Contr.* 1.4.6. For an example of *oportere* in requesting or prefacing a juristic *responsum*, see the question put to the jurist, Alfenus, in *D.*6.1.58.

lege agi Legal terminology, 'an action to be conducted at law'; see *OLD s.u. ago* 44a and *TLL* I 1396.65–1397.26. Though the MSS report *legem*, the idiom uses the form *lege*, which may be an old locative. Cf. *Mur.* 25, *Ver.* II.2.29, and Var. *L.* 6.31.

The law, whether expressed by *lex* or *ius*, was closely associated in the Roman mind with the physical place in which that law was exercised – i.e. a court; hence *in ius ire* or *in ius uocare*. See further DeWitt (1940) 88–89. Cf. Ter. *Ph.* 984: *lege agito ergo*!

19.2 sit constituta Along with *oportere* the repetition of these words and phrases from the beginning of §17 gives a sort of ring composition to C.'s legal argument; see nn. *ad loc.*

Sicilia tota The primary position of the subject outside of the protasis lends emphasis. For *tota*, see §2 *cuncti* n.

si una uoce loqueretur A *fictio personae* or *prosopopoeia*, whereby non-personal things are given a voice and other elements of personified behaviour, is used to personify a collective entity such as regions and cities – in this instance, the island of Sicily and its inhabitants. The device injects a sense of vivacity and variation into a speech, and after C. has made an argument regarding statutory construction, affords the listener a moment of reflection. For examples, see Greenidge 156. For personification, see Lausberg §§820, 826–829. Cf. the personification of Rome in *Cat.* 1.18 with Dyck *ad loc.*, where C.'s imagined speech of the *patria* takes the form of a prayer. For Quintilian's analysis of *prosopopoeia* and his comment on *Cat.* 1.27–29, see *Inst.* 6.1.25, 9.2.31–32; cf. Pl. *Cri.* 50a–54d. For the need to set apart such a passage with a change of intonation, see Quint. *Inst.* 1.8.3. On the use of a fictitious scenario to strengthen one's argument, see §6 *quodsi* ... n.

Given the content of the following statement and C.'s discussion of legal avenues, it is tempting to see in this depiction a reference to the judicial process of *fictio* in which a non-Roman was granted access to a Roman civil procedure (see §18 *ciuili* ... *actione et priuato iure* n.). In that case the praetorian *formula* would be preceded by a contrafactual condition, e.g. *Si Aulus Agerius* ... *heres esset* .... This personification therefore underscores two main tenets of C.'s argument: first that Sicily is unable to prosecute Verres through a civil procedure, and since the criminal court is its only venue for redress, it is its prerogative to find a suitable speaker (see n. below); second that some collective representation is required if the island is going to be able to speak *una uoce.* It is tempting to think that the *diuinatio* process arose in relation to offences which affected more than one person. As a practical consequence, it forced potential litigants either through their own mutual agreement or through the intervention of a court to combine their claims into a kind of class action; see Introduction §III.

19.3 quod auri, quod argenti, quod ornamentorum The statement uttered here by the imaginary personification of Sicily resembles ritualized language used before a magistrate by which the plaintiff would identify the person accused and the nature of the charge. Several features of this imagined dialogue suggest that this is a recreated legal performative statement. The first part of the charge against Verres relates to money and items of monetary value; the second half (*quod … beneficio … iuris habui*) involves flagrant disrespect for the laws and charters which govern the province, whether or not these alleged infractions resulted in financial loss. The statement includes all of the information required to bring an accusation: the name of the defendant (*C. Verres*), the charges (a request for 100 million sesterces), an assertion of the plaintiff's rights under the law (*ex lege*), and an official laying of the charge (*quo nomine … repeto*). In a legal action, all of these statements, if accepted by the magistrate, would form the basis of the *intentio* in the praetorian formula in civil procedure; see Greenidge 150–152. For the formula in the *legis actio sacramento,* see Kaser (1996) 81–85 and Greenidge 58–59. That there would be a similar proclamation required at the *nominis delatio* of a criminal recovery court is not surprising, since a recovery court was a blend of public and private legal procedure; see Greenidge 461. **ornamentorum** Artwork was covered under the items that could be recovered in a *quaestio de repetundis* and subsumed under the general term '*pecunia*'; see §18 *ereptae pecuniae* n. See Miles (2002) on concepts of cultural property, and the extensive commentary by Baldo (2004) on *Ver.* II.4. Whether the plaintiff(s) received the stolen artwork or simply financial restitution is unclear.

19.4 urbibus, sedibus, delubris C. cites locations representative of the various spheres of social life: the civic, private, and religious;

cf. §11 *ciuitates ... domos ... fana*. As far as temples are concerned, land in the provinces could not be designated as legally 'sacred' even though it might be treated as such: Gaius *Inst.* 2.7 *etiamsi non sit religiosum, pro religioso habetur: item quod in prouinciis non ex auctoritate populi Romani consecratum est, proprie sacrum non est, tamen pro sacro habetur.* These repetitions caught the attention of Gellius; see citation of Gel. 13.25.9–11 at §11 *Siciliam prouinciam* ... n.

fuit (*PM* Gel.13.25.9 : *om.* γ) Though the Italian family is often guilty of accretions, *fuit* finishes the first tricolon, which refers to physical objects, while the next verb, *habui*, applies to the legal privileges afforded to various communities in Sicily; see *beneficio* n. below. The inclusion of the verb also gives a molossus-cretic ending.

quod ... iuris A second class of grievances that are not strictly of monetary value, though many of Verres' manipulations of the provincial justice system were used for monetary gain. *Iuris* is a partitive genitive with *quod*.

in una quaque re 'in each and every instance'.

19.5 beneficio Similar to *priuilegia* or προνόμια, 'a benefit conferred by law, edict, legal status, etc'. See *OLD s.u.* 3 and *TLL* II 1886.20, and cf. *Ver.* II.3.123. A hallmark of Roman expansion, Sicily was allowed to maintain many of its laws and institutions that had existed prior to the imposition of a Roman administration. Although Sicily had been conquered in the mid-third century, it was finally organized as a province by the consul P. Rupilius (*RE* 5, *MRR* 1.497–498, cos. 132; *Ver.* II.3.125) in 132/1, after he quelled the First Servile War. This charter conferred certain economic and legal benefits. A key feature of the so-called *lex Rupilia* was the preservation of the *lex Hieronica*, which regulated tithe-collection during the Hieronic kingdom. Established sometime after 265/4, the tax system under Hiero required a tenth of one's entire harvest of cereal grains and probably wine, oil, and minor crops as well; see *Ver.* II.2.32 *Inter aratores et decumanos lege frumentaria, quam Hieronicam appellant, iudicia fiunt.* Individual *ciuitates* retained some independence inasmuch as they were granted the authority for collecting these revenues. Under the *lex Rupilia*, these communities also kept their own laws and courts regarding civil matters. On judicial arrangements, see the citation of *Ver.* II.2.32 in the introduction to §§52–58. For discussion of the *lex Rupilia*, see *Staats.* 3.745–746, Greenidge 114–115, and Carcopino (1919) 71–72, 144–145. Scramuzza (1937) 246–248 argues that the new charter was also intended to decrease the size of large estates and discourage further slave uprisings. On a similar charter, see A. J. Marshall (1968). On Rupilius' reorganization of Sicily, see *Ver.* II.2.32–44, 59, 90, 125, and Val. Max. 6.9.8. For more on the *lex Hieronica* and Verres' transgression of this traditional agreement, see Pritchard (1970) and A. J. Marshall (1967). For an analysis of *Ver.* II.2.35–50 and the function of the *lex Rupilia*, see López (1972) and Broggini (1964). For more on the procedure of establishing provincial organization, see Willems (1883) 2.703–712 and Künkel (1995) 2.342–534.

senatus populique Romani In the earlier portions of the speech, C. has been highlighting tensions between the senatorial order and the Roman people; cf. §§7–8. He only tends to refer to the *SPQR* collective when mentioning senatorial motions and decrees. Here the headword of the genitives is *beneficio*; cf. *Ver.* II.2.114, 4.69, *Dom.* 17, and *Deiot.* 6. Ritschl (1853) 494–495 defends the form *senati* on the evidence of Charisius, citing Pliny the Elder (see app. crit. *ad loc.*). The vague reference to the *Diu. Caec.* could also refer to §32 *ex senatus consulto.*

id mihi tu, C. Verres At a *nominis delatio,* the speaker must identify the person against whom he is laying a charge. It is appropriate on such formal occasions to call the defendant by his full name; see §3 *C. Verres* n. When nominative first- or second-person pronouns are expressed, there is often a contrast; see Spevak (2010) 92–93. The tension here may not be so much between Sicily and Verres as it is between Verres and the enactments of the *senatus populique Romani.* This particular cluster of pronouns is not found elsewhere in Latin, but the phenomenon is common; e.g. *Vat.* 15 *id tu tibi, Quinct.* 56 *tu id tibi,* and *Ver.* II.2.206 *ego hoc tibi. Mihi* receives the least stress in secondary position; see Spevak (2010) 94–96. On pronoun placement more generally, see Adams (1994b).

19.6 eripuisti atque abstulisti The quasi-synonymous pair in final position lends emphasis, though there are nuanced differences between the two verbs. *Eripere* implies a blatant and/or violent theft; Schol. Gronov. (330.10 Stangl) *subripit qui clam aliquid tollit; eripit qui palam et per uim. In aliis ergo subripuisse dixit, de Verre eripuisse*; *D.* 2.7.4.pr *eripere enim est de manibus auferre per raptum*; see further *TLL* V 2.788.73. *Auferre* has a basic sense of 'remove' or 'dispossess' and echoes the wording of the *lex de repetundis*: *ablatum ... siet*. For this *iunctura* again in emphatic final position, see *Ver.* II.4.14 *eripuisse atque abstulisse* with Baldo *ad loc.* and 4.134. For quasi-synonymous pairs, see §1 *causam rationemque* n.

quo nomine 'on these grounds'. With regard to possessions or rights, *nomine* indicates the grounds of an accusation; see *OLD s.u. nomen* 25, Heumann–Seckel 1d, and Berger *s.u. nomine*. This legal term was also probably a part of the official statement for laying a charge; see *quod auri, quod argenti ...* n. above.

abs te Only with the personal pronoun *te* does C. use *abs*, and even this is primarily confined to his earlier writings; cf. §21. After the year 54, he prefers *a te* exclusively except for epistolary writing. Although fairly common in his early speeches, *abs* may suggest that this passage is a direct imitation of a *nominis delatio* and the legal proclamation made before a praetor, which often preserved archaic forms. For *abs te*, see *TLL* I 3.12–25, Wölfflin (1933) 108, Neue-Wagener 2.828–830, Parzinger 2.57–64, and Berry on *Sul.* 3.

19.7 sestertium miliens An elliptical expression for *miliens centena milia sestertium*, i.e. 100 million sesterces. During the trial itself, C. would estimate the damages at 40 million sesterces; see *Ver.* I.56. Several explanations have been put forward to explain this discrepancy. First, as the scholiast notes, C. had not yet undertaken his exploratory journey to Sicily to gather evidence, so this may be an exaggerated estimate. Or the figure could take into account the practice of double restitution under the *lex Cornelia de repetundis*. At any rate, an exact figure would only be determined after the trial during a separate procedure for the assessment of damages (*litis aestumatio*).

ex lege 'according to the law'; see *TLL* V 2.1108.50. The entire phrase (along with *beneficio senatus populique Romani iuris habui*) is reminiscent of the legal utterances used in the *legis actio sacramento*: '*eum ego ex iure Quiritium meum esse aio*' ('which I declare is my property according to Roman law'); see further *TLL* V 2.1108.45. For this dialogue, see Greenidge 58–59 and Kaser (1996) 81–85.

repeto 'to reclaim extorted property'; see Berger and Heumann–Seckel *s.u.*

si uniuersa *Expolitio*/ *commoratio*. C. dwells on the issue that Sicily is unable to speak for herself and repeats with almost direct correspondence the phrase before the *prosopopoeia*.

ut dixi C. again uses this parenthetical phrase to mark the resumption of his own voice after the *fictio personae* in *Cat.* 1.19: *Haec si tecum, ut dixi, patria loquatur, nonne impetrare debeat, etiam si uim adhibere non possit?* On *expolitio*, see introduction to §§20–22.

19.9 harum rerum actorem *Res* here means 'the charges'; *OLD s.u.* 11 and Heumann–Seckel *s.u.* 1d. On the meaning of *actor* in a proper legal sense, see §12 *actorem* n.

idoneum Recalls C.'s comment at §16 and prepares the audience for him to explain why the Sicilians think Caecilius unsuitable; see §§20–22 below.

Confirmatio I, resumed (§§20–22)

Caecilium Siculi plane nolunt

Cicero's clients know Caecilius and would rather be left without an advocate than depend upon his services. Why they have such a poor estimation of him, it is unnecessary to say. He should defer in favour of C. rather than violently deprive the province of its last shred of hope for restoring its fortunes.

In the conclusion to the first part of the *confirmatio*, C. turns attention from himself to his opponent. Most of the passage is a recapitulation (*expolitio*), though with some emotive development, of the material that he already presented in the *narratio*, viz. that the

Sicilians do not want Caecilius to lead the prosecution against Verres and that Caecilius himself has committed some wrongs against them; see *Rhet. Her.* 4.54 *Expolitio est, cum in eodem loco manemus et aliud atque aliud dicere uidemur.* Rhetorical precept suggests that, in addition to repeating the idea in different words, the speaker should intensify the message through a fictitious soliloquy (*sermocinatio*) or an emotive address to the audience (*exsuscitatio*) strengthened by *interrogatio*; see *Rhet. Her.* 4.55 *Tertium genus est commutationis, quod tractando conficitur, si sententiam traiciemus aut ad sermocinationem aut exsuscitationem.* In this portion of the *Diu. Caec.*, C. embraces both options. The Sicilians are given a *sermocinatio* (§20), and C. himself deploys a barrage of nine emotive questions at Caecilius (§§21–22). On *expolitio* and emotive modification, see *Rhet. Her.* 4.54–56; Lausberg §§830–842, 839–841. There is an underlying *complexio*: either the Sicilians do not know anything about Caecilius and prefer someone they do know, or, more damning, they know Caecilius and purposefully oppose his appointment. Either way, according to this depiction, his petition to lead the prosecution is an indication of his poor character and disregard for Rome's allies and her laws.

§20

20.1 tam impudens See §13 *impudentiae meae* n.

reperietur Passives such as *reperietur* and *inueniuntur*, followed by a relative clause of characteristic in the subjunctive, denote the existence of a thing and are more or less the equivalent of *est*; see K-St. 2.2.303–304. During this rhetorical question, one could imagine that C. would redirect his critical gaze toward Caecilius, whom he soon addresses.

20.2 alienam causam In representing a person or party other than oneself, one was acting *in alieno nomine*; see §11 *cognitorem… actorem* n.

inuitis iis Under other versions of the *lex de repetundis*, if a non-Roman had a charge accepted and was assigned a legal representative by the praetor (either by choice or out of legal necessity), there seems to have been a right of repudiation; see *Statutes* 1.66. In this instance, though, both C. and Caecilius have entered the *postulatio* in their own name and not as a representative; therefore the Sicilian delegations would not have the right to reject the outcome of the *diuinatio.* See further §64 *quod eum sibi Achaei patronum adoptarant* n.

quorum negotium C. conveniently omits the possibility that Caecilius has a reasonable grievance himself. On *negotium,* see §27 *quid negoti* n.

20.3 accedere aut aspirare audeat *Accedere* here, 'to occupy oneself with', especially in a legal obligation; *OLD s.u.* 9a and *TLL* I 260.47–58. C. uses *aspirare* in his orations almost exclusively in the sense of 'to hanker after' or 'aspire to'; see *OLD s.u.* 9a and *TLL* I 841.80–842.8, and cf. §51 *me inuito aspirare possit.* For this collocation, cf. *Ver.* II.1.142 *quisquam ad meam pecuniam me inuito aspirat, quisquam accedit?* Both verbs give the sense here of an unwanted incursion, i.e. 'sticking one's nose where it does not belong'. The assonance and nigh pleonastic expression here are a characteristic of the heightened emotion in the passage.

Q. Caecili Caecilius' *praenomen* may have been added in the MS tradition; see §22 *Caecili* n.

20.4 hoc Siculi dicerent *Sermocinatio*; see Lausberg §§820–825. Though not distinguished by all rhetoricians from *prosopopoeia, sermocinatio* is concerned with real persons and the other with non-personal things. Representing a collective (e.g. Greeks or Sicilians) is a borderline case; see further Lausberg §824. This device produces much the same effect as *euidentia*; even though the dialogue is fictitious, the orator puts himself and the audience in the place of eyewitnesses to the conversation; see Quint. *Inst.* 8.3.61 and 9.2.40. On the difference between *expolitio* and *commoratio* in some rhetoricians, see Lausberg §830.

te Emphatic primary position; see Adams (1994b) 105.

non nouimus, nescimus qui sis, numquam te antea uidimus A *tricolon crescens* with an alliteration and asyndeton that convey a sense of exasperation, which will be heightened by the *interrogatio* in §21. On alliteration, see §6 *furta atque flagitia* n. **qui sis** See §37 *qui sis* n.

20.5 fortunas See §2 *fortunis* n.

defendere The imagined dialogue resumes the leitmotif of 'prosecution as defence' which played a prominent role in the outset of the speech in §§1–7. By having the Sicilians revive this notion themselves in an imagined dialogue, C. is suggesting that they too view this legal action as defensive.

20.6 fides Essentially a recapitulation of §11 *meam fidem, quam habent spectatam iam et cognitam.* On *fides*, see §13 *fide atque praesidio* n.

nonne id dicerent The apodosis of the present counterfactual sentence that started with *si … Siculi dicerent* above. *Nonne* anticipates a positive answer; see H-Sz. II.462.

20.7 cuiuis probare deberent 'ought to come to be favourably regarded by anyone'; see *OLD probo* 6b. Although *probare* has judicial and juristic overtones, *deberent* also implies a legal or moral obligation; see §1 *una et id … probabit, et …* n. For indirect speech following direct speech, see *Sul.* 3 with Berry *ad loc.*

nunc hoc dicunt 'but as it is, they actually say that …'. *Nunc* does not convey a temporal sense but rather 'introduces a fact or consideration opposed to a previous speculation', namely the imagined *sermocinatio* above; see *OLD s.u. nunc* 11. Rather than lapse into another direct discourse as he has done above, C. changes to indirect discourse for variation.

utrumque se nosse C. repeats a similar adumbration from §4 *nam illi multo mihi hoc facilius remisissent si istum non nossent, aut si iste apud eos quaestor non fuisset.*

20.8 defensorem See *defendere* n. above.

alterum plane nolle On the colloquial intensifier, *plane*, see Hofmann §69; cf. *Att.* 13.13–14.4 *id ego plane nolo.*

§21

21.1 etiamsi taceant, satis dicunt C. is fond of this oxymoron; cf. *Cat.* 1.18 and 21 with Dyck *ad loc.*, *Sest.* 40, and *Sul.* 82 with Berry *ad loc.*: *tacita grauitas et fides de uno quoque loquitur.* By constructing a meaning for silence, C. is able to impose his own interpretation. In effect it allows him to present an argument or opinion without evidence. For similar oxymora in the Greek orators, see Büchner (1951). **taceant** C. frequently uses *etiamsi* to introduce a concessive clause governing a potential subjunctive in the present tense, which is the reading transmitted by *P* and γ; for this construction, see *OLS* 1.484, K-St. 2.2.439, and H-Sz. 671–672. Cf. *Prou.* 8 *itaque omnia illa quae et saepe audistis, et tenetis animis etiamsi non audiatis, praetermitto, Cat.* 1.19 *Haec si te cum ita, ut dixi, patria loquatur, nonne impetrare debeat, etiamsi uim adhibere non possit?* The paradosis is to be preferred over the imperfect subjunctive *tacerent* in *M*, but as Pinkster notes, 'It is often difficult to distinguish a potential of the past from a present counterfactual'; see *OLS* 1.487. The lemma of the scholiast alone has the present indicative *tacent*, which is ruled out by *uerum non tacent.*

uerum non tacent C. does not follow up this statement with any details but only continues to refer to the Sicilians' distrust of Caecilius – either in character or ability – and to suggest that Caecilius himself could face prosecution (*te ipsum ... ulciscantur*). Cf. again at §28 *Quare negent ex me non audies: hos patere id suspicari quod necesse est.* Normally, when completely omitting information (*reticentia*), C. gives the audience reasons for the omission: brevity, relevance, absence of proof, common knowledge, etc. The scarcity of truth or evidence is the primary reason for using this rhetorical device. On *reticentia* and *occultatio*, see §28 *plura non dicam* n.

21.2 tamen ... ? tamen ... ? tamen ... ? tamen ... ? cur ... ? cur ... ? cur ... ? cur ... ? The remainder of the section is an extended *interrogatio.* Lausberg §§767–770: 'No answer is expected, since in view of the situation, from the point of view of the speaking party, the answer is supposed to be self-evident. The impatient and emotive couching of the statement in the form of a question is intended to humiliate the opposing party'; see also Quint. *Inst.* 9.2.7–8. The series of rhetorical questions becomes longer and longer and builds into an emotional, exasperated crescendo. The verbs are carefully varied. At first the audience sees an image of Caecilius as a volunteer (*te offeres*) and a defender (*defendes ... defensorem*) ready to pledge his services, though unwanted. The presentation becomes more violent as he is depicted as wrenching away their hope (*ui extorquere*), physically impeding and ruining the Sicilians (*te interponis ... euertere*), and robbing them of every ounce of their power (*adimis potestatem*). Over the course of C.'s line of questioning, Caecilius goes from offering an unwanted defence to outright assault on the people of Sicily and is recast, in a degree, as a miniature Verres. The emotive effect of an *interrogatio* was a rhetorically acknowledged method of allowing the speaker to linger on a particular argument; see introduction to §§20–22 on *expolitio.*

iis inuitissimis See §20 *inuitis iis* n.

te offeres 'to offer one's services voluntarily'; *OLD s.u. offero* 10 and *TLL* IX 2.509.47. Peterson's apparatus fails to mention that *offers* is the reading found in all manuscripts. Only a deletion in the first hand of *O* and a supralineal correction in *G* give the future tense *offeres,* which most editors have adopted. Though there is no conceptual difficulty with the present tense, in this series of syntactically parallel questions in which every other verb is in the future tense, it would be strange if the leading verb alone were in the present. Only if he is chosen as the prosecutor will Caecilius then offer his services to the Sicilians and speak at Verres' future trial (*loquere*). The reading of *O* has not been properly or accurately reported. The initial correction appears to be in the first hand: *sat(is)* ~~*dic*~~' *dicunt* *utr(um) offeres* | *puto* [*uerum* in margin in a second hand] *n(on) tace(n)t t(ame)n his i(n)uitissi(im)is te offers.* The inserted verb, *puto,* may indicate that the scribe was copying a conjecture in his exemplar, as he only later noticed.

aliena causa See §20 *alienam causam* n.

21.3 loquere There may be a subtle jab at Caecilius in C.'s choice of words: *loqui* is usually used to denote unadorned everyday speech and rarely proper oratory, for which *dicere* is more common. Cf. §37 *familiariter tecum loquar* and *Ver.* I.20 *Vere loquar, iudices*; see *TLL* VII 2.1673.63–73. C. prefers this older second person ending in the future and imperfect indicative and in subjunctive forms; he more commonly uses the *-ris* termination in the present tense for disambiguation, especially if the verb is deponent; cf. §21 *conaris*. The future tense, furthermore, with a long penultimate syllable, provides a Ciceronian trochaic metron. See further Neue-Wagener 3.204–206 and K-St. 1.675–676.

defendes Even when speaking about Caecilius' plea to prosecute Verres, C. presents it as a defence so as to keep this concept fresh in the minds of the jury. For the conceit to be valid, it has to hold true for both C. and Caecilius.

desertos ... defensos The alliterative antithetical pair are placed in contrast to one another.

21.4 potius ... esse malunt The combination of *potius* and *malle* is pleonastic and rarely found in C., and *esse* is frequently omitted; see Schmalz *s.u. malle.* Cf. *Balb.* 19 *ut ... hominis ipsius ornamenta adiumento causae potius quam impedimento esse malitis*, *Cael.* 19, and *Fam.* 4.3.1. Among a series of verbs in the future tense (*loquere*, *defendes*, etc.), *malunt*, *uult*, and *conaris* are verbs often used in the present tense with an infinitive as a circumlocution for the future; see H-Sz. 312–314.

abs te See §19 *abs te* n.

21.5 pollicebere *Polliceberis* is the reading in *E* and may originally have stood in *S*. However *-re* is C.'s usual second-person termination in the future tense; see *loquere* n. above.

uelle sua causa *Velle* with *causa* means 'to have someone's well-being or interests at heart'; see *OLD s.u.* 15b. Cf. *Att.* 11.8.1 *per eos qui nostra causa uolunt*, and *Ver.* II.2.64 *Repente coepit dicere se omnia Verris causa uelle.* The accusative, *suam causam* ('to want their case'?), would be unparalleled in C. Among the *deteriores* with *causam*, v[2] has a marginal notation to insert *defendere* before *nec*; O[2] likewise wrote *defendere* before *posse*, though this correction was deleted by a third hand.

21.6 posse arbitrantur '... who think that you neither have their best interests at heart, nor, if you actually did, that you would be able to do them any good'. An enthymeme *ex pugnantibus*;

see Iulius Rufinianus 30 (*RLM* 45.32) ἐνθύμημα *fit cum periodos orationis ex contrariis sententiis astringitur.* See further Lausberg §371 and Quint. *Inst.* 5.10.1–4. *Posse* can be used absolutely to indicate efficacy or achievement; e.g. *Q. fr.* 2.15.4: … *plus unus Cato potuerit quam omnes leges omnesque iudices.* See *TLL* X 2.137.74–138.21.

eorum spem exiguam reliquarum Here *spem* takes both a subjective and objective genitive. For the use of two genitives with a single substantive, see further K-St. 2.1.416–417, and Berry at *Sul.* 82 *cuiusquam … orationis.* **reliquarum** esp. with *spes*, that 'which is left for the future'; see *OLD s.u.* 5. Hence, 'their meagre hope of future happiness'.

21.7 habent … positam For the perfect passive participle with *habeo*, see §11 *habent spectatam iam et cognitam* n.

in legis et in iudici seueritate Judicial corruption becomes the major theme of the first speech against Verres; see §8 *iudiciorum seueritatem desiderant* n. C. will expand upon it briefly in §§23–24 regarding Hortensius' supposedly unsavoury tactics.

21.8 ui extorquere A strong, physical verb with militaristic overtones, *extorquere*, is nicely juxtaposed with an abstract object, *spem.* The metaphor latent in *extorquere* is confirmed and enhanced by *ui*; see Ernout–Meillet *s.u. torqueo* and *TLL* V 2.2041.59, 2045.76–2046.24.

te interponis *Interponere* used reflexively to mean 'interfere'; see *OLD s.u.* and *TLL* VII 1.2248.55–72.

quibus … lex consultum esse uult The perfect passive infinitive with *uolo* is found primarily in C.'s early speeches; see Landgraf on *Rosc. Am.* 2 *praereptam uelim*, K-St. 2.1.173–174, and H-Sz. 352. C. bases this statement on his interpretation of the *lex de repetundis*; see the introduction to §§17–18. In what seems like a personification of the law, he again reveals a framework for interpreting law based on legislative intent. What he really means is not 'law' but 'those who drafted the law', i.e. the senate and people of Rome.

21.9 in prouincia On Caecilius' tenure in Sicily, see Introduction §II.

21.10 non optime es meritus Litotes in an idiomatic construction: *mereor* with an adverb and *de* meaning 'to conduct oneself ... towards' and specifically here, 'to do one's duty'; see *OLD s.u. mereor* 6a and *TLL* VIII 809.53. The construction is embedded in the Roman political vocabulary and associated with ideas of *beneficium* and *officium*. 'The most frequent form is the passive participle with an active meaning: *bene* (*optime*) *meritus de aliquo*; i.e. "the one who has fulfilled his *officia*" and who consequently "has rendered service to someone", *male meritus* "he who has not fulfilled it". [La forme la plus fréquente est le participe passé à valeur active : *bene (optime) meritus de aliquo* ; c'est donc «celui qui s'est acquitté de ses *officia*» et qui par conséquent «a rendu service à quelqu'un», *male meritus* «celui qui ne s'en est point acquitté».]' See further Hellegouarc'h 169–170; cf. *Mil.* 99 *Non enim inimici mei te mihi eripient, sed amicissimi, non male aliquando de me meriti sed semper optime.* C. does not offer details here but only implies that Caecilius failed in some of his obligations as quaestor; later he will implicate him in Verres' crimes (§28).

fortunis omnibus ... euertere *Euertere* with the ablative: 'to expel' someone from his possessions; see *OLD s.u.* 6, and *TLL* V 2.1028.59–68. *Fortunis omnibus evertere* is found several times in the Verrines (*Ver.* II.1.155, 2.43, 3.16, 3.197) but is not attested elsewhere. When C. uses *omnes fortunae*, the context is almost invariably negative, in which a calamity is threatened or realized; cf. §56, *Quinct.* 6, 47, 76, 95, *Planc.* 40, *Pis.* 41, *Flac.* 81, 96, and *Dom.* 45. The verb has a strong visual and physical element; cf. the uprooting of trees at Verg. *G.* 1.256 and Stat. *Theb.* 6.107. For *fortunis evertere* (without *omnibus*), see *Flac.* 11.

21.11 persequendi iuris sui *Ius persequi* – 'to pursue or assert one's rights'; see *OLD s.u. persequor* 5b and *TLL* X 1.1695.26, 55. Cf. Plaut. *Capt.* 492: *nunc barbarica lege certumst ius meum omne persequi*, and §29 *fratrem tuum, ... tecum tuas iniurias persequi. TLL* X 1.1695.55.

deplorandae calamitatis *Deplorare* is a favourite of C.; see Merguet *s.u.* Cf. *Phil.* 11.6 *Quis est qui pro rerum atrocitate deplorare tantas calamitates queat?* See further *TLL* V 1.574.65–575.22. On *calamitas*, see §11 *calamitatum* n.

§22

22.1 nam A 'forward-linking' *nam*. 'It not only provides subsidiary information with regard to the preceding discourse unit, but at the same time introduces a new thematic unit'; Kroon (1995) 156. This is similar to the function of δέ; cf. *Ver.* II.4.126 *Nam Sappho quae sublata de prytanio est dat tibi iustam excusationem, prope ut concedendum atque ignoscendum esse uideatur.* Cf. the 'backward-linking' *nam* at §18.

te actore See §28 *te actore* n.

22.2 adfuturum C. implies that if Caecilius is selected to lead the prosecution the Sicilians would neither come out to show their support through their presence at the trial nor be forthcoming as witnesses. See also §29 *non adesse* n.

intellegis While *putare* has the nuance of 'supposition' or 'idea', *intellegere* indicates 'full understanding or perception'; see *TLL* VII 1.2096.79–2097.9 and X 2.2760.1–15. 'Which of them do you suppose would come forward to support you when you know full well that …'. C. now accuses Caecilius of knowing that he discharged his duties poorly during his quaestorship and that the Sicilians are anxious to prosecute him as well. This is a bold and purely rhetorical accusation. The historical record preserves no indication that the Sicilians ever brought charges against Caecilius. Furthermore, Caecilius could have been prosecuted after he left office in 72. For Marinone's inferences on the quaestors serving with Verres, see Introduction §II.

ut per te alium sed ut per alium aliquem te ipsum *Commutatio* (ἀντιμεταβολή) in which words are repeated in transposed order; cf. *Clu.* 5: *denique illa definitio iudiciorum aequorum … ut in iudiciis et sine inuidia culpa plectatur et sine culpa inuidia ponatur.* For additional examples, see *Phil.* 4.8, *Quinct.* 49, Quint. *Inst.* 9.3.85, Rutil. 1.6, and Isid. 2.21.11; see further Lausberg §801. Rhetorical handbooks call for such a play on words to be used sparingly, but when used moderately they enliven discourse with their ornamentation; see *Rhet. Her.* 4.32. **per alium aliquem** There are other examples in C. of this pleonastic construction; cf. *Corn. fr.* ([Asc.] 75C) *Quid ego nunc tibi argumentis respondeam posse fieri* *ut alius aliquis Cornelius sit qui habeat Philerotem seruum*, *Sest.* 53 *expulsus non alio aliquo sed eo ipso crimine*, *De orat.* 2.36, *Fin.* 2.109, 4.46, and *Inu.* 1.15, 2.58. Such instances of pronominal pleonasm are often archaizing; see H-Sz. 801 and *TLL* I 1608.76–80. The Italian tradition must have omitted *alium* by *saut du même au même*. **te ipsum** after the phrase is inverted, *te* is accompanied by an intensifying adjective.

22.3 ulciscantur As C.'s criticisms of Caecilius have mounted over the course of the rhetorical questions, he has begun to accuse Caecilius of committing the same crimes that he has ascribed to Verres: theft and deprivation of hope (*ui extorquere*), detriment to the Sicilians' well-being (*eos … fortunis omnibus conaris euertere*, etc.), and disregard for their rights under the law (*te interponis* …). In short, C. begins to attack Caecilius as though he were Verres himself. On the notion of retributive justice, see §11 *ultorem* and §54 *qui possit ulcisci* with nn. *ad loc.* A verb of uncertain etymology, which may share a common root with *ulcus* (ulcer, sore), 'to avenge oneself upon'; Ernout–Meillet *s.u.*

laborare 'to exert oneself' followed by a final clause; see *TLL* VII 2.803.11 and *OLD s.u.* 2.

Confirmatio II (§§22–26)

The Candidate Least Desirable to the Accused

Now that it is clearly established that the Sicilians want Cicero to represent them – not Caecilius – it still leaves another important consideration unanswered in this proceeding: whom does Verres least want to prosecute him? The former governor's associate, Hortensius Hortalus, has been cajoling jurors in order to influence the outcome of the diuinatio. *He remains confident that if Caecilius is chosen, Verres will easily be acquitted of the charges. Otherwise, Hortensius will have to change his tactics in the courtroom and espouse more honest techniques and eschew the safe havens of bribery and political wheeling and dealing.*

C. turns to the second consideration that he set out in his *partitio* (§10): whom does the accused least want to prosecute him? On the broadest level, the argument is derived from an enthymeme by which the jury can easily deduce that C. is the least desirable candidate for the defence since Verres' advocate, Hortensius, is 'canvassing' so vehemently for Caecilius' selection. Though Cicero never calls him by name, Hortensius' cajoling of the jurors is presented to the audience through a lively *sermocinatio* (§23), and then Cicero reminds the jurors of Hortensius' former methods of bribery and jury-tampering (§24). Verres' defence comes to epitomize the back-handing and corrupt dealing that Cicero claims characterize the Roman criminal courts under senatorial control, and the vignette also contributes to C.'s suggestion that the vote in the *diuinatio* is tantamount to the final verdict on Verres.

22.4 at enim This marks the beginning of the second section of the *confirmatio*, which C. begins with a summary of the argument from §§11–22. On *at enim*, see §15 *at enim* n.

solum id est … 'but this is simply to say that …'. C. concludes his first major argument of the speech, §10 *quem maxime uelint actorem*. The argument in §§11–22 has done very little to advance this claim, and so he ends the discussion with the same assertion that he made from the outset. He will now turn his attention to the other half in §§22–26 (*a quo Verres minime se accusari uelit*). *Id* and *illud* refer to these two halves of the *argumentum* respectively. An explicative *ut* clause (*ut … uelint*) defining the subject matter is summarized in *id*; for this construction, see H-Sz. 645.

alterum illud, credo, obscurum est The parenthetical *credo*, 'I suppose', signals irony. Cf. *Phil.* 1.11 *Solusne aberam, an non saepe minus frequentes fuistis, an ea res agebatur ut etiam aegrotos deferri oporteret? Hannibal, credo, erat ad portas aut de Pyrrhi pace agebatur …*, Pl. *Rud.* 397, and Ter. *Eun.* 98. Such parenthetical expressions are important in the written version of a speech in places where the irony is not so obvious but could have been indicated through inflection during the actual delivery. Since the statement has been marked out as ironic, the phrase conveys the same sense as *perspicuum* and *non dubium*, which were often repeated in the first part of the *confirmatio*; see §15 *cum id ita perspicuum sit …* n. In addition to linguistic variation, the reference to *obscuritas* also contrasts with Verres' and Hortensius' flagrant and egregious efforts to influence the outcome of the *diuinatio* (*palam* … *uehementer* … *aperte*). On irony and humour, which are rarer in this *diuinatio* than in the rest of the Verrines, see Haury (1955) 81, 117.

22.5 minime C. recalls the *contentio* (ἀντίθετον) that he set out in the *propositio*; see §10 *quem maxime* … *quem minime* … n.

22.6 ecquis often connotes impatience in direct questions, especially when paired with words such as *umquam* and *tandem*. Cf. *Font.* 37 *Ecquis umquam reus* …, *Rosc. Am.* 46 *Ecquid tandem tibi uidetur* …, and *Phil.* 2.14.

tam palam … tam uehementer Contrasted with *obscurum*; see *alterum illud, credo, obscurum est* n. above. The anaphora and asyndeton underscore the sense of strenuousness and repetition in their attempts to influence the jury.

honore 'public office'; here used more or less synonymously with *magistratus*; see *OLD s.u.* 5 and *TLL* VI 2926.27–2927.22. Running for high political office was notoriously expensive and time-consuming – a fact that the senatorial jury would know well, and one not lost on C. himself, who was currently standing for the aedileship; see Introduction §I. Hortensius likewise was a candidate for the consulship; see §23 *magnus ille defensor* … n. For electioneering tactics, see the *Commentariolum Petitionis*, Yakobson (1999), and Tatum (2007). For bribery during these elections, see Lintott (1990). On a broader understanding of *honos*, see Hellegouarc'h 383–387.

22.7 contendit governs the prepositional phrases with *de* (*de honore* … *de sua salute*) and the negative purpose clause introduced by *ut ne*. For *breuiloquentia*, see H-Sz. 822–828.

ille atque illius amici Verres and 'his associates'; see *TLL* I 1908.45–60. *Amici* is tantalizingly vague, though the audience comes to learn that one of them is Verres' advocate, Hortensius Hortalus; see §23 *magnus ille defensor* … n. During the trial, C. would also include the other co-consul-elect, Q. Metellus Creticus, among Verres' supporters. On the bonds and duties associated with *amicitia*, see §6 *causa tantae necessitudinis* n.

ut ne γ simply reads *ne*, where both branches of the Italian family read *ut ne*. The pleonastic construction *ut ne*, more common in C.'s earlier speeches, has an archaic sound that imparts solemnity and is therefore found in urgent requests, orders, and important reminders; see Parzinger 2.3, see further 2.1–4. Cf. §14 *ut … ne*, *Rosc. Am.* 54, *Ver.* II.1.123, 4.64, 5.174. C. has been emphasizing the concerted efforts of Verres and Hortensius in such a way that this expression would not be out of place. C., however, only has one other instance in which a negative purpose clause depends upon *contendere*, and in that instance only *ne* is used: *Ver.* II.5.2 *pro suo iure contendet ne patiamini* ….

haec … delatio detur The *diuinatio* convened after the *postulatio* but before the *nominis delatio*, when the accused would be officially indicted. For an outline of the legal procedure, see Introduction §III. Though unattested elsewhere (see *TLL* V 1.416.44–61), *delationem dare* may have been a fixed legal phrase; cf. §§10, 49 *cuicumque uos delationem dedissetis* n.

22.8 sunt See §13 *sunt* n.

in me *In* expressing an abstract location indicating who has a particular power or capacity (*esse in aliquo*); *OLD s.u. in* 26 and *TLL* VII 1.772.48–63. Cf. *Rosc. Am.* 111.

22.9 Caecili (γ*PMF*[1] : Q. Caecili *cett. deteriores*) Peterson (1905) 412: 'This phenomenon seems not to have been sufficiently noticed: there may have been a tendency on the part of copyists to include a *praenomen*.' After having addressed Caecilius by two names, it is not a mark of disrespect or contempt for C. to use only his *nomen* here. So Adams (1978) 146 notes: in the law courts, 'sustained double naming is not usual, except in the address of the *iudex* …. [Additionally] a sort of camaraderie among advocates seems to have led to the practice of referring to opposing counsel by single name only'. After addressing the jury briefly (*at enim … delatio detur*), C. again speaks to Caecilius directly.

non esse The final position after the vocative is emphatic.

in utroque nostrum See *in me* n. above.

22.10 sint (*γP*: sunt *M*) The subjunctive is required for the indirect question. For other examples of *commemoro* with indirect questions, cf. *Ver.* I.23, II.5.140, and Merguet *s.u.*

paulo post commemorabo C. will return to his analysis of his qualities and those of Caecilius in a large portion of the speech; see §§27–35. This forecasting feature with *paulo post* is again used at *Planc.* 41 *Quam ob rem paulo post de isto plura dicam* ….

§23

23.1 nunc Used adversatively, 'but for now …'.

23.2 tacitus tu … assentiare *Assentior* carries a sense of the middle voice, though the active form is also attested in C.; cf. *Q. fr.* 2.1.2, *Fam.* 1.2.1, and 1.9.21. See further Schmalz *s.u.* and Neue-Wagener 3.19–20. On this second-person termination, see §21 *loquere* n. There is perhaps a touch of the meta-rhetorical here; the reading audience would not have had a copy of Caecilius' speech – even in the literary tradition, he is *tacitus.* On this oxymoron, see §21 *etiamsi taceant, satis dicunt* n.

nullam … nullam … The short σύγκρισις/*comparatio*, which anticipates the longer comparisons to come, is presented with anaphora and syntactic parallelism. C. favours the repetition of *nullus* and *nihil*; see §43 *nihil … nihil … nihil.* See further Pease on *N. D.* 1.75.

23.3 contemnat Cf. §39 *noli haec contemnere.* I.e. Verres will have to give serious attention to his trial if C. is the one conducting it.

pertimescat C. frequently affords forms of *pertimesco* the final position in its clause since it provides a desirable prose rhythm such as the trochaic metron here; see Laurand 179. C. would prefer *extimesco* in his later speeches, and all compounds with *per-* are more frequent in the early speeches. In the later speeches, they tend to be reserved for passages in a more colloquial register; see Laurand 263–276. However, this may be due to the fact that more legal speeches are extant from C.'s earlier career. Consequently, this may simply be part of a generic difference between legal and deliberative orations – the former preferring more 'old Latin' forms; see von Albrecht (2003) 106–107.

23.4 magnus ille defensor et amicus eius Q. Hortensius Hortalus (*RE* 13, *MRR* 2.131, cos. 69), the foremost orator of his day, praetor in 72, and the leader of Verres' defence counsel. By the time of Verres' trial in early August, Hortensius would be consul-elect for the year 69. During the *diuinatio* proceedings in early January, however, he had yet to lay hold of that political clout. Elections for 69 only took place around 27 July – a fortunate turn of events for Verres as the first hearing against him took place around 5 August. C. offers another small vignette of Hortensius in the *actio prima* after the consular election; see *Ver.* I.18–21. Hortensius' co-consul, Q. Caecilius Metellus Creticus, would also lobby on Verres' behalf; see *Ver.* I.26–29. For a timeline of these events, see Introduction §III.

This extended passage about Hortensius also typifies a practice of 'non-naming'. Even though C. speaks at length about Hortensius, even attributing a short dialogue to him, he never refers to him by name. This avoidance of naming can indicate contempt and hostility; cf. the remarkable passage at *Sest.* 15–25, where C. speaks of Clodius, Gabinius and Piso, none of whom are ever named. See further Adams (1978) 164. Hortensius is not mentioned by name until *Ver.* I.18. **magnus** normally precedes the noun which it describes, while *ille* would tend to take the primary position in the phrase. The inversion of adjective and demonstrative here focuses emphasis on *magnus*, perhaps to draw attention to Hortensius' reputation as an orator; on this word order, see Marouzeau 3.94, 112–117.

tibi suffragatur 'is campaigning for you'. The verb is most commonly used to describe canvassing for an election; *OLD s.u.* Hortensius also had an ongoing bid for the consulship; see n. above. **suffragatur** It was a common practice among some scribes to write the name of referenced individuals in the margins (even if referenced obliquely as in this case). The parent of the *deteriores* must have incorporated into the text the name of Hortensius, which is absent from P^1 and γ though a second hand has included it as a supralineal gloss in *P* and *D*.

me oppugnat 'he opposes me'; *OLD s.u.* 2a. There may be some physical overtones; for legal representation as physical combat, see §1 *defenderim multos, laeserim neminem* n. For *oppugnare* applied to forensic or political clashes, see *TLL* IX 2.802.63–72. Cf. *Ver.* I.24, *Sul.* 3, and *Clu.* 170.

23.5 aperte Cf. §22 *tam palam ... tam uehementer* n.

ab iudicibus If editors and MSS can be trusted, C. uses both *a* and *ab* before a consonantal *i*. Cf. *Ver.* II.3.72 *ab iudiciis petiuisse*; *Flac.* 69 *a iudicibus oratio auertitur.* On the judges, see §1 *iudices* n.

petit C. may suggest some comparison between the Sicilians' entreaty that he take up their case against Verres and Hortensius' coaxing of the judges that they choose Caecilius; cf. §14 *Hi sciunt hoc non modo a me petitum esse sed ita saepe et ita uehementer esse petitum ut aut causa mihi suscipienda fuerit aut officium necessitudinis repudiandum.* C. has already revealed his supposed motives as altruistic and guided by social values, while Hortensius' appeals exemplify the type of behaviour which undermines the public perception of the court. The verb *petere*, repeated emphatically below (*peto ... peto ... peto ...*), is commonly used of soliciting votes; see Hellegouarc'h 211 and *TLL* X 1.1967.3–60.

anteponare In the *exordium* §1, C. uses the verb *praeponere*, but *anteponere* in §59 and in the *peroratio* at §73. Metrical considerations may be at play, since *anteponare* provides a favoured cretic-trochee rhythm.

23.6 honeste ... inuidia ... offensione Hortensius draws upon words deeply embedded in the Roman political, social, and civic vocabulary. One who acted *honeste* was acting with due regard for his fellow citizens and in accordance with moral rectitude; C. devotes the first book of *De officiis* to determining whether an action is *honestus* or *turpis*. For *honestus* in philosophical vocabulary and for the Greek τὸ καλόν, see Liscu (1930) 148. Although frequently used to denote jealousy, *inuidia* here suggests the sort of anger directed against those with power. '*Inuidia* therefore is more associated with a social or political position than *odium*, which is a more personal and visceral feeling [*Inuidia* donc davantage lié à la position sociale ou politique que l'*odium*, sentiment plus personnel et instinctif]'; see Hellegouarc'h 196, 194–199. A similar sense can be detected in *offensio*, which is 'the hostility resulting from previous acts of enmity .... But above all it seems that *offensio* is a more momentary feeling that does not have the same permanent state of mind as *odium* [l'hostilité résulte d'actes antérieurs d'inimitié .... Mais surtout il semble bien que l'*offensio* soit un sentiment plus momentané, qu'il n'ait pas le caractère d'état permanent de l'âme qui est celui de *odium*]'; see *ibid.* 194–195. If so, Hortensius may be trying to make his request sound nigh inconsequential. For the *inuidia* that Hortensius (and C.) can stir up against Caecilius, see §46 *inuidiam* n.

23.7 inquit C. enlivens the scene by inserting another *sermocinatio*, in which Hortensius is depicted as bribing or hounding one of the jurors voting in the *diuinatio*. Of course, the scene could be entirely fictitious; see Stroh (1975) 177 n. 16. Yet as mentioned above, a *sermocinatio* makes no claims of representing actual events – they need only be plausible. **enim inquit** Not found in γ. The omission of *enim*, however, is a common error. *Inquit* seems necessary to indicate the transition to direct speech and is also found in the lemma of the scholiast. Cf. *Q. Rosc.* 26, 46, *Ver.* II.1.25 '... *Causam enim' inquit 'cognosci oportet'* and elsewhere.

quod soleo ... impetrare Bribery was common but perhaps not as common as C. would lead us to believe; see further *LGRR* 28–30. In this example, Hortensius is depicted as habitually engaged in offering bribes, though C. never mentions it explicitly here. *Impetrare*, 'to obtain by entreaty' (*OLD s.u.*; *TLL* VII 1.599.81), may be etymologically related to religious language; see Ernout–Meillet *s.u. patro*.

uehementius contendi The scholiast alleges that this phrase suggests bribery; see [Asc.] 107 (192 Stangl) *'Cum uehementius contendi': cum pecuniam iudicibus dedi.* The *TLL* IV 664.40–42 cites this scholiast and the passage to assert the interpretation as well, but this is an inference rather than something inherent in the diction; *vehementius contendere* is regular Latin and is used elsewhere without a hint of bribery. Cf. §22, *Ver.* II.1.150, *Caec.* 97, *Att.* 1.10.2, *Fam.* 13.19.2, and 15.13.2. A distinctive trait of Ciceronian syntax is the use of the perfect and pluperfect tenses to express a repetitive action in a subordinate clause. This use stops after C. and Caesar and will give way to the subjunctive; see Lebreton 222–223.

23.8 reus The defendant in a civil or criminal trial. By placing *reus* outside of its clause, Hortensius is emphasizing that the matter over which he is trying to have some influence does not concern an indicted individual but simply the choice of the lead prosecutor; see *sine ullo tuo periculo* n. below. The etymology of the term is uncertain. C. suggests that it may come from *res*, i.e. whom the matter at hand concerns. See *De orat.* 2.321 *reos appello quorum res est*; cf. 2.183. Others have suggested that it originates from a sense of obligation and debt (χρέος), particularly relevant in civil cases; see Berger *s.u.*

potius ... quam The tmesis is avoided in *PM*, but the order of γ puts additional emphasis into the contrast of *hoc* and *illo*. Cf. *Q. Rosc.* 2 *Cur potius illius quam huius credetur?*

23.9 da mihi hoc; concede ... The plaintive phrases carry a colloquial and almost comedic tone. Cf. Pl. *Trin.* 244 *da mihi hoc, mel meum, si me amas, si audes*, and *Ver.* II.2.151 *Da mihi hoc; iam tibi maximam partem defensionis praecideris.*

23.11 cum dederis Here *cum* marks the equivalence of two actions or events, when one produces the other; e.g. *cum tacent, clamant.* On the particular use of the future perfect here with *cum*, see Lebreton 335. For the indicative in *cum identicum* clauses, in which the affairs of the main clause and subordinate clause coincide, see *OLS* 1.611–615 and H-Sz. 622–623.

sine ullo tuo periculo 'without any danger to yourself of legal retribution'. On this meaning of *periculum*, see §25 *magno multorum periculo* n. The senatorial jury may not have been in danger of facing charges of bribery since, during a *diuinatio*, the jurors were not sworn in nor was there any consequence of a *diuinatio* that deprived someone of wealth or life. Attempting to influence the jurors at a *diuinatio* may have been a common tactic for influential politicians. For Pompey potentially meddling in a *diuinatio*, see *Q. fr.* 3.2.1 *apud Catonem erat diuinatio in Gabinium futura inter Memmium et Ti. Neronem et C. L. Antonios M. f.. putabamus fore ut Memmio daretur, etsi erat Neronis mira contentio. quid quaeris? probe premitur, nisi noster Pompeius dis hominibusque inuitis negotium euerterit.* **sine ... sine** The insistence conveyed by the anaphora and the repetition of *honeste ... honestum, inuidia ... inuidiosa* cast suspicion on Hortensius' pleas and constant reassurances that jurors can accede to his request without consequences.

sine infamia *Infamia* is the resentment targeted against those who abuse their power – in this instance, senatorial misconduct in the courts; cf. §9 *iudiciorum infamia*, §42 *infamia C. Verris* with nn. *ad loc.*, and *Ver.* I.2: *inuidiam senatus ... inflammare.* On *infamia*, see Hellegouarc'h 195–199.

23.12 ut Even in this small vignette, Hortensius seems to have made the same appraisal of the *diuinatio* that C. has, viz. that the outcome of the *diuinatio* is tantamount to the outcome of the trial itself.

laboro is often completed with a prepositional phrase governed by *causa*; see *TLL* VII 2.802.54. Cf. *Rosc. Am.* 98.

§24

24.1 ait C. returns from direct discourse to indirect discourse: *esse, esse, ferre, constituere,* and *dari* are all infinitives introduced by *ait.* The *sermocinatio* provides a kind of *euidentia* that allows the jurors to see and hear Hortensius' attempts to manipulate the *diuinatio*; see §20 *hoc Siculi dicerent* n.

idem Viz. Hortensius. On non-naming, see §23 *magnus ille defensor ...* n.

aliquis metus It is unclear what sort of reprisal a non-compliant juror could expect after he had taken a bribe but failed to keep up his end of the bargain. The modifier *aliquis* conveys a threatening tone. According to C. at the trial of Oppianicus in 74, the defendant had hoped to secure his acquittal by bribing 16 of the

32 jurors; when he called for an open vote, however, only five voted to acquit. See *Clu.* 73–76.

24.2 ad gratiam The repetition of the preposition already attached to a compound verb (*adiunctus*) was indicative of an older style of speech. *Gratia* here refers to Hortensius' political influence and pressure; see *OLD s.u.* 5c and Hellegouarc'h 202–209.

certos ... in consilio 'there are certain members of the jury ...'. C. accuses Hortensius of bribery and jury-tampering even during the *diuinatio.* C. would like us to imagine that Hortensius has found a few trustworthy members of the jury who will act as his enforcers to ensure that all of the bribed jurors vote accordingly.

24.3 perfacile For words intensified with *per-* in C.'s early style, see §23 *pertimescat* n. The adjective *perfacilis* is rare in C. and only used here and in *Cael.* 24, 51, 62 – a speech in which C. uses a wide variety of *per-* compounds; see Austin at *Cael.* 25 *perattente.* The register of *per-* compounds may suggest that Hortensius is assuming a casual and familiar tone with his fellow senators.

non enim singulos ferre sententias 'because they do not vote one by one ...'; see *OLD s.u. fero* 27a.

24.4 uniuersos constituere Procedure in the *quaestio de repetundis* as constituted under the law on the Tabula Bembina had jurors voting *singillatim*; see *lex repet.* l. 52 [*iudex ita inducito*] *eamque sortem ex hace lege apertam bracioque aperto lit<t>eram digiteis opertam pala*[*m in eam sitellam*] *coicito d*[*eque tribunali descendito; i*]*temque in eos ceteros singilatim iu*[*dices* —vac *sententiae quo modo pronontientur.* vac *quei*].

ceratam ... tabellam Waxed tablets must have been used for voting in the *diuinatio,* though the precise method is unclear. Voting procedures for an actual trial under the *lex* on the Tabula Bembina (ll. 44–56) stipulated that jurors use 'boxwood ballots four fingers long, marked in ink with C for *condemno* on one side and A for *absoluo* on the other. [They] obliterated the letter that they did not want – or both if they wished to record a no-vote – and then in turn cast them into a jar with their arm bare but any surviving letter covered with their fingers'; trans. Lintott (2004) 71.

A foreman was selected by lot to pull the ballots one at a time from the jar and announce the result aloud before passing it along to another juror and then to the presiding praetor. By C.'s time, it appears that jurors used wax tablets rather than these boxwood ballots. Certainly, wax tablets (or boxwood ballots) made sense during the actual trial, when there were only three voting possibilities (*absoluo, condemno,* and *non liquet* – the latter denoted by removing both markings on the tablet). During a *diuinatio,* however, these terms were not applicable and how jurors used the wax tablets is unclear. If there were only two candidates, the wax tablets could have been inscribed with the names of the two competing prosecutors – the juror would simply erase the name of the undesired candidate. Some other procedure must have been followed if there were more than two.

Any procedural details on voting stipulated in the *lex Cornelia de repetundis* have been lost, but from this passage it seems that the voting method for the trial and *diuinatio* differed. In the trial, the jurors would vote one by one, while votes were cast simultaneously in the *diuinatio* (*non enim singulos ferre sententias sed uniuersos constituere*). [Asc.] 108 (Stangl 193) also remarks that the votes were cast into a traditional ballot box (*in cistam*). It is tempting to suggest that the votes were reported and recorded in a manner similar to that used in passing legislation and electing magistrates in the *comitia,* for which see Sis. *hist.* 118, *Rhet. Her.* 1.21, Plin. *Nat.* 33.31, and [Asc.] 108 (Stangl 193) *In diuinationis causis et in aliis maioribus uniuersi iudices in cistam tabulas simul coniciebant suas, easque insculptas litteras habentes <A>, absolutionis; C, condemnationis; cum de alicuius capite agebatur, N et L, ampliationis; his enim litteris significabant 'non liquere' .... Singuli autem sententiam de tabula pronuntiabant in leuioribus causis, et ob id ipsum neque nota neque custode opus fuit, cur corruptor iudicum adiungeret metum ad gratiam iudicantis.* The method outlined by the scholiast, however, should not hold for a *diuinatio* for reasons stated above; see further Introduction §III.

24.5 cera legitima C. alludes to the trial of a Terentius Varro, who had ascended the political ladder during the Sullan regime but in 75 was arraigned by Ap. Claudius Pulcher (*RE* 297, cos. 54, cens. 50) on charges of extortion for some misdeed in Asia.

It appears that the trial did not go forward that year but was postponed until 74. [Asc.] 108–109 (193 Stangl):

> <M.> Terentius Varro, consobrinus frater Hortensi, reus ex Asia apud L. Furium praetorem primo de pecuniis repetundis, deinde apud P. Lentulum Suram, est accusatus; absolutusque est a Q. Hortensio, qui corruptis iudicibus hunc metum adiunxit ad gratiam, ut discoloribus ceris insignitas iudices tabulas accipiant et timeret unusquisque eorum ne fidem pactionis non seruare uideretur, si non in tabula, quam unicuique datam meminisset Hortensius, ex nota cerae scilicet discoloris, absolutum Varronem reperiret.

Since jurors voted by secret ballot, Hortensius cleverly had the wax in the voting tablets marked with distinct colours to ensure that those jurors whom he bribed followed through with acquittal.

This incident became infamous – perhaps through C. himself, who mentions it several times over the course of the Verrines to heighten the perception of a corrupt judiciary; see *Ver.* I.17, 35, 40, 47, *Clu.* 130; see further *LGRR* 30–33. See also Porphyrio on Hor. *S.* 2.1.49, *ORF* 92.VIII, and 130.I. The defendant's *praenomen* is uncertain – perhaps Aulus or Marcus; Stangl emended the text of the scholiast to read *M. Terentius Varro.* Our other sources only preserve the *nomen* and *cognomen.* Even if this is the correct reading, he is not to be confused with the famous antiquarian mentioned in *Brut.* 60, 205. A. Terentius Varro had been a legate in c. 85–82 and may have served as propraetor in Asia; see Brennan (2000) 558. For modern accounts and uncertainty regarding his name, see Magie (1950) 1.249, 2.1125 n. 42. For additional references, see *TLRR* 144, 158. Each tablet presumably had a distinct mark, *contra* Vince (1893).

atque This and *ac* at the head of their clause introduce something unexpected in continuation; cf. καὶ μήν. There may be a slight adversative sense in *atque*; cf. *Cat.* 2.3 *ac si quis est talis qualis esse omnis oportebat* .... For examples of both, see *Clu.* 11, 20, 43, 56 with Fausset *ad loc.* For a fuller discussion, see Seyffert 1§14.

24.6 tam ... quam The idiom contrasts *propter Verrem* with *quod eum ... delectat*; cf. *Ver.* II.3.155 *non hoc mihi tam molestum est Apronio suadere Timarchidem, quam quod hoc idem patrono suo praecipit*, and *Lael.* 15; Liv. 37.11.4–5 *cum diem non tam apparatu absumpsisset quam quod conspici proficiscentem classem nolebat*, and Liv. 26.6.4 *tam armati ... quam quod ... arcebant* with Oakley (1983).

24.7 a pueris nobilibus Conducting a criminal trial could be a catalysing event (*illustris accusatio*) for young men with political aspirations and seems to have been socially acceptable. C.'s idols, whom he mentions momentarily, L. Licinius Crassus and M. Antonius, both undertook such a prosecution, as did Sulpicius, the Luculli, and Julius Caesar; see *Off.* 2.49–50, *Cael.* 47, 73–74, *Pis.* 82, *Ver.* II.3.1–3. Such accusations could engender enmity and were consequently only conducted once; see *Ver.* II.5.180. See further Mitchell (1979) 147 n. 106, Wiseman (1971) 120–121, and Dugan (2005) 8. Cf. §70 *ea iam aetate, cum aedilitatem petat?* There is still debate concerning the conditions under which one could be labelled a *nobilis* and which offices one's ancestor would need to have attained. It is agreed that all patricians were *nobiles* but disputed whether any curule office ennobled plebeians or just the consulate, dictatorship, consular tribunate, and (perhaps) mastership of the horse. For a bibliography on the debate, see *N-P s.u. nobiles*, Brunt (1982), and Shackleton Bailey (1986). On the verb *elusit*, see §45 *sit elusurus* n.

24.8 a quadruplatoribus 'profiteers'. The contemporaneous author of the *Rhet. Her.* 2.41 cites the quip: *Quadruplator, ut breuiter scribam, capitalis est: est enim inprobus et pestifer ciuis.* Concerning the etymology of the term, the scholiasts offer two different explanations: they are so named because they either receive a fourth of the goods claimed during the trial or they routinely accused those who had to pay a quadruple fine; see [Asc.] 110 (194 Stangl); Schol. Gronov. 326 Stangl. The name came to be more broadly applied to those who undertook prosecutions for profit and reveals a general suspicion about a prosecutor's *ratio accusandi.* On *quadruplatores*, see Rutledge (2001) 37–39, J. Kelly (1966) 168–171, and Bettini (1977). The low esteem in which these profiteers were held well before C.'s time is clear from the rant of Saturio, the parasite, in Pl. *Pers.* 62–76; see with Woytek *ad loc.*, Danek (1988), Partsch (1910), and Paoli (1954). C. recapitulates this theme at §68 *illius modi quadruplatores.*

24.9 pro nihilo putauit *Pro nihilo* is used with *putare* or other verbs of mental estimation; see *TLL* X 2.2763.61–67. C. frequently uses the phrase in a pleonastic construction with verbs such as *contemno, sperno, respuo,* and *despicere*; cf. *Caec.* 56, *Vat.* 64, *Phil.* 13.21, *Tusc.* 3.36, *Off.* 1.28, 71, and *Mil.* 64 *immo uero ut contempsit ac pro nihilo putauit, quae neque maximo animo nocens neque innocens nisi fortissimus uir neglegere potuisset!*

uiros fortes spectatosque homines *Spectatus* comes to mean 'of observed merit or worth; distinguished'; see *OLD s.u.* 2. C. revisits this idea toward the conclusion of the speech; see §68 *per homines honestissimos uirosque fortissimos.* Being *fortis* is a characteristic of those possessing *uirtus*; see further Hellegouarc'h 248.

24.10 diutius dominari For the metaphorical image of the orator ruling over the courtroom and the jury as a supreme ruler, see *Quinct.* 94 and Quint. *Inst.* 2.5.8 with Reinhardt and Winterbottom (2006) *ad loc.* At the time, Hortensius was Rome's most famous orator and would be active for 44 years all told, though his *dominatio* would end with the trial of Verres; see *Brut.* 229–230, 320.

§25

25.1 huic ego homini Viz. Hortensius; on non-naming, see §23 *magnus ille defensor* … n. The demonstrative *huic* acts as a host for the enclitic personal pronoun, which brings it into sharper focus; cf. *Cat.* 3.17 *hunc ego hominem tam acrem, … nisi … compulissem.* See further, with examples, Adams (1994b) 122–124, 141–151, Adams (1999), and *OLS* 1.741–742.

denuntio Though the verb can be used in a generic sense of giving notice (*TLL* V 1.554.9), it is also employed frequently in the spheres of political, religious and juridical terminology for a declaration or announcement; see *TLL* V 1.555.11–556.62 and Berger *s.u. denuntiare.* C.'s diction may suggest a veiled threat of legal repercussions for Hortensius' alleged impropriety.

25.2 causam hanc Cf. §5 *onus hoc … mihi suscipiendum* n.

agi See §16 *ad agendum* n.

rationem … defendendi Only here does C. use this gerund with *ratio* rather than *defensionis*; cf. *Ver.* II.3.190, 5.4.

25.3 mutandam … mutandam The epiphora (Lausberg §§631–632) provides emphasis and 'epexegetical supplementation', i.e. how Hortensius must modify his defence tactics.

et ita [tamen] mutandam (*MP*²) Though the agreement of *P*¹ and γ would normally give the paradosis, here the omission of the entire phrase, which gives good Ciceronian idiom, could have been caused by *saut du même au même.* Cf. §14 *petitum esse … et ita uehementer esse petitum, Ver.* II.5.72 *dicam … et ita dicam ut …, Dom.* 36 *ut et is adoptet …, et ita adoptet ut ne …, Mur.* 53 *ornata in prouincia petisset diligenter, et ita petisset ut …, Man.* 7 *regnat, et ita regnat ut …,* and *Man.* 10 *sed de Lucullo dicam alio loco, et ita dicam, Quirites, ut ….* See further Introduction §VI. Elsewhere C. uses *atque ita* rather than *et ita*; cf. *Caecin.* 24 *qui confitetur atque ita libenter confitetur ut …, Fam.* 7.5.2 *Mitto igitur ad te Trebatium atque ita mitto ut …, Rab. Perd.* 8, and *Mur.* 15. Peterson, who did not appreciate the value of the *deteriores*, concluded that 'the whole clause should probably go out. It may have resulted from an attempted inversion, *esse totam* for *totam esse*, and from dittography – to which latter cause we may with great probability ascribe at least the appearance of *tamen* after *ita*'; Peterson (1903) 198. About *tamen*, which does not convey the right sense, he is likely correct. *O* and some other *deteriores* read *causam* for *tamen*, which could be a slip or correction since the abbreviations for the two words are similar and often confused.

meliore … condicione On *honestus*, see §23 *honeste … inuidia … offensione* n.

25.4 uult uti The text here is undoubtedly corrupt, and several approaches have been espoused to correct the passage. In C.'s speeches, *condicio* is frequently used in the ablative with either *utor* or *sum*; see Merguet *s.u.* One approach, printed by Zumpt, accepts a variant in the tradition of [Asc.] (though Stangl bracketed it), which provides *sit* after *condicione* and retains the reading of the Italian family, which universally includes *esse* in the relative clause: *ut meliore … condicione sit, quam qua ipse esse uult.* He follows *O* et al. in omitting the second *ut* and construes *imitetur* as jussive. Otherwise, the ablative pronoun *qua* needs explanation. Therefore, other editors, including Peterson, have emended *ut imitetur* to *uti, imitetur* and assumed that the archetype of the MSS tradition omitted the *i* by haplography; cf. *Ver.* II.1.150, *Clu.* 150, *Agr.* 2.6, *Cael.* 57, *Pis.* 4, *Quinct.* 85; see further Peterson (1905b). Peterson's solution is simple and idiomatic and provides a cretic-spondee rhythm. Others besides, including Thomas, Jordan, and Müller, have adopted the reading of *D* (*condicione, quam qua ipse uult, imitetur*) on their assumption that *ut* has been unnecessarily repeated.

imitetur Imitation of other orators was a method of rhetorical training; see *Rhet. Her.* 1.3 *Haec omnia tribus rebus adsequi poterimus: arte, imitatione, exercitatione. … Imitatio est, qua impellimur cum diligenti ratione ut aliquorum similes in dicendo ualeamus esse.* This advice prefigures the 'rhetorical education' that C. will offer Caecilius in the subsequent sections, though here C. is not giving advice on how to speak but how to behave.

homines eos quos *Is* in postposition performing a cataphoric rather than anaphoric function. Perhaps the pronoun is attracted to the relative; see Spevak (2010) 239–241.

25.5 ipse uidit Hortensius had already led a prosecution *de repetundis* in 95 during the year of Crassus' consulship; see *TLRR* 90.

L. Crassum et M. Antonium L. Licinius Crassus (*RE* 55; *MRR* 2.11, 17; 3.18; Sumner R104; *cos.* 95, *cens.* 92) and M. Antonius (*RE* 23 and suppl. 1; *MRR* 2.1, 6–7; 3.19; Sumner R103; *cos.* 99, *cens.* 97) were the renowned orators of recent memory; both came to forensic and political prominence at the turn of the century. Here the two men are cited for their respect of the judicial process, since, when representing their clients, they relied on their eloquence rather than other methods of physical or financial coercion. On Hortensius' previous shenanigans, see §24 *cera legitima* n.

Much of what is known about their oratorical accomplishments comes from C.'s *De oratore*, in which they appear as the primary interlocutors, and *Brutus*, which C. wrote upon the news of Hortensius' death. Crassus had arranged C.'s education and selected his course of study and teachers; perhaps for this reason he holds Crassus in even higher regard than Antonius. Since Crassus died before C. was yet 16, he may never have heard him speak in court; he did, however, have the opportunity to see Antonius in action; see *Tusc.* 5.55. Outside of his rhetorical treatises, C. mentions the men frequently, and the two of them together five times in the surviving speeches, where they typically serve as *exempla* of eloquence; see *Quinct.* 80, *Ver.* II.2.191, *Clu.* 140, *Rab. Perd.* 26, and *Planc.* 33. Although they receive C.'s highest praise, no examples of their oratory survive save a few citations of Crassus. At the time, publication of speeches was rare, and Antonius intentionally left his speeches unpublished; see the episode regarding publication at *Clu.* 140–141. On the careers of Crassus and Antonius, see also Fantham (2004) 26–48, Scholz (1963), and Rawson (1971).

25.6 iudicia causasque On this common collocation, §1 *causis iudiciisque publicis* n.

fidem et ingenium The good faith and talent of Crassus and Antonius stands in contrast to Hortensius' back-handed dealing.

25.8 magno multorum periculo *Periculum* is particularly associated with the endangerment of the *reus* in a criminal trial; see *OLD s.u.* 3 and *TLL* X 1.1462.10–42. The term implies that C. would vigorously prosecute any juror suspected of corruption during Verres' trial for extortion. For *periculum* as a characteristic of *causae publicae* as opposed to *priuatae*, see *Sul.* 2, *Man.* 2, *Rosc. Am.* 85 with Landgraf *ad loc.*, and Quint. *Inst.* 6.1.36. In Greek, the associated term is κίνδυνος; cf. Lys. 24.1.

§26

26.1 ego The primary position of the personal pronoun carries an adversative sense, 'But I …'. Cf. §§10, 30, 35, 41, and 70; see further H-Sz. 102. The first contrast implied is between

Hortensius, who attempts to subvert the course of justice in favour of his client, and C. This gives C. the opportunity to end the *confirmatio* with a short recapitulation of the personal and civil motives that led him to prosecute Verres, which he had discussed extensively in §§5–9. This then forms the first half of a *comparatio* between C. and Caecilius in §§26–27.

in hoc iudicio In its most elastic form, *iudicium* refers not just to the *diuinatio* proper but to the entire procedure and subsequent trial. See Berger *s.u. iudicium.*

receptam ... susceptam Both words have legal overtones of contractual obligation and guardianship. *Recipere* means 'to assume an obligation for oneself or another'. *Suscipere* similarly means 'to assume a unilateral obligation' – i.e. without reciprocal obligation and gratuitously accepted. Berger *s.u.*; Heumann–Seckel *s.u.* Both terms underscore C.'s sense of responsibility. Schol. Gronov. 326 Stangl *recipimus rogati, suscipimus sponte, aut recipimus diuites, suscipimus autem aequales uel minores*; cf. *Ver.* II.2.1, 5.183 with Thomas *ad loc.*, and *Orat.* 2.101.

26.2 non unus modo improbus There is an implied contrast with *sed omnino* below – and in C. this is usually provided by *non modo.* The reading of *S* may have been difficult to see and presumably abbreviated, since the descendants of *S* invariably have a word after *non* but with variants such as *nisi* (*DET*), *modo nisi* (*N*), and *tantum* (*H*). Given *N*'s tendency to report original readings and corrections within the main body of its text, *modo* may have been the correction in *S*, though it is strange that *D* did not report it since it seems an obvious choice. Since the scholiast's lemma omits *homo*, Peterson (1903) 198 recommended *non unus modo improbus*, which gives good emphasis to *unus.* Cf. *Marc.* 32 *restat ut omnes unum uelint qui habent aliquid non sapientiae modo sed etiam sanitatis.* On conventions of non-naming, see §23 *magnus ille defensor* ... n.

improbus ... improbitas Although *malus* may be the opposite of *bonus* in moral discourse, *improbus* is the preferred term in the political sphere. The opposition of the *boni* and the *improbi* is a common dichotomy in Ciceronian speeches and political dialogue. See *Lael.* 74 *nec ob aliam causam ullam boni improbis, improbi* *bonis amici esse non possunt, nisi quod tanta est inter eos, quanta maxima potest esse, morum studiorumque distantia. Improbitas* represents a violation of *fides*, and is a leading trait of those who undermine the *res publica*; see *Mur.* 9 and Clodius in *Att.* 2.9.1. The term is applied frequently to Verres and also to dishonest judges; see *Clu.* 85. The scholiast suggests that *improbitas* refers to the purported corruption of the Roman judicial system. For more on *improbus* and *improbitas*, including those whom C. so accuses, see Hellegouarc'h 528–530.

26.3 opprimendus *Opprimere* denotes a violent and instant suppression (*OLD* 6) and is figuratively applied; see *TLL* IX 2.789.7–41. Here it is used in parallel with *exstinguenda atque delenda*; see n. below. The diction may infuse the passage with fire imagery, which likens *improbitas* to a consuming flame. The metaphor is prevalent in C. and is often used to describe a pestilence, an army, or any other force that presents widespread danger. The comparison to fire would be potent; along with flooding, fire was the greatest natural threat to Rome. For fire imagery, see Fantham (1972) 7–11, 130, Pöschl (1964) 474–475, and *Sul.* 3 with Berry *ad loc.* Additionally, *exstinguere* may be a natural or gradual suppression; see *Rosc. Am.* 36 with Landgraf *ad loc.* Although C. may be able to squelch Verres in a single trial, the process of suppressing and completely obliterating corruption is longer and more thorough. For these combined images, cf. *Har.* 6 *T. Annius ad illam pestem comprimendam, exstinguendam, funditus delendam natus esse uidetur et quasi diuino munere donatus rei publicae.*

sed omnino omnis (omnino ω : omnis [Asc.] N^{2sl}) Although the phrase does not appear in the rest of Ciceronian oratory, Peterson (1903) 198 declared that '*omnino omnis* is certainly right', and it is found elsewhere; cf. *Inu.* 1.25, 86, 2.17, 161 *Amic.* 78, *Tusc.* 1.97, 4.53, *Leg.* 1.44, and *De orat.* 2.1. The MSS have the adverb, while the scholiast's lemma and the second-hand supralineal notation in *N* provide the adjective. The paradosis *sed omnino* is easily defendable as it is commonly used after *non modo*; cf. *Rosc. Am.* 81 *qui non modo Romae non fuit sed omnino quid Romae ageretur nesciuit.* But the dichotomy of *omnis* / *unus* is also frequent throughout the speech; cf. §3 *uno praetore per triennium.*

26.4 quod populus Romanus ... flagitat C. continues to put the *diuinatio* into a political context of latent social upheaval. *Flagitare* is used to denote the loud, incessant demand of popular unrest; see *TLL* VI 839.32 and §8 *efflagitata* n. On the iterative characteristic of the verb, Walde–Hofmann *s.u.*

26.5 exstinguenda atque delenda *Exstinguenda and delenda* parallel with *opprimendus*, and the two are often paired; see *Ver.* II.4.120, *Cat.* 1.30, 4.7, *Mur.* 80, *Har.* 6, *Sul.* 3, and *Sest.* 17. All applications of this metaphor are martial; the objects of these verbs are literally (or by extension) cities or opposing forces. Here the metaphor gives a physical presence to the abstract notion of *improbitas* which Verres himself will come to embody; see also §42 *audientiam ... improbitas illius factura sit.* For the imagery of the phrase, see *opprimendus* n. above. The intervening clause (*id quod ... flagitat*) emphasizes the core sentiment of these gerundives. For *atque* followed by a consonant, see §2 *populati atque uexati* n.

quid eniti aut quid efficere possim *Eniti* denotes strenuous effort, and *efficere* suggests that the goal of those efforts is also obtained; Ernout–Meillet *s.u. facio.* In later speeches, C. will create a common motif whereby his efforts on behalf of the Roman people form the basis for the *beneficia* that they bestow upon him in the form of political office. 'By setting up a reciprocal relationship between the People's benefits and his own efforts, Cicero creates the impression of a close connection between him and the People, in which the People also have an active part'; Manuwald *ad Phil.* 4.16. So strong is the sense of *efficere* in the civic arena that Isidore falsely thought that *officium* derived from it; see *Etym.* 6.19.1 and Hellegouarc'h 152. C. will finally mention his candidacy for the aedileship in §70.

26.6 malo ... ponere A *praeteritio* that continues the careful syntactic parallelism used above. C.'s new emphasis on talent and ability presents a challenge. The orator must avoid incurring the *odium* of arrogance at all costs, or else risks losing the *beneuolentia* of the audience; see *Inu.* 1.22 *Beniuolentia ... comparatur, si de nostris factis et officiis sine arrogantia dicemus*, and Quint. *Inst.* 4.1.8–10. C. clings to a modicum of modesty through *praeteritio* and implied *comparationes* with Caecilius rather than discussing his own accomplishments directly. The efficacy of C.'s modesty caught the attention of several later Latin rhetoricians: Grillius 1.22 (*Jakobi* 94.15–17) [*Cicero*] *meritum suum sine arrogantia praedicauit*, and Martianus Capella, *De Rhetorica* 28 (*RLM* 470.14) *non superbe sed moderate loquitur*. For an analysis of Cicero's rhetorical techniques and Greek models for modest self-praise, see Tempest (2010). On avoiding the pitfalls associated with self-praise, see Lausberg §275β and Rutherford (1995). On Demosthenes' handling of the problem in the *De corona*, see Yunis (2001) 109 and Wankel (1979) 127–129. Only in this speech is the phrase *in oratione non ponere* (or virtually negated as here) used for a *praeteritio*; cf. §16 *in oratione mea non pono*.

aliorum refers to both Sicilians and Romans on the basic level of the text. The phrase *in oratione ponere* (§16), however, also suggests a hint of the meta-literary, in which case the *alii* would be those reading or hearing the speech after publication, and their *spes* will be realized in the following six published orations.

Digressio (§§27–47)

On the Ideal Prosecutor

But what can Caecilius possibly accomplish? Has he ever given anyone an indication of what kind of speaker he is? Has he even considered what a monumental task it is to conduct a criminal prosecution? Since this is Caecilius' first opportunity to learn how many qualities a successful prosecutor must have, Cicero will take the time to explain it to him, and if Caecilius recognizes even one of these traits in himself, then C. will yield the role of prosecutor to him. First, a prosecutor must be of unassailable character, honest and blameless. Second, he must have excellent training in rhetoric and experience in oratory. While C. is loth to express his own accomplishments in these areas, it will be clear that Caecilius has succeeded in none of them.

The digression in §§27–47 is presented, at first glance, as an ancillary discussion on the qualities of an ideal criminal prosecutor to explain why Cicero, and not Caecilius, would be the most desirable prosecutor for the Sicilians and the least desirable for Verres. C. addresses the moral character of the orator (§§27–35), rhetorical training and ability (§§35–40), and education and experience (§§40–43), and then concludes by describing the potential showdown between Hortensius and the prosecutor-to-be (§§44–47); further details are given at the head of each subsection. Within each topic there is a direct or implied σύγκρισις / *comparatio* between Caecilius and C. in which C. is shown to be superior in every regard.

This miniature lecture on rhetoric and oratory fulfils both immediate forensic and long-term literary goals and is so extended that it changes the colour and timbre of the entire speech. At first, it functions as a humiliating and patronizing invective against Caecilius' moral, intellectual, and professional qualities. When the digression begins, Caecilius is put into the position of an ὀψιμαθής, receiving much-needed instruction (albeit too little, too late) on the requirements of oratorical training and performance (*hoc primum tempus discendi nactus es*). The first lesson on moral character puts Caecilius under suspicion of collusion and/or incompetence, which would undermine any prosecution he might bring. In the second, C. ridicules Caecilius' substandard education, scant training, and utter lack of rhetorical proficiency and physical stamina. These may be hard to attain, but as Caecilius learns in the third lesson, any grounding in rhetoric and oratory must also be put into practice to be honed and improved. As the jury eavesdrops on this denigrating lesson, both they and Caecilius are finally compelled to picture Verres' trial itself, with the eager throngs in attendance, the weight of expectation, and the mastery of the defence counsel, parrying, dodging, and undercutting Caecilius' every move. The emphasis on rhetorical skill or oratorical ability shifts the focus of the *Diuinatio* away from the allegations of the injured parties as a selection criterion and foregrounds the proficiency of the speaker as the most important factor for the aggrieved, the accused, and, by extension, the jury, in choosing the most acceptable prosecutor. As a result, C. re-characterizes the *diuinatio* procedure, not as a *prima facie* presentation of grievances, but as an adversarial rhetorical contest (§37 *contentionem certamenque*).

What is even more remarkable about this embedded rhetorical handbook is the extent to which C. not only lays bare the rhetorical methods of persuasion (among them *dispositio, actio, enargeia, complexio,* and *amplificatio*; see nn. *ad loc.*) but also demonstrates them and uses them upon his opponent while the jury and spectators listen. One of the widespread tenets of rhetorical education emphasized that 'in speaking, the orator uses his skill to disguise his artistry so that it is not conspicuous and noticed by all'; see *Rhet. Her.* 4.10 *in dicendo, ne possit ars eminere et ab omnibus uideri, facultate oratoris occultatur,* and the additional references to *dissimulatio artis* below. In short, there was an art in the appearance of artlessness. And furthermore, 'art should be concealed not only to avoid the suspicion of cleverness and of insincerity, but also to avoid an air of pedantry and the classroom, which is a different thing altogether'; Andersen (1996) 77. Yet C. precisely turns the courtroom into the classroom – for invective, entertainment, and education. C. assumes the role of his rival's *rhetor* and mockingly refers to Caecilius' primary school teacher, who has accompanied him to court (§47 *magister ludi nescioqui*). Undoubtedly there was some entertainment and delight for C.'s rhetorically trained audience (as his senatorial jury would have been), who heard C. recite fundamental aspects of oratory and watched him ensnare his opponent in the process; see Quint. *Inst.* 2.4.7 *namque ea sola in hoc ars est, quae intelligi nisi ab artifice non possit.* As a literary production, the *Diu. Caec.* and this passage in particular function as an extension of C.'s rhetorical works and highlight the didactic purposes of published oratory. Unlike the hapless Caecilius, C.'s reading audience will come to understand and anticipate the arguments and tactics that he will deploy in the subsequent speeches against Verres and be able to picture more fully his battle with Hortensius.

On *dissimulatio artis,* see Arist. *Rhet.* 3.2.3–4, *Rhet. Her.* 2.17, 2.47, 4.10, 4.32, *Inu.* 1.25, 1.98, *De orat.* 2.156, 2.177, *Brut.* 37, 139, *Orat.* 38, and Quint. *Inst.* 1.11.3, 2.5.7, 4.1.8–9, 4.1.54–60, 4.2.59, 4.2.126–127, 8.3.2, 9.4.144, 11.2.47. The idea became such a trope in late Republican and early Imperial rhetoric that the concealment in and of itself became an object of spectacle; see Andersen (1996).

Ethical Qualities of a Good Prosecutor (§§27–35)

C. lectures Caecilius on the moral rectitude required of a prosecutor. This common theme was already established in Greek rhetoric; see Arist. *Rhet.* 1366a. Cf. Quint. *Inst.* 12.1.1, 3 *Sit ergo nobis orator quem constituimus is qui a M. Catone finitur uir bonus dicendi peritus, uerum, id quod et ille posuit prius et ipsa natura potius ac maius est, utique uir bonus ... Neque enim tantum id dico, eum qui sit orator uirum bonum esse oportere, sed ne futurum quidem oratorem nisi uirum bonum.* As C. dilates on the topic here, he launches an *ad hominem* attack against Caecilius and impugns his character by implicating him in Verres' various embezzlement schemes when Caecilius was serving under him as quaestor. C. alleges that Caecilius' complicity, or at the very least complacency, would prevent him from levelling several serious charges against his former commander. The *argumentum ex uita* was traditionally the first in a *confirmatio* and thus assumes an appropriate position in this long *comparatio*; see Berry (1996) 46. The treatment of this material also prepares C.'s reading audience for the extensive discussion of Verres' management of grain collection and taxation in the third speech of the *actio secunda.*

§27

27.1 tu uero ... quid potes? A figured question that does not seek to acquire information but to emphasize a point; see Quint. *Inst.* 9.2.7 *figuratum autem quotiens non sciscitandi gratia adsumitur sed instandi.* This form of *interrogatio* is often used to antagonize or humiliate the opposing party; see Lausberg §§762–770 and Quint. *Inst.* 9.2.6–16; cf. §21. *Vero* underscores the adversative sense of the primary position of the pronoun and gives these initial rhetorical questions a confrontational tone; see §26 *ego* n. **potes** see §21 *posse arbitrantur* n.

Caecili After the first instance, advocates would typically address each other by a single name with no sense of disdain implied. On this naming convention, see §4 *dicebam habere eos actorem Q. Caecilium* n.

quo tempore aut qua in re The full extent of Caecilius' previous forensic activity is unknown. On his career, see Introduction §II.

27.2 specimen aliquod 'any indication at all'. C. typically prefers the noun *exemplum*, and *specimen* is relatively uncommon in his speeches; cf. *Pis.* 95, fr. 8 *specimen ... ingeni. Specimen* may be considered a species of the genus *exemplum* and indicates an observable example (**specio*); see Ernout–Meillet *s.u. specio* and Forcellini *s.u. exemplum*. The indefinite adjectival forms of *aliquis* normally stand before their substantive unless particular stress is being placed on the item it modifies, i.e. 'any ... at all'; cf. *unum aliquod* below. See also H-Sz. 408 and Marouzeau 1.168. For similar use of *specimen*, cf. *Tusc.* 5.55 and *N. D.* 3.80.

tute tui Polyptoton. C. likes to combine different forms of the same pronoun, e.g. §16 *haec in hac. Tui* is required rather than *tuum* when used as an objective genitive, and it carries a dative sense, i.e. 'danger for yourself'; see K-St. 2.1.597. C. uses the pronominal suffix *-te* more frequently in his earlier speeches; for another example, see §31. In both instances, the suffix seems to have a reflexive quality. On *tute*, see further H-Sz. 173 and Dunkel (2006). On pronominal parataxis, see Parzinger 1.48–51 and Marouzeau 3.145.

27.3 periculum fecisti C. questions Caecilius' experience and willingness to undertake challenges in an *argumentum a persona* regarding habit or custom. See *Inu.* 1.35 *habitum autem [hunc] appellamus animi aut corporis constantem et absolutam aliqua in re perfectionem, ut uirtutis aut artis alicuius perceptionem aut quamuis scientiam et item corporis aliquam commoditatem non natura datam, sed studio et industria partam*, and [Incert. Auct.] *RLM* 306.35 *Nam licet orator plenus sit perceptione ipsius artis, tamen aliquantum argumento detrahit, si neges in eadem exercitatione uixisse, ut ipse* [*Cicero*] *contra Caecilium, quia aufert uictum, infirmat habitum, cum dicit: quando tute tui periculum fecisti.* For more on *argumenta a persona*, see *Inu.* 1.34–36 and Lausberg §376. This use of *periculum*, indicating a personal trial or test, should be distinguished from that above in §25 *magno multorum periculo*; for *periculum facere* with a reflexive, see *TLL* X 1.1459.26.

in mentem tibi non uenit A common expression in comedy with a colloquial colouring. This change in register also suggests that C. is assuming a patronizing tone with Caecilius, a technique that further denigrates his opponent. The phrase often introduces a rhetorical question; cf. Ramsey *ad Phil.* 2.18, 40, Berry on *Sul.* 19, and K-St. 2.1.472. **mentem** The ablative form in γ must be wrong as the idiom securely uses the accusative; Flavius Caper (*GLK* 92) *in mentem uenit, non in mente.*

quid negoti *Negotium* originally meant the absence of *otium* (leisure) but came to take on a more positive connotation, 'business', and can refer to a variety of duties including forensic activity, political responsibilities, and military service. In later Latin, *negotium* will come to mean 'trial'; see Quint. *Inst.* 5.12.13 and *Cael.* 1 *forensibus negotiis* with Austin *ad loc.* For further references, see *N-P s.u.*

27.4 causam publicam As opposed to *causae priuatae* (civil trials). Unlike civil disputes, criminal trials garnered more attention and gave orators the opportunity to win renown; see *Opt. Gen.* 9–10. C. returns to this theme in §§50ff.; on *causae publicae,* see §1 *causis iudiciisque publicis* n.

sustinere This metaphor with *causa* only occurs in C. at §§35, 39, and *Sest.* 14; see *OLD s.u.* 5a. The collocation is more common in the letters and so may suggest a more colloquial tone.

uitam alterius totam The defendant's *uita ante acta* was far from extraneous in Roman courts and was used to establish the probability (or improbability) of his guilt. Rutledge (2001) 18: 'The strengths and weaknesses of a case would occasionally depend not on how well a [prosecutor] could prove legal transgressions, but on how effectively he could impugn the character and life of the defendant, and argue based not on fact but on the probability that the defendant was guilty as charged.' In the *actiones in Verrem,* C. will not only discuss Verres' tenure in Sicily but also his urban praetorship and other aspects of his personal life not strictly germane to the allegations against him. There were also practical legal considerations for specifying acts of extortion during his other magistracies. Once tried in the *quaestio de repetundis,* a defendant could not be brought back to court for any actionable conduct committed before the trial; see Alexander (1982) and Lintott (1992) 30–31. On character in the Roman courts, see the introduction to the *exordium*; see further Riggsby (2004) 167–185 and May (1988).

explicare ... exponere Cf. *Rosc. Am.* 34 *totam causam, iudices, explicemus atque ante oculos expositam consideremus*; see also §39. The phrase *uitam ... explicare* may have a meta-literary aspect – 'to unroll a written biography' as though reading a scroll; see *TLL* V 2.1727.69. Meanwhile, *exponere* can refer both to the process of *narratio* and to publishing a written work; cf. Quint. 8.4.22 and *De orat.* 1.227, respectively, and see *TLL* V 2.1764.4–40. On the alternative meanings for *uita*, see *OLD s.u.* 6a–b; cf. Sen. *Suas.* 6.21.

27.5 in oculis conspectuque The process of vivid description; a rhetorical device identified by a host of terms, including ἐνάργεια, ἔκφρασις, *descriptio, phantasia,* and *demonstratio.* See *Ver.* II.1.7 *Intellegit me ita paratum atque instructum in iudicium uenire ut non modo in auribus uestris sed in oculis omnium sua furta atque flagitia defixurus sim.* This technique was a valuable asset in providing *euidentia* but is not fully explicated in Roman rhetorical handbooks. For a full discussion, see Innocenti (1994), Vasaly (1993) 104, Webb (2009) 131–166, and Quint. 6.2.29. See further Lausberg §810.

27.6 sociorum salute ... grauitatem iudiciorum defendere The prosecution again styled as a defence; C. has already pledged help for the welfare of the province and its inhabitants in §3, the *grauitas* of the courts in §§8–9, and the *uis legum* in §§17–18. C. leads the reader/audience to anticipate all these themes throughout the Verrines.

27.8 quoniam hoc primum tempus Caecilius is pejoratively presented as an ὀψιμαθής (late-learner) – someone who overvalues his scant education and 'pursues activities for which he is too old'; see the colourful description at Theophrastus *Char.* 27 with Diggle (2004) *ad loc.* Cf. *Fam.* 9.20.2, Gell. *N.A.* 11.7.3, 15.30.1, Lucian *Salt.* 33, and Isoc. 10.2 νῦν δὲ τίς ἐστιν οὕτως ὀψιμαθὴς ὅστις οὐκ οἶδε .... For the character in Latin literature, see Hor. *Ep.* 1.1.53–69 with Reckford (2002) and Hor. *S.* 1.10.21.

27.9 oporteat Only *O* and some of the minor *deteriores* have the correct form of the verb, which could easily have been a correction. The erroneous *oporteant* is found in every branch of the MS tradition and suggests another error from synesis (*constructio ad sensum*), viz. construing *multa* as a plural subject, in the archetype of all extant manuscripts; cf. §1 *miratur* transmitted as *mirantur. F* has the correct reading here, but there are indications that an abbreviation bar was erased (*oporteãt*).

ex quibus si unum aliquod ... C. makes a similar wager regarding Verres' theft of artwork; cf. *Ver.* II.1.61 *Vnum ostende in tabulis aut tuis aut patris tui emptum esse: uicisti.* **aliquod** is absent from the French tradition, but it provides a worthwhile point of emphasis on *unum*; on this emphatic position, see §27 *specimen aliquod* n.

27.10 ipse istuc *Istuc* is a strengthened form of *istud* which includes the deictic suffic *-ce* and contributes to C.'s challenging tone here; see Neue-Wagener 2.398–400 and H-Sz. 183–184. *Ipse* is one of the few corrections in the second hand of *P* present in the French family (γ) but absent from all members of the *deteriores.* Perhaps the corrector of *P* was following a less corrupt relative of an ancestor of *M*; see Reeve (2016) 49–50.

27.12 integritatem ... innocentiam singularem In an expression ascribed to Cato, the orator was a *uir bonus dicendi peritus*; see Quint. *Inst.* 12.1.1–45 with Austin, Sen. *Contr.* 1 praef. 9, and *De orat.* 2.85. The need for moral excellence must be understood against the backdrop of the debate regarding rhetoric and philosophy; cf. Plat. *Grg.* (particularly 520a–b) and *De orat.* 1.41–47 with May and Wisse *ad loc.* See further Michel (1961). On the moral orator in Quintilian, see Reinhardt and Winterbottom (2006) xlvi–l and Winterbottom (1964). Quint. *Inst.* 2.15.26–29 goes on to endorse Plato's tenet in *Gorgias* that true rhetorical skill can only be obtained by the good, just man: τὸν μέλλοντα ὀρθῶς ῥητορικὸν ἔσεσθαι δίκαιον ἄρα δεῖ εἶναι καὶ ἐπιστήμονα τῶν δικαίων, *ut appareat Platoni non rhetoricen uideri malum, sed eam ueram nisi iusto ac bono non contingere.*

Integritas and the adjective *integer* are typically paired with another positive attribute; see §70 *integerrimos diligentissimosque* with n. *ad loc. Innocentia* indicates an abstention from immoral behaviour, and this is precisely the quality of a good administrator, such as a provincial governor; see *Ver.* II.3.21, 217, and *Q.fr.* 1.2.7. For these terms, see further Hellegouarc'h 282–283. C. has already self-identified as *integer* in §9, and he suggests that the Sicilians' approval of his tenure as quaestor demonstrates his administrative honesty. This pairing was favoured for its alliteration; cf. *Ver.* II.4.7, *Phil.* 3.25, *Rosc. Com.* 26, and *De orat.* 1.229.

nihil est ... 'for there is nothing more unbearable than someone demanding an account for another's life when he cannot possibly give one for his own'. A *tu quoque* argument, i.e. an allegation of hypocrisy; see Dahlman and Feteris (2013) 67. C. alludes to some wrongdoing during Caecilius' tenure as quaestor and again, more explicitly, later on in the speech. His involvement in provincial mismanagement will make him an unsuitable prosecutor; see §§31–32. C. reverses this *tu quoque* argument in his defence of M. Caelius; i.e. Caelius' litigious zeal demonstrates that he must be of good character. See *Cael.* 78 *Non enim potest qui hominem consularem, cum ab eo rem publicam uiolatam esse diceret, in iudicium uocarit ipse esse in re publica ciuis turbulentus; non potest qui ambitu ne absolutum quidem patiatur esse absolutum ipse impune umquam esse largitor.*

§28

28.1 hic 'at this point'; *OLD s.u. hic*[2] 6. C. will make other allegations later in the speech to impugn Caecilius' character.

28.2 plura non dicam By suggesting that he is omitting additional ways in which Caecilius does not live up to the standard of *integritas* and *innocentia*, C. appears to have more evidence at his disposal than he may in fact have. The arguments that C. does enumerate, however, are unconvincing: that Caecilius means to abscond with evidence, that he is implicated in Verres' crimes, and that his familial and political connections prevent him from being an earnest prosecutor. *Occultatio* 'is ... used to present material which would, if critically examined by an alert jury, be found false or refutable. It enables a statement to be made and mentally noted by the jury in a speaker's favour; but because he seems to regard it as unnecessary for his argument or irrelevant, they do not examine it too closely. By this means, weak arguments and false evidence could be introduced with confidence under the pretence of omitting them'; Usher (1965) 176. On *reticentia* and *occultatio* with further examples, see Usher (1965), *Rhet. Her.* 4.37, and *Sul.* 73 *quid ... commemorem* with Berry *ad loc. Occultatio*, in which some items are mentioned but no evidence is given, is similar to *praeteritio*, which serves to emphasize what is dismissed, and *reticentia*, wherein the orator actually passes over information leaving the impression that more could have been said. These techniques are ubiquitous in these sections, in which C. alleges some sort of wrongdoing on Caecilius' behalf, and suggest a true paucity of evidence; cf. §28 *quare negent ex me non audies*, §29 *nec ea dico ..., quibus ego nunc non utor*, and §33 *sunt alia magis occulta furta ....*

animaduertere The reading of the French family and *M. P*'s *animum aduertere*, which is used by C. and Sallust as an archaism, may be correct since *P* has preserved some archaic spellings (§54 *maxumam*) and uncorrupted forms (§49 *moratorum*). See Schmalz *s.u. animadvertere*. For the double accusative with composite verbs, see K-St. 2.1.292–293 and H-Sz. 44–45.

28.3 adhuc a nullis 'up to now no one except the Sicilians has been able to get to know you'. The import of this statement is debated. Sherwin-White (1939) 307n remarks: 'Nothing in Cic. *Diu. in Caec.* 4 and 20 suggests that Q. Caecilius was more than a resident of Sicily by economic connection or remote servile origin'; cf. Plut. *Cic.* 7.6. If this sceptical interpretation is right, C. may simply mean to point out that Caecilius has held no magistracies other than his quaestorship in Sicily. The scholiast and some later scholars, however, have suggested that this statement means that Caecilius was himself a Sicilian; see *RE* 101, [Asc.] 98 (185 Stangl) *Q. Caecilius Niger, domo Siculus*, and in reference to this passage, 112 (195 Stangl) *quia aut Siculus ipse est aut quia nisi quaestor in Sicilia nihil aliud fuit Caecilius in quo nosceretur 'quid hominis' esset.* The latter interpretation gains some credence simply because C. is so vague. If Caecilius is indeed Sicilian, C. would not want to draw attention to this close connection with the island. On Caecilius' career, see Introduction §II. On character and conduct in political office, see Yakobson (1999) 109. For political office as the place of moral evaluation, see Dem. 19.247 citing Soph. *Ant.* 175–190.

28.4 tu te inimicum esse dicis The repetition of the pronoun and the verb underscore C.'s incredulity, and *te* and *esse* may act as focusing clitics for *tu* and *inimicum.* Cf. §12 *cui te inimicum esse simulas.* On the attraction of the same noun in different cases, see §27 *tute tui* n.

28.5 te actore An ablative absolute with conditional force, 'if you were the prosecutor'. The ablative absolute as a sociative phrase (pronoun and predicate noun-complement) is one of its oldest uses. This construction is formed by analogy with the Greek genitive absolute; see K-St.2.1.779–780 and H-Sz. 138. Frequent in C. are ablatives absolute that denote the 'chief agent' in a forensic setting, i.e. defence, prosecution, or jury; cf. §22 *te actore, Ver.* II.1.52 *Samiis accusantibus,* and *Cael.* 4 *neque his iudicantibus* ... *neque defendentibus nobis.* On these ablative absolutes, see further Laughton (1964) 100–107.

ad iudicium non adfuturos A large contingent of provincials at an extortion trial in no way guaranteed success. Foreign witnesses were frequently attacked as untrustworthy, and reference to ethnic stereotypes was rife in forensic rhetoric – C. himself resorts to it frequently in extortion trials: cf. Asian Greeks in *Pro Flacco,* Sardinians in his defence of Scaurus, and Gauls in *Pro Fonteio.* See also the discussion of *argumenta a persona* at Quint. 5.10.24. On the presentation of foreigners in the aforementioned speeches and the Verrines, see Vasaly (1993) 191–243. For broader considerations of ethnicity, see Syed (2005) and Balsdon (1979). On *adsum,* see §29 *non adesse* n. Knowing how to support or discredit witnesses was an important skill for the successful advocate; see Arist. *Rhet.* 1376a and *Rhet. Her.* 2.9.

quare negent ex me non audies *Quare* not infrequently refers to a plural idea; cf. *Rosc. Am.* 41, 94 with Landgraf *ad loc.*, and Caes. *BG* 1.33.2, 5.31.5, and *Fam.* 10.21.1. C. may suggest that the

Sicilians have many reasons for denying support to Caecilius; on *reticentia*, see *plura non dicam* n. above.

28.6 hos sc. the jury. C. is still addressing Caecilius directly, hence *patere*. Cf. C.'s questioning of Decianus at *Flac.* 70 *Primum patere me esse curiosum.*

illi quidem *Quidem* correlates with *sed* to contrast the two indirect statements, *in Verrem deportare uelle … asportare te uelle.* And while the particle *quidem* typically follows the contrasted word, 'so powerfully do *quidem* and pronouns attract one another that they often distort the logic of expression: *quidem*, displaced from the word it should follow, is put next to the pronoun instead'; see Solodow (1978) 36–40. *Quidem* preceded by *ille* is particularly common in C.; see e.g. §§35, 44.

28.7 hominum genus nimis acutum et suspiciosum C. speaks similarly of the Sicilians in *Ver.* II.3.20 and 5.71. For the most part, throughout the Verrines C. downplays many of the cultural differences between his Roman audience and his Sicilian clients. Instead, he asserts that morals and customs are better indicators of cultural similarity than nationality and language; see *Off.* 1.55 *Sed omnium societatum nulla praestantior est, nulla firmior, quam cum uiri boni moribus similes sunt familiaritate coniuncti; illud enim honestum, quod saepe dicimus, etiam si in alio cernimus, tamen nos mouet atque illi in quo id inesse uidetur amicos facit.* Therefore, in the *Diu. Caec.*, C. highlights cultural similarities such as religious institutions and veneration (§3), respect for Roman governmental institutions and laws (§18), and faculties of reasoning (§§14, 28).

But here the pronoun *illi* in contrast with *hos* and the allusion to stereotypes separate the Sicilians as 'other'. This is a strategic manoeuvre. By drawing attention to a perceived stereotype, C. may be subtly questioning the notion of a cultural divide. As he goes on to describe Caecilius' involvement and complacency during Verres' praetorship, he compels the audience to ratify the Sicilians' shrewdness. In showing similar faculties of analysis and judgement, the Roman jurors would effectively take a further step in removing a perception of 'otherness' from the Sicilians.

This assimilating portrayal of the Sicilians is more subdued than the one presented in *Ver.* II.2.1, in which their culture is compared to that of a virtuous agrarian proto-Roman society. At *Ver.* II.2.2–11, 149, C. specifically mentions the un-Hellenic nature of Sicily and its similarity to native Roman virtues and cultural identity. For much the same characterization of Sicilians as shown here, cf. *Brut* 46 *itaque, ait Aristoteles, cum sublatis in Sicilia tyrannis res priuatae longo interuallo iudiciis repeterentur, tum primum, quod esset acuta illa gens et controuersiae nata, artem et praecepta Siculos Coracem et Tisiam conscripsisse.* The characteristic of being *acutus* does not seem to be pejorative, but rather indicates good judgement; cf. Col. 1.3.9 on the Carthaginians. On the Roman presentation of the Sicilians, see Lintott (2008) 95. For an overview of C.'s imagined communities and fluctuating cultural boundaries, see Gildenhard (2011) 126–140. For the process of defining fictive cultural boundaries in the ancient world, see Koschorke et al. (2007), Gruen (2006), and Gotter (2000). On discrediting witnesses through ethnic stereotypes, see *ad iudicium non adfuturos* n. above.

28.8 litteras 'documentary evidence', here especially financial accounts as this would have been Caecilius' purview as quaestor. *Litterae* can refer to a host of official documents such as financial sureties and legal papers; see *TLL* VII 2.1521.24 and *OLD s.u.* 6a. Cf. *Ver.* I.33 *nunc hominem tabulis, testibus, priuatis publicisque litteris auctoritatibusque accusemus.* Such forms of evidence could be impounded by law, and the prosecutor had the right to compel delivery. If the owner refused to comply with the request, the prosecutor could make a formal visit to obtain them; see *Ver.* II.1.50 and 3.154. Once acquired, these papers were sealed to prevent forgery, and when the time for collecting evidence had expired, they had to be deposited with the presiding magistrate of the court within three days. At the time of the trial, they could be passed around the jurors for inspection. They were presented during the course of speeches and read aloud by the court *scriba*, unlike personal testimony, which was given after the speeches were delivered; see Greenidge 488–489, 493–495 with references to the documents collected by C. for his prosecution of Verres. Though documentary evidence was classed as an inartistic proof, i.e. not relying on rhetorical discovery, its effectiveness was still subject to rhetorical manipulation and could be diminished by casting suspicion on its authenticity. On the *genus inartificiale*, see Lausberg §§351–354.

deportare … asportare In the period after the *nominis receptio*, the prosecutor was granted time to gather evidence. In many trials, it had to be a minimum of ten days; see [Asc.] *In Corn.* 59. The *crimen repetundarum*, however, was allotted at least 30 days, if not more, since evidence was probably overseas; see *Vat.* 33. After this *diuinatio*, C. requested 110 days for evidence-gathering, although he only used 60; cf. [Asc.] 125 (205 Stangl). For the complete procedure, see Introduction §III.

This play on prefixes is a kind of *annominatio*/paronomasia. Cf. *Rosc. Am.* 5 with Landgraf *ad loc.*, 107 *obtulerint … tulerunt*; *Sul.* 47 *tulisse … retulisse* with Berry *ad loc.*, 63 *ferebat … referebat*, etc. See *Rhet. Her.* 4.30, and see further Holst (1925) 70–76 and Lausberg §§637, 638.1a. There is a nuanced difference between the verbs. *Deportare* indicates removal with a destination in mind – Rome in particular; see *OLD s.u.* 2a and *TLL* V 1.588.41–72 – while *asportare* in this instance indicates removal of evidence with no intention of bringing it to Rome, 'to abscond with'; see [Asc.] 112 (195 Stangl) *Asportare aliquid ut intereat, deportare ut mutet locum*, and Schol. Gronov. 326 Stangl *deportamus proprie cum oportet portare, asportamus cum non oportet.* For more on the play on prefixes, see *Rhetores Graeci* 3.36.14–25 Spengl and MacLeod (1979) 23. This sort of wordplay was criticized by Quintilian (*Inst.* 9.3.72) and Seneca (*Suas.* 7.11).

28.9 consignata sit 'attested, recorded' (see *OLD* 2 and *TLL* IV 436.74), but also a play on words since seals were affixed to documentary evidence to avoid tampering or forgery (see *OLD s.u.* 1 and *TLL* IV 436.51) See *litteras* n. above. On seals, see *N-P s.u. seals.*

§29

29.1 firmum uerumque Both adjectives refer to the moral qualities of the *accusator* and so act as a continuation of the *uir bonus* discussion initiated at §27 *integritatem atque innocentiam. Firmus* is frequently associated with *constantia*, the resistance to outside influence; cf. Hellegouarc'h 284. C. remarks in *Part.* 117: *deinde etiam argumento firmo, quia tamen saepe falsum est, posse recte non credi, uiro bono et firmo sine uitio iudicis non posse non credi.* The notion of *uerus* relates to the intent of the advocate, not the truth-value of what he says. Even a morally upstanding orator could find himself needing to be deceptive; see *De orat.* 1.229–230 and Quint. *Inst.* 12.1.36–37, and see further May and Wisse (2001) 9–12. For the moral overtones of *uerus,* see *OLD s.u.* 9 and *TLL* VI 817.25–47, 818.18–37. It is C.'s contention that Caecilius is unduly influenced by external considerations and shows indications of a *falsus accusator.* C. will again revisit the need for outstanding moral character before his own discussion of Verres' management of the grain tithe; see *Ver.* II.3.1–5. For this collocation, cf. *Fin.* 3.48, *Tim.* 28, Plin. *Ep.* 2.11.19 *uir pro ueritate firmissimus,* and 4.22.3.

eum ego si... non posse The remote protasis has concessive force, '*even* if'.

29.3 nec ea dico *Occultatio*; see §28 *plura non dicam* n.

infirmare non possis The physical metaphor of *infirmare* is a favourite of C.; cf. §44 *infirmare conabitur,* and *Sul.* 78.

te The hyperbaton provided by the intervening temporal clause (*antequam … decesseris*) lends emphasis to *te.*

29.4 decesseris Not only upon departing from Sicily but also leaving political office; cf. §2 *ex ea prouincia decessissem* n. C. uses *decedo* with both *ex* and *de*; the former applies solely to provinces with the exception of *Font.* 13–14, while the latter may be used with figurative objects. See the syllepsis at *Balb.* 11: *qui de ciuitate decedere quam de sententia maluit.*

in gratiam redisse cum Verre Although the expression concedes the notion of a row between Caecilius and Verres (§52 *id quod dictitas, iniuriam tibi fecisse Verrem*), C. asserts that they have reconciled their differences. As evidence, he notes that Verres has retained Caecilius' *scriba* and is entertaining his brother, Marcus; see nn. below. C. will return to the theme of a reconciliation in §58 after he has explained the origin of the dispute (§§55–57) and further alleges that the two men have visited one another and dined together; see nn. *ad loc. Gratia* implies the bonds of *amicitia* between two people and encompasses a certain disposition toward aiding the other person through *beneficia*; see Hellegouarc'h 202–208. For the phrase *in gratiam redire cum aliquo*, see §58, *Ver.* II.1.2, *Sest.* 130, and *Prou.* 18 with Grillo *ad loc.*

29.5 Potamonem, scribam L. Papirius Potamo (*RE* 71), *scriba* to Caecilius, was retained by Verres after Caecilius left office to assist in judicial and fiscal matters; see *Ver.* II.3.137, 154, 4.44. It has been argued that Potamo would no longer have been officially a *scriba quaestorius* after Caecilius' term concluded and that 'Papirius Potamo and Maevius undoubtedly served Verres as *librarii* after they had left their posts as quaestorian *scribae*. The conditions for recruiting these men to less well-regarded positions were probably more flexible than those which regulated the system of decuries. To understand their continued service under the governor of Sicily, one readily imagines that Verres hired them directly and under his own personal responsibility. [Ce fut sans doute en effet comme librarii que Papirius Potamon et Maevius servirent Verres après qu'ils eurent quitté leur poste de scribe questorien. Les conditions de recrutement à ces postes moins bien considérés étaient probablement plus souples que celles qui régissaient le système des décuries. Pour comprendre la continuité de leur affectation auprès du gouverneur de Sicile, on imagine volontiers que Verres les avait embauchés directement et sous sa seule responsabilité]'; David (2006) 48. When C. refers to him during his service under Verres, he calls Potamo *amicum tuum* (4.44), not his *scriba*. For other members of Verres' cohort, see Pittia (2006).

Scribae were the highest-ranking non-elected officials (*apparitores*). The most well compensated among them were the *scribae quaestorii*, two of whom were assigned to quaestors to assist them during their magistracy, and who would, as a matter of course, also work closely with the quaestor's commander. Even when C. attacks the *scribae* in Verres' cohort, he goes to great lengths to distance himself from offending the *ordo* as a whole, who represented an influential force; see *Ver.* II.3.182. As C. remarks of *scribae* in *Dom.* 74: *qui nobiscum in rationibus monumentisque publicis uersantur*; cf. *Mur.* 42. For more on the office and prosopography of *scribae*, see Purcell (1983), David (2006), Badian (1989), Damon (1992), and *N-P s.u. scriba.*

C. refers to Potamo here by *cognomen* alone. Though people associated with the opposition frequently only receive one name (see Dickey (2002) 51), it is hard to attach any definitive import to this instance of naming as C. varies his references to Papirius Potamo throughout the corpus: *cognomen* alone (*Ver.* II.4.44), the more formal *nomen* + *cognomen* (*Ver.* II.3.137), and the non-prestigious form of *praenomen* + *nomen* (*Ver.* II.3.154). The simple *cognomen*, being the last name to be established and originally used only by the aristocracy, could be a way of informally acknowledging acceptance into the higher social class; see Adams (1978) 150.

familiarem See §13 *familiariter* n.

retentum esse Caecilius only served during the first year of Verres' tenure as governor; see Badian (1984) and Introduction §II. The verb need not imply that Potamo maintained his status as a *scriba*, but that he was appointed by Verres to his staff in some other capacity since the propraetor did not have the authority to assign decurial *scribae*; see *Potamonem, scribam* n. above with David (2006). The observation hardly suggests that Caecilius maintained strong ties to Verres after his term of office. Perhaps the audience is meant to infer that Caecilius and his staff were wilfully complicit in Verres' schemes.

29.6 M. Caecilium (*RE* 17) Caecilius' brother; nothing more is known of him. Early on in the manuscript tradition, the name was corrupted to *Caelium.*

29.7 lectissimum atque ornatissimum For the sense of the superlative, see §13 *uiri clarissimi* n. Irony must be implied, though this pairing is not used sarcastically elsewhere; cf. *Ver.* II.1.15 and 4.79.

non adesse *Adesse* here means 'to give support by one's presence in court'; see *OLD s.u.* 12 and *TLL* II 923.20–36. Why Caecilius' brother should be with him in the court is unclear – a flimsy argument on C.'s part. It was common for family members of plaintiffs or defendants to come to public trials, which would allow an advocate to showcase them in an appeal to the jury's emotions; cf. *Cael.* 79–80. Their absence could arouse suspicion and be used by the opposing party; cf. Roscius with Dyck (2003) 236. The *diuinatio*, however, is simply a pre-trial hearing, but C.'s assertion is meant to cast suspicion on Caecilius. At the very least, it suggests that the influence of his familial connections with Verres would not allow him to conduct a thorough prosecution.

29.9 et haec et alia ... quibus ... non utor *Praeteritio.* C.'s indications of prevarication are weak at best. *Praeteritio* and the phrase *et haec et alia* are used in this instance to indicate a surfeit of evidence when in fact there is none. For the phrase *et haec et alia,* cf. *Clu.* 100, *Orat.* 174, *Att.* 15.22.1, and L. Valerius speaking of M. Cato at Liv. 34.5.6. On *praeteritio* and related techniques, see §28 *plura non dicam* n.

29.10 falsi accusatoris Viz. *praeuaricator*; see §58 *utrum te perfidiosum an praeuaricatorem existimari mauis?* n.

signa permulta *Signum* indicates presumptive rather than demonstrative evidence; cf. Quint. *Inst.* 5.9.1–16 *Diuiduntur autem in has primas duas species, quod eorum alia sunt, ut dixi, quae necessaria <sunt, alia quae non necessaria>. Priora illa sunt quae aliter habere se non possunt, quae Graeci* τεκμήρια *uocant .... Alia sunt signa non necessaria, quae* εἰκότα *Graeci uocant.* The latter are the equivalent of Aristotle's σημεῖον; see *Rhet.* 1357a. These *signa non necessaria* form the basis of an enthymeme, which indicates probability rather than established proof; see Lausberg §§358–365, especially §359 '*signa* are not intrinsically concerned with the facts to be treated in the trial – their connection with the facts is established only through a cognitive process'. The postposition of *permulta* provides emphasis and a desirable cretic + trochee rhythm.

29.11 hoc dico, te ... uerum accusatorem esse non posse C. often uses the phrase *hoc dico* after a negative or *praeteritio*; cf. *Ver.* II.1.34, 1.53, 2.111, 4.109, *Planc.* 93, *Mur.* 69, *Phil.* 5.17, and *Clu.* 100 *omitto et haec et alia permulta quae illo iudicio in*

Staienum dicta sunt; hoc dico .... The ring composition, going back to *accusatorem firmum uerumque*, encapsulates C.'s suggestion that Caecilius' relationship with Verres is far from strained. In the following sections, C. will examine additional reasons why Caecilius' prosecution will be weak (to hide his own misdeeds) or a total sham (to protect his pre-arranged agreements with Verres).

As with *te, antequam* ... above, the postposition of the conditional clause, *si maxime cupias*, adds emphasis to *te*. The word order of the Italian family (*esse non posse*) ends the sentence with a desirable cretic-trochee clausula and avoids the homeoteleuton found in the French tradition.

§30

30.1 permulta esse crimina The copula often splits predicates and subjects and places emphasis on a host that denotes quantity, such as *permulta*; cf. Caes. *Gal.* 5.41.3 *omnem esse in armis Galliam*, and *Fam.* 7.18.1 *non tibi maiori esse curae* ... *quam mihi*. For additional examples, see Adams (1994a) 19–24. *Crimen* here is a 'matter for accusation or blame' (*OLD* 2; *TLL* IV 1193.52) as opposed to 'indictment, charge' (*OLD* 1; *TLL* IV 1190.40).

C. introduces material here in the *Diuinatio* that he will develop fully in the third speech of the *actio secunda* (*de frumento*), in which he will allege that Verres had issued an edict that contravenes the usual method of assessing and collecting the grain tithe under the Hieronic law. In part of this extortionate scheme, Verres sold the tithe-collecting contracts for an exceptionally high rate and then gave the collector *carte blanche* to demand both an amount of grain well in excess of a tenth and money in lieu of additional grain. The speech *de frumento* will give a litany of various Sicilian communities and the amounts exacted from each as well as Verres' subversion of the judicial appeal process available to farmers. Other outrages concern disbursements from the state treasury that were to be used for additional purchase of grain and for the maintenance of the governor and his staff. According to C., Verres kept most of this money for himself or found ways of profiting by lending out the money at a high rate of interest to public contractors; see nn. below. This passage in the *Diu. Caec.* calls into question the thoroughness of any future prosecution by Caecilius and also impugns his trustworthiness and record of public service.

30.2 societas may imply a partnership for nefarious purposes; hence C. implicates Caecilius in a criminal conspiracy; cf. *Ver.* II.3.42 *societatem furtorum tuorum,* and 3.140. C. uses *societas* frequently in *Rosc. Am.* (21 *et passim*) to describe the arrangement between Chrysogonus, Magnus and Capito. See also *OLD s.u.* 1, Achard (1981) 107–108, and W. Spencer (2011). Cf. on the first triumvirate Tac. *Dial.* 5.3 *Caesar et Pompeius et Crassus iuncta societate imperium Romanorum possidebant.* For the financial and legal overtones of the word, see Berger *s.u.* On a more positive use of the term, see §61 *societatem* n.

30.3 attingere non audeas *Attingere* does not indicate a full exposition of the charge but rather the slightest mention; see *OLD s.u.* 9a, and *TLL* II 1145.84. C. uses it to denote real or feigned brevity; cf. *Rosc. Am.* 123, *Scaur.* 21, and *Dom.* 40 *quae ego nunc perbreviter attingo.* C. implies that Caecilius fears self-incrimination. Supposing that Caecilius was complicit in and subsequently benefited from some form of extortion, even if he were not prosecuted directly, he could still be held liable for punitive damages during the *litis aestimatio* after Verres' conviction. As an elected magistrate, however, he was also liable to prosecution; see Damon and Mackay (1995).

queritur Sicilia tota C. mentions none of these accusations against Caecilius in the prosecution of Verres; [Asc.] 13 *non intelligunt haec ad tempus commode adiungi: quae uicto Caecilio non sunt necessaria.* On personification of a city or state, see §19 *si una uoce loqueretur* n. On the exaggeration of *tota Sicilia,* see §2 *cuncti* n.

ab aratoribus The *arator* was the head of the farm, who interacted directly with the *decumani.* On the interaction between Verres and the farmers, see Pritchard (1971). Sicilian grain production was so vital to the large urban population of Rome that endangering those supply lines through mismanagement would have been of grave concern to the senate.

30.4 frumentum ... in cellam Grain purchased with public funds for the maintenance of the governor and his staff. In addition to the grain acquired by tithes and requisitions under the *lex Terentia Cassia frumentaria*, Verres was legally entitled to extract a certain amount of grain for personal use. The price paid per *modius* differed among these various mandates for purchase. Under the *lex Terentia Cassia* of 73, Verres was instructed to purchase the second tithe at 3 sesterces per *modius*, and a further 800,000 *modii* of wheat at 3½ sesterces; see *Ver.* II.3.163. For the *frumentum in cellam*, the price was set at a generous 4 sesterces per *modius* of wheat and 2 for barley; see *Ver.* II.3.188.

A custom existed whereby a farmer might pay a monetary tax in lieu of a grain contribution to the governor – a practice which would alleviate transportation costs and/or offer the farmer a higher net profit on his produce. From his personal allocation, Verres sought to net 12 sesterces per *modius* (*duodenos sestertios*) by asking for money from the farmers instead of grain at the price of 8 sesterces per *modius* and keeping the original maintenance money (4 sesterces per *modius*) allotted to him by the senate. In the *actiones in Verrem*, C. manages to breathe some life into a dull topic through a spirited *sermocinatio*; see *Ver.* II. 3.196–197. On the governor's maintenance, see also Tac. *Agr.* 19.4, Mommsen, *Staatsr.* 1.297–298, Mann (1985), and Pritchard (1971). On the grain market and corn supply, see Erdkamp (2005) 206–225 and Rickman (1980). For the ways in which C. incorporates allegations normally connected with embezzlement into an extortion charge, see Frazel (2009) 187–221.

30.5 tritici modius HS II Grain would sell, on average at this time, for approximately 2½ sesterces per *modius*. This may have been a low estimate on C.'s part. He later moderates his price estimate; see *Ver.* II.3.189 *hoc reprehendo, quod, cum in Sicilia HS binis tritici modius esset, ut istius epistula ad te missa declarat, summum*

HS ternis, id quod et testimoniis omnium et tabulis aratorum planum factum antea est, tum iste pro tritici modiis singulis ternos ab aratoribus denarios exegit, and 3.194.

singulos 'price per unit' in financial transactions. For the total sum of 12 sesterces per *modius*, see *frumentum* ... *in cellam* n. above.

30.6 exegisse 'exacted'; see *OLD s.u.* 8a and *TLL* V 2.1453.24, 78.

magnum crimen ... iniuria non ferenda μεταβολή; Julius Rufinianus *RLM* 76.18 *iteratio unius rei sub uarietate uerborum*, followed by a citation of this sentence. Cf. *Clu.* 41, 167. See further Lausberg §645. For the isolated emphatic nominative, see H-Sz. 29.

30.7 ego ... tu For the adversative sense of the initial position, see §26 *ego* n. The initial personal pronouns *ego* and *tu*, frequently juxtaposed, often introduce *comparationes* between C. and Caecilius. The one that follows demonstrates how each of them would deal with Verres' extortion and embezzlement scheme mentioned above. C. could use it alone to obtain a conviction; Caecilius, C. alleges, will have to omit it altogether because of his personal involvement in provincial administration; see §31.

hoc uno crimine C. suggests that this infraction alone is enough to render a guilty verdict. A trial *de repetundis* was not broken down into various counts – a defendant was either found guilty or acquitted. Individual counts would be assessed separately during the *litis aestimatio*; see Lintott (2008) 91. On C.'s novel method of presenting counts with their respective witnesses separately, see Vasaly (2009) 110–113.

30.8 condemnem necesse est 'to cause to be condemned'; see *OLD s.u. condemno* 2 and *TLL* IV 125.34–46. For *necesse est* with the subjunctive without *ut*, see H-Sz. 531.

§31

31.1 utrum ... an The disjunctive rhetorical question introduces a dilemma (*complexio*): either Caecilius must overlook a serious charge against Verres or implicate himself in criminal activity.

This part of C.'s argument anticipates a portion of the *reprehensio* (§§ 59–65) in which C. explains why Caecilius' former relationship with Verres as his quaestor should debar him from leading the prosecution. Here he admits that Caecilius' interaction with Verres would have made him privy to information that could prove damning for Verres, but C. contends that not only should Caecilius have prevented these crimes in the first place but that he was also complicit in them. Caecilius is therefore unlikely to pursue these charges since he would implicate himself in the process. Caecilius' vulnerability to *complexiones* will form part of C.'s meta-rhetorical discussion of Hortensius' tactics; see §45. By the use of dilemma, C. reinterprets Caecilius' involvement in Verres' administration as a disadvantage and an indication of suspicious behaviour. On this particular dilemma, see Craig (1993) 59. On *complexio* as an argument from enthymeme, see *Top.* 54–55 with Reinhardt *ad loc.*

31.2 obicies? Si obicies Legal terminology; 'to charge a person with a crime'. See Berger *s.u.*, Heumann–Seckel *s.u.* 2, and *TLL* IX 2.56.26. The anadiplosis provides logical progression; see Lausberg §619.

alteri crimini Predicative dative; see K-St. 2.1.344.

31.3 quod eodem tempore in eadem prouincia tu ipse fecisti The anaphora and homeoteleuton of *idem* underscores Caecilius' supposed involvement in Verres' embezzlement scheme. Caecilius, C. contends, would be susceptible to an *anticategoria* in which the defence counsel could allege that the prosecutor himself was guilty of the same crime. Lausberg §197: 'as a reply to the prosecutor's accusation of *Fecisti*, the defendant thus charges the prosecutor with *Fecisti* – the same particular (identical) *crimen*'. See Quint. *Inst.* 3.10.4 *Id si et ipsum uocari debet* ἀντικατηγορία *(nam proprio caret nomine), duo genera erunt eius: alterum quo litigatores idem crimen inuicem intentant, alterum quo aliud atque aliud: cui et petitionum condicio par est,* and 7.2.9 *Interdum enim substituitur mutua accusatio, quam Graeci* ἀντικατηγορίαν *uocant, nostrorum quidam 'concertatiuam'.*

31.4 ut quominus ... possis 'that you could not object to your own condemnation?' *Ut* followed immediately by *quominus* is rare. For the only other instance in C., cf. *Red. Sen.* 12 *ut quominus occulte uestrum malum gemeretis nihil diceret.* In negative clauses, *recusare* regularly completes its meaning with a noun clause introduced by *quin* or *quominus*; see Schmalz *s.u.* and *OLD* 3c. Cf. *Phil.* 1.27 *quominus mihi inimicissimus sit non recusabo.*

31.5 condemnere The subjunctive is required, contrary to the reading of many MSS.

praetermittes 'leave out, omit'; see *OLD s.u.* 3, and *TLL* X 2.1032.8–40. The parallelism with *audebis* and *erit* shows that the future tense of M must be right.

31.6 tua ista The close semantic relationship of *iste* with the second person is frequently demonstrated in its collocation with the second-person possessive adjective in the phrase *iste tuus.* The word order here is less common but gives a more favourable molossus-cretic rhythm and is not without parallel; cf. *Cat.* 1.22, 25, *Ver.* I.34, and *Phil.* 2.101. See further H-Sz. 183.

domestici periculi metu 'from fear of self-endangerment'. For *domesticus* as 'one's own', see *TLL* V 1.1870.10, and *OLD s.u.* 4. On *periculum*, see §25 *magno multorum periculo* n.

certissimi 'undeniable, irrefutable'; see *OLD s.u.* 5 and *TLL* III 912.25–55.

31.7 susceptionem Previous editors noticed that the contrast implied by *non modo … uerum etiam* was too weak with the MS reading, *suspicionem*, and suggested an array of emendations (*subscriptionem* Madvig : *sponsionem* Peterson : *susceptionem* Eberhard : *expositionem* Luterbacher : *suspicionem* and *mentionem* trans. Pluygers). Peterson (1903) 198–199 outlines the rationale for most of them except Eberhard's. None of them, however, knew of the existence of *E*, which reports *suspectionem.* Though late and un-Ciceronian in itself, it suggests that the original reading was in fact *susceptionem*, and that the reading of the Italian family was a correction to a spoonerism in the hyparchetype. Elsewhere C. uses the phrase *crimen suscipere*, 'to take up or accept an allegation'; see *Sul.* 68 *Neque enim istorum facinorum tantorum, tam atrocium crimen, iudices, P. Sullae persona suscipit,* and *Rab. Per.* 18 *ego autem, si mihi esset integrum, susciperem hoc crimen, agnoscerem, confiterer.* He uses *susceptio* to refer to taking up a case; cf. *Mur.* 2 *ipsa susceptio causae reprensa est.* The nominal construction provides a memorable homeoteleuton. One should understand '... which out of concern for personal endangerment is terrified not only of including this grievous and undeniable charge but of even the very mention of it'.

31.8 pertimescat See §23 *pertimescat* n.

§32

32.1 ex senatus consulto In addition to collecting the tithe, Verres was instructed by a *senatus consultum* and the *lex Terentia Cassia* of 73 BCE to purchase a second tithe and some additional grain besides; see *Ver.* II.3.163, 5.52, and *pecunia* ... n. below. A *senatus consultum* was a recommendation from the senate to a magistrate in the form of a resolution. During the Republic, these resolutions were not legally binding but were so in practice. On *senatus consulta* and their language, see Talbert (1984) 303–305, 431–435, Sherk (1969) 7–13, and Sherk (1970) 59–63. On the *lex Terentia Cassia,* see Rotondi (1912) 366. For a survey of *leges frumentariae,* see Virlouvet (1994).

frumentum ... quo frumento Duplication. The repetition of the noun within its relative clause gives the passage a bureaucratic tone that imitates the phrasing of a *senatus consultum.* Cf. §2 *tempus* ... *quo tempore.* On the style of *senatus consulta,* see n. above.

praetore *Praetor* and *populus Romanus* were similarly abbreviated in MSS (*pr*) and are frequently confused when a copying hand or annotator expands the abbreviation.

32.2 pecunia omnis soluta non est 'payment has not been made in full'; see *OLD s.u. soluo* 19b. Verres had received a disbursement from the Roman treasury of 120,000 sesterces over his three-year tenure to purchase additional grain at a fixed price. C. maintains that Verres devised three schemes to profit from this influx of funds. The first was to loan out the public money at interest to those corporations (*societates*) that were designated to collect the additional grain and then keep the interest for himself rather than return it to the state. The second was simply not to pay the Sicilian communities for the additional wheat, while the third was to levy various administrative fees on any funds that he did disburse. Such crimes would leave Verres liable to face charges of embezzlement. For C.'s narrative of these events, see *Ver.* II.3.163–182.

32.3 graue ... graue The anaphora gives way to a *correctio* whereby C. amends or qualifies his initial statement: 'This is a *serious* charge against Verres, or should I say, only serious if I am the prosecutor ....' On this device, see Lausberg §784. It is also identified by Quint. *Inst.* 9.2.18 as *reprehensio* (self-correction). Cf. *Mur.* 80 *Atque haec ciues, ciues, inquam, si eos hoc nomine appellari fas est.*

hoc crimen A charge additional to the one that C. has already mentioned; see §30 *frumentum ... in cellam* n.

graue me agente, te accusante nullum Berry on *Sul.* 2: '[Leeman (1963) 22] has pointed out that in Greek and Latin it is the order A B A B which is artificial and rhetorical: the order A B B A was not thought worthy of comment until the second century AD at the earliest ([Hermog.] *Inu.* 4.3, and Sch. Isoc. 12.47), when it was termed "chiasmus".'

32.4 eras *Eius* in *E* and *N* may have been the original reading in *S*; the two forms are easily confused. But although there are parallels (cf. *Flac.* 46, and *Opt. Gen.* 15 *Sed exorietur Thucydides; eius enim quidam eloquentiam admirantur*), the first *tu* would be lacking a verb. Furthermore, a reader would have no way of understanding *tu quaestor* in the past tense without a verb being expressed. *t* reads *eras*, which is the only evidence in this text that suggests it was not descended from *E*, but the reading may be a lucky slip or correction in *t* or its intermediary; see Introduction §VI.

enim A consensus-building particle: 'you must admit'. Although *enim* is often thought of as marking 'causal' relationships between clauses, it more properly indicates an 'appeal to consensus'. See *Fam.* 3.1 in which a 'potentially challengeable utterance ... is toned down by a justificatory clause containing a commonsense argument'; Kroon (1995) 196–197.

tu ... tu Repetition of the personal pronoun underscores Caecilius' involvement in Verres' regime, and his responsibility and vulnerability.

quaestor On the date of Caecilius' quaestorship, see Introduction §II.

pecuniam publicam 'money belonging to or owed to the state treasury. *Pecunia publica* could be lent to private individuals only on interest and with real security'; Berger *s.u.* Caecilius' responsibility for public funds could make him open to a charge of *peculatus* (embezzlement); see *pecunia omnis soluta non est* n. above. In establishing his case against Verres, C. will look back to Verres' own term as quaestor and impugn his method of book-keeping and allege that he had previously embezzled public funds; cf. *Ver.* II.1.36. For the terms of *peculatus*, see *D.* 48.13.1–16.

tractabas 'you were the one managing the public funds'; *OLD s.u.* 6a. For the verb used concerning a magistrate's particular duties, see *Font.* 5, Tac. *Hist.* 4.9.1, and *CIL* II 1964.5.

32.5 etiamsi cuperet praetor An exaggeration on C.'s part; the statement is softened; see *magna ex parte* n. below.

deductio A reduction in the amount that should have been paid; in this instance, the various administrative fees deducted from payments made to Sicilian farmers so that Verres could keep the money for himself. When he recounts these charges in the trial proper, however, C. pinpoints the *scriba* as one of the beneficiaries; see *Ver.* II.3.181 *Ex omni pecunia quam aratoribus soluere debuisti certis nominibus deductiones fieri solebant, primum pro spectatione et collybo, deinde pro nescioquo cerario. Haec omnia, iudices, non rerum certarum sed furtorum improbissimorum sunt uocabula.*

... *Scribae nomine de tota pecunia binae quinquagesimae detrahebantur*. These are the only two instances of the financial sense of the term in C. For other examples, see Gaius *Inst.* 4.65, and *TLL* V 1.283.45.

32.6 magna ex parte 'to a large extent' (*TLL* X 1.457.38–56), a phrase which softens C.'s statement that the quaestor maintained complete control over the provincial purse. The quaestor was subordinate to the praetor and so would have little recourse to a higher authority to deny the orders of his superior.

tua potestas The official power designated to Caecilius by virtue of his office; *OLD s.u.* 3, and Heumann–Seckel *s.u.* 1a. This, however, is a misrepresentation, as Verres would have possessed the *maior potestas* in relation to his quaestor and so had the right of intercession; see §35 *summam ... potestatem* n. For *potestas* introducing a negative prohibitive clause, see *TLL* X 2.317.81; cf. Sen. *Ben.* 3.22.4.

32.7 silebitur The impersonal passive emphasizes the notion of 'silence'. Not only will Caecilius not bring up the charge, but there will also be no mention of it from witnesses and evidence. On the impersonal passive and promotion of the action, see Pinkster (1992).

32.8 mihi crede confirms a statement and occasionally reinforces advice; cf. §39, *Cat.* 1.6. For the *sententia* with *mihi crede*, cf. Ov. *Am.* 1.9.1–2 *Militat omnis amans, ... Attice, crede mihi.* See further Shackleton Bailey (1956–1957) 13–14.

32.9 non potest ... defendere is qui ... coniunctus est When a gnomic *sententia*/γνώμη assumes the final position after a longer train of thought, especially in a *confirmatio*, it is called an *epiphonema*; see Quint. *Inst.* 8.5.11. Cf. §71 *itaque semper ii diligentissime laboriosissimeque accusarunt* with n. *ad loc.*, and *Ver.* II.5.119. For further discussions of this device, see Quint. 8.5.1–35, Julius Victor (*RLM* 412), [Hermog.] *Inu.* 4.9, and Lausberg §879. A maxim of this type is not always universally applicable but is often derived from the peculiar circumstances of the case; see [Arist.] *Rhet. Alex.* 430b, and Lausberg §877. **uere defendere ... Manci-** is omitted by the scribe of *N*. The exemplar of *N* may have been written, as was *S*, in a single column of 60–70 characters per line, but there may have been an intermediary between *S* and *N*; see Introduction §VI. **uere** renews the emphasis on a *uerus accusator*; see §29.

cum reo criminum societate C. returns again to the language of conspiracy; see §30 *societas* n.

§33

33.1 mancipes were typically contractors (*redemptores*) who, either through auction or through some other means, had entered into an agreement with the state to provide public services – e.g. maintenance of public businesses, army supplies, or in this instance, grain collection and transportation. In the provinces, the provincial governor would usually administer the letting of public contracts or have them conducted under the supervision of the quaestors; see *Ver.* II.3.18. C. narrates Verres' embezzlement scheme at *Ver.* II.3.163–176, though C. goes on to say at the end of that passage: *Quid est, Verres? ne illam quidem tibi defensionem reliquam fecisti, mancipes in istis rebus esse uersatos, mancipes frumentum improbasse, mancipes pretio cum ciuitatibus decidisse, et eosdem abs te illarum ciuitatum nomine pecunias abstulisse, deinde ipsos sibi frumentum coemisse, nihil haec ad te pertinere?* For the letting of public contracts by provincial governors, see Broughton (1929). Festus *s.u. Manceps dicitur qui quid a populo emit conducitue quia manu sublata significat se auctorem emptionis esse.* Etymologically, *manu -*ceps* is 'one who takes something by hand'; see further *N-P s.u.*, Nicolet (1972) 264–268, and Mateo (1999) 25–32.

a ciuitatibus *Ciuitas* is 'especially used with regard to foreign *ciuitates* in the sense of a large group of free individuals living together and organized as a legal social unit'; Berger *s.u.* From C.'s comments at *Ver.* II.2.133–137 one can infer that at this time there were 65 of these administrative units in Sicily.

33.3 solum The final position is emphatic: 'did this happen *only* when Verres was praetor?' The common Ciceronian pairing of *non solum ... sed etiam* led to the transposition of *solum* and *non* in some later Italian *deteriores.*

non gives the passage a conversational style when used alone for a negative response; see Hofmann §46.

quaestore Caecilio A reversal of the word order name–title such as is found in *Verre praetore* above. Caecilius' name in the final position is emphatic and provides a more metrically pleasing cretic and resolved spondee. On this form of the ablative absolute, see §28 *te actore* n.

quid igitur? The question adds a discursive tone similar to a *sermocinatio,* in which an interlocutor seeks to understand the relevance of the preceding statement, and more specifically here signals a *ratiocinatio* (an indirect form of *amplificatio*) in which the consequences of 'attendant circumstances ... are amplified'; see Lausberg §405. In this instance, C. explains how Caecilius' previous relationship with Verres precludes him from making an allegation in which he may be implicated. In C., *quid igitur?* is almost invariably followed by a longer, fuller question; cf. *Rosc. Am.* 122 *Quid igitur? Chrysogonus suine malefici occultandi causa quaestionem de eis haberi non uolt?* See Seyffert 1§49 and *Rosc. Am.* 2 with Landgraf *ad loc.* Other instances in C. include *Ver.* I.20, II.2.106, 5.9, *Caec.* 60, *Flac.* 55, 88, *Phil.* 1.38, *Tusc.* 1.61, 5.13, and 5.22.

33.4 daturus es For the future participle with the present tense of *sum* as a periphrasis for the future tense, see H-Sz. 312 and *OLS* 1.429–435. The periphrastic construction is common in early Latin and has a tinge of purpose, although it becomes a simple future in later colloquial Latin and the Church Fathers; cf. Petr. 45.4. On the future participle in C., see Laughton (1964) 118–124.

huic Viz. Verres; a vivid deictic. C. uses a proximate pronoun to refer to Verres even though he was certainly not present at the *diuinatio.* The reference here is not purely intratextual, that is to say, recalling 'Verres' mentioned a few sentences previous, but also proximate in a mental/psychological sense, which treats

Verres as being at the forefront of a juror's mind. For deixis in Latin pronouns, see Bernini and Schwartz (2006) 215–221. For a similar use of the deictic, see *Lig.* 5 with Gotoff *ad loc.* and *Deiot.* 8. For the predicative dative, see §31 *alteri crimini* n.

et potuisti ... et debuisti The verbs stress Caecilius' ability and obligation to control finances and tax collection. *Debeo* is given the final position to underscore Caecilius' shirked moral obligation.

33.5 an totum id relinques? C. again uses the same *complexio* tactic he had earlier; cf. §31 *utrum ... an* n. *Relinquere* may refer to the abandonment of a charge or accusation; see Heumann–Seckel *s.u.* 3.

ergo introduces the probable conclusion to the *ratiocinatio* introduced by *quid igitur?* above.

33.6 faciebat The iterative imperfect draws attention to Verres' repeated violations.

quem ad modum defensurus esset non reperiebat *Reperire* can refer to rhetorical *inuentio.* C. depicts Verres as planning for an extortion trial long before he finished his term of office as though it were an inevitability; see *Ver.* I.4–5. For *reperire* with an indirect question, see *Rosc. Am.* 124 *de quo, iudices, neque quo modo dicam neque quo modo taceam reperire possum* with Landgraf *ad loc.*

33.8 atque Used in transition to a new line of argument; see Seyffert 1§15.

quae in medio posita sunt 'those issues that are common knowledge'; *OLD s.u. medius* 3b and *TLL* VIII 594.16–595.7.

33.9 occulta *Occultatio*; see §28 *plura non dicam* n. Throughout this ethical attack on Caecilius, C. alludes to other damning evidence against Caecilius without substantiation. These cryptic statements allow him to give the impression of possessing incriminating evidence. In his prosecution of Verres, Caecilius will be implicated in none of them. Perhaps C. simply makes good on his statement at §35 *ego etiam quae tu sine Verre commisisti Verri crimini daturus sum.*

istius Caecilius is not infrequently denominated with the pejorative *iste*; see §§4, 31, 47, *passim.*

credo The parenthetic *credo* tells the reader that C. does not actually mean to suggest that Caecilius is truly angry with Verres; see §22 *alterum illud, credo, obscurum est* n.

animos atque impetus 'violent mental impulses'; *OLD s.u. impetus* 5a and *TLL* VII 1.607.68–608.16 (as well as 608.63–610.11). Here expressed as a hendiadys; *animus* would normally stand in the genitive; cf. *Inu.* 2.17, *Mur.* 65, and *Cael.* 76 *de impetu animi.*

33.10 benignissime cum quaestore suo (*ΠγP*: *cum quaestore suo benignissime M*) The fifth-century papyrus fragment is legible enough at this point to confirm the reading in *P* and the French family. *Benignitas* is frequently demonstrated through physical gifts of monetary value. The implication here is that Caecilius will have received money (and artwork perhaps?), although C. modifies this suggestion in the subsequent sentence. On *benignitas*, see Q. Cic. *Pet.* 41–44, and see further Hellegouarc'h 218.

communicauit indicates co-ownership or a division of shared goods and proceeds, and returns to the notion of a criminal conspiracy between Caecilius and Verres; see §30 *societas* n. and *TLL* III 1957.63. On the legal implications of common ownership, Berger *s.u. communio.*

§34

34.1 scis Only used 11 times in the second-person singular in C.'s extant speeches – and usually aimed at an opponent whom C. wants to portray as being wilfully misleading or irrational. The technique arouses the suspicion of the jurors about other information that his opponent may be unwilling to disclose or acknowledge; cf. e.g. *Rosc. Am.* 147 (against Chrysogonus), *Sul.* 11 (Torquatus), *Flac.* 66 (Laelius), *Vat.* 16 (Vatinius), and *Phil.* 2.91 (M. Antonius).

ad me (*ΠPM* : *a me* γ) The French family makes C. the agent of the passive infinitive and would imply that he has already brought allegations against Caecilius, which is incompatible with the sense of the following conditional statement.

esse delata *Deferre* has a legal meaning that particularly relates to the disclosure of information that would lead to a prosecution; see *OLD s.u.* 8, 9. The passive construction allows C. to avoid naming an informant. The implication, however, is surely that the Sicilians, who have approached C. about leading the prosecution, have also told him about Caecilius' wrongdoings and complaisance during his tenure as quaestor. This, in turn, allows C. to present himself as informed about particular illegal activities in the province, even before he has secured the position as prosecutor and gone to collect evidence. But C. fails to mention any further specific allegations of collusion – giving good reason to think they are entirely fabricated.

quae si uelim *Praeteritio.* For another similarly phrased example, cf. *Ver.* II.5.21 *Relinquo haec omnia; quae si uelim persequi, facile ostendam tua crudelitate in alios omnis tibi aditus misericordiae iudicum iam pridem esse praeclusos.* Cf. *Rosc. Am.* 135, and *Ver.* II.1.155.

proferre Legal terminology, 'to present as evidence in court'; see *TLL* X 2.1682.38, and Berger and Heumann–Seckel *s.u.* This diction suggests the summoning of witnesses or the production of documents, which would presumably be out of place in a *diuinatio*; see §13 *testes* n. Again, C. artificially assumes the role of a prosecutor even in this pre-trial hearing by levelling an attack on Caecilius as he would do on a defendant.

34.2 uobis inter uos Pleonasm. The repetition of the pronoun draws attention to the supposed bond between Caecilius and Verres. Some editors, following Eberhard, have sought to remove *uobis.* C. also uses the repetitive phrasing of the dative and *inter* with the pronoun again at *Ver.* II.3.98: *Vos autem, iudices, putare debetis esse quiddam nobis inter nos commune atque coniunctum.* Cf. *Att.* 1.17.4, and *Fam.* 9.8.2. On the attraction of pronouns to one another, see §27 *tute tui* n.

uoluntatem fuisse coniunctam 'a common purpose has been forged between you ...'. In Roman political vocabulary, *uoluntas* indicates an outlook, inclination, or disposition that results in an action; see Hellegouarc'h 181–185. This shared opinion or purpose is a key aspect of a political relationship; see *OLD s.u. coniungo* 7. In the other instances in which C. uses *uoluntas* with verbs denoting a 'bonding' or 'joining' (*Deiot.* 39 and *Quinct.* 52) he immediately emphasizes the social obligations inherent in those connections. For example, C. speaks of his shared *uoluntas* with Deiotarus and remarks that along with their *amicitia* and *familiaritas* it establishes *necessitudo* between them. Similarly, Caecilius is characterized as sharing various kinds of connection with Verres that imply social obligations to one another, e.g. *familiaritas* (§13) and *necessitudo* (§§46, 61). For similar wording used to describe the relationship between Laelius and Scipio, see *Amic.* 15. For the *contentio*, see *diuisam* n. below.

34.3 praedam Calling the money or items removed from Sicily *praeda* casts Caecilius and Verres in the role of looting soldiers or brigands; see *TLL* X 2.523.2–59, 524.42–69. They have become the sort of thieving politicians mentioned by Cato at Gel. 11.18.18: *Sed enim M. Cato in oratione quam de praeda militibus diuidenda scripsit uehementibus et inlustribus uerbis de inpunitate peculatus atque licentia conqueritur. Ea uerba quoniam nobis inpense placuerant, adscripsimus: 'Fures' inquit 'priuatorum furtorum in neruo atque in compedibus aetatem agunt, fures publici in auro atque in purpura'.*

adhuc Caecilius would have been out of office two years at this point. C. may want to indicate that the two men share a deep level of trust, or that perhaps a sham prosecution to ensure Verres' acquittal is part of their agreement. In either case, the suggestion seems untenable and certainly unsubstantiated.

diuisam The two parallel isocola conclude with antonymic pairs (*coniunctam* and *diuisam*) and form a *contentio* (ἀντίθετον). This particular form, in which the contrasting words occur at the end of their clause, Quintilian 9.3.82 labels a *distinctio*. Cf. *Clu.* 80 *ut quod in tempore mali fuit nihil obsit, quod in causa boni fuit prosit.* On *contentiones* generally, see §10 *quem maxime ... quem minime ...* n.

Cf. §§35, 61 and nn. *ad loc.* For contrasting pairs in C., see further Kirby (1997).

34.4 indicium … dari 'to be given leave to turn informant'; this also implies a grant of immunity in return for testimony about crimes in which the witness was complicit; see *OLD s.u. indicium* 2b, *TLL* VII 1.1151.7, Berger *s.u. index.* Cf. *Att.* 2.24.4 with Shackleton Bailey *ad loc.* Normally, if a witness gave testimony in which he acknowledged some sort of joint guilt or complicity, he could not claim any exemption from prosecution; see *Dig.* 48.18.1.26, and *Cod.* 9.2.17.1. But if he had reached a special agreement beforehand (*fide publica data*), a witness could obtain immunity (or a slave his freedom) if his testimony, though self-incriminating, also supported the prosecution of his accomplice.

Under the Republic, immunity from prosecution, *fides publica*, in return for giving testimony seems to have been solely the purview of the senate and not the presiding magistrate; see Livy 8.18, 39.19, and *Rab. Perd.* 28 *quae fides, Labiene, qui potuit sine senatus consulto dari?* The senate could, however, extend this authority to magistrates; see Livy 39.19 *de ceterorum indicum impunitate praemiisque consulibus permissum est*, and the immunity C. offers to T. Volturcius: *Cat.* 3.8 *fidem publicam iussu senatus dedi* with Dyck *ad loc.* On granting immunity in general, see Mommsen *Straf.* 456–458 and Ulpian at *Dig.* 48.18.1.26. For other examples of *fides publica*, see *TLL* VI 669.50. The term also has a wider semantic range beyond the granting of immunity; see Fernández de Buján (2001) 190, Morgan (2015) 93–94, and *Prou.* 3 with Grillo *ad loc.*

The term *index* could be used pejoratively, and these informants were often from a lower social class; see *N-P s.u. index.* On this passage, [Asc.] 114 remarks:

> There are certain instances in which immunity is granted to an informant: in the case of treason (*proditio*), impinging on the majesty of the Roman people (*maiestas*), and charges of that sort. There are also certain people who are able to be informants. Therefore, neither is an extortion case typically conducted through informants, nor is a person of senatorial rank able to give evidence without contravening the laws. An informant who is himself an accomplice

> of that crime reveals subterfuge in return for immunity. The sense of the passage here however is: 'You can be an informant, if you are allowed; but be a prosecutor – that's what we are debating here – you cannot.' Sufficiently abusive to censure Caecilius as an untrustworthy man.

The *deteriores*, *E*, and *t* report *iudicium* – a far more common word – for *indicium*. The two minims of *n* and *u* are frequently and easily confused. The reading *indicium* is found in the oldest medieval manuscript, *P*, and the fifth-century papyrus fragment, *Π*, which prompted a later scribe to write in the margin *nam legibus uetitum erat senatorem ferre indic*[*ium*], followed by a longer, somewhat confused text in Greek. Roberts (1938) 76 ventures to offer a translation:

> There was a law among the Romans to the effect that when two men, being private persons, committed a crime such as murder, if one of those who committed the crime gave information about it, saying *I have committed this crime with this man*, then the informant was not punished, but as a reward for the information received a pardon; but he who was denounced was punished. If, however, two senators committed a crime, then the informant was also punished … because it was his duty to give information. Do you (i.e. Caecilius) wish … to take up the case seriously? I (i.e. Cicero) shall be willing to speak your part for you. Does not the law prevent you, as a senator, from receiving pardon? For, as a senator, you ought not to have committed this crime … But do you, on the ground that you yourself are acting for the Sicilians, wish to conduct the prosecution, or do you prefer to hand it over to a man who is in a position to prosecute well and frankly? For I have a clear conscience. You are unable to prosecute him; for you were a partner in his crimes.

dari (ω : *fie*[*ri*] *Π*) The phrase *indicium fieri* is found at *Flac.* 40, 'but where, as here, *indicium* means "permission to give evidence (against an accomplice)" rather than "evidence", *dare* is obviously more suitable'; see Roberts (1938) 76.

postulas In a legal context, *postulare* refers to an official request before a magistrate; see §64 *delationem nominis postularet* n. C. uses a complementary infinitive with this verb, as he does here, primarily in his earlier writing, perhaps through the influence of Greek syntax; see H-Sz. 346.

quod tecum una fecerit The crimes committed by Verres during Caecilius' quaestorship in 73 BCE, to which Caecilius could bear witness and for which he would be excused for turning state's witness. C. has already mentioned the misappropriation of funds intended for grain-purchasing and the money demanded from taxpayers in lieu of grain; see §§30, 32–33. For *facere* as 'committing a crime', see *OLD s.u.* 21b and *TLL* VI 127.16.

34.5 concedo With a legal colouring, 'to concede, grant another a right'. See Berger *s.u.* and *TLL* IV 17.23–59.

si id lege permittitur On the origin of *lege*, §19 *lege agi* n. Not all people were allowed to give evidence as witnesses. Younger family members were generally disqualified, as well as freedmen if the matter involved their *patronus*; see Paul. *Sent.* 5.15.3. Those who were ineligible to bear witness were delineated by the individual statute that constituted the court. For example, anyone convicted of a criminal charge could not give evidence in a trial under the *lex Iulia de ui*; see *Dig.* 22.5.3.5. Greenidge 483 writes: 'Different laws establishing *quaestiones* may also have contained a list of persons disqualified *propter notam et infamiam uitae* such as was found in the *lex Iulia de ui*, for the category is thoroughly republican, and might quite as well have been found in laws of the Ciceronian as in those of the imperial period'. If the scholiasts are correct, then Caecilius would have been barred from presenting evidence in a *quaestio de repetundis*; see *indicium … dari* n. above.

sin autem de accusatione dicimus 'But if we are actually having a discussion about the right to conduct a prosecution, …'.

34.6 concedas oportet *Oportet* introduces a clause in the subjunctive without *ut*; see K-St. 2.2.236-237. In this case, the subordinated verb, *concedas*, precedes it and *oportet* acts as an emphasizing focuser: 'then surely you must concede that …'. See also *concedo* n. above.

34.7 alterius peccata The genitive coming before its noun usually signifies a contrast with a previous possessive – in this case, *suo* above; see Marouzeau 1.133–136.

demonstrare See §44 *ipsam causam … demonstrare* n.

§35

35.1 ac uide A colloquial Latin phrase that is a combination of an imperative and an exclamatory interjection; see Hofmann §45 with examples from Greek (ἰδοῦ, vel sim.), Roman comedy, and C.'s letters, e.g. *Att.* 11.21.3. The register is again appropriate to the imagined back-and-forth between C. and Caecilius; cf. §61 and similarly *Ver.* II.5.85. In almost all instances in which C. begins with *ac uide,* he is pointing out a contrast between two items; cf. §61 and *Dom* 84.

interfuturum sit introduces a *contentio* (ἀντίθετον); see §10 *quem maxime … quem minime …* n. Cf. §§34, 61. On this use of the subjunctive, see §42 *sit allatura* n., and for the future periphrastic, see *Verri crimini daturus sum* n. below.

tuamque is the reading in *P* and the six descendants of *S* used in this edition; *M* has *atque tuam.* Another descendant of *S,* Wolfenbüttel Extrav. 265.2, reads *et tuam,* and many editors, including Klotz, Müller, Zumpt, and Thomas, have given it pride of place. Zumpt dismisses the reading of *M* (in nullo meliorum librorum est) and writes *ad loc.* 'Optio datur, utrum velis *et tuam,* quod est in Guelf. pr. [Wolfenbüttel Extrav. 265.2], an *tuamque,* quod exhibet Guelf. 2. [*G*] Leid …. Mihi quidem coniunctio adiunctiva *que h.l.* prorsus displicet, eam ipsam ob causam quod adiungit, non, dum opponit, coniungit'. There are other examples of *-que* being used in this sense, however; cf. *Ver.* II.3.42 *Vide inter importunitatem tuam senatusque bonitatem quid intersit,* and 5.85 *Vide quid intersit inter tuam libidinem maiorumque auctoritatem.* The condition of the papyrus is such that *tuamque* is probable rather than certain.

35.2 ego … tu Disjunctive parallelism. The pronouns are both placed in the primary position for emphasis within their own clause and to contrast with one other.

etiam An additive particle that 'signals the addition of an element to a set' and is anteposed. Here it intensifies the relative clause *quae* ... *commisisti* and is paralleled by *ne* ... *quidem* below. On these particles, see Spevak (2010) 51, 53 respectively.

quae ... commisisti 'those offenses you committed', *OLD s.u. committo* 17a and *TLL* III 1910.45–1912.37. It is unclear if C. has anything in mind here at all, and perhaps he is only making a misleading adumbration; see [Asc.] 114. He will go on to mention the Agonis Affair (§§55–57) but nothing further. **tu sine Verre** 'without Verres' aid or assistance'; *OLD s.u. sine* 4.

Verri crimini daturus sum 'I am going to allege against Verres'; see *OLD s.u. do* 17b and *TLL* V 1.1691.79–1692.10. C. goes on to fulfil his intention; see *Ver.* II.3.225 *Vellem etiam hoc posset dicere, nihil ad se istam rationem pertinere, per quaestores rem frumentariam esse administratam. Ne id quidem ei licet dicere, propterea quod ipsius litterae recitantur ad ciuitates de ternis denariis missae.*

C. uses the periphrastic future more frequently in his letters than in other genres, and it would come to take on more prominence in colloquial language since it did away with the need to determine if a verb formed its future in *-bo* or *-am*. Even so, there would appear to be a difference in meaning between the periphrastic future used here and the simple future, *obicies*, below. In the periphrastic version, C. says what he *intends* to do, whereas, in the ordinary future tense, he presents what Caecilius would do at a trial as a certainty. The periphrastic future 'had already developed five distinct uses [in early Latin]: representing an act as intended, on the point of happening, destined to occur, and expressing resolve, and mere futurity'; see Lease (1919) 270–273. For this periphrastic construction, see also H-Sz. 312, and K-St. 2.1.760-762; see further *OLS* 1.429–435.

35.3 summam ... potestatem In public law, *potestas* referred to the official powers, rights and duties of a Roman magistrate and served as a point of reference in the political hierarchy. Officials vested with *maior potestas* could cancel or forbid the actions of a lower magistrate with *minor potestas*. Among the provincial magistrates, the governor would possess the *maior potestas* over all his other subordinates. In this particular case, a praetor could overrule the actions of his quaestor. For this reason, C. contends that Verres' greater power also entails greater responsibility for the actions of his staff, and says that he will consequently hold him accountable for any wrongdoing by Caecilius. The legality of this statement is questionable. While C. does express this general notion that a praetor should be responsible for his underlings at *Q. fr.* 1.1.10–11 (*his autem in rebus iam te usus ipse profecto erudiuit nequaquam satis esse ipsum has te habere uirtutes, sed esse circumspiciendum diligenter ut in hac custodia prouinciae non te unum sed omnis ministros imperi tui sociis et ciuibus et rei publicae praestare uideare* ...), it also seems from *Fam.* 2.18.2–3 (... *sin quid offenderit, sibi totum, nihil tibi offenderit*) that quaestors are responsible for their own conduct. In both passages from C.'s letters, however, the emphasis seems to be on protecting one's personal reputation rather than having to confront some legal action. C. threatens to ascribe Caecilius' crimes to Verres more for rhetorical effect than for legal argument, *pace* Brennan (2000) 837. If Caecilius had used his position or any delegated *imperium* for extortion, or if he had received money as a result of Verres' misconduct, then he would be liable himself under the *lex de repetundis.* However, one must wonder to what extent this provision would apply, since, as C. himself admits, *omnes intellegent ... ne praedam quidem adhuc esse diuisam.* C. perhaps obscures the notions of *potestas* for the purposes of *inuentio*; cf. §32 *tua potestas* n. and *reperiare* n. below. On *potestas*, see *N-P s.u.*, Kunkel and Wittmann (1995) 2.21–2, 207–224, and Berger *s.u.* On the liability to prosecution of those *quo ea pecunia peruenerit*, see Damon and Mackay (1995).

This adjective–noun combination is also part of a long-range hyperbaton as the noun and its modifier are separated from each other by *ipse haberet*; see Powell (2010a) 174–176. In such hyperbata, the first element is usually a determiner or a quantifier – in this case, the latter – and receives additional emphasis. Powell (2010a) 184 also explains that this sort of hyperbaton does not characterize a passage as rhetorical or colloquial, but rather bestows upon it 'a generalised *oral* feature which surfaces in those kinds of written prose texts (letters, dialogues, and the less formal parts of speeches) which approach most closely the character of a reasonably close imitation or evocation of oral discourse', and therfore all the more fitting here in a part of the *diuinatio* in which C. portrays himself as conversing with Caecilius; §37 *familiariter tecum loquar.*

35.4 contra Following the second of two adversative pronouns in primary position; cf. *Phil.* 8.16 *Ego P. Clodium arbitrabar perniciosum ciuem, sceleratum, libidinosum, impium, audacem, facinerosum, tu contra sanctum, temperantem innocentem, modestum, retinendum ciuem et optandum*; also *B. Afr.* 22.4, Sen. *Dial.* 4.34.5, and with *ille, Ver.* II.4.109, and Ter. *Ad.* 44. See further *TLL* IV 739.72.

ne quae ille quidem C. presumably uses this phrase in lieu of *ne ea quidem quae ille* for the sake of symmetry. For the attraction of *quidem* to *ille*, see §28 *illi quidem* n.

obicies See §31 *obicies? Si obicies* n.

35.5 coniunctus The notion is repeated for rhetorical effect from §32 *coniunctus est* and §34 *uoluntatem … coniunctam* above. The implication is one of criminal collusion. The perfect tense also suggests that the effect of the action is still ongoing; see K-St. 2.1.130-131.

reperiare This short digression on the collection of the grain tithe is framed with mirrored phrasing; *daturus es huic crimini … Verri crimini daturus sum*; *potuisti prohibere … te non prohiberet*; *quem ad modum defensurus esset non reperiebat … coniunctus cum eo reperiare.* C. has anticipated a line of argument from Caecilius to the tune that his tenure under Verres would give him inside knowledge of the governor's misdeeds, especially with regard to misappropriation of public funds. C. instead portrays this inside knowledge as a liability, since, in C.'s estimation, Caecilius must share the responsibility with Verres. C. goes on to present this liability in a false dilemma: either Caecilius must incriminate himself, or he must impair his prosecution by omitting serious charges against his former *propraetor*; see §31 *utrum … an* n.

If one considers the *Diuinatio* as a pedagogical product, this passage, while ostensibly discussing the moral character of the ideal Roman advocate, demonstrates methods of *inuentio* – and the verb *reperire* may be a play on this idea. C. begins with a *res* (a fact or statement that we shall accept as true), namely that public funds for the purchase of grain have not been distributed (§32) and that some other unspecified malfeasance has occurred (§33 *alia magis occulta furta*). Through a process of *inuentio* and an implicit application of status theory, C. devises arguments aimed at two possible conclusions, wherein either Caecilius and Verres (§32), or just Verres alone (§35), should be held culpable for the misdeed. On the first line of argumentation, C. establishes that Caecilius had power over the public purse (*pecuniam publicam tu tractabas*), and therefore he could be considered part of a criminal conspiracy (*qui cum reo criminum societate coniunctus est*). On the second line of argumentation, he does not ask if Caecilius had *potestas* but rather who had the *maior potestas*. With that second approach, he claims, he could pin on Verres the embezzlement of public funds as well as any misdeeds committed by Caecilius alone.

C. employs both these lines of argument in his denunciation of Verres in the *actio secunda*. On the one hand, Verres is held culpable for his actions as quaestor (*Ver.* II.1.39 *Nullae sunt occultiores insidiae quam eae quae latent in simulatione offici aut in aliquo necessitudinis nomine*) and on the other, he is to be held responsible for the actions normally entrusted to quaestors during his praetorship (*Ver.* II.3.225).

Rhetorical Education, Oratorical Ability and Experience (§§35–43)

'To sustain a case of this magnitude, a good orator must have some training and experience in public speaking, politics, and administration. And I realize that I am getting into dangerous territory when talking about one's gifts, education, and abilities, so I will not speak about myself. But Caecilius, do you really have the mental and physical ability to present a compelling description of all of Verres' crimes and outrages over the course of his entire political career? Maybe you could have managed it if you were better educated, but as it is, you learnt Greek and Latin in Sicily and not in Athens and Rome. Such a highly visible and anticipated trial will require the finest focus, memory, strength, voice, and powers of public speaking. I would not dare say that I have all of

these qualities, but at least I have devoted my entire life to developing them; even so the thought of conducting such a high-profile prosecution makes me shudder.'

C. resumes the discussion initiated in §27 on the qualities of a good orator. After focusing on the moral qualities and behaviour requisite to successful prosecution (*uir bonus*), he explains that the orator must have some forensic experience as well as abilities in argumentation and public speaking (*dicendi peritus*).

35.6 quid? ... Caecili C. marks the transition to a new line of argument in a lively and attention-grabbing style with the interrogative and a vocative, both of which are commonly so used. For the vocative, see §2 *iudices* n. For the interrogative to mark a rhetorical transition, see Seyffert 1§27, and *OLD s.u. quis* 12b. Cf. *Mil.* 43, where it is also followed by a vocative, and *Rosc. Am.* 43 with Dyck *ad loc.*

illa ... contemnendane tibi uidentur esse *Illa* remains in the neuter plural even though the multiple nouns to which it refers are all feminine. The pronoun here is anticipatory and looks forward to the discussion of *facultas, dicendi,* etc. in the following sentence. On anticipatory *ille,* see H-Sz. 413. The enclitic *-ne* is only rarely attached to forms of *ille* and attaches itself most logically to the pivotal idea in the sentence; see H-Sz. 461. **uidentur** signals an embedded secondary focalization that offers the point of view assigned to Caecilius. This point of view is one of naïveté and short-sightedness and is used to further C.'s characterization of Caecilius.

35.7 sustineri See §27 *sustinere* n.

nullo modo potest A mannerism of C.'s. He uses it more often than all other writers of classical Latin combined. In the Verrines alone, cf. *Ver.* II.3.35, 5.45, 5.170.

35.8 aliqua ... aliqua ... aliqua The anaphora and tricolon *crescens* emphasize the paucity of thought Caecilius has given to the skills required of a successful prosecutor. See *OLD s.u. aliquis*[2] 2, and on anaphora, see Lausberg §629.

facultas agendi ... dicendi consuetudo *Facultas*, with its roots in *facio*, implies an ability to lead a trial, while *consuetudo* focuses on habituation and practice. This pairing of ability and experience is mirrored in *ratio* and *exercitatio*; see n. below.

in foro, iudiciis, legibus An understanding or experience in political life, the courts, and issues at law was vital for the forensic orator. As part of his education, a young man with ambitions for public life would have embarked upon a kind of apprenticeship that would have introduced him to the business of the Roman Forum and to individuals with judicial experience and knowledge of political life. C. followed M. Antonius and L. Licinius Crassus, who took an interest in his theoretical education, and the famed jurist Q. Mucius Scaevola, who taught C. about Roman law. Caecilius may not have had access to such exceptional education. On the so-called *tirocinium fori*, see *Brut.* 304–305, Corbeill (2007) 70–77, and White (2023).

35.9 aut ratio aut exercitatio *Ratio* refers to cognition and theoretical knowledge, while *exercitatio* indicates practice and exercise that lead to proficiency; see *OLD s.u.* and *TLL* V 2.1382.7–25 (and 1381.17–29). Much of this section of the speech addresses the traditional triad of natural ability (*ingenium/natura*), theory (*ars*), and practice (*exercitatio/usus*) as the necessary elements for eloquence. The relative merits of each of these became the subject of debate, particularly between natural ability and theory; see *De orat.* 1.113–159, 2.74–98, and Quint. *Inst.* 2.19. C. also remarks to his brother Quintus at *De orat.* 1.5: *solesque non numquam hac de re a me in disputationibus nostris dissentire, quod ego eruditissimorum hominum artibus eloquentiam contineri statuam, tu autem illam ab elegantia doctrinae segregandam putes et in quodam ingeni atque exercitationis genere ponendam.* C. wades into this debate in this speech and implies that an effective orator must possess all three of these elements. Although he can scarcely remark on his natural ability (§36) without seeming arrogant, he demonstrates it throughout the speech, and he also mentions his extensive experience and devotion to the study of rhetoric (§41, *passim*). Caecilius, on the other hand, is shown to be deficient in all of them.

§36

36.2 scopuloso difficilique in loco uerser In C. *scopulosus* appears only here in the speeches, and otherwise only in *De orat.* 3.69, where it is not used figuratively. However, the nautical metaphor of the orator dealing with difficult topics as a ship would navigate rocks and rough seas is common; cf. *Cael.* 51 *Sed quoniam emersisse iam e uadis et scopulos praeteruecta uidetur oratio mea, perfacilis mihi reliquus cursus ostenditur.* This particular phrase from the *Diu. Caec.* must have resonated with the author of [Quint.] *Decl.* 259.12: *Intellego, iudices, quam difficili ac uelut scopuloso loco uersetur oratio mea.* On nautical metaphors, see Aßfahl (1932) 66–69 and the bibliography in Pöschl (1964) *s.u. Schiff.* On metaphors more generally, see Quint. *Inst.* 8.6.4–18, and see further Lausberg §§558–564. A second hand in *P* has made a supralineal correction of *scopuloso* to *scrupuloso*, a word which C. only uses at *Tusc.* 4.33: *ex quibus quoniam tamquam ex scrupulosis cotibus enavigavit oratio.* The correct reading, however, is not in doubt. The rare use of *scopulosus* is confirmed by the later hand in *Π* that wrote '*scopuloso*' in large letters at the top-left of the folio.

cum ... tum ... 'every sort of arrogance is distasteful, but it is especially off-putting when it comes to intelligence and talent'. See §2 *cum summum ... tum non nullum* n.

arrogantia Discussing the difficulties and downfalls of self-praise is a common topic of rhetorical education; see *Inu.* 1.22 *Beniuolentia quattuor ex locis comparatur ... ab nostra, si de nostris factis et officiis sine arrogantia dicemus,* and Dem. 5.4 Ἀκριβῶς δ' εἰδώς, ὦ ἄνδρες Ἀθηναῖοι, τὸ λέγειν περὶ ὧν αὐτὸς εἶπέ τις καὶ περὶ αὑτοῦ παρ' ὑμῖν ἀεὶ τῶν πάνυ λυσιτελούντων τοῖς τολμῶσιν ὄν, οὕτως ἡγοῦμαι φορτικὸν καὶ ἐπαχθὲς ὥστε ἀνάγκην οὖσαν ὁρῶν ὅμως ἀποκνῶ. See also Quint. 11.1.15–28. On the *odium* of self-praise, see the introduction to §§2–5.

36.3 odiosa 'distasteful'. The word is commonly used with this meaning in colloquial language; cf. Pl. *Cur.* 45; Ter. *Ph.* 937. It is used nigh synonymously with *molestus* here, and this collocation with *molestus* is not uncommon in C.; cf. *Sen.* 47, *Rosc. Am.* 47 with Landgraf *ad loc.*, and *Flac.* 13. Gradations of meaning do exist between the two words, as he makes a distinction between them at *Att.* 13.52.2: ἐπισταθμείαν *odiosam mihi, dixi, non molestam.* Acknowledging social norms and expected behaviour also advances C.'s status as an orator. Rhetorical education and good oratory were not simply about producing compelling speeches, but also about learning and demonstrating social expectations. For decorum in oratorical speech, see *Off.* 1.132.

ingeni atque eloquentiae C. moves on from rhetorical education and practice to the element of natural talent; see §35 *aut ratio aut exercitatio* n. This collocation occurs mostly in C.'s rhetorical works. In fact, in speaking of the trials against Verres, he says at *Brut.* 318 *sed omni huic sermoni propositum est, non ut ingenium et eloquentiam meam perspicias, unde longe absum, sed ut laborem et industriam.* Similarly, at *Rosc. Am.* 34, they are the desirable characteristics of a *patronus* and an *orator*, respectively; cf. also *Brut.* 59 *ut enim hominis decus ingenium, sic ingeni ipsius lumen est eloquentia.* But *ingenium* and *eloquentia* as objects of praise are not particularly pleasing to the audience in a laudatory speech; see *De orat.* 2.344.

multo molestissima An alliterative end to the sentence with a double cretic rhythm. On the persuasive implications of recognizing social expectations, see *odiosa* n. above.

36.4 nihil dico *Praeteritio.* Cf. *Quinct.* 30, *Ver.* II.1.157, 5.11. C. frequently uses the phrase *nihil dico amplius.* Cf. *Arch.* 8, *Dom.* 17, *Planc.* 17, 88. **dico ... dicere ... dicerem** polyptoton. The repetition may have suggested the dichotomy of *facere non dicere.* C.'s speech here is a demonstration of his *ingenium* rather than an empty discussion. C. says of Hermagoras in *Inu.* 1.8 *nam satis in ea uidetur ex antiquis artibus ingeniose et diligenter electas res collocasse et nonnihil ipse quoque noui protulisse; uerum oratori minimum est de arte loqui, quod hic fecit, multo maximum ex arte dicere, quod eum minime potuisse omnes uidemus.*

§37

37.1 De te, Caecili C. expands and contracts the narrative spaces throughout the *Diuinatio.* First, he addressed not just the jurors but also the attendant crowd (§1); then he spends much of his time addressing only the empanelled jurors. In this passage, he contracts the narrative space to focus on one addressee, his opponent. He would seem thus to be suspending the fiction of the *diuinatio* and initiating an extra-discursive conversation directly with Caecilius, which continues until §47 *putemus.* The listening and reading audience is compelled to look upon this episode as an outside observer. To create this more intimate narrative space, the linguistic register changes to a more colloquial style; C. signals this change by saying that he is going to 'have a conversation' (*loquar*), as opposed to speaking formally (*dicere*); on register change, see the following notes.

Thomas *ad loc.* construes the prepositional phrase *de te* as depending on *existimes* far below. The preposition *de*, however, can introduce a looser connection and indicate a change of subject; cf. *Fam.* 12.30.5 *de Attio Dionysio nihil puto esse.* It may here be performing a kind of double duty in which the reader would at first understand it as a change of topic and then only later construe it with *existimes.*

The later Latin rhetorician, Julius Rufinianus, cites this passage as an example of *communicatio,* or ἀνακοίνωσις, construed as a mode similar to *dubitatio,* in which the speaker asks a series of fictitious deliberative questions about the proper method of speaking that he should follow (10 = *RLM* 41.9). See further Lausberg §779, and Quint. 9.2.20–25. Cf. *Rab. Per.* 22 *Tu denique, Labiene, quid faceres tali in re ac tempore?*

mehercule This colloquial exclamation was an abbreviated form of *me hercules adiuuet* or *me hercule adiuues,* only properly used by men, although there are some exceptions; see Gellius *NA* 11.6 *Nusquam igitur scriptum inuenire est apud idoneos quidem scriptores aut 'mehercle' feminam dicere aut 'mecastor' uirum.* C. says at *Orat.* 157 that he prefers the sound of *mehercule* over *mehercules,* and he uses it almost exclusively in his later oratory except at *Deiot.* 17; see the latter with Gotoff *ad loc.* As for its position in the sentence, it is never the first word 'in mustergültiger Prosa'; see Landgraf *ad Rosc. Am.* 58. The shortened form, *hercle,* perhaps came from southern Italian dialects, and *mehercle* 'ist eine frühe Kreuzung von *hercle* und *mehercules*'; Hofmann §36 and see also Schulze (1966) 310–312. See also the full-length study by Gagnér (1920). The tone suggested here is hard to judge; perhaps one of feigned exasperation, especially when paired with the anacoluthon below; see *de maximis acerbissimisque rebus* n. below.

extra hanc contentionem certamenque The change in register is consonant with the sort of narrative space that C. wants to create. One style of speech is appropriate to oratory, another to conversation between friends; see *Off.* 1.132 *Et quoniam magna uis orationis est, eaque duplex, altera contentionis, altera sermonis, contentio disceptationibus tribuatur iudiciorum, contionum, senatus, sermo in circulis, disputationibus, congressionibus familiarium uersetur, sequatur etiam conuiuia.* **certamen** It is part of C.'s rhetorical strategy in this particular *diuinatio* to represent the procedure as an oratorical contest rather than an inquiry into the motives or grievances of the would-be prosecutor; see Introduction §IV. Alliterative pairs are more common in C.'s earlier speeches; for this alliterative pair, see also *Ver.* II.1.3 and *Leg.* 3.1. For the metaphor of forensic activity as military engagement, see §1 *defenderim multos, laeserim neminem* n.

37.2 familiariter Speaking 'as amongst friends' is a mark of a *sermo* as opposed to an *oratio*; see n. above. The conversational tone continues to affirm the image of this scene as an interaction between teacher and student. 'The personal relationship ... was at the center of classical notions of instruction'; see Konstan (1993) 11. For more on teacher–student interaction, see Maurice (2013) 95–101.

loquar As opposed to *dicam*, see §21 *loquere* n.

tu ipse *Ipse* by its nature is an intensifying pronoun, but postposition provides additional emphasis. Changing the position of *ipse* relative to the noun that it modifies for the sake of intensification varies from author to author. For example, postposition is rare in Caesar but far more common in C., as here; see Marouzeau 1.185–187.

quem ad modum existimes 'how you have formed an opinion of yourself'. On the hyperbaton, see *de te, Caecili* n. above.

37.3 uide etiam atque etiam 'carefully consider'; see *OLD s.u.* 1c and *TLL* V 2.930.18–63. Cf. §46. The phrase is slightly less common in later speeches. This interaction between C. and Caecilius allows C. to demonstrate, in the *Diuinatio*, methods for confronting Hortensius in the trial proper and prefigures *Ver.* II.5.174, in which C. addresses Hortensius: *Quam ob rem te quoque, Hortensi, si qui monendi locus ex hoc loco est, moneo uideas etiam atque etiam et consideres quid agas, quo progrediare, quem hominem et qua ratione defendas.*

tu te collige 'come to your senses'; see *OLD s.u. colligo*[1] 17a and *TLL* III 1614.52–1615.9. On the juxtaposition of the same pronoun in different cases, see §27 *tute tui* n.

37.4 qui sis (*PM* : *quis sis* γ) The reading in the French family is attributable to dittography and/or correction. The first *s* is commonly dropped for the sake of euphony and *qui sit* (*sim, sis*) is a particularly common construction; cf. §20 *nescimus qui sis*, and *Ver.* II.2.188 *qui sit is Verrucius.* See further Löfstedt (1956) 2.84.

putasne … putasne … putasne The first of a series of three ascending rhetorical questions (the others coming at 38.1 and 38.5) that artistically follow the three imperatives above, *uide … collige … considera.* In fact, despite the colloquial tone of this passage, rhetorical elements and balanced groupings are in full effect. In the third iteration, *te* is absent before *posse* in all manuscripts of authority, but the repetitive phrasing suggests that Thomas was right to supply it.

de maximis acerbissimisque rebus A slight anacoluthon. The thought seems to be completed by *tot res … sustinere* below, which has no clear syntactical relationship to this prepositional phrase. C. changes construction after the intervening *cum* clause. Anacoluthon is one of those linguistic features that are a 'deliberate evocation of the spoken word'; see Powell (2014) 49. However, Mayer (2005) 203 finds these features problematic, noting that '[anacoluthon] does not appear to be a rhetorical device. Sometimes it may be purely conversational, but anacolutha in periodic sentences are lapses from the strictly controlled syntax we find elsewhere, and cannot be so defended'. See his article for more examples of anacolutha in C. Here, however, when seen in the context of the other linguistic features, the evocation of a conversational tone is undeniable.

37.5 causam sociorum fortunasque prouinciae As a sort of ring composition, C. reiterates the points that he has brought up in §27 *in mentem ... defendere.* See also §2 *fortunis* n.

37.6 ius populi Romani In particular, the extortion from, in addition to the torture and execution of, Roman citizens. This will be the main theme of the fifth speech of the *actio secunda,* though C. makes it clear throughout the second hearing that Verres mistreated Sicilian provincials as well as Roman citizens; cf. *Ver.* II.3.59. For the meaning of *ius,* see §18 *ius* n.

grauitatem Also mentioned at §§8 and 27 and closely associated with the idea of *seueritas,* which C. mentions in connection with the courts at §§8 and 21. *Grauitas* is also a particular virtue of the senatorial order, whose control of the criminal courts would come to an end this same year; see Hellegouarc'h (1972) 283, 290. The reading preserved in the French family is *grauitatemque,* but in these series of rhetorical questions, C. prefers asyndeton between discrete units. Here he invokes provincial concerns, national interest, and the prerogative of the senate.

iudiciorum The MSS unanimously report *iudici,* but Shackleton Bailey (1979) 241 convincingly argues: 'Verres' prosecutor would be upholding the judicial system, not this particular tribunal. All analogy calls for *iudiciorum legumque*; cf. §27 *uim legum, grauitatem iudiciorum,* §35 *in foro, iudiciis, legibus,* §68 *leges iudiciaque,* §70 *ad legum defensionem iudiciorumque auctoritatem.*' To these one might add §8, *Verr.* 1.82, 5.186, *Mil.* 18, *Phil.* 8.10, and 11.

37.7 tot res tam grauis tam uarias 'so many issues of such gravity and variety'. Cf. *Rosc. Am.* 43 *tot praedia, tam pulchra, tam fructuosa, Sul.* 40 *tot res tantas, tam uarias, tam repentinas,* and *Phil.* 2.67 *uix uidetur tot res tam dissipatas, tam distantibus in locis positas tam cito absorbere potuisse.*

uoce Demosthenes is reported to have uttered the famous dictum that the three most important features of oratory were delivery, delivery, delivery. And among the aspects of delivery, voice was considered the most important; see *De orat.* 3.213–225 with Fantham (2004) 292–298. For this reason, Quintilian 11.3.1 notes that *pronuntiatio* was one of the most prominent terms for 'delivery'. The orator was obviously constrained to some extent by the voice that nature had given him, but other aspects of it could be strengthened, such as stability and vocal flexibility, through declamation and with the aid of professional voice coaches, φωνασκοί. The voice also had to be modulated to match the material presented and was a key component in moving the emotions of the audience. The *Diuinatio* itself would have provided C. with various material to demonstrate his vocal mastery and appropriate use of modulation. During this discussion of oratory, the conversational tone (*sermo*) would have been most appropriate, and within this subcategory, the explicative conversation (*demonstratio*) requires a calm voice (*remissa uoce*); see *Rhet. Her.* 3.23. For rhetorical handbooks on voice, see Arist. *Rhet.* 3.1, Quint. 11.3.15–65, and *Rhet. Her.* 3.20–25, which has a longer discussion than that in *De orat.*, where C. puts more emphasis on gesture and expression. On voice coaches, see *N-P s.u. phonaskoi.* Quint. 11.3.8 says that Hortensius' written speeches give no grounds for his outstanding reputation and concludes that his high regard must be due, in no small part, to his delivery. Both *pronuntiatio* and *actio* encompass both voice and gesture; on the latter, see §46 *gestu ipso ac motu corporis* n.

memoria was added to the *officia oratoris* by the Rhodian or Pergamene School, but an interest in it surfaces already in the Sophists. It became a vital skill when speakers had to address an assembly or court without notes. Orators at either end of the spectrum of memory were noted: C. Scribonius Curio's was said to be horrible (*Brut.* 217 *memoria autem ita fuit nulla, ut aliquotiens, tria cum proposuisset, aut quartum adderet aut tertium quaereret*). Hortensius', on the other hand, was exceptional (*Brut.* 301 *primum memoria tanta, quantam in nullo cognouisse me arbitror, ut quae se cum commentatus esset, ea sine scripto uerbis eisdem redderet quibus cogitauisset*). For a further discussion on memory, see *De orat.* 2.350–360, and Quint. *Inst.* 11.2.1–51.

37.8 consilio *Consilium* was the overall strategic approach of one's speech that encompassed aspects of *inuentio, dispositio,* good judgement, stasis theory, etc.; see Quint. 6.5.3–11 and *TLL* IV 456.73. In fact, Quintilian cites C.'s strategy of delivering a short speech in the *actio prima* to avoid having the trial of Verres pushed over into the next year as an excellent example of *consilium*; see Quint. 6.5.11 *Illud dicere satis habeo, nihil esse non modo in orando sed in omni uita prius consilio, frustraque sine eo tradi ceteras artis.* In an echo of this passage in the *peroratio,* C. asks the judges to choose the individual whom they regard as able to *magnitudinem causae ... sustinere ... consilio.* Though here the particular rhetorical meaning is more prominent, its collocation with *ingenium* is not uncommon; cf. §44, *De orat.* 1.184, *Sest.* 47, and *Har.* 40.

ingenio Innate ability or native talent that must be maintained by rigorous study (*industria*) and is often discussed in opposition to theoretical learning; see §35 *aut ratio aut exercitatio* n.

sustinere See §27 *sustinere* n.

§38

38.2 quaestura Verres first served as quaestor in 84 and was assigned by the senate to the consul Gnaeus Papirius Carbo (*MRR* 2.57, 60, 64; *RE* 38) in Picenum. Carbo was serving his second term as consul alongside L. Cornelius Cinna, who would die in a mutiny that year, and stayed on as the sole consul for the remainder of the year. In 83 he became the proconsul of Italy and Cisalpine Gaul as he prepared to oppose Sulla upon the latter's return from the East. Verres stayed on, presumably as *proquaestor,* under Carbo, but must have correctly gauged the unfolding political and military situation and so defected to Sulla. During this time, he is accused by C. of absconding with 600,000 sesterces of public money intended for Carbo that was neither returned to the public treasury nor handed over to Sulla. In return for his political allegiance, Sulla let Verres have the property of proscribed individuals in the area of Beneventum. For C.'s account of Verres' tenure as quaestor, see *Ver.* II.1.34–40 and 3.177.

legatione Verres was dispatched in 80 as a legate for Cn. Cornelius Dolabella (*MRR* 2.80; *RE* 135), who was proconsul of Cilicia in 80 and 79, and assumed the position of *legatus pro quaestore* after the death of Dolabella's quaestor, Gaius Publicius Malleolus (*RE* 19). Verres had been Malleolus' guardian (*tutor*), and C. alleges that he more or less kept his ward's estate for himself; see *Ver.* II.1.41–102, and 3.177. Upon Dolabella's return to Rome, Verres testified in 78 against his former commander during an extortion trial in which Dolabella was convicted; see *TLRR* 135. C. suggests that Verres pinned a number of his own crimes on Dolabella to escape prosecution himself; see *Ver.* II.1.95–97. See also *in Achaia, Asia Pamphyliaque* n. below. On the relationship between a quaestor and his commander, see the introduction to §§59–65.

The general duties of a *legatus* were malleable; Varro *L.* 5.87 says that they were those *qui lecti publice, quorum opera consilioque uteretur peregre magistratus, quiue nuntii senatus aut populi essent.* For more on the position of *legatus*, see *Staats.* 2.696–701, Schleussner (1978), and *N-P s.u. legatus.* For prorogation, see §3 *per triennium* n.

praetura Verres had been *praetor urbanus* in 74, and the discussion of his tenure constitutes a substantial portion of the first speech of the *actio secunda.* C. alleges that Verres perpetrated several miscarriages of justice to defraud heirs of their patrimony and let out government contracts for frivolous building works; see *Ver.* II.1.103–158. For example, Verres issued an *edictum perpetuum* that retroactively applied an inheritance statute, the *lex Voconia,* which prohibited women from being named heirs, in one instance in order to strike up a deal with the next of kin, who would be due to receive the estate of the deceased; see *Ver.* II.1.104–114. On other occasions, Verres found reasons to overturn bequests and profit from the new arrangements. The fact that Verres then omitted these clauses from his praetorian edict in Sicily, C. suggests, proves his inconsistency in applying the law and consequently his intent to defraud. Among his other injustices, C. also claims that Verres accepted an outrageously high bid to straighten the columns on the Temple of Castor and Pollux (this being unnecessary and impossible work, according to C.) in an embezzlement scheme; see *Ver.* II.1.129–150. This story would have been particularly effective if the *actio secunda* had actually taken place, since the temple façade was visible from the location of the Extortion Court; see Introduction §III. For the general duties of the *praetor urbanus*, see Brennan (2000) 98–108, 396–398, 630–633.

38.3 Romae ... Italia The sites, respectively, of Verres' urban praetorship and his quaestorship under Dolabella; see *praetura* n. above and *quaestura* n. above.

in Achaia, Asia Pamphyliaque Verres travelled through these territories on his way to meeting Dolabella in Cilicia and then later while on assignment from his commander. C. outlines his various depredations and outrages; most involved art-theft, others extortion and miscarriages of justice. **Achaia** Here Verres is supposed to have tortured a local magistrate, stolen gold from Athens, and made off from Delos with sacred art, which he was forced to return by a kind of divine intervention; see *Ver.* II.1.44–48. Achaia is 'the official name for the Roman province of Greece, commemorating Rome's defeat of the Achaean Confederacy in 146 BCE'; see *OCD s.u.* Its boundaries fluctuated, and early on it seems to have included Epirus and Thessaly. *Achaia* is the proper spelling of the Roman province, not *Achaea*; see Oliver (1983) 152 n. 6. **Asia** C. accuses Verres of extorting meals, horses and other gifts. In particular, he is cited for stealing artwork from Chios, Erythrae, Halicarnassus, Tenedos, and the Temple of Juno at Samos; see *Ver.* II.1.49–52. A central narrative episode in the first speech of the *actio secunda* also occurred in Asia – the so-called Episode at Lampsacus; see *Ver.* II.1.63–85 with Steel (2004). In another vignette, Verres, after demanding a ship and an escort from the community of Miletus on his way to Myndus, kept the ship, forced the crew to walk back, and then eventually sold it back to two Milesian residents to turn a profit; see *Ver.* II.1.86–90. **Pamphylia** Verres is likewise alleged to have stolen famous statuary from Aspendus and Perga; see *Ver.* II.1.53–55. Pamphylia was on the southern coast of Asia Minor, northeast of Lycia, in the Roman province of Cilicia; see *AAW* 65. The name of the province, as well as the provincial boundaries, changed over time; see *N-P s.u.* For these locations, see the map in Appendix B. Mentally situating Verres' crimes both temporally and geographically may have helped in memorizing and organizing them; see *n.* below.

38.4 locis temporibusque diuisa sint C. has just mentioned the temporal periods marked by Verres' series of offices and his physical whereabouts during each phase. In continuing Caecilius' rhetorical education, C. reminds him that the orator must also focus on the proper structure of his oration and the arrangement of his arguments; for *dispositio* or *collocatio*, see *Inu.* 1.9, *Rhet. Her.* 3.16, and Quint. 3.3.1. See further Lausberg §443–452. The orator should choose whichever arrangement best serves *utilitas*; see Quint. 7.1.1. What C. says here also prefigures the organizing principle for the *partitio* of the *actio secunda*, for which he will use Verres' aforementioned progression of offices; see *Ver.* II.1.34 *Hi sunt anni consumpti in quaestura et legatione Asiatica et praetura urbana et praetura Siciliensi; quare haec eadem erit quadripertita distributio totius accusationis meae.* With such a dizzying array of evidence and detail, the Verrines must have been a model of how to structure and present a series of complex observations, allegations and evidence. In them, C. broadly adopts the *modus per tempora*, which arranges items in a temporal sequence; see Fortun. 3.1 (*RLM* 120–121), and Mart. Cap. 30 (*RLM* 471–472).

38.5 criminibus et oratione distinguere Loosely, 'to organize these points in your speech and assign the appropriate charges to each'. The infinitive here is more or less synonymous with *diuidere* and refers to *dispositio*; see n. above. C. calls attention to the difficulty of deciding which charge should be levelled against Verres' various misdemeanours in the *actio secunda*; see *Ver.* II.4.88 *Vnum hoc crimen uidetur esse et a me pro uno ponitur, de Mercurio Tyndaritano; plura sunt, sed ea quo pacto distinguere ac separare possim nescio.*

38.6 in eius modi reo 'when dealing with a defendant of this sort'; *OLD s.u. in* 42.

38.7 libidinose ... nefarie ... crudeliter Tricolon. The phrase looks forward to *Ver.* I.56 *Dicimus C. Verrem, cum multa libidinose,* *multa crudeliter in ciuis Romanos atque socios, multa in deos hominesque nefarie fecerit, tum praeterea quadringentiens sestertium ex Sicilia contra leges abstulisse.* **libidinose** C. uses the positive degree of this adverb only in the Verrines in reference to Verres' general demeanour; cf. *Ver.* II.5.85. For other examples of Verres' sexual misconduct, see II.1.64–67. 5.28, 31, 34, 81–82.

aeque … uideantur A move toward compassion which requires the audience to assume the point of view of the sufferer. Compassion is discussed in rhetorical works under several headings, including *conquestio, commiseratio,* and *miseratio*; see Lausberg §439. The fullest explication of arousing compassion in the audience is given at Arist. *Rhet.* 1385b13–1386b. There Aristotle requires that the suffering be (1) serious, not trivial, (2) not caused by the person's culpable action or, if deserved, disproportionate, and (3) similar to suffering that the observer can experience as well. It is an important part of the persuasive process in obtaining justice for the aggrieved; see Nussbaum (1996) 37. On enargeia, see *uisa sunt* n. below.

acerba et indigna 'painful and undeserved'. The adjectives correspond to the Aristotelian requirements that the impact upon the sufferer is painful (λυπηρός) and unwarranted (κἂν οἴωνταί τινας εἶναι τῶν ἐπιεικῶν· ὁ γὰρ μηδένα οἰόμενος πάντας οἰήσεται ἀξίους εἶναι κακοῦ); see n. above. C. will go on to demonstrate in the Verrines the method for arousing pity by fulfilling the third Aristotelian requirement for individuals to be able to identify with the sufferers – namely that they or their friends may suffer something similar; see *Ver.* II.1.112 *Atque ego non dubito quin, ut mihi, cui mea filia maxime cordi est, res haec acerba uidetur atque indigna, sic uni cuique uestrum, qui simili sensu atque indulgentia filiarum commouemini.* Cf. *Ver.* II.2.95. The collocation of these adjectives is common in the Verrines; cf. II.1.137, 4.100, 5.31.

38.8 his … illis Referring to the jurors in Rome and the victims in Sicily, respectively. The separation implied by the deictic pronouns *hic* and *ille* also tacitly recognizes a perceived separation both between Romans and provincials and between the jury and the victims; see §28 *hominum genus…* n. The act of evoking compassion is a key mechanism by which that distance is shortened.

uisa sunt The focalizing verb (*uideri*) does not need to be repeated except to indicate a change in tense. More importantly, the repetition emphasizes the focalization through the eyes of the victims; see *aeque … uideantur* n. above. C. is highlighting the process of vivid description (*euidentia*, ἐνάργεια), which places the speaker and the audience in the position of eyewitnesses; see further Lausberg §§810–819.

§39

39.1 magna This entire concluding section of the 'miniature rhetorical handbook' is imbued with a condescending, magisterial tone. *Magna*, though given some added emphasis in primary position, still retains a banality that colours this passage, as though C. were talking down to Caecilius; see Marouzeau 1.91. To keep up the nigh derisive tone, C. uses *magnum* again below.

mihi crede Another colloquial injection, which in this context is not only informal but also patronizing. With this passage obviously in mind, Don. Ter. *Ad.* 101 remarks *quasi imperito dicit 'mihi crede', non 'me intellege'. quod imitatus Cicero sic Caecilium exagitat …; hic enim et auctoritas dicentis et contemptus ostenditur audientis.* Cf. §32 *mihi crede* n.

noli haec contemnere C. similarly urges the jurors not to spurn the testimony of a Sicilian delegation at *Ver.* II.4.113 *Quas illorum querimonias nolite, per deos immortalis, aspernari, nolite contemnere ac neglegere, iudices!*

39.2 dicenda, demonstranda, explicanda Homeoteleuton. On *explicare*, see §27 *explicare … exponere* n. Cf. *Clu.* 104 *dicta et exposita et demonstrata sunt omnia.*

39.3 exponenda … agenda *Exponere* means to state the facts, presumably without persuasive embellishment (see §27 *explicare … exponere* n.), as opposed to the sense of argument inherent in *agere*: 'a case cannot simply be stated, but it must be firmly and eloquently argued'. For this sense of *exponere*, see *Pis.* 7 *Exposui breuiter consulatum meum.* **agenda** C. speaks of *actio* – the actual performance of the speech, in other words, delivery.

copioseque Used with regard to eloquence, see *TLL* IV 915.81–916.59. Cf. *Planc.* 37, *Ac.* 2.63, and *Cael.* 29 *res tamen ipsa et copiose et graviter accusari potest.*

39.4 proficere is the authoritative reading of *γPM*[1] and perhaps *O* before it was corrected; the other *deteriores* have *perficere.* The manuscripts upon which this tradition relies abbreviate *pro-* and *per-* on most occasions, and in some hands the two are so similar as to be easily misunderstood for the other. Alternatively, the scribe may have had *perficiendum* in mind. *Proficere* has the more compelling sense 'to achieve something' or 'be successful' as opposed to the sense of mere completion implied by *perficere*; for this use of *proficere* in reference to rhetoric and forensic speech, see *TLL* X 2.1699.63.

39.5 libenter studioseque With these adverbs, C. more or less makes the distinction in English between 'hear' and 'listen', the latter implying a willing cognitive engagement, i.e. to render the audience attentive and well disposed. Since this was a primary purpose of the *exordium* (see introduction to §§1–9), C. will demonstrate in the following sections (§§41–42) the emotive figures that he often employs in *exordia* to command his audience's attention, both in speaking of his own trepidation at conducting such an onerous prosecution and in describing the expectations and size of his potential audience. For the epiphora of *audiant ... audiant*, see Lausberg §631. For *studiose audire*, cf. *Inv.* 1.2, 24, *Sest.* 36, *Brut.* 96, 156, *Lucull.* 12, Quint. *Inst.* 3.1.17, Sen. *Con.* 2.2.8, and Tac. *Dial.* 2.1.

39.6 natura 'innate talent'; one part of the triad that included theoretical knowledge and practice mentioned earlier; see §35 *aut ratio aut exercitatio* n. C. will expand upon these three elements in the following sections of his speech.

optimis ... disciplinis atque artibus C. considered the *artes* to consist in the 'reading of literature, grammar, geometry, astronomy, music, and rhetoric'; cf. *Marc.* 4 with Gotoff *ad loc.* and *De orat.* 1.6, 8, 128, 149–159, 187–190. See further Morgan (1998) 35–36. The content of C.'s ordinary education (*enkyklios paideia*) would not have differed markedly from that of Caecilius. In fact, there seems to have been a uniformity of basic educational structure in the Hellenistic and Roman world, and literate education would have proceeded along the same lines over a wide range of times and places. As Morgan (1998) 24 writes: 'Some part of ancient society found education useful for defining and maintaining a common culture and identity. ... It is one of the places where it is possible to see how strongly, despite all local variations of politics, bureaucracy, culture and social structure, a sector of the ancient world regarded itself as an entity.' For C.'s particular course of study in his youth, see Treggiari (2015) 241–243. Beyond basic literate education, Caecilius would certainly have reached the same elite levels of education that C. had, namely those that entailed the study of grammar and rhetoric. C. does not make a distinction about the content of his education in comparison with Caecilius, but he does emphasize duration and location as important factors; see respectively *a pueritia* n. and *Athenis* n. below.

a pueritia One's initial education would have started at home, but around the age of seven, children may have attended a public school or studied at home with tutors, either a hired teacher or an educated slave; see Quint. *Inst.* 1.2 and Bonner (1977) 20–33. C. would seem to imply that Caecilius did not start his studies at the appropriate age.

Of C.'s education before the age of 15, we have scant information. His education certainly began in his hometown of Arpinum, where he was presumably taught by a household slave. When he was ten, his father relocated his children to Rome to further their education, at which point C. was received into the house of L. Licinius Crassus (*RE* 55), who gave him his entrée into the world of Roman politics and oratory; see *De orat.* 2.1–9. He also speaks warmly at *Arch.* 1 of the role at this point in his training played by Archias, who may have been his *grammaticus* for Greek. While this stage of his education would not have focused as intensely on rhetoric as his later studies did, perhaps C. mentions this instruction from the earliest stage of life to highlight his traditional elite education as superior to Caecilius' out in the provinces and to reiterate how long he has been laying the groundwork for a forensic career. A short narrative of C.'s education is given at Plu. *Cic.* 2–3. For modern descriptions, see Clarke (1968), Gelzer (1969) 1–28, and Rawson (1975) 1–28. On Roman education for this time of life in general, see Bonner (1977) 10–89. Generally speaking, boyhood would encompass a young male's life up to the point when he assumed the *toga uirilis*, which C. received in the year 91. On other ways of reckoning *pueritia* and *adulescentia*, see §4 *ab ineunte adulescentia* n.

39.8 litteras Graecas Students under the tutelage of a *grammaticus* may have studied Greek literature first with a focus on pronunciation, grammar, and facility of exegesis; see Quint. *Inst.* 1.4.1, 1.1.12–14. Passages from Homer would have been the first port of call (1.8.5, 10.1.46–50), and other poets and prose authors would follow (10.1.51–84). C. is referring, however, to a later stage of his education and the study of Greek literature, language, and philosophy at a much higher level; see *Athenis* n. below. As for the role of literary studies in education and the training of an orator, Morgan (1998) 94–95 notes:

> One's impression on reading Quintilian, and even more on reading other elite writers, is that they recommend virtually the whole of Greek and Latin literature, for a bewildering range of purposes. Among the other functions assigned to literature are the conveyance of practical information, the provision of role models, the reflection of real life, the formation of character, the training of memory, instruction in characterization, elementary instruction in other disciplines, the demonstration of correct language, and the presentation of paradigms of every type of rhetorical figure, trope, argument and genre.

The authors chosen for the earliest stages of literate education evidently have a strong moral component, while later authors are more directly applicable to oratory. In practice, it seems that teachers used a core set of texts, such as Homer, which they then supplemented with a variety of 'peripheral' texts; perhaps more arcane secondary texts would be part of a more elite education;

see Morgan (1998) 85–89. For more on the use of poetry in oratorical training, see North (1952). [Plut.] *Mor.* 14D–37B demonstrates how students might learn from expounding passages of poetry, albeit in the service of learning philosophy rather than oratory.

Athenis Athens had long been a destination for further education in philosophy and rhetoric. C. himself journeyed in 79 to Athens, where he remained for six months. Along with his brother Quintus and other associates, he studied under the Platonic philosopher Antiochus of Ascalon, the Epicurean philosophers Zeno of Sidon and Phaedrus, and the rhetorician Demetrius of Syria, who was perhaps the author of Περὶ ἑρμηνείας; see *Brut.* 314–316, *Fin.* 2.16, 5.1, *Leg.* 2.36, *N. D.* 159, and *Tusc.* 3.38. Upon his departure, he moved on to Asia Minor and Rhodes in 78 and 77. For his activities during this period with ancient and modern sources, see Marinone (1997) 59.

Since C. wants to make a distinction between himself and Caecilius, he suggests that his education was of greater intensity (*in his elaborasses*) and longer duration (*a pueritia … studuisses*), and now, with a mention of location, insinuates that his education was of higher quality. While many aspects of their education were similar, a different location would mean different teachers and pedagogical presentations. Elite centres of learning, such as Rome, Athens, Pergamum, and Alexandria, were at the forefront of pedagogical development, and only later did these changes make their way to smaller centres of learning. Furthermore, the reputation of these cultural capitals also attracted the most highly regarded teachers.

More important than the quality of his education, however, may be the social implications. C.'s further education in Athens marks him out as a member of the social and intellectual elite; his superior education also occasions a superior social status. For C. the *diuinatio* is not just an oratorical contest but also inherently a social and political one. Yet he conveniently skips over the tradition that the legendary founders of Greek rhetoric, Corax and Tisias, were from Sicily; see Quint. *Inst.* 3.1.8.

Lilybaei Lilybaeum, modern Marsala, is located on a promontory on the far western coast of Sicily; see map in Appendix A. Originally established by the Carthaginians in the early fourth century, it came under Roman control in the treaty of 241 at the end of the First Punic War. It was the seat of Roman provincial administration of the island, probably at first overseen by a quaestor and after 227 by a praetor. When the Roman capital moved to Syracuse in 211, Lilybaeum remained an important centre for maritime trade and naval operations as well as the residence of a second quaestor. As a trading hub, the city would undoubtedly have had some educational facilities, as would any major city in the Roman world.

The western part of Sicily had been under Roman control longer than the east, and, as Tribulato (2012) 34 states, '[w]e are used to thinking that east Sicily preserved its Greek culture for longer; yet most official inscriptions produced in Syracuse after the foundation of the *colonia* were in Latin, as seems to have been the case in the other major cities of the east. Conversely, west Sicily – which was more intensively Romanized from the very start – reserves some surprises: Lilybaeum ... shows a predominance of public inscriptions in Greek'. Some inscriptions found in Lilybaeum dating from the mid-second century show that 'Latin was mostly used by those involved in the provincial administration and in commerce, with a possible addition of the few Sicilians who had frequent contacts with them. West Sicily was an area of intensive contacts, and Lilybaeum provided a linguistically varied context in which Greek, Latin and Punic all mixed'; Tribulato (2012) 34.

C.'s comments about Caecilius' education in Lilybaeum raise some interesting questions. Is he suggesting that Caecilius received his proper education in Lilybaeum – in which case, such a biographical detail would suggest that he was raised in Sicily – or is this comment meant as a slight – i.e. that Caecilius took no pains for his education until after he had assumed the quaestorship? C. is perhaps intentionally vague; see Introduction §II.

Latinas The evidence for the Latin literature most commonly studied in Roman education comes from literary sources and papyri of a much later period, by which point Virgil was well established as the most popular; see Quint. 10.1.85–131, and Morgan (1998) 97. As for C.'s education, he demonstrates an extensive knowledge of Greek and Latin authors too lengthy to rehearse here. For the role of literature in early education and rhetorical training, see *litteras Graecas* n. above.

Romae Although he had been born in Arpinum, C. was sent to Rome around the age of 15 to continue his education; see *a pueritia* n. above.

39.9 in Sicilia If Caecilius had been raised in Sicily and learnt Latin there, he may have had a detectable accent. [Asc.] 115 (197? 24–26 Stangl): *Dicit illum Graecas litteras, simul Latinas in Sicilia didicisse, in ea insula quae neutra bene utatur.* See Woytek *ad* Plaut. *Pers.* 394–395.

magnum See *magna* n. above.

39.10 expectatam C. may be exaggerating the public's anticipation of this trial, but this is also an effective meta-rhetorical flourish meant to engage the interest of his reading audience; see *libenter studioseque* n. above.

diligentia consequi The *diligentia* of the prosecutor is mentioned repeatedly, and especially in the *peroratio*; cf. §§51, 67, 70–73. It refers to the scrupulous attention to detail and energy that one applies to a particular *officium*; see Hellegouarc'h 251–252. Antonius is made to remark at *De orat.* 2.147–148 *Et sic, cum ad inueniendum in dicendo tria sint: acumen, deinde ratio, quam licet, si uolumus, appellemus artem, tertium diligentia, non possum equidem non ingenio primas concedere, sed tamen ipsum ingenium diligentia etiam ex tarditate incitat; diligentia, inquam, quae cum omnibus in rebus tum in causis defendendis plurimum ualet.* He continues through 2.150 to say that many aspects of forensic oratory are all a matter of diligence, using the constant refrain *diligentia est,* and so concludes, *complectar uno uerbo, quo saepe iam usi sumus, diligentia; qua una uirtute omnes uirtutes reliquae continentur.*

memoria complecti 'to remember'; *OLD s.u. complector* 4b and *TLL* III 2086.77–79. On memory in oratory, see §37 *memoria* n. In hyperbolic fashion, C. will go on to say that Verres' crimes are so numerous that even he cannot remember them all; see *Ver.* II.4.57 *nullo modo possum omnia istius facta aut memoria consequi aut oratione complecti.*

39.11 expromere (*γP*: exponere *M*) The rarer *expromere* is the correct reading ('reveal'). See *OLD s.u.* 3, and *TLL* V 2.1805.55. Cf. *Rab. Perd.* 8: *An de peculatu facto aut de tabulario incenso longa oratio est expromenda?* The other reading, *exponere*, though more common in C., was perhaps in the scribe's mind from §39 *causa* ... *exponenda* above; cf. *Ver.* II.1.32.

uoce ac uiribus sustinere For the voice of the orator, see §37 *uoce* n. above. Without electronic amplification of the voice, addressing a large crowd with a lengthy speech required physical stamina; see *De orat.* 1.149, 156. C. remarks with this same collocation at *Ver.* II.1.31 *uererer ne mihi crimina non suppeterent, ne oratio deesset, ne uox uiresque deficerent* .... The notion of bodily strength and the voice are also closely connected by the fact that in the medical science of the day air was thought to have travelled through the arteries; cf. *Brut.* 313–316, and *Nat.* 2.138. See also Calboli (1983) 23–56 for a fuller discussion of air circulation in the body and the appropriate power of the voice in different types of speaking. **ac** is the reading of *γP* and thus stands on better authority than *et* in *M* and the *deteriores.*

§40

40.1 fortasse dices *Anticipatio* in ascribed *oratio recta*; cf. *Sul.* 84–85 with Berry *ad loc.* After a heavy-handed critique of Caecilius' education and rhetorical training, C. uses this imagined objection as a transitional element to turn the conversation to his own education (§40) and his forensic preparation and experience (§41). Linguistic and syntactical elements in the passage, such as repeated phrasing and adversative pronouns, invite direct comparison between C. and Caecilius; see nn. below. C. does not state his educational and forensic accomplishments outright; rather he establishes his relative merit vis-à-vis Caecilius. This tactic is akin to developing an argument from the *locus a comparatione*, which 'relates unequally ranked concepts [or persons] to one another'; see Lausberg §§395–397, and Quint. *Inst.* 5.10.86–93. In other words, though C. may not be the embodiment of the ideal orator, his superior education and extensive experience at the bar make him more suitable than Caecilius to lead a prosecution. This argumentative approach, combined with a *sermocinatio* that adds some liveliness and levity, allows C. to moderate his position and avoid the impression of *arrogantia* even if the humility is feigned; see introduction to §§2–5 on the *odium* of self-praise.

quid ergo This and *quid igitur?* are common expressions in *ratiocinatio*, in which the speaker poses and answers his own questions; cf. §33 *quid igitur?* with n. *ad loc.*, and *Rosc. Am.* 2, 36 with Landgraf *ad loc.* On this expression, in which *quid* is used to change subjects, see also Hofmann §66 and Ferri and Probert (2010) 37 on Donatus.

omnia Hyperbaton; separation from *haec* and its final position in the sentence convey an emphatic incredulity.

utinam quidem essent A contrafactual wish that at least gives a nod to humility; see K-St. 2.1.184. The insertion of *quidem* gives the response a colloquial tone; cf. C.'s use of the same expression at *Sul.* 54 and *Phil.* 1.20 in a *sermocinatio* to respond to an objection.

40.2 mihi a pueritia est elaboratum 'from childhood a great deal of effort on my part has been expended …'. To prompt the comparison between himself and Caecilius, C. echoes his diction (§39 *si … a pueritia … in his elaborasses*). And yet, by switching to the impersonal passive construction, the syntax puts emphasis on the action of the verb rather than the agent and thereby softens the statement so that it appears less boastful. The dative of agent is used often with the periphrastic constructions of the perfect passive participle, especially when close to a prepositional phrase with *a(b)* and the ablative that is not expressing agency; see K-St. 2.1.324. On C.'s early education, and elementary learning in general, see §39 *a pueritia* n.

40.3 quodsi often has an adversative force as here: 'yet if I have been unable to …'. See §54 *quodsi* n.

ego See §41 *ego* n.

haec ... assequi 'to attain to these qualities'; see *OLD assequor* 3, and *TLL* II 860.46.

propter magnitudinem rerum ac difficultatem C. uses almost exactly the same phrase to describe the rigours of rhetorical education at *De orat.* 1.16 *Quid enim quis aliud in maxima discentium multitudine, summa magistrorum copia, praestantissimis hominum ingeniis, infinita causarum uarietate, amplissimis eloquentiae propositis praemiis esse causae putet, nisi rei quandam incredibilem magnitudinem ac difficultatem?* In the subsequent sections of *De orat.* 1.17–18, C. summarizes the qualities of an ideal orator – much of which he covers in the *Diu. Caec.*

40.4 in omni uita A typically Ciceronian exaggeration. On his earlier forensic activity, see §1 *tot annos* n.

40.5 quam longe tu te ab his rebus abesse arbitrare 'do you realize how utterly deficient you are in all these respects?' While C. has been in the process of *actively* improving his skills (*mihi ... est elaboratum*, and *nihil aliud egi*), Caecilius has failed to give them any thought whatsoever (*cogitasti* and *suspicari*) so that C. calls him, not to action, but to a simple recognition of his deficiencies. This rhetorical question gives the conclusion to the *locus a comparatione*: though C. may not possess all the qualities of an ideal orator, he certainly has them to a greater degree than Caecilius; see *fortasse dices* n. On the juxtaposition of the same pronoun in different cases, see §27 *tute tui* n. In addition to implying contrast, the personal pronouns here may contribute to the colloquial tone of the passage; see Hofmann §95. C. generally prefers the form *arbitraris*; on the second-person singular passive ending in C., see §21 *loquere* n.

40.6 antea numquam C. continues to develop the image of Caecilius as an ὀψιμαθής; see §27 *quoniam hoc primum tempus* n.

40.7 ingrederis 'to begin to deal with (a topic)'; see *OLD s.u.* 4b and *TLL* VII 1.1572.35–47. Cf. *Phil.* 2.88.

quae et quantae sint correlates in inverse order to *magnitudem* and *difficultatem* above, which call attention to the nature and extent of leading a prosecution. Note the consonance and homeoteleuton of the interrogatives and the sibilance of *sint suspicari potes.*

suspicari denotes a shallower sense of mental engagement than *cogitasti* above; e.g. 'to have even the vaguest notion of …'; see *OLD s.u.*

§41

41.1 ego The repeated use of nominative personal pronouns in the previous section emphasizes the direct contrast between C. and Caecilius, and here the pronouns assume the primary position, making the contrast even starker. This *ego* is mirrored by the primary adversative position of *tu* in §43: 'For my part, I …. But you ….' The direct confrontation makes spectators of the senatorial jury and helps solidify C.'s depiction of the *diuinatio* as an oratorical battle – one which builds in a crescendo to the imagined showdown with Hortensius in §§44–47. What follows in this section will demonstrate the contrast between C.'s state of mind about assuming the prosecutorial role against Verres (§§41–42) and that of Caecilius (§43). The disparity is further emphasized by the syntax and rhetorical devices; see §43 *tu nihil metuis, nihil cogitas, nihil laboras* n. below.

41.2 sicut omnes sciunt A 'prompting gesture', aimed primarily at the judges in the *diuinatio* (but also involving the *corona* and reading audience), to remind them of his previous experience at the bar. Such parenthetical asides achieve two main goals: first, to involve the audience in the speech and keep their attention; second, to remind the listeners of information which may not be as patently obvious as the speaker suggests. These gestures normally occur in the second-person plural, but since this particular periphrasis is embedded in a direct address to Caecilius, C. refers to his listening audience in the third person. For such prompts, see *Sest.* 6 *ut plerique meministis* with Kaster *ad loc.*, 74, 82, 124, *Cael.* 10, *Mil.* 37, 47, *Phil.* 2.69, 7.4, 14.15, and *Flac.* 73.

in foro iudiciisque ita uerser C. returns to some themes from the exordium; see §1. *Forum,* by association with the place of legal activity, also came by metonymic shift to signify not just the physical location for trials but also 'forensic practice' or 'the bar'; see *OLD s.u.* 5 and *TLL* VI 1204.33. C. is fond of the expression *in foro uersari*; see *TLL* VI 1199.29. The present tense of the verb suggests that his activities as an advocate are ongoing. The relative clause has a concessive sense, as signalled by *tamen.* The verbs *uerser* and *consumam* are in the subjunctive although it was not strictly necessary; see H-Sz. 559–560. **iudiciisque** the Italian MSS (*PM*) and (independently) *t* repeat the preposition; both could have arisen through dittography. Zumpt, who also omits the second preposition in his edition, noted the difficulty in selecting between the variants and suggested that there is no definitive rule about the repetition of prepositions in such phrases; see his n. *ad loc.* Even so, given the nigh pleonastic sense of the pair, the consensus reading of the French family seems more fitting. Cf. *Rosc. Am.* 88 *propter fori iudiciorumque insolentiam.*

eiusdem aetatis C. had probably just turned 36 a few days before this hearing. See timeline in Introduction §III. For the genitive of quality, see K-St. 2.1.454.

41.3 aut nemo aut pauci pluris causas defenderint Of those advocates whose names are recorded, C.'s upcoming opponent, Q. Hortensius Hortalus, also made innumerable court appearances; see *TLRR* 220. The diction would suggest a subtle reinforcement of the notion of 'prosecution as defence' (§5 *defensio est existimanda*), but it must also be noted that *defendere causam* means 'to plead a case, not necessarily for the defence, and must be distinguished from *defendere aliquem*'; see *Sen.* 38 with Powell *ad loc.* For C.'s other known forensic activity up to this point, see §1 *tot annos* n. **defenderint** The perfect subjunctive is not found in the primary MSS but is required by sense and the sequence of tenses.

41.4 omne tempus quod liberum mihi ab amicorum negotiis datur The reading of all MSS, *quod mihi ab amicorum negotiis datur* is deficient, and the problem is perhaps ancient. The separative use of *ab* requires an adjective for its meaning to be clear; see *OLS* 1.220–221, 226. Though [Asc.] comments on the phrase (*quod mihi licet per amicorum negotia, quibus occupatus <sum>*), his lemma has been lost, and a textual difficulty may have prompted his note. The phrase was imperfectly healed in the citation from Victorinus 1.4 (Ippolito 32.106 *et qui omne reliquum tempus, quod mihi ab amicorum negotiis datur*); although *omne reliquum tempus* is Ciceronian (cf. *Man.* 9), the position of *reliquus* outside of the subordinate clause is problematic, and it is not used in this sense; *TLL* I 12.12–42. Sydow (1932) 458 suggested *quod ⟨liberum⟩ mihi …* citing *Rab. Perd.* 17 *liberum tempus nobis dabitur* and *Leg.* 1.8 *si mihi ullum tribueretur uacuum tempus et liberum.* This conjecture, as it fits both the sense and Ciceronian idiom, as has been accepted.

C. subtly reinforces his *ethos* as a speaker attentive to the *officium* owed to family, friends, and country, wherein, in Ciceronian parlance, *negotium* most commonly means the business of forensic oratory; see §27 *quid negoti* n. For the importance of developing eloquence in the dispatch of these obligations, cf. *Inu.* 1.5 *hinc* [*ab eloquentia*] *amicis quoque eorum certissimum et tutissimum praesidium comparator.* On the expectations associated with *amicitia*, see §6 *causa tantae necessitudinis* n.

41.5 in his studiis laboribusque I.e. in theoretical study and rhetorical training. C. uses this pairing elsewhere when discussing the efforts required for being a good orator; cf. *De orat.* 2.633 *quod semper statui neminem sapientiae laudem et eloquentiae sine summo studio et labore et doctrina consequi posse,* and 1.260–263 in the discussion of Demosthenes.

paratior … promptiorque C. speaks of his thorough preparation at *Ver.* I.32 *Si utar ad dicendum meo legitimo tempore, mei laboris industriae diligentiaeque capiam fructum, et hac accusatione perficiam ut nemo umquam post hominum memoriam paratior, uigilantior, compositior ad iudicium uenisse uideatur.* The candidate who depends on oratorical prowess is also admonished to keep his skills sharp; see Q. Cic. *Pet.* 3 *eius facultatis adiumenta, quae tibi scio esse seposita, ut parata ac prompta sint cura et saepe quae de Demosthenis studio et exercitatione scripsit Demetrius recordare.*

ad usum forensem Cf. §47 and C.'s description of Caelius' education at *Cael.* 72 *Cuius prima aetas disciplinae dedita fuit eisque artibus quibus instruimur ad hunc usum forensem, ad capessendam rem publicam, ad honorem, gloriam, dignitatem.*

41.6 deos ... propitios A conventional prayer; cf. *Ver.* II.5.37 *ita mihi omnis deos propitios uelim,* and *CIL* IV 1679. See *TLL* X 2.2054.13–24 (also 25–43). This language of invocation was common to *exordia* and is part of a larger meta-rhetorical strategy in which C. demonstrates the ways of garnering the attention and goodwill of one's audience; see §39 *libenter studioseque* n. This subtle invocation is meant to be compared with Caecilius' hackneyed expression; see §43 *'Iouem ego Optimum Maximum'* n. As C. begins to proffer an image of how the trial would unfold under his supervision, he employs other language and motifs commonly found in *exordia*; see *commoueor animo ... toto corpore perhorresco* n. below. See also *Cael.* 42 with Dyck *ad loc.* Cf. Quint. *Inst.* 10.1.48 on the rhetorical quality of Homer: *Age uero, non utriusque operis ingressu in paucissimis uersibus legem prohoemiorum non dico seruauit sed constituit? Nam et beniuolum auditorem inuocatione dearum quas praesidere uatibus creditum est et intentum proposita rerum magnitudine et docilem summa celeriter comprensa facit.*

41.7 ut, cum The completion of the explanatory clause introduced by *ut* is delayed by the interjection of the *cum* clause. The effect is one of heightened anticipation. The scholiast [Asc.] has the lemma *ita mihi deos uelim propitios ut commoueor animo ac toto corpore perhorresco, cum illius diei mihi uenit in mentem quo die citato reo,* which gives a syntax less complicated and less expressive.

illius temporis mihi (γM: *illius mihi temporis P*) The textual uncertainty here may be ancient since Priscian cites this passage four times, twice agreeing with γM (*GLK* 3.355.12–13, 369.11–12), and twice with *P* (188.5–8, 352.17–20). The reading in *P* places *mihi* in its usual unstressed position and *ille* is a common host; cf. *Ver.* I.35 *Nam illud mihi nequaquam dignum industria conatuque meo uidebatur,* and *Agr.* 2.6 *Accedit etiam ille mihi summus labor ac difficillima ratio consulatus gerendi.* The reading of γM, however, has more to recommend it. The order may be more emphatic and appropriate to the anaphora of *mihi* which is repeated four times in this sentence. In other examples of this construction from C., he does not split the genitives with the ethical dative even when *illius* could host; see below. Furthermore, of the other later authors who cite this passage, both have *mihi* after the two genitives. Don. *ad* Ter. *Ad.* 681 has *illius temporis*; [Asc.] has *diei* for *temporis*, which is perhaps an error of anticipation caused by *quo die*. The deictic pronoun here has a temporal rather than spatial sense.

uenit in mentem For the register of this phrase, see §27 *in mentem tibi non uenit* n. For the genitive with this construction, see K-St. 2.1.472. Cf. *Ver.* I.51 *fac tibi paternae legis Aciliae ueniat in mentem* and *Ver.* II.4.110 *Venit enim mihi fani, loci, religionis illius in mentem*; II.5.124.

41.8 citato reo 'when the defendant is summoned'; see *OLD s.u. cito* 4a, and *TLL* III 1200.38–1201.16. In imagining the start of Verres' trial, C. is prompting his audience to do the same, and in the sections that follow they are encouraged to visualize the start of the trial in two different guises, one with C. as lead prosecutor, the other with Caecilius; see the introduction to §§44–47.

The *citatio* was the official summoning of the defendant to trial; see Heumann–Seckel *s.u. citare.* Cf. *Clu.* 49–50, *Ver.* II.2.98. Unlike the *nominis delatio*, the presence of the defendant was not required. Greenidge 473 remarks: 'The objection to the trial of an absentee, which seems to have prevailed at the earlier stage of the *nominis delatio*, appears to find no place at this stage of the procedure. Whether the non-appearance of the accused be due to voluntary exile or to contumacy, the case goes on to its legitimate end. Milo and many others convicted in 52 BC were condemned in absence.' Verres' trial would begin on 5 August; see Introduction §III.

commoueor animo … toto corpore perhorresco The motif of the distraught advocate persists throughout the Ciceronian corpus and is a method of arousing *pathos* in his audience; see Quint. *Inst.* 6.2, and Lausberg §357.3. In rhetorical prescription it is most at home in the *peroratio* or *exordium*; cf. *Mil.* 1, *Deiot.* 1, *Rosc. Am.* 9 with Landgraf *ad loc.*, *Clu.* 51, and especially *Quinct.* 1 *Quae res in ciuitate duae plurimum possunt, eae contra nos ambae* *faciunt in hoc tempore, summa gratia et eloquentia; quarum alteram, C. Aquili, uereor, alteram metuo. Eloquentia Q. Hortensi ne me in dicendo impediat, non nihil commoueor, gratia Sex. Naeui ne P. Quinctio noceat, id uero non mediocriter pertimesco.* As the passage continues in our speech, C. conveys this fearful and heightened emotional state through diction and syntax – anaphora (*quantam … quantam … quantam*), tricolon *crescens*, asyndeton, and a possible anacoluthon (*pro offensione … dignum*).

At first it would appear that expressing fear at the prospect of delivering a speech against Verres would undermine C.'s claim to be the better choice for prosecutor, but C. is demonstrating mastery of a common trope and hence his superiority to Caecilius. At §39, C. told Caecilius that an orator must make his audience listen *libenter studioseque*, and in this passage he uses tropes found in *exordia* to demonstrate how an orator can go about it in practice. C. would have Crassus remark at *De orat.* 1.120–121: *ut enim quisque optime dicit, ita maxime dicendi difficultatem uariosque euentus orationis exspectationemque hominum pertimescit. Qui uero nihil potest dignum re, dignum nomine oratoris, dignum hominum auribus efficere atque edere, is mihi, etiamsi commouetur in dicendo, tamen impudens uidetur. Non enim pudendo, sed non faciendo id quod non decet, impudentiae nomen effugere debemus. Quem uero non pudet – id quod in plerisque uideo – hunc ego non reprehensione solum sed etiam poena dignum puto. Equidem et in uobis animum aduertere soleo et in me ipso saepissime experior, ut et exalbescam in principiis dicendi et tota mente atque artubus omnibus contremiscam.*

As for this collocation, *animo commoueri … corpore perhorrescere*, C. uses it again at *Ver.* II.4.110 *Qui tandem istius animus est nunc in recordatione scelerum suorum, cum ego ipse in commemoratione eorum non solum animo commouear uerum etiam corpore perhorrescam?* **perhorresco** in C.'s speeches, one frequently finds *perhorrescere* as the latter of two verbs of fearing or emotional agitation; cf. *Ver.* II.4.78, *Agr.* 2.101, *Cael.* 60, *Mil.* 42, and 67. Its secondary position is due to its greater intensity compared to other more common verbs of fearing that precede it. In this instance, 'not only is my mind shaken but my entire body is racked with fear'. On *per-* compounds, see §23 *pertimescat* n.

§42

42.1 iam nunc 'even now', i.e. well before the actual trial. With this particular use of *iam*, the 'speaker indicates … that a certain state of affairs starts or takes place earlier than is somehow expected'; see Kroon and Risselada (2002) 65. C. repeats the phrase again below in an attempt to bring the effect of these future events into the present moment. It also underscores the characterization of the *Diuinatio* as tantamount to Verres' trial itself; see §12 *praeiudicium … plane iudicium* n.

mente et cogitatione prospicio 'I can clearly see in my mind's eye …'; *OLD mens* 4b. C. feigns emotional and mental distress at the thought of facing the attentive throngs that will attend Verres' trial and the expectations that they will have for the lead prosecutor. In proffering his own mental vision of Verres' forthcoming trial, C. progresses from his internal emotional state in §40 and now compels his audience to imagine the broader emotional and physical atmosphere from the advocate's perspective. This tactic demonstrates for the jurors his ability to stir emotions, and as a literary artefact, this section of the speech heightens the expectation of the reader for the subsequent *orationes in Verrem.* **mente et cogitatione** the pairing of *mens* and *cogitatio* is found throughout C.; cf. *Ver.* II.4.67, 5.35, *Clu.* 69, *Flac.* 3, *De orat.* 2.175, 186, *Orat.* 8, *Luc.* 143, *T. D.* 1.38, 55, and *Off.* 1.95. See *TLL* III 1457.44–45. On quasi-synonymous pairs, see §1 *causam rationemque* n.

42.2 quae … quantam … quantam … quantam The asyndeton along with the anaphora of *quantam* and the *tricolon crescens* provides a linguistic picture of C.'s agitation and helps to engender this same response in his audience. See §41 *commoueor animo … toto corpore perhorresco* n.

concursus The scene that C. only imagines here is depicted as becoming reality in the *actio prima*; see *Ver.* I.4 *Neque tantum me exspectatio accusationis meae concursusque tantae multitudinis, quibus ego rebus uehementissime perturbor, commouet …*, and *Ver.* I.15 *haec multitudo.* This image does not just convey the excitement and expectation of the populace and the apprehension felt by the prosecutor but also the potential danger of unrest and mob violence. While *concursus*, taken alone, has a neutral valence ('throngs'), its latent meaning ('uprisings, uproars, or tumult') is lurking just beneath the surface and awakened in the presence of *concitare* and *multitudo*; cf. *Ver.* II.5.52, 94; *Clu.* 137; *TLL* IV 115.78–116.26 (*contra* 115.11, where this passage is listed). Thus, in setting the stage for the upcoming trial by describing the size and emotional state of the audience, C. reminds his senatorial jury of the popular unrest – whether real, perceived, or projected – arising from senatorial misconduct that he previously mentioned in §§8–9, and of its potential to erupt into violence. Rioting famously erupted around the trial of Milo; see *Mil. passim* with [Asc.] 30–43C. For a list of violent outbreaks from 287 to 50 BCE, see Lintott (1968) 209–216.

42.3 exspectationem A meta-rhetorical flourish. In describing the anticipation for Verres' trial, C. provokes a similar expectation in his reading audience. Cf. *Rosc. Am.* 11 *Quanta multitudo hominum conuenerit ad hoc iudicium uides; quae sit omnium mortalium exspectatio, quae cupiditas ut acria ac seuera iudicia fiant intellegis*, and *Ver.* I.30.

magnitudo iudici 'the gravity of this trial'; *OLD s.u.* 6, and *TLL* VIII 118.58–75. C. draws attention to what he suggests are the possible consequences of Verres' trial for the Roman public and his clients, and particularly for the senatorial order, who may lose their control over the judiciary.

sit allatura 'Latin lacks a synthetic subjunctive form of the future, and the use of the periphrastic expressions in these contexts might therefore be regarded as mere suppletion of a gap in the paradigm'; *OLS* 1.433. See further Pinkster (1987) 194.

42.4 auditorum multitudinem The consonance of 'm' sounds may suggest the murmuring of the crowd. See *concursus* n. above. On the *corona populi*, see §1 *eorum qui adsunt* n.

infamia has both a legal and moral meaning and is another example of C.'s manipulation of legal terminology; e.g. §12 *praeiudicium.* As a moral term, it refers to the bad reputation acquired by those who engage in reprehensible acts or who belong to a category of people known for unsavoury behaviour, such as actors or prostitutes. From this moral meaning, the term comes to denote a legal condition in which one is entirely or partially deprived of certain legal capacities, such as holding public office or voting. This legal dimension of *infamia* was always inherent in a conviction for a criminal offense; see *Dig.* 48.1.7 *Infamem non ex omni crimine sententia facit sed ex eo quod iudicii publici causam habuit.* In attributing *infamia* here to Verres, C. presents the public perception of Verres' misdeeds as well as a proleptic implication of his future conviction. In other words, the proper outcome of the trial will result in the moral judgement against Verres becoming a legal one. For ancient legal discussion of *infamia,* see also *Dig.* 3.2.1–4. For a complete discussion of *infamia* and *ignominia,* see Kaser (1956), Santalucia (1998), and Greenidge (1894) 18–40. There has been debate, however, as to whether the penalty under the *lex Cornelia* was capital; see Sherwin-White (1949). See also, §71 *de capite ac fortunis* n.

concitatura *Concitare,* along with *concursus* above, belongs to a nexus of words denoting social unrest; cf. *Flac.* 96, *Sest.* 105, *Ver.* II.1.83. See also *TLL* IV 67.38 (where this passage is mislabelled as *Ver.* II.1.42). For the insinuation here, see *concursus* n. above.

42.5 audientiam An uncommon word in classical Latin and one that appears only here in C.'s extant speeches. Except at Apul. *Met.* 3.4, it is always construed with *facere* and usually describes the duty of a herald; cf. *Cato* 28 with Powell *ad loc.*, Plaut. *Poen.* 11, *Rhet. Her.* 4.68, and Liv. 43.16.8.

orationi meae By using the personal pronoun, C. subtly forces his audience to visualize him giving the prosecutorial speech rather than Caecilius. The previous clauses have set a visual and emotional scene, and here C. places himself within it.

improbitas 'outrageous behaviour'. Cf. §26 *improbus* ... *improbitas* n.

illius The scansion of the second syllable of *illius* was not consistent among Latin authors. It could be short in the epic and lyric poets, but sometimes long, as C. says in his discussion of prose rhythm at *De orat.* 3.183. See further Ritschl (1868) 683–689 and McKeown *ad* Ov. *Am.* 1.14.14.

factura is the reading of the Italian family as well as *D* and *t* of the French. *N* often incorporates apparent marginalia or corrections from *S* (here lost) and thus reads *factura uel futura. Futura* must have been a variant in *S*, which E^1*HG* have wrongly taken over. There may have been a correction in the intermediary between *E* and *t.* The correct reading is not in doubt; see *audientiam* n. above.

42.6 iam nunc See *iam nunc* n. above.

timeo Followed here by an indirect question introduced by *quidnam.* C. expresses a similar concern about being unable to meet the expectations of those who have been wronged by Verres considering the sheer number of crimes he has committed; see *Ver.* II.1.103. On the motif of fear, see §41 *commoueor animo … toto corpore perhorresco* n.

pro offensione … exspectatione … magnitudine The syntax of this phrase is not clear at first glance. *Pro offensione* must be understood adnominally with *quidnam*; cf. *Planc.* 69, *Phil.* 8.30 (*aliquid*), *Off.* 2.74. *Exspectatione* and *magnitudine* depend on *dignum.* Prepositional phrases introduced by *pro* and dependent on *dignus* are a rare construction, and this would be the only one in C.; see K-St. 2.1.516. Cf. Sal. *Cat.* 51.8: *nam si digna poena pro factis eorum reperitur, nouom consilium adprobo.* Other uses of *dignus* followed by *pro* are mainly confined to poetry; cf. Verg. *A.* 2.537, 9.250; see *TLL* V 1.1148.3–19. **pro offensione hominum** *offensio* used in the objective sense here 'in due proportion to the mistreatment of these men …'. While *hominum* would logically refer to the Sicilians, C. does not name them. In the homogenizing term *homines,* C. can magnify Verres' crimes as affecting a larger swath of the population.

42.7 inimici infensique The disposition of the Sicilian farmers toward Verres is described similarly with a striking elision in examples; cf. *Ver.* II.2.149 *infenso animo atque inimico.* On alliterative pairs, see §6 *furta atque flagitia* n. **inimici** For *inimicitia* and its meaning, see Hellegouarc'h 186, and C.'s concise explanation at *Ver.* II.3.6. **infensi** applies to a group that has been wronged and therefore angered; Hellegouarc'h 189–190.

42.8 dignum I.e. fitting and apposite for the expectations of the occasion. See *Orat.* 70 *ut enim in uita sic in oratione nihil est difficilius quam quid deceat uidere.* πρέπον *appellant hoc Graeci, nos dicamus sane decorum.* For *dignus* as applied to public speaking, see Hellegouarc'h 390–391, and more fully 388–411, and Balsdon (1960).

eloqui refers to the speaking register of the orator (*TLL* V 2.420.53–64); see *Orat.* 61 *sed et Graece ab eloquendo* ῥήτωρ *et Latine eloquens dictus est.* On the other hand, *loqui* is generally used of more common speech; see §21 *loquere* n., and Agroecius (*GLK* 7.124.18f.) *loqui hominis est, obloqui obtrectatoris, … alloqui suadentis uel hortantis aut iubentis, eloqui oratoris.*

§43

43.1 tu … nihil metuis, nihil cogitas, nihil laboras C. abruptly pivots to Caecilius, who shares none of the anxieties and attention to training and preparation that C. has just described. The primary adversative position of the pronoun ('but you') mirrors §41 *ego* (see n. *ad loc.*) and is followed by a tricolon with emphatic anaphora and asyndeton. In describing himself in §§41–42 as a cautious man who understood the magnitude of this case, C. had used complex sentence structure and subordination. Caecilius' simple-mindedness is correspondingly conveyed in §43 by short unadorned sentences.

43.2 ex uetere aliqua oratione Perhaps from a speech of Cato or Gracchus; see n. below. Lifting phrases from another speech may not have been uncommon among young orators. Suet. *Jul.* 55 says of the young Julius Caesar: *genus eloquentiae dumtaxat adulescens adhuc Strabonis Caesaris secutus uidetur, cuius etiam ex oratione quae inscribitur 'pro Sardis' ad uerbum nonnulla transtulit in diuinationem suam.* This may be a subtle admonition to C.'s readers not to mine his published oratory for fixed phrases and witty retorts, but to study these passages for his deployment of rhetoric and argumentative strategy. *Aliqua* also suggests that Caecilius is not particularly choosy about the speeches he lifts from. Both phrases C. mentions would typically come from *exordia*; see nn. below.

43.3 'Iouem ego Optimum Maximum' uel 'Vellem, si fieri potuisset, iudices' The invocation of Jupiter Optimus Maximus seems already to have been a well-worn tactic in the generation before C. and now somewhat hackneyed; see V. Max. 1.pr1 *nam si prisci oratores ab Ioue optimo maximo bene orsi sunt*, and Serv. *A.* 7.259, 11.301 *more antiquo: nam maiores nullam orationem nisi inuocatis numinibus inchoabant, sicut sunt omnes orationes Catonis et Gracchi; nam generale caput in omnibus legimus. unde Cicero per inrisionem ait 'si quid ex uetere aliqua oratione "Iouem ego optimum maximum"'*. Nevertheless, C. himself occasionally indulges in this invocation. Those of his speeches that contain this phrase, however, suggest that this sort of old-fashioned language was appealing to the public at large rather than the educated elite; cf. *Mur.* 1, *Rab. Perd.* 5, *Red. Pop.* 1, and *Corn.* 1 fr. 2 *ut ab Ioue optumo maximo ceterisque diis deabusque omnibus opem et auxilium petam.* This invocation could have additional efficacy when delivered in a proceeding that was taking place in the Roman Forum, as the Temple of Jupiter Optimus Maximus would be clearly visible on the lower crest of the Capitoline Hill; see L. Richardson (1992) 221–224. Defendants, for example, would call upon Jupiter Best and Greatest in their time of need; cf. *Ver.* II.4.71. For the oratory of Tiberius Gracchus, see Flower (2013) with further notes on Gaius. This practice of invocation at the outset of a speech perhaps draws upon the Greek oratorical tradition, although it was relatively less common; cf. Dem. 18 πρῶτον μέν, ὦ ἄνδρες Ἀθηναῖοι, τοῖς θεοῖς εὔχομαι πᾶσι καὶ πάσαις, and Lycurg. εὔχομαι γὰρ τῇ Ἀθηνᾷ καὶ τοῖς ἄλλοις θεοῖς καὶ τοῖς ἥρωσι τοῖς κατὰ τὴν πόλιν καὶ τὴν χώραν ἱδρυμένοις. C. has already shown an awareness of this rhetorical technique but deploys it with more subtlety and deftness; §41 *deos … propitios* n. **'Vellem, si fieri potuisset, iudices'** had also become a predictable oratorical opening. In fact, C. uses similar ones himself at *Phil.* 9.1 *uellem di immortales*, and *Sul.* 1 *Maxime uellem, iudices*; see Manuwald and Berry *ad loc.*, respectively. A similar phrase had been a standard opening in Greek oratory as well; cf. Is. 10, Dem. 14, 16, 32, 33, and 45. Cf. Ov. *Met.* 13.128–30 for unfulfilled condition as an opening.

Victorinus, in explicating a Ciceronian precept, finds fault with these phrases because they are so generally applicable and are therefore not tailored to any particular cause; see *Inu.* 1.26 (Ippolito 83.116) *'uulgare est, quod in pluris causas potest accommodari.' Id est, quod dicitur generale principium et quod non unius sed omnium potest esse causarum, si sic incipias 'Iouem . . .' aut 'Vellem . . .'.* From this point of view, employing these trite phrases could be indicative of shallow preparation – and this is certainly part of the criticism of Caecilius. But C.'s attack on Caecilius here is perhaps more nuanced than these later rhetoricians allow, though it is an interesting point in the *Nachleben* of the *Diu. Caec.* that Victorinus is clearly reading this speech as partly a rhetorical treatise. The critique is not so much that these phrases are to be avoided – as one can see, C. occasionally has recourse to both expressions, timeworn though they may be – but that Caecilius fundamentally misunderstands the preparation required for a strong oratorical performance. They therefore succinctly betray his total inexperience, poor training, and educational shortcomings.

Furthermore, in C.'s characterization of him, Caecilius repeatedly demonstrates the improper way to consume, understand, and employ published oratory in the preparation of his case and in the furtherance of his rhetorical ability. See §52 *hunc librum* n. for the meta-rhetorical valence of these comments.

43.4 ediscere Memorization of passages from other speeches was certainly a part of rhetorical training but only a preliminary one; see *De orat.* 1.157 and *Rhet. Her.* 3.39–40. The image of Caecilius simply memorizing or lifting phrases or passages wholesale from other speeches and treatises furthers his characterization as a late-learner; see §27 *quoniam hoc primum tempus* n.

Combating Hortensius (§§44–47)

Even if Caecilius would not have to face an opponent, he still lacks the ability to put forward a solid prosecution. But as it is, he would have to engage in rhetorical battle with an extremely eloquent and well-prepared orator – Hortensius. C. can appreciate Hortensius' eloquence without being pinned down since he knows all of his methods of attack from prior experience. C. imagines how Hortensius will dodge Caecilius' attacks, how he will land a few rhetorical punches, and then ensnare Caecilius in a false dilemma. Poor Caecilius will be dizzied and confused. What will he do as Hortensius dismembers his arguments, places the blame on him, and even makes him question his own case? How will he endure the hatred that Hortensius will stir up against him? Hortensius' onslaught of words will be complemented by his dazzling delivery, and Caecilius will be left beaten and bewildered. How can Caecilius hope to match up against such a sharp opponent when he is still getting his arguments from school textbooks?

C. now introduces another tacit consideration in the choice of prosecutor: namely, who best matches up with the potential defence advocate, in this case, Q. Hortensius Hortalus. The language of imagination and visualization, which C. had introduced in describing the *corona* of spectators (§42), continues (§45 *uidere iam uideor*, §46 *mihi enim uidetur*, §47 *iam continuo uideo futurum*), whereby he prompts his audience to imagine a showdown with Hortensius, first with C. as his opponent (§44) and then with Caecilius (§§45–47). Colour and verve are added to the imagined scene by the use of an extended metaphor which compares the courtroom showdown to heavy combat sports (e.g. *pugnandum certandumque sit … opprimet … peruertet … labefactare atque infirmare conabitur, transigere, expedire, absoluere … praestringat aciem … in hac prolusione … in ipsa pugna*; see nn. *ad loc.*), thereby further adding to C.'s agonistic characterization of the *diuinatio.* Modern commentators have not agreed upon the precise metaphorical reference. Some point to wrestling and others to gladiatorial sword-fighting. There does seem to be an amalgamation of the two. C.'s bout with Hortensius is more akin to the former; Caecilius' bout with him, the latter. (See nn. *ad loc.*)

In this rhetorical sparring, C. depicts himself as fully aware of his opponent's talents and therefore able to counter them successfully (*noui omnis hominis petitiones*). Caecilius, however, or so C. contends, will be outmatched. He then describes the rhetorical tricks and line of argument that Hortensius would use if Caecilius were to face him, viz. the false dilemma, demolishing the coherence in Caecilius' arguments, and an *ad hominem* attack against Caecilius that stirs up enmity by demonstrating his disregard for social norms and religious institutions. While this analysis allows C. to demonstrate his familiarity with Hortensius' tactics and establish his fitness to challenge him, it is more importantly a meta-rhetorical treatment of the *Diuinatio in Caecilium* itself. The very tactics that Hortensius would be inclined to use in the course of his defence are the same arguments that C. himself will use in his own *reprehensio*: the false dilemma (§58), separating and dismissing Caecilius' potential arguments (§§52, 59), and stirring up *inuidia* against Caecilius for breaching the quasi-parental relationship of quaestor and commander (§§59–65; for a further discussion, see the introduction *ad loc.*)

For C.'s reading audience, other meta-rhetorical and pedagogical considerations are at play. This line of argumentation is also used to demonstrate C.'s ability to create a vivid image for his audience and evoke an emotional response – a skill which he has already identified as vital for a successful prosecutor (§§27, 39). Furthermore, in his careful game of not actually mentioning Hortensius by name, C. has to some extent assimilated himself to Hortensius, or at the very least, has shown himself to be Hortensius' equal. A match-up between these two orators is a contest that others should want to see – another invitation for C.'s audience to anticipate the speeches *in Verrem*. As he would say at *Ver.* II.1.14 *non uereor ne … a me ullum munus aedilitatis amplius aut gratius populo Romano esse possit.*

§44

44.1 ac si tibi nemo responsurus esset 'and even if no one was preparing to respond to you …'. Nutting (1925) 144 remarks 'Whatever may be said of the logic of a "future contrary to fact", such a category must be recognized.' Cf. *Fin.* 4.62 *Rogarem te, inquit, ut diceres pro me tu idem, qui illis orationem dictauisses, uel potius paulum loci mihi, ut iis responderem, dares, nisi et te audire nunc mallem et istis tamen alio tempore responsurus essem, tum scilicet, cum tibi.* See further H-Sz. 662, Hoppe (1875) 20–25, and Landgraf on *Rosc. Am.* 52.

ipsam causam ... demonstrare Viz. to establish a *prima facie* case and its most basic rationale, not to prove it conclusively; cf. *Quinct.* 34. In this collocation with *demonstrare, causa* indicates the fundamental basis for the charge irrespective of any defensive arguments; see *Rhet. Her.* 2.28, and *Inu.* 1.23. C. suggests that Caecilius cannot plead effectively as he does not even know the basic allegations against Verres from the aggrieved party. Compare Quint. *Inst.* 2.21.16 *nam et litigator rusticus inlitteratusque de causa sua melius quam orator qui nesciet quid in lite sit: sed accepta ... a litigatore, melius orator quam ipse qui docuerit.* See further Lausberg §51. If the basic case had not been proven, in addition to the possible verdicts of *absoluo* and *condemno*, a judge could also give the verdict of *non liquet*, which indicated that the case was still in doubt; see §24 *ceratam ... tabellam* n. In earlier forms of the recovery court, a verdict of *non liquet* seems to have been common and was the grounds for establishing the procedure of two separate actions; see Introduction §III.

ut ego arbitror A colloquial parenthetical expression. Though more common in C.'s letters than orations, when he uses it in the latter, it acts as a filler phrase to add more weight to the words or phrases that follow; cf. *Sest.* 16, *Har. Resp.* 48, and *Pis.* 68. Here it conveys a sense of incredulity and emphasizes *demonstrare non posses*; see n. above.

44.2 illud The cataphoric use of the pronoun referring to the whole phrase that will follow, namely the accusative and infinitive construction *tibi ... esse certamen* and the indirect question *quicum ... disserendum, ... altercandum, ... pugnandum certandumque sit.*

44.3 cum homine disertissimo et ... paratissimo Hortensius; see §23 *magnus ille defensor ...* n.

44.4 certamen Cf. *Brut.* 319 *cum igitur essem in plurumis causis et in principibus patronis quinquennium fere uersatus, tum in patrocinio Siciliensi maxume in certamen ueni designatus aedilis cum designato consule Hortensio.* For other uses of *certamen* to describe forensic contests, cf. *Ver.* II.1.3, 2.177. See also *TLL* III 885.29–887.31, and Quint. *Inst.* 5.12.22 *Igitur et ille quem instituimus adulescens quam maxime potest componat se ad imitationem ueritatis, initurusque* *frequenter forensium certaminum pugnam iam in schola uictoriam spectet, et ferire uitalia ac tueri sciat, et praeceptor id maxime exigat, inuentum praecipue probet.* For the import of this extended metaphor, see the introduction to §§44–47.

quicum C. prefers the older form, *quicum,* to *quocum* generally; see Neue-Wagener 2.461–465. *Cum quo* appears to have been a gloss in *S*; the supralineal reading in *D* appears to be in the first hand, while the scribe of *N* nonsensically wrote both (*qui cum quo cum*). In the fragmentary papyrus, *Π*, the C scribe also wrote *cum quo* as a supralineal gloss, presumably for a non-native speaker of Latin.

disserendum In its meaning as 'argue, dispute', rather than its more common sense 'to set in order' or 'to discuss'; see *TLL* V 1.1462.19. *Disserere* usually has an adverb such as *contra* or *aduersus,* but here C. has sacrificed the typical construction for the tricolon; for its regular use, cf. *De orat.* 1.85, *Acad.* 1.7, *Fam.* 3.8.25 *disputabant, ego contra disserebam; dicebant, ego negabam.* It is only construed with *cum* here, *Off.* 3.26, and Vulg. *Acts* 17.18 (as a translation for συνέβαλλον αὐτῷ). See also *modo altercandum* n. below.

modo altercandum is entirely absent from the medieval tradition of the *Diu. Caec.* It is preserved, however, in *Π*. Roberts (1938) 77 summarizes the argument for its inclusion succinctly:

> It might be argued (1) that *altercandum,* either in its non-technical sense of 'wrangle, quarrel', or in the technical sense of *altercatio,* the sharp question and answer of opposing counsel, does occupy a middle place between *disserendum,* which implies no more than 'discussion', and *pugnandum,* and further that, as the text stands in the MSS., the transition is abrupt; (2) that *altercari* is a rare word – it occurs only twice in Cicero [*Brut.* 159, 173] – and so is unlikely to have crept into the text as a gloss on the common *disserendum*; (3) that even if it is a gloss, we have to assume a double error to account for the *modo.*

One might also add that it would mirror nicely the tricolon of *numquam* ... *numquam* ... *numquam* below. For this sense of *altercor,* cf. *Brut.* 159, 173, Plin. *Ep.* 3.9.24; see *TLL* I 1751.25

For *altercatio*, see Greenidge 478–479. For rhetorical precepts on this quick back-and-forth between orators, see Quint. *Inst.* 6.4.1–22. For the repetition of *modo* to support the inclusion of this phrase, cf. *Font.* 12 *modo ab nostris imperatoribus subacti, modo bello domiti, modo triumphis ac monumentis notati, modo ab senatu agris urbibusque multati sunt ....*

44.5 omni ratione 'by every means possible'. The wide semantic range of *ratio* allows for an understanding which befits both the cognitive machinations of oratorical *inuentio* and the movements and approaches of a physical attack; cf. §35 *aut ratio aut exercitatio* n. and *OLD* 14.

pugnandum certandumque The tricolon, if the reading of *Π* is accepted, concludes with the homeoteleuton and doublet of the strongest and most physical of the gerunds. While *certare* points to a competitive engagement, *pugnare*, with its martial meaning more to the fore, more vividly evokes physical combat; see *TLL* III 891.83 and X 2.2552.33–39, respectively. On quasi-synonymous pairs, see §1 *causam rationemque* n.

44.6 ingenium Innate talent required of an orator; see §35 *aut ratio aut exercitatio* n. See also *TLL* VII 1.1523.24.

laudo The scholiast remarks *Cur hoc Tullius dicit?* and goes on to suggest that it is meant to allay the fears of the Sicilians, who have heard so much about Hortensius; see [Asc.] 116 (198 Stangl). C.'s praise for Hortensius in the midst of a speech recurs in later speeches; cf. *Sul.* 12, *Rab. Perd.* 18, *Mur.* 48, *Flac.* 41, *Sest.* 3, 14, and *Planc.* 37. It would in fact be the death of Hortensius in 50 BCE that would prompt C. to compose his *Brutus*. He remarks at the outset of that treatise on famous orators: *Cum e Cilicia decedens Rhodum uenissem et eo mihi de Q. Hortensi morte esset adlatum, opinione omnium maiorem animo cepi dolorem. ... Dolebamque quod non, ut plerique putabant, aduersarium aut obtrectatorem laudum mearum sed socium potius et consortem gloriosi laboris amiseram* (*Brut.* 1). In praising the skill of his opponent, C. not only shows that Caecilius is not up to the task but also elevates the status of his achievement over Hortensius in the trial proper. See further Tempest (2011) 150.

pertimescam C. sang a different tune in his previous extant encounter with Hortensius; *Quinct.* 2 *uerum ita se res habet, ut ego, qui neque usu satis et ingenio parum possum, cum patrono disertissimo comparer.* On fear, see §41 *commoueor animo ... toto corpore perhorresco* n.

probo: 'to esteem'; *OLD s.u.* 2, and *TLL* X 2.1464.4–36. For its more moral or legal valence, see §1 *una et id ... probabit, et ...* n.

44.7 delectari facilius quam decipi The contrast between the two infinitives is highlighted by their alliteration. *Delectatio* was one of the three main goals of oratory and generally refers to the delight or entertainment given to the audience; see *De orat.* 2.115, *Orat.* 69, *Brut.* 185, 276, and *Opt. Gen.* 3. *Decipere,* on the other hand, implies 'duping' or 'cheating' (*TLL* V 1.174.73). In other words, C. can appreciate Hortensius' performance but, with full awareness of his tactics, he will not be deceived. On Hortensius' style of delivery, see §46 *gestu ipso ac motu corporis* n. below.

44.8 numquam ... numquam ... numquam Anaphora and asyndeton in a tricolon *crescens* draw attention to the weapons in Hortensius' arsenal (*consilium, artificium,* and *ingenium*), underscore the rapidity of the action, and advance the image of a trial as a physical contest. Pseudo-Hermogenes advises that the language and style of vivid passages should be similar to that of the subject they describe; see Webb (2009) 57 with n. In some branches of the MSS tradition, *numquid* is written for *numquam* in one or more instances, perhaps owing to the propensity to abbreviate in the exemplars. The statements with *numquam* fit better into the flow of C.'s argument than a series of incredulous questions.

opprimet consilio A metaphor of physical combat. Initially, the listener may have thought of the verb's common usage in military language – i.e. 'to take by surprise, catch unawares'; see *OLD s.u.* 7a and *TLL* IX 2.788.53–789.6. Quint. *Inst.* 12.9.20 remarks on the ability of an orator who is well prepared to avoid being caught by surprise: *Sed siue in respondendo fuerit subito dicendum, siue quae alia ita exegerit ratio, non oppressum se ac deprensum credet orator cui disciplina et studium et exercitatio dederit uires etiam facilitatis: quem armatum semper ac uelut in procinctu stantem non* *magis umquam in causis oratio quam in rebus cotidianis ac domesticis sermo deficiet.* As C. continues with the metaphor, however, the comparison seems to be with wrestling; see nn. below. *Opprimere*, for example, could suggest a wrestling hold, common at the outset of a match, in which one contestant would try to gain control of his opponent with a headlock or waistlock; see *TLL* IX 2.784.56–75, and Poliakoff (1987) 33–40. For other wrestling metaphors, see *Clu.* 52 and *Sul.* 47 with Berry *ad loc.* For the understanding of *consilium*, see §37 *consilio* n.

ullo artificio peruertet An *artificium* is generally a 'trick or cunning device'; see *OLD s.u.* 4a and *TLL* II 706.29–61. As with *consilium* above, the double-entendre contributes to the metaphorical use of *peruertet.* As it applies in the field of public speaking, an *artificium*, such as the artistic proof, is the product of the orator's status as *artifex* and master of rhetorical τέχνη. Compare Quint. *Inst.* 2.17.2 *Quod quidem adeo ex iis qui praecepta dicendi tradiderunt nemo dubitauit ut etiam ipsis librorum titulis testatum sit scriptos eos de arte rhetorica, Cicero uero etiam quae rhetorice uocetur esse artificiosam eloquentiam dicat*, and 3.3.12 *artificis est persuadere.* As C. depicts him here, Hortensius possesses those qualities of a good orator that C. had expounded previously: sound rhetorical preparation and strategy (*consilium*), the ability to put theory into practice (*artificium*), and innate ability (*ingenium*); cf. §§35–36. Within the wrestling metaphor, this could be any surprise move or tactic. **peruertet** 'to overturn, upset, knock down (persons, esp. in a fight)'; see *OLD* 1b and *TLL* X 1.1860.49 (or perhaps, more concretely, 'to turn around'; see *OLD* 3). In the context of a wrestling match, this could imply knocking one's opponent to the ground by throwing him backwards, or assuming a waistlock in which the opponent was turned around. For images of this latter tactic depicted on Greek pottery and in statuary, see Poliakoff (1987) 41–43.

44.9 ingenio me suo A 'short-range' hyperbaton. Cf. von Albrecht (2003) 113: 'if placed after its noun, the possessive can be separated from it. Cicero increasingly uses this artificial type of word order up through the *Caesarian Orations*, where a culmination is reached; in the *Philippicae* he reverts to his earlier style.'

A possessive in postposition and separated from its headword places emphasis on the enclosed word(s); see Powell (2010) 176. For a full study of hyperbaton with possessive pronouns, see Menk (1925). For *ingenium*, see §35 *aut ratio aut exercitatio* n.

labefactare atque infirmare 'cut my legs out from under me'; pleonasm. *Labefactare*, an intensive form of *labefacere*, literally means to make someone fall or slip and is a favourite expression of C. (cf. *Clu.* 194), and one which he frequently uses as the first in a pair of verbs; cf. *Ver.* II.3.182, *Rab. Perd.* 3, *Fin.* 3.70, and *Fam.* 5.13.2. He uses the collocation of *peruertere* and *labefactare* (and *conquassare*) again at *Vatin.* 19 in reference to the effect of Vatinius' tribunate on the Roman state. For the etymology of *labefactare*, see Ernout–Meillet *s.u. labo*; for its scansion, see K-St. 1.1031–1032. During a wrestling bout, after hemming up one's opponent in a lock or forcing him to place all his weight on one foot, a competitor could force him to trip and fall with a sweep of the legs or by knocking him behind the knee; see Poliakoff (1987) 33–34. See, for example, the wrestling match between Ajax and Odysseus at Hom. *Il.* 23.700–737, especially 711–713. In formal Greek wrestling, a competitor won a bout by forcing his opponent to fall in such a way that his shoulders or back touched the ground. The first contestant to win three bouts was the winner, and so in Greek literature the metaphor of the 'third fall' came to symbolize a total defeat; cf. Pl. *Euthyd.* 277d ἐπὶ τὸ τρίτον καταβαλῶν. For other examples of this metaphor in Greek literature, see Krause (1841) 424. In a gladiatorial bout, losing one's footing would be an obvious disadvantage; see *TLL* VII 2.766.12–14, which remarks that *labefactare* is used here *per translationem e sermone gladiatorio factam.*

44.10 conabitur In saying that Hortensius would not dare to attempt these manoeuvres (*TLL* IV 346.52), C. may imply that he and Hortensius share a kind of mutual respect for one another, though at such an early juncture in C.'s career it may not have been requited.

omnes … petitiones rationesque dicendi C. continues the metaphor of oratory as wrestling or armed combat. For this meaning of *petitio*, cf. *Cat.* 1.15, and Serv. *A.* 9.437 *petitiones enim proprie* *dicimus impetus gladiatorum*; see *TLL* X 1.1941.18. The C scribe of *Π* also noticed the wordplay when he wrote in the margin of his text *proprie petitiones ad gladiatores pertinet*; see Roberts (1938) 75. C. also uses this metaphor at *De orat.* 3.206 to describe figures of speech: *Orationis autem ipsius tamquam armorum est uel ad usum comminatio et quasi petitio uel ad uenustatem ipsam tractatio*, and *Orat.* 228.

44.11 saepe in isdem saepe in contrariis causis C. had represented Publius Quinctius in his civil case against Sex. Naevius in 81; Hortensius defended Naevius successfully. See *TLRR* 126, and Kinsey on *Quinct.* No other trials in which both advocates appeared, either on the same or opposing sides, are recorded, though C. does make reference to earlier forensic activity at *Quinct.* 4. After Verres' trial, Hortensius and C. would appear together as defence advocates in seven other trials, for Rabirius, Murena, Sulla, Flaccus, Sestius, Plancius, and Scaurus. See *TLRR* 221, 224, 234, 247, 271, 293, and 295, respectively.

uersati sumus See *OLD s.u.* 13a, and cf. §1 *in causis iudiciisque publicis ita sim uersatus.*

44.13 de suo ingenio iudicium As with the *Diuinatio* and Caecilius, C. also imagines Verres' trial as a rhetorical contest between himself and Hortensius. This is another small indication that the *Diu. Caec.* may have been published after the conclusion of Verres' trial – not only does this statement raise the stakes for Hortensius, but it also contributes to C.'s accolades in besting his adversary. See Q. Cic. *Pet.* 2 *uenito quasi in singulis causis iudicium de omni ingenio futurum sit.*

§45

45.1 te uero, Caecili C. directs his comments again squarely at Caecilius. For the adversative primary position, see §41 *ego* n.

45.2 sit elusurus 'give you the slip'; another verb that evokes the metaphor of physical combat. Cf. Don. Ter. *Eun.* 55 *eludere proprie gladiatorum est*, and *Opt. Gen.* 17 *Non enim in acie uersatur nec ferro, sed quasi rudibus eius eludit oratio. A me autem, ut cum* *maximis minima conferam, gladiatorum par nobilissimum inducitur, Aeschines tamquam Aeserninus, ut ait Lucilius, non spurcus hom, sed acer et doctus.* See further *TLL* V 2.429.65–79. C. has already used it to describe Hortensius' handling of inexperienced young nobles at §24, and here he imagines that the same fate would befall Caecilius. Although he uses this metaphorical meaning of *eludere* elsewhere (cf. *Rosc. Am.* 128 and *Ver.* II.3.92), the underlying notion of physical combat is made more prominent here than in other instances through the collocation of other such metaphors; see the introduction to §§44–47.

quam omni ratione iactaturus 'how he will throw himself at you with every trick in the book'. Although the image usually given by this verb is that of being buffeted by the waves, collocations here evoke the image of aggressive sport; cf. *Tusc.* 2.56 *pugiles uero, etiam cum feriunt aduersarium, in iactandis caestibus ingemescunt.* See also *TLL* VII 1.54.52–55.12. For *ratio* as 'contrivance', see *OLD s.u.* 14b.

45.3 uidere iam uideor The phrase can be used to indicate a vision, prophecy, or imagination; cf. Ter. *Adel.* 384, *Lael.* 41, *Cat.* 4.10 with Dyck *ad loc.* Visualization through vivid description could play an important role in the act of persuasion. The invitation to imagine an unfolding scene of a forensic battle with Hortensius relies more heavily on metaphor than *enargeia*, but is still sufficient to conjure up a vivid picture. According to Aristotelian rhetorical precepts, a metaphor which conveys action and motion (such as the physical combat C. describes here) conveys even greater vivacity; see Arist. *Rhet.* 1411b–1412a. The audience would mentally 'fill in the picture' to complete the scene with details not mentioned by the speaker; see Webb (2009) 84–87, 107–109 on Quint. *Inst.* 8.3.64–65.

quotiens ille tibi potestatem optionemque facturus sit ut eligas utrum uelis ... An almost textbook definition of a false dilemma (*complexio*), a method of entanglement which would have been a standard component in Hellenistic rhetorical education. Here C. acknowledges Hortensius' mastery of the rhetorical device, but as the analysis of the *exordium* has shown, he has already deployed this technique subtly on a much broader scale against his audience (see introduction to §1), and rather blatantly against Caecilius in §§12–13 and §§30–31. He will do so again at §58 and §60. This has the effect of simultaneously demeaning Caecilius, demonstrating his rhetorical skill, and entertaining his educated audience with a sophisticated joke at his opponent's expense; see further Craig (1985). Furthermore, C.'s explanations and demonstrations of effective rhetoric in the *Diuinatio* guide his reading audience in appreciating the subsequent speeches against Verres.

The technique has gone by several names; see *Inu.* 1.45 *complexio est, in qua, utrum concesseris, reprehenditur, ad hunc modum: 'si inprobus est, cur uteris? si probus, cur accusas?'.* Meanwhile Quint. *Inst.* 5.10.69 treats it as a type of *diuisio*, and the author of *Rhet. Her.* also addresses it not only as a *diuisio* (4.52) but also as a *duplex conclusio.* Our term is taken from Hermogenes and the later Greek rhetoricians, who call it a διλήμματον; see further Lausberg §393.

45.6 aestus … error … tenebrae The metaphor of combat is continued but raised to the level of an epic encounter. *Aestus* refers to the imagined anxiety that Caecilius would experience when confronting Hortensius, but its usage is generally poetic and denotes the swell of a stormy sea or the motions of flames and throws of fever (*OLD s.u.*); see *quam … iactaturus* n. above. C. only uses the word four times in his extant speeches, and twice it refers to the fluctuations of the popular assembly; cf. *Mur.* 35, and *Planc.* 15. For metaphorical uses of *aestus*, see *TLL* I 1121.45. *Error* and *tenebrae*, likewise, have transferred meanings that refer to mental confusion and ignorance (as they are often used in Lucretius), but this collocation brings their more physical meanings to the fore and suggests a labyrinthine or underworld scene; see *OLD s.u. error* 1c and *TLL* V 2.815.34. In this evocative image, there may also be aspects of a deathly duel as 'the outcome of fatal encounters in the amphitheatre was predictably ritualized in terms of the transition to the underworld'; see Coleman (1990) 67. Caecilius, confronting an overpowering opponent that will dismember his prosecution, is clearly doomed; see *membra diuidere* n. below. Of course, in the time of

C., gladiatorial shows were staged with temporary structures in the Roman Forum; thus the comparison is even more apt.

di immortales The quasi-epic invocation of the gods mid-sentence heightens the bathos of the scene.

homini minime malo This final ironic flourish completes the pathetic picture of Caecilius. The fight envisioned between Caecilius and Hortensius is unfair; the former is undoubtedly outmatched, and his demise is quick in coming. The spectacle, therefore, would be poor. A more prolonged and fiercely fought battle provided better entertainment; see *Dig.* 48.19.31 with Coleman (1990) 57. For this expression, cf. *Ver.* II.3.106 *docuerunt uos quid lucelli fecerit homo non malus, familiaris praetoris, Apronius.*

45.7 quid? The succession of three rhetorical questions gives the impression of Hortensius' attacks coming at multiple angles.

membra diuidere The double-entendre of *membra* is obvious. In addition to a body part, it can also be used to refer to a part of a speech; see *OLD s.u.* 5b and *TLL* VIII 644.50–645.18. Cf. *Part.* 118 *Atque haec accusationis fere membra sunt*, and *Top.* 30. The speech-as-body motif is also familiar from Socrates' characterization; cf. Plt. *Phaed.* 264c ἀλλὰ τόδε γε οἶμαί σε φάναι ἄν, δεῖν πάντα λόγον ὥσπερ ζῷον συνεστάναι σῶμά τι ἔχοντα αὐτὸν αὑτοῦ, ὥστε μήτε ἀκέφαλον εἶναι μήτε ἄπουν, ἀλλὰ μέσα τε ἔχειν καὶ ἄκρα, πρέποντα ἀλλήλοις καὶ τῷ ὅλῳ γεγραμμένα. While the phrase is used metaphorically elsewhere, for instance at Sen. *Ep.* 89.1, the more visceral meaning here comes to the fore. Compare C.'s citation of a Latin version of *Medea* at *N. D.* 3.67 *puerum interea obtruncat membraque articulatim diuidit / perque agros passim dispergit corpus.*

45.8 in digitis suis Apparently this was a remarkable feature of Hortensius' delivery; see Quint. *Inst.* 4.5.24 *Nec inmerito multum ex diligentia partiendi tulit laudis Q. Hortensius, cuius tamen diuisionem in digitos diductam nonnumquam Cicero leuiter eludit.* Quintilian may have been echoing C.'s *elusurus sit* above, in which case, it is a clever turn in which C. is shown to have the upper hand. C. also remarks of Hortensius at *Brut.* 303 that he *rem complectebatur memoriter, diuidebat acute.*

singulas partes causae constituere For the organization of a *refutatio*, Quintilian advises that one must decide whether to address the points of the prosecution all at once or one by one. The 'divide and conquer' method is advisable when the cumulative force of a prosecution is strong; see Quint. *Inst.* 5.13.13 *urgent uniuersa: at singula quaeque dissolueris, iam illa flamma, quae magna congerie conualuerat, diductis quibus alebatur concidet, ut si uel maxima flumina in riuos diducantur qualibet transitum praebent*; cf. *Inu.* 1.30. C. himself has less to say about the arrangement of arguments within the *refutatio*; cf. *De orat.* 2.313–314, 331–332. The reader is prompted to analyse how C. will frame his arguments in the trial proper. In the speeches against Verres, he comments on his novel method of arguing his case (*Ver.* I.55, II.1.29), and Vasaly (2009) 111 notes that

> what is *nouum* is that he will treat each charge as a miniature case, with its own small-scale introductory oration, followed by corroborating witnesses; the only difference between his procedure and what is normally done, therefore, will be that in the latter, the oratorical treatment of *all* the charges (*omnia*) precedes the introduction of the witnesses, while in Cicero's method witnesses to each particular issue (*in singulas res*) will follow introduction of that charge.

For *constituere* as 'to set forth a case or argument', see *OLD s.u.* 10 and *TLL* IV 519.49–50. Nevertheless, undertones of the latent physical meaning of the verb are certainly present.

45.9 transigere, expedire, absoluere *Transigere* has the connotation of 'piercing with a weapon' (*OLD s.u.* 1) and *expedire* of 'freeing oneself from a hold' (*TLL* V 2.1605.64, 1607.57). *Absoluere* here means to 'finish off' or 'to do away with' an argument; see *OLD s.u.* 5b, *TLL* I 176.65, and cf. *Rhet. Her.* 1.27. C. has omitted the finite verb *coeperit*, which should be understood from the sentence above. This process of omitting words, which Quintilian calls *detractio*, along with asyndeton imbues the narrative with brevity and variation. Here it underscores the rapidity with which Hortensius could dismantle Caecilius' prosecution of Verres.

45.10 periculum facessieris An uncommon verb. With *periculum*, it means 'to bring a case against someone'; see *OLD s.u.* 2, and *TLL* VI 139.49. Priscian *GLK* 2.535 *'facesso' uero et [alia uerba] quae possumus desideratiua dicere (significat enim 'facesso' 'desidero facere'); frequentatiua enim esse non possunt, cum primae coniugationis non sunt*; in contradiction to Serv. *A.* 4.295, 9.44. The spelling *facessieris* is attested only in *P* in the medieval tradition, but the variant is ancient; Priscian, in his discussion of the morphology of these desiderative verbs in the perfect tense, cites this sentence with *facesseris*, the reading of *Π* and the other medieval manuscripts, but then notes *inuenitur tamen in quibusdam codicibus 'facessieris'*. The reading in *P* offers the more Ciceronian cretic and resolved trochee ending *-ūm făcēssĭĕris*, though *facesseris* is by no means unacceptable in providing a hypodochmiac. For other verbs of this type, see Neue-Wagener 3.390–399. For *periculum* as it relates specifically to endangerment in a criminal trial, see §25 *magno multorum periculo* n.

§46

46.1 commiserari, conqueri C. briefly outlines the emotional appeals that Hortensius could make in his defence of Verres and the effect it would have on Caecilius' prosecution: viz. the shifting of *inuidia* from Verres to Caecilius, and the latter's disregard for social norms such as *necessitudo*. The verbs denote the two elements of emotional appeal (*amplificatio*); see *Rhet. Her.* 4.69. *Commiseror*, an uncommon verb in classical Latin (see *TLL* III 1899.77–1900.9; cf. Quint. *Inst.* 11.3.58), refers to an appeal to pity (*commiseratio*), while *conquestio* aroused the audience's anger against one's opponent (see *TLL* IV 350.80). In essence, C. has moved sequentially through the parts of Hortensius' defence since *amplificatio* is most often found in the *peroratio/conclusio*; see *De orat.* 2.125, 3.219, *Rhet. Her.* 2.50, and Quint. *Inst.* 10.1.107. The style here also reflects the substance. Alliteration and asyndeton are common in emotionally charged passages. C., in discussing how Hortensius' speech will shift animosity and stir emotions, inserts these elements of emotive language to affect his audience and Caecilius. On *amplificatio* and common components of a *conclusio*, see the introduction to §§71–73.

ex illius inuidia See *inuidiam* n. below.

deonerare 'to offload'; an exceptionally rare verb in extant Latin literature, and this is its only preserved use in the classical period. *TLL* V 1.558.61–70 shows only a single instance in a few scholiasts and one use at Ammianus 24.6.4, who uses the verb literally in reference to unloading ships. *Demere* or *adimere* would have been a more classical choice. The rarity of the verb may have led to the other manuscript readings and the insertion of the later Latin verb *dehonorare*. The correct reading is found in *M* and *Π*.

46.2 traicere Another word with martial overtones, such as 'thrusting or piercing with a weapon', but here 'to transfer' from one person to another; see *OLD s.u.* 5a. This process of transferring blame from one to another, *translatio criminis*, was a necessary skill; cf. Quint. *Inst.* 9.2.4 *Quae delectatio aut quod mediocriter saltem docti hominis indicium nisi … scierit, remouere a se, in alium traicere … ?* The technique amounted to an *anticategoria* – an attack on the jurisdiction of the prosecutor on the grounds that he was guilty of a crime himself.

46.3 necessitudinem In Roman political vocabulary, *necessitudo* represents a stronger but more limited version of *amicitia* that established a quasi-familial relationship between two individuals. It could result from, for example, joint military or political service. According to C., Caecilius, in suing for the prosecution of his former praetor, transgresses this established social norm of Roman republican politics. While Hortensius could exploit this prior relationship in any future showdown, it will form a key part of C.'s *reprehensio* at §§59–65; see the introduction to those sections for a full discussion of this instance of *necessitudo* and a critique of C.'s argument.

Personal attacks in regard to *necessitudo* will also form a part of C.'s tactics in *In Verrem*. Such disregard for social norms, C. maintains, only serves to demonstrate that Verres is a threat to the stability of the Roman state. Cf. *Ver.* II.1.38 *Omnium est communis inimicus qui fuit hostis suorum*; see also *Ver.* I.11, and II.1.34–43.

morem maiorum Hortensius could depict Caecilius' prosecution of Verres as a contravention of the *mos maiorum*, yet it is C.

himself who will use this argument against Caecilius in §§61–65. This label of 'ancestral custom' came to summarize 'the set of moral rules, or code of behaviour, applicable to both private as well as public life, centred around essential values such as *auctoritas, dignitas, libertas, gratia,* [and] *honos*'; Arena (2014) 217. While it is often appealed to as a static set of long-standing values, it was remarkably flexible and adaptable. What *mos maiorum* meant or how it might manifest itself in action was an area of constant debate and negotiation, and it could be invoked to support various and sometimes contradictory courses of action; see the debate on Pompey's command at *Man.* 60. For the pragmatic orator, the point was to know how and when to invoke it. To demonstrate that one was acting according to the *mos maiorum* could win that side approval, while showing one's opponents' actions as contrary to it would be tantamount to exiling them from the normative boundaries of Roman civilization. The bibliography for studies of *mos maiorum,* both generally and within the Ciceronian corpus, is extensive; see further Arena (2014) 234–238.

morem ... religionem is the reading of all manuscripts of authority. Gronovius suggested reading *more ... religione* as ablatives with *constitutam*; Halm, Klotz, and Müller adopted it. The reading of *Π*, in which *constitutam* is omitted in the first hand and *more* emended to *morem* in a later hand, suggests that the textual difficulty is ancient. Roberts (1938) 77 writes

> The omission [of *constitutam*] is probably accidental, as if *more* and *religione* are read, *constitutam* is essential. But another hand [perhaps the E scribe] has added an *m* to *more* and may have done the same in the next line to *religione* .... It might be argued that the reading *morem ... religionem* arose as an attempt to make sense of a text from which, as in *[Π]*, *constitutam* had already been lost. The evidence of the papyrus is interesting as showing that both readings were current in the fifth century.

For this edition, the MSS reading has been retained on balance for two reasons. First, while it is conceptually true that C. will argue that *necessitudo* between quaestor and commander has been established according to social and religious custom (and hence the possibility of admitting these nouns as agents in the ablative), here he is listing those areas of the Roman moral code to which Caecilius' actions would be an affront. Therefore, it is more powerful and direct if *mos* and *religio* stand on an even syntactic ground with *necessitudo*, since this allows the moral breach to proceed in ascending order, first from an individual relationship to a broader social one, and finally to a divine one. Second, if *more* and *religione* were admitted as correct, the asyndeton between these two agents, particularly in final position, would seem odd, if not un-Ciceronian.

46.4 sortis religionem Perhaps best rendered as 'the sanctity of the lot'. Quaestors were generally given their assignments by lot, though occasionally they could be appointed *extra sortem ex senatus consulto*; cf. Laelius under Scipio Aemilianus at Livy 30.33.2; on this procedure, see Introduction §II. For the notion of religious obligation implied by sortition, see the discussion on 'Quaestors and the *Causa Necessitudinis*' at the introduction to §§59–65, where C. deploys this line of invective against Caecilius.

eius orationis The conceptual relationship between *orationis* and its headword, *inuidia*, is strained and demonstrates the assertion that 'the scope of possible relations [between a genitive and its headword] is infinite and no restrictions seem to apply'; see *OLS* 1.1000. C. is referring to the *inuidia* that Hortensius' speech would engender amongst the members of the audience. Greenwood, in his Loeb translation, renders the whole sentence as 'Can you face the hostility [*inuidiam*] that such arguments will arouse against you?' When *inuidia* indicates the hostility which results from such an action, the accompanying genitive usually refers to the offending deed; cf. *Sul.* 1 *ambitionis* and *Fam.* 1.1.1 *largitionis*; see further Hellegouarc'h 197–198. For an extensive discussion of the uses of the genitive, see de Groot (1956). Cause adjuncts are generally in the ablative case or prepositional phrases; see *OLS* 1.902–904 with examples. **orationis** (ω : *orationi* [Asc.]) Richter prints *poterisne eius orationi subire? [Inuidiam]* on the following grounds: 'The dative with *subire* in the sense of *resistere, non succumbere* is cited by ancient grammarians with this example. Otherwise, Cicero associates it as a synonym of *suscipere, excipere, sustinere* with an accusative. The manuscripts have added *inuidiam* to the spurious genitive *orationis* from its earlier use above. (And *inuidia* does not belong with *uide modo* since its object is in the preceding question.) [Den Dativ bei *subire* in der Bedeutung von *resistere, non succumbere* belegen alte Grammatiker mit diesem Beispiel. Sonst verbindet C. es als Synonymen von *suscipere, excipere, sustinere* mit einem Accusativ. *inuidiam* setzen die Handschriften zu dem fehlerhaften Genitiv *orationis* aus dem Früheren hinzu. Zu *uide modo* gehört es nicht, denn dessen Object liegt in der vorhergehenden Frage.]' The ancient grammarian he references must be Nonius Marcellus (4.404.2 Mercier = 2.649.3 Lindsay). The paradosis, however, is defensible; cf. *Part.* 66 *De honestate sic, ut honestumne sit pro amico periculum aut inuidiam subire*, and *Fam.* 15.4.2. *Π* would seem to have *orationis*, and although it is damaged here along the left side, the number of characters missing would require a word such as *inuidiam*; see Roberts's edition.

inuidiam in broad terms, is the feeling aroused when an individual observes someone else exceeding the limits imposed by social norms or by his own ability and is therefore related to a sense of jealousy arising from feelings of inferiority and humiliation. It is similar in meaning to *odium*, though the latter is more personal, while the former arises as a result of someone's social or political position. Hellegouarc'h 197 goes on '*Inuidia* is not only a state of mind; it is expressed by acts of hostility and … it is also displayed by words and *inuidia* then takes on the meaning of "reproach". [*invidia* n'est pas seulement un état d'âme, elle s'exprime par des actes d'hostilité et… elle se manifeste aussi par des paroles et *inuidia* revêt alors le sens de «reproche».]' For this sense of reproach, cf. *Planc.* 75. In this instance, Caecilius will arouse indignation and scorn by disregarding the norms of *necessitudo*; see the introduction to §§59–65. At the outset of the *actio prima*, the object of *inuidia* will not be Verres, but the senatorial order itself; see *Ver.* I.1.

46.5 etiam atque etiam See §37 *uide etiam atque etiam* n.

46.6 obruat Another word that evokes an image of physical combat; see *TLL* IX 2.151.64–75. Cf. *Off.* 3.48 for an example of stoning. C. is fond of the metaphorical meaning in his speeches; cf. *Ver.* II.1.20 *his criminibus, his testibus, et urbanis et prouincialibus, sic obrutus atque oppressus est ut … nemo istum comperendinatum sed condemnatum iudicaret,* and 2.151. In both examples from *In Verrem,* it is Verres that is being overwhelmed, suffering the fate that would have been Caecilius' were he to have faced Hortensius.

gestu ipso ac motu corporis Hortensius, about whom C. frequently speaks favourably in his rhetorical treatises, was apparently notorious for his excessive gestures, and C. may be making fun of him here; cf. *Ver.* II.3.49 *tamenne putamus patronum tuum in hoc crimine ceruiculam iactaturum …?.* C. says of Hortensius at *Brut.* 303 *uox canora et suauis, motus et gestus etiam plus artis habebat quam erat oratori satis*; see also Quint. *Inst.* 1.8.2. A sharper criticism is found in Gell. *NA* 1.5.2–3, where Hortensius is mocked for looking like an actor and resembling a female mime-artist or a dancing girl; see further Berry (1996) 24–26 with notes.

As for C.'s treatment of gesture and bodily movement elsewhere, he briefly addresses their use at *Orat.* 59 and *De orat.* 3.220: *Omnis autem hos motus subsequi debet gestus, non hic uerba exprimens scaenicus, sed uniuersam rem et sententiam non demonstratione sed significatione declarans, laterum inflexione hac forti ac uirili, non ab scaena et histrionibus sed ab armis aut etiam a palaestra; manus autem minus arguta, digitis subsequens uerba, non exprimens; bracchium procerius proiectum quasi quoddam telum orationis; supplosio pedis in contentionibus aut incipiendis aut finiendis.* Other movements of the body that C. mentions involve hitting one's forehead or slapping one's thigh to stir the emotions of the audience; see *Brut.* 278. C.'s rather short treatment of gesture and movement in his rhetorical treatises is typical of the tradition that he inherited from previous generations. Aristotle only made brief comments at the outset of book 3 of the *Rhetoric,* and the subject is not addressed in *Rhetorica ad Alexandrum. Rhetorica ad Herennium* likewise treats it as a novel topic; see 3.19, 26–27. It is Quintilian that most fully codifies the gestures appropriate for oratory at *Inst.* 11.3.65–184, and 'there are good reasons for supposing that the hand gestures described by Quintilian would in all likelihood have been familiar to Cicero as well. ... [L]ively gesticulation was a prominent feature of the Roman culture heritage'; see further Hall (2004). For a full discussion of gesture and acclamation in Roman oratory with illustrations, see Aldrete (1999) and Graf (1991). Maier-Eichhorn (1989) provides a commentary on *Inst.* 11.3 with illustrations of hand gestures. On the meaning of *gestus*, see Corbeill (2004) 17–18, 107–139. For other ancient references to *pronuntiatio* or *actio*, which both denoted a combination of voice and gesture, see Lausberg §1091. For voice, see §37 *uoce* n.

All ancient discussions of gesture and movement concern themselves with its effect on the audience – how these actions contribute to clarity, emphasis, and persuasion – and not its effect on one's opponent. This makes this passage in the *Diuinatio* unique. C. makes the argument here that Hortensius' delivery was so enthralling that it would distract even the opposing counsel, though it is impossible to say whether this was an additional intent or simply a felicitous by-product. The passage from *De orat.* 3.220 cited above is notable for C.'s use of martial imagery in discussing gesticulations, which mirrors the extended metaphor used here in §§44–47. Perhaps this was an image used in rhetorical pedagogy that was familiar to C.

46.7 praestringat aciem 'to blunt', as with the edge of a weapon, but transferred to the senses; *OLD s.u. praestringo* 3b, and *TLL* X 2.940.43–61. Cf. *Phil.* 12.3 and *Rab. Post.* 43.

46.8 abducat This figurative use, 'to bewilder', is found elsewhere; see *TLL* I 62.16–84, and cf. *Leg.* 1.47.

§47

47.1 huiusce rei This fossilized phrase, like *huiusce modi*, contains the original form of *hic*, *hicce*, which includes the deictic suffix *-ce*. For more on this form, see K-St. 1.599, H-Sz. 468, Neue-Wagener 2.414, *OLD s.u. -ce*, and *TLL* III 719.8–39. C.'s preference for it declines after 63; see *Rosc. Am.* 5 and 6 with Landgraf and Dyck, respectively.

47.2 iam continuo 'immediately'. For *continuo* as a marker of colloquial language, see *Rosc. Am.* 94 with Landgraf.

47.3 uideo See §45 *uidere iam uideor* n.

isto libro The deictic pronoun implies a derisive gesture toward an educational textbook that Caecilius has to hand that he did not even bother to conceal. C. mentions it again at §52 *hunc librum* and may be deliberately misleading about the text Caecilius has brought with him. For the sort of book indicated by C., see *ex alienis orationibus compositum* n. below. For the practice of using a speech written by others, cf. Suet. *Rhet.* 2 *hunc eundem* [L. Plotium Gallum] – *nam diutissime uixit – M. Caelius in oratione quam pro se de ui habuit significat dictasse Atratino accusatori suo actionem.* For another possibility, that Caecilius had a manuscript to hand, consider the example of C. at *Planc.* 74 as discussed by Vössing (2008).

magister ludi typically denotes a primary school teacher and is therefore a dismissive term for Caecilius' instructor. The image also furthers the depiction of Caecilius as an ὀψιμαθής, who has not even advanced past the most elementary level of education; see §27 *quoniam hoc primum tempus* n. The *ludi magister* 'occupied the lowest place in the educational hierarchy of ancient Rome' and would typically teach students from humble backgrounds; see Maurice (2013) 4–10. A two-tiered system of education that corresponded to social status was prominent, particularly in large metropolitan areas. On the etymology of *ludus* as 'school', see Bonner (1977) 56–57. Given the nexus of vocabulary denoting combat, C. may be making a pun on *ludus* as a *ludus gladiatorius.*

47.4 nescioqui A colloquial marker of disdain; cf. *De orat.* 1.91, where Antonius is calling into question the tradition of rhetorical education: *usque a Corace nescioquo et Tisia,* and *Phil.* 11.12, *Pis.* 1, *Deiot.* 23, *Amic.* 87. See also H-Sz. 537.

ex alienis orationibus compositum The exclamations in §43 might suggest a copy of speeches by the Gracchi or Cato (see §43 *ex uetere aliqua oratione* n.), or given C.'s depiction of Caecilius' nascent rhetorical training, one may imagine a book of declamations or *controuersiae*, such as the later books of Seneca or those ascribed to Quintilian. In C.'s time they would have been known simply as *causae*; see Sen. *Conu.* 1. *pr.* 12 *Declamabat autem Cicero non quales nunc controuersias dicimus, ne tales quidem quales ante Ciceronem dicebantur, quas thesis uocabant. hoc enim genus materiae quo nos exercemur adeo nouum est ut nomen quoque eius nouum sit. controuersias nos dicimus: Cicero causas uocabat.* Teachers of rhetoric would instruct their students by using models of published oratory, and C. himself had a keen awareness that his work would be used in an educational setting; see Bonner (1977) 309–310.

uerbo uno 'by even a single word'. The postposition of *unus* is emphatic; see Marouzeau 1.207–208. Cf. *Ver.* II.4.8 *uerbo uno repellar*, *De orat.* 2.109, 3.189, and *Att.* 3.12.2.

47.5 discesseris 'to depart or deviate from an established text'; see *OLD s.u.* 6c and *TLL* V 1.1288.24.

47.6 in hac prolusione 'in this warm-up bout'. Bonner (1977) 57: '[T]he words *proludere* and *prolusio*, which C. jestingly uses as a play on *ludus*, retained a particularly military connotation, that is, preliminary practice for battle.' C. uses the same diction for an image of gladiatorial combat in discussing *exordia* at *Orat.* 2.32: *Atque eius modi illa prolusio debet esse, non ut Samnitium, qui uibrant hastas ante pugnam, quibus in pugnando nihil utuntur, sed ut ipsis sententiis quibus proluserint uel pugnare possint.* Serv. *A.* 12.106, where this passage is cited, glosses *prolusio* as a *praemeditatio certaminis.*

47.7 nihil fueris 'you're a nobody', with an implication of incompetence; see *OLD s.u. nihil* 8b. Cf. C.'s self-deprecating remarks at *Fam.* 7.33.1 *nos enim plane ... nihil sumus*, and *Att.* 1.19.4 with Shackleton Bailey *ad loc.* Cf. §48 *ut tu tamen aliquid esse uideare* n.

in ipsa pugna 'in the actual fight'. In its literal sense, *pugna* could refer to fights between gladiators, boxers, and the like. For a similar comparison with declamations as a preliminary exercise before the 'bout' in the courtroom, cf. Quint. *Inst.* 5.12.17 *quia declamationes, quibus ad pugnam forensem uelut praepilatis exerceri solebamus ....* For this meaning of *ipse*, *OLD s.u.* 5 and *TLL* VII 2.339.4–19.

cum acerrimo aduersario Viz. Hortensius. *Aduersarius* has both a martial and legal meaning; *OLD s.u.* and *TLL* I 843.28–49. In the *actio prima*, it is C. that takes on the role of the *acerbus aduersarius* of senatorial corruption; see *Ver.* I.36 *Quoniam totus ordo paucorum improbitate et audacia premitur et urgetur infamia iudiciorum, profiteor huic generi hominum me inimicum accusatorem, odiosum, adsiduum, acerbum aduersarium.* For this *iunctura*, cf. *Quinct.* 37, *Har.* 34, *Tusc.* 5.76, *Ac.* 12, *Att.* 10.8.8, and Liv. 2.61.2.

47.8 putemus By shifting from the first-person singular, *arbitrabor*, to the first-person plural, C. is co-opting the jury into sharing his point of view; see §72 *a nobis* n. Cf. *Rosc. Am.* 54, and *Ver.* II.2.141.

Confirmatio III (§§47–51)

The 'Troupe' of Subscriptores

Someone might say that Caecilius' shortcomings will be shored up by his assistant prosecutors. But he has second-rate supporters: Appuleius, who is long in the tooth but short on training, and Alienus, who has shown himself to be a robust shouter but has never given any indication of oratorical skill. In any event, Caecilius' assistants would have to suppress whatever abilities they do have so as not to outshine the chief prosecutor – it is like actors in a Greek play; the supporting cast should never upstage the lead actor. Just imagine what a performance this will be when even mediocre speakers will have to hold themselves back to make Caecilius look better. He may find another assistant from this troupe of loiterers looking for an opportunity. They ought to have no part in C.'s prosecution. He has his own friends that he can rely upon if necessary. These profligate pleaders should spend their time with the other spendthrifts. C. is far too circumspect and committed to the Sicilians' cause to let a spy, in the guise of a guardian, slip into his confidence.

This portion of the *Diuinatio* on assistant prosecutors is appended to the discussion of Caecilius' rhetorical ability and yet constitutes a discrete subject within the *confirmatio.* C. first assails the experience and skill of Caecilius' would-be *subscriptores,* L. Appuleius and (T. or A.) Alienus, and their role in Caecilius' potential prosecution and then goes on to address the issue of his own assistant prosecutors. C., perhaps to his detriment, has none. His discussion of *subscriptores* – especially his reluctance to accept any not of his own choosing – is allusive (*ad ea quae dixerint*) and interrupts the flow of his argument. This disjointedness suggests compulsion. From it one may infer that potential prosecutors were expected to discuss this issue when bringing a charge before a praetor or making their case at a *diuinatio.* The process of subscription is not well documented or studied, and much must be extrapolated from C.'s comments here.

Subscriptores, so called because they would sign their name underneath the signature of the lead prosecutor on the *inscriptio* (also called a *subscriptio*), could join a prosecution either through the acceptance of the chief prosecutor or by judicial appointment, or through a combination of the two. In the first instance, a lead prosecutor would come, either to the *diuinatio* or before a magistrate at the *nominis delatio,* with a set of supporters of his own selection. These would normally be chosen from among his political allies or patrons or other interested parties; see Alexander (2002) 99. In the second instance, an assistant or assistants could be appointed, upon petition, by the jury at a *diuinatio* or, presumably, by the magistrate that admitted the charge if no *diuinatio* were necessary (Gel. 2.4.1). Potential *subscriptores* for appointment could come from among the unsuccessful candidates at a *diuinatio* (*Ver.* II.1.15 *ne subscribendi quidem, cum id postularet, facerent potestatem*) or from those who only wanted an assistant's role, perhaps being motivated by injury or potential gain (§49 *qui subscriptionem sibi postularunt cuicumque uos delationem dedissetis*). These potential assistants may also have expressed a desire to work under a particular lead prosecutor (§51). And while the lead prosecutor could express his opinion about these assignments, he may have had no choice in the matter (§50). The *subscriptor*'s role became official at the *nominis delatio.* It was not uncommon for major prosecutions to have at least three assistant prosecutors. While undertaking a prosecution without an assistant prosecutor was infrequent, it was not unheard of; e.g. Erucius seems to have been the only speaker for the prosecution of Roscius, and M. Tuccius was the sole prosecutor of C. Sempronius Rufus (*Fam.* 8.8.1).

One would normally have to assume that the duties of the *subscriptor*, especially when chosen by the lead prosecutor, were to assist in the prosecution as a speaker and/or an aide in the collection, organization, and presentation of material evidence and witnesses. Other injured parties may have been able to speak to another aspect of the alleged crime that had not been covered or investigated by the chief prosecutor. In addition to these practicalities, assistant prosecutors may have brought other assets with them, such as political influence or different oratorical strengths. In the case of the latter, an assistant may have had parts of the prosecution assigned to him accordingly. For example, when M. Plaetorius Cestianus led the prosecution of Fonteius, he was assisted by M. Fabius, whose connection to Q. Fabius Maximus Allobrogicus offered some political clout (see *Font.* 36, and Alexander (2002) 62–63). Likewise, Herennius, a more experienced orator, assisted the much younger Atratinus in his prosecution of Caelius, and assumed the important role of speaking last (see Alexander (2002) 221). Caecilius supposedly had two *subscriptores* in mind, L. Appuleius and Alienus; a potential third, C. suggests, could be procured from those wanting to assist whichever prosecutor the jury chose. This last unnamed potential *subscriptor* in the passage is portrayed as envisioning his role as a *custos*, but the implications of this characterization are unclear, and it may have been purely a Ciceronian invention; see §51 *'custodem … Tullio me apponite'* n.

At one point in this discussion, C. expresses concern about the competence or trustworthiness of any *subscriptores* that could be assigned to assist him; see §51. While a *subscriptor* could be a liability (cf. *Flac.* 81–82), C.'s abundance of caution and somewhat misleading suggestion that he has *subscriptores* in mind may be a ploy to cover for his lack of assistants, and to discourage the jury or magistrate from assigning one to him; see nn. *ad loc.* C. espouses a metaphor throughout which plays upon the semantic range of *actor* and compares these hopeful assistants to theatrical stereotypes; see §48 *ut in actoribus Graecis* n. below. One must be cautious in generalizing about the role of a *subscriptor* from what C. says here, and some scholarship on the matter is not sufficiently circumspect. See further (with caution) *RE s.u.*,

A. Jones (1972) 63–64, *Straf.* 372–373, 385–386, and Greenidge 465, 475–476. Each chapter that discusses a trial in Alexander (2002) also introduces what is known of the prosecutorial team and its connection to the defendant.

47.9 esto C. turns back to address the jury directly. *Esto* is a colloquial transition marker that signals a *concessio,* similar to εἶεν; 'very well then' or 'so be it' and may have a sarcastic undertone; see Risselada (1993) 115, 134–135. Cf. Pl. *Ps.* 935a and Ter. *Hau.* 572. For similar uses of *esto* in C., cf. *Rosc. Am.* 73 with Landgraf *ad loc., Ver.* II.5.42, and *Deiot.* 30; see also Hor. *S.* 1.6.19. On other marks of *concessio,* see further Seyffert 1§69.

nihil ... nihil The anaphora, asyndeton, and abrupt parataxis impart further emphasis to C.'s derisive and dismissive tone toward Caecilius. Cf. *nihil fueris* n. above.

at is frequently used to introduce an imagined objection that the speaker will proleptically address; for this rhetorical device, see §1 *si quis ... miratur* n. Here C. responds to the idea that Caecilius' oratorical shortcomings can be overcome by his cast of supporting prosecutors.

subscriptoribus 'assistant prosecutors'; for more on the process of *subscriptio,* see the introduction to §§47–51.

47.10 tamen ... tametsi Although *tametsi* is a concessive particle, it is more often found with the indicative than the subjunctive. C. frequently correlates *tametsi* with *tamen,* though he would eschew this pleonasm in his more mature style; see Parzinger 2.26–29. Here the typical arrangement of the correlating clauses is reversed; cf. Q. Cic. *Pet.* 32 *neque id tamen satis est, tametsi magnum est, si non sequitur spes utilitatis atque amicitiae, ne nomenclator solum sed amicus etiam bonus esse uideare.* For the pleonastic construction *tametsi ... tamen,* see further H-Sz. 672, and Landgraf at *Rosc. Am.* 49.

47.11 princeps in agendo The lead prosecutor; see *OLD s.u. princeps*², and *TLL* X 2.1279.67. Though as C. introduces an extended metaphor of Caecilius and his *subscriptores* as stage performers, the meaning of *princeps* as 'the leader of an acting troupe' will come to the fore; see §48 *princeps* n. For *ago,* see §19 *lege agi* n.

47.12 ornatissimus 'excellently prepared'; cf. *Ver.* II.3.186: [*Siculi*] *non, quem ad modum sperasti, tardiores fuerunt, sed ornatiores tuo iudicio ad testimonia dicenda uenerunt.* The image perhaps suggests someone prepared for battle; see *TLL* IX 2.1033.26. Cf. *Font.* 16 *exercitus … maximus atque ornatissimus.*

L. Appuleium (*MRR* Suppl. 23) Appuleius would become praetor in 59 and proconsul of Macedonia in 58. He was a non-noble and was 'said to be the first in his family to reach curule office (though not necessarily the senate). When Cicero was thrown into exile in 58, he eventually headed to [Appuleius'] *prouincia.* There Appuleius' quaestor (and relative) Cn. Plancius harbored Cicero in his official residence at Thessalonica from at least July through late November 58. When Cicero defended Plancius on the charge *de sodaliciis* he is tacit about Appuleius' role in all this, except to say that the governor "harbored the same fears as the others" who refused their aid'; Brennan (2000) 535, and *Planc.* 28, 99. He does not have the cognomen 'Saturninus' as some sources say. The *RE* and *MRR* 2, as printed, have incorrect information, but see Shackleton Bailey (1976) 14–15, (1992) 17 and Syme (1964) 111.

47.13 proximum 'next in line, second', with reference to ability or standing; see *TLL* X 2.2043.57–2044.7. Cf. *Clu.* 152.

hominem non aetate sed usu forensi atque exercitatione tironem A *tiro* was a trainee undergoing comprehensive instruction either as a military recruit or as a young man looking to embark on a legal and political career; see §35 *in foro, iudiciis, legibus* n. A tinge of ambiguity can be detected here, since C. has just deployed an extensive metaphor of heavy combat sports. At any rate, C. portrays Appuleius, like Caecilius, as a late-learner; see §27 *quoniam hoc primum tempus* n. On *usus* and *exercitatio,* see §35 *aut ratio aut exercitatio* n. and *Sul.* 47 *usu … robustior* with Berry *ad loc.* On chiasmus, see §32 *graue … graue* n.

§48

48.2 ut opinor 'if I remember correctly'. C. frequently uses this colloquial parenthetical expression to avoid the appearance of pedantry when discussing art, geography, or chronology. Here it breaks up his laundry list of names and adds to the conversational style of the passage, but it also implies a dismissive tone toward Alienus as a potential *subscriptor*. For *ut opinor* in C., see *Rosc. Am.* 46 with Landgraf, and *TLL* IX 2.724.67–725.30.

Alienum (*RE* 1) Some have believed this word to be the noun *alienus*, but the deictic *hunc* and specifying comments make it clear that C. is using a proper name; see [Asc.] 118. The possibility of confusion may have injected some humour into the reference – a form of *adnominatio*. The name is uncommon and is usually spelled as *Allienus* in inscriptions. Shackleton Bailey (1976) 8, 14 addresses the issue of haplography: 'A praenomen is evidently missing. *T.* would easily fall out after *habet*, but the praenomen of C.'s friend A. Allienus would fall out with equal ease. Despite the uncomplimentary nature of the reference [at *Diu. Caec.* 48], this could be the same person, since his friendly relations with Cicero are not attested until many years later.' This should remain an open question, however; C. may have bucked naming conventions to make an intentional play on Alienus' name; he certainly does so at §50 *ex quibus alienissimis hominibus* below. He will similarly make a play on Verres' name (pig, boar) in this speech at §57 and in the *actiones* proper; cf. *Ver.* II.1.121, 2.19, 191, 4.53, and 95. For more on name play, see Corbeill (1996) 57–98.

a subselliis 'from the crowd of onlookers'. *Subsellia* were the oblong narrow seats found in a variety of domestic and political contexts. Here C. refers specifically to those of the courtroom that were used by everyone except the presiding magistrate. In its plural form, *subsellia*, the word was so closely associated with legal proceedings that it was used as a metonym for the courts themselves; see *OLD* and *RE s.u.* With this latter meaning, C. speaks disparagingly of those who 'hang around the court'; cf. *De orat.* 1.264 *qui habitaret in subselliis neque quicquam amplius adferre quam quod causarum necessitas postularet.* The scholiast makes a supposition about C.'s reason for mentioning this detail: [Asc.] 118 *Vtrum hoc ad contemptum an ad genus laudis pertinet? Ego quasi ad laudem dictum accipio, ut maior irrisio sit Caecilii, <qui> nec a subselliis* *fuerit aliquando*. That explanation seems unsatisfactory. C. is more likely drawing attention to Caecilius' lack of preparation in that he hastily had to find a *subscriptor* among those present.

48.3 in dicendo ... in clamando Alienus is depicted as a noisy, boorish orator. Cf. *Brut.* 182 *ego tamen ita de uno quoque dicam ut intellegi possit quem existimem clamatorem, quem oratorem fuisse*, and *De orat.* 3.81 *clamatores odiosi ac molesti*. The verb *clamare* is also used of those hired audiences who shout and clap at trials. See Plin. *Ep.* 2.14.4–13, where he laments the practice, though he speaks approvingly of it at *Ep.* 6.2.3. For *dicere* used of elevated, oratorical speech, see §21 *loquere* n.

48.4 quidem The asyndeton and adversative *quidem* create a strong contrast between *in dicendo* and *in clamando*. Cf. *Ver.* II.1.25, 4.72, and *Orat.* 210 *id nos fortasse non perfecimus, conati quidem saepissime sumus*. See further Solodow (1978) 75–84.

bene robustum atque exercitatum 'well developed and experienced'. For *robustus* in this context, see Quint. *Inst.* 1.8.12: *Verum priora illa ad pueros magis, haec sequentia ad robustiores pertinebunt*; also *Sul.* 47 and *Cael.* 7 with Austin *ad loc.* For *exercitatum* see §35 *aut ratio aut exercitatio* n. For this coupling, see *Cat.* 2.20, Cels. 5.26.22, and Quint. *Inst.* 5.10.82 (contrasting).

in hoc spes tuae sunt omnes The postposition of *omnis* is uncommon in C. and emphatic; see Merguet 1.172. 'In him, you have put every last one of your hopes.'

48.5 actor Perhaps in anticipation of the metaphor; see *ut in actoribus Graecis* n. below. For the use of *actor* in Plautus and Terence to designate a 'leading actor', see Brown (2002) 228–229. The comparison of an advocate to a stage actor is found elsewhere in C.; see esp. *De orat.* 3.213–227.

48.6 iudicium (*PM* : *om.* γ) The reading of the French family deserves consideration. *Iudicium* could have been supplied by a scribe to fill out the meaning of *totum* according to regular parallels (e.g. §27 *causam publicam sustinere*; *Cael.* 70). Given the use of *actor* above and the comparison with Greek actors below, the double-entendre of *sustinere* as 'shoulder the task of' and 'sustain the role of (a character *uel sim.*)' would be more effective without *iudicium* expressed.

contendet The notion of competition remains (see *OLD s.u.* 4), yet this time between actors; see *Quinct.* 77, where C. compares himself to someone facing Roscius the actor: *qui uero cum ipso [Roscio] contenderent, eos, etiam si quid antea recti aut uenusti habere uisi essent, id amittere.*

48.7 consulet laudi et existimationi tuae 'have regard for *your* esteem and reputation'; *OLD s.u. consulo* 6b, and *TLL* IV 578.21. C. refers not to the *laus* and *existimatio* that Caecilius has currently but rather to the accolades that he hopes to gain from the prosecution of Verres. This would affirm the notion that both men's tacit motivation is simply to improve their standing in the social and political hierarchy. *Laus* implies 'the conscious desire to elevate and exalt ['la volonté consciente d'élever et d'exalter']'; Hellegouarc'h 366. It is an inheritable quality of the *nobiles*, but it can be acquired, among other activities, through legal advocacy; see Q. Cic. *Pet.* 38 *Praeterea magnam adfert laudem et summam dignitatem, si ii tecum erunt qui a te defensi et qui per te seruati ac iudiciis liberati sunt.* Later C. will claim that Caecilius can win *maiorem laudem* by dropping his suit altogether; see §60. *Existimatio,* on the other hand, refers to an impression that an individual has made upon his peers and the opinion that others have of him. The term has a neutral valence on its own (i.e. one can have both a *bona* and *mala existimatio*). Therefore, to evoke a positive connotation, it is often paired with another positive term; cf. *Ver.* II.1.5, and Caes. *Ciu.* 1.26.4 with *laus* (which is always positive), or in a phrase where the meaning is clear such as §72, where C. speaks of his own reputation. Political reputation (*existimatio, fama,* etc.) will become a key issue in the *conclusio*; see §§70–73. On *existimatio* and *laus* in Roman political vocabulary, see Hellegouarc'h 362–363 and 365–369, respectively. Although C. twice mentions that it may be problematic for the speaking ability of *subscriptores* to outshine the lead prosecutor, this seems to be a characteristic concern of unscrupulous prosecutors; see *Flac.* 82.

48.9 ut tu tamen aliquid esse uideare Both here and in §49 (*se aliquid futurum putet*), Caecilius' hoped-for importance is only a superficial appearance (*uideare*) or his own delusion (*se … putet*). *Esse aliquem* and *esse aliquid* are colloquial ellipses ('so that you may at least seem to be *something*', i.e. a person of importance). See *OLD s.u. aliquis* 11, *TLL* 1.1614.48–59, and Hoffman §154 n. Cf. *Att.* 3.15.8. For the use of neuter pronouns in this bathetic, derogatory sense, cf. §47 *ipse nihil est.*

ut in actoribus Graecis C. compares the proposed prosecutorial team under Caecilius to a troupe of actors, and in doing so he exploits the wide semantic range of the term *actor*; see *actor* n. above and cf. §1 *actorem* n. There is no scholarly consensus on C.'s exact reference here. Long, in his commentary, thought that C. must be referring to ethnically Greek actors in Greek plays. Thomas, Halm, and Richter, for example, follow the scholiast in construing *Graecus* as a transferred epithet, viz. that these are actors in *fabulae palliatae*, Roman adaptations of Greek plays, as opposed to the Atellan farce; see [Asc.] 119 *Palleatarum scilicet fabularum. In his enim, etiamsi Latinae sunt, Graeca omnia seruantur. Nam Latinae fabulae per pauciores agebantur personas, ut Atellanae, togatae et huiusmodi aliae.* (See further on Atellan farce Brown (2002) 227–228; Liv. 7.2.12.) Finally, the scholiast Porphyrio clearly thought that C. was referring to mime when he cites this passage in reference to Hor. *Ep.* 1.18.13–14: *ut puerum saeuo credas dictata magistro / reddere uel partis mimum tractare secundas.* These salacious productions were growing in popularity during the late Republic, and there could be multiple actors. The lead actor, the *archimimus*, was sometimes supported by a second actor who would parody the leader's movements and utterances; see Mayer *ad* Hor. *Ep.* 1.18.13–14. Or alternatively, C.'s reference may have been unclear to his audience when they first heard it.

However, C. has just explained that Caecilius' *subscriptores* would need to be attuned to the praise and reputation (*consulet laudi et existimationi tuae*) sought by the lead prosecutor. This notion of deference finds a parallel in the competition instituted in Athens in 449 BCE that gave an award to the best leading actor. Although there was an evolution in the number of actors that performed in classical Greek drama, tragedies were typically performed with only three speaking actors: a *protagonist*, a *deuteragonist*, and a *tritagonist*. In tragedies composed after 449, 'it is important to notice the regular presence of a leading character, whose prominence in the action of the play would almost certainly have justified the attribution of that role to a leading actor, who was in competition with other leading actors'; Ley (2006) 36. There was no award for the best supporting actor. As a result, a secondary actor may have tempered his talents in order the better to shine a spotlight on the protagonist. C.'s learned audience would have known about the lead roles of Greek tragedy, and the prominence of a single character, even if not for the sake of competition, may have been maintained in the Latin adaptations of Greek originals.

As for the *fabulae palliatae* of authors like Plautus and Terence, there are references to lead roles; cf. Ter. *Ph.* 26–27 *Latini Phormionem nominant / quia primas partis qui aget is erit Phormio.* The necessity to give way to another actor may not have arisen from any competition but from sociological changes in the perception of actors in the late Republic. 'The last century BC was the century of the individual … [and] counterbalancing the decline in importance of the dramatic poet was the rise in influence of the individual stage artists who were presented not only on the public stage but also in private houses, a factor which in the long run greatly contributed to their high profile in Roman life … the actors were more in the public eye; they were stars'; Jory (1988) 78. In fact, more names of stage artists are known from the period of C. than from any earlier period, and notable figures such as Sulla, Antony, and even C. himself were known to keep the company of performers. Marius was thought unsophisticated because he did not have actors over for dinner; see Sal. *Jug.* 85.39. In the staging of *fabulae palliatae*, the rise of actors' stardom may have had the effect that well-known actors were given the leading roles and those in more minor roles were expected to keep a lower profile. The lead actor exercised a degree of control over the supporting cast, but 'evidence for the way in which a Roman *actor* controlled his company is not plentiful …. It has sometimes even been claimed that the other members of the company were typically slaves owned by the *actor*'; Brown (2002) 234. For a register of Roman Republican actors, see Garton (1972) 231–265. C. also uses the metaphor of a play at *Ver.* II.2.18 *qualis iste in quarto actu improbitatis futurus esset?*

48.10 secundarum aut tertiarum partium 'a second or third role'. *OLD s.u. secundus* 10b and *pars* 9b, and *TLL* X 1.464.7–22, 465.31–46. Demosthenes uses δευτεραγωνιστής in the sense of a supporting speaker in a trial; see D. 19.10; and τριταγωνιστής as a pejorative; see D. 18.209, 19.247. See also §49 *primas … partes* n.

48.12 submittere 'lower his voice'; *OLD s.u.* 9a. The accusative and infinitive after *fieri* is rare in classical Latin, though there are other examples; cf. *Q. fr.* 1.3.6 *illud quidem nec faciendum est nec fieri potest, me diutius quam aut tuum tempus aut firma spes postulabit in tam misera tamque turpi uita commorari …*; K-St. 2.2.240. Perhaps *submittere* was construed as being more dependent on the verb of seeing, *uidemus.*

princeps C.'s extended metaphor now conjures up the other meaning of *princeps* as 'the leader of an acting troupe'; cf. Suet. *Cal.* 58.1; *TLL* X 2.1287.6. C. speaks of Hortensius playing the lead role though Cotta was nominally the lead prosecutor; see *Brut.* 317 *cum Cotta princeps adhibitus esset, priores tamen agere partis Hortensium.*

48.13 sic faciet Alienus 'Alienus will play his role like this'. For this meaning of *facere*, see *TLL* VI 95.22–44. Cf. Pl. *Epid.* 581 *ego lenocinium facio qui habeam alienas domi atque argentum egurgitem domo prorsus?*

tibi seruiet, tibi lenocinabitur After the comparison of Caecilius and his *subscriptores* to a troupe of actors, the etymological pun is unmistakable. Though *seruire* has a range of meanings and is commonly used in C. to mean 'have regard for', its literal meaning 'to be a servant for' is evoked here; cf. Pl. *Ps.* 610. The wordplay is confirmed by *lenocinari*, which is only found here in C., and which must take on an even more colourful meaning than 'to pander to', as is suggested by its etymological root, *leno*; see *TLL* VII 2.1153.28. Both the *leno* and the *seruus* were stock characters in *fabulae palliatae.* In this linguistic play on words, Alienus is cast in the role of both servant and brothel-keeper. Since role-doubling does not seem to have been a component of Roman comedy as it was in traditional Greek tragedy, the fact that he is having to play multiple roles underscores Caecilius' helplessness. Meanwhile the repetition of *tibi* in emphatic position and the asyndeton give the sentence a tone of mockery. The pun on *leno* itself gives the section a touch of comedic flair; see Welsh (2005) with references for a pun in Plautus on *leno.* For wordplay in Plautus generally, see Brinkhoff (1935), Mendelsohn (1907), and E. B. T. Spencer (1906). For the etymology of this verb, see Ernout–Meillet *s.u. leno.* For the role of the *leno* in comedy, see Arnold (1998).

minus aliquanto *Aliquanto* usually follows the comparative on which it depends and means 'a significant amount, a good deal'; cf. §18 *arcem, minus aliquanto nunc quidem munitam quam antea.*

14 48. contendet See *contendet* n. above.

§49

49.1 considerate, cuius modi accusatores … simus habituri C. continually shifts the grammatical subjects in these sections to good psychological effect. After speaking to Caecilius (*tibi*), he invokes the jurors with the imperative *considerate,* and then includes himself as a member of the jury and other onlookers in this first-person plural verb. This careful shifting implies that C. and his audience share the same critical point of view toward Caecilius and his supporters. On the future participle with the subjunctive, see §42 *sit allatura* n.

49.3 ex ea facultate C. softens the suggestion that Alienus possesses any sort of speaking ability with *si quam habet,* having already stated above that he has never seen him in the capacity of an advocate; §48 *qui quid in dicendo posset numquam satis attendi.* On *facultas,* see §35 *facultas agendi … dicendi consuetudo* n.

49.4 tum denique C. prefers this formulation to *tum demum.* For *tum denique* with conditional sentences, see H-Sz. 659.

aliquid futurum See §48 *ut tu tamen aliquid esse uideare* n.

49.5 uehemens The forceful orator is one that can move the emotions of his audience; cf. *Orat.* 69 *sed quot officia oratoris tot* *sunt genera dicendi: subtile in probando, modicum in delectando, uehemens in flectendo; in quo uno uis omnis oratoris est.* Such vehemence was not suited to the *exordium* and may suggest that Alienus would also need to cede the role of final prosecuting speaker; see *De orat.* 2.317. C. himself often spoke last among his fellow advocates, as this was the most important position for appealing to the emotions of the jury; see *Brut.* 190, and *Orat.* 130.

sibi ($D^{2mg} r^2 v^2$: tibi γPM) The transmitted reading, *tibi*, cannot be correct. In this section, C. has shifted to addressing the jury directly (e.g. *hoc considerate, Caecilius ... putet,* and *dedissetis*). The correction *sibi,* in stemmatically remote codices, is surely a conjecture but a good one. The reflexive must refer back to Caecilius (the subject of *putet*) rather than the subject of its own clause, Alienus; see K-St. 2.1.600.

primas ... partes 'the leading role', especially one in a play, and usually found in the plural; see *OLD s.u. pars* 9, *TLL* X 1.465.3, and similarly X 1.464.71. Cf. *Brut.* 317, and Ter. *Ph.* 26–27. For more on this comparison to theatrical roles, see §48 *ut in actoribus Graecis* n. Paradoxically, among a group of advocates, it would be the one most accomplished at swaying the jury that would speak last; see *uehemens* n. above.

49.6 quartum C. counts total prosecutors here, not simply *subscriptores.* A major trial could be expected to have as many as four prosecutors, as was the case at the trials of Scaurus, Murena, and Caelius; see also §47 *subscriptoribus* n. The defendant could have still more *patroni,* although this was rare; see [Asc.] *Sc.* 18C: *defenderunt Scaurum sex patroni, cum ad id tempus raro quisquam pluribus quam quattuor uteretur: at post bella ciuilia ante legem Iuliam ad duodenos patronos est peruentum.* For the number of advocates allowed under different statutes, see Greenidge 476.

49.7 ex illo grege *Grex* was also the technical term for an acting troupe; *OLD s.u.* 3b, and *TLL* VI 2333.45–57. Cf. Pl. *As.* 3; *Cas.* 22; *Ps.* 1334; Ter. *Hau.* 45; *Ph.* 32. [Asc.] 119: *Et non recessit a translatione scaenicorum, qui sunt tragici et comici, dicendo quartum actorem et gregem.* The deictic *ille* along with the preceding *non uideo* suggests that C. is glancing sardonically around the court and gesturing towards these individuals. 'The *actor* was not only the leading actor but the man in charge of the company (*grex*)'; Brown (2002) 229.

moratorum is an uncommon word and jokingly plays on the similarly sounding *oratorum*; on paronomasia / *annominatio*, see Lausberg §637. Both scholiasts identify them as a group of potential speakers, but [Asc.] 119 goes further: *obturbatores quosdam sordidosque causidicos significat, qui adhibebantur ad moram faciendam, dum meliores aduocati recrearentur et se denuo compararent ad dicendum.* The *OLD s.u.* 1 follows this active understanding as 'one who hinders or delays', viz. here to allow the leading orator some recovery time. That meaning, while possible, seems inadequate, and the scholiast may have been making a guess based on etymologies. The medio-passive sense of 'loiterer' seems more appropriate and characterizes these potential *subscriptores* as undesirable opportunists lingering around the Forum and looking for work; cf. the painted warning from *CIL* IV 813: *OTIOSIS LOCVS HIC NON EST, DISCEDE MORATOR*. The rarity of the term led to its corruption in the *deteriores* to the orthographically proximate and more common *oratorum.* The correct reading is preserved in *P* and the scholiasts, while the French family transmits *meatorum* ('passerby'? see *TLL* VIII 5.11.58) and the incomprehensible *meato,* which prompted a corrector of *D* to postulate *mercatorum* and another word which is illegible.

subscriptionem 'the role of assistant prosecutor'; *OLD s.u.* 5.

postularunt There are not enough examples of *subscriptio* with its above meaning to show if *subscriptionem postulare* was a fixed legal phrase, though it would seem likely; cf. *Ver.* II.1.15. For *postulare* as 'to make application (to the praetor or other magistrate) for', see *OLD s.u.* 2, and *TLL* X 2.261.67–84. This would suggest that there was an official procedure before the jury in the *diuinatio* or the presiding magistrate to express interest in a position as an assistant prosecutor.

49.8 cuicumque uos delationem dedissetis 'to whomever you grant the right to act as prosecutor'. The phrase *delationem dare* is related to the *nominis delatio* – or what is sometimes referred to as the *criminis delatio* – which was the next step in the pre-trial process after the *diuinatio*; cf. §10. At that point, the lead prosecutor went before the president of the court to specify the accused and state the alleged offence. For the full procedure, see Introduction §III.

§50

50.1 ex quibus alienissimis hominibus 'but from this group of men totally alien to you', viz. men who had expressed interest in supporting the prosecution – whether the lead prosecutor be C. or Caecilius – since C. goes on to suggest that someone from this same group could be assigned to assist him. An additional pun is made on the name of Alienus, whose name he has repeated four times in a short section of speech; see §48 *Alienum* n. This prepositional phrase is separated from the result clause to which it properly belongs for emphasis and is a partitive attribute of *hospes aliquis*; see *OLS* 1.1034.

50.2 hospes aliquis As *aliquis* normally precedes its noun, postposition emphasizes its headword; see Marouzeau 1.165–168. *Hospitium*, properly speaking, can only exist between strangers; see Hellegouarc'h 51–52. Caecilius must depend upon a *hospes*, while C. has *amici*. The distinction between *amicitia* and *hospitium*, blurred in some cases, is set in contrast here.

50.3 non sum tantum honorem habiturus The phrase *honorem habere alicui* means 'to pay someone tribute', though in modern parlance, one would say here 'I would not do them the honour of …'; *OLD s.u. honos* 3, and *TLL* VI 2920.45–51. Cf. *Ver.* II.1.38. See further Hellegouarc'h 384.

ad ea quae dixerint The context and content of these supposed statements is unclear. Though C. claims that he is going to deal with this issue in short order, the statements of these potential *subscriptores* still seem to merit attention. A complete fabrication on C.'s part would serve no apparent rhetorical purpose, since it detracts from the flow of his argument. Instead, therefore, this may allude to an unknown part of the pre-trial subscription process during which other interested parties expressed a desire to be a *subscriptor* before the *diuinatio.* The only statement that C. recounts explicitly is the request of an anonymous interlocutor (discussed below) to be assigned to the trial, so that he can 'keep guard' over C., who gives scant reason why he should be rejected. C.'s remarks are simply dismissive and somewhat abusive; see nn. below.

50.4 certo loco A defined section within a speech; cf. *Rhet. Her.* 3.16. See *TLL* VII 2.1592.43–1593.22.

singillatim For a similarly phrased *praeteritio,* cf. *Ver.* II.3.53 *Etenim quoniam summam ac numerum iniuriarum uobis, iudices, non possum expromere, singillatim autem de unius cuiusque incommodo dicere infinitum est, genera ipsa iniuriarum, quaeso, cognoscite,* and 5.143. For the orthographical variations of *singillatim,* see Neue-Wagener 2.560.

50.5 breuiter … quasi praeteriens 'briefly … more-or-less skipping over them'. C signposts the rhetorical technique of *praeteritio,* in which the speaker states his intention to leave certain points out of his speech. The effect of the *praeteritio* is threefold: first, C. can skip over arguments, perhaps valid ones, for assigning some other prosecutors to assist him; second, his dismissive attitude belittles these potential assistants; and third, in telling his audience that he is going to abbreviate this part of his speech, he can gain an even stronger interest from them in the sections that follow. On this method of garnering interest, see Quint. *Inst.* 9.2.55. On *praeteritio,* see Lausberg §§882–886. C. shows much the same disdain for any other potential *subscriptores* as he showed toward Apuleius and Alienus; see §48 *ut opinor* n.

50.6 tantane … inopia … tanta inopia The anaphora juxtaposes C., who has plenty of eloquent supporters, with the would-be *subscriptores,* who are simply looking for someone to prosecute.

uobis C. shifts to address the whole group of unnamed would-be *subscriptores,* i.e. litigators awaiting the outcome of the *diuinatio.* It is the only time in the *Diuinatio* that C. addresses a group that is not the jury.

50.7 ex his quos mecum adduxerim The reference is unclear, though C. would have gestured in the direction of his supporters. Among them may have been his cousin, Lucius, who travelled with him on his trip to Sicily to obtain evidence against Verres and may have been a *subscriptor*; see *Ver.* II.4.25, 145. If he did not want to share the spotlight during the prosecution, he may misleadingly suggest that he has other *subscriptores* in mind.

50.8 addatur The use of the passive has clouded this legal procedure, but it suggests that a *subscriptor* could be appointed even if the lead prosecutor was unwilling. For *addere* as 'assign in an official capacity', see *OLD s.u.* 4, and *TLL* I 582.25.

50.9 praeripere A problematic argument, since the same could be said of C.; cf. §4 *dicebam habere eos actorem Q. Caecilium* n.

50.10 ad columnam Maeniam A column at the north end of the Roman Forum, which may have been visible from the location of the *diuinatio.* If so, C. could have gestured towards it. In addition to its use as a time-keeping gnomon (Plin. *Nat.* 7.212), this column was used at the time of C. for displaying the names of debtors; see Schol. Bob. *ad Sest.* 18 *Dicit factum Gabinium superbiorem illo praecipue, quod esset aere alieno defaeneratus. Et utitur ambiguis locorum nominibus: nam puteal uocabatur locus in uicinia fori, ubi erat columna etiam Maenia, aput quam debitores a creditoribus proscribebantur.* Creditors would use these proscriptions (*proscriptiones debitorum*) to advertize publicly the names of insolvent debtors; see Berger *s.u.* and Weiss (1949). The action of posting the names may not have been a legal sanction proper but rather public ridicule and an indication of a debtor's lack of creditworthiness; cf. Q. Manlius at *Clu.* 39. According to [Asc.] 119, the *tresuiri capitales*, under whose purview came slaves and lower-order freedmen, would inflict their punishments in the vicinity of this column: *uestra defensione condignos, uelut fures et seruos nequam, qui apud triumuiros capitales ad columnam Maeniam puniri solent.* With one proverbial stone, C. assails both the oratorical ability and the socio-economic status of these other potential assistant prosecutors by implying that they are only suited for unimportant trials and are perhaps impoverished themselves; see n. below. On the proscription of debtors, see further Hinard (1985) 25–27, Cascione (1996), and *Sest.* 18 with Kaster *ad loc.*

Although there are conflicting stories about the origin of this monument, the modern scholarly consensus is that it was erected in 338 in honour of C. Maenius' defeat of the Latins; see Plin. *Nat.* 34.20. The other origin story is told by [Asc.] 120 (201 Stangl) and Porphyrio *ad* Hor. *Sat.* 1.3.21, who report that Maenius sold his house in the Forum but reserved a single column for himself so that he could watch the gladiatorial combats staged there. Richardson rejects this explanation (*NTDAR s.u. columna Maenia*) on the grounds that houses large enough to require columns of this size would have been extremely rare at this date. The conflicting stories, he theorizes, may have arisen from the lack of an inscription or crowning statue. For its location, see Carandini (2017) 158, 161, table 21; and the illustration in Introduction §III. On political spaces in oratory, see Vasaly (1993) and Morstein-Marx (2004) 92–107. **ad columnam Maeniam** The lemma of [Asc.] leaves no doubt as to the proper name of the column, which was later corrupted to *aenea* and *aerea* in the medieval manuscript tradition. The ablative construction of the medieval MSS (*a columna*), however, has merit: *a columna Maenia* ('from the Maenian column'), i.e. with some help from the information provided by the Maenian column.

uestri ordinis reos reperiatis 'find defendants of your own ilk'; *OLD s.u. ordo* 5. C. insultingly suggests that these would-be *subscriptores* are financially destitute; see *ad columnam Maeniam* n. above. Calling them an *ordo* was surely a sarcastic slight as this was a term usually reserved for classifying the social standing of senators and *equites*; see *TLL* IX 2.961.31–53. The insult was perhaps highlighted by the alliterative cretic-spondee ending to the clausula.

§51

51.1 'custodem ... Tullio me apponite' *Sermocinatio* from an imagined petitioner. The relationship implied by *custos* could be either collaborative or adversarial. The term ranges in sense from a protector/guardian, who ensures safety and well-being, to a guard/overseer, such as a gaol-keeper or nightwatchman, who keeps watch over a person or situation that is a potential threat; cf. *Ver.* II.5.12 *custos defensorque prouinciae*, and Pl. *Aul.* 556 *Argus … quem quondam Ioni Iuno custodem addidit*; e.g. *carceris custos.* In the first sense, the *subscriptor* would look out for C.'s interests in preparing the prosecution; in the latter, he would ensure C.'s proper handling of the trial and be on the lookout for *praeuaricatio.* At first glance, this second role seems farcical; presumably a *diuinatio* jury would not appoint a prosecutor who seemed untrustworthy. But if one considers the fact that C. had no prior connection with Verres and suffered no injury, it stands to reason that some other person or party may have requested to join the suit to ensure that due diligence was done.

C. initially suggests that this assistant would be so incompetent as to disclose or steal his prosecutorial strategy and evidence, but his continued characterization imputes more nefarious motives to the assistant prosecutor and draws upon the more adversarial sense of *custos.* The *subscriptor*, he contends, would conduct advance espionage and tamper with evidence to ensure, not C.'s success, but Verres' safety and acquittal. Nowhere else is a *subscriptor* characterized as a *custos*, and this representation may have been a Ciceronian invention to evoke for his audience the image of the guardian from Roman comedy; see Pl. *Merc.* 90–92, and Ter. *Phorm.* 287–288. If this was in fact a turn of phrase used by a potential *subscriptor*, C. certainly latched onto it for comic effect. He uses *custos/custodire* four more times in this section to solidify the characterization. **Tullio** Over the course of C.'s career, he shifts from referring to himself by his *nomen*, Tullius, to his *cognomen*, Cicero; see Shackleton Bailey (1992) 95. For *apponere*, 'to appoint (a person esp. to someone else in a specific capacity, e.g. as a guard)', see *OLD s.u.* 7, and *TLL* II 301.54–57.

51.2 ad meas capsas A *capsa* was a cylindrical container, often made of beech wood, that was used for storing and transporting objects, particularly documents, in which capacity it was synonymous with a *scrinium*; see Plin. *Nat* 16.299, and *N-P s.u. scrinium.* In other instances, a *capsa* could be used for storing fruit; see Plin. *Nat.* 15.82, Mart. 11.8.3, Dig. 33.7.12.1, and *RE s.u.* These multiple uses of a *capsa*, combined with the image of Caecilius needing to take in a fourth speaker as a guest (*hospes*), cast this unnamed speaker in the comedic role, not of the guardian (*custos*), but rather of the parasite (*parasitus*). The stock character of the parasite as found in the plays of Plautus and Terence is generally characterized by opportunism, a lack of wealth, and a dependence upon his patron for food. The loitering potential *subscriptor* has all the trappings of a parasite in search of dinner: 'The parasite of Greek comedy would scout out an establishment at which a special meal was being made ready – by keeping an eye on who was hiring cooks in the agora (Alexis 259) ... – and present himself at the hospitably open front door'; Damon (1997) 28–29. Greenwood's Loeb translates *capsas* as 'cupboards' and Morabito as *cassetto*, both of which preserve the double-entendre better than Fuhrmann's *Aktenbehälter* and Fiocchi and Marinone's *cassette dei mei documenti.* For the general characteristics of the parasite, see Damon (1997) 23–36, and 195–251 for parasites in C. Martianus Capella 522 (*RLM* 477.27) seems to have found fault with C.'s spondaic *capsas* before *admisero,* but there seems to be a lacuna in the text of Mart. Cap.; see Stahl and Johnson (1977) *ad loc.* In any case, the two words form a perfectly acceptable molossus and cretic ending.

51.3 enunties ... auferas The implication seems to be that a *subscriptor,* be it inadvertently or intentionally, might disclose information (*enuntiare*) about the evidence or prosecutorial strategy to the public or defence counsel, or even worse, that he would abscond with evidence; cf. §28, where the Sicilians have the same concern about Caecilius. For *enuntiare* in the sense of disclosing confidential information, see *TLL* V 2.623.49–80; cf. *Rosc. Am.* 110, and *Mur.* 25. Unlike some modern judicial systems, the Roman system had no right of discovery, and the prosecution would not have to disclose evidence before the trial; see Riggsby (2010) 198.

51.4 sed de isto 'custode' toto 'about this whole "guardian" business'. For *istuc totum* as a kind of dismissive summarizing phrase with a quotation, cf. *Tul.* 26 *At istuc totum 'DOLO MALO' additur in hoc iudicio eius causa qui agit* .... When a declinable noun is quoted or commented on, it is normal idiom to adapt the word to the syntax of the context, as is done here (*custode*). Cf. Ov. *Met.* 9.528 *scripta 'soror' fuerat; uisum est delere 'sororem',* but this is not without exception; cf. Plin. *Ep.* 3.2.2 and Cat. 86.3. See further Adams (2013) 220–221.

breuissime respondebo That C. must respond further suggests that these were petitions put before the praetor before the *diuinatio.* Cf. §50 *breuiter ... quasi praeteriens* n.

51.7 me inuito There is an implication that a *subscriptor* could be appointed by the jury in the *diuinatio* even if the lead prosecutor wanted otherwise, but it may have been a common component of a *diuinatio* speech for a potential prosecutor to express his opinions about *subscriptores.* For more information on the appointment process, see §47 *subscriptoribus* n.

aspirare Cf. §20 *accedere aut aspirare audeat* n.

fides ... diligentia The asyndeton and rigidly parallel clauses, with the repetition of *-em re-* at the end of each, give the phrase a kind of aphoristic and moralizing quality. Moreover, C. concludes the discussion of *subscriptores* with a clever twist. Under normal circumstances, one might think that refusing to accept assistants or include other interested parties in the prosecution would arouse suspicion. However, rather than having this accrue to his detriment, C. asserts that his circumspection is actually a firm indication of his reliability and attentiveness. C. has been emphasizing his *fides* throughout and reiterates at the *conclusio* the necessity of *fides* and *diligentia* in a prosecutor; see §§67, 73. C. was fond of pairing *fides* and *diligentia*; in this corpus alone, see *Ver.* I.34, II.1.19, 1.135, 2.179, and 3.64. On *fides*, see §5 *officio, fide, misericordia* n.

51.8 speculatorem The revelation is a fitting conclusion to C.'s extended metaphor on theatrical performers; in a genre so full of mistaken identities, he purports to remove the mask and uncover the person beneath the *persona.* The potential *subscriptor,* in the guise of a *custos,* is in fact a spy. In the late Republic, in addition to delivering messages and scouting, *speculatores* were used in reconnaissance and espionage; see *B. Afr.* 35.4. When they were captured, rather than being held as prisoners of war, they were usually summarily executed; see *B. Hisp.* 13.3, 20.5. Clodius is so characterized at *Dom.* 18, but otherwise in his speeches, C. employs its literal sense; cf. *Ver.* II.5.164–165, and *Man.* 46. The use of *speculator* activates the more adversarial sense of *custos*; see *'custodem ... Tullio me apponite'* n. above. Cf. *Cat.* 1.6 *Multorum te etiam oculi et aures non sentientem, sicut adhuc fecerunt, speculabuntur atque custodient.* For a full discussion of the term *speculator* and the evolution of its role, see Dubuisson (1996). On espionage in the late Republic, see Sheldon (1987) 51–139, esp. 129–132.

REPREHENSIO (§§52–71)

After the digression on *subscriptores*, Cicero passes from his *confirmatio* to the *reprehensio* – the part of the speech in which an orator attempted to weaken the arguments of his opponent; see *Inu.* 1.78 *Reprehensio est, per quam argumentando aduersariorum confirmatio diluitur [aut infirmatur] aut eleuatur.* In this regard, the *reprehensio* was akin to a defence, and for that reason, it could be more challenging than the *confirmatio*; see Quint. *Inst.* 5.13.3. The defence counsel, in the normal course of a criminal proceeding, was at an inherent disadvantage inasmuch as one had to wait for (or anticipate) the arguments of the prosecution to formulate a response; cf. *Ver.* I.55, II.1.4–25, and see Powell (2010b). The prosecution, meanwhile, could plan an entire case in advance and had an opportunity to respond, to some extent, to the arguments of the defence during the presentation of witnesses and evidence. But in a *diuinatio* proceeding, the first speaker had only one opportunity to present his case. To borrow Quintilian's metaphor (see above), C. is having to parry an attack before his opponent's sword is even drawn.

Even so, C. could anticipate Caecilius' likely angle of attack. According to Quintilian, *diuinationes* generally present two main arguments: the speaker discusses his *maior causa* and establishes the likelihood that he will bring the more genuine and robust prosecution (one characterized by *industria, uis*, and *fides*); see the introduction to §10. Considering the retributive nature of Roman justice to which C. appeals (§58 *iniuriae ... impunitae atque inultae*), it stands to reason that competing litigants in a *diuinatio* would state the nature and severity of their injuries and relationship to the accused. C. responds as though Caecilius will fall back on this traditional approach. He constructs counterarguments in support of the claim that Caecilius has been personally injured by Verres (§§52–58) and then presents the negative implications of Caecilius' service as Verres' quaestor (§§59–65); see introductions *ad loc.*

What is perhaps most innovative and intriguing about this portion of C.'s speech is that the *Diuinatio in Caecilium* contains a *reprehensio* at all. In presenting their arguments in a *diuinatio*, potential prosecutors may have made a passing reference to the greater gravity of their claims versus those of other would-be prosecutors (e.g. a person who had lost the entirety of his property and his station in life would be a more energetic and diligent prosecutor than the man who had only lost a set of silver plate). But an extensive counterargument may have come as a surprise. While the *reprehensio* does put the *Diu. Caec.* into a more forensic mould and demonstrates C.'s rhetorical prowess in a judicial context, it also betrays his inherently defensive position, open as he was to allegations of political opportunism. By all normal measures, Caecilius has the better claim to lead the prosecution against Verres. C. cannot claim that Verres has committed any illegal act against him or that he had any prior relationship with him whatsoever. He is therefore obliged to dismantle the more traditional strengths of Caecilius' case (§§52–58) and find ways to make Caecilius' familiarity with Verres into a liability of its own (§§59–65).

For more on *reprehensiones* generally, see Lausberg §430 and Berry on *Sul.* 36–45. Not all rhetorical theorists treat the *reprehensio* and the *probatio* as separate parts of the speech; some prefer to speak generally of the *argumentatio*/πίστις since they use the same method of argument; see Arist. *Rh.* 2.26, 3.17 δεῖ δὲ καὶ ἐν συμβουλῇ καὶ ἐν δίκῃ ἀρχόμενον μὲν λέγειν τὰς ἑαυτοῦ πίστεις πρότερον, ὕστερον δὲ πρὸς τἀναντία ἀπαντᾶν λύοντα καὶ προδιασύροντα. See also *Inu.* 1.78–96, *Rhet. Her.* 1.4, 2.3–12, *De orat.* 2.331, *Part.* 44–45, and Quint. *Inst.* 5.13.1–60, esp. 5.13.18, which mentions the argument in §§59–65.

Reprehensio I

Iniuria non facta (§§52–58)

Perhaps Caecilius will claim that he has been injured by Verres. That certainly seems possible given that everyone else in Sicily has been. But these other Sicilians have found someone to avenge the wrongs done to them. Meanwhile, in vainly pursuing his own self-interest, Caecilius will allow these other crimes to go unpunished and unavenged. Surely he will concede that the lead role for the prosecution should be given to the person who has suffered the greatest injustice. The wrongs committed against an entire province must inevitably outweigh the misfortune suffered by one man. And once the nature of this supposed 'injustice' has been described, it will be clear that there is no injustice at all.

In the first part of his refutation, C. challenges Caecilius' rationale for prosecuting Verres. C. postulates (since Caecilius has yet to speak) that Caecilius will try to demonstrate that he is motivated by an *iniuria* that Verres committed against him. C. adheres closely to rhetorical precepts which recommend that a speaker deny his opponent's claims, or else grant their claims but deny the validity of the conclusions drawn from them. C. at first concedes the notion that Caecilius is motivated by an illegal act committed against him by Verres (§54 *quod si* ...; §55 *at* ...) and later denies the categorization of the act as unlawful (§58). Verres' alleged deed (*factum*) will be analysed in three discrete sections that evaluate the magnitude of the deed, the nature of the supposed offence, and whether the *factum* should be classified as an *iniuria*.

C.'s method of argumentation draws upon the Hellenistic rhetorical theory of stasis (στάσις, *constitutio, status*). According to this theory, the rhetorician pinpointed the area of disagreement and formulated the precise question (*quaestio*) that should be the focus of the judges' inquiry. Rhetorical theorists tended to explain the basic outline of this approach in reference to a criminal defence (as this was the most natural application). So, for example, when a plaintiff alleges that the defendant committed some act (*fecit*), the defendant could simply deny the allegation (*non feci*). In that case, the point of disagreement concerns whether or not the defendant committed the act, and the jury is confronted with the question, 'Did he do it or not?' (*an fecerit*), an example of a *quaestio* from the *status coniecturae.* If the defendant admits that he committed the act, he can attempt to qualify his admission (*feci sed …*) by claiming (1) that what he did should not be classified as a crime (*status finitionis*), or (2) that he acted with legal justification (*status qualitatis*), or (3) that he is being tried in an inappropriate legal venue (*status translationis*). These *status* have the corresponding *quaestiones*: *quid fecerit, an iure fecerit,* and *an actio iure intendatur.* Depending on the case at issue, the appropriate *quaestio* or *status* could change as the argument progresses, as happens in C.'s line of argument in §§52–58; see further Lausberg §93.

C. first turns to the *status quantitatis,* whereby the deed is admitted but is shown to be quantitatively less important than had been alleged (*quantum sit?*; §54). Rather than give a description of the *factum* at the outset of his counterargument, C. argues the question of severity by comparison: Verres has committed injustices throughout the island of Sicily and so the injuries suffered by an entire province, which C. claims to represent, must outweigh any particular loss – whatever it may be – suffered by an individual; see §54 *maximam … iniuriam* n. This comparison is followed by C.'s exposition of the supposed *iniuria,* the Agonis Affair, which is rooted in the *status qualitatis* and explores the nature of the deed (*quale sit?*; §§55–57). In this particular instance, C. concludes that Verres did deprive Caecilius of property, but since these goods were illegally acquired in the first place, Verres acted lawfully and in accordance with moral and religious scruple; i.e. '*fecit sed iure*'; Lausberg §§123–130, and *Inu.* 1.18. This justification of Verres' actions allows C. to move to a question of definition (*quid sit?*; §58). The *status finitionis* presents the question of whether or not the facts of the case are labelled 'correctly and objectively in legal terms'; i.e. '*feci sed aliud*'; Lausberg §§104–122, 166–170. C. therefore restricts and more clearly defines *iniuria* in the judicial context. From an etymological view, a deed can only be called an *iniuria* if it is done *non iure*; see §52 *iniuriam* n. C. then goes on to engage in an onomastic argument: since Verres' actions in the Agonis Affair have been demonstrated to be just, Caecilius' deprivations may be called a 'loss' but not an *iniuria*; see §58 *laesum … iniuriam* n. The argument is tantamount to a denial (or, at the very least, a *translatio*) of the initial proposition and a rejection of Caecilius' stated motivation.

As a result, C. gives a rather full defence of Verres concerning this one episode and finally has to soften his position; see §57. In spite of that, this first refutation is a *tour de force* of progressive rhetorical argument and demonstrates quite clearly for the audience C.'s claim: *noui omnis hominis petitiones rationesque dicendi* – and that he can deploy them himself.

For an outline of stasis theory in increasing detail and complexity, see Lausberg §§79–223. Among the ancient sources, the fullest theoretical exposition was that of Hermagoras of Temnos, a second-century BCE Greek orator whose work influenced later rhetoricians; see *Inu.* 1.10–19, and Quint. *Inst.* 3.6.1–104. Cf. *Rhet. Her.* 1.18–27, whose system is considerably different. Many Hellenistic rhetorical handbooks do not admit the *status quantitatis*, or treat it as a species of the *status qualitatis*; see Lausberg §§128, 178, and Quint. *Inst.* 7.4.41–44, 3.6.48 *Fecerunt alii totidem* [quattuor] *status, sed alios, an sit, quid sit, quale sit, quantum sit, ut Caecilius et Theon.* For another evaluation of kind and quantity, cf. *Ver.* II.3.203 *ea res quam ego dico et ea quam tu fecisti inter se genere iniuriae, non magnitudine pecuniae differat.* For more on the Agonis Affair, see the introduction to §§55–57.

§52

52.1 uerum ut ad te, Caecili, redeam Now that C. has dealt with the issues of potential *subscriptores* for both himself and Caecilius, the transition to the *reprehensio* begins by returning to Caecilius' shortcomings as an orator, which had been discussed at length in the *probatio* (§§27–47). *Verum* signals a *reditus ad propositum*; cf. *Ver.* II.4.35 *Verum ut Lilybaeum … reuertatur* and *Rosc. Am.* 91 *Verum ut coepi dicere.* For other examples, see Seyffert 1§42. Likewise, the vocative *Caecili* marks a shift in the line of argumentation; see §2 *iudices* n. *Redire* can mean to return to an argument in progress; cf. *Planc.* 76 *ut redeam ad Plancium.* C. resumes the attack on Caecilius' oratorical ability interrupted by the *anticipatio* on *subscriptores*; see §47 *at* n.

quam multa ... quam multa C. was fond of this initial repetition and asyndeton; cf. *Font.* 38, *Clu.* 150, *Man.* 32, *Orat.* 223, *Luc.* 75, *Fin.* 4.5, and *Diu.* 2.99. The sentences also echo §27 *Cognosce ex me, quoniam hoc primum tempus discendi nactus es, quam multa esse oporteat in eo qui alterum accuset,* and this sentence bookends C.'s 'oratorical education' for Caecilius.

52.2 uides 'you appreciate'; *OLD s.u.* 14c.

52.3 cupiat A primary objective established by C. in the *partitio* (§10) was to determine *quem minime uelit is qui eas iniurias fecisse arguatur.* C.'s change in diction signals a move from an expression of preference (*uelit*) to one of outright desire. *Cupiat* highlights the extent to which Caecilius fails this test.

profecto iam 'surely now'; see §1 *profecto* n. For *profecto* as an amplifier, see *TLL* X 2.1671.10–18.

quid ad haec dici potest C. usually levels questions of this sort when starting an *anticipatio* to respond to potential retorts from his opponents; cf. *Ver.* II.3.169, and 5.147. The expression is frequently personal such as at *Quinct.* 55 *Quid ad haec Naeuius?* and *Ver.* II.3.205 *Quid ad haec Hortensius?* C. uses the passive construction as a jibe against Caecilius, which he explains in the following vignette – viz. by saying Caecilius is relying on a rhetorical textbook and his advisor to formulate his response. **haec** (*PM* : *hoc* γ*O*) The use of the plural pronoun is regular in this fixed phrase, while *h(a)ec, hoc,* and their abbreviations can easily be misread.

52.4 quid tu dicturus sis See §42 *sit allatura* n. **tu** is omitted in the French family, but the pronoun provides an emphatic contrast with *hunc librum.*

52.5 hunc librum C. recapitulates the motif of Caecilius as a late-learner and the insinuation that he has a rhetorical teacher and textbook to hand to help him craft his speech; see §§43, 47 with nn. *ad loc.* The scene takes on added humour through C.'s quasi-personification of the book. Underlying this invective against Caecilius is the meta-rhetorical lesson that presents Caecilius as an apotreptic *exemplum* and demonstrates to the reader of the

Diuinatio the incorrect way to employ written speeches in rhetorical training; see Introduction §V.

monitor tuus hic Perhaps the same person as the *magister ludi nescioqui* in §47. In its most basic sense, a *monitor* was someone who offered advice; see Ernout–Meillet *s.u. moneo*, and Schol. Gronov. 327 Stangl [*monitor*] *dicitur qui uel propria dicenti suggerit uel aliena.* However, if one needs recourse to a *monitor* in the midst of a proceeding, this is generally a sign of poor preparation; Quint. *Inst.* 6.4.8–9. Moreover, in addition to its being a further slight against Caecilius, the image of a *monitor* may revive the conceit of Caecilius and his *subscriptores* as actors; cf. §§48–51. Fest. p. 138M *<monitores> qui monent histriones in scaena.* It is possible that these disparaging remarks about an unnamed *monitor* – and earlier, a *magister* – conceal the fact that Caecilius has supporters with him at the *diuinatio.* C. has simply reinterpreted the meaning of their presence. The penultimate position of the deictic *hic* adds emphasis. On these meanings of *monitor*, see *TLL* VIII 1420.61–69.

52.6 recte monere The phrase is common in Plautus (cf. *Men.* 346–347, *Mos.* 842, *Bac.* 330, *Per.* 603, *Ps.* 1050, and *Rud.* 829) and may suggest a colloquial tone that plays on the etymology of *monitor* above; cf. *De orat.* 2.97, and *Ver.* II.4.5 *recte admones.*

discedas C. exploits the semantic range of *discedere*, which can mean both 'to withdraw as a party from a trial' and 'to depart from a written example'; cf. Berger *s.u. discedere* and §47 *si ab isto libro ... uerbo uno discesseris.* There seems to be no procedural restriction that would have prevented Caecilius from dropping his bid for the prosecution before responding to C.'s speech.

52.7 neque When a positive *ut* clause is followed by a negative one, C. and other classical authors generally prefer *neue*, but C. does occasionally use *neque*, as here; cf. *Ver.* II.3.115, *De orat.* 2.350 *adiungam etiam de memoria, ut labore Crassum leuem neque ei quicquam aliud de quo disserat relinquam nisi ea quibus haec exornentur.* See further *OLS* 1.718–719, and K-St. 2.1.192–193. *Neque* would become more common in post-classical authors.

uerbum ullum The postposition of *ullus* is emphatic; 'not a single word'. Cf. *Ver.* II.4.133 *signum ullum.* On the relative placement of *ullus,* see Marouzeau 1.165–172.

52.8 an can mark a question that is 'an ironic or depreciative continuation of a preceding question, especially a rhetorical one'; see *OLS* 1.330–333, K-St. 2.2.519, and Seyffert 1§51. Cf. *Prou.* 9 *an uero in Syria diutius est Semiramis illa retinenda?*

dictitas Caecilius would presumably have made known his grievance with Verres at the *postulatio*; see Greenidge 459.

iniuriam C. suggests that Caecilius is using the term *iniuria* in a loose sense (i.e. 'mistreatment'), but later he will insist upon a narrower legal definition; see §58 *laesum … iniuriam* n. The lack of juristic texts on public law means that further explication must be found from civil jurisprudence. After the advent of the formulary procedure, jurists more carefully defined the concept of *iniuria* and what it constituted; see Schulz (1953) 50–51 and Lenel (1927) §190. Republican jurists would commonly analyse legal terms through etymologies, and therefore an *iniuria* must be an action that is *non iure*; see *D.* 47.10.1.pr.

> *Iniuria ex eo dicta est, quod non iure fiat: omne enim quod non iure fit iniuria fieri dicitur …. Interdum iniuriae appellatione damnum culpa datum significatur, ut in lege Aquilia dicere solemus: interdum iniquitatem iniuriam dicimus, nam cum quis inique uel iniuste sententiam dixit, iniuriam ex eo dictam quod iure et iustitia caret, quasi non iuriam.*

They also recognized the imprecise nature of the term; *Inst.* 4.4.pr.:

> *Generaliter iniuria dicitur omne quod non iure fit: specialiter alias contumelia, quae a contemnendo dicta est, quam Graeci* ὕβριν *appellant, alias culpa, quam Graeci* ἀδίκημα *dicunt, sicut in lege Aquilia damnum iniuria accipitur, alias iniquitas et iniustitia, quam Graeci* ἀδικίαν *uocant. Cum enim praetor uel iudex non iure contra quem pronuntiat, iniuriam accepisse dicitur.*

Furthermore, when a plaintiff alleges that an *iniuria* has been committed against him, the nature of the offence should be specified; see *D.* 47.10.7.pr.: *Praetor edixit: 'qui agit iniuriarum, certum dicat, quid iniuriae factum sit'.* C. will turn his position as the first speaker in the *diuinatio* to his advantage by attributing a flimsy claim to Caecilius; see §55 *qualis iniuria dicatur* .... On etymological exegesis in the Roman jurists, see Schulz (1953) 67, 336, and Lausberg §466. On the semantic and legal range of *iniuria,* see Heumann–Seckel *s.u.*

fecisse A charge was traditionally formulated with the accuser saying '*Fecisti*'; see Quint. *Inst.* 3.6.5.

arbitror Used absolutely, 'I reckon so!'; see *OLD s.u.* 4c, and *TLL* II 418.32. Cf. the use of *uideo* and *audio* at *Ver.* II.5.69.

52.9 ueri simile 'plausible', here introducing a subordinate accusative and infinitive construction (*te … fuisse*); see *OLD s.u. similis* 3. Like *probabile,* the phrase signals an argument from plausibility; cf. *Rosc. Am.* 92, *Ver.* II.4.11, and *Inu.* 1.9. This form of argument requires the audience to accept the premise to the conclusion: here, that Verres has committed outrages against all Sicilians. There is a subtle psychological manipulation in presenting a contentious issue (the extent of Verres' nefarious behaviour) as a generally accepted truth. On εἰκός arguments, see introduction to §1.

52.10 illi sc. Verres. On syntax, see n. below. This is another example of derogatory anonymity; cf. §23 *magnus ille defensor* … n.

eximium A rare but classical use in which the verbal force of the adjective prevails and in which it is nigh synonymous with the perfect passive participles *exemptus* and *exceptus*; cf. Ter. *Hec.* 66, Quint. *Inst.* 8.2.8, and Liv. 9.34.11 *tu unus eximius es in quo hoc praecipuum ac singulare ualeat?* See *TLL* V 2.1492.16–27. The verbal quality of *eximium* is so strong that the dative dependent upon it, *illi,* may be thought of as a dative of agent; see H-Sz. 96–97, *OLS* 1.247–249, 296–297; *pace* Suárez (2001), who would style it as a possessive dative. Hence: 'that you alone should have been picked out by him for special consideration'.

consuleret Cf. §48 *consulet laudi et existimationi tuae* n.

§53

53.1 ceteri Siculi The phrasing implies that Caecilius is also Sicilian – or at least has a greater connection with the island than his term as quaestor; see Introduction §II.

53.2 ultorem See §11 *ultorem* n.

tu dum tuas iniurias per te … persequi conaris The build-up of forms of the second-person singular pronoun, *tu … tuas … te,* underscores C.'s depiction of Caecilius' prosecution as selfish. The audience will also find an intentional ambiguity in the personal adjective, *tuas,* as to whether it is possessive or objective in meaning: 'the injustices you suffered' or 'the injustices you inflicted'. C. has already introduced the notion that the Sicilians may want to seek retribution against Caecilius as well; see §22. On the primary position of *tu,* see §26 *ego* n. **per te** 'by your own efforts'; see *OLD s.u. per* 15b, and *TLL* X 1.1159.24. **persequi** 'to seek requital or restitution for'; see *OLD s.u.* 3 and *TLL* X 1.1695.46–64. On revenge in the criminal court, see §11 *ultorem* n.

53.3 id agis ut The syntactic ambiguity of the clause as potentially either purpose or result leaves open the question whether Caecilius is simply unaware of the consequences of his actions or wilfully obstructing the Sicilians' case against Verres. C. will phrase the dilemma more explicitly; see §58 *utrum te perfidiosum an praeuaricatorem existimari mauis?* n. On the ambiquity of clauses introduced by *ut,* see Cabrillana (2011) 67–73. For another example, cf. *Ver.* II.5.116 *sed secum <cum> ipse certat, id agit ut semper superius suum facinus nouo scelere uincat.*

ceterorum quoque *Quoque* can act as a 'focusing particle'; here it signals a contrast between two constituents, *tuas* and *ceterorum.* See further Spevak (2010) 49–51.

53.4 iniuriae sint impunitae atque inultae Homeoteleuton and a loose form of alliteration (since the initial repetitive sound relies upon a prefix; see Wölfflin (1933) 227). Cf. *Ver.* II.5.149 *inultam impunitamque,* and Tac. *Hist.* 4.77.3. C. is being somewhat misleading here. It is true that if Caecilius' prosecution was unsuccessful or if the grievances of the Sicilians were not taken into account during the *litis aestimatio*, Verres would no longer be liable to prosecution under the *lex Cornelia de repetundis*, since a previous version of the statute, the *lex Acilia*, 'enacted that no accusation should be made on a matter already judged under the law, whether the accused has been condemned or acquitted. The same rule was doubtless enacted in each of the laws constituting *iudicia publica*'; A. Jones (1972) 79. As a result, no financial restitution may be made to the Sicilians from the extortion court, but vengeance may be exacted by other means – especially if the alleged offence was also prosecutable under a different law. In fact, C. himself is quick to point this out at *Ver.* II.1.11–14.

hoc te praeterit 'but this you have failed to notice'; see *OLD s.u. praetereo* 8a, and *TLL* X 2.1023.61–75. Cf. *Ver.* II.3.11, *Clu.* 17, *Caec.* 101 *non me praeterit*, *Att.* 7.3.6 *hoc te praetermisisse miror.* What is phrased as a slight against Caecilius is also a reminder to the jurors about the paradigm they should use in evaluating the two speakers at the *diuinatio. Hoc* is cataphoric and summarizes the infinitive phrase that follows.

53.5 non id solum spectari solere, qui debeat, sed etiam illud, qui possit ulcisci Here C. legitimizes his novel approach to a *diuinatio* by arguing that the assessment of oratorical ability (*qui possit*) is not a new consideration for a *diuinatio* but one that is necessary, fundamental, and indeed inherent in the traditional manner of choosing who ought to (*qui debeat*) lead the prosecution. Desire and fervour (*quid is uelit*) cannot be taken into consideration until ability (*quid facere possit*) has been established. C.'s attempt at establishing the legitimacy of his approach is bolstered by a tinge of legalistic language; *posse* and *debere* are not an uncommon collocation in juristic texts, 'that someone is able and should ...'. Cf. *D.* 26.7.8.pr. *si potuit et debuit* ..., 17.1.59.4, 36.1.27.pr., and 47.4.1.4.

53.6 eum superiorem esse I.e. if someone has both the desire and the ability. C. also covers the other side of the argument to give the impression of exhaustive reasoning; cf. §61 *si superior omnibus rebus esses....*

53.8 solere C.'s repeated use of *solere* alerts his audience to the fact that he is about to address a customary line of argumentation in a *diuinatio*. See the introduction to the *partitio* (§10) and nn. below.

§54

54.1 quodsi signals a *concessio* in the form of a *praeparatio*, i.e. a concession to a line of argument likely to be espoused by one's opponent in a subsequent speech; see Lausberg §§854, 856. In this manoeuvre, C. ostensibly lays to one side the question of speaking ability and turns to an argument not particular to Caecilius, but rather more characteristic of *diuinationes* generally: *cui maior iniuria est facta?* Upon first consideration, C. loses in this head-to-head comparison with Caecilius. C. had no prior relationship with Verres, and he had never sustained any loss or injury at Verres' hands. Caecilius' claim, whatever it may be, should easily convince the judges that he is the more aggrieved party. C., however, has 'sprinkled seeds' in anticipation of this argument by constantly representing his advocacy as a direct manifestation of the will of the majority of Sicilians. See particularly in §19 *quoniam id non poterat, harum rerum actorem quem idoneum esse arbitrata est ipsa delegit.* The rest of the outrages committed against the rest of the Sicilian population, C. reckons, should clearly outweigh an injury suffered by an individual; see *maximam ... iniuriam* n. below. On *quodsi* in oratorical argumentation, see Seyffert 2§32.3; cf. *Arch.* 17 *Quodsi ipsi haec neque attingere neque sensu nostro gustare possemus ....*

censes 'are you advising that ...?' L&S *s.u. censeo*: is 'very frequent, especially in C., when a question, rhetorical or real, is addressed to a second person, often referring to erroneous opinions'. In this case, Caecilius' opinion is correct but will tell against him; cf. *censes* later in this sentence. The verb is typically of a high register and often refers to official resolutions by political bodies and individuals invested with some authority, e.g. censors or military commanders; Heumann–Seckel *s.u.*, and *TLL* III 792.13, 793.39–77. The use is ironic in passages such as these; cf. *Rosc. Am.* 38.

oportere See §19 *oportere* n.

54.2 maximam ... iniuriam C. evaluates Caecilius' claim to the prosecution on more traditional grounds: on whom has Verres inflicted the greatest injury? C. deploys a stasis theory of quantity (*quantum sit?*) or relation (*ad aliquid*); see Quint. *Inst.* 3.6.51 *Hoc ultimum* [the status *ad aliquid*] *maxime in comparatiuo genere uersari putat, quoniam melius ac peius, maius et minus nisi alio relata non intelleguntur.* On stasis theory generally, see introduction to §§52–58. The short hyperbaton stresses *maximam*; see Marouzeau 1.174.

54.3 utrum tandem This dialectical method also has juristic and legal overtones to it, which give an impression of logical reasoning on C.'s part, though see *quodsi* n. above. On **tandem**, see §6 *quis tandem* n.

54.4 laesum A careful choice of verb that C. explains later in a *status finitionis*; see §58 *laesum ... iniuriam* n.

uexatam ac perditam 'utterly devastated'. *Vexare* frequently refers to the act of ravaging and pillaging (see *OLD s.u.* 3), while *perdere* conveys the final result, i.e. complete and irrecoverable loss (see *OLD s.u.* 1 and *TLL* X 1.1265.45–68 in relation to states and communities). For this pairing, cf. *Ver.* I.12, *Vat.* 7, and *Off.* 2.28. The final position of this phrase in its clause mirrors the position of *laesum* and underscores the antithesis between Caecilius' injury and the devastation of Sicily. C.'s rhetorical question builds to a crescendo with homeoteleuton and internal rhyme. On quasi-synonymous pairs, see §1 *causam rationemque* n.

54.5 opinor Parenthetical, but not signalling irony, as it frequently does; cf. *Rosc. Am.* 52 *nam illa, opinor, tu quoque concedis leuia esse atque inepta.* Instead, it softens the statement; see Barrios-Lech (2016) 142–154. For the use of *opinor* in C., see Laurand 87–89.

concedes ... concede The first use of *concedere* is construed along the lines of a verb of speaking – 'you will admit that'; the second use emphasizes a desired result – 'you grant that ...'. On this nuance of meaning, see K-St. 2.2.224–225, Landgraf *ad Rosc. Am.* 54, and *TLL* IV 16.4, 54–55. The collocation of *opinor* and *concedere* seems to occur at weaker points in C.'s argumentation – especially when he wants the audience to accept an unproven supposition or condition; cf. *Quinct.* 68, *Rosc. Am.* 52, *Ver.* II.3.114, and *Cat.* 1.17.

grauius ... grauius The repetition (*conduplicatio*) of *grauius* in this section has a reinforcing emotive function and prompts the audience to weigh up the relative wrongs suffered by Caecilius and the Sicilians. On *conduplicatio*, see Lausberg §612.

ab omnibus I.e. not just the jurors but the broader public and Caecilius himself; the issue is a moral rather than a judicial one.

54.6 igitur C. gives the impression of logical reasoning with the use of conclusive language; cf. *Lig.* 4 with Montague (1992) 566–567.

in accusando prouincia; nam prouincia accusat ... A chiastic anadiplosis in which the last two members of a syntactical group are repeated inversely at the start of the next. The *geminatio* of *prouincia* serves as an emphatic reinforcement and diminishes Caecilius' claims to lead the prosecution for personal retribution. On *anadiplosis*/ *reduplicatio*, see Lausberg §§619–622. The explicative particle *nam* signals that C. is going to state the assumption in the previous argument: that if the Sicilian representatives have chosen him as their advocate (see §11 *me defensorem calamitatum suarum, me ultorem iniuriarum, me cognitorem iuris sui, me actorem causae totius esse uoluerunt*), then he is speaking not for himself but for all Sicilians (§19). C.'s entire *ratio*/ *causa* for acting as prosecutor, as stated from the outset, is predicated on the idea that he will represent – by proxy – the voice of the plaintiffs. Yet this is a glaring weakness in C.'s case, as this notion of 'representationality' was hardly a standard concept in Roman legal advocacy. As the remaining text of the *lex repetundarum* suggests, a Sicilian could have been the *nominis delator* and an advocate could have been chosen or appointed later to act for him; see *lex repet.* ll. 9–12 and Lintott (1992) 18–20, and see Ulpian at *D.* 3.1.1.4 for the principle of assigning an advocate. In that case, an advocate would be acting as the vicarious voice, but the original *delator* would presumably receive the reward for a successful conviction. In suing to be the *nominis delator* himself, however,

C. is not a mere messenger for the Sicilians, and any claim that he makes to speak for them is his own creation. Moreover, any *praemia* awarded would have gone to C., not to the Sicilians, 'on whose behalf' he has supposedly argued; see further Crook (1995) 161–162. C., however, is able to import this concept of representation, well known from his defence speeches, by continually emphasizing that his prosecution is more appropriately thought of as a defence of the Sicilians. On the idea of the advocate as 'representative', see Crook (1995) 158–163. For a similar use of *nam*, see §18 *nam* n. Underpinning C.'s notion of collective representation is his interpretation of the *lex repetundarum*; see introduction to §§17–18, and §65 *lex ipsa* … n. In many respects, C. tries to turn this case into a civil action in which he acts as a *uindex*, who was an actual 'representative' in *legis actiones* and 'entered into the whole legal position of the person on whose behalf he intervened. If there was a condemnation, [the *uindex* himself] was condemned'; Crook (1995) 158. On the ability of non-Romans to initiate charges under the *lex Cornelia de repetundis*, see §64 *quod eum sibi Achaei patronum adoptarant* n.

54.9 totius The postposition is emphatic; see Marouzeau 1.172, 175.

adoptauit 'has selected or secured as'; see *TLL* I 809.39–41. See further §64 *quod eum sibi Achaei patronum adoptarant* n.

The Agonis Affair (§§55–57)

Caecilius may claim that he should be chosen as prosecutor because he has been personally injured by Verres. But he would be a fool to mention the exact nature of this so-called injury. Cicero will therefore tell the story. There was a wealthy resident of Lilybaeum, Agonis, a freedwoman of Erycinian Venus. When a prefect of Antonius requisitioned her musicians for use in the Roman fleet, she sought to forestall this seizure of property by referring to herself and her goods as 'the property of Venus'. The news of this altercation came to Caecilius, who then summons Agonis to court and asks a jury to determine 'if she had referred to herself and her goods as the property of Venus'. The jury inevitably found that this had been the case and so Caecilius not only seizes her property but also enslaves her once more to Venus. He then liquidates her assets and keeps the proceeds for himself. When Verres later comes to Lilybaeum, he orders Caecilius to return the money.

Indeed, Verres looked like a veritable Mucius Scaevola! What could be more considerate, chivalrous, and noble? But like a man sipping from the cup of Circe, Verres was transformed back into his true self; he only returned a small part of the money to Agonis and pocketed the rest. Though Verres may have offended Caecilius, he certainly did not act unlawfully in this instance. If Caecilius truly believes he was wronged, surely no one else would have judged Verres more harshly. But what would one say if it came to light that he later came back into Verres' good graces, and that he later stayed for some time at Verres' house, and that they dined together? One must consider Caecilius either a trickster or a false prosecutor. He can choose whichever title he prefers.

Cicero pre-emptively counters the claim that Caecilius is acting out of personal injury by telling his own version of this supposed incident; for its place in the larger rhetorical argument in the *reprehensio* and the *status qualitatis*, see the introduction to §§52–58. Though he will later say that Caecilius *ab isto laesus inimicitias iustas persequeretur* (*Ver.* II.1.15), the considerations of expediency for winning the *diuinatio* must have prompted the unflattering characterization presented here. He portrays Caecilius as an unscrupulous magistrate and trivializes the supposed injury he suffered at Verres' hands. In many regards, Cicero assimilates Caecilius to a junior version of Verres – an opportunist, greedy administrator who abuses his position and authority for personal gain.

The nature of the case involving Agonis is far more convoluted than Cicero's straightforward narrative makes it appear. Upon a first impression, Caecilius' actions look preposterous, although this is precisely the point. A more complete and plausible story can be posited that incorporates the disparate elements Cicero carefully selects. A reconstruction must first consider the fate of the musicians, since, one must believe, this is the property which precipitated the legal action that followed. It has often been assumed that a suit was filed against Agonis to force her to turn over the slaves since she is made the defendant in the *intentio* drafted by Caecilius; see §56 *si paret* … n. below. It stands to reason, however, that the prefect successfully requisitioned the musicians despite Agonis' protest. First, as a matter of practicality, a prefect on assignment to requisition supplies would not have instigated a suit to do so (unlike a tax-collector; see J. Kelly (1976) 52); he had might and precedent on his side. Second, even in Cicero's story, there is no indication that the prefect actually brought suit, but only that Agonis' protest 'was announced to Caecilius'. Finally, there is no mention of the musicians being seized as a result of the verdict against Agonis. The phrasing *pauca mancipia … retinere uult* further suggests that, by the time Agonis' issue came to court, the musicians were well on their way to keeping time for Antonius' rowers. It is far more probable that after her servants were requisitioned, Agonis brought a suit before a Roman magistrate to have her slaves returned or restitution made.

In reorganizing the province, Rome established the procedures by which these disputes would be adjudicated depending on the citizenship status of the parties involved. These fall into six categories that C. sets out at *Ver.* II.2.32:

1. Cases between two fellow citizens should be tried in their home city and by their own laws.
2. For cases between two Sicilians of different cities, the praetor should appoint judges by lot in accordance with the decision of Publius Rupilius made on the advice of the ten legates, which is known among them as the *lex Rupilia.* [Three judges in total; see *Ver.* II.2.42]
3. When an individual sues a community or a community an individual, a council of some city is appointed to try the case, after a city has been rejected by each side in turn.
4. When a Sicilian is sued by a Roman citizen, a Sicilian is appointed as a judge.
5. When a Roman citizen is sued by a Sicilian, a Roman citizen is appointed as a judge.
6. In other cases, the regular procedure is to nominate judges from the *conuentus* of Roman citizens.

Scholars have generally looked to Agonis' case to explicate the sixth category and have inferred that trials involving *liberti* must have been subject to Roman judges. While it may be true that litigants who were freedmen were treated under this last category, that inference cannot be drawn from Agonis' example. Agonis was not simply a *liberta*; she was the freedwoman of Venus Erycina, and this is a crucial distinction; see §55 *liberta Veneris Erycinae* n. Moreover, the judicial inquiry initiated by Caecilius, as Cicero presents it, appears at first to be entirely unrelated to the dispute over Agonis' slaves. To conjure up an image of a blatant miscarriage of justice, Cicero has omitted important connections. When Agonis brought suit, as the freedwoman of a goddess, there may have been a legitimate question about the proper judicial procedures to follow and how her claim should be resolved. This uncertainty also explains why she appears nominally as a defendant in this vignette, since the language of the *intentio* strongly suggests a *formula praeiudicialis*, viz. that Caecilius has instigated a pre-trial inquiry to determine the legal status of an individual claiming to be the freedperson of a deity; cf. Berger *s.u. causa liberalis.* Thus, the Agonis Affair is not an example of the *lex Rupilia* in practice but rather an inquiry into how the *lex Rupilia* might apply in her case. This also explains why *recuperatores* were empanelled to make a ruling: this sort of question fell within their purview; see §56 *iudicant recuperatores* n. As for taking possession of Agonis' goods, the quaestor at Lilybaeum had oversight of the finances of the Temple of Venus at Eryx (as C., having served there himself, would have known).

The narrative of the story of Agonis is not strictly germane to the question of who should be the prosecutor, but its introduction here is nonetheless pertinent. It falls into the second category of *narratio* that C. outlines at *Inu.* 1.27: *alterum* [genus narrationis], *in quo digressio aliqua extra causam aut criminationis aut similitudinis aut delectationis non alienae ab eo negotio, quo de agitur, aut amplificationis causa interponitur.* Cf. Victorinus *ad loc.* (Ippolito 85.22) *Haec narratio extra causam est; agitur enim qui magis debeat accusare: sed tamen ad causam facit; locus enim introducitur in quo se Caecilius iniuriam a Verre passum esse commemorat, qua se laesum accusare debere contendit.* The Schol. Gronov. 327 Stangl calls it a *subnarratio*: *non legitimae causae narratio.* On its use as a *relatio criminis*, see §55 *proferatur* n. Cicero's misleading narrative is bolstered by the simplicity of his style. His unadorned prose moves into the historic present and employs asyndeton to suggest a seamless chain of events. On the application of the *lex Rupilia*, see Kantor (2010) (especially 192–194 on this case).

§55

55.1 at C. leaves aside the issue of the relative importance of Caecilius' loss (*status quantitatis*) and addresses its exact nature (*status qualitatis*). On *at* used to signal a transition, see §15 *at enim.*

eam … iniuriam The hyperbaton emphasizes the demonstrative and, in this case, raises doubt: 'this injury, such as it is, …'. On this kind of separation, see Marouzeau 1.154. Cf. Caes. *Gal.* 1.18.9 … *sed etiam de ea quam habeat gratia desperare.*

quoque See §53 *ceterorum quoque* n.

55.2 animos … alieno incommodo commouere? C. has already emphasized the importance of compelling the audience to empathize with the injured party; see §38 *aeque … uideantur* n. He will manipulate the story involving Agonis in such a way as to both trivialize Caecilius' complaint and demonstrate that this supposed 'injury' is roundly deserved for his immoral and extortionate behaviour. Caecilius will also be at pains to demonstrate that these alleged offences meet a level of criminality that warrants treating them as a public offence; otherwise the matter could be held in a civil court; cf. *D.* 47.10.7.1. For the collocation of *commouere* and *incommodum*, cf. *Ver.* II.3.144 *Quodsi quis sociorum incommodis minus commouetur* ….

minime Peterson prints the preceding sentence as indicative rather than interrogative, but *minime* is usually a response to a rhetorical question when placed in the primary position; cf. *Ver.* II.4.146, and 5.69.

55.3 ad rem pertinere 'to be relevant'; see *OLD s.u. pertineo* 4c, and *TLL* X 1.1808.34–53.

qualis iniuria dicatur C. manifestly signposts a new line of argument based on the *status qualitatis* (*quale sit?*).

55.4 proferatur *OLD s.u.* 5b 'to bring up (a fact or circumstance) in support of a contention', though it often has a specific legal sense, 'to produce (documents or witnesses) in evidence'; see *OLD s.u.* 5a, Heumann–Seckel *s.u.*, and *TLL* X 2.1682.38–61. C.'s narrative digression that follows (§§55–56) will serve as a kind of *euidentia* by which the jury can judge the nature of the *iniuria* Caecilius supposedly suffered. The overall effect of the narrative will be a *relatio criminis*, which 'consists in the victim of the deed's being regarded as the guilty party: by his/her own (different) culpable act the victim of the deed established the precondition for our thereby justified deed'; see Lausberg §179, and *Inu.* 2.78–86. C. recommends a vivid narrative for this purpose; see *Inu.* 2.78 *res expressa uerbis ante oculos eorum qui audiunt ponitur, ut ipsi se quoque idem facturos fuisse arbitrentur si sibi illa res atque ea faciendi causa per idem tempus accidisset*, and *Rhet. Her.* 2.49. The technique is more commonly used by a defendant, and C. will have to backtrack from exculpating Verres entirely. On *narrationes* generally, see the introduction to §§2–5.

cognoscite ex me For *cognosco* with *ex*, see K-St. 2.1.400, and *TLL* III 1510.65–1511.26. Cf. *Ver.* II.1.130.

55.5 plane See §20 *alterum plane nolle* n.

proferet See *proferatur* n. above.

55.6 Agonis An otherwise unknown freedwoman of Venus Erycina; on her status, see *liberta Veneris Erycinae* n. below. The name Ἀγωνίς, however, is attested elsewhere. The Greek comic playwright, Alexis, wrote a play about a love intrigue entitled Ἱππίσκος but which was also known by the name of its lead character, Ἀγωνίς. An entry in the *Suda s.u.* reads Ἀγωνίς· ὄνομα ἑταίρας. But as Arnott (1996) 52 notes 'the ultimate source of this entry is not likely to have been the passage in Cicero [*Diu. Caec.* 55], but rather one of the *hetairai* lists compiled by Hellenistic scholars. Other non-literary attestations of the name also come from an Alexandrian vase from 298 or 260 BCE (see Courbey (1922)

216) and inscriptions from Athens, Arcadia, and Acarnania (see *LGPN* IIA and III *s.u.*).

quaedam est A common beginning to a Ciceronian narrative. In telling the tale, C. anticipates the manner of the *actio secunda*; cf. *Ver.* II.1.27, 64, 115, 2. 53, 65, 128, 169, 4.30, *Pis.* 86; and in narrative more generally, see Apul. *Met.* 4.28 with Kenney *ad loc.*

liberta Veneris Erycinae The status implied by being the 'freed-person of a god(dess)' and the nature of 'sacral manumission' continues to be debated. Besides this reference in C., there are only eight other examples in both Greek and Latin sources of someone being described as a *libertus dei* or (ἀπ)ελεύθερος θεοῦ. This relative scantiness could indicate that the designation was infrequent; see Ricl (2001b) 290–291. Moreover, the epigraphic evidence is so geographically and chronologically diverse that any conclusions drawn must necessarily be tentative.

It is generally agreed that to become an (ἀπ)ελεύθερος θεοῦ, one originally had to be consecrated to a god(dess) at a sanctuary by one's master in an act of sacral manumission. The implications of this consecration are far from clear, and three interpretations have been advanced as to the level of freedom that it implied. Some scholars have treated (ἀπ)ελεύθερος θεοῦ and ἱερόδουλος as interchangeable and simply as a matter of perspective, and so in other words the individual was free from the viewpoint of the former owner, but a slave of the sanctuary; see Petsas et al. (2000) 111. Other interpretations view this as an intermediary step in becoming an (ἀπ)ελεύθερος θεοῦ. Ricl (2001a) 143 remarks:

> The donated slave, who is not a free person in the eyes of the law until the Goddess decides to set him free, is nonetheless protected from abuse, sale, arbitrary seizure and all forms of alienation from the Goddess, the protection being additionally enforced by the threat of heavy fines against all possible transgressors. He formally and legally belongs to the Goddess who keeps all his documents in her archives as proof of her ownership. Although we cannot consider him legally free, no more so than prior to

> his consecration when he was bound to a human master, we can fully understand how his new status constituted an improvement: it was inferior to that of the slaves liberated through Greek or Roman forms of 'secular manumission', but it meant having a milder master and being personally free with respect to the world outside the sanctuary. Finally, all the consecrated slaves could own and dispose of their movable and immovable property as they wished.

According to this formulation, to become an (ἀπ)ελεύθερος θεοῦ, the temple slave, who had become an ἱερόδουλος through consecration by his original master, would need to be released by the sanctuary from the obligations that had been imposed upon him at his initial consecration. From that point on, he would be free to worship his patron god without mandatory service on the god's 'customary days'; Ricl (2001a) 142; cf. *SEG* 50: 189.

Still others argue that the initial act of sacral manumission was a true manumission; Caneva and Pizzi (2015) 171–172:

> Nothing permits us to think that ἱεροί actually *belonged* to a sanctuary. It is more correct to speak of them as individuals with a specific relation to a specific sanctuary. The reference to a sanctuary was part of a dissuasive strategy aimed at preventing other people from using as slaves these newly manumitted persons with a precarious status, which was a potential risk. The fact that any contraveners would be guilty of ἱεροσυλία or ἱεροφορία does not allow us to think, as Darmezin [(1999) 224] does, that '*ces affranchis sont donc deuenus des biens sacrés, ils appartiennent au dieu*'. It should be seen as a sanction against someone who would disrespect their new status rather than as a proof that such persons are devoid of freedom .... Similarly, the objects possessed by the freedmen do not belong to the sanctuary but are put in relation to it, be this relation as it is. On the same level, lists of freedmen kept by priests in their archives are not a list of goods *per se*, but rather come from the need to know who has been consecrated.

But on a practical level, 'sources allow us to conclude that, despite the formal distinction implied by the language used, little or hardly any practical difference with regard to status existed between a ἱερόδουλος whose service was restricted to a sanctuary and a freedman who had to serve therein'; Caneva and Pizzi (2015) 184.

Out of these interpretations, a common element emerges that stresses the importance of the sanctuary in protecting and strengthening the status of the consecrated individual, either as temple property or as a guarantor and witness to the manumission. In the latter instance, a freed person generally had reduced civil rights and a precarious social status that could be exploited or abused by more powerful people in their society; the act of consecration put the individual in a relationship with the sanctuary that served to safeguard him against the seizure of his property and forced re-enslavement; see Ricl (2001a) 146–147, and Caneva and Pizzi (2015) 187–188.

Whatever Agonis' obligations to the cult of Erycinian Venus, she was most likely not a citizen of her community, for unlike the rules of Roman law, which could give freedmen *domicilium* and certain rights, freedpersons in the Greek *poleis* were consistently denied full citizenship rights. Since she would have regarded the sanctuary of Venus Erycina as the primary protector of her rights and property, it is altogether understandable that she would have invoked her status when faced with unlawful alienation; see *ut mos in Sicilia est …* n. below. Though C. often misleadingly presents Sicily as a homogenous state, it was composed of 65 *ciuitates*, and all these may have had different laws and local customs; see *Ver.* II.2.133–137, and Pfuntner (2015). The cult of Venus of Eryx, however, was so widely revered that it could have been appealed to as a safeguard for Agonis' status throughout the island.

The bibliography for these issues is extensive. The bulk of the evidence for sacral manumission and consecration comes from the inscriptions from Leucopetra in Macedonia, just southwest of Mount Bermion; cf. *I.Leukopetra* 43. On these inscriptions and for an overview of the debate, see Petsas et al. (2000) 32–35, 52 and Harper (2011) 369 n. 11. Caneva and Pizzi (2015) advance more arguments on the nature of the relationship between the dedicatee and the temple and offer a substantial list of sources.

For a still fuller discussion, see Bömer (1960) 1–207. A funerary inscription from Sicca Veneria, which was said to be founded from the Venus/Astarte cult on Eryx, also mentions a *C. Iulius Optatus Veneris libertus*; see *CIL* VIII 27580. Buckland (1970) 447–448 gives a short comparison with Greek practices and the Roman *manumissio sacrorum causa.*

Veneris Erycinae The shrine of Venus on Mount Eryx in Sicily was a major religious site located on the northwest corner of the island; see the map in Appendix A. From prehistoric times, it seems to have been a religious site for the Phoenician goddess Astarte, and it was subsequently associated with Aphrodite by the later Greek inhabitants. The Romans, who captured the temple in 249 BCE, associated this site with the temple founded by Aeneas for his mother, Venus, and so they held it in high esteem. So Diod. Sic. 4.83.6 remarks οἱ μὲν γὰρ καταντῶντες εἰς τὴν νῆσον ὕπατοι καὶ στρατηγοὶ καὶ πάντες οἱ μετά τινος ἐξουσίας ἐπιδημοῦντες, ἐπειδὰν εἰς τὸν Ἔρυκα παραβάλωσι, μεγαλοπρεπέσι θυσίαις καὶ τιμαῖς κοσμοῦσι τὸ τέμενος, καὶ τὸ σκυθρωπὸν τῆς ἐξουσίας ἀποθέμενοι μεταβάλλουσιν εἰς παιδιὰς καὶ γυναικῶν ὁμιλίας μετὰ πολλῆς ἱλαρότητος, μόνως οὕτω νομίζοντες κεχαρισμένην τῇ θεῷ ποιήσειν τὴν ἑαυτῶν παρουσίαν. In 215, Q. Fabius Maximus Verrucosus dedicated a shrine to Venus Erycina inside the pomerium on the Capitoline Hill, and in 181 another shrine was founded by L. Porcius Licinus in front of the Colline Gate. The original site on Mount Eryx continued to be venerated and was restored under Tiberius in 25 CE; see Tac. *Ann.* 4.43.4. On the temple's foundation, see Str. 6.2.6, Diod. Sic. 4.83.1–7, and Wilson (1990) 283–285. On the tentative locations of the shrines in Rome with citations from the ancient sources, see Carandini (2017) 1.160, 454, respectively.

Verres evidently cultivated a close relationship with the temple (which could also explain his intervention in this legal quandary with Agonis). Within his administration, C. alleges, *serui Venerii* served as henchmen and tithe contractors, some of whom C. mentions by name (Diognetus, Bariobalus, and Symmachus); see *Ver.* II.3.86, 89, and 92, respectively, and Scramuzza (1936). A close association with the temple could offer

Figure 4: The shrine of Venus Erycina as commemorated on a silver denarius of C. Considius Nonianus in 57 BCE; RRC 424/1.

practical benefits: considering 'the high prestige of Venus Erycina throughout Sicily and the far-reaching spread of the cult of Eryx, it is understandable that Verres relies on the sanctuary to govern (and rob) the entire island *Veneris nomine.* [il grande prestigio di Venere Ericina in tutta la Sicilia e l'ampia diffusione del culto di Erice, è logico quindi che Verre si appoggi al santuario per governare (e depredare) Veneris nomine tutta l'isola.]'; Della Corte (1979) 227. Furthermore, this interaction may have offered the added benefit of strengthening ties between Sicily and Rome; see Martorana (1979). So close was Verres' relationship with the cult that when C. invokes all the gods from whom Verres has stolen, Venus is conspicuously absent. Vasaly (1993) 214 n. 35 summarizes: 'Cicero solves the problem [of Verres' close connection with Venus Erycina] by focusing on the Sicilan cult of Ceres at Henna and by depicting Verres' devotion to Venus and Cupid as a mask for his greed and an expression of his libidinousness.' For more on *serui Venerii* in the Verrines, see Della Corte (1979) and Eppers and Heinen (1984). At *Ver.* II.5.141, a person described as a *seruus Venerius* is able to bring a charge against the Roman citizen C. Servilius. In other words, either C. is drawing attention to Verres' complete disregard for the temple slave's status or something about his position as a *seruus Venerius* allowed him to have standing at law. The notion that the slaves of Venus Erycina engaged in sacred prostitution has largely been debunked; see Lindner (2009), Beard and Henderson (1998), and especially Budin (2008) 184–191.

55.7 mulier was 'a neutral term designating a specific woman whose qualities need not necessarily be under discussion', while *femina* in Republican prose is used as 'a respectful term denoting a woman of moral or social distinction'; see Adams (1972). For a former slave, *mulier* is certainly a more appropriate appellation.

ante hunc quaestorem In many ways, C.'s miniature prosecution of Caecilius in the *Diuinatio in Caecilium* is echoed and expanded in *In Verrem*; cf. *Ver.* II.2.35, 3.67 *ante hunc praetorem* ..., and 4.46 *ante istum praetorem.* See Introduction §IV.

copiosa plane et locuples The pleonasm stresses her affluence. The vignette between Caecilius and Agonis will be like many of those between Verres and other wealthy inhabitants of Sicily. Throughout his prosecution of Verres, C. will frequently describe the governor's victims as *locuples* as a sign of Verres' contempt for their dignity; cf. *Ver.* II.2.68 and 4.29; see Merguet *s.u.* The adjective is often paired with a form of *honestus* or with another positive attribute, such as *nobilis.* For this coupling, see *Ver.* II.4.50, *Man.* 65, and Fro. *Ep.* 3.8.1 (van den Hout p. 41). For *plane,* see §20 *alterum plane nolle* n. **locuples** since the tendency was for 'x' [ks] to simplify to 's' in later Latin, *locuplex* in many MSS is a hypercorrection from analogy with *simplex* and *duplex*; see Appendix Probi 186 *locuples non locuplex* with Baehrens *ad loc.*

55.8 praefectus ... quidam An unnamed prefect of M. Antonius; see n. below. A prefect was a Roman functionary appointed by a magistrate with responsibilities designated for a particular task or period of time but with no official legal authority; see *N-P s.u.*, and *Staats.* 3.557.

Antoni M. Antonius Creticus (*RE* 29; *MRR* 2.101, 111), son of the orator/consul of 99 mentioned at §25 and father of the triumvir. As the praetor of 74, he had been given an extraordinary command to combat piracy throughout the Mediterranean. He started his operations in the west, in particular just off the coast of Italy, to secure the supply lines for grain coming from Sicily. He turned his attention in 72 and 71 to Crete, where he was defeated and died. C. has nothing good to say about him; see

Ver. II.3.213 *Antonium, cum multa contra sociorum salutem, multa contra utilitatem prouinciarum et faceret et cogitaret, in mediis eius iniuriis et cupiditatibus mors oppressit.* The damning assessment is echoed in [Asc.] 122 (202 Stangl), and Sall. *Hist.* 3.2–3 *Qui orae maritimae, qua Romanum esset imperium, curator <nocent>ior piratis .... Perdendae pecuniae genitus et uacuus a curis nisi instantibus*; for a discussion see McGushin *ad loc.* His exploitation of the provinces may have been due in no small part to insufficient funding provided by an internally divided senate. At any rate, the reputation stuck. [Asc.] 176 (239 Stangl) calls him a *dissolutissimus largitor* and says that he along with his *comitibus pessimis* ([Asc.] 122 (202 Stangl)) exploited provincials. C. discusses him more in depth in his connection to grain requisition from Sicily; see *Ver.* II.3.213–216, and 2.8. Vell. Pat. 2.31.3–4 says that he received power similar to Pompey's under the *lex Gabinia* and had *imperium aequum* with respect to other provincial governors in the region. For his campaign against the pirates, see de Souza (1999) 141–148 and Brennan (2000) 406–407. The location of his fleet of Lilybaeum is a key factor in determining the dates of Caecilius' quaestorship under Verres; see Introduction §II. For *prouinciae* overlapping with other magistrates, see Drogula (2015) 320. The cognomen *Creticus* ascribed to him in imperial times may have been pejorative; see Linderski (1990).

symphoniacos seruos [Asc.] 122 (202 Stangl) *Cani remigibus celeuma per symphoniacos solebat et per assam uocem, id est ore prolatam, et, ut in Argo naui, per citharam. Sed quia hic 'in classe' dixit, possumus intelligere ad hoc symphoniacos capi solere, ut in classe pugnantibus classicum canant: unde ipsi tibiae classicae nomen impositum est 'classicum'.* Casson (1971) 310 notes that 'Rome adopted the traditional Greek organization ... officers and ratings were taken over with little change – as could be expected in a navy whose ships were largely Greek in design and whose first crews were largely drawn from the Greek-speaking parts of the Mediterranean.' The *symphoniacus* was a ship's flautist (the equivalent of the αὐλητής or τριηραύλης in Greek), who would pipe the time for rowers at a pace set by the *celeuma* (κελευστής). The role is recorded as an occupation in *ILS* 2874, and musicians were also repossessed by Verres during his tenure in Sicily; see *Ver.* II.5.64,

73. In the Roman navy, this type of musician was occasionally joined or supplanted by a *pitulus*, who beat the time with a mallet. On officers and men in the ancient navy, see Casson (1971) 300–321. Scramuzza (1936) 327 assumes that these were also temple slaves, but to judge from C.'s description here, they were the property of Agonis, who looked to the temple to maintain her status and property rights.

55.9 abducebat Requisitioning, involving the involuntary seizure of property and generally termed *postulatio*, was a regular practice for supplying and maintaining the Roman army. Any commander with *imperium* had the right to compel civilians to provide for the military – sometimes without compensation. Food and supplies were the most commonly seized items, but pack animals and slaves were also subject to seizure; see Sal. *Cat.* 29.3 *ea potestas per senatum more Romano magistratui maxuma permittitur: exercitum parare, bellum gerere, coercere omnibus modis socios atque ciuis, domi militiaeque imperium atque iudicium summum habere.* Perhaps intentionally, C. is vague as to whether Antonius' legate was operating under orders, but *abducere* usually suggests seizure that is unlawful – as *per iniuriam* would suggest – or disingenuous if done under orders; see *OLD s.u. abduco* 5a, and *TLL* I 61.18–32. For requisitioning in the Roman army, see Roth (1999) 141–148 and Kissel (1995) 82–112.

55.10 ut mos in Sicilia est ... C. implies that Agonis' use of local idiom has been wilfully misconstrued by Caecilius; see *dixit ... esse* n. below. For *mos* meaning 'popular idiom', cf. *Opt. Gen.* 23. 'Cicero correctly makes the important distinction (not always respected by Roman authorities) between (*serui*) *Venerii* and *ii qui a Venere se liberauerunt*'; Ricl (2001b) 294, and see also Budin (2008) 186–188. The phrase *ut mos est* has a colloquial tone; cf. *Ver.* II.5.27, *Tusc.* 5.103, and *Att.* 1.16.4. See further, *TLL* VIII 1528.67–74, and H-Sz. 634.

55.11 praefecto illi The postposition of *ille* can be found in a narrative when its substantive was mentioned so far back in the story that the audience may need reminding or if (as it is in this instance) the substantive has not been explicitly designated; see Marouzeau 1.155–162. Cf. *Phil.* 1.1 *ciuitas illa.*

religionem … obiceret 'might bring forward a matter of religious scruple as a hindrance or disincentive to some action'; see *OLD s.u. obicio* 9a, and *TLL* IX 2.57.22. Cf. Pl. *Mer.* 881 *Religionem illic <mi> obiecit.* Schol. Gronov. 327.5 Stangl *religio est timor cum ueneratione.*

55.12 dixit et se et sua Veneris esse Agonis would presumably have spoken in Greek rather than Latin. In addition to the complexity of Agonis' relationship with the cult of Venus Erycina, the language denoting that relationship may have been misunderstood – especially in translation. Inscriptions that commemorate sacral manumissions have been found in which the manumitted individual(s) are described as being 'of the sanctuary' (τῶ ἱαρῶ) and 'free' (ἐλευθέρων). Yet 'the genitive does not denote *stricto sensu* the possession of the freedmen by the sanctuary – why would they then be called ἐλευθέρων? – but rather a relation to the sanctuary'; Caneva and Pizzi (2015) 172. Scramuzza (1936) 327 concludes that 'this claim implies two things … first that they were no longer slaves, but free; second, that no individual, no city-state, not even the Roman people has authority over them. In other words, they were not under secular law.' Caecilius and the *recuperatores* may have been able to interpret this as a performative rather than descriptive utterance, viz. that she was actively, at that moment, committing herself to the temple; see Budin (2008) 184.

§56

56.2 uiro … aequissimo Sarcasm.

56.3 iubet As befits the vivid narrative style, C. uses a simple parataxis with the historic present to convey a sense of brevity, verve, and veracity.

iudicium dat 'he allows a hearing on the following question'; see *OLD s.u. iudicum* 5d, and *TLL* V 1.1678.8–18.

56.4 SI PARET EAM SE ET SVA VENERIS ESSE DIXISSE A conditional statement, known as the *intentio*, used in the Roman formulary procedure to embody the claim of the plaintiff; see

Greenidge 150–161. 'The *intentio* is expressed in the form of a condition "if it appears (*si paret*)", upon which the condemnatory judgement depends, because, if the condition does not materialize (*si non paret* = if it does not appear), the judge must absolve the defendant. In certain exceptional cases, the whole formula consists only of an *intentio*, as in *formulae praeiudiciales* in which no specific claim is expressed but only a question is posed (for instance, whether one is a freedman …) which is preliminary to a subsequent legal measure'; Berger *s.u. intentio.* Of course, there were *causae liberales*, in which the liberty of the individual was the primary issue to be determined and not a pre-trial inquiry; on these legal formulae and the *causa liberalis*, see Lenel (1927) 377–387 and Crook (1967) 58–62. Cf. *D.* 18.1.5.1 *quia difficile dinosci potest liber homo a seruo.*

In this version of the story, the drafting of this *intentio* and an unavoidable verdict is Caecilius' wrongdoing. In this regard, he is once again assimilated to a version of Verres, who is also accused of drafting *intentiones* to achieve an outcome to his own advantage. See *Ver.* II.2.31 *Si uero illud quoque accedit, ut praetor in ea uerba iudicium det ut uel L. Octauius Balbus iudex, homo et iuris et offici peritissimus, non possit aliter iudicare, – si iudicium sit eius modi ….* But what may be happening here, if one gives Caecilius the benefit of the doubt, is a Roman magistrate encountering difficulty in understanding a foreign institution.

Paret - the correct legal formula, not in doubt - seems to have caused some confusion for copyists. *P* has *parret* with a deletion mark under the first 'r', while the French family has *parretheam* for *paret eam.* Among the *deteriores, M* alone appears to have had *paret*; there is a stroke over the 'e' which is not as bold or deliberate as other abbreviation marks in the first hand and seems to come from the hand of a corrector who also wrote some marginalia. *pare(n)t* is the first-hand reading of the other *deteriores.* For other examples of *si paret*, see *Ver.* II.2.31, Gaius *Inst.* 3.91; 4.4, 37, 41, 46, 47, 60, 64, and 86.

iudicant recuperatores *Recuperatores* were panels of three to five judges who acted in the place of a single *iudex* in certain civil (and criminal) procedures. Recuperatorial competence centres on issues of high public interest, viz. issues of liberty (*causae liberales*), public fines, offences that threaten public order and safety, and physical *iniuria*. It is also generally believed that their court could act more quickly than other judicial processes, since they could convene on days outside the normal forensic calendar, e.g. *dies nefasti*. Otherwise, their origin, role, uniformity, and function in Roman judicature remain a controversial issue; Johnston (1987) 67–70 gives a concise overview. The more widely accepted opinion suggests that the recuperatorial institution arose from a need for international adjudication in which citizens sought to recover goods or property (as their name suggests) lost in war and that the system was only later incorporated into the internal legal framework; see Fest. 342 L. *s.u. reciperatio*, and Schmidlin (1963). The contrary position asserts that *recuperatores* were initially part of the internal legal system and 'represent force rather than speed [of adjudication]', since they could enforce their judgements, which put *causae liberales* within their purview; see J. Kelly (1976), esp. 54–57. A closer reading of this passage in the *Diu. Caec.* weakens Kelly's position, since it appears that the power to enforce a judgement lies in the hands of the magistrate. C. accuses Verres of using *recuperatores* of his own choosing to assure his desired verdict; see *Ver.* II.3.35. In Agonis' case, it is unsurprising that *recuperatores* should be appointed either to determine her status at law or to rule on lost property.

56.6 iste The vituperative *iste* will be reminiscent of C.'s prosecution of Verres, all too fitting as this vignette portrays Caecilius' administration in a similar light to Verres'. C. will similarly mention Verres' failure to administer civil trials appropriately during his praetorship; see *Ver.* I.12.

in possessionem bonorum … intrat As Verres would have delegated power to his quaestor to administer justice, Caecilius had the right to grant *possessio bonorum*; see *D.* 2.1.1 *Ius dicentis officium latissimum est: nam et bonorum possessionem dare potest et in possessionem mittere*. But Caecilius presumably came into possession of Agonis' property himself in his capacity as quaestor, as it seems to have been the responsibility of the quaestor at Lilybaeum to administer temple revenues; see *Ver.* II.2.22 *Itaque* *adponit* [Verres] *qui petat Veneri Erycinae illam hereditatem. Non enim quaestor petit, ut est consuetudo, is qui Erycum montem obtinebat: petit Naeuius Turpio quidam ….* 'To come into possession', however, is not synonymous with ownership; see *D.* 41.2.10.1 *aliud est enim possidere, longe aliud in possessione esse: denique rei seruandae causa, legatorum, damni infecti non possident, sed sunt in possessione custodiae causa.* See further Heumann–Seckel *s.u. possidere*, and Costa 1.123–125. **intrat** *in possessionem* is a legal phrase frequently construed with verbs such as *mittere, uenire* or *ire*; cf. *Quinct.* 83 with Kinsey *ad loc.* and Brassloff (1928) for a full survey of constructions in Roman jurists. This, and the similar number of minims, may explain why a form of *mittere* has entered both the Italian tradition and some of the descendants of S. The regular phrase, however, cannot work here as *mittere in possessionem* requires someone different from the subject to take possession. For *intrare in possessionem*, see *D.* 41.2.1.19, 41.3.4.22.

56.7 in seruitutem Roman law does acknowledge a formal reduction in legal status, *capitis deminutio*, to varying degrees (*maxima, media, minima*), which corresponds to a loss of freedom, citizenship, or family affiliation; see Gaius *Inst.* 1.159–163, and *D.* 4.5.1–11. If, however, the legal procedure that C. is actually describing here is a *praeiudicium* to determine Agonis' free status, the verdict of the *recuperatores* does not change her standing at law but rather acknowledges what it is. Unless a slave was granted *peculium*, he could not own property.

adiudicat Legal terminology; see Heumann–Seckel *s.u. zu erkennen durch richterlichen Ausspruch.* The term was particularly used in the division of property; see *TLL* I 702.25–69.

56.8 pecuniam redigit See *quam ex Agonidis bonis redegisset* n. below. Here Caecilius' actions become less defensible, and the thread of the actual events may be lost. As noted above, *possessio bonorum* does not imply ownership; while it may grant usufruct, it does not necessarily give the possessor the right to sell or liquidate his or her assets. This in turn raises the question of the precise nature of the quaestor's relationship to the cult of Venus Erycina and whether he had the power to make such financial decisions.

dum … retinere uult The verb of desire suggests that Agonis was unsuccessful in preventing the requisitioning of her slaves; see the introduction to §§55–57.

pauca mancipia sc. the *serui symphoniaci. Mancipium* was originally a technical legal term that expressed power over persons or objects, and was sometimes synonymous with *mancipatio* – the conveyance of ownership by a prescribed ritual in which, among other acts and utterances, the new owner seized the property with his hand (*manu capere*). Later it came to denote the property itself, especially slaves; see Berger *s.u. mancipium*, Ernout–Meillet *s.u. manceps*, and *TLL* VIII 255.33–256.38.

Veneris nomine Agonis ac religione When *ac* is used to connect two syntactically equivalent words or phrases, non-modifying words do not seem to intervene. '*Agonis*' should not be an otiose gloss since there has been a change of subject between *redigit* and *uult*; rather its position prevents '*Veneris*' as being understood ἀπό κοινοῦ with both *nomine* and *religione.*

56.9 fortunas omnes libertatemque suam C. draws a contrast above between her initial loss (*pauca mancipia*) and the loss of her property and status here; see *in seruitutem* n. above.

56.10 Lilybaeum Verres uenit Roman governors travelled extensively within their provinces to conduct both military campaigns and judicial assizes. Sicily was a peculiar case in the Roman provincial system. Even in the absence of a military campaign, the governor of Sicily spent part of his summer on tour, since there was a 'need for military supervision of the slaves at harvest time. Furthermore, unlike his eastern counterparts, the Sicilian governor was responsible for the actual sale of the tithe contracts, and to this end he had to travel during the summer to assess the value of the crop …. [During Verres' tenure,] Sicily was then endangered by the remnants of the Sertorian war and of the servile rebellion, and by the standing menace of piracy, so that Verres had to inspect and organize his defences'; A. J. Marshall (1966) 240, and *Ver.* II.5.29. The other major component of gubernatorial responsibility was the administration of justice through local assizes throughout the province – these being usually relegated to the winter months in provinces with ongoing military campaigns. Assize centres were usually larger cities that were conveniently located on the road network and provided the venue for adjudication for the surrounding area. Within Sicily, assizes were held in the same locations on a usually annual basis. Among them were Syracuse, Lilybaeum, Messana, Agrigentum, and Panhormus; see Carcopino (1919) 157, Liv. 31.29.8, *Ver.* II.2.63, 3.27, 38, and 5.16. Though C. attempts to present him as a lazy, drunken official, whiling away the winter in Syracuse, 'Verres, in fact, appears in cities all over Sicily with suspicious frequency and regularity, hounding, robbing, and carousing, but never, of course, attending to his official duties'; A. J. Marshall (1966) 23. *Ver.* II.5.26 depicts him staying inside all winter, but cf. 4.86, where he is seen in Tyndaris in the depths of winter. Verres' reason for coming to Lilybaeum is not specified, but C.'s diction implies that he took official judicial cognizance of the matter; see n. below.

56.11 rem cognoscit, factum improbat The arrival of Verres is narrated, like Agonis' loss of status and property, in the historic present and in simple syntax with parataxis and asyndeton; see *in possessionem bonorum … intrat* n. above. Crook (1967) 85:

> The governor of a province, as fount of all procedural law, was entitled simply to *cognoscere*, try a case, which (as opposed to the *ius dicere* of the praetors) meant to try it completely before himself with any procedure he saw fit – summon the parties, determine the issue, hear the evidence, pronounce the judgement, and see to its execution. This right he had with respect to the Roman citizens in his sphere no less than the peregrines.

Cf. *Ver.* II.2.26 *Verres calumniatorem adponebat, Verres adesse iubebat, Verres cognoscebat, Verres iudicabat; pecuniae maximae dabantur; qui dabant causas obtinebant. Improbare,* meanwhile, implies an official rejection by a superior magistrate; see Heumann–Seckel *s.u.*, and *TLL* VII 1.687.34, 688.9–12. Cf. *D.* 2.8.10.1 [*Iudex*] *qui ex causa improbat ab arbitro probatos.* On what may have been legitimate attempts by Verres to quell judicial corruption in Sicily, see Verres' edict at *Ver.* II.2.33 and A. J. Marshall (1967).

C. is light on details. The effect is one of unassailable simplicity, but it may be whitewashing the truth. One would like to know if an official appeal was made. Even as a slave, Agonis may have had some legal recourse; see *D.* 49.1.15 *sin uero neque dominus neque alius pro domino appellauerit, ipsi seruo qui sententiam tristem passus est auxilium sibi implorare non denegamus.* It would seem that an appeal could be made from the findings of the *recuperatores* and that Caecilius (as the appointing magistrate) or Verres (as the magistrate that entrusted jurisdiction to Caecilius) could serve as the appellate; see *D.* 49.3.1–3.

cogit quaestorem As the magistrate with *imperium*, Verres could enforce his judgement. Cf. *D.* 43.2.1.1 *Ait praetor: 'Quorum bonorum ex edicto meo illi possessio data est, quod de his bonis pro herede aut pro possessore possides possideresue, si nihil usucaptum esset, quod quidem dolo malo fecisti, uti desineres possidere, id illi restituas'. Hoc interdictum restitutorium est et ad uniuersitatem bonorum, non ad singulas res pertinet et appellatur 'quorum bonorum' et est apiscendae possessionis uniuersorum bonorum.* Verres' concern may not have been so much with the slight to Agonis as with the infringement upon the cult of Venus Erycina in its right to protect Agonis' liberty.

56.12 pecuniam ... eam ... omnem The hyperbaton gives the sense 'every last penny'.

quam ex Agonidis bonis redegisset 'which he had realized from the sale of Agonis' property'; see *OLD s.u. redigo* 5, and Heumann–Seckel *s.u. redigere* 4.

56.13 annumerare et reddere 'to pay back ... and to make full restitution'. Though *reddere* in its most simple sense means 'to give back, return', here it would seem to be synonymous with the more legal term, *restituere,* meaning 'to reinstate into a former condition'; see Berger *s.u. restituere.* A *restitutio in integrum* would reinstate Agonis to her formal legal position, i.e. the status of a freed person. 'This was an extraordinary praetorian remedy (*auxilium*) granted at the request of a person who had suffered an inequitable loss .... A thorough investigation of the case (*causae cognitio*) preceded an *in integrum restitutio* as a result of which the praetor could annul through a decree (*decretum*) a transaction valid according to the *ius ciuile*'; see Berger *s.u. restitutio in integrum.* On quasi-synonymous pairs, see §1 *causam rationemque* n.

§57

57.1 id quod often acts like a modern set of dashes to mark off a parenthetical statement; cf. §53 *id quod non potes.*

uos omnes ammirari uideo Imputing surprise to his audience is a common method used in introducing and dispelling a paradox; cf. §1 *si quis ... forte miratur ...* with notes *ad loc.* In purporting to see and read the faces of those around him, C. is constructing a persuasive mechanism whereby he can reflect back an image of the spectators to themselves that may not be a true likeness but one to which they are compelled to assimilate themselves. In this instance, if they had not felt a sense of bewilderment at Verres' uncharacteristic behaviour, they now do, and C. has set the expectations for the joke that follows. Speaking directly to the jurors has the added benefit of allowing C. to grab the attention of his audience after a narrative digression.

57.2 Q. Mucius Quintus Mucius Scaevola. There were two men by this name who were prominent in the two previous generations and who both held the governorship of Asia. For convenience they are distinguished by the titles *Augur* and *Pontifex.*

The first, Scaevola Augur (c. 170–87 BCE; *RE* 22; cos. 117), was a famed jurist. He was such an outstanding lawyer that his name became proverbial for excellence at the bar. C. remarks at *Brut.* 102 *is oratorum in numero non fuit, iuris ciuilis intellegentia atque omni prudentiae genere praestitit*; cf. Hor. *Ep.* 2.2.89. He was charged by T. Albucius (see §63 *T. Albucium* n.) for extortion after his praetorship in Asia, but was acquitted. He went on to become consul in 117, and in his later years, C. was counted among his pupils. His written legacy was only in the form of legal *responsa*, but C. would make him a key character in his dialogues, *De oratore*, *De re publica*, and *Laelius de senectute.*

The second, Scaevola Pontifex (c. 140–82 BCE; *RE* 22; cos. 95), excelled at law and oratory. It was probably after his consulship in 95 alongside L. Licinius Crassus that he became the governor of Asia. His administration was lauded for its fairness; see *Att.* 5.17.5 *et simul hanc gloriam iustitiae et abstinentiae fore illustriorem spero si cito decesserimus, id quod Scaeuolae contigit, qui solos nouem mensis Asiae praefuit.* See also *Ver.* II.2.29, *Planc.* 33, V. Max. 8.15.6, Diod. Sic. 37.5 ὅτι Κόιντος Σκαιουόλας μεγίστην εἰσηνέγκατο σπουδὴν διὰ τῆς ἰδίας ἀρετῆς διορθώσασθαι τὴν φαυλότητα τοῦ ζήλου. On his governorship in Asia, see Brennan (2000) 549–552 and Badian (1956). There is some debate as to the date of his tenure, 97 or 94; see Ferrary (2000) 163–165 and Lewis (2006) 110–112, who both argue for the earlier date. C. had studied under him as well; see *Amic.* 1.1, and Schulz (1953) 57 n. 1, 334.

Many believe that C. is referring to the latter, Scaevola Pontifex; among them, see [Asc.] 122 (202 Stangl) and Shackleton Bailey (1992) 70. Zumpt *ad loc.* agrees but not without doubt. To muddy the waters further, C. would also refer to the two men together and praise their common traits; cf. *Rab. Per.* 26 *duos Mucios.*

The uncertainty of this identification does not, however, pose a problem from a rhetorical point of view. After a narrative in which Verres has been the righteous judge, C. quickly has to dispel any suggestion that Verres ever conducted himself appropriately as governor, and so he swiftly shatters this image. This type of humorous irony makes for an effective form of invective. Among his six types of irony, Rufinianus *de figuris* (*RLM* 39.25) calls this διασυρμός, *cum rem aliquam aut personam eleuamus.* On *ironia,* see Lausberg §§582–585, 902, Quint. *Inst.* 8.6.54–56. For a general discussion of humour and irony in this speech, see Haury (1955) 117, though he does not see as much humour in C.'s lecturing of Caecilius as others might. For irony in C. with examples and a brief discussion, see Canter (1936). C. introduces briefly here the sorts of jibes and puns that he will use more widely in the *actiones in Verrem*; see *aliquo Circaeo poculo factus est Verres* and *uertit* nn. below. For more on the Mucii and their contribution to jurisprudence, see Frier (1985) 143–144 and *passim.*

57.3 elegantius ... aequius ... uehementius ... Tricolon. *Elegans* refers to 'observing the proprieties of conduct, scrupulous, punctilious'; see *OLD s.u.* 2b. Cf. *Att.* 5.20.6 *moriar si quicquam fieri potest elegantius. Vehementius* is used here in a positive sense; see *OLD s.u.* 2.

ad hominum existimationem The lack of a gerundive in the first colon has prompted conjecture. Eberhard and Pluygers suggest *ad <colligendam> hom. exist.*, and Peterson, though he does not print it in his Oxford Classical Texts edition, *ad hom. exist. <conciliandam>*. The paradosis, however, is sound Latin. *Ad* can be used in a purpose adjunct without a gerund(ive), especially with abstract nouns that have a prevailing verbal sense; cf. *Fat.* 10 *neque haec scribunt uituperantes, sed potius ad laudem, Ver.* II.2.157 *Hos homines tu persuadebis ad honorem atque amplitudinem tuam pecunias maximas uoluntate sua contulisse?* See further, *OLS* 1.905–908, and *TLL* I 530.13–62 (for this passage, I 537.52). For *existimatio*, which can refer to the forming of an opinion or, as it does here, the (favourable) opinion that is had of someone, see §48 *consulet laudi et existimationi tuae* n., and *OLD s.u.* 2.

57.4 quaestoris libidinem C. assimilates Caecilius into a version of Verres, whom he frequently characterizes as an insatiable tyrant with unrestrained lusts and desires; see Vasaly (1993) 122–124 and Frazel (2009) 166–185. Cf. §9 *libidine* n. and §38 *quae ille libidinose … fecerit.*

57.6 e uestigio *secl. Halm*, but the reading is cited by both Priscian 3.373 *GLK* and Schol. Gronov. 327 Stangl. It would be more plausible, however, to delete *repente*, which neither source includes; it may have been incorporated into the text as a gloss for an unfamiliar phrase. There is no other instance of a pleonastic *repente* in C.

57.7 aliquo Circaeo poculo factus est Verres Both a mythological reference and a pun. C. refers to the story from the *Odyssey* in which Circe turns Odysseus' followers into swine; Hom. *Od.* 10.237–240 αὐτὰρ ἐπεὶ δῶκέν τε καὶ ἔκπιον, αὐτίκ᾽ ἔπειτα / ῥάβδῳ πεπληγυῖα κατὰ συφεοῖσιν ἐέργνυ. / οἱ δὲ συῶν μὲν ἔχον κεφαλὰς φωνήν τε τρίχας τε / καὶ δέμας, αὐτὰρ νοῦς ἦν ἔμπεδος, ὡς τὸ πάρος περ. The image is particularly apt since *uerres* was also the word for an uncastrated male pig; see

OLD s.u., Var. *R.* 2.4.21, and Plin. *Nat.* 18.322. C. was fond of this play on the name of Verres; cf. *Ver.* II.1.121, 2.191, 4.53, Quint. *Inst.* 6.3.55, and Plut. *Cic.* 7.6. He combines it again with a mythological reference at *Ver.* II.4.95 *aiebant in labores Herculis non minus hunc immanissimum uerrem quam illum aprum Erymanthium referri oportere.*

Corbeill (1996) 68: 'In Republican Rome names could *denote*, in the strongest sense of this verb. That is, names could be elicited not simply as empty signifiers but as labels that provided direct access to internal content.' A significant number of Roman *cognomina* are pejorative and frequently comment on some sort of physical attribute of the holder, e.g. *Rufus* (red-headed), *Verrucosus* (full of warts), *Varus* (bow-legged), etc. Another subset of names originated from animals, such as *Scrofa* (sow), *Musca* (fly), and *Asinus* (ass). Roman notions about the connection between character and name meant that these could be exploited for invective or corroboration of guilt. C. himself recommends as much; see *Inu.*2.28 *nam et de nomine nonnumquam aliquid suspicionis nascitur – nomen autem cum dicimus, cognomen quoque intellegatur oportet; de hominis enim certo et proprio uocabulo agitur, ut si dicamus idcirco aliquem Caldum uocari quod temerario et repentino consilio sit; aut si ea re hominibus Graecis inperitis uerba dederit quod Clodius aut Caecilius aut Mutius uocaretur.* Cf. *Phil.* 13.27 for a pun on the name *Mus.*

For another Odyssean reference, see *Ver.* II.5.146. Despite the examples discussed, mythological allusions are infrequent in C.'s speeches and most refer to the Trojan cycle. Since these stories were so well known, such references would not come across as tedious or pedantic. Other literary references include *Ver.* II.1.46, 48, 4.52, 72, and 105–107. For literary references in C.'s other speeches, see Radin (1911). For pejorative cognomina used as a mechanism for stability among the Roman elite, see Corbeill (1996) 57–98, with 79, 91–95 on Verres. Still helpful for wordplay in C. is Holst (1925) 47–51, 116 (though he assumes some emendations that are not generally accepted). C. makes other puns from the similarity of Verres' name to the verb *uerrere*; see *uertit* n. below. **Circaeo** (*PM* : *circe* γ : *circes* [Asc.]) the Italian family provides the adjectival *Circaeo*, which is supported by the quotations from Rufinianus and Priscian; cf. Verg. *A.* 7.10, 793, and see further *TLL Onom.* II 455.10–33. Both the French family and [Asc.] give a form of the genitive: *Circ(a)e* (cf. Verg. *A.* 3.386, Prop. 3.12.27; see further *TLL Onom.* II 454.36–40) and *Circes* (cf. Ov. *Met.* 4.205, 13.968, 14.10, 69, 71, 247, 294, Petr. 134.10; see further *TLL Onom.* II 40–44), respectively. The first hand of *O* has been obliterated, and a second hand has perhaps written the genitive *circeṣ* in the margin, which has been partially obscured through rebinding. On the morphology of Greek names in Latin, see Charisius *Gramm.* 5 (77.27–78.4 Barwick); see further Housman (1910).

Halm, in his edition of Rufinianus, who cites this sentence as an example of διασυρμός, prints *epoto Circaeo*, based on his chief manuscript, but then notes in his apparatus that 'Rufinianus seems to have written *poculo Circaeo*'; see *RLM* 39. It is not impossible that *epoto* has fallen out; cf. *Clu.* 168 *epoto poculo.* On διασυρμός, see Lausberg §583.

57.8 uertit Emendation to *uerrit* has been suggested to make another pseudo-etymological play on the name of Verres by its affinity with *uerrere* ('to sweep, brush away'); in a modern American idiom, perhaps 'the one who will clean you out'. Cf. *Ver.* II.2.18–19 *O praeclare coniectum a uulgo in illam prouinciam omen communis famae atque sermonis, cum ex nomine istius quid iste in prouincia facturus esset perridicule homines augurabantur! … uidete satisne paratus ex illo omine urbano ad euerrendam prouinciam uenerit.* Other passages have been similarly marked out for emendation to preserve a pun: 3.137 *auertentem* > *auerrentem*; 4.53 *auertere* > *auerrere*; cf. 2.52 *euersum.* These emendations, all of which are generally accepted by Holst (1925) 116, have some support from Quint. *Inst.* 6.3.55: *Multa ex hoc <genere> Cicero in Verrem, sed ut ab aliis dicta: modo futurum ut omnia uerreret [cum diceretur Verres].* Even without accepting all the suggested emendations, the audience was already attuned to plays on Verres' name and may have detected this one as well. On the connection between names and character and on wordplay in C., see *aliquo Circaeo poculo factus est Verres* n. above.

57.9 quantulum uisum est 'whatever trifling amount he thought suitable'. C. cannot get round the fact that Agonis did receive some form of restitution. Only here in C.'s speeches is *quantulus* found as a subordinating relative. At *Ver.* II.3.3 and *Agr.* 2.66 it is used as an interrogative. The diminutive, though often a feature of colloquial language, conveys in itself some contempt; on this and diminutives in C., see Laurand 248–262.

Iniuria non facta, resumed (§58)

§58

58.1 laesum ... iniuriam C.'s *narratio* of the Agonis Affair has demonstrated the nature of the supposed *iniuria* against Caecilius (*quale sit?*). He now pivots to another line of argumentation from stasis theory – *status finitionis* (*quid sit?*). The aim of this question is to describe the facts of the case in correct legal terminology. See *Inu.* 1.11 *Nominis est controuersia, cum de facto conuenit et quaeritur, id quod factum est quo nomine appelletur. quo in genere necesse est ideo nominis esse controuersiam, quod de re ipsa non conueniat; non quod de facto non constet, sed quod id quod factum sit aliud alii uideatur esse et idcirco alius alio nomine id appellet.* The question therefore has two areas of concern: the action (*factum*) and the law (*lex*). According to C., Caecilius would be permitted to say that he is *laesus*, but Verres' intervention in Agonis' loss of status and property does not meet the legal definition of an *iniuria*; see §52 *iniuriam* n. The scholiasts draw out the distinction between the two: [Asc.] 123 *Iniuria semper iniusta est; laedi aliquis etiam iuste potest: nam et qui iure damnantur laeduntur, sed non iniuria*; cf. Schol. Gronov. *ad loc. laeditur qui contra uoluntatem suam patitur aliquid, etiamsi iuste patiatur damnum.* However, this semantic difference is not always borne out in the extant literature; see *TLL* VII 2.868.69, where *laedere* is the equivalent of *iniuriam facere.* Moreover, it seems that, in this instance, C. makes *iniuria* a more particular subset or species of the genus *laesio* as elsewhere people are said to be *laesi iniuria*; cf. *Ver.* II.3.1, 109. When questions of definition succeed with the judge, the result is usually an implied *translatio*, i.e. the issue at hand is not being adjudicated in the appropriate venue. Or in other words, whatever happened to Caecilius, the *quaestio de repetundis* is not the appropriate arena for redress; see Lausberg §131. This analysis of Caecilius' claim, however, is tantamount to an outright rejection of the proposition.

For a similar onomastic argument, cf. Quint. *Inst.* 3.6.49 *'sustuli, sed non furtum feci', 'percussi, sed non iniuriam feci'.* C. calls this question of definition from stasis theory the *constitutio definitiua,* though it is variously entitled elsewhere as *finitio* (Quint. *Inst.* 3.6.5) and *definitio* (*Rhet. Her.* 1.21; Quint. *Inst.* 3.6.4); see further Lausberg §89. For detailed references to this question in stasis theory, see Lausberg §§104–122, 166–170.

dices The manuscript tradition is nigh unanimous on the future tense *dices,* while only the first hand of *P* and the scholiast read the present tense *dicis. P,* however, is not to be set aside lightly, and the evidence of the scholiast gives further room for hesitation. Despite the conviction of previous editors, both readings are defensible. Neither form presents much difficulty in the context of a conditional protasis. The employment of the present tense in the protasis with a future in the apodosis is most common with *si uis, si uoltis,* and *si sapis;* cf. Pl. *As.* 453 *si uoltis, faciam.* But for other verbs, cf. *Fam.* 5.12.10 *si enim suscipis causam, conficiam commentarios rerum omnium; sin autem differs me in tempus aliud, coram tecum loquar,* and Sal. *BC* 58.9 *si uincimus, omnia nobis tuta erunt.* See further Bennett (1910–1914) 1.62, and H-Sz. 660.

The final considerations are syntax and morphology. C. has constructed such precisely parallel conditional statements that one would expect the tense of *dicere* to match that of the following protasis. *Quereris,* however, is morphologically ambiguous. C. tends to use *-re* for the second-person passive except with the present tense, when he will use *-ris* (and this was Zumpt's reason for printing *dicis*). But he is not consistent in these morphological choices – in fact, K-St. 1.676 notes this passage as an example of *-ris* with the future passive. Rhythm favours the future, *querēris.* The long penultimate syllable, which distinguishes it from the present tense, provides a more Ciceronian trochaic metron. Furthermore, since Caecilius has yet to speak, the future tense is certainly logical.

On the second-person passive ending in C., see §21 *loquere* n., where similar difficulties have suggested emendation.

patiar et concedam ... defendam et negabo Two sets of parallel quasi-synonymous pairs that emphasize the contrast between *laedere* and *iniuriam facere*; see *laesum ... iniuriam* n. above. The absolute use of *defendere*, 'to rebut', is rare and somewhat strained here. C. is resurrecting the metaphor of physical combat; see *uideo esse necesse alterutrum* n. below. In stasis theory, a statement about which both sides agree is called *confessum*; see Quint. *Inst.* 7.1.5–6.

58.2 quereris Used of a legitimate complaint; cf. §11 *queruntur Siculi uniuersi*, §30 *queritur Sicilia*, and Plin. *Ep.* 3.4.2. On the tense, see *dices* n. above.

denique A marker of a progression within the same argument; see Seyffert 1§12. Cf. *Ver.* II.1.149, 2.167, 5.11, and 69.

58.3 grauiorem iudicem 'a more severe judge'; cf. *Sul.* 3 *grauius iudicium.*

58.4 si tu cum illo postea in gratiam redisti In a neatly arranged tricolon, C. attempts to provide more corroborating evidence that Verres and Caecilius have re-established a bond of *amicitia.* He has previously intimated charges of *praeuaricatio*, and this section revisits the theme he developed in §29; see nn. *ad loc.* These indications, while suggestive, are far from conclusive, and he couches all of them in conditional statements; see nn. below. On *praeuaricatio*, see *utrum ... mauis?* n. below.

58.5 domi The Roman home was a locus for social interaction and public life among the elite and their clients; see Grahame (2000) 48–74. Guests calling upon Rome's elite would range from their close friends to clients and dependants, though C. clearly means to intimate the former; see Wallace-Hadrill (1988) 55. Verres' primary residence during his tenure would have been in Syracuse, which had become the seat of government for Roman administration of the province.

aliquotiens 'on several occasions', while lacking specificity, implies some frequency.

58.6 cenauit Commensality was an important aspect of Roman social and political relations and could occur in a variety of contexts.

The sort of occasion envisioned here is the more intimate *conuiuium*, i.e. 'dinner party', as opposed to the more formal *cena recta. Conuiuia* allowed the host to establish and maintain an affiliation with his guests; cf. C.'s advice to Paetus at *Fam.* 9.24.3, or Cato's dinners at *Sen.* 46 and Plut. *Cat. Ma.* 25.2. In general, however, the relationship between guest and host was frequently unequal, and our limited evidence suggests that those with a higher social position received more invitations than they issued; see D'Arms (1984). Note, for example, that Caecilius is depicted as entertaining Verres for dinner in his home (*apud te*), but Verres only receives Caecilius into his (*domi*) with no indication that a meal was shared.

When it came to entertaining magistrates or other high-ranking officials, some potential hosts may have felt obliged to receive them; see C.'s reception for Caesar: *Att.* 13.52.2 *hospes* [Caesar] *tamen non is cui diceres 'amabo te, eodem ad me cum reuertere'.* Conversely, at Plut. *Cat. Min.* 12 Cato remarks upon not being suitably received during his travels in Asia. While 'the larger institutional context in which much of Roman social dining indubitably occurred is that of the private *hospitium*' (D'Arms (1984) 331), C. wants others to view this dinner not as an obligation but as a token of *amicitia.* Yet it is not surprising that Caecilius would need to receive Verres either during his term of office as quaestor in Lilybaeum or if he maintained a residence in Sicily. Though some towns and cities would have designated lodgings for visiting dignitaries, many did not, and hosting responsibilities fell to others in the community; see Nicols (2011) 431. Even if he was only a back-bench senator, Caecilius' actions in this instance are consistent with those of a man who wanted to move up the ladder socially and politically. Sabotaging his relationship with his praetor while Verres was still immune from prosecution would not have been politically expedient. His attempt to prosecute Verres could be seen as an attempt to re-energize his political career; see Introduction §II.

Conuiuia set the scene for one of Verres' more colourful depredations; cf. the episode at Lampsacus, *Ver.* II.1.63–69 with Steel (2004). For *cenare* used of *conuiuia* and not *cena recta*, cf. *Tusc.* 5.100. On *hospitium* in the strict sense, see Nicols (2011); on social aspects of the Roman house, see *domi* n. above.

utrum te perfidiosum an praeuaricatorem existimari mauis? In this dilemma, Caecilius must be either disregarding the bonds of *fides* and *amicitia* between himself and Verres or colluding with the defence. On the one hand, he would show himself to be of bad character; see *Rhet. Her.* 4.25 *Nam, quem in amicitia perfidiosum cognoueris, eum quare putes inimicitias cum fide gerere posse?* On the other hand, he would be guilty of *praeuaricatio* – a prosecutable offence that constituted collusion between the prosecutor and the defendant in a criminal trial to secure the latter's acquittal. In the case of the latter, another trial would be convened in the same court, first, to determine if there had been a *praeuaricatio* in the first proceedings, and second, to try the case again. The *praeuaricator* faced severe punishments and *infamia*, i.e. a loss of citizenship rights; see Berger *s.u. praeuaricatio.* See also *D.* 47.15, Heumann–Seckel *s.u. praeuaricari, Straf.* 501–503, Santalucia (1998) 180–181 with notes, Levy (1933) 177–233, and Alexander (1982) 142–144. On *fides*, see §5 *officio, fide, misericordia* n.

58.7 uideo esse necesse alterutrum gives the dilemma the illusion of logical, mutually exclusive reasoning.

58.8 pugnabo recalls, along with *defendam*, the extended metaphor of physical combat that C. used throughout his description of Caecilius' imagined rhetorical battle with Hortensius in §§44–47. *Pugnare* is rarely, and only here in C., followed by a clause of prevention introduced by *quominus.* Cf. Ov. *Ep.* 19.120 *quoque minus uenias, inuida pugnat hiemps.* See further *TLL* X 2.2558.6, though it does not cite this passage. On the original relative function of *quo* as seen here by *in eo … quo*, see H-Sz. 680–681.

utrum uelis eligas C. claimed that if Caecilius were to face Hortensius in court, Caecilius would be ensnared by a false dilemma; see §45 *quotiens … uelis …* n. In deploying his own *complexio*, C. brazenly recalls this earlier discussion with nigh verbatim signposting, and in one short stroke, he calls into question Caecilius' motives, shows himself to be a proper match for Hortensius, and provides an example of his rhetorical acumen for the jurors and his reading audience.

Reprehensio II

Quaestor eius qui accusatur (§§59–65)

Since Caecilius has suffered no wrongdoing at the hands of Verres, what other grounds could he have for being a more suitable prosecutor than Cicero? That he was Verres' quaestor? That would be an outrageous argument. A good quaestor should endure any hardships inflicted upon him by his commander, since their political relationship is a sacred one – akin to that of a child and parent. Even if Caecilius had cause and the law on his side, it would be an ethical violation to prosecute his superior. In previous diuinationes, *quaestors bidding to sue their commander have almost always been rejected.*

Since Cicero has demonstrated in the first part of the *reprehensio* that Caecilius has no justifiable motive for prosecuting Verres, in the second part (§§59–65) he argues that his attempt to do so now is tantamount to a breach not only of Roman values but also of divine sanction. He bolsters this argument by citing the precedent of other quaestors who have attempted to prosecute their superior officers and were subsequently refused the right to do so, on the ground that allowing such a prosecution would systematically undermine the Roman values that ensured the proper functioning of the state. Demonstrating Caecilius' disregard for these fundamental ideals of Roman society serves as a kind of invective that challenges his claim to lead the proscution and further ostracizes him from the Roman community. In doing so, C. espouses a line of attack that he claimed Hortensius would employ during Verres' trial if Caecilius were leading the prosecution; see §46 *commemorare quaestoris cum praetore necessitudinem constitutam, morem maiorum, sortis religionem? poterisne eius orationis subire inuidiam?* Again, C. shows himself as a skilful rhetorician and worthy match for his future opponent.

The argument appeals to a common rhetorical strategy in which positive law – i.e. that which is established by custom and statute – is shown to be in conflict with natural or divine law. See *Rhet. Her.* 2.19 *Natura ius est, quod cognationis aut pietatis causa obseruatur, quo iure parentes a liberis et a parentibus liberi coluntur. Lege ius est id quod populi iussu sanctum .... Consuetudine ius est id quod sine lege aeque ac si legitimum sit usitatum est* ..., and Quint. *Inst.* 7.4.5; see further Lausberg §176. Thus, while Caecilius may have the positive legal ability to prosecute Verres under the *lex repetundarum*, in doing so he would violate social norms imbued with divine force since they reflect the obligations of natural law. This application of the *legum contrariarum status*, sometimes called *purgatio*, is a kind of 'norm-evaluation conflict' in which C. has identified two competing 'laws' – one divine and the other positive – and forces the question *utra lex potentior*; see Lausberg §§138, 187, 220. The technique is usually one appealed to in a defence, in which a defendant may admit to an action and even its illegality but nevertheless claim that he acted in accordance with natural law. C. inverts the strategy here. He is ready to concede that Caecilius may be acting legally (*iure*) but maintains that he is acting in contravention of a higher standard of divine law (*non pie*); see §62 and the discussion below.

Quaestors and the Causa Necessitudinis

The norm to which C. appeals in this section of the *reprehensio* has already played a central role in the *Diuinatio in Caecilium*. This is the bond between individuals or between an individual and a community known as *necessitudo*, and it carriers a further consideration of the moral imperatives and social expectations that it imposes. C. invokes the mandates of this 'special bond' as one of his primary motives for seeking the prosecution (§6 *causa tantae necessitudinis* and §14 *officium necessitudinis*) and, here, as one of the leading reasons why Caecilius should be rejected(§§46, 59–61). In his analysis of *necessitudo*, Hellegouarc'h classes it as a stronger but more limited version of *amicitia*. See Festus p. 162M: *Necessari sunt, ut Gallus Aelius ait, qui aut cognati aut adfines sunt, in quos necessaria officia conferuntur praeter ceteros.* While it was a bond that naturally arose among blood and married relationships, it also pertained to the quasi-familial relationship between two individuals that could be established, among other ways, through joint military or political service. This sense of loyalty and obligation between commander and quaestor is made analogous to that between a parent and his child, and this characterization of the relationship between a quaestor and his commander-in-chief is too frequently mentioned elsewhere to be a 'groundless ideal'. (Cf. §§61, 63, 65, *Ver.* II.1.40, *Fam.* 2.17.6, 13.10.1, *Red. Sen.* 35, and *Planc.* 28 *L. uero Apuleius hunc tanti facit ut morem illum maiorum qui praescribit in parentum loco quaestoribus suis praetores esse oportere officiis beniuolentiaque superarit.* See further Thompson (1962a) 340, *Staats.* 2.563–564, and Hellegouarc'h 72.) Consequently, *necessitudo* is often associated with *familiaritas*, but while the latter simply points to the state and nature of a relationship, *necessitudo*, Hellegouarc'h continues, 'emphasises the obligations which result from it or which have given rise to it [insiste sur les devoirs qui en résultent ou qui en ont été l'origine]'. It is this special bond that, Cicero claims, should preclude Caecilius from prosecuting Verres.

But what were these obligations that *necessitudo* demanded? Most studies tend to look to instances in which an individual explains or justifies his course of action on the grounds of *necessitudo*. Generically speaking, services rendered run the gamut: helping a neighbour with his harvest (*Off.* 1.59), passing along news (*Fam.* 1.9.25, 13.77.1, 15.6.1), intervening on someone's behalf with a person in power (Caes. *Ciu.* 3.82.4), offering support in an election (*Pet.* 56), and others still further. Yet chief among them – perhaps owing to the bias of our sources – was defending someone in court; see *Rab. Post.* 41, *Deiot.* 39, *Sul.* 2 with Berry *ad loc.*, and Rowland (1970) 195 n. 10. The range of this application is easily understandable on several grounds, not the least of which is that not all *necessitudo* was the same. An awareness of the semantic range for this term, or any vague term about social values, is vital for understanding the ways in which they may be deployed or exploited. As many ancient and modern politicians are wont, C. can invoke a generally recognized social value or political ideal, even when the implications for action that the value entails are constantly under debate and negotiation. That a cultural norm is invoked to justify a course of action does not necessarily mean that the action undertaken is an inherent part of the stated norm. And so while it is helpful, and sometimes necessary, to mention only the core elements of particular abstract Roman terms such as *amicitia*, *necessitudo*, and *hospitium* (as has been done in this commentary), what Brunt says of *amicitia* is applicable more generally to its subgenres: 'The term ... is indeed ambiguous within a wide range. To determine its exact nuance in any particular context requires tact and discrimination, and it is often found where we have not sufficient knowledge of the circumstances to discriminate.' As with *amicitia*, there were 'gradations in quality and degree' of *necessitudo* – and, one may suspect, different attendant expectations in due proportion; see Brunt (1965) 7. Cf. Gel. 5.13.1–6.

The quaestor–commander version of *necessitudo* has its nuances with its own practical applications. It seems as though this special bond was thought to be established as soon as a quaestor was assigned, usually by sortition, to his commanding officer. For example, when C. is assigned C. Coelius Caldus as his quaestor by lot, he immediately assumes that a bond of *necessitudo* has been established as a matter of course, but the nature of the relationship is defined as an official connection and not yet a close personal one (*consuetudo*); see *Fam.* 2.19.1 *Cum optatissimum nuntium accepissem te mihi quaestorem obtigisse, eo iucundiorem mihi eam sortem sperabam fore quo diutius in prouincia mecum fuisses. magni enim uidebatur interesse ad eam necessitudinem quam nobis fors tribuisset consuetudinem quoque accedere.* As C.'s letter to Coelius makes clear, this *necessitudo* existed on a spectrum and could move from one of mere official connection to a more personal one. This has led to the distinction between *necessitudo publica* and *necessitudo priuata* and a corresponding distinction of the obligations associated with it; see Rowland (1970) 194 and Thompson (1962a) 348–349:

> The *necessitudo* [*publica*] seems to have been merely a matter of official etiquette, not an intimate personal relationship .... It may be concluded that the relationship between quaestor and commander-in-chief, as prescribed by public policy and custom, was an entirely official relationship. The quaestor was required to show a certain reverence, courtesy, and loyalty towards his superior during their official connexion. This held good also for other members of the commander's staff who did not happen to be friends

> or clients of the commander. Public policy and custom also imposed on the commander the moral obligation to treat his juniors correspondingly.

This 'reverence' for the commanding officer can be seen in action when C. excuses the behaviour of Cn. Sallustius, then quaestor under M. Bibulus, as reported at *Fam.* 13.10.1 *petis a me ut Bibulo te quam diligentissime commendem. in quo mihi uoluntas non deest, sed locus esse uidetur tecum expostulandi. solus enim tu ex omnibus qui cum Bibulo sunt certiorem me numquam fecisti quam ualde Bibuli uoluntas a me sine causa abhorreret. … quod ego officio quaestorio te adductum reticere de praetore tuo non moleste ferebam, quamquam quem ad modum tractarere audiebam.* C. respects Sallustius' 'quaestorial obligation' and consequently his silence on Bibulus' attitude toward C. But this letter provides further evidence that the relationship between a quaestor and his commander was initially professional rather than personal, as Sallustius still feels compelled to request a *commendatio* from C. in order to foster a closer relationship with Bibulus.

The relationship, even if an official one, with its specific reciprocal responsibilities, was taken seriously. In fact, if quaestors were assigned a commander to whom they felt they could not show due loyalty, they were expected to refuse the appointment, as M. Piso did in 83 and M. Junius Brutus in 53 (see *Ver.* II.1.37 and [Aurelius Victor] *Ill. Vir.* 82.3, respectively with Stewart (1987) 418, 424–426). However, once in office, the quaestor was expected to maintain the deferential and collegial relationship associated with a *necessitudo publica*; [Asc.] 167 (233 Stangl) *potuisti enim et debuisti, si nolles, repudiare illam sortem, aut susceptam tueri.* Failure to do so left him subject to censure. Cato the Elder, for example, who was serving as quaestor to Scipio Africanus in Sicily in 204, abandoned his *prouincia* because of his disapproval of Scipio's extravagant lifestyle; see Nep. *Ca.* 1.3 *quaestor obtigit P. Africano consuli, cum quo non pro sortis necessitudine uixit: namque ab eo perpetua dissensit uita.*

The extent to which a disregard for quaestorian–praetorian *necessitudo* constituted a religious infraction is up for debate. C. certainly speaks here about this violation in religious language, describing it as an *impietas.* Stewart (1987) has argued that the act of sortition was used to indicate the *iudicium deorum* and to sanctify the special bond between a quaestor and his commander. Therefore, from this point of view, any violation was a rejection not just of human but also of divine institutions. On the other hand, this relationship and the congeniality it mandated by custom may simply have been one of public policy and not grounded in religiosity. Depicting it in such overt religious tones could be a rhetorical hobbyhorse brought out whenever the situation suited. As Thompson (1962a) 345 writes, 'the doctrine of *sortis religio* would seem to have been a piece of religious fiction designed to give a quasi-religious sanction to the principle of *quaestoris cum praetore necessitudo.* It must have been considered a convenient doctrine for use in politics and the law-courts. ... In Cicero's time, it was clearly part of the stock-in-trade of Roman advocates: mere rhetorical humbug.'

The bounds and duration of *necessitudo* were also nebulous. While some instances of *necessitudo* are thought to have been long-term and hereditary, others may have been more fleeting. In particular, there seems to be a question of whether the bond between a quaestor and his commander was imagined as extending beyond their term of office together. For example, when C. says *cum is tibi parentis numero fuisset* (§62), the pluperfect tense implies a natural conclusion of the quasi-familial relationship. But when C. mentions his former quaestor, T. Fadius, he depicts this bond between magistrates as enduring even after the term of office is over and, in this instance, also being hereditary; see *Red. Sen.* 21 *T. Fadius, qui mihi quaestor fuit, M. Curtius, cuius ego patri quaestor fui, studio amore animo huic necessitudini non defuerunt.* But the discrepancy on this occasion can be explained. It may be that the deference implied by the phrase *in loco parentis* was no longer an important aspect of the relationship after the term of office and gave way to a more equal association between the two men. The nature of this subsequent relationship would depend on how far along the spectrum of *necessitudo* the relationship had developed. But the official relationship of mutual respect and obligation, insofar as it was mandated by tradition, could lapse at the conclusion of the period of joint service.

In his philosophical treatises, C. opines that any subsequent bonds of *amicitia* (and *necessitudo*) should endure some personal injuries (*Off.* 1.33), but they could be severed for just cause. For example, the well-being of the *res publica* must always come first; see *Off.* 3.53 *Maxime autem perturbantur officia in amicitiis, quibus et non tribuere quod recte possis et tribuere quod non sit aequum contra officium est .... At neque contra rem publicam neque contra ius iurandum ac fidem amici causa uir bonus faciet, ne si iudex quidem erit de ipso amico,* and *Amic.* 42 *praecipiendum est igitur bonis ut, si in eius modi amicitias ignari casu aliquo inciderint, ne existiment ita se alligatos ut ab amicis in magna aliqua re publica peccantibus non discedant*; see also *Amic.* 35–43, 63, and *Off.* 1.31. Furthermore, other Roman ideals, such as justice, were acknowledged to take precedence regardless of personal relationships; see *Off.* 3.43 and §59 *iustam* n.

In this context, however, C. is speaking among the jurors of the court and not the philosophers of the Stoa; he can develop a hierarchy of values and their relative obligations to suit his purposes. Moreover, while showing an acute awareness elsewhere in his oeuvre of the importance of establishing definitions of terms (in this speech, see §58 *laesum ... iniuriam* n.), he also appreciates the ability to exploit the semantic range of culturally defined terms such as *necessitudo.* 'In his rhetoric of truth, constitutional facts and prevalent norms and values are consigned to a chimerical world of appearance and falsehood, whereas his own, idiosyncratic views of things acquire definitive ontological substance'; Gildenhard (2011) 141–143. In this instance, the importance of the *causa necessitudinis* is magnified to such a degree that it becomes the foundation of Roman political stability, which reflects the proper order of the human and divine world. Its violation invites chaos.

This survey of *necessitudo* and its substantiation in the quaestor–commander relationship as well as C.'s own musings on the subject allows one to see that C.'s attack on his opponent here is tendentious at best. He manipulates the imprecise nature of *necessitudo,* which allows him to imply that Caecilius' relationship with Verres is at one end of the spectrum, when in fact it may have been at the other; see e.g. §58. But even so, Caecilius could counter his claims of impropriety or impiety: first, by saying that the special bond established between him and Verres as a matter of his appointment had expired with his term of office; second, that regardless of the nature of their relationship, Verres had nullified it by committing an outrage against him, though he would now be at pains to state the nature of the injury; and third, by maintaining that his concern for the *patria* outweighed any possible consideration of their prior relationship.

Nevertheless, to reaffirm his description of the sanctity of the bond between a quaestor and his commander and how this relationship should impact *diuinatio* proceedings in practical terms, C. provides *exempla* of other quaestors who have sued for the right to lead a prosecution against their former superior as a kind of judicial precedent (see §63 with prosopographical notes *ad loc.*). In every instance, C. claims that former quaestors were rejected *ne libido uiolandae necessitudinis auctoritate iudicum comprobaretur.* This interpretation, however, is complete fabrication or, at the very least, unfounded supposition. Even in standard hearings in a *quaestio perpetua* – much less a *diuinatio* – the jury did not issue any sort of written judicial reasoning, and so the Roman criminal court system had no way of validating particular legal arguments over others. Interpretation of previous legal proceedings became the purview not of the jurist, but of the rhetorician; see *Inu.* 1.79 *iudicatum aliam in partem traducitur.* In the *diuinationes* that C. cites, there could have been other factors which led the jury to award the prosecution to another party. It may very well be that the other parties were chosen because they had suffered a greater *iniuria* rather than that quaestors were categorically refused in some attempt to affirm the traditional etiquette between (former) quaestor and commander. C.'s evidence is self-destructive. If there had been such a general stigma about prosecuting a former quaestor, he would certainly not be able to muster so many examples among the previous generation. Furthermore, he subtly admits that there must have been instances in which quaestors were appointed; see §62 *neque fere umquam.* The 'special bond' between quaestor and commander may not be as durable and sacrosanct as C. makes it out to be; see Quint. *Inst.* 5.13.18 *Petit accusationem in Verrem Q. Caecilius, quod fuerat quaestor eius: ipsum Cicero ut pro se uideretur effecit.*

On *amicitia*, see Brunt (1988) 351–381. On *necessitudo*, see Hellegouarc'h 71–76; Thompson (1962a); Rowland (1970) 193–198. For further references to quaestorian *necessitudo*, see *Ver.* II.1.41 and *Fam.* 13.26.1.

§59

59.1 quodsi is used to indicate that C. is picking up a previous line of questioning from §52, namely what reason Caecilius can give for wanting to prosecute Verres. C. assumes that the previous argument, that Caecilius has not suffered what may strictly be understood as an *iniuria*, has been accepted. It is now anticipated that Caecilius will argue that he should be preferred because he was Verres' quaestor. The implications of this former political service under Verres will constitute the main discussion in §§59–65. On this use of *quodsi*, see Seyffert 1§75; cf. §54 *quodsi* n.

ne iniuriae quidem ... causa The hyperbaton of the genitive from its headword puts even greater stress on *iniuria*; see Marouzeau 1.128. On C.'s narrow meaning of *iniuria*, see §58 *laesum ... iniuriam* n.

facta sit C.'s repetition of this clause begins to take on a mocking tone.

59.3 quod dicturum te esse audio Perhaps a complete fabrication on C.'s part, though it may have been a fair assumption that Caecilius would mention that his tenure under Verres would allow him to proceed without much time for collecting evidence or interviewing witnesses; see n. below. **te** omitted in the first hand of *P* and added above the line in front of *dicturum.* Peterson, who was able to collate *P* by autopsy rather than from microfilm, believed the correction to be in the first hand, though the letter formation of the 'e' would suggest otherwise. In any event, the agreement of γ and *M* offers good authority. It is a good example, however, of Peterson's theory that many transpositions are the result of a corrected omission; see Peterson (1907b) 151.

59.4 quaestorem illius fuisse Caecilius' presentation at the *diuinatio* would presumably involve his stating his relationship to the accused. C. must turn this prior relationship into a disadvantage, since he himself had no direct connection to Verres whatsoever. What cannot be known is whether this would have made up a primary component of Caecilius' argument. At the very least, his tenure under Verres would have exposed to him the nature of Verres' administration and provided him with some inside knowledge of Verres' conduct. Even though he was only one of two quaestors, Caecilius may have been privy to some aspects of Verres' commercial dealings in the province and in possession of a copy of Verres' financial records. Though the quaestor and the governor kept separate accounts, the governor's records were subject to the quaestor's scrutiny; see C.'s justification of his accounts to his own quaestor at *Fam.* 5.20. Caecilius may have had more detailed knowledge than C. of the disbursements for grain purchases mentioned in §§30–33, where C. has already turned Caecilius' service under Verres into a liability rather than an asset. On the dates of Caecilius' quaestorship, see Introduction §II.

grauis 'compelling', a sense extractable from its meaning of 'having weight or authority, influential'; see *OLD s.u.* 13, and *TLL* VI 2285.9. For *grauis causa*, cf. §§6, 61, *Clu.* 82, *Ver.* II.2.109, *Inu.* 2.175, *Off.* 1.71, *Att.* 1.10.2, 7.7.3, and Caes. *Ciu.* 1.44.3. Its sense of prompting one to action has an affinity with *necessitudo*; see Nonius 315.29 '*Graue*', *necessarium* ....

si certares ... in contentione C. postpones the protasis of the conditional statement for effect. 'What a compelling reason that would be, *if* ...'. The diction also subtly maintains the characterization of the *diuinatio* as an oratorical contest; in this part of the speech alone, cf. §62 *in contentionem de accusando* and §63 *contendit.* For *certare* introducing an indirect question, see *OLD s.u.* 4, *TLL* III 899.11, 897.8; cf. *De orat.* 2.335.

59.5 amicior (*P* : *amicitior* γ*M*) *Necessitudo* can be thought of as a more specialized kind of *amicitia*; see the introduction to §§59–65. Bringing a suit or testifying against someone severed ties of *amicitia* and established personal enmity (*inimicitia*); see Brunt (1988) 370. Though the form found in the *deteriores* and the French family is also attested in the MSS of other texts (cf. *Att.* 8.11D.8, *Fam.* 3.2, 3.3, Sal. *Iug.* 10.5; see *TLL* I 1902.44), Schmalz (*s.u. amicus*) labels this longer form as *neulateinisch,* i.e. after 600 CE, and it may be a hypercorrection (under the influence of *amicitia*?); see further Reisig (1881) 247 n. 199.

59.6 suscipiendarum inimicitiarum The clash of genitive plural endings was often a reason for construing the phrase with a gerund and an object, though there are exceptions; see §60 *eas ferendo ... quam ulciscendo* n. There are cases in which scribes corrupted a gerund into the more common gerundival expression; cf. Ov. *Am.* 1.11.63 with McKeown *ad loc.*

ridiculum est In a negative sense, 'absurd'; *OLD s.u.* 2. C. masks the nuanced reality of the situation with the claim of absurdity; see introduction to §§59–65.

59.7 causam necessitudinis See introduction to §§59–65.

ad inferendum periculum See §25 *magno multorum periculo* n. For *inferre* in this sense, cf. *Rhet. Her.* 4.47 *accusatoris officium est inferre crimina*; see *TLL* VII 1.1386.42–1387.5.

iustam C. will appeal to the notion of *iustum/iniustum* throughout this portion of the speech; cf. §60 *causam ... iustam,* §61 *iustiorem ... causam,* §62 *iniustum ... bellum,* and §63 *causa iustissima.* Establishing the *maior causa* as the *iustior causa* may have been a common argument in *diuinationes*; cf. the case of L. Piso in §64. For more on *iustitia,* see *Off.* 3.28, and Hellegouarc'h 265–267. The assessment of a cause as just or unjust is a fundamental tenet of Aristotelian rhetoric in the *genus iudiciale*; see Arist. *Rhet.* 1.3, and Lausberg §61.

§60

60.1 si plurimas ... iniurias accepisses Though C. has suggested that Caecilius received no injury from Verres (§§55–58), he goes on to argue that even if he had suffered many, Caecilius should endure (*ferendo*) rather than avenge (*ulciscendo*) them. C.'s use of the past contrafactual protasis allows him to deny at once that Caecilius suffered any injuries, and to present an anticipatory counterargument if Caecilius should make convincing claims to the contrary. The hyperbaton emphasizes the adjective of quantity; see Marouzeau 1.174. Cf. *Inv.* 1.67; *Sul.* 23 *Nemo istuc M. illi Catoni seni, cum plurimos haberet inimicos … obiecit umquam*; Caes. *Gal.* 5.13.3 *complures praeterea minores obiectae insulae existimantur.*

60.2 eas ferendo … quam ulciscendo The gerund with an object accusative is generally a feature of archaic and post-classical Latin, unless the author wants to emphasize the concept of the verb or avoid 'die schwerfällige Genitivendung *-orum*'; see H-Sz. 373. Cf. Caes. *Gal.* 1.52.3 *spatium … pila coniciendi.* Both Caesar and C. have their exceptions; cf. §59 *suscipiendarum inimicitiarum.* An emphasis on the action of the verb may explain why the gerund with object accusative is more common with an instrumental ablative; see H-Sz. 379, and Bennett (1910–1914) 1.445, 450–452. On retributive justice, see §11 *ultorem* n.

maiorem laudem C. suggests that Caecilius is primarily motivated by the procurement of *laus*; cf. §48 *consulet laudi et existimationi tuae* n.

mererere There may have been a correction to a haplography in *S* as some descendants give the present indicative (*merere*). The fact that *O* shares the same error here is not remarkable in itself, but see n. below. On morphology, see §58 *quereris* n. For *mereor* with an inanimate object, especially *honor* and *laus*, see *TLL* VIII 804.1–47.

60.3 nullum illius in uita The printed reading is common to *D* and almost every member of the Italian family. *S* must have been corrected here. *E* reads *in illius uita nullum*, while *N*, which frequently incorporates what must have been marginal or supralineal corrections in *S*, reports *nullum nullius illius uita.* The outlier in the Italian family is *O*, which shows contamination from the older French tradition – a fact which may not come as a surprise given the composite nature of the manuscript; see Introduction §VI. The position of *illius* in *E* and *O* removes ambiguity and associates the possessive genitive with *vita*, which is the correct instinct, but C. rarely admits a genitive between *in* and *vita* with occasional exceptions for *eorum*, *hominum*, and *eiusmodi*; though cf. *Ver.* II.3.5 *in istius unius vita*. C. was fond of pairing *in vita* with expressions containing *nullus* and *nihil*; in the speeches, cf. §40, *Ver.* II.3.213, *Clu.* 18, *Arch.* 14, *Cael.* 39, *Mil.* 96, and *Mur.* 14.

60.4 iniuriam appellas *Appellare* can be used in speaking of the *status finitionis*, in the sense of 'labelling'; cf. *Rhet. Her.* 1.21; *TLL* II 274.51–275.8. C. has challenged this categorization; see §58 *laesum ... iniuriam* n.

hi statuent The deictic shifts the responsibility of the decision to the jurors, and the verb, used of judicial decisions generally (cf. §71), also carries the notion of establishing precedent; see *OLD s.u.*

ne in alio quidem probarent Caecilius has been shown to be so lacking in rhetorical proficiency that the jurors would not make an exception for him. See §1 *una et id ... probabit, et ...* n.

60.5 iustam See §59 *iustam* n.

ad necessitudinem uiolandam Verres is likewise accused of violating the bonds of *necessitudo* during his term as quaestor under Cn. Carbo; see *Ver.* I.11 *Cuius ut adulescentiae maculas ignominiasque praeteream, quaestura, primus gradus honoris, quid aliud habet in se nisi Cn. Carbonem spoliatum a quaestore suo pecunia publica, nudatum et proditum consulem, desertum exercitum, relictam prouinciam, sortis necessitudinem religionemque uiolatam?* See also generally *Ver.* II.1.34–43. In the same way that this line of argument is meant to stain Verres' character, so C. attacks Caecilius'. *Violare* almost always has moral overtones and implies the desecration, outrage, or pollution of something sacred. This choice of verb also re-emphasizes C.'s characterization of *necessitudo* as sacrosanct; see *OLD s.u. uiolo*. For *necessitudinem violare*, cf. §63, *Sul.* 2.

60.6 uideri The rhetorical question ends with an alliterative trochaic metron.

summam iniuriam According to C., a serious injury would only mitigate the inappropriateness of Caecilius' proposed prosecution of Verres, and he would still be open to public ridicule; see n. below. This counterargument anticipates an argument from Caecilius based on the *status quantitatis*. C. can claim that, regardless of the scope of the supposed injury, social norms should prevent Caecilius from levelling charges against Verres. On the *status quantitatis*, see introduction to §§52–58.

60.7 sine ulla uituperatione *Vituperatio* is etymologically related to *uitium*, which seems to have its origins in augural language. A physical defect in the body under analysis by the augurs was taken to indicate a break in the natural order. Hence its connection to a moral failing; see Ernout–Meillet *s.u. uitium*. Thome (1992) 77 explains 'defect, a word including rather technical mistakes as well as moral guilt, vice, not legally punishable, but in spite of that (or rather in consequence of that) subject to moral condemnation of the community and liable to the judgement of the censors'; see also *Tusc.* 4.39 *Quo modo autem in corpore est morbus, est aegrotatio, est uitium, sic in animo.* Frequently translated as 'invective', which is not always apt, *uituperatio* is more akin to 'adverse criticism' and denoted the act of censure and public shaming directed at transgressors of normative Roman behaviour. In rhetorical treatises on epideictic speech, it is identified as the opposite of *laus*; cf. *Rhet. Her.* 2.44; *Inu.* 2.12, 2.177. Such acts of shaming usually addressed the qualities of an individual's body (*corpus*), mind (*animus*), or external circumstances (*externa*) and were used for maintaining proper behaviour and order; see *Rep.* 5.6 *Nec uero [optumi] tam metu poenaque terrentur, quae est constituta legibus, quam uerecundia, quam natura homini dedit quasi quendam uituperationis non iniustae timorem*; see also *Rhet. Her.* 3.10 with Caplan (1954) *ad loc.* By calling into question Caecilius' character (*animus*) and adherence to proper social norms, C. (or any other future opponent) could impugn the honesty of his motives and thereby undermine the efficacy of his prosecution. On *uituperatio* and invective, see Corbeill (2002) and Koster (1980).

60.8 sine scelere Although the etymology of *scelus* is uncertain, it clearly comes from religious language and indicates both the offence and the resulting pollution. From its earliest uses, it tends to denote 'exceptionally vile crimes such as malicious murder, sacrilege and high treason', with an 'element of something fatal and pernicious, of being under a curse'; Thome (1992) 77. Lennon (2013) 40 says 'Such serious offences went against Roman custom (*mos*) and sense of right (*fas*), and appear to have had strong ties to religion .... Offences that caused *scelus* also offended the gods, upsetting the *pax deorum* and requiring expiation.' See further, *ibid.* 39–41. Though he exaggerates here, C. asserts that, because of the bond connecting a praetor with his quaestor, if Caecilius were to prosecute Verres without the provocation of an *iniuria*, then this would constitute a religious violation. Verres' actions towards his commander-in-chief are likewise styled as *scelera*; see *Ver.* I.11. On the uncertain etymology of *scelus*, Ernout–Meillet *s.u.*, Rocca (1995), and Devoto (1933) 238–239.

60.9 incertum (γP : inceptum M : iam certum *Eberhard*) Some editors have rejected the reading from the French family and *P* as out-of-place backtracking, since C. has been specific about the scope and nature of Caecilius' supposed *iniuria*; see §§52–58. However, he may be intentionally hedging his bets. The praetor granted Caecilius an action at the *postulatio*, so one should expect that he will present some serious *iniuria* when he speaks. But C. can state here that he has done enough, in his telling of Agonis' mistreatment, to cast some suspicion on Caecilius' grievances. 'For that reason, since there may be some uncertainty regarding (the nature of) the alleged wrong ...'. While *certum* (with *est de* ...) can convey the sense of 'substantiated' or 'exactly determined' in legal terminology (cf. Ulpian at *D.* 47.10.7.pr. and 2: *Praetor edixit: 'qui agit iniuriarum, certum dicat, quid iniuriae factum sit': quia qui famosam actionem intendit, non debet uagari cum discrimine alienae existimationis, sed designare et certum specialiter dicere, quam se iniuriam passum contendit .... Praeterea illo spectat dici certum de iniuria, quam passus quis sit, ut ex qualitate iniuriae sciamus, an in patronum liberto reddendum sit iniuriarum iudicium*), *incertum* (with *est de* ...) means 'uncertain' rather than 'unproven'; cf. *D.* 40.12.7.5 *cum de hoc incertum est* ...; 16.3.1.40 *si de quantitate ponderis incertum est. Inceptum* does not fit with the sense of the phrase and is rarely used in C.

60.11 discedere 'to withdraw [from contention]'; Heumann–Seckel *s.u.* 2. As suggested at §52, it appears that Caecilius would have been able to withdraw his petition to lead the prosecution before speaking. The *TLL* perhaps gets the wrong sense here and compares it to the use of *discedere* at §71; see n. *ad loc.*, although one may detect a syllepsis here that employs the verb in both the literal and legal (figurative) sense.

§61

61.1 differat introduces a *contentio* (ἀντίθετον); see §10 *quem maxime ... quem minime ...* n. In the two sentences that follow, C. uses close parallel word-order to highlight the difference between how Caecilius and C. think that Caecilius' previous service under Verres should influence the jury's decision. In each sentence, the personal pronouns *tu* and *ego* are in primary adversative position and separated from the main verb by a subordinate clause. For other *contentiones*, cf. §§10, 34, 35, *Ver.* II.5.75 *Vide quid intersit utrum faciendum fuerit: in illo reprehensio nulla esset, hic defensio nulla est*, and *Phil.* 8.15 *Ego nolo quemquam ciuem committere ut morte multandus sit; tu, etiam si commiserit, conseruandum putas.*

61.2 hac una in re The ablative of respect is generally expressed without a preposition, though there are exceptions; see H-Sz. 132–133, 125–127. Some editors omit the preposition, but C. may have sacrificed the more natural construction in favour of parallelism with *hanc unam ob causam.* On isocola in *contentiones*, see §10 *quem maxime ... quem minime ...* n.

61.4 omnibus (γ : *ceteris PM*) The MS tradition is evenly split. While it could be argued that *omnibus* is a *Perservationsfehler* from *omnibus rebus inferior* above, C. has carefully constructed a parallel *contentio*; see *differat* n. above. Symmetry in all other respects makes the contrast between *inferior* and *superior* sharper.

accusatorem *secl. Halm* The capacity in which a person is rejected (*repudiari*) can either be specified or inferred from context; see *OLD s.u. repudio* 2. C. explicitly expresses the capacity here to emphasize its incompatibility with *quaestor illius* above and perhaps to recall the language of the *lex de repetundis*; see n. below.

61.5 repudiari I.e. to be rejected on moral grounds; see Festus p. 350M and Heumann–Seckel *s.u.* 2. This is the verb used in the *lex de repetundis* of the Tabula Bembina for rejecting a patron; *lex repet.* 11 *de patrono repudiando* (see *Statutes* 66, and Lintott (1992) 90, 115–116).

oportere One of three instances of this verb in quick succession. C. makes a repeated appeal to moral rather than strictly legal authority, which also hints at a juxtaposition of natural and positive law; see *sic enim a maioribus nostris* n. below. For the valence of this verb, see §19 *oportere* n.

sic enim a maioribus nostris C. is continually at pains both here and in the subsequent sections of the speech to situate his motives for prosecuting Verres within the *mos maiorum* and depicting Caecilius' as contrary to them. Here he argues that the nature of the quaestor–commander relationship is one established by Roman ancestral custom and that it is to be understood as analogous to a child–parent relationship. The latter would have been understood as governed by a kind of natural law, viz. as a close relationship with concomitant duties and obligations which would have been regarded as universal; see *Rhet. Her.* 2.19. The quaestor–commander relationship is thereby presented as a cultural institution equivalent to a *ius naturale.* Thus, in this context, contravention of the *mos maiorum* is tantamount to a violation of natural law and the closely associated virtues of *pietas* and *fides*; see Quint. *Inst.* 7.4.5, and Lausberg §176. In short, Caecilius' legal rights under positive Roman law are at odds with his obligations under natural law. This conflict will be developed further; see §62 *iure ... pie* n. On the traditional aspect of the quaestor–commander relationship, see introduction to §§59–65. On C.'s bid and its context within the *mos maiorum*, see the introduction to §§66–71. On *mos maiorum* generally, see §46 *morem maiorum* n. *Sic* is frequently used with *maiores*; cf. Cato *Agr.* praef. 1, *Ver.* II.2.8, *Balb.* 39, *Fin.* 2.118, Var. *L.* 9.16.

61.6 parentis loco See introduction to §§59–65. For this use of *locus*, see *TLL* VII 2.1586.1–33.

61.7 iustiorem ... grauiorem See §59 *iustam* and *grauis* nn., respectively.

causam necessitudinis 'ties of friendship'; see *OLD s.u. causa* 12, and *TLL* III 688.4–24.

61.8 coniunctionem sortis See Thompson (1962a) 339: '*Sortis necessitudo* need mean no more than "provincial connexion" or "bond between magistrates serving in the same province" ... [f]or *sors* was regularly used as a synonym of *prouincia* (cf. Livy 9.42.1)'; see §46 *sortis religionem* n.

prouinciae ... offici ... publici muneris In the assignment of duties to magistrates, *prouincia* originally designated an area of cognizance and responsibility rather than a geographic zone itself. A *munus publicum* signified one's obligation to the state; see *OLD s.u. munus* 2, *TLL* VIII 1665.20–47, and Heumann–Seckel *s.u. munus* 1. Cf. *D.* 50.16.239.3 *Munus publicum est officium priuati hominis, ex quo commodum ad singulos uniuersosque ciues remque eorum imperio magistratus extraordinarium peruenit.* All three taken together give a fairly rounded impression of a magistrate's duties and responsibilities in his assigned area. The term *prouincia* began to shift from this initial sense to a more geographic one, and this evolution is well documented in the Verrines; see J. Richardson (2008) 82–84.

61.9 societatem 'An intense bond of *fides.* An infringement made the party liable to a particular sanction that was not dissimilar to one that would apply to an unfaithful guardian, trustee, or representative. [un intenso vincolo della *fides,* la cui infrazione espone il socio ad una speciale sanzione, non dissimile da quelle che colpiscono il tutore, il fiduciario ed il mandatario infedeli]'; see Costa 1.186–187. *Societatem* seems redundant with *coniunctionem* and makes it unclear which accusative goes with *prouinciae* and *offici.* Its inclusion or exclusion does not impair the rhythm of the clausula; *publici muneris* provides a double cretic, *muneris societatem* either a resolved cretic and trochee or double trochee. Though *societatem* could be a gloss on the phrase, it may have been thought of as the result of the *coniunctio sortis.* C. also uses the phrase *muneris societas* again at *Fam.* 5.2.1 to describe his political partnership with Q. Metellus Celer. See §30 *societas* n. for a more pejorative sense of the term.

§62

62.2 iure ... pie C. states explicitly what had been intimated above, namely that, even though there is no statutory prohibition that prevented Caecilius from filing a suit against Verres, doing so would constitute a breach of *pietas*, i.e. a dereliction of duty toward a kinsman, the state, and the gods; see *Rep.* 6.16, *N. D.* 1.116, and *Inu.* 2.66 *pietatem, quae erga patriam aut parentes aut alios sanguine coniunctos officium conseruare moneat.* In a disparity between what is afforded by human law (*lege ius*) and natural law (*pietas, ius naturale*), the latter takes precedence; see Lausberg §176 and Beard (1993) 56.

eum posses (*PM* : *trans.* γ) The order in the Italian tradition offers a better quasi-enclitic position for *eum.*

numero 'a category, class'; see *OLD s.u.* 11, and Schmalz *s.u.* Cf. *Brut.* 78 *numero eodem fuit S. Aelius*; *Ver.* II.4.41 *Iste etiam tum patrem, si non in parentis, at in hominum numero putabat.*

62.3 fuisset The pluperfect tense implies that this quasi-parental relationship was coterminous with their office; see introduction to §§59–65.

neque ... et Was rarely used to combine sentences or phrases in older Latin but became the norm with C.; see H-Sz. 517.

iniuriam See §58 *laesum ... iniuriam* n.

62.4 periculum crees For *periculum creare*, cf. *Rosc. Am.* 85, *Ver.* II.2.90, *Flac.* 2, *Balb.* 41, and *Har.* 40 *NE PER OPTIMATIVM DISCORDIAM DISSENSIONEMQVE PATRIBVS PRINCIPIBVSQVE CAEDES PERICVLAQVE CREENTVR.* The use of the phrase in a response of the haruspices may suggest that this expression was an archaism; see Landgraf on *Rosc. Am.* 85, and Beard (2012) 27. On *periculum* as particularly associated with *iudicia publica*, see §25 *magno multorum periculo* n.

fatearis Frequently in a negative sense, 'to admit a fault' or in a legal sense 'confess'; see Heumann–Seckel *s.u.*, Ernout–Meillet *s.u.*, and Berger *s.u. confessio.* Cf. §9 *fateor* n. On morphology, see §58 *quereris* n.

62.5 iniustum impiumque bellum In a hyperbolic extension of the scope of *periculum*, C. employs a metaphor, common in forensic oratory, to compare Caecilius' potential prosecution of Verres to war – albeit, in this instance, an unjust and unholy one. C. evokes a concept, firmly rooted in the Roman ethos, that all military campaigns should be a part of a *bellum iustum*. A just war required that there be a particular cause for action, and the proper procedures must be followed in making a declaration of war; see *Rep.* 3.35 (Isid. *Etym.* 18.1.2–3) *Illa iniusta bella sunt quae sunt sine causa suscepta. Nam extra <quam> ulciscendi aut propulsandorum hostium causam bellum geri iustum nullum potest .... Nullum bellum iustum habetur nisi denuntiatum, nisi indictum, nisi repetitis rebus*, and *Off.* 1.36 with Dyck *ad loc.* This was the task of the priestly college of *fetiales*, who, through an archaic ritual, first offered the offending polity the opportunity to make restitution for wrongs committed. Only after these procedures had been duly performed would the gods judge an act of war to be justified, marking the point after which one could call the war *pium*; see Nonius 529M *nec bella indicebantur, quae tamen pia uocabant, priusquam quid fuisset fetialibus denuntiatum. Pietas* and *ius(titia)* are closely associated; cf. *Clu.* 42 *iuste pieque, Phil.* 13.37 *o conseruandus ciuis cum tam pio iusto que foedere!, Sest.* 4, and *Rep.* 2.31. See further Liv. 9.1.10 with Oakley *ad loc.*

Here the analogy attempts to underscore C.'s characterization of Caecilius' prosecution as one which has not been motivated by *iniuria*, and which was not simply a *faux pas* but also represented a quasi-religious violation. On the procedures of the *fetiales*, see D. H. 2.72.1–9; *N-P s.u.*; see also A. Watson (1993), who compares the fetial ritual to Roman legal procedure. For more on *bellum iustum*, see *Phil.* 13.35, *TLL* II 1847.79–1848.13, and see further Harris (1979) 163–171.

ista quaestura ad eam rem ualet 'The bearing that your quaestorship has on this case is that ...' with Heumann–Seckel *s.u. ualere* 3. The rhetorical tactic is one in which the speaker takes an admitted fact, viz. that Caecilius was Verres' quaestor, but uses the process of invention to determine how this admitted fact should be applied to the case at hand. In this instance, C. says that Caecilius' quaestorship is pertinent inasmuch as it provides a hindrance which Caecilius must overcome, not a justification which he can invoke. On deriving a contrary conclusion from an opponent's argument, see Arist. *Rh.* 2.25.1–4, 12–14. The derisive *iste* also reminds the jurors of Caecilius' behaviour with Agonis and the grain tithe.

62.6 in ratione reddenda A financial metaphor, 'to render an account'; see *OLD s.u. reddo* 13b and *TLL* XI 2.155.48–70. Cf. *Cael.* 35. This is an all too apt metaphor given Caecilius' service as quaestor. See also §1 *causam rationemque* n.

62.7 qui *pler. codd.* In the absence of any strong argument to the contrary, the majority reading of the MSS has been accepted; 'you who had been his quaestor' with the unexpressed subject of *accuses* as the antecedent of *qui.* The way in which the relative clause in the following sentence, *qui quaestor fuisset,* mirrors this one also supports the reading. The lack of a direct object for *accusare* presents no difficulty – it is used absolutely at §§8, 32, 65, 71. Jordan and Thomas follow the correction in *r*, *eum cui.* Cf. §65 *Accusaui eum cui quaestor fueram.*

62.8 postulandum On *postulatio,* the initial approach to a magistrate to start a criminal accusation, see Introduction §III.

62.9 fere umquam C. qualifies his statement, which leads us to believe that in the period under discussion at least one quaestor was awarded the prosecutorial role in a *diuinatio.* The historical record provides no examples until the prosecution of Granius Marcellus by Caepio Crispinus in the early Principate; see Tac. *Ann.* 1.74.1. In any case, the reasons for the person being rejected at the *diuinatio* may have had nothing to do with the fact that they had been the accused's quaestor. Even so, legal precedent need not have any valence during a *diuinatio,* but it does demonstrate a method of argumentation necessary in forensic oratory.

uenit in contentionem A standard idiom, 'to become the subject of dispute'; *OLD s.u. contentio* 4b, and *TLL* IV 673.54–56. C. is reaffirming his characterization of the *diuinatio* as an oratorical contest; cf. §59.

§63

63.1 itaque signals a result or inference from the preceding argument; cf. §71 *itaque semper* .... C. now goes on to provide three examples of quaestors who made a bid to prosecute their former commanders. The choice of *exempla* suggests that there was not as much widespread disapproval as C. implies; see below *ut tu mecum* n. *Itaque* normally comes in the first position in C.; see Schmalz *s.u.*

neque ... neque ... neque... The anaphora, polysyndeton, and strict parallelism in these three clauses give the impression (almost certainly false) that C. can muster numerous *exempla* to prove his assertion.

63.2 L. Pithioni *Badian.* Perhaps an otherwise unknown individual by the name of L. Sempronius Pithio. The correct name here has been the subject of discussion. Peterson adopted the reading of the *deteriores*, the cognomen *Philo.* In an attempt to associate him with a known *gens*, Münzer hesitantly assigned him to the Veturii given the name of the consul of 206, L. Veturius Philo; see *RE* Veturius 21. Badian (1984) 291–296 noted that Klotz and Peterson did not accurately report the reading of several manuscripts, and he suggested that more credence should be given to the readings *pythoni* and *pitioni.* However, Badian neither saw *P* nor knew of other important manuscripts, such as *E*, whose readings nevertheless confirm his suspicion. He makes the conjecture that this individual is the son or grandson of L. Sempronius Pitio, who was a *monetalis* in 148; see RRC 216. The legend on the obverse of his coins reads PITIO, but it was not common to show the aspiration of *tenues* at that time, and manuscripts of Latin authors regularly add aspirants; see *Orat.* 160 and H-Sz. 1.160. By the time of C., however, it could well have been 'Pithio'. Regardless of his name, if the conjectures set out below about his praetor, C. Servilius, are correct, he was a quaestor in Sicily in 102.

On the order in which C. mentions these trials, see [Asc.] 122 (203 Stangl) *Propiora exempla et magis similia posteriora ponenda sunt.* 'The scholiast is pointing out that Cicero in *Diu. Caec.*

saves his closest (qualitative, not chronological) parallel for last'; see *TLRR* 70.

C. Seruilium C. Servilius Vatia (*RE* 12, cf. 11) was probably the propraetor in Sicily for the year 102 during the Second Slave War. His term of office was unsuccessful, and he largely blamed his predecessor, L. Lucullus; see Diod. Sic. 36.9. But there remain uncertainties about the correct identification of this Servilius and the date of the trial in question.

According to Badian's reconstruction of the events, there are two men named Servilius who were involved in a judicial tit-for-tat in the late-second or early-first century: C. Servilius Vatia and Servilius the Augur. The latter was a relative of the former and prosecuted L. Lucullus. C. Servilius Vatia was subsequently prosecuted in retribution; see *TLRR* 70. Both men were convicted. Later, this relative, Servilius the Augur, was also tried by L. Lucullus (*RE* 104) and M. Terentius Varro Lucullus (*RE* 109) but was acquitted; see *Off.* 2.50, Plut. *Luc.* 1, *TLRR* 71–72. Münzer and Mommsen treat C. Servilius Vatia and 'Servilius the Augur' as one and the same person, while Shackleton Bailey (1992) 87 remains in doubt. Equating the two men presents difficulties. For the Luculli to be a plausible age to prosecute, the trial in question would need to have taken place some ten years after Servilius' term, around the year 91, and so either Diodorus or Plutarch must be wrong about its outcome (unless, of course, there was more than one prosecution). For the timeline, individuals involved, and feud between the Servilii and Luculli, see Badian (1984) 301–306.

nominis deferendi potestas Granting of the *nominis delatio*; see Introduction §III on legal procedure.

63.3 M. Aurelio Scauro (*RE* 216; *MRR* 3.32) Perhaps the son of M. Aurelius Scaurus (*RE* 215, cos. suff. 108). He became a quaestor sometime between 95 and 90 and served under L. Valerius Flaccus in Asia. Consensus makes him the same individual as the Scaurus mentioned at *Ver.* II.1.85 *nuper M. Aurelio Scauro postulante, quod is Ephesi se quaestorem ui prohibitum esse dicebat quo minus e fano Dianae seruum suum … abduceret …* and the Scaurus on the now lost pair of inscriptions from Delos; see *ILLRP* 378, Badian (1984) 298–301, and Sumner (1973) 80–82. In that case, this *diuinatio* would have taken place around 94 or 93. The moneyer by this name of RRC 282/1, struck in 118, cannot be our quaestor, *pace* Broughton *passim.* On the meaning of *nuper* in relation to *Ver.* II.1.85, see §67 *nuper* n.

L. Flaccum L. Valerius Flaccus (*RE* 178; *MRR* 3.212; cos. suff. 86) had been a curule aedile in 99 or 98 and may have become a praetor in 96 or 95, which was followed by his governorship of Asia in 95 or 94. The fullest account of his governorship is a portion of C.'s speech in defence of his son almost three decades later; see *Flac.* 55–59. The nature of Flaccus' offences in Asia is unknown, but C. explains that money from all around Asia (*pecunia a tota Asia*) was deposited in Tralles for festival games in Flaccus' honour. It appears, however, that these games were never held, and so it is possible that Flaccus took some of the money for himself. 'In normal conditions, it is difficult to see how the diversion of funds for a praetor's games would escape the notice of subsequent governors. Of course once the Sullan government did gain control, it will not have taken any pains to see that this individual received his due, which helps explain why that fund for the Flaccus festival was eventually all but forgotten .... [When Flaccus was prosecuted for extortion,] the question of those missing funds may have come into it'; Brennan (2000) 553–554.

Cn. Pompeio Cn. Pompeius Strabo (*RE* 45; *MRR* 3.165–166; cos. 89), father of Pompeius Magnus, whose military and political success would establish a path to power for his son, had a career that is well recorded. His quaestorship in Sardinia, to which C. refers here, is now dated to 106 rather than 104, since in the latter year he was tribune of the plebs; see Badian (1984) 306–309. His unsuccessful attempt to become the prosecutor of his former governor, T. Albucius, may have been an attempt at an *illustris accusatio* during his canvass for the tribunate. He went on to become praetor in or before 92 and governor of Macedonia. C. had served under him as a new army recruit at the same time as Catiline and Pompeius Magnus; see *Phil.* 12.27, and *ILLRP* 515.

63.4 T. Albucium (*RE* 2; *MRR* S14) was propraetor in Sardinia in 106 (or less likely 104; see previous n.) and may have served for more than one year while fighting against uprisings. He threw his own triumph-like celebration in Sardinia, and it was perhaps for this reason that he was refused a *supplicatio* by the senate; see *Prou. Cons.* 15. Expenses for his provincial 'triumph' may have compelled him to plunder his province, and he faced *repetundae* charges upon returning to Rome. His former quaestor, Pompeius Strabo, lost the lead prosecutorial role to C. Iulius Caesar Strabo Vopiscus (see below), who successfully prosecuted him; see *Pis.* 92, *Scaur.* 40, and *RPCC* 171–173. C., who lampooned Albucius for his sloppy oratory and Epicureanism, calls him *Graecus T. Albucius uel potius paene Graecus*; see *Brut.* 131. He fittingly moved to Athens in his exile and studied Epicurean philosophy; see *Tusc.* 5.108. See further Brennan (2000) 476–477, Wiseman (1971) 210–211, Badian (1984) 306–307, and Gruen (1964) 101–106; *TLRR* 67 has some errors. Other anecdotes, references, and a bibliography can be found in Castner (1988) 1–6. For the prosopography of exiles and Albucius in particular, see G. Kelly (2006) 175.

propter indignitatem *Indignitas* is 'the quality of those who cannot be trusted' and so may suggest suspicions of *praeuaricatio.* Thompson (1969) argues that these attempted prosecutions by quaestors were attempts at *praeuaricationes* to protect their former commanders, but if that had been the general suspicion, C. would surely have deployed these examples to underscore that point. On *indignitas*, see Hellegouarc'h 393.

When providing *exempla*, it is the duty of the speaker to demonstrate how they relate to the subject at hand; see Lausberg §411. C. has therefore to assert that these prosecutorial applicants were rejected precisely because they were former quaestors and not on other grounds. The force of this assertion is tendentious at best.

63.5 auctoritate iudicum comprobaretur Elsewhere C. argues that judicial decisions set a precedent for what is legal; see *Ver.* II.3.219 *id prouidete, ne auaritiae, quae antehac occultis itineribus atque angustis uti solebat, auctoritate uestra uiam patefaciatis inlustrem atque latam. Nam si hoc probatis et si licere pecunias isto nomine* *capi iudicatis, certe hoc, quod adhuc nemo nisi improbissimus fecit, posthac nemo nisi stultissimus non faciet. Improbi sunt qui pecunias contra leges cogunt, stulti qui quod licere iudicatum est praetermittunt.* This argument goes a step further. Inherent in this comment is the supposition that judicial action actually serves to validate or encourage non-legally prescribed normative behaviour, and that jurors should consider, in addition to strictly legal arguments, the broader effects of their verdicts on social values.

63.6 Cn. Pompeius Some French MSS omit *Pompeius.* Though it is possible that the whole name is a gloss on *ille*, the reference may not have been clear enough after *quorum nemo.* On this individual, see *Cn. Pompeio* n. above.

C. Iulio C. Iulius Caesar Strabo Vopiscus (*RE* 135; *MRR* 2.26, 3.109; aed. cur. 90) defeated Cn. Pompeius Strabo for the right to prosecute T. Albucius and won the subsequent trial. C. appreciated his humour and wit and calls him a *specimen … humanitatis salis suauitatis leporis* (*Tusc.* 5.55), and he would have him deliver the excursus on wit in *De orat.* 2.216–290. Despite his oratorical ability, he may have been selected as the prosecutor for his political connections to his stepbrother Q. Lutatius Catulus and the latter's extensive social circle; see *RPCC* 172. His political career was cut short as he tried to seek the consulship illegally and was later killed by Marians during civil unrest in 87; see *Har. Resp.* 43, *Phil.* 11.11, *Brut.* 307, and [Asc.] 25C. For additional praise of his conversational style, see *Brut.* 177, *Off.* 1.133, *De orat.* 2.90, and 3.30. In addition to being an orator, he was highly regarded as a tragic poet; see [Asc.] 25C, and Val. Max. 3.7.11. On his agnomen, see *N-P s.u.* On his run for the consulship, see Katz (1977) 45–63. Julius Caesar reputedly used parts of this *diuinatio* speech in one of his own; see Suet. *Iul.* 55.2.

63.7 ut tu mecum C. is at pains to make the similarity between his historical *exempla* and the current *diuinatio* as clear as possible. He repeats this comparison again at *Off.* 2.50 *non est saepe faciendum nec umquam nisi aut rei publicae causa, … ut nos pro Siculis, pro Sardis [in Albucio] Iulius.* Prag (2013) 271–272 writes 'Strikingly, at some twenty-five years distance, this repeats Cicero's justificatory comparison in the *Diuinatio* of his prosecution of Verres with that of Albucius by Strabo. This might suggest that good examples of patronal prosecution on behalf of provincial clients were rather thin on the ground.' And although the justification may have been similar, the comparison is not entirely apt as Strabo, who held the quaestorship sometime before 96, seems to have been much younger and at an earlier stage in his political career when he prosecuted Albucius.

Though C. has spoken to Caecilius directly in large sections of the speech, this is the last time that he will address him in the second-person singular. From this point onward, he will turn his attention more directly to the jurors and signal the final segment of his speech (§71 *iudices*).

63.8 auctoritatis See *C. Iulio* n. above.

63.9 ab Sardis Sardinia was conquered by T. Sempronius Gracchus (cos. 238) and became a Roman province in 227, though rule was periodically resisted. On the island's subjugation, see Liv. 23.40.1–41.7. See C.'s unflattering description of the Sardinians, *Scaur.* 38.

63.11 semper haec causa ... semper haec ratio accusandi At the end of the *Diuinatio*, the transitions in C.'s arguments become subtler. This sort of aphorism acts as a pivot, in that C. intentionally obscures the progression of his argument as he approaches the most damning aspect of his bid to prosecute Verres: that, in the lack of any personal loss, he must be motivated by political opportunism; see introduction to §§66–71. For another example of C.'s grand generalizing with *semper*, see *Mur.* 39 (also on Cato's attacks on Galba) *Semper in hac ciuitate nimis magnis accusatorum opibus et populus uniuersus et sapientes ac multum in posterum prospicientes iudices restiterunt.* Cf. *Sest.* 96, and *Deiot.* 40.

The anaphora, asyndeton, and paratactic parallelism of this last part of the section elevate the register of the passage, and they are followed by a series of *tricola crescentia*: (1) *pro sociis*, (2) *pro salute prouinciae*, (3) *pro exterarum nationum commodis*; and (1) *inimicitias suscipere*, (2) *ad periculum accedere*, (3) *operam, studium, laborem interponere.*

63.12 honestissima See §65 *honestius* n.

§64

64.1 probabilis 'commendable'; see *TLL* X 2.1445.57–1446.10. C. is picking up on language from the *exordium*. Cf. §1 *una et id ... probabit, et ...* n.

64.2 qua in re dolori suo, non rei publicae commodis seruiunt A weak argument. Although C. makes them mutually exclusive, arguably the Roman criminal system, insofar as it depends on a private individual rather than a public prosecutor to initiate charges, only functions in the interest of the state as a consequence of private action.

64.4 grata 'welcomed', i.e. worthy of bestowing *gratia* on; see *TLL* VI 2261.14. On *gratia*, see Hellegouarc'h (1972) 202–208. Cf. §7 *quid est quod aut populo Romano gratius esse debeat.*

nulla priuatim accepta iniuria After going to great lengths to argue that Caecilius has suffered no *iniuria* (§§52–58), C. takes the easily assailable position that the most honourable prosecution comes from those who have suffered no personal injury but are moved by the plight of Rome's allies. Without the motivation of any personal loss, the prosecutor may have been open to attack from the defence counsel; cf. *Ver.* II.3.1 *Omnes qui alterum, iudices, nullis impulsi inimicitiis, nulla priuatim laesi iniuria, nullo praemio adducti in iudicium rei publicae causa uocant prouidere debent non solum quid oneris in praesentia tollant, sed quantum in omnem uitam negoti suscipere conentur. Legem enim sibi ipsi dicunt innocentiae continentiae uirtutumque omnium qui ab altero rationem uitae reposcunt, atque eo magis si id, ut ante dixi, faciunt nulla re commoti alia nisi utilitate communi.* And further, in a passage redolent of the *exordium* of the *Diu. Caec.*, see *Ver.* II.3.6 *Et in hoc homine saepe a me quaeris, Hortensi, quibus inimicitiis aut qua iniuria adductus ad accusandum descenderim.* In other contexts, C. will place personal retribution higher on the hierarchy of justifications for prosecution; see *Off.* 2.50.

64.6 nuper See §67 *nuper* n.

P. Gabinium (*RE* 13; *MRR* 3.98) Another prosopographical uncertainty. The date of his praetorship is debated as either 89 or

88. He is mentioned as one of the praetors at *Arch.* 9 that enrolled new Roman citizens under the *Lex Plautia Papiria.* Given the date of the passage of the law, Badian assigns Gabinius and other praetors to the year 88; see Badian (1964) 74–82. Other scholars, including Broughton, think 89 more probable; see Keaveney and Madden (1983) and Brennan (2000) 377–378. On this chronology, it was assumed from the passage here that he was a propraetor in Macedonia of unknown duration. This 'phantom Macedonian command' has been justifiably called into question; see Brennan (2000) 377 n. 181, 527–528. According to Lactantius *Diu. Inst.* 1.6.14, a Gabinius was one of the three *quindecimuiri sacris faciundis* in 76 that were sent to receive an oracle from the Erythrean Sibyl. Since Gabinius was eventually condemned and exiled – if this is the same Gabinius – his trial cannot have occurred before this deputation. In fact, it may have been Gabinius' behaviour during the trip to Erythrae that led to his trial and conviction: 'The legation to Asia of the year 76 offers a plausible enough context for the offences against the Achaeans .... In modest support of this reconstruction, one notes that we also never hear again of Gabinius' fellow *XVuiri s.f.*, though both *nobiles*: all three *legati* may have been disgraced'; Brennan (2000) 528. The date of the trial is also disputed but must have been sometime between 76 and 70, the *Diu. Caec.* itself providing the *terminus ante quem*; see *TLRR* 174.

64.7 L. Piso Either L. Calpurnius Piso Caesoninus (*RE* 90; cos. 58, cens. 50) or L. Calpurnius Piso Frugi (*RE* 98; *MRR* 3.48; pr. 74). Badian (1964) 82, 100 argues for Caesoninus:

> It is in this political context [of the weakening of the Sullan settlement] that we must place the prosecution of P. Gabinius, not long before 70, by that *uir fortissimus et innocentissimus* L. Piso – almost certainly Caesoninus, just back from service in the East (where the Achaeans had come to know him) and just of the right age to acquire renown by a political prosecution .... At the time of the Social War, Piso was *grandis iam puer* (*Pis.* 87). If he got his consulship *suo anno,* he was born in 101 and would become eligible for the quaestorship in 71 – which makes excellent sense.

> Cicero's compliment implies military service; and taking it together with the fact that the Achaeans asked him to be their *patronus*, we may without hesitation place that service in the East.

He would, of course, receive scathing treatment from C. in his *In Pisonem*, in which he is unflatteringly compared to T. Albucius as they were both denied triumphs by the senate (see §63 *T. Albucium* n.); see *Pis.* 92. On his Epicureanism (which he also shared with Albucius), see Castner (1988) 16–23.

While the identification with Caesoninus is plausible, as Badian argued, it is far from being certain. C. refers to an L. Piso two more times in *In Verrem*, and in both cases, he refers to Frugi, the praetor of 74; see *Ver.* II.1.119, 4.56. 'That inclines the balance toward this same man'; Gruen (1968b) 162 and see also Shackleton Bailey (1992) 30. Frugi is notable for having served as a praetor at the same time as Verres and hearing cases which Verres refused; see Brennan (2000) 446–448.

delationem nominis postularet On the Roman criminal procedure of *postulatio* and *nominis delatio*, see Introduction §III. Here *postulare* is used in the strict legal sense; see *TLL* X 2.261.67–84.

64.8 Q. Caecilius An otherwise unknown individual. Many modern sources focused on history tend to equate this Caecilius with C.'s opponent in the *Diuinatio*; see Brennan (2000) 527, *TLRR* 174, and B. A. Marshall (1977a) 84. Commentators are more circumspect; if this were one and the same individual, surely C. would have made more of the fact that he had lost a previous *diuinatio* while claiming the same rationale for prosecuting, namely that he was avenging a private wrong. It would have strengthened his characterization of Caecilius as an inexperienced advocate and *praeuaricator*. David (1992) 758–759 suggests that this is Q. Caecilius Metellus Creticus; see further Prag (2013) 272 and Shackleton Bailey (1992) 25.

inimicitias ... susceptas 'long-standing enmity'. This would have been the more typical justification for conducting a prosecution; see *Off.* 2.50. *Inimicitia* is found with *suscipiere*; see *TLL* VII 1.1622.43–47. Cf. §59, *Cat.* 2.11, and *Sest.* 72.

64.9 auctoritas et dignitas C. has to acknowledge that there were other reasons why Piso would have been chosen over Q. Caecilius, who had the more traditional motivation for prosecution. See §17 *auctoritatis* n. and §73 *dignitate* n. **et** (γ : *ac PM*) the two terms are closely associated, but the usual connector is *et* or *-que*, cf. *Ver.* II.2.107, and *Pis.* 64.

64.10 causa iustissima On *cum* ... *tum*, see §2 *cum summum* ... *tum non nullum* n. On the *causa iusta*, see §59 *iustam* n.

quod eum sibi Achaei patronum adoptarant *Patronus* applies to Piso 'in the social and non-legal sense of the term, and before the accusation brought against Gabinius. *Patronum cooptare* is the usual formula in inscriptions, but this [phrasing] is ignored by Cicero, who always uses the "*patronum adoptare*" [to describe] the choice of a patron by a community in a non-judicial context [au sens social et non judiciaire du terme, et avant l'accusation introduite contre Gabinius. "*Patronum cooptare*" est la formule usuelle dans les inscriptions, mais elle est ignorée de Cicéron, qui en revanche utilise toujours "*patronum adoptare*" pour le choix d'un patron par une communauté dans un contexte non judiciaire]'; Ferrary (1998) 25, and see also Prag (2013) 270; *pace* Lintott (1980) 386.

The title of *patronus* with respect to the Roman criminal court seems to have emerged from a similarity with the *patronus–cliens* relationship. Though the nature of the role evolved as new statutes were passed, 'the institution (of the *patronus*) was a typical part of the trial for extortion throughout its history [l'istituto (del *patronus*) rimase tipico del processo *repetundarum* in tutti i tempi]'; Serrao (1956) 511. In the earliest instance of provincial complaints, the non-Roman plaintiffs legally required the assistance of citizen *patroni*, either because Rome had yet to establish a criminal system to handle these complaints or because the legal process in use was one from civil procedure; see Gruen (1968a) 10–16, Lintott (1981) 172–175, and (1992) 15–20. The latter appears to be the case with the first statute, the *lex Calpurnia*, based on the *legis actio sacramento*, in which 'formally, the *patroni lege agebant* in their own name, but in essence they represented the interests of foreign victims [formalmente i *patroni lege agebant* in nome proprio, ma sostanzialmente rappresentavano gli interessi dei danneggiati stranieri]'; Serrao (1956) 479. As foreign litigants were afforded the right to initiate legal proceedings against Roman magistrates, a *patronus* became a kind of judicial assistant, appointed by the presiding magistrate after the *postulatio*; see *lex repet.* l.9 *quei ex h.] l. pequniam petet nomenque detulerit ... sei eis uolet sibei patronos in eam rem darei ....* These men held an officially recognized position before the court, but they were no longer a legal necessity, and they were not arguing the case in their own name. That is, Serrao argues, until the *lex Cornelia de repetundis*, under which Verres would be tried, reversed the populist programme of the Gracchan legislation and removed the rights of non-Romans to initiate the legal process.

Despite these assertions to the contrary, it is unlikely that the *lex Cornelia* barred foreign litigants. The *lex de repetundis* on the Tabula Bembina (123/2) explicitly allows foreign litigants, and a close reading of the *SC Caluisianum* implies that this right must have existed under the *lex Julia* of 59 BCE; see Ferrary (1998) 26 and Brunt (1961) 193 n. 16. In fact, the *SC Calu.* (ll. 90–93) refers to this right as an ancestral custom: τῶν προγόνων τῶν ἡμετέρων δίκας χρημάτων [ξετη] ἀπαιτήσεως νομοθετησάντων, ὅπως ῥᾷον οἱ σύμμαχοι ὑπὲρ ὧν ἂν ἀδικηθῶσιν ἐπεξελθεῖν καὶ κομίσασθαι χρήματα ἀφαιρεθέντες δύνωνται (*SEG* IX.8, Ehrenberg and Jones (1976) no. 311, de Visscher (1940) 137–138). Given this statement and the relatively conservative nature of Roman legislation, it seems odd, despite Sulla's pro-senatorial reforms, that this ability should have been specifically removed and then reinstated so quickly. Finding a senatorial patron should not be viewed as a legal necessity but a practical one. Negotiating the language, culture, and legal system, presenting appropriate arguments, and persuading fellow senators to convict one of their own would more-or-less force Roman subjects to choose a champion of senatorial rank to argue their case. C.'s intentional blurring between the lines of legal *patronus* and social *patronus* is so convincing in this speech that historians of Roman law assumed a fundamental shift in the functioning of the *lex de repetundis.* However, Ferrary is undoubtedly right about Piso's role as a social rather than legal *patronus*, since he was the one who initiated the charge, as indicated by the phrase *delationem nominis postularet.*

§65

65.1 lex ipsa de pecuniis repetundis sociorum atque amicorum populi Romani patrona sit In the previous *exemplum* of the *diuinatio* between L. Piso and Q. Caecilius, C. has once again stressed the importance of the jury selecting an advocate that has the backing of the aggrieved provincials. He had dilated upon this issue earlier in §§12–16 and followed it, as he does here, with an interpretation of the *lex repetundarum.* His argument from §§17–18 relies on a 'purposive' interpretation to contend that the statute was enacted to provide Rome's allies with an avenue for legal redress, and that, as a consequence, the jury should choose the prosecutor whom the members of those communities have backed to be their legal counsel. Here C. comes to the same conclusion about the intent (*uoluntas legislatoris*) but by different means, namely by appealing to *aequitas*; see n. below.

In the metaphor at §18, C. had characterized the law as an *arx* (fortress), since he wanted to stress there that the protection afforded to the allies by the law was their only line of defence. The unique metaphor here depicts the law as a *patrona* (protectress) and thereby associates it with the moral obligations associated with a *patronus–cliens* relationship to defend the client and represent their best interests; see n. above. On the *status generis legalis*, see Lausberg §§198–223. For the nuances of C.'s legal argument, see introduction to §§17–18. *Ipse* can be positioned before or after its noun without a significant change in meaning and seems to be dependent on author; postposition is rare in Caesar but relatively frequent in C.; see Marouzeau 1.186.

65.3 iniquum est 'it is unjust'. An argument from the *loci aequitatis* (appealing to *aequitas* as a natural law) can be used to determine the *uoluntas* of a *legislator.* Cf. Isid. *Orig.* 10.7 *aequus est secundum naturam iustus dictus, Top.* 90, and Quint. *Inst.* 3.6.43. *Aequitas* denotes a kind of fairness that includes benevolence and goes beyond *iustitia*, which guarantees only what was strictly required according to the law; cf. Galba at *De orat.* 1.240. The *honestior causa* can be shown to be the *aequior causa*; see *Inu.* 2.156 *nam placet in iudiciali genere finem esse aequitatem, hoc est partem quandam honestatis*, and *Part.* 66.

legis iudicique actorem When it means 'advocate' or 'legal counsel', *actor* is usually found with *causae* or by itself; cf. §11 and below. Only here is it delimited by *lex* and *iudicium*. C. means to strengthen the connection between the intent of the law and its effect on the choice of prosecutor, denoting 'the most suitable advocate for their rights under the law and their representation before the court'. On the term *actor*, see §1 *actorem* n.

65.4 socii looks at first to be oddly placed between two accusatives connected by *-que* and their genitive modifiers. But the positioning is emphatic and occurs at the end of a clausula with a cretic and resolved spondee.

65.5 an ... See §52 *an* n. A difficult phrase whose clarity is sacrificed to achieve parallelism as is frequent with *contentiones*; see §§10, 34, 34, and 61. Marinone, Fiocchi, and Vottero (1992) preserves it best in Italian: 'o forse ciò che è onorevole da ricordare non deve sembrare di gran lunga il più giusto da approvare'.

65.6 honestius Cf. *Inu.* 1.21 *sin autem partem turpitudinis, partem honestatis habebit, beniuolentiam captare oportebit, ut in genus honestum causa translata uideatur.* Through a subtle progression throughout the speech, C. is able to present his case as an honourable one though his rhetorical tactics in the *exordium* are appropriate to those of the *genus admirabile* or *anceps.* He also convinced the scholiast, [Asc.] 99 (186 Stangl), who says of the *Diu. Caec.*: *genus causae honestum.* On the rhetorical strategy of the *exordium* and the *genera causarum*, see introduction to §§1–9.

65.7 aequius See *iniquum est* n. above.

splendidior ... illustrior The two adjectives are quasi-synonymous (both related to brightness and shine) and come to denote a quality which attracts attention or admiration; cf. §6 *causam ... tam illustrem.* It is important to note here that the idea of perception is inherent in both, i.e. regardless of one's actual motives, what course of action looks more admirable? Of the two adjectives, *illustris* is the stronger and therefore comes second. Both would eventually become honorifics, especially for the equestrian order; see Hellegouarc'h 458–463.

65.8 commemoratio C. ventures into more traditionally deliberative (rather than judicial) topics; see *Rhet. Her.* 3.7 *Laudabile est quod conficit honestam et praesentem et consequentem commemorationem .... Cum igitur erit demonstratum rectum esse, laudabile esse demonstrabimus aut ab idoneis hominibus – ut si qua res honestiori ordini placeat, quae a deteriore ordine improbetur – aut quibus sociis aut omnibus ciuibus, exteris nationibus, posterisque nostris.*

accusaui ... accusaui ... Another *contentio.* The two statements summarize the conflict C. has presented between his *causa necessitudinis,* which compels him to take up the prosecution, and Caecilius', which should prevent him from doing so; see introduction to §§59–65.

65.9 sors consuetudoque maiorum See n. below.

deorum hominumque iudicium This clause explains the implications of the *sors consuetudoque maiorum.* C. presents the 'sanctity of the lot' as both a human and a divine institution, which allows him to imply that Caecilius' attempted prosecution of Verres is a breach of both. The suggestion is that the sortition (*sors*) revealed the will of the gods, while the *consuetudo maiorum* constituted the collective will of Roman society. See *Inu.* 1.101 *primus locus sumitur ab auctoritate, cum commemoramus quantae curae res ea fuerit iis quorum auctoritas grauissima debeat esse: diis inmortalibus, qui locus sumetur ex sortibus ....* Cf. §46 *sortis religionem* n. This characterization may have been mere rhetorical flourish; see introduction to §§59–65.

65.10 rogatu sociorum ... Summarizes the *narratio*; see §§2–5.

65.12 dubitare ... All manuscripts in the French family are unified in their omission of the text, presumably by *saut du même au même,* until its resumption at §66 *M. Catonem.*

65.13 apud quos quaestor fueris C. sacrifices the strength of his argument for the elegance of parallelism; cf. §34, 35, and 61. The statements above (*accusaui … accusaui …*) were mutually exclusive; the former applied only to Caecilius, the second only to C. However, in this final comparison of *causae*, both C. and Caecilius had served as quaestors in Sicily, and so Caecilius could just as easily make this argument for his case. There is nothing preventing Caecilius from offering multiple reasons for his indictment of Verres; C. himself has claimed both personal obligations to Sicily and civic obligations to the Roman state.

Digressio (§§66–71)

Consuetudo maiorum

Great men at the height of Roman civilization thought it one of the most fitting and becoming actions they could undertake to ward off harm from their friends and allies and to defend the fortunes of nations under Roman rule. Marcus Cato came to the aid of the Spaniards; Gnaeus Domitius indicted Silanus for the injuries committed against a single man. Nothing alarms wicked men so much as the renewal of the long-dormant custom of allies bringing their just complaints to a man of power who can muster his faculties to defend their fortunes and the transition of the courts of law from the hands of inexperienced youth and opportunists to brave and honest men. Rome's forefathers found no fault with this custom when Publius Lentulus and Scipio Aemilianus, both excellent men at the height of their public careers, conducted their own prosecutions. That was a glorious time when the name and majesty of the empire carried great sway. And though no one was surprised at them, someone may wonder why Cicero is trying to make a name for himself as a prosecutor at this stage in his career – and at the age when he is running for aedile. But defending the downtrodden is a duty, not just for men like Cicero, but for even older men of higher rank.

Our country is gravely ill and infected by the contagion of a few men. That men of high character should once again take control of the courts of law is the only hope of remedy. And there is nothing more salubrious for our nation than that accusers fear for their reputation and esteem as much as the accused fear for their lives. The most vigorous and scrupulous prosecutors are those who think that they are putting their own reputations on the line.

The next section of the *Diu. Caec.* appears to stand outside the *reprehensio* as a discussion *extra causam.* It is here that C. finally addresses his bid to prosecute Verres in the context of his canvass for the aedileship. In response to a potential critique that he is older and better established than a typical prosecutor and is therefore only taking up this case for the sake of political advancement, C. presents two new counterarguments: first, that the conduct of prosecutions not by *imperiti adulescentuli* but by eloquent senior statesmen, who litigate collectively on behalf of provincials, is an established Roman tradition, even if it has fallen out of fashion for some time; second, that, as the previous examples demonstrate, the state only flourishes when it has a judiciary manned by prosecutors who have a reputation and legacy to uphold. Therefore, his candidacy for the aedileship, as he will go on to argue (§72), should not be viewed as a motivating factor so much as a surety that guarantees his diligence and trustworthiness in the prosecution. The implication is that the purpose of the *diuinatio* is to ensure not the quality of the motive but the quality of the result. This is the *coup de grâce*, in which C. takes his greatest liability and makes it into his greatest asset.

He does not, however, confront the topic directly. While clear delineations between parts of a speech and progressions of argument can permit the audience to follow the speaker carefully, obscuring transitions can also serve persuasive ends by facilitating a more indirect approach to a difficult subject. This is a case in point. C. dovetails the transition to this topic by mirroring the argumentative pattern of *argumentum–exempla* used in the previous section. For Caecilius, C. had named quaestors who lost bids to prosecute their former commanders. Here C. begins by placing himself among a parade of older Roman notables who supposedly undertook or supported prosecutions on behalf of provincials, including Cato the Elder, Publius Lentulus, and Scipio Aemilianus. He will use their example to argue that sympathy for the allies is a better motive that personal injury (§64), that prosecutions on behalf of provincial clients are part of the old tradition of the Roman courts (§§66–67), and that it is the role of learned, established politicians to lead these prosecutions (§69); see discussion below.

The process of *inductio* whereby C. explains the relevance of these *exempla* to the issue at hand comes in the form of a response to an unnamed interlocutor, reminiscent of the imagined observer from the *exordium*: *'Quid sibi iste uult? accusatoremne se existimari, qui antea defendere consueuerat, nunc praesertim, ea iam aetate, cum aedilitatem petat?'* (§70). Even then the accusation is more concerned with C.'s age than his candidacy – the reference to the aedileship seemingly being used as a point of reference for his age. The issue of age, however, is a red herring and simply an oblique method used for addressing the suspicion that C. is undertaking this prosecution solely for political advancement; see §70 *ea iam aetate* n. The senior rank and age of Aemilianus in particular is used as grounds for C.'s following the argument from the *locus a comparatione* (§70 *et aetatis* … n.), viz. that defending the downtrodden and pursuing the wicked is a task particularly appropriate for those even older and more prominent than him. In conclusion, he distils a *sententia* from his *exempla*: the most sincere and diligent prosecutors have always been those that risk their reputation to lead a prosecution (*itaque semper … accusarunt*). An application of this *sententia* to himself and Caecilius will form the bulk of the *conclusio*.

'We should not feel that the start of a peroration is always to be precisely pinned down'; Winterbottom (2004) 219. Though C. clearly signposts his concluding remarks (§71 *quam ob rem* … n.), important functions of the *conclusio*, such as recapitulation of arguments (*enumeratio*) and emotional appeals (*amplificatio*), are embedded in this portion of the speech. C. subtly reminds the jury of the components he introduced at the *partitio*, namely that he is the preferred advocate of the Sicilians, whose case he has accepted at their request and out of obligation (§67), and that he is a skilled and effective orator that the defence would especially fear (§68). His emotional appeal manages to incorporate both disgust and sympathy. The *indignatio* aroused against Caecilius in these final sections is somewhat muted, since it has been provoked at other places in the speech in which his character, motivation, and ability have been called into question; in C.'s final remarks, Caecilius is reduced, perhaps even more damningly, to irrelevance. Rather, hostility is briefly directed against those few (§70 *paucorum*) that infect the nation's courts with their vices and shamelessness. The appeal to pity, however, is more sustained. While it would be common in defence speeches to locate the source of pity in the character of the defendant – by referring to his contributions to society, the plight of his family, or the importance he represents to the state – at the conclusion of the *Diuinatio*, the defendant and object of pity becomes the *res publica* (or at least the *status quo*) and to some extent C. himself. In an extended allegory, C. represents the republic as desperately ill and suffering from a cancer infecting her courts with only one possible remedy available (cf. the conceit introduced in §9 *hoc unum … remedium*). C.'s style towards the end of the *digressio* similarly anticipates the *conclusio*. On *conclusiones* generally, see §§71–73 introduction. For an argument *extra causam* before the *peroratio*, cf. *Mil.* 92 with Winterbottom (2004) 217–219. On transitions in C.' s speeches, see Fotheringham (2004) and (2006), and Steel (2009) 86, who notes that 'C. complicates his transitions in order to give a speech a more compelling and persuasive overall unity.'

Exceptional Exempla

To build up to his final assertion that there is a tradition of senior statesmen conducting prosecutions for provincials, C. points to Cato the Elder, Domitius Ahenobarbus, Publius Lentulus, and Scipio Aemilianus. The surface correspondences are clear. But even a small peek beneath the surface reveals glaring disparities regarding their legal venue, their purported motivation, and the final outcome of their suits.

C. claims to be renewing a long-disused custom – and *longo interuallo* it must have been. Of the examples that C. can summon, none come from the previous decade or were adjudicated under the *lex Cornelia de repetundis*. In fact, the attempted indictments of Philus and Galba precede altogether the initial founding of the extortion court in 149. Ahenobarbus' prosecution of Silanus appears to have been *apud populum*; see §67 *diem dixisse* n. The suits led by Lentulus and Scipio Aemilianus are the last known trials to be led by senior statesmen, the most recent of which was some 45 years previous, and both under different versions of the statute; see Prag (2013) 271 and Ferrary (1998) 44–45. Second, while C. lets his audience infer that these advocates are representing Rome's allies against injustices perpetrated by unscrupulous administrators, only one of these instances at best – Cato's action against Philus – can be viewed as collective representation. There is nothing to suggest that, in the attempted prosecution of Galba, Cato was acting at the behest of provincials; see §66 *M. Catonem illum sapientem* n. The delay in Domitius' prosecution of Silanus casts serious doubt on the altruistic portrayal of his motives, and even in the best of lights, C. says elsewhere that this trial was a paradigm for 'the defence of an individual, not a collective'; Prag (2013) 270, and cf. *Ver.* II.2.118. Finally, and perhaps most notably, all the actions advocated by the aforementioned statesmen were failures: Philus simply left Rome before any action was taken against him, and the attempt was abandoned. Galba got off scot-free. And the other three trials against Silanus, Aquilius, and Cotta all ended in acquittal; see nn. *ad loc.* The reasons for failure range from a rejection of the overwhelming political influence of Cato the Elder and Scipio Aemilianus to outright bribery. In fact, the trials of Aquilius and Cotta (if this is the same trial) are treated by Appian as some of the blatant miscarriages of justice in the senatorial courts that precipitated the Gracchan reforms. App. *BC* 1.22:

> [Γάιος Γράκχος] τὰ δικαστήρια, ἀδοξοῦντα ἐπὶ δωροδοκίαις, ἐς τοὺς ἱππέας ἀπὸ τῶν βουλευτῶν μετέφερε, τὰ ὑπόγυα μάλιστα αὐτοῖς ὀνειδίζων, ὅτι Αὐρήλιος Κόττας καὶ Σαλινάτωρ καὶ τρίτος ἐπὶ τούτοις Μάνιος Ἀκύλιος, ὁ τὴν Ἀσίαν ἑλών, σαφῶς δεδωροδοκηκότες ἀφεῖντο ὑπὸ τῶν δικασάντων, οἵ τε πρέσβεις οἱ κατ' αὐτῶν ἔτι παρόντες σὺν φθόνῳ ταῦτα περιιόντες ἐκεκράγεσαν. ἅπερ ἡ βουλὴ μάλιστα αἰδουμένη ἐς τὸν νόμον ἐνεδίδου· καὶ ὁ δῆμος αὐτὸν ἐκύρου.

In short, these are poor examples for precedent or justification, and there may simply have been few examples of litigation which could possibly be construed in this light. As has recently been noticed, the image of patronage painted in the Verrines – and in the *Diuinatio* in particular – is misleading. The patron–

client relationship as cultivated between Roman administrators and provincial elites/cities tended to manifest itself in the form of a defence for the former magistrate, not a prosecution. After an administrator-cum-patron's term of office, provincials would use this new relationship to represent their interests before the senate. If a former administrator were convicted on criminal charges of extortion, much of that effort would have been for nought. Furthermore, magistrates, aware of the danger of political persecution in the courts, may have tried to establish a history of patronage in provincial cities during their tenure to safeguard against these potential *repetundae* indictments. Provincials may have abandoned their relationship with a former magistrate only if the prosecuting side offered more political clout, as C. suggests is the case with the Sardinians turning on Scaurus; see *Scaur.* 36. 'In other words, *patrocinium* of the provinces as claimed in the Verrines by Cicero was not so much an old custom, as almost a non-custom, invented by Cicero for the occasion'; Prag (2013) 274.

This choice of *exempla* may also send a coded message to his senatorial audience. At points throughout this speech and the *actio prima*, C., no stranger to the 'rhetoric of crisis', reminds the senators of popular agitation for judicial reform and the restoration of tribunician powers; this trial, he contends, is a decisive moment in the assertion of the power of the Roman senate; see §§8, 73. The cases he invokes come at similarly important junctures. The actions against Philus and Galba took place before a permanent court existed for extortion, at which time, the *comitia* were the only institutions of any permanence that allowed for the prosecution of these types of criminal charges. The *lex Calpurnia* of 149, in addition to regularizing a mechanism for legal redress, has also been understood as an attempt to re-exert the senate's ability to police their own members; see *RPCC* 12. Meanwhile, the trials of Aquilius and Cotta, coming just before the Gracchan reforms, also represent another tipping point in the balance of influence. These cases come at crucial junctures in the assertion of senatorial control, and they likewise serve as reminders for the senatorial jury that their privileges and ability to self-regulate were in jeopardy.

Assimilating himself to Lentulus and especially Aemilianus, both outspoken opponents of the Gracchan programme, is also an exercise in self-fashioning in which C. can demonstrate his membership in the senate and assert its prerogatives. Even so, he admonishes them that these prerogatives must be earned and preserved through responsible, honest stewardship. While looking like a crusader against corruption during his canvass, he can also signal to the jury that he is a staunch supporter of senatorial authority. The platform for exposure offered by an extortion trial was too good for C. to pass up. But he had to cater to divergent audiences – to the masses that elected him and the senatorial ranks he hoped to ascend. For a further analysis of these *exempla* in relation to provincial patronage, see Prag (2013). On campaign rhetoric, see Tatum (2013) 138–145.

§66

66.1 clarissimi uiri The adjective *clarissimus* is applied to members of the senatorial class; see Dickey (2002) 316 and Hellegouarc'h 227–229. All of the men C. mentions in the following *exempla* were members of the senate.

temporibus optimis Referring to a past time in a grand narrative of decline. The trials mentioned here all come from the mid- to late second century BCE, though when C. uses the phrase again at *Sest.* 6 he refers to the early first century after 'the suppression of Saturninus and before the outbreak of the Social War and the civil wars that followed'; see Kaster *ad loc.* The phrase may be more situational than temporal and used to describe a time of senatorial control; see introduction to §§66–71. For other events in the mid- to late second century described as *optima tempora*, cf. *Font.* 39, and *Clu.* 95.

66.2 amplissimum pulcherrimumque 'most glorious and honourable'; see *OLD s.u.* 7 and 3a, respectively. Both adjectives also convey a similar sense to *splendidus* and *honestus*; see *TLL* I 2009.28–31, 2011.36–38 and X 2.2566.55–74, respectively. For this collocation, in respect to his prosecution of Verres, see *Ver.* I.36 *hoc munus aedilitatis meae populo Romano amplissimum pulcherrimumque polliceor.*

hospitibus clientibusque *Hospitium*, generally speaking, signified a guest–host relationship analogous to the Greek concept of προξενία and took two forms, *priuatum*, which involved a connection between individuals, and *publicum*, a relationship with a collective. It was similarly understood in quasi-religious terms and with reference to natural order; cf. *Ver.* II.2.110, and Plin. *Nat.* 2.144. Verres, of course, would be notorious for violating terms of *hospitium*; e.g. *Ver.* II.5.109.

The duties and obligations associated with *hospitium* varied depending on the nature of the relationship; cf. *necessitudo* in the introductory section to §§59–65, and Nicols (2011) 433–434. While some discussions of *hospitium* treat the term *hospes* as simply a polite form of *cliens* (e.g. Badian (1958b) 154–155), the Romans do not seem to have thought of these two relationships as mutually exclusive. In other words, one could simultaneously be both a *hospes* and a *cliens/patronus* 'even though the former sort of bond could be seen as assuming equality between the two parties involved, and the latter inequality .... One may guess that the circumstances dictated (in a fashion perfectly clear to a Roman) whether one responded as a guest-friend, as a patron, or as a client'; Nicols (2011) 433. The kind of relationship could be further defined by the words with which *hospes* was paired. Here, in a pair with *cliens*, the relationship implied is more one-sided, the Roman obviously providing a greater service to the provincial *hospes* than vice versa. Cf. §67 where Aegritomarus is styled as a *hospes* and *amicus*. There, *amicus* implies that Aegritomarus was a prominent individual who enjoyed close, equitable connections with influential Romans. On *clientela* and *amicitia*, see further P. J. Burton (2003) 344. On *hospitium*, see further Mommsen (1864).

66.3 in amicitiam populi Romani dicionemque There is some debate over the nature of international relationships between Rome and other communities that are described as *amicitiae*. Some would identify *amicitia* as a political euphemism that avoided reminding a client state of its inferiority. Badian (1958b) 12–13 writes 'Just as, in private usage within Rome, *amicus* can now be a polite term for an inferior (or, conversely, a superior) – i.e. a client or patron – , so in the wider sphere, where there are no equals left to Rome as a great power – or to a Roman senator as an individual – , *amicitia* necessarily becomes another term for clientship'. Gruen (1984) 54–95, 75 abjures and suggests that calling the arrangement between Rome and other communities an *amicitia* signalled its informal nature and that it was 'a conventional way of expressing favor or even signifying protection by a great power for a weaker one', albeit one which was otherwise loose and frequently ignored. Still others argue that the aspects of Roman interpersonal *amicitia* better describe the relationship between states than the *patronus–cliens* model. P. J. Burton (2003) 365, for instance, writes

> The Romans carried over into the international sphere not just the discourse, but also the practices and behaviors associated with interpersonal *amicitia* .... The mutual exchange of gifts and favors, the efforts to build international consensus, the moralizing and empathetic language of diplomatic interactions, status fluctuations between partners, the maintenance of independent foreign policy agendas, and even reprimands and punishment of perceived betrayals of loyalty – all of these bespeak friendship and its processes.

Regardless of its exact nature, C. surely means to invoke the kind of obligations and actions associated with personal relationships that compel established senators to act on behalf of provincials. Total surrender, *deditio in dicionem* ('surrender to the jurisdiction of Rome'), seems to have been the same in effect as *deditio in fidem* or *deditio in potestatem.* For other interpretations along the lines of Badian, see further P. J. Burton (2003) 342 n. 53 with references. For a further discussion of international relations, see P. J. Burton (2011) and Heuss (1933). **in -am ... -emque** though *in dicionem* vel sim. is frequently used with verbs such as *uenire* and *redigere,* when the verb is *esse* the prepositional phrase is typically construed with *in* and the ablative; see *TLL* V 1.962.4–963.14, especially, 962.64–74. Cf. *lex repetund.* 1 *quoiue in arbitratu dicione potestate amicitiau*[*e populi Romani* —]. The MS tradition, however, unanimously reports the accusative, and this use where one would expect the ablative is attested in other formulaic and legal phrases with *esse*; cf. *Quinct.* 22 *ex eo tempore res esse in uadimonium coepit*, *Ver.* II.2.67 *ut nomine iudiciorum omnium bona atque fortunae in istius unius essent potestatem?*, and 5.98 *quod, qui illam partem urbis tenerent, in eorum potestatem portum futurum intellegebant.* See further Gellius *NA* 1.7.16–18, *TLL* VII 1.795.15–61, H-Sz. 276–278, and *Statutes* 18.

66.4 iniurias propulsare C. would later state that a failure to ward off offences was an act of *iniustitia* itself; see *Off.* 1.23 *Sed iniustitiae genera duo sunt, unum eorum qui inferunt, alterum eorum qui ab is quibus infertur, si possunt, non propulsant iniuriam.*

eorumque fortunas defendere C. has avoided typical *ABBA* word-order and places *defendere* in an emphatic final position. He is reemphasizing the conceit of prosecution-as-defence (see §5) and continues to do so throughout this passage; cf. §§67, 70.

66.5 M. Catonem illum sapientem M. Porcius Cato (*RE* 9; cos. 195), often referred to by other appellations such as *Sapiens*, *Censorius*, and *Maior*, was a vigorous politician and heralded as the founder of Latin prose. His illustrious career is well known. C. may be referring to two incidents here in which Cato represented the interests of Spanish provincials; see [Asc.] 124 (203 Stangl) *Cato hic accusauit Sergium Galbam pro direptis Lusitanis et P. Furium pro iisdem, propter iniquissimam aestimationem frumenti.*

In 171 a delegation from both provinces in Spain arrived at the Roman senate to protest against maladministration and extortion by Roman officials. Five senatorial assessors (*recuperatores*) were appointed for every former magistrate from whom the Spaniards wanted restitution (Furius was among them), and the Spaniards were asked to choose Roman patrons to be their advocates – those of Hispania Citerior chose Cato and Publius Scipio.

The passage here also anticipates the conclusion of the *actio secunda*, in which C. again compares himself to Cato; see *cum … gessisse* n. below.

The text of the French family resumes at this point; see §65 *dubitare …* n.

66.6 prudentissimum *Prudentia* implies a knowledge gained from experience that imparts the ability to make wise decisions and is a quality of the ideal statesman; cf. *Rep.* 2.45. C. elsewhere describes Cato as exemplifying *prudentia*; see *Lael.* 5, and *Brut.* 294. For *prudentia* generally and its associated qualities, see Hellegouarc'h 256–267.

cum multis graues inimicitias gessisse 'had serious grievances with many men'. This passage is the only indication that there was any backlash from Cato's representation of Hispania Citerior in the accusations against Furius Philus or his support of the tribune's *rogatio* against Galba, though C. certainly makes the implication again at *Ver.* II.5.180: *Venit mihi in mentem M. Catonis, hominis sapientissimi et uigilantissimi; qui cum se uirtute non genere populo Romano commendari putaret, cum ipse sui generis initium ac nominis ab se gigni et propagari uellet, hominum potentissimorum suscepit inimicitias, et maximis laboribus suis usque ad summam senectutem summa cum gloria uixit.* C.'s phrasing here is also an elegant periphrasis to avoid the fact that in neither instance was there an actual trial. The plural *inimicitiae* is always used unless referring to an abstract concept; see *Cael.* 32 with Austin *ad loc.* For *gero* with abstract terms such as *inimicitiae* and *amicitia*, see *TLL* VI 1934.16–23.

66.7 accepimus 'we have learned that …'; see *OLD s.u.* 18 and *TLL* I 307.31–308.32.

propter Hispanorum … iniurias P. Furius Philus (*RE* 82; *MRR* 1.494) was praetor in Hispania Citerior in 174; see Livy 41.21.3. The scope of Furius' crimes is alluded to at [Asc.] 124 (203 Stangl); see *M. Catonem illum sapientem* n. above. See also Livy 43.2.12: *in futurum tamen consultum ab senatu Hispanis quod impetrarunt ne frumenti aestimationem magistratus Romanus haberet neue cogeret uicensumas uendere Hispanos quanti ipse uellet, et ne praefecti in oppida sua ad pecunias cogendas imponerentur.* Furius' case was deferred and when it resumed he had reportedly gone into exile in Praeneste, though *fama erat prohiberi a patronis nobiles ac potentes conpellare*; see Livy 43.2.1–12.

The second case which C. refers to here is Cato's support for the prosecution of Servius Sulpicius Galba (*RE* 58; *MRR* 1.455–457; cos. 144). Galba was assigned to Hispania Ulterior first as praetor in 151 and then prorogued in 150. His offences were notorious and often recounted. In the final year of his tenure, he invaded Lusitania, and he subsequently agreed to come to terms with the inhabitants and to settle them on arable land. Once they were separated into three groups and surrendered their weapons, he ordered his men to surround each group with a ditch to prevent escape and then slaughter them. Around 8000 of them were massacred, and others were enslaved. So Appian remarks of Galba: ἀπιστίᾳ μὲν ἄρα ἀπιστίαν μετιών, οὐκ ἀξίως δὲ Ῥωμαίων μιμούμενος βαρβάρους. A notable survivor was Viriathus, who would run raids and create havoc for the Romans from 147 to 139. For more on the massacre, see *Brut.* 88, App. *Hisp.* 59–60, Liv. *Ep.* 49, Suet. *Gal.* 3, V. Max. 9.6.2, *MRR* 1.456–457, Simon (1962) 60–67, and Brennan (2000) 174–175 with notes.

Upon Galba's return to Rome in 149, the tribune L. Scribonius Libo introduced a *rogatio* against him and proposed that a *quaestio* be established to try him on charges of maladministration. The *lex Calpurnia* had yet to establish a permanent extortion court, and this was becoming a common method of dealing with provincial grievances and mismanagement. Cato, now 85 and in the final year of his life, spoke in favour of the motion to try Galba, but Galba seems to have secured defeat of the tribune's proposal through impressive oratory, histrionics, and (perhaps) bribery. Tearful, Galba paraded his children and foster child before the people and commended them to the protection of the Roman republic; see *Brut.* 89–90. There are some who think that Galba was actually brought to trial and acquitted; for them, see Gruen (1968a) 13 n. 11, and *TLRR* 1. Cato would include details of the episode and his speech against Galba in the final book of his *Origines*; on which speech, see *ORF*³ 196–199, V. Max 8.1.2, Gruen (1968a) 12–13, and Astin (1978) 111–113. C. mentions this trial again at *Mur.* 59–60, but working under different circumstances, he suggests that Cato's enthusiasm for having Galba convicted was rejected because Cato had too much personal power and influence; see also *Inu.* 1.5. It may have been the failed indictment that prompted a tribune of 149, L. Calpurnius Piso, to establish the first standing criminal court at Rome under the *lex Calpurnia* (not to be confused with the L. Calpurnius Piso at §64).

The hyperbaton in this sentence is striking. In both this and the following sentence, *iniurias* is separated from its genitive by a subordinate clause for emphasis and reserved for the final position. C. uses this matching sentence structure and epiphora to bring out the correspondence between the two trials. This may also be a final jab to remind the jury that Caecilius' misfortune at the hands of Verres does not qualify as an *iniuria*; see §58 *laesum … iniuriam* n. On epiphora, see Lausberg §631.

apud quos consul fuerat Cato had been the consular commander in 195 in Hispania Citerior, where he suppressed uprisings. He later celebrated a triumph for these accomplishments, and it explains his connection with the Iberian peninsula; see Liv. 34.8–21, and Astin (1978) 28–50, 302–310. C. wants to suggest that Cato's connections with Spain are analogous to his own connections with Sicily, but the comparison is far from complete. In the accusations against Furius, Cato was under compulsion by the senate, and the delegation from Spain was obliged to choose *patroni* as it could not speak for itself. As for the attempted prosecution of Galba, Cato may have had other compelling reasons to support it besides the welfare of the Spanish provincials.

§67

67.1 nuper is not to be understood in an absolute sense ('recently'), but to point to 'the contrast between older and more recent *exempla*'; see Oakley *ad* Liv.9.34.14. Ahenobarbus' prosecution of Silanus is separated by over 40 years from the example of Cato, but still over 30 years prior to the date of the *Diuinatio*. Cf. §63 *M. Aurelio Scauro* n., *Ver.* II.1.85, and *Off.* 2.58 (for an event 35 years prior) with Dyck *ad Off.* 1.25. A more recent *exemplum* was sometimes thought to be more efficacious than a distant one, though a skilled orator could find ways to exploit both; see *Rhet. Her.* 3.4, *Orat.* 169, and *Part.* 96 *uterque uero ad augendum habeat exemplorum aut recentium, quo notiora sint, aut ueterum, quo plus auctoritatis habeant, copiam.* For additional examples with *nuper*, see further Oakley *ad* Liv. 9.34.14.

Cn. Domitium (*RE* 21; *MRR* 1.559; cos. 96, cens. 92) Cn. Domitius Ahenobarbus' term as tribune of the plebs was litigious. He conducted two high-profile trials that were both unsuccessful. In late 104, he prosecuted M. Iunius Silanus for either *perduellio* or *maiestas*; see n. below. Then, in the following year, he levelled charges for some religious misdemeanour against M. Aemilius Scaurus (*RE* 140, cos. 115, cens. 109) in a trial before the people. In the later episode, he may have been motivated by his failure to be co-opted into the college of pontiffs upon the death of his father. In response, he passed a measure that made appointment to the priestly colleges subject to a vote of the 17 tribes. It was probably through this new law that in late 103 he was appointed *pontifex maximus*, a position that he would hold for the rest of his life; see *RPCC* 173–174, and *MRR op. cit.* He continued to ascend the Roman political ladder to become consul in 96, and during his term as censor in 92 with L. Lucinius Crassus he would enact an edict against teaching rhetoric in Latin; see Gell. *N.A.* 15.11.2, *De orat.* 3.24.93, Quint. *Inst.* 2.4.42, and Tac. *Dial.* 35.1. He died around the year 89. On the dating of the trial, see Sumner (1973) 97–100, Marshall *ad* [Asc.] 80–81C, and *MRR* 3.82.

M. Silano M. Iunius Silanus (*RE* 169; *MRR* 1.545; cos. 109) had served both as a consul and proconsul in Transalpine Gaul and suffered a humiliating defeat at the hands of the Cimbri. Normally, in such circumstances, he would have been prosecuted upon his return to Rome, as happened to Popillius Laenas in 107. Instead he was only prosecuted for waging war without public sanction some years later by Cn. Domitius Ahenobarbus; see [Asc.] 80C *M. Silanus quinquennio ante consul fuerat quam Domitius tr.pl. esset, atque ipse quoque aduersus Cimbros rem male gesserat: quam ob causam Domitius eum apud populum accusauit. Criminabatur rem cum Cimbris iniussu populi gessisse, idque principium fuisse calamitatum quas eo bello populus accepisset; ac de eo tabellam quoque edidit. Sed plenissime Silanus absolutus est; nam duae solae tribus eum, Sergia et Quirina, damnauerunt.* See further *TLRR* 63. On the exact nature of the charge, B. A. Marshall (1977b) 422–423 remarks:

> Either the case was brought primarily over the injuries to Aegritomarus, and Silanus' earlier defeat was dragged into the trial, possibly because the case against Silanus was not strong; Ahenobarbus might have chosen to prosecute Silanus before the people (rather than to use the normal extortion court) in order to take advantage of the current popular dissatisfaction with senatorial commanders. Or the charge of making war against the Cimbri without authority was the main one, reinforced by general accusations of maladministration, of which the injuries to Aegritomarus were an instance.

These professed reasons may have masked Ahenobarbus' real motives. Gruen is tempted to see this trial as part of a larger jockeying for position among Roman political groups. Silanus may have been closely aligned with the Metelli, and this prosecution could have been an attack on their weakened 'faction'; Gruen (1964) 108–110. The delay between the supposed offences and the prosecution does suggest some ulterior motive other than the noble, altruistic obligations of *necessitudo* and *amicitia* that C. presents. Regardless of this, B. A. Marshall (1977b) 419 suspects that the evidence against him was simply too weak as the margin of acquittal demonstrates. On C.'s comparison in the *actio secunda*, see *Aegritomari* n. below. C. also mentioned the trial at *Corn.* fr. 2.7 with no mention of Aegritomarus. **M. Silano** The MS reading has the praenomen *D.* or *Decimo* and various forms of the cognomen. The other historical references above provide a sure correction.

diem dixisse A technical legal phrase which refers to the summoning of the accused before the *iudicium populi* by a magistrate in an older form of criminal procedure; see *TLL* V 1.1050.18–32, *Strafr.* 163–164, 324, 388, Berger *s.u. dicere diem*, and Greenidge 329–331, 344–349, 351.

67.2 propter … iniurias For the hyperbaton and epiphora, see §66 *propter Hispanorum … iniurias* n.

Aegritomari An otherwise unknown resident of Transalpine Gaul, who was supposedly treated unlawfully by M. Silanus during the latter's tenure in the province. Domitius apparently claimed that he was prompted, at least in part, to prosecute Silanus on Aegritomarus' behalf. The delay between Silanus' magistracy and the prosecution (see *M. Silano* n. above) does bring Domitius' purported motives into question. Nevertheless, C. will compare Domitius' acting on behalf of Aegritomarus with his prosecution of Verres on behalf of Sthenius; see *Ver.* II.2.118 *fecerunt hoc multi apud maiores nostros, fecit etiam nuper homo clarissimus, Cn. Domitius, qui M. Silanum, consularem hominem, accusauit propter Aegritomari Transalpini hospitis iniurias.*

paterni amici atque hospitis *Paternus* implies the heritable nature of *amicitia* and *hospitium*; see *TLL* X 1.698.60–69. For example, on *tesserae* that commemorate the establishment of *hospitium*, the names of the individuals involved are listed along with 'their intention to formalize a relationship, and the intention that the relationship should continue to future generations (... *liberis posterisque*)'; Nicols (2011) 428–429. See further §66 *hospitibus clientibusque* n.

Domitius' father of the same name (*RE* 20 with Suppl. 3.349, cos. 122, cens.115) had campaigned extensively in southern Gaul against the Allobroges and built the *uia Domitia* among other Roman installations in the region. Domitius himself had been one of the *duouiri* at the provincial foundation of Narbo in 118/7; see *N-P s.u.* I.3. This connection with the province could explain the origins of Domitius' relationship with Aegritomarus. 'One may presume that prominent Romans enjoyed such relations with many individuals and families in the provinces they had once governed'; Nicols (2011) 431.

67.5 longo interuallo Even C. must admit that this practice had abated. His most recent example, Cn. Domitius Ahenobarbus, was over 30 years earlier; see nn. above. C. was fond of this phrase and uses it 18 times in his extant orations.

repetita ac relata *Repetere* is used when referring to distant *exempla*; cf. *Ver.* II.3.182. Here the pleonastic alliterative pair, preceded by homeoteleuton, ends the clausula in a trochaic metron (*āc rĕlātă*).

querimoniae 'grievances'. As the basis for a criminal charge, see Heumann–Seckel *s.u.*

67.6 delatae 'entrusted'; see *OLD s.u.* 10a.

non inertissimum Litotes, i.e. 'highly skilled'. *Iners* is a negated form from *ars*; see Ernout–Meillet *s.u. ars.* The implication is one skilled in the *ars* or τέχνη of rhetoric and reinforces C.'s paradigm that one's speaking ability is the most crucial factor in the selection of a prosecutor. On litotes, see Lausberg §§586–588.

qui uidebatur Cf. §10 *quem maxime uelint actorem esse ii quibus factae esse dicantur iniuriae.*

67.7 fide diligentiaque sua Cf. §§51, 73; C. is obviously speaking about himself.

§68

68.1 hoc ... hoc ... hoc ... Tricolon and asyndeton highlight the frustration of the *nocentes.* C. primarily recapitulates the statements he made in §24 that established and honest public figures should initiate prosecutions rather than inexperienced young men and profiteering informants.

laborant 'they are anxious'; cf. §43 *nihil laboras,* and see *OLD s.u.* 7.

atque adeo 'or rather'. C. wants to stress that his prosecution is not a novel approach, but one which he has restored after a period of disuse. The phrase marks a *correctio* after the present infinitive *institui* and has the same meaning as *uel potius*; see Parzinger 2.34, and Seyffert 1§16. C. uses this phrase frequently in the Verrines and his early speeches. In his later style, he will replace these 'forceful expressions ... with more subjective and therefore less offensive expressions such as *uel dicam*; *uel si mauis*; *siue etiam*; *uel etiam* (*si uis*); *uel ut uerius dicam*'; von Albrecht (2003) 112. On *correctio,* see Lausberg §785; cf. §5 *non potius accusatio ....*

68.2 referri ac renouari Both verbs convey a sense of restoration; see *OLD s.u. refero* 16 and *renouo* 5a. If any nuanced difference can be pinpointed, *referre* could denote reinitiating an old practice and *renouare* could suggest overseeing that practice's vigorous revitalization; on quasi-synonymous pairs, see §1 *causam* *rationemque* n. On alliterative pairs, see §6 *furta atque flagitia* n. The doubling and alliteration are particularly suited for the recommended style of a *conclusio.* See also §67 *longo interuallo* n.

moleste ferunt C. repeats the phrase again at §69, and perhaps the audience is meant to associate the direct speech there with a *homo nocens,* who now, in a turn of fortune, is the aggrieved one, not C. (§4 *tuli grauiter et acerbe*). **ferunt** (*PM* : *fertur* γ) the reading of the Italian family is surely correct. The tricolon has kept the same third-person plural subject throughout, as does the subsequent clause (*putant*). The error could arise from an errant or misunderstood abbreviation mark.

68.3 serpere Usually used to describe negative conditions or activities. Cf. *Ver.* II.2.53 *iniuria et peccandi consuetudo.* Elsewhere in C.'s speeches the verb is only found with *malum* and *rumor* as subjects; see Merguet *s.u.* The conditional statement would therefore seem to be focalized through the eyes of the *nocentes homines.*

prodire The image is that of a serpent creeping in and emerging; see further *TLL* X 2.1601.4–14.

68.4 imperitos adulescentulos Cf. §24 *a pueris nobilibus.* The diminutive, in general, is neither infrequent nor necessarily pejorative, as it seems to be here. See C.'s self-reference at *Caec.* 97 *Atque ego hanc adulescentulus causam cum agerem contra hominem disertissimum nostrae ciuitatis ... probaui,* and in regard to the age he was when writing the *Inu.* at *De orat.* 1.5. On diminutives in C. generally, see Laurand 248–262.

68.5 quadruplatores See §24 *a quadruplatoribus* n.

68.6 amministrentur In reference to managing affairs of state or administering laws, see *OLD s.u.* 4 and *TLL* I 732.36.

§69

69.1 consuetudinis atque instituti C. will elaborate with *exempla* on what was only adumbrated in the *propositio,* §5 *adductus sum ... uetere consuetudine institutoque maiorum.* This pleonastic collocation is only found in the Verrines among C.'s speeches;

see §5, *Ver.* II.3.15, 131, and 143. Though both are sometimes defined in terms of one another (see *TLL* IV 553.40), *consuetudo* suggests a practice which has become permanent through habitual reiteration, while *institutum* can imply intentional establishment (see *TLL* VII 1.1994.19), i.e. it was both a repeated practice and one thought worthy of maintaining. On the genitive of the exciting cause with impersonal verbs of emotion such as *paenitebat*, see H-Sz. 82, and *OLS* 1.132–135. On quasi-synonymous pairs, see §1 *causam rationemque* n.

69.2 P. Lentulus P. Cornelius Lentulus (*RE* 202) was the son and grandson of the former consuls of 199 and 237 and became suffect consul himself in 162. To judge from the year of his aedileship in 169, he must have been born around 206, and was therefore about 80 years old when he prosecuted Manius Aquilius in 125 or 124; see Sumner (1973) 60 and *TLRR* 23. [Asc.] 124 (204 Stangl) names the charge as extortion. His motive for prosecuting Aquilius is unclear, but he failed; see *M'. Aquilium* n. below. Sumner (1973) 60 writes: 'Perhaps what galvanized him into his astonishing burst of senile hyperactivity was his lection as *Princeps Senatus* by the censors of 125', but it is not at all clear that Lentulus had been chosen as *princeps senatus* at the time of the trial. C.'s comment, *is qui …*, may simply serve to provide identifying rather than temporal information. At any rate, he was clearly a senior statesman at the time. C. mentions him as a sufficiently skilled orator and politician; see *Brut.* 108, and *De orat.* 1.211. On references to Lentulus' term as *princeps senatus*, see Ryan (1993) 311–313. He was also well known for his resistance to C. Gracchus in 121; see V. Max 5.3.2, and *Phil.* 8.14.

69.3 princeps senatus At the peak of this position's importance in the third and second centuries, the *princeps senatus* was generally the longest serving senator of censorial rank, who was appointed to this position by the censors and whose name was listed first on the *album senatorium.* The position had no set duties or *imperium,* but the holder was considered to be the leading voice of the senate and would be consulted first on matters up for senatorial debate. Though the *princeps senatus* was expected to have held the censorship, if no *censorius* were available, an appointee of consular rank was acceptable – as was the case with P. Cornelius Lentulus; see n. above. Political considerations certainly played a role when there were several senior statesmen in contention; see Mora (2003). The other qualifications associated with the post are less clear. In particular, Mommsen's insistence that the *princeps senatus* must come from a patrician *gens maior* (*Aemilia, Claudia, Cornelia, Fabia, Valeria,* and perhaps *Manlia*) has been called into question; see Ryan (1993) 338–365. The official position seems to have slowly fallen into abeyance after the Sullan reforms, during which time it lost senatorial precedence to the *consules designati.* Suolahti suspects that from that point onward senior senators with significant *auctoritas* were only informally called *princeps senatus* or simply *princeps.* C. wants to demonstrate that even the most senior and well-respected magistrates used to initiate prosecutions. See further Suolahti (1972) and Ryan (1993) 285–408, 420–439.

M'. Aquilium (*RE* 10; cos. 129; *MRR* 1.504, 509) after his consulship, Aquilius was the governor from 128 to 126 of Asia, a territory which had only recently been formed from Attalus III's bequest of the kingdom of Pergamum to Rome in 133. The two previous governors, P. Crassus Mucianus and M. Perperna, had worked to pacify the new territory, but both died in the province: the first, after he was captured, the second, after he captured the pretender Aristonicus (Eumenes III) but before being able to return home. Aquilius finished this pacification, and along with ten senatorial *legati* established the organizational framework of the province. In 126 he returned to Rome for a triumph on 11 November. Sometime later he was charged with extortion and accused of accepting bribes from Mithridates V to persuade him to hand over Phrygia; see App. *Mith.* 57, *TLRR* 23, J. Richardson (1987) 12, and [Asc.] 124 (204 Stangl) *de pecuniis repetundis accusatus est.* Flor. *Epit.* 1.35, however, suggests that the charge was *maiestas* related to his conduct in the Asiatic war. Although guilty, he was notoriously acquitted. Bribery seems to have been at play, and his acquittal is cited as a factor in the transfer of the courts to the *equites* under the Gracchan reforms; see introduction to §§66–71. For his tenure in Asia, see further Brennan

(2000) 232–235 and ancient sources in *MRR*. On the trial and its implications for C. Gracchus, see *RPCC* 76–78.

69.4 P. Rutilio Rufo (cos. 105) The textual tradition reports the praenomen *C.*, and later editors have referred to him as an otherwise unknown member of the Rutilii (*RE* 33). Unless there was a relative of this unattested Gaius among the jurors, it is unclear why C. should mention him here, especially as he was only a *subscriptor*. It is much more likely, among this parade of famous Romans, that C. would mention the well-known Publius Rutilius Rufus. He had been born on or before 158 and had served as a military tribune to Scipio Aemilianus in Spain 134–132; see *Rep.* 1.17 and App. *Hist.* 382. He must have been praetor by 118 since he ran unsuccessfully for the consulship in 115; see *De orat* 2.280. Depending on his date of birth, at the time of Aquilius' trial he would have been 33 years old if not older, and perhaps at an appropriate juncture to canvass for aedile, though this is purely speculative. Though he was later convicted for extortion in the late 90s, Marius was thought to have influenced the vote of partisan equestrian jurors; see Cass. Dio *fr.* 97; *TLRR* 94. This reference to P. Rutilius Rufus may also be a subtle reminder to C.'s audience about the peril facing his senatorial jury should the courts be reformed; see introduction to §§66–71. C. had met him in Smyrna in 78 (*Brut.* 85) and lauded him as a model of virtue and honesty (*Rab. post.* 27). On his trial, see further Kallet-Marx (1990) 122–139. This emendation is further supported by the observation that the republican Rutilii seem to use the *cognomen* rather than the *praenomen* to identify themselves; the Rutilii Calvus, Lupus, Nudus, and Rufus were all Publii. On *subscriptores*, see the introduction to §§47–51.

P. Africanus P. Cornelius Scipio Africanus Aemilianus (*RE* 335; cos. 147, 134; cens. 142), the adopted grandson of the elder Scipio Africanus, and famed military leader and conqueror of Carthage in his own right, prosecuted L. Aurelius Cotta on charges of extortion; see *TLRR* 9. For the trial and its outcome, see *L. Cottam* n. below. On the dating of the trial, see *posteaquam bis consul et censor fuerat* n. below. Potentially relevant for C.'s own political self-fashioning is Aemilianus' opposition to populist

Gracchan reforms and land redistribution; see Briscoe (1974) and Beness (2005). For a full treatment of his life and accomplishments, see Astin (1967).

69.5 amplissimus The vocative would become an honorific title in later Latin, frequently with *consul*; see Dickey (2002) 310. For *amplus* as a quality of the senatorial class, see Hellegouarc'h 229–231.

posteaquam bis consul et censor fuerat Aemilianus' final consulship is securely dated to 134, and C. also mentions this trial at *Mur.* 38 with the same contextualizing statement: *Bis consul fuerat P. Africanus et duos terrores huius imperi, Carthaginem Numantiamque, deleuerat cum accusauit L. Cottam.* Even so, the modern scholarly consensus has assumed that C. is either wilfully misleading here or simply incorrect according to a fragmentary reference to a row between Scipio and Cotta in 138 by the epitomator of Livy at *Per. Oxy.* 55: *P. Africanus cum L. Cottam [accu]sar[et . . . . | magnitudinem nom[inis..] . cae[. . . . .* ; see Grenfell and Hunt (1909) 101. Schlesinger, in his Loeb edition, offered the reconstruction: *P. Africanus cum L. Cottam [accu]sar[et, iudices ob] magnitudinem nom[inis eum] cad[ere noluerunt.].* If these reconstructions are correct, then Scipio Aemilianus waited over five years from the time of Cotta's consulship to prosecute him. The reasons for the delay may have been logistical as he was busy with his duties as censor, defending himself in court, and then away as a member of a senatorial commission; see Badian (1958c) 216. Scipio may have been spurred into action only later when in 138, or more likely 139, Q. Pompeius, his associate, was unsuccessfully prosecuted for extortion by leading members of the Metelli. It was therefore in retribution that Scipio prosecuted Cotta, who was defended by Q. Caecilius Metellus Macedonicus (*RE* 94; cos. 143, cens. 131) – who had also been one of the leading accusers of Pompeius; see further *RPCC* 37–38 with notes.

However, given the speculative restoration of *Per. Oxy.* 55, the date of the trial should remain an open question. Though C. is no historian, Scipio's previous political offices are central to his point here. Mendacity would undermine rather than serve his purposes. Since Scipio's second consulship, during which he subdued Numantia, was in 134, his prosecution of Cotta would need to be dated after Scipio's return in 132. If Macedonicus' duties as censor were as onerous as some have suggested, one should date the trial of Cotta to 130 or 129. For a reconsideration of these sources with bibliography, see Watson (2019).

69.6 L. Cottam L. Aurelius Cotta (*RE* 98; cos. 144) is remembered as 'a disgraceful example of prodigality and insolvency'; Badian (1958c) 216, and see also Lucil. 11.440–442, and V. Max. 6.4.2, 6.5.4. During his tribunate, he had apparently tried to use the sacrosanctity of his position to avoid paying off his creditors. Even so, he was elected to the consulship of 144 along with Ser. Sulpicius Galba; on the latter, see §66 *propter Hispanorum … iniurias* n. According to V. Max. 6.4.2, he and Galba contended for the command of Spain, but Scipio Aemilianus saw to it that neither of them received it. The allegations levelled against Cotta by Aemilianus in his later extortion trial are far from clear. If the charges related to Cotta's consulship, it is hard to find a province that he would have been sent to. 'Spain … was at this time the only part of the Empire that needed a consular governor for major warfare. Consuls, at this time, were not normally sent to perfectly peaceful provinces'; Badian (1958c) 217. Since we know that he was not sent there, Badian goes on to suggest that Italia may have been assigned as his province, and therefore the prosecution related to offences committed against *socii*. But this conjecture, based on the silence of the Livian epitomators, is questionable. A range of other ancient sources refer to the trial; see *Mur.* 58, *Brut.* 81, Liv. *Per. Oxy.* 55, V. Max. 8.1.abs.11, and Tac. *Ann.* 3.66.1–2. The references at *Font.* 38 and App. *BC* 1.22 could refer to this trial or to another trial of L. Aurelius Cotta (*RE* 99; *cos.* 119). See further J. Richardson (1987) 12, Brennan (2000) 176–177, and Astin (1967) 258. On his birth date, see Sumner (1973) 43–44.

iure … iure In a broader sense, 'deserved, warranted'; see *TLL* VII 2.698.69–699.6. Cf. the narrower, legal sense, §62 *iure … pie* n.

69.7 auctoritas huius imperi ciuitatisque maiestas *Auctoritas* can be applied to a group of people as a whole but more often refers to the influence, power, and prestige of the senate and its members. C. may therefore be alluding to the senate's ability to regulate itself and the state since 'to express the superiority of the Roman people, the authority and influence they enjoyed over other people, Latin has a special term: *maiestas* [pour exprimer la supériorité du peuple romain, l'autorité et l'influence dont il jouit sur les autres peuples, le latin possède un terme spécial: *maiestas*]'; Hellegouarc'h 314. *Maiestas* expresses a kind of moral and physical superiority with religious undertones and is often associated with the Roman people as distinct from the senate; cf. *Phil.* 3.13, and *Sest.* 83. See further Hellegouarc'h 313–320. Taken together, the two terms express the prestige of the *senatus populusque Romanus.* On chiasmus, see §32 *graue* ... *graue* n. On *imperium*, see J. Richardson (1991): 'The earlier significance [of *imperium*], the right of command within the Roman state ... was never lost, but in addition the meaning "empire", in an increasingly concrete, territorial sense came to be a normal usage.' Cf. *Man.* 55 *omnis socios in ultimis oris auctoritate nostri imperi saluos praestare poteramus*, *Dom.* 133, *Mur.* 58, and V. Max. 2.2.2.

69.8 nemo mirabatur in Africano illo Cf. §1 *si quis uestrum* ... *aut eorum* ... *forte miratur.* C. begins to echo the language and issues presented in the *exordium.* The comparison is misleading; Aemilianus was not in the midst of an electoral campaign. Even so, it is with him that C. most wants to associate himself, though see n. below.

69.9 homine paruis opibus ac facultatibus praedito This self-deprecatory statement should not be understood absolutely but as an expression of modesty when comparing himself to Scipio Aemilianus. C. may be older and more influential than the typical prosecutor (an *adulescentulus* or *quadruplator*), but it is bold for him, not yet an aedile, to suggest a similarity between himself and one of the most celebrated of all Romans.

In this collocation, *opes* – the singular form is rarely found – and *facultates* denote a combination of political and social influence and financial means. Hellegouarc'h 237 writes 'In accordance with the general meaning of abstract words used in the plural, *opes* has a corresponding concrete definition and indicates everything at the disposal of the politician to exercise his influence. [Conformément au sens général des mots abstraits employés au pluriel, *opes* a donc le sens concret correspondant et désigne tout ce dont dispose l'homme politique pour exercer son influence.]' Cf. *Quinct.* 2 *P. Quinctius, cui tenues opes, nullae facultates*, and *Amic.* 55. These qualities are the opposite of those found in the inexperienced youth, who is lacking in standing, and the opportunistic and money-hungry *quadruplator.*

69.10 simulant sese mirari To suggest that the unnamed interlocutor's surprise is feigned rather than genuine undermines his *ethos* as deceptive and discredits the statement to follow (*quid sibi iste uult?* ...). The implication is that anyone who suggests that C.'s attempted prosecution is surprising is in fact hiding an ulterior motive and looking for a flimsy reason to disregard his bid.

ferunt Also the reading in *O*, though many editors misreport it.

§70

70.1 quid sibi iste uult? ... Virtual *oratio recta* introduced by *moleste ferunt.* The tone is decidedly accusatory: 'What is he after?' For *uelle* with a reflexive dative of interest, see *OLD s.u.* 16 with further examples at *L&S s.u.* I.E.4b; cf. *Dom.* 29. The expression becomes rare in post-Augustan authors. The direct speech gives voice to the anonymous observer from §1 (*si quis uestrum ... aut eorum qui adsunt, forte miratur* ...). The first half of this anonymous interlocutor's question corresponds to concepts from the initial vignette: *ita sim uersatus ut defenderim multos, laeserim neminem* with *qui antea defendere consueuerat* and the adverbs *subito nunc* with *nunc praesertim.* C. finally makes explicit the unspoken concern from the *exordium*: the coincidence of this bid to prosecute Verres and his canvass for the aedileship. Recapitulating an argument through direct speech at the conclusion of an oration is recommended at *Inu.* 99: *nam tum ex tua persona enumerare possis, ut, quid et quo quidque loco dixeris, admoneas; tum uero personam aut rem aliquam inducere et enumerationem ei totam attribuere.*

70.2 accusatoremne se existimari 'to make a reputation as a prosecutor', not represented in the *OLD* or *TLL*, and more closely allied to the idea of developing a reputation, *existimatio*; see §71 *de laude* ... n.

defendere consueuerat See §1 *defenderim multos, laeserim neminem* with n. *ad loc.* on C.'s earlier forensic activity, and cf. §5 *manere in instituto meo uideor.* **consueuerat** the MS tradition is unhelpfully divided on the spelling. Though the perfect tense of *consuescere* is commonly syncopated (Neue-Wagener 2.483–486), the full form offers a choriambus and cretic rhythm (*dēfēndĕrĕ cōnsuēuĕrat*) and is not without parallel; cf. *Brut.* 10 *ut consueuerat.* See further *TLL* IV 550.81

70.3 ea iam aetate C. had probably turned 36 just recently, but the issue of age is a red herring. Though he has mustered examples of established politicians leading prosecutions or speaking out against provincial maladministration, his absolute age should pose no trouble. The minimum age for the quaestorship, established by the *lex annalis*, was 30. Therefore, if the timeline associated with the quaestors serving under Verres is correct (see Introduction §II), the earliest Caecilius could have been born was 104 to stand for election in 74. This would make him C.'s junior by only two years, and they would both have attained the same position on the *cursus honorum.* The issue of age only has meaning when combined with a charge of political opportunism in the midst of a campaign for higher office. There may have been more tolerance for young men looking to embark upon a political career – hence C.'s repeated emphasis on inexperienced youth leading suits against senators; cf. §24 *a pueris nobilibus* and §68 *imperitos adulescentulos.*

cum aedilitatem petat C. finally addresses the issue which had loomed large from the outset. Only after a long delay and by an oblique route does he finally approach this potentially disagreeable topic; see Stroh (1975) 186, *pace* Tatum (2013) 144. By this point, however, he had mustered every other argument in his favour, and so can take an ambitious approach in which he offers his candidacy as a sure sign of his sincerity and scruple. By the trial proper in early August, C. would be aedile-elect; cf. *Ver.* II.5.36. On the dates of elections, see *Staats.* 1.580–588. For *petere*, 'to be a candidate for (an office)', see *OLD s.u.* 9a, and *TLL* X 1.1967.12.

ego uero The adversative positioning of the pronoun combined with *uero* signals that C. is going to present an alternative point of view that challenges the suppositions of the interlocutor.

70.4 et aetatis non modo meae sed multo etiam superioris et honoris amplissimi C. has just cited examples of men who were in the final years of their life when they spoke out against or accused another senator (Cato, Lentulus, Aemilianus). He now expresses a sentiment which initiates the process of *inductio* (relating the *exempla* to this particular *causa*) that will be completed below; see §71 *nulla salus* .... The method of argumentation is derived from the *locus a comparatione* – if men such as these can lead prosecutions for provincials, surely someone of lesser stature should also be allowed. On the *locus*, see Quint. *Inst.* 5.10.87, and Lausberg §395. *Superior* here connotes both higher rank and age; see *OLD s.u.* 4. *Honor amplissimus* refers to the highest political standing – in the Roman political context, censorial or consular rank; see §69 *amplissimus* n. On the genitive of characteristic or *genitiuus proprietatis*, see K-St. 2.1.454, H-Sz. 62, and *OLS* 1.774–775, where it is treated as a possessive with respect to the infinitives *accusare* and *defendere*. **et aetatis** *et* was omitted in *M* and the *deteriores* by haplography, *ae-* normally being written as *e-* in the MS tradition.

70.5 accusare improbos et miseros calamitososque defendere On chiasmus, see §32 *graue me agente, te accusante nullum* n. For the *iunctura* of *miser* and *calamitosus*, which was a favourite of C., cf. *Rosc. Am.* 77, *Ver.* II.1.82, *Mur.* 62, and *Fam.* 9.13.3. *Calamitosus* can be used in both an active (destruction-inflicting) and, as here, passive meaning (damage-suffering); see *TLL* III 121.22, 40. On *improbi*, see §26 *improbus ... improbitas* n. Cf. §67 *defendere*.

70.6 profecto The emotive particle anticipates the following *amplificatio*; see *aegrotae* ... n. below. More generally, see §1 *profecto* n.

hoc remedium C. is recapitulating an image of illness and sense of urgency and unrest that he had already suggested earlier; cf. §9 *hoc unum ... remedium.* The allegory of sickness and cure used to depict an emotional, moral, or political crisis has a long tradition in classical literature going back to Homer. C. was fond of comparing the *res publica* to an ailing body and developed the image frequently in reference to the Catilinarian conspiracy; see e.g. *Sul.* 76 with Berry *ad loc.*, *Cat.* 1.31, 2.11, and *Phil.* 8.16. See further Pöschl (1964) 507–508, Aßfahl (1932) 50–52, *s.u. Medizin*, and Fantham (1972) 14–18. Fantham stated that C. 'uses *remedium* only in the context of personal grief ... [but] *medicina* is more general, of national and personal ills'. This passage should dispel so strict a dichotomy. For the orator as physician, cf. *Clu.* 57. For this metaphor in Demosthenes, see Wooten (1979). In ancient rhetorical theory, an allegory was a metaphor (which usually only applied to one word) extended over an entire sentence or more; see Quint. *Inst.* 8.6.44, 9.2.46. This image of the ailing republic is an incomplete allegory (*permixta apertis allegoria*) in which 'part of the expression is lexically on the level of the serious idea'; see Lausberg §§895–901, esp. §897.

70.7 aegrotae ac prope desperatae rei publicae The *res publica* takes the place normally assumed by the forlorn defendant or his family in the emotional appeal (*amplificatio*); see §§66–71 introduction. The form *aegrotus* is rarer than *aeger*, and C. may have chosen it to provide a resonant homeoteleuton with *desperatae*; see *TLL* I 955.50–71. In a medical sense, *desperatus* can mean 'terminally ill' (hence the moderating adverb, *prope*); see *TLL* V 1.740.52–73. But when applied to individuals, it can be suggestive of latent unrest; see Hellegouarc'h 534. Compare its use for Clodius at *Dom.* 13, Piso at *Sest.* 33, the Catilinarian conspirators at *Cat.* 2.5, 10, and the rebels at Caes. *Gal.* 7.3.1. A tinge of the latter may be detectable here since C. has already mentioned the public agitation for reform; see §8. C. revives the allegory again at *Ver.* II.1.5 *Itaque mihi uideor* [*iudices*] *magnam et maxime aegram et prope depositam rei publicae partem suscepisse.*

iudiciisque corruptis et contaminatis Both participles are used to indicate decay and sickness, both moral and physical; see *OLD s.u.*, *TLL* IV 1054.74–1056.34, and 629.47–630.81. This alliterative pair is only found here in C. **et** C. avoided *ac* before 'c', where *atque* is used over 90 per cent of the time. There are exceptions, however; see *Ver.* II.1.45, and II.5.34 with Thomas *ad loc.* **contaminatis** the incorrect reading in *P* and the French family may have arisen from dittography of a Tironian *et* (7). The proper reading is an easy correction.

70.8 paucorum uitio ac turpitudine C. introduces the 'few bad apples' approach and, in doing so, exonerates some of the jury from the charges of bribery and extortion that threaten senatorial control over the criminal courts. *Pauci* is frequently a pejorative in C. and refers to that oligarchic inner core of the *nobilitas* that exercises nigh tyrannical control, prefers wealth to virtue, and opposes the rise of *homines novi*; see Hellegouarc'h 443–446. This is consonant with C.'s *nouus homo* rhetoric throughout the Verrines. Cf. §70, *Ver.* I.36 (cited below), II.1.155, 3.145 *o inuidiosum offensumque paucorum culpa atque indignitate ordinem senatorium!*, and 5.126–127.

Appropriately here, since C. refers to the health of the state as though it were a living body, both *uitium* and *turpitudo* originally indicated a physical defect and later assumed their moral sense; see Ernout–Meillet *s.u.* *Turpitudo* is the characteristic of a person who does not attend to his responsibilities with strictness, accuracy, and honesty; see Hellegouarc'h 388. For its meaning as the opposite of *honestas*, cf. *Cat.* 2.25. For this collocation, see the description of Apronius: *Ver.* II.3.23 *gurges uitiorum turpitudinumque omnium.*

70.9 auctoritatem The term suggests a defence of senatorial control; see §69 *auctoritas huius imperi* ... n.

quam honestissimos et integerrimos diligentissimosque *Integritas* and *integer* are usually paired with another admirable quality, since it is a kind of 'threshold virtue' (Kaster) of a person's disposition and constancy; cf. §9 *idonei atque integri* and §27 *integritatem atque innocentiam.* The accompanying adjectives in this instance stress the respect and scrupulousness of the men in question. *Diligentia* is the quality of a prosecutor or other person in public service, such as a magistrate or military commander, that is demonstrated in the energetic, faithful, and scrupulous discharge of his duties (*officia*). It constitutes one aspect of the *uirtus* of a civically engaged individual; see Hellegouarc'h 251–252. See further Kaster (2005a) 134–148.

70.11 prodesse In reference to curing or relieving ailments, see *OLD s.u.* 3, and *TLL* X 2.2243.38–74. The alliterative sequence also heightens the pathos of the image. Cf. §7 *in quo ego rei publicae plus hoc tempore prodesse possim.*

medicina For this use with application to a 'sick' society, see *TLL* VIII 541.80–542.26. Cf. *Sest.* 43, and 135. On the metaphor, see *hoc remedium* n. above.

§71

71.1 nulla salus This sententious statement forms the basis of an enthymeme, whose conclusion will be deduced below (*itaque* ...). This gnomic statement also completes the process of *inductio* that more clearly defines how the *exempla* (of Cato, Lentulus, and Aemilianus) relate to the present debate, viz. that the state flourishes only when men of standing take up cases and feel that their reputations are at stake when they undertake prosecutions. The aphorism is neatly phrased in two parallel relative clauses. See also Quint. *Inst.* 6.1.2 *Quae autem enumeranda uidentur, cum pondere aliquo dicenda sunt et aptis excitanda sententiis et figuris utique uarianda.* On the repetition of *nulla ... nulla*, see n. below. On the metaphor, see §70 *hoc remedium* n. and cf. §9 *salutis omnium causa.*

71.2 de laude, de honore, de fama sua These terms exist in a nexus of words that describe the recognition, actively or passively, of an individual's standing in society. They relate more broadly to the political capital that allows an individual to ascend the ranks of the Roman magistracies. Taken individually, they have various nuances. On *laus*, see §48 *consulet laudi et existimationi tuae* n. *Honos* is the homage due to someone who has performed his duty (*officium*) and implies an act of recognition. In a narrow sense this recognition will become manifest in the conferment of a magistracy (hence the association of the word *honos* with political office; cf. §72 *honorem*). *Fama* here is synonymous with *existimatio* in the objective sense of 'reputation', though in other texts it does have a pejorative colouring; see Ernout–Meillet *s.u.* Hellegouarc'h 365 tries to make a distinction: '*Existimatio* indicates the "reputation" that results from a personal judgement based on the opinion that one has of an individual's character; *fama* implies a collective opinion elicited through important and conspicuous actions. [*Existimatio* désigne la « réputation » qui résulte d'un jugement personnel, fondé sur l'opinion que l'on a de la personnalité d'un individu; *fama* implique une opinion collective provoquée par des actions importantes, éclatantes.]' See, however, Yavetz (1974) 48–50. On these terms, see Hellegouarc'h 365–369, 383–387, and 364–365, respectively. The anaphora of the preposition is appropriate to the heightened style of a *conclusio.* On the accumulation of prepositions as part of the Attic style, see Laurand 301–302.

71.3 de capite ac fortunis suis *Caput,* which can refer broadly to one's 'life' (*TLL* III 416.31, 417.31), denotes the civil status of a Roman citizen; see *TLL* III 420.27, and Berger *s.u.* The punishments associated with conviction in the criminal courts varied by charge but could include loss of citizenship (*capitis deminutio*) and loss of property; on change of status, see §56 *in seruitutem* n. An *interdictio aquae et ignis* could be pronounced by the senate or a magistrate, if the accused went into exile before the sentence was passed. In practice this entailed loss of citizenship and property. Though the *lex Iulia* would set a capital penalty for conviction in the *quaestio de repetundis,* earlier penalties – including that under the *lex Cornelia* – may have been pecuniary in the first instance with the possibility of further punishment; see Sherwin-White (1952).

71.4 pertimescere See §23 *pertimescat* n.

itaque semper ii diligentissime laboriosissimeque accusarunt C. concludes his counterargument with a *sententia*; see Quint. *Inst.* 8.5.2 *consuetudo iam tenuit ut mente concepta sensus uocaremus, lumina autem praecipueque in clausulis posita sententia* (sometimes called an *epiphonema* when occurring at the end of an argument as it does here). *Semper* highlights the universal character appropriate to a *sententia,* while *itaque* gives the impression that this statement has been deductively reasoned from the preceding statement: in short, those who have a reputation to protect will be better prosecutors than those who have nothing to lose. This is the *volta* in C.'s argument whereby he turns the issue of his candidacy from a liability into an asset; see §§66–71 introduction. Furthermore, it gives the jury another way of evaluating one of the typical issues at a *diuinatio*: *uter plus industriae aut uirium sit allaturus ad accusandum*; see Quint. *Inst.* 7.4.33, and see further §10 introduction. In the *conclusio*, this principle will form the basis for a final *comparatio*, in which C. will demonstrate how it applies to Caecilius and himself, respectively. On *sententia*, see §32 *non potest* ... n. On C.'s fondness for generalizing with *semper*, see §63 *semper haec causa* ... n. On this method of reasoning, see Lausberg §371 on *ratiocinatio*.

71.5 in discrimen existimationis C. suggests that a trial is a critical and decisive moment for a prosecutor upon which hinges his entire career and reputation. In a careful turning of the tables at the outset of the trial proper, C. explains that it is not so much he that has reached this turning-point, but the Roman senatorial order itself; cf. *Ver.* II.1.2 *Nunc in ipso discrimine ordinis iudiciorumque uestrorum.* This dovetailing may suggest at least simultaneous publishing of the *Diuinatio* and the *actio prima*; see Introduction §V. Similarly, at the conclusion of the final speech of the *actio secunda*, Hortensius is reminded that, despite his election to the consulship, he must still be concerned for his own reputation as Verres' lead attorney; cf. *Ver.* II.5.174–177, esp. 175 *Quod enim te liberatum iam existimationis metu, defunctum honoribus designatum consulem cogites, mihi crede, ornamenta ista et beneficia populi Romani non minore negotio retinentur quam comparantur.* On *existimatio*, see *de laude* ... n. above.

CONCLUSIO (§§71–73)

The judges should realize that Caecilius will not conduct a vigorous and forceful prosecution. He has no prior reputation to uphold nor any expectations for future advancement. Simply put, were he to mismanage Verres' trial, he would stand to lose nothing. But Cicero will fight tooth and nail. His political career, his hopes for the future, and his hard-won reputation are all in the hands of the Roman people. His only safeguard is in the diligent discharge of his duties – one false step, and everything that he has worked for will be lost. Therefore, the judges must decide who will be able to conduct such a momentous prosecution with faithfulness and attentiveness. If the judges prefer Caecilius, Cicero will not think that he has lost for any worthy reason. But the jury should be wary: the Roman people may think that the jurors do not want a vigorous prosecution – and that the senatorial order never will.

Rhetorical precept allotted two primary objectives to the final portion of a speech, which C. called the *conclusio*, others, the *peroratio*: first, to offer a brief summary (*enumeratio*), and second, to stir the emotions of the audience (*amplificatio*). The emotional appeal could be further subdivided into stirring up vitriol toward one's opponent (*indignatio*) and arousing pity for one's own side (*conquestio*); the former was more suited to prosecution, the latter to defence. C. was regarded as the undisputed master of the *conclusio* and was usually assigned the role of the final speaker if he was arguing before the court as one of several advocates; see *Brut.* 190, and *Orat.* 130. The peroration of the *Diu. Caec.* is concise and does not display the typical rhetorical components to their fullest degree. In fact, many of these traditional functions of the *conclusio* are found in the preceding sections; see introduction *ad loc.* But, as is often stressed, this is not strictly a forensic speech, and what similarity it does display to the forensic genre proper is often C.'s invention.

Enumeratio est per quam res disperse et diffuse dictae unum in locum coguntur et reminiscendi causa unum sub aspectum subiciuntur; see *Inu.* 1.98. If any summary can be detected at the conclusion of the *Diu. Caec.*, it is indeed brief and markedly different from the main points of discussion presented at the *partitio* (§10). Firstly C. briefly reminds his audience that rhetorical ability is a first-order consideration in the selection of a prosecutor (*facillime posse magnitudinem causae ac iudici sustinere*), and as for the typical qualities emphasized at a *diuinatio* (*industria*, *fides*, and *uis*), he argues that the greatest guarantors of diligence and sincerity are not the injuries suffered by the plaintiff but the effect of the trial on the social and political reputation of the prosecutor. The emotional appeal normally found in *conclusiones* (which has already been initiated in the prior sections) is built upon the final σύγκρισις / *comparatio* in the speech in which the stakes for Caecilius and C. are compared, respectively (§§71–72). Caecilius, with no ongoing campaign and with no prior reputation for oratorical ability and political promise, stands to lose nothing (§71). It is not so much a call for indignation as a declaration of his irrelevance. C., on the other hand, in a more vivid and emotive passage, arouses some sympathy for his plight: he is wagering all his accrued accomplishments and future ambitions on the successful prosecution of Verres and in a single stroke could lose everything that he has spent his life trying to achieve (§72). The two passages comparing Caecilius and C. have nigh direct correspondences and each echoes the language of the other, e.g. *opinio* and *existimatio*, *spes*, *deperdo* and *perdo*, etc. On the *amplificatio per comparationem*, see Quint. *Inst.* 8.4.9–14, and Lausberg §§420.2, 423.

In a shift of the power dynamic (and what could be construed as a piece of electioneering), it is revealed that the arbiter of this reputation and the gatekeeper to political advancement is not the jury or its decision but the perception and assessment of the Roman people. In his final words, C. alludes to the proposed judicial reforms that would break up the senatorial monopoly of the juries in the criminal courts. In selecting C., the jury (and the senatorial class in general) can indicate to the *populus Romanus* their willingness and desire to administer a just and exacting criminal judiciary. His senatorial audience are therefore compelled to see that their own interests align with C.'s and that their reputation too is already at stake now in the *diuinatio* (§§72–73). The last chord that C. strikes is not one of pity but rather one of admonishment; see §73 *prouidete* n. And it is this theme that he will expand upon and amplify in his first speech against Verres. But for now, though this is only a pre-trial hearing, the Roman public is watching and waiting to pass a judgement of its own.

Rhetorical treatises are replete with *loci communes* that can be used in *conclusiones*; see e.g. C.'s own youthful catalogue at *Inu.* 1.101–109. C. further heightens these emotive appeals by invoking virtues and high-minded Roman qualities such as *diligentia*, *seueritas, fides, dignitas, fama/existimatio, honos, officium.* See *Inu.* 1.109 *nam saepe uirtus et magnificentia, in quo grauitas et auctoritas est, plus proficit ad misericordiam commouendam quam humilitas et obsecratio.* The stylistic features of the passage are in keeping with rhetorical precept. Asyndeton is particularly recommended along with repetition, iteration, hendiadys, and a sort of natural style also filled with weighty words; see *Part.* 53–54. Most of these features are immediately identifiable in the conclusion of the *Diu. Caec.* and are noted *ad loc.* On *conclusiones* generally, see Arist. *Rh.* 3.19, [Arist.] *Rh. Al.* 36, *Inu.* 1.98–109, *Rhet. Her.* 1.1, 2.47–50, *De orat.* 2.332, *Part.* 52–60, *Orat.* 122, Quint. *Inst.* 4.1.28, and 6.1.1–55; see further Lausberg §§431–442. For other occasions on which C. broadens the implications of the outcome at the conclusion of a speech, cf. *Rosc. Am.* 152, *Ver.* II.5.172, 175, *Caec.* 103; see also Quint. *Inst.* 6.1.13.

71.7 quam ob rem hoc statuere, iudices, debetis 'and for this reason, you necessarily ought to conclude that …'; see *OLD s.u. statuo* 13. *Quam ob rem* and the vocative, *iudices*, signal the start of the *conclusio/peroratio* proper. 'The way the judges should vote is commonly presented as the logical consequence of what has been said and done to persuade them. Cicero may accordingly use phrases like "this being so" or "wherefore" to introduce his exhortation to them to act as he wishes'; Winterbottom (2004) 229. Cf. *Sul.* 86 *quam ob rem.* Other words of logical transition are found at *Mur.* 86 and *Arch.* 32 (*quae cum ita sint*), and *Caec.* 104 and *Dom.* 147 (*quapropter*); see *ibid.* 229 n. 64. The obligatory sense of *debere* also underscores the notion that C. is logically demonstrating how the *sententia* from the previous section applies to Caecilius (§71) and himself (§72); see *itaque … accusarunt* n. above. *Hoc* is cataphoric and looks forward to the accusative and infinitive construction *Q. Caecilium … (esse) acturum.*

In the *partitio*, C. had given the jury a novel rubric for selecting a prosecutor: §10 *haec duo in primis spectari oportere: quem maxime uelint actorem esse ii quibus factae esse dicantur iniuriae et quem minime uelit is qui eas iniurias fecisse arguatur*; see nn. *ad loc.* Those considerations, it seems, are superseded by the aforementioned *sententia* or, at the very least, give another method by which the jury can reasonably determine who would be the more energetic and diligent litigator.

71.8 de quo ... qui The relative clauses express a causal relationship with the conclusion; see H-Sz. 559.

nulla In the high style, the passage is replete with negations and anaphora (*nulla ... nullaque, neque ... neque, non nimis* (three times), *nihil ... nihil*) and performs the recapitulatory function of the *conclusio* to remind the jurors of Caecilius' lack of experience, ability, and ambition (§47 *ipse nihil est, nihil potest*). This style is appropriate to the emotive function of the *conclusio*; cf. *Orat.* 69 *uehemens in flectendo.* On the *genus grande*, see Lausberg §1079.3.

opinio Caecilius has no prior reputation (*opinio ... ante collectam famam*) that he would need to uphold. As C. has already mentioned, the Sicilians, who alone have been able to evaluate his character, hold a decidedly unfavourable opinion of him; cf. §28 *te adhuc a nullis nisi ab Siculis potuisse cognosci.* C. essentially repeats the same thought in succession to linger on the point; see Quint. *Inst.* 8.4.27 *Potest adscribi amplificationi congeries quoque uerborum ac sententiarum idem significantium. Nam etiam si non per gradus ascendant, tamen uelut aceruo quodam adleuantur .... Simile est hoc figurae quam* συναθροισμόν *uocant, sed illic plurium rerum est congeries, hic unius multiplicatio.* For *opinio* used positively without a modifier, see *OLD s.u.* 5, and *TLL* IX 2.720.72–721.40. On *fama*, see *de laude* ... n. above. At the outset of the *actio prima*, C. will also address *opinio* and *existimatio* – not his own but that of the state and the senatorial order; cf. *Ver.* I.1–2 *Inueterauit enim iam opinio perniciosa rei publicae uobisque periculosa .... Adduxi enim hominem in quo reconciliare existimationem iudiciorum amissam ... possetis* (Peterson; but see §73 *nostro* n.).

nullaque Negative declarative clauses are usually coordinated with *nec* and *neque*; see *OLS* 1.713–716, and H-Sz. 448–450. But C. uses a less common construction here to preserve the repetition and symmetry of the phrase. Cf. Landgraf on *Rosc. Am.* 96 *si nullum iam ante consilium de morte ac de bonis eius inieras nullamque societatem neque sceleris neque praemi cum homine ullo coieras.*

71.9 exspectatio The performance during the trial proper is a crucial moment that both looks backward to validate one's own reputation (*opinio*) and looks forward by demonstrating an individual's potential. This characterization of trials as the venue for making or breaking one's reputation is consistent with and confirms the way in which C. advanced his career through legal advocacy rather than military engagement.

neque ut ... neque uti C. will occasionally use this older form of *ut* seemingly for the sake of variation; see H-Sz. 632. Cf. *Font.* 18 *non ut culpam in alios transferamus, sed uti doceamus ....*

71.10 conseruet The parallelism is also complemented by two alliterative pairs of verbs at the end of the cola: *conseruet ... confirmet, deperdat ... discedat.* C. will take the image of preservation and safety to an even higher degree in what follows by comparing his hopes and accomplishments to hostages; see §72 *obsides* n.

reliqui temporis spem See *exspectatio* n. above. Cf. §72 *spem quam propositam nobis habemus,* and *Flac.* 3 *tantum a uobis petimus ut omnia rei publicae subsidia, totum statum ciuitatis, omnem memoriam temporum praeteritorum, salutem praesentium, spem reliquorum in uestra potestate, in uestris sententiis, in hoc uno iudicio positam esse et defixam putetis.*

laborat C. demonstrated earlier how Caecilius has given no attention to his education or to his trial preparation. His apparent lack of effort here is consistent with that previous characterization; see e.g. §43 *nihil laboras.* C. highlights his future efforts with the more colourful expression *omni ratione erit dimicandum* (§72).

71.11 non nimis ... seuere ... accurate ... diligenter Tricolon with anaphora of the litotes *non nimis. Seueritas* denotes an uncompromising moral strictness and is often applied to Stoics like Cato. In addition to these connotations of steadfast morality, in a judicial context, it also suggests a prosecution impervious to bribery and malign influence; see Hellegouarc'h 281–282. C. has already called Caecilius' sincerity into question and suggested *praeuaricatio*; cf. §59. *Accuratio* signifies painstaking attention to detail; see *TLL* I 342.16–23, 343.41–64. C. has already mentioned the difficulty in organizing and presenting the number of crimes Verres has committed and the range of evidence against him; see §39. Cf. *Att.* 14.9.4 *accurate agam de Buthroto,* and *Brut.* 238 [on C. Macer] *at in inueniendis componendisque rebus mira accuratio, ut non facile in ullo diligentiorem maioremque cognouerim.* For the collocation of the nigh-synonymous adverbs, *accurate* and *diligenter,* cf. *Fin.* 2.31, *N. D.* 1.15

71.12 nihil ... in offensione deperdat Mirrored in §72 *si tantulum offensum titubatumque sit,... uno tempore uniuersa perdamus.* By *offensio,* C. implies losing the trial against Verres; see *OLD s.u.* 2, and *TLL* IX 2.497.49. **nihil** The similarity of the abbreviations for *nihil* and *in hoc* caused the error in *E* and *t*; see Introduction §VI.

71.13 ut turpissime flagitiosissimeque discedat I.e. even if Caecilius conducted the trial against Verres without regard for honesty, uprightness, or any sense of shame. Doing so, however, would put him in the same category as those who have corrupted the criminal justice system and imperilled the state; cf. §70 *paucorum uitio ac turpitudine* n. C. was fond of this pairing – particularly in the Verrines, applying it to Verres' behaviour (cf. §6, *Ver.* II.1.32) and to the corrupt court system; cf. *Ver.* I.45 *Idem* [*C. Pompeius*] *in eadem contione cum dixisset ... iudicia autem turpia ac flagitiosa fieri ... tum uero non strepitu sed maximo clamore suam populus Romanus significauit uoluntatem.* As a parting shot, C. encourages his audience to imagine that Caecilius could behave with all the characteristics which make Verres so dangerous and which combine to erode confidence in the Roman criminal system; unscrupulous and unskilled prosecutors like him would only serve to perpetuate these problems.

The *ut* introduces a concessive clause. Bertocchi and Maraldi (2011) 171 write 'This type of *ut*-clause tends to ... function as the protasis of a concessive conditional period. Here the *ut*-clause formulates a supposition which is characterized as extreme'; it always precedes the main verb. For other examples, cf. *Phil* 12.8, *Lig.* 27. See further Maraldi (1998). When *discedere* is paired with an adverb or adverbial prepositional phrase, it often means 'to come off as' and approaches the sense of 'to be'; see *TLL* V 1.1281.71, and cf. §60. This use may anticipate the martial images to follow, since the verb is used to describe the manner or condition in which one leaves a battle, and is 'transferred beyond the military sphere, frequently into the judicial sphere, on account of its analogy to the former'; see *L&S s.u.*

de suis ueteribus ornamentis 'from his former honours'; see *OLD s.u.* 6, and *TLL* IX 2.1011.25. A touch of irony here, since Caecilius has none except his senatorial rank. In general, *ornamenta* could refer to previous successes at the bar or in elections and were a mark of *nobilitas*. Cf. *Mur.* 15 *Summam uideo esse in te, Ser. Sulpici, dignitatem generis, integritatis, industriae ceterorumque ornamentorum omnium quibus fretum ad consulatus petitionem adgredi par est.* See also Hellegouarc'h 234. In particular, *ornamenta* could be the distinctive insignia used to mark someone's rank or office; see *Sul.* 50 with Berry *ad loc.*, and *Clu.* 154. See further *Staats.* 1.455–467, and *TLL* IX 2.1012.11.

71.14 requiret (*P*: -it γ*M*) Despite the agreement of *M* with the French family, *ueteribus* is written with respect to future time and informs the proper tense of the verb. The progression of tenses from the present to the future also parallels the preceding sentences. The reading adopted is also in the scholiast's lemma: *Hoc est enim 'nihil requiret': non sentiet sibi deesse aliquid ex his rebus quas nunquam habuit*; see [Asc.] 124 (204 Stangl).

§72

72.1 a nobis Commonly called the 'rhetorical plural' or 'sociative plural', in which the speaker uses the first-person plural pronoun to refer to himself or his own actions; see *OLS* 1.1119. Latin grammarians also describe it as the *pluralis modestiae*, though 'not all instances do reflect modesty' (*OLS* 1.1119). Its use seems to be motivated by an intent not to call attention to oneself entirely and to assume that one's audience shares a certain point of view as well; see K-St. 2.1.87–88, and H-Sz. 19–21. While the prepositional phrase is placed in primary adversative position in order to contrast the respective risks and rewards for Caecilius and C. (cf. the comparisons in §§41–43), these general statements also apply more broadly to the senatorial order as a whole. Should senators also fail to show their sense of duty and diligence toward the Roman people, they will lose the privileges associated with their order; see introduction to the *conclusio*. On the use of *nos* for *ego*, see also Pieroni (2010). See also §73 *uos … ego … populus Romanus* n., where C. abandons this manner of speaking.

obsides Literally 'hostages' but meant in the metaphorical sense of *pignus*, a 'pledge, assurance'; see *TLL* IX 2.219.8–29. The martial allegory depicts the Roman social contract as a lopsided relationship in which the ultimate power is in the hands of the *populus Romanus*. Allen (2006) 44–46:

> In domestic politics … both the language and the practice of hostage-taking were evident in the formation of coalitions, the settlement of disputes, and the easing of tensions, all with the same coercive quality of the institution's foreign manifestations. … Cicero identified the phenomenon of hostage obligation as a catalyst for the smooth workings of Republican institutions, where power is loaned out based on the figurative collateral of a statesman's family and position. … Just as a foreign enemy would respect the terms of a treaty when there were hostages, likewise a consul (or praetor, or tribune) would only avoid corruption and maintain order when something they valued was out of their hands. … As Cicero sees it [in *Diu. Caec.* 72], the Roman people have lent him his status, and by holding his title, rights and privileges as figurative hostages, they ensure that he does work that is in keeping with their conception of a public servant.

C.'s senatorial audience are also meant to see their prerogatives in this same context and realize that the powers they exercise can also be withdrawn.

For the same image in a *conclusio*, cf. *Cat.* 4.9, *Clu.* 83, and, with Austin *ad loc.*, *Cael.* 78 *Habet a M. Caelio res publica, iudices, duas accusationes uel obsides periculi uel pignora uoluntatis.* On this metaphor, see Aßfahl (1932) 75 and Pöschl (1964) 539 *s.u. Rechtswesen.* C. goes on to list these *obsides* as *honos*, *spes*, and *existimatio*; see nn. below. For hostages and hostage-taking, see Allen

(2006) with bibliography. Metaphors such as this are appropriate to the high style; see §71 *nulla* n.

habet populus Romanus In the previous section, C. has outlined what Caecilius does not have (*habet … nihil*). In a stroke of modesty and by way of enlarging the implications of the jury's decision, the centre and true owner of social and political capital is not C., as one might expect from the previous comparisons, but the *populus Romanus*. Its invocation here by C. is a shrewd one. He can sing a more populist tune while also presenting himself as a potential defender of the senate's current prerogatives. It was election season after all, and 'Roman elections … were the traditional environment for an annual collision between the paired and dynamic principles of the Republic, the people's majesty, and the aristocracy's authority'; Tatum (2013) 133.

72.2 conseruare, tueri, confirmare ac recuperare On the emotive accrual of synonyms, see Quint. *Inst.* 9.3.46; see further Lausberg §655. *Recuperare* is the appropriate verb for the recovery of hostages; cf. Caes. *BG* 3.8.2–5 *ab his fit initium retinendi Sillii atque Velanii et si quos intercipere potuerunt quod per eos suos se obsides, quos Crasso dedissent, recuperaturos existimabant …. Omni ora maritima celeriter ad suam sententiam perducta communem legationem ad Publium Crassum mittunt, si uelit suos recuperare, obsides sibi remittat.*

72.3 omni ratione erit dimicandum C. extends the allegory of warfare started above; see *obsides* n. The phraseology here briefly recalls the extended allegory of oratory as physical combat; cf. §44 *omni ratione pugnandum certandumque sit.* For *dimicare* used to describe forensic debates, see *TLL* V 1.1201.69–83. Cf. *Sest.* 1, and *Balb.* 5. Such a comparison has a way of equating the glory won through combat with the renown procured through victory in the courts.

habet … habet … habet … Anaphoric tricolon *crescens*; see Lausberg §629. The asyndeton adds verve and rapidity appropriate to a *conclusio* and reemphasizes the status of the *populus Romanus* as the ultimate arbiter of political power; see notes on style in the introduction to §§71–73, and *habet populus Romanus*

n. above. On the Demosthenic aspects of this feature, see von Albrecht (2003) 130.

72.4 honorem 'political office', sc. in C.'s case the aedileship. See also *OLD s.u.* 5, *TLL* VI 2926.41, and §70 *cum aedilitatem petat* n.

spem quam propositam nobis habemus Also used of an expectation of future office; cf. *Sul.* 30 *spe proposita amplissimae dignitatis.* See further *TLL* X 2.2068.40. For *proponere* with *spes* vel sim., see *TLL* X 2.2068.36–73. Cf. *B. Hisp.* 22.7 *neque sibi ullam spem uictoriae propositam habere.*

72.5 existimationem See §48 *consulet laudi et existimationi tuae* n. For the reference to the *existimatio* of the courts in *Ver.* I.1, see §71 *opinio* n.

sudore Always paired with *labor* or *sanguis* in C.'s speeches; cf. *Font.* 12, *Agr.* 2.16, and 69. The image of physical toil and watchfulness also strengthens the allegory of combat.

72.6 ut could introduce the result clauses in both apodoses (*possimus* ... *perdamus*), but the period becomes so long that C. repeats it below; see H-Sz. 808.

officium In addition to a social obligation, the term can encompass the 'sense of one's obligation, dutifulness'; see *OLD s.u.* 3d. Cf. §4 *tempore atque officio coactus.*

diligentiam On *diligentia,* see §70 *quam honestissimos* ... n.

72.8 incolumia ac salua 'safe and sound'; the pleonasm adds emphasis, provides a cretic and spondee rhythm, and renews the allegory of hostages as surety; see *obsides* n. above. This pairing of these adjectives (or their respective nouns) is common in C. (cf. *Inu.* 2.169, *Ver.* II.5.153, *Pis.* 33, *De orat.* 3.178, and *N. D.* 3.87) and in Caesar and Livy, particularly in military contexts; cf. Caes. *Ciu.* 1.72.3, 2.32.12, Liv. 23.42.4, 29.27.1, 41.28.9.

si tantulum offensum titubatumque sit 'if there is even the slightest slip or stumble'. C. is fond of the emotive diminutive *tantulum,* which here softens *offensum.* The consonance of *t* and the lumbering homeoteleuton give the phrase an onomatopoetic quality that replicates the sound of someone tripping over an obstacle – *titubo* perhaps being an onomatopoeia itself; see *OLD s.u.* Both verbs, initially with physical meanings, are used metaphorically in a moral sense. Cf. *Rhet. Her.* 1.12 *eo diligentius omnis eius partis perscrutati sumus, ut ne paruula quidem titubatione aut offensatione impediremur.* On quasi-synonymous pairs, see §1 *causam rationemque* n.

72.9 singillatim See §50 *singillatim* n.

uno tempore uniuersa perdamus At the end of the *actio secunda,* it will be Hortensius who is depicted as losing his position and authority; cf. *Ver.* II.5.175 *sed quo die populo Romano tribuni plebi restituti sunt, omnia ista uobis, si forte nondum intellegitis, adempta atque erepta sunt.*

The final clause of the sentence is built upon a chiastic arrangement of antonyms: *singillatim* (A) … *diu* (B) … *uno tempore* (B') *uniuersa* (A'). The alliteration of *un-* highlights the juxtaposition and imbues the line with pathos. The image of coming to utter ruin through one misstep in just a single day evokes an Aristotelian sense of tragic pity, which wins sympathy for C. and has his senatorial audience recognize their own precarious situation; cf. *Inu.* 1.106 *Conquestio est oratio auditorum misericordiam captans. … qua oratione habita grauiter et sententiose maxime demittitur animus hominum et ad misericordiam conparatur, cum in alieno malo suam infirmitatem considerabit.* See further Lausberg §439.

§73

73.1 quapropter, iudices The vocative signals the final remarks of the *conclusio*; see §72 *quam ob rem* … n.

quem existimetis facillime posse magnitudinem causae ac iudici sustinere In his final remarks, C. once again recapitulates the evaluative paradigm that he has been suggesting throughout the *Diuinatio,* namely that the best prosecutor is first and foremost the most able speaker; cf. §§27, 37, 67. *Existimare* is also used in the formal language of the senate and so befits the senatorial jury; cf. *Phil.* 3.37; see *OLD s.u.* 3, and *TLL* V 2.1523.74–1524.2.

On the pairing of *causa* and *iudicium*, see §1 *causis iudiciisque publicis* n. On the competing perspectives in this final section, see *arbitretur* n. below.

73.2 fide, diligentia, consilio, auctoritate The asyndeton is characteristic of a *peroratio*; see §§71–73 introduction. The first two terms used in traditional *diuinationes* blend considerations of *fides* and *industria*, while the others suggest preparation and social standing. On *diligentia*, see §70 *quam honestissimos* ... n. On *consilium*, see Hellegouarc'h 254–258.

73.3 uos ... ego ... populus Romanus In the previous passage, C. had used the first-person plural to indicate a kind of shared system of values; see §72 *a nobis* n. Here he reverses course and potentially puts himself at odds with the jurors. All three nouns are put in emphatic primary position, underscored even further by the fact that *uos* and *populus Romanus* have been displaced from their respective clauses. See §72 *habet populus Romanus* n.

73.4 dignitate Ablative of respect. Compare *Inu.* 2.166 *dignitas est alicuius honesta et cultu et honore et uerecundia digna auctoritas.* Kaster (2005a) 144–145: '*Dignitas* – etymologically related as it is to thought of comely and fitting appearance (*decus*) – is first and foremost something that others ascribe to you, according to the way your behaviour appears to them.' The implication is that C. has successfully communicated to the jury the justness of his cause and his oratorical ability. Therefore, if the jurors reject him, it would indicate that the senatorial order does not want a rigorous prosecution. See further Hellegouarc'h 388–411, and Balsdon (1960) 43–46.

arbitrabor See *arbitretur* n. below. [Asc.] 124 (204 Stangl) *Hoc quidem uidetur plane dicere, sed latenter hoc significat, prauo de se iudicio magis iudicibus haesuram turpitudinem quam sibi.*

73.6 placuisse ... placere Regularly used of resolutions and decisions by authoritative bodies, here the jury, elsewhere of the senate; see *OLD s.u.* 5b, and *TLL* X 1.2263.56–75.

nostro *DE*[1]*HPMFb (uestro NGtOvlar)* The confusion of *uos/nos* and *n(oste)r/u(este)r* is common; the crossbars connecting the two minims may be imperceptible. C. has somewhat defiantly separated himself from his audience (*uos* … *ego* above), but it seems too adversarial a note to strike at the very conclusion; cf. *Sul.* 93 with Berry *ad loc.* The *actio prima* starts with a similar discussion, but here the textual tradition is not unanimous, though variants are not reported at all by Peterson:

Ver. I.1 nostri ordinis *γPMFlrv* : uestri ordinis *GO Peterson.*

The choice for some editors may come down to notions about C.'s self-representation at this point in his career. The most authoritative MSS have *nostro*, which I have adopted cautiously. The postposition does not necessarily imply an *ego/ uos* separation but rather places emphasis on *ordini*, and so magnifies the implications of the jury's vote for the entire senatorial class; see Marouzeau 1.136.

arbitretur *Arbitrari* suggests, to a greater extent than *existimare*, an opinion or judgement based on sight and emphasizes the role of perception; see Ernout–Meillet *s.u. arbiter.* The jurors are compelled to think about how the public at large will construe the jury's actions if C. is not selected as the prosecutor. This final exhortation in §73 has been built around three divergent points of view: firstly, that of the jurors, who must assess the relative merits of the potential prosecutors; secondly, that of Cicero, who will not think less of himself if he is refused the leading prosecutorial role by a corrupt system; and thirdly, that of the *populus Romanus*, who will develop a strong impression of the senatorial order in response to their vote. This final deviant focalization through the eyes of the *populus Romanus* mirrors the same device from the *exordium*, but this time the object of the observer is not C. but the jury itself. They, however, cannot offer a different interpretation or motive for their actions – that remains the sole prerogative of the orator.

73.7 prouidete C.'s final admonishment to the senators offers hope and fear in due measure. In the final words of the *Diuinatio*, they are the ones caught in a dilemma: fear of losing their prestige and privilege if they choose Caecilius, but in C. a hope of retaining both. This final emotive passage fits well within the *genus deliberatiuum*; cf. Isid. *Orig.* 2.4.4 *In suasoria autem duae sunt quae plus ualent: spes et metus. Prouidere* is used when urging the senators to act in their own and the state's interests; cf. *Ver.* I.43, II.3.219, *Cat.* 4.18, *Flac.* 104, and *Rab. Post.* 15. See *TLL* X 2.2325.50–60, 21–37. The clausula ends with a trochaic metron and the sentence itself contains antitheses and repetitions, which may have prompted the audience's applause. On the emotive effect of this rhythm, see *Orat.* 213–214, and on tricola, see Morstein-Marx (2004) 137 and Atkinson (1984) 48. On clausula in final words of speeches, see *Sul.* 93 with Berry *ad loc.*

APPENDIX A
MAP OF SICILY

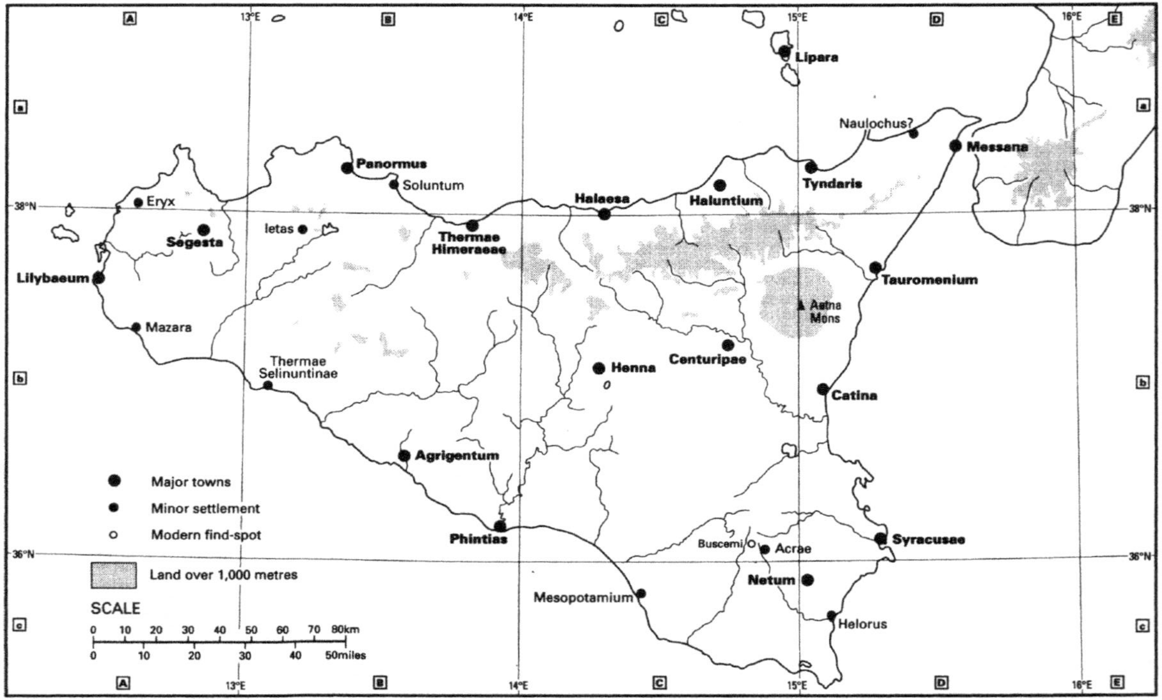

Map 1 Map of Sicily

APPENDIX B
MAP OF ROMAN TERRITORY IN 70 BCE

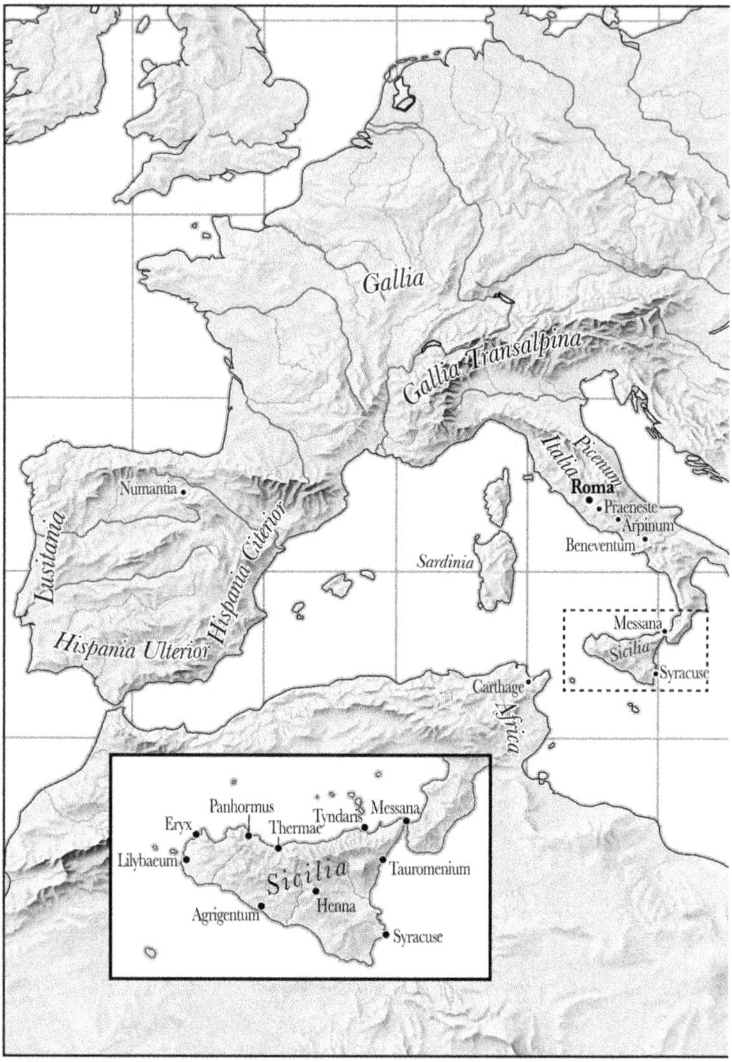

Map 2 Map of Roman territory in 70 BCE
(Joe LeMonnier, https://mapartist.com/)

Macedonia
Asia Minor
Lampsacus
Tenedos
Pergamum
Phrygia
Graecia
Smyrna
Tralles
Chios
Miletus
Asia
Erythrae
Myndus
Pamphylia
Achaia
Cilicia
Delos
Halicarnassus
Syria
Aspendus
Lycia
Samos
Perga
Creta
Sidon
Ascalon
Alexandria
Aegyptus

BIBLIOGRAPHY

Accame, S. (1946), *Il dominio romano in Grecia dalla Guerra acaica ad Augusto* (Rome).

Achard, G. (1981) *Pratique rhétorique et idéologie politique dans les discours de Cicéron* (Leiden).

Adams, J. N. (1972), 'Latin Words for "Woman" and "Wife"', *Glotta* 50: 234–255.

(1978), 'Conventions of Naming in Cicero', *CQ ns* 28.1: 145–166.

(1994a), 'Wackernagel's Law and the Placement of the Copula *Esse* in Classical Latin', *PCPS Supplement* 18.

(1994b), 'Wackernagel's Law and the Position of Unstressed Personal Pronouns in Classical Latin', *TCPS* 92.2: 103–178.

(1999), 'Nominative Personal Pronouns and Some Patterns of Speech in Republican and Augustan Poetry', in J. N. Adams and R. G. Mayer, eds., *Aspects of the Language of Latin Poetry* (Oxford), 97–133.

(2013), *Social Variation and the Latin Language* (Cambridge).

Albrecht, M. von. (2003), *Cicero's Style: A Synopsis* (Leiden). *Mnemosyne Supplement* 245.

Aldrete, G. (1999), *Gestures and Acclamations in Ancient Rome* (Baltimore, MD).

Alexander, M. C. (1982), 'Repetition of Prosecution, and the Scope of Prosecutions, in the Standing Criminal Courts of the Late Republic', *CA* 1: 141–166.

(1985), '*Praemia* in the *Quaestiones* of the Late Republic', *CPh* 80: 20–32.

(1990), *Trials in the Late Roman Republic: 149BC to 50BC* (Toronto).

(2002), *The case for the prosecution in the Ciceronian era* (Ann Arbor, MI).

Allen, J. (2006), *Hostages and Hostage-Taking in the Roman Empire* (Cambridge).

Allen, W. (1954), 'Cicero's Conceit', *TAPA* 85: 121–144.
Ames-Lewis, F., ed. (1992), *Cosimo 'il Vecchio' de' Medici, 1389–1464: Essays in Commemoration of the 600th Anniversary of Cosimo de' Medici's Birth* (Oxford).
Andersen, Ø. (1996), '*Lingua suspecta*: On Concealing and Displaying the Art of Rhetoric', *Symbolae Osloenses* 71: 68–86.
Ando, C. (2015) 'Fact, Fiction, and Social Reality in Roman Law', in M. Del Mar and W. Twining, eds., *Legal Fictions in Theory and Practice* (Cham). *Law and Philosophy Library* 110: 295–323.
Arnold, P. (1998), *The* Pornoboskos *and* Leno *in Greek and Roman Comedy*. DPhil thesis, University of Oxford.
Arnott, W. G., ed. (1996), *Alexis: The Fragments: A Commentary* (Cambridge and New York).
Aßfahl, G. (1932), *Vergleich und Metapher bei Quintilian* (Stuttgart).
Astin, A. E. (1967), *Scipio Aemilianus* (Oxford).
(1978), *Cato the Censor* (Oxford).
(1982), 'The Censorship of the Roman Republic', *Historia* 31: 174–187.
(1985a), 'Censorships in the Late Republic', *Historia* 34: 175–190.
(1985b), 'Cicero and the Censorship', *CPh* 80: 233–239.
Atkinson, M. (1984), *Our Masters' Voices: The Language and Body Language of Politics* (London).
Austin, R. (1948), *Quintiliani Institutionis Oratoriae Liber XII* (Oxford).
Bablitz, L. (2007), *Actors and Audience in the Roman Courtroom* (London).
Badian, E. (1954), 'Lex Acilia repetundarum', *AJPh* 75: 374–384.
(1956), 'Q. M. Scaevola and the Province of Asia', *Athenaeum* 34: 104–123.
(1958a), 'Notes on Provincial Governors from the Social War down to Sulla's Victory', *PACA* 1: 1–18.
(1958b), *Foreign Clientelae: 264–70 BC* (Oxford).
(1958c), 'Mam. Scaurus Cites Precedent', *CR* 8: 216–220.
(1964), *Studies in Greek and Roman History* (Oxford).
(1983), 'The Silence of Norbanus', *AJPh* 104: 156–171.
(1984), 'Three Non-Trials in Cicero: Notes on the Text, Prosopography, and Chronology of *Diuinatio in Caecilium* 63', *Klio* 66: 291–309.
(1989), 'The *scribae* of the Roman Republic', *Klio* 71: 582–603.
Baehrens, W., ed. (1922), *Sprachlicher Kommentar zur vulgärlateinischen Appendix Probi* (Halle).
Bal, M. (1985), *Narratology: Introduction to the Theory of Narrative* (Toronto).

Baldo, G. (2004), *In C. Verrem Actionis Secundae Liber Quartus* (Florence).

Balsdon, J. P. V. D. (1938), 'History of the Extortion Court at Rome 133–70 BC', *PBSR* 14: 98–114.

(1939), 'Consular Provinces under the Late Republic', *JRS* 29: 57–73.

(1960), '*Auctoritas, Dignitas, Otium*', *CS ns* 10: 43–50.

(1962), 'Roman History, 65–50 B.C. Five Problems', *JRS* 52: 134–141.

(1979), *Romans and Aliens* (London).

Barendt, P. O. (1902), 'Ciceronian Use of *nam* and *enim*', *CR* 16: 203–209.

Baronowski, D. (1990), '*Sub Umbra Foederis Aequi*', *Phoenix* 44.4: 345–369.

Barrios-Lech, P. (2016), *Linguistic Interaction in Roman Comedy* (Cambridge).

Batstone, W. W. (1994), 'Cicero's Construction of Consular Ethos in the First Catilinarian', *TAPA* 124: 211–266.

Bauman, R. A. (1983), *Lawyers in Roman Republican Politics: A Study of the Roman Jurists in their Political Setting 316–82 BC* (Munich).

Beard, M. (2012), 'Cicero's "Response of the *haruspices*" and the Voice of the Gods', *JRS* 102: 20–39.

Beard, M. and Henderson, J. (1998), 'With This Body I Thee Worship: Sacred Prostitution in Antiquity', in M. Wyke, ed., *Gender and the Body in the Ancient Mediterranean*, (Oxford), 56–79.

Begley, C. (1988), *'Voluntas' in Cicero.* PhD thesis, University of North Carolina at Chapel Hill.

Beness, J. L. (2005), 'Scipio Aemilianus and the Crisis of 129 BC', *Historia* 54: 37–48.

Bennett, C. (1910–1914), *Syntax of Early Latin* (Boston, MA). 2 volumes.

Berger, A. (1953), *Encyclopedic Dictionary of Roman Law* (Philadelphia, PA). *TAPS* 43.2.

Bernard, J-E. (2000), 'Philosophie politique et antijudaïsme chez Cicéron', *SCI* 19: 113–131.

Bernini, G. and Schwartz, M., eds. (2006), *Pragmatic Organization of Discourse in the Languages of Europe* (Berlin).

Berry, D. H. (1996), *Cicero: Pro Sulla Oratio* (Cambridge).

(2000), *Cicero: Defence Speeches* (Oxford).

Bers, V. (1997), *Speech in Speech: Studies in Incorporated 'Oratio Recta' in Attic Drama and Oratory* (London).

Bertocchi, A. and Maraldi, M. (2011), 'Conditionals and Concessives', in P. Baldi and P. Cuzzolin, eds., *Complex Sentences, Grammaticalization, Typology* (Berlin). New Perspectives on Historical Latin Syntax 4: 93–194.

Bettinetti, S. (2001), *La statua di culto nella pratica rituale greca* (Bari).

Bettini, M. (1977), 'Il parasito Saturio, una riforma legislativa e un testo variamente tormentato', *SCEO* 26: 83–104.

Bloomer, W. M., ed. (2015), *A Companion to Ancient Education* (London).

Blösel, W. (2000), 'Die Geschichte des Begriffes mos maiorum von den Anfängen bis zu Cicero', in B. Linke and M. Stemmler, eds., *Mos Maiorum: Untersuchungen zu den Formen der Identitätsstiftung und Stabilisierung in der römischen Republik* (Stuttgart), 25–97.

Boklenstein, M. (1998), 'Between Brackets: (Some Properties of) Parenthetical Clauses in Latin: An Investigation of the Language of Cicero's Letters', in R. Risselada, ed., *Latin in Use: Amsterdam Studies in the Pragmatics of Latin* (Amsterdam), 1–18.

Bömer, F. (1960), *Untersuchungen über die Religion der Sklaven in Griechenland und Rom, Teil II: Die sogenannte sakrale Freilassung in Griechenland und die* (δοῦλοι) ἱεροί (Mainz).

Bona, F. (1980), 'L'ideale retorico ciceroniano ed il "ius civile in artem redigere"', *SDHI* 46: 282–382.

Bonner, S. (1977), *Education in Ancient Rome: From the Elder Cato to Pliny the Younger* (London).

Bourdieu, P. (1984), *Distinction: A Social Critique of the Judgement of Taste* (Cambridge, MA), trans. R. Nice.

Bowman, D. A. (1989–1990), 'The Formula Sociorum in the Second and First Centuries BC', *The Classical Journal* 85: 330–336.

Brassloff, S. (1928), *Possessio in den Schriften der römischen Juristen. Ein Beitrag zur Kenntnis der römischen Rechtsprache* (Vienna).

Brennan, T. C. (2000), *The Praetorship in the Roman Republic* (Oxford). 2 volumes.

Brinkhoff, J. (1935), *Woorspeling bij Plautus* (Nijmegen).

Briscoe, J. (1974), 'Supporters and Opponents of Tiberius Gracchus', *JRS* 64: 125–135.

Broggini G. (1964), 'Fictio civitatis, strumento dell'arbitrio giurisdizionale di Verre?', in *Synteleia V. Arangio-Ruiz* (Naples), 934–943.

Broughton, T. R. S. (1929), 'The Inscription of Phileros', *AJPh* 50: 279–285.

(1951–1960), *Magistrates of the Roman Republic* (New York). 3 volumes.

Brown, P. (2002), 'Actors and Actor-Managers at Rome in the Time of Plautus and Terence', in P. Easterling and E. Hall, eds., *Greek and Roman Actors* (Oxford), 225–237.

Brunt, P. (1961), 'Charges of Provincial Maladministration under the Early Principate', *Historia* 10: 189–227.

(1965), '*Amicitia* in the Late Roman Republic', *PCPS* 11: 1–20.

(1971), *Social Conflicts in the Roman Republic* (London).

(1980), 'Patronage and Politics in the Verrines', *Chiron* 10: 273–289.

(1982), '*Nobilitas* and *Novitas*', *JRS* 72: 1–17.

(1986), 'Cicero's *Officium* in the Civil War', *The Journal of Roman Studies* 76: 12–32.

(1988), *The Fall of the Roman Republic and Related Essays* (Oxford).

Büchner, H. (1951), *Das Oxymoron in der griechischen Dichtung* (doctoral thesis, University of Tübingen).

Budin, S. (2008), *The Myth of Sacred Prostitution in Antiquity* (Cambridge).

Burkert, W. (1985), *Greek Religion* (Cambridge, MA).

(1988), 'The Temple in Classical Greece', in M. Fox, ed., *Temple in Society* (Winona Lake, IN), 27–47.

Burton, G. P. (1975), 'Proconsuls, Assizes and the Adminstration of Justice under the Empire', *JRS* 65: 92–106.

Burton, P. J. (2003), '*Clientela* or *Amicitia*? Modeling Roman International Behavior in the Middle Republic (264–146 B.C.)', *Klio* 85: 333–369.

(2009), 'Ancient International Law, the Aetolian League, and the Ritual of Surrender during the Roman Republic: A Constructivist View', *The International History Review* 31: 237–252.

(2011), *Friendship and Empire: Roman Diplomacy and Imperialism in the Middle Republic (353–146 BC)* (Cambridge).

Butler, S. (2002), *The Hand of Cicero* (London).

Butzmann, H. (1964), *Die Weissenburger Handschriften* (Frankfurt). *Kataloge der Herzog August Bibliothek Wolfenbüttel: Neue Reihe.* Volume 10.

Cabrillana, C. (2011), 'Purpose and Result Clauses', in P. Baldi and P. Cuzzolin, eds., *Complex Sentences, Grammaticalization, Typology* (Berlin). *New Perspectives on Historical Latin Syntax* Vol. 4: 19–92.

Calboli, G. (1983), 'Oratore senza microfono', in A. Ceresa-Gastaldo, ed., *Ars Rhetorica Antica e Nuova* (Genoa), 23–56.

Calderini, A. (1945), *Papiri latini: Appunti delle lezioni di papirologia* (Milan).

Cameron, A. (1998), 'Black and White: A Note on Ancient Nicknames', *AJPh* 119: 113–117.

Caneva, S. and Pizzi, A. (2015), 'Given to a Deity? Religious and Social Reappraisal of Human Consecrations in the Hellenistic and Roman East', *CQ* 65.1: 167–191.

Canter, H. (1936), 'Irony in the Orations of Cicero', *AJPh* 57: 457–464.

Caplan, H., ed. (1954) *Ad C. Herennium. De ratione dicendi (Rhetorica ad Herennium)* (Cambridge). Loeb Classical Library.

Carandini, A. and Carafa, P., eds. (2017), *The Atlas of Ancient Rome: Biography and Portraits of the City* (Princeton, NJ).

Carcaterra, A. (1987), 'Euristica e logica nel processus iuris', *SDHI* 53: 219–269.

Carcopino, J. (1919), *La Loi d'Hiéron et les Romains* (Paris). [Though the cover lists 1919, the title page indicates 1914].

Cascione, C. (1996), '*Bonorum Proscriptio apud Columnam Maeniam*', *Labeo* 42: 444–455.

Casson, L. (1971), *Ships and Seamanship in the Ancient World* (Princeton, NJ).

Castner, C. (1988), *Prosopography of Roman Epicureans from the Second Century B.C. to the Second Century A.D.* (Frankfurt). *Studien zur klassichen Philologie* 34.

Cavenaile, R. (1958), *Corpus Papyrorum Latinarum* (Wiesbaden).

Chahoud, A. (2010), 'Colloquial Language in Literary Studies', in E. Dickey and A. Chahoud, eds., *Colloquial and Literary Latin* (Oxford), 42–64.

Chalkomatas, D. (2007), *Ciceros Dichtungstheorie* (Berlin).

Chatelain, E. (1884–1900), *Paléographie des classiques latins* (Paris). 14 volumes.

Christ, M. R. (1998), *The Litigious Athenian* (Baltimore, MD).

Clark, A. C. (1918), *The Descent of Manuscripts* (Oxford).

Clarke, M. (1968), 'Cicero at School', *G&R* 15: 18–22.

Classen, C. (1980), 'Verres' Gehilfen in Sizilien', *Ciceroniana* 4: 93–114.

(1985), *Recht–Rhetorik–Politik* (Darmstadt).

Coleman, K. M. (1990), 'Fatal Charades: Roman Executions Staged as Mythological Enactments', *JRS* 80: 44–73.

Coleman-Norton, P. R. (1950/1), 'Cicero's Contribution to the Text of the Twelve Tables', *CJ* 46: 51–60, 127–34.

Coleman-Norton, P. R. et al. (2003), *Ancient Roman Statutes: A Translation with Introduction, Commentary, Glossary, and Index* (Austin, TX).

Corbeill, A. (1996). *Controlling Laughter: Political Humor in the Late Roman Republic* (Princeton, NJ).

(2002), 'Ciceronian Invective', in J. May, ed., *Brill's Companion to Cicero: Oratory and Rhetoric* (Leiden), 197–217.

(2002b), 'Rhetorical Education in Cicero's Youth', in J. May, ed., *Brill's Companion to Cicero: Oratory and Rhetoric* (Leiden), 23–48.

(2004), *Nature Embodied: Gesture in Ancient Rome* (Princeton, NJ).

(2007), 'Rhetorical Education and Social Reproduction in the Republic and Early Empire', in W. Dominik and J. Hall, eds., *A Companion to Roman Rhetoric* (Malden, MA), 69–82.

Corbett, P. E. (1970), 'Greek Temples and Greek Worshippers: The Literary and Archaeological Evidence', *BICS* 17: 149–158.

Costa, E. (1927), *Cicerone giureconsulto* (Bologna). 2 volumes.

Coudry, M. (2004), 'Contrôle et traitement des ambassadeurs étrangers sous la République romaine', in C. Moatti, ed., *La mobilité des personnes en Méditerranée de l'Antiquité à l'époque moderne: procédures de contrôle et documents d'identification* (Rome), 529–565.

Covino, R. (2005), *The Magistrates of Republican Sicily* (PhD thesis, University of St Andrews).

Craig, C. P. (1981), 'The *Accusator* as *Amicus*: An Original Roman Tactic of Ethical Argumentation', *TAPA* 111: 31–37.

(1985), 'Dilemma in Cicero's *Diuinatio in Caecilum*', *AJP* 106: 442–446.

(1993), *Form as Argument in Cicero's Speeches* (Atlanta, GA).

Crawford, J. (1984), *Marcus Tullius Cicero: The Lost and Unpublished Orations* (Göttingen).

(1994), *Marcus Tullius Cicero: The Fragmentary Speeches* (Atlanta, GA).

Crawford, M. H. (1996), *Roman Statutes* (London). 2 volumes.

Crook, J. A. (1967), *Law and Life of Rome* (Ithaca, NY).

(1995), *Legal Advocacy in the Roman World* (London).

Dahlman, C. and Feteris, E., eds. (2013), *Legal Argumentation Theory: Cross-Disciplinary Perspectives* (Dordrecht).

Damon, C. (1992), 'Sex. Cloelius, Scriba', *HSCP* 94: 227–250.

(1997), *The Mask of the Parasite: A Pathology of Roman Patronage* (Ann Arbor, MI).

Damon, C. and Mackay, C. S. (1995), 'On the Prosecution of C. Antonius in 76 B.C.', *Historia: Zeitschrift für Alte Geschichte* 44.1: 37–55.

Danek, G. (1988), 'Parasit, Sykophant, Quadruplator: Zu Plautus *Persa* 62–76', *WS* 101: 223–241.

D'Arms, J. (1984), 'Control, Companionship, and *Clientela*: Some Social Functions of the Roman Communal Meal', *EMC* 28: 327–348.

Darmezin, L. (1999) *Les affranchissements par consécration en Béotie et dans le monde grec hellénistique* (Nancy). Études Anciennes 22.

Daube, D. (1956), *Forms of Roman Legislation* (Oxford).

David, J-M. (1992), *Le patronat judiciaire au dernier siècle de la république romaine* (Rome).

(2006), 'Ce que les Verrines nous apprennent sur les scribes de magistrats à la fin de la République', in J. Dubouloz and S. Pittia, eds., *La Sicile de Cicéron: lectures des Verrines* (Paris), 35–56.

Davies, J. (1968), 'Molon's Influence on Cicero', *CQ* 18: 303–314.

Degrassi, A. (1963), '*Veneria*', *Latomus* 22: 436–439.

Delisle, L. (1864), *Le cabinet des manuscrits de la Bibliothèque Nationale* (Paris). Volume 1.

(1874) *Le cabinet des manuscrits de la Bibliothèque Nationale* (Paris). Volume 2.

Della Corte, F. (1979), '*Servi Venerii*', *Maia* 31: 225–235.

Devoto, G. (1933), 'I Problemi del più antico Vocabolario giuridico romano', *Annali della R. Scuola Normale Superiore di Pisa. Lettere, Storia e Filosofia* 2.2: 225–240.

DeWitt, N. (1940), 'Semantic Notes to Latin Etymologies', *Language* 16.2: 88–94.

Dickey, E. (2002), *Latin Forms of Address from Plautus to Apuleius* (Oxford).

Dickey, E. and Chahoud, A. (2010), *Colloquial and Literary Latin* (Oxford).

Di Franco Lilli, M. C. (1970), *La Biblioteca Manoscritta di Celso Cittadini* (Vatican). *Biblioteca Apostolica Vaticana: Studi e Testi* 259.

Diggle, J., ed. (2004), *Characters* (Cambridge and New York).

Dihle, A. (1982), *The Theory of Will in Classical Antiquity* (Berkeley, CA).

Dilke, O. A. W. (1980), 'Divided Loyalties in Eastern Sicily under Verres', *Ciceroniana* 4: 43–56.

Dominik, W. J., ed. (1997), *Roman Eloquence: Rhetoric in Society and Literature* (London).

Dominik, W. J. and Hall, J., eds. (2007), *A Companion to Roman Rhetoric* (Oxford).

Drogula, F. (2015), *Commanders and Command in the Roman Republic and Early Empire* (Chapel Hill, NC).

Drumann, W. and Groebe, P. (1899–1929), *Geschichte Roms in seinem Übergange von der republikanischen zur monarchischen Verfassung* (Berlin). 6 volumes.

Dubouloz, J. and Pittia, S. (2006), *La Sicile de Cicéron: Lectures des Verrines* (Paris).

Dubuisson, M. (1996), 'Renseignements, espionnage et services secrets dans l'armée romaine', *Ktèma* 21: 305–312.

Dugan, J. (2001), 'How to Make (and Break) a Cicero: *Epideixis*, Textuality, and Self-Fashioning in the *Pro Archia* and *In Pisonem*', *Classical Antiquity* 20: 35–77.

(2005), *Making a New Man: Ciceronian Self-Fashioning in the Rhetorical Works* (Oxford and New York).

(2009), 'Rhetoric and the Roman Republic', in E. Gunderson, ed., *The Cambridge Companion to Ancient Rhetoric* (Cambridge).

Dunkel, G. E. (2006), 'Latin *egomet* and *tute*', in R. A. Bombi et al., eds., *Studi linguistici in onore di Roberto Gusmani* (Alessandria), volume 3: 677–692.

Dunkle, J. R. (1967), 'The Greek Tyrant and Roman Political Invective of the Late Republic', *TAPA* 98: 151–171.

Dyck, A. (1981), 'On Panaetius' conception of μεγαλοψυχία', *MH* 38: 153–161.

(1996), *A Commentary on Cicero, De Officiis* (Ann Arbor, MI).

(1998), 'Narrative Obfuscation, Philosophical *Topoi*, and Tragic Patterning in Cicero's *Pro Milone*', *HSCP* 98: 219–241.

(2003), 'Evidence and Rhetoric in Cicero's *Pro Roscio Amerino*: The Case against Sex. Roscius', *CQ* 53: 235–246.

(2008), *Cicero: Catilinarians* (Cambridge).

Easterling, P. and Hall, E., eds. (2002), *Greek and Roman Actors: Aspects of an Ancient Profession* (Cambridge).

Eckstein, A. (1995), 'Glabrio and the Aetolians: A Note on *Deditio*', *TAPA* 125: 271–289.

Edwards, M. (2004), 'Oratory', in I. de Jong et al., eds., *Narrators, Narratees, and Narratives in Ancient Greek Literature* (Leiden).

Ehrenberg, V. and Jones, A. H. M., eds. (1976), *Documents Illustrating the Reigns of Augustus and Tiberius* (Oxford). Second edition.

Eilers, C. (2002), *Roman Patrons of Greek Cities* (Oxford).

(2009), *Diplomats and Diplomacy in the Roman World* (Leiden).

Enos, R. L. (1988), *The Literate Mode of Cicero's Legal Rhetoric* (Carbondale, IL).

Eppers, M. and Heinen, H. (1984), 'Zu den *servi Venerii* in Ciceros Verrinen', in V. Giuffrè, ed., *Sodalitas: Scritti in onore di Antonio Guarino* (Naples), volume 1: 219–232.

Erdkamp, P. (1998), *Hunger and the Sword: Warfare and Food Supply in Roman Republican Wars (264–30 BC)* (Amsterdam).

(2005), *The Grain Market in the Roman Empire: A Social, Political and Economic Study* (Cambridge).

Fabbri, Q. (1932), 'Q. Cecilio e la Diuinatio', *Historia: studi storici per l'antichità classica* 6: 292–296.

Fallu, E. (1973), 'La questure de Cicéron. Examen de la fonction questorienne dans le domaine de la fiscalité en Sicile', *CEA* II: 31–54.

Fantham, E. (1972), *Comparative Studies in Republican Latin Imagery* (Toronto). *Phoenix* Supplement 10.

Roman Literary Culture: from Cicero to Apuleius (Baltimore, MD).

(2002), 'Orator and/*et* Actor', in P. Easterling and E. Hall, eds., *Greek and Roman Actors: Aspects of an Ancient Profession* (Cambridge), 362–376.

(2004), *The Roman World of Cicero's 'De Oratore'* (Oxford).

Fedeli, P. (1980), 'Cicerone e Lilibeo', *Ciceroniana* 4: 135–144.

Fernández de Buján, A. (2001), '*Fides Publica* e *Instrumenta Publice Confecta* en Derecho romano', *RELat* 1: 189–200.

Ferrary, J. (1998), '*Patroni* et accusateurs dans le procédure *de repetundis*', *RHD* 76: 17–46.

(2000), 'Les gouverneurs des provinces romaines d'Asie Mineure (Asie et Cicilie), depuis l'organisation de la province d'Asie jusqu'à la première guerre de Mithridate (126–88 av. J.-C.)', *Chiron* 30: 161–193.

Ferri, R. and Probert, P. (2010). 'Roman Authors on Colloquial Language', in E. Dickey and A. Chahoud, eds., *Colloquial and Literary Latin* (Cambridge and New York), 12–41.

Feteris, E. (2008), 'Models for the Analysis of Legal Argumentation', *Informal Logic* 28.1: 1–5.

Frier, B. W. (1985). *The Rise of Roman Jurists* (Princeton, NJ).

Finley, M. (1979), *Ancient Sicily* (London). Third edition.

Flach, D. (1994), *Die Gesetze der frühen römischen Republik: Text und Kommentar* (Darmstadt).

Flower, H. I. (2013), 'Beyond the *Contio*: Political Communication in the Tribunate of Tiberius Gracchus', in C. Steel and H. van der Blom, eds., *Community and Communication: Oratory and Politics in Republican Rome* (Oxford), 85–100.

Fotheringham, L. (2004), 'Repetition and Unity in a Civil Law Speech: The *pro Caecina*', in J. Powell and J. Paterson, eds., *Cicero the Advocate* (Oxford), 253–276.

(2006), 'Gliding Transitions and the Analysis of Structure: Cicero's *Pro Archia*', in C. Deroux, ed., *Studies in Latin Literature and Roman History* (Brussels), 32–52.

Fowler, D. (1983), 'Lucretius on the *clinamen* and "Free Will" (II 251–93)', in *Syzetesis: studi sull'epicureismo greco e romano offerti a Marcello Gigante* (Naples), 329–352.

(1990), 'Deviant Focalisation in Virgil's *Aeneid*', *PCPS* 36: 42–63.

(2002), *Lucretius on Atomic Motion: A Commentary on* De Rerum Natura *Book Two, Lines 1–332* (Oxford).

Fox, M., ed. (1988), *Temple in Society* (Winona Lake, IN).

Fraenkel, E. (1968), *Leseproben aus Reden Ciceros und Catos* (Rome). *Sussidi Eruditi* 22.

Frank, H. (1992), *Ratio bei Cicero* (Frankfurt-am-Main).

Frati, L. (1909), *Indice dei codici latini conservati nella R. Biblioteca Universitaria di Bologna* (Florence). *Studi italiani di filologia classica* 17.

Frazel, T. (2004), 'The Composition and Circulation of Cicero's *In Verrem*', *CQ* 54: 128–142.

(2009), *The Rhetoric of Cicero's* In Verrem (Göttingen).

Frost, M. (2005), *Introduction to Classical Legal Rhetoric: A Lost Heritage* (Aldershot).

Fuhrmann, M. (1980), 'Tecniche narrative nella seconda orazione contro Verre', *Ciceroniana* 4: 27–42.

(1995), *Die Reden gegen Verres* (Zurich).

Gagnér, A. (1920), *De 'hercle', 'mehercle', ceterisque id genus particulis priscae poesis Latinae scaenicae* (Greifswald).

Gallazzi, C. (1984), 'P. Mil. Vogl. Inv. 1190. Frammento di Cicero, In C. Verrem Act. Sec. Lib. V', *ZPE* 54: 21–26.

Gardner, J. (1998), *Family and Familia in Roman Law and Life* (Oxford).

Garton, C. (1972), *Personal Aspects of the Roman Theatre* (Toronto).

Geeraerts, D. (2002), 'The Scope of Diachronic Onomasiology', in V. Agel et al., eds., *Das Wort. Seine strukturelle und kulturelle Dimension. Festschrift für Oskar Reichmann zum 65. Geburtstag* (Tübingen), 29–44.

Gelzer, M. (1969), *Cicero: Ein biographischer Versuch* (Wiesbaden).

Genette, G. (1980), *Narrative Discourse* (Oxford).

Georgescu, V. (1936), *Le mot* causa *dans le latin juridique* (Bucarest).

Gilbert, N. W. (1963), 'The Concept of Will in Early Latin Philosophy', *JHPh* 1: 17–35.

Gildenhard, I. (2011), *Creative Eloquence: The Construction of Reality in Cicero's Speeches* (Oxford).

Glucker, J. (1984), 'Chapter and Verse in Cicero', *GB* 11: 103–112.

Gordon, R. L. (1979) 'The Real and the Imaginary. Production and Religion in the Graeco-Roman World', *Art History* 2: 1–34.

Gotoff, H. C. (1979), *Cicero's Elegant Style: An Analysis of the Pro Archia* (Urbana, IL).
(1993), *Cicero's Caesarian Speeches* (Chapel Hill, NC).
Gotter, U. (2000), 'Akkulturation als Methodenproblem der historischen Wissenschaften', in W. Eßbach, ed., *Wir/ihr/sie. Identität und Alterität in Theorie und Methode* (Würzburg), 373–406.
Graf, F. (1991), 'Gestures and Conventions: The Gestures of Roman Actors and Orators', in J. Bremmer and H. Roodenburg, eds., *A Cultural History of Gesture from Antiquity to the Present Day* (Oxford), 36–58.
Grahame, M. (2000), *Reading Space: Social Interaction and Identity in the Houses of Roman Pompeii: A Syntactical Approach to the Analysis and Interpretation of Built Space* (Oxford). BAR International Series 886.
Greenidge, A. H. J. (1894), Infamia*: Its Place in Roman Public and Private Law* (Oxford).
(1901), *The Legal Procedure of Cicero's Time* (Oxford).
Greenough, J. B. (1899), 'Some Questions in Latin Stem Formation', *HSCP* 10: 1–17.
Grenfell, B. P. and A. S. Hunt, eds. (1904), *The Oxyrhynchus Papyri* (London). Volume 4.
Grethlein, J. and Rengakos, A., eds. (2009), *Narratology and Interpretation. The Content of Narrative Form in Ancient Narrative* (Berlin). *Trends in Classics* Supplementary Volume 4.
Grillo, L. (2015), *Cicero's* De Provinciis Consularibus Oratio (Oxford).
Groot, A. W. de (1956), 'Classification of the Uses of a Case Illustrated on the Genitive in Latin', *Lingua* 6: 8–66.
Grube, G. M. A. (1961), *The Greek and Roman Critics* (London).
Gruen, E. (1964), 'Politics and the Courts in 104 BC', *TAPA* 95: 99–110.
(1968a), *Roman Politics and the Criminal Courts 149–78 BC* (Cambridge).
(1968b), 'Pompey and the Pisones', *CSCA* 1: 155–170.
(1974), *The Last Generation of the Roman Republic* (Berkeley, CA).
(1984), *The Hellenistic World and the Coming of Rome, I–II* (Berkeley, CA).
(2006), 'Romans and Others', in R. Morstein-Marx and N. Rosenstein, eds., *The Blackwell Companion to the Roman Republic* (Oxford), 459–477.
Gunderson, E. (2009), *The Cambridge Companion to Ancient Rhetoric* (Cambridge).

Habermas, J. (1975), *Legitimation Crisis* (Boston, MA).
Hachtmann, K. (1895), *Die Verwertung der vierten Rede Ciceros gegen C. Verres, de signis* (Bernburg).
Hadot, P. (1971), *Marius Victorinus: recherches sur sa vie et ses oeuvres* (Paris).
Haffter, H. (1934), *Untersuchungen zur altlateinischen Dichtersprache* (Berlin).
(1956), '*Superbia* innenpolitisch', *Studi Italiani di Filologia Classica* 27–28: 135–141.
Hafner, G. (1968), 'Cn. Naevius und M. Claudius Marcellus', *MDAI (R)* 75: 64–73.
Hall, J. (1996), 'Social Evasion and Aristocratic Manners in Cicero's *De Oratore*', *AJPh* 117.1: 95–120.
(2004), 'Cicero and Quintilian on the Oratorical Use of Hand Gestures', *CQ* 54.1: 143–160.
Halm, C. (1863), *Rhetores Latini Minores* (Leipzig).
(1874), *Ciceros Rede gegen Q. Caecilius und der Anklagerede gegen C. Verres viertes und fünftes Buch* (Berlin).
Hammer, D. (2014), *A Companion to Greek Democracy and the Roman Republic* (Oxford).
Happ, H. (1967), 'Die lateinische Umgangssprache und die Kunstsprache des Plautus', *Glotta* 45: 60–104.
Harper, K. (2011), *Slavery in the Late Roman World, AD 275–425* (Cambridge and New York).
Harries, J. (2004), 'Cicero and the Law', in J. Powell and J. Paterson, eds., *Cicero the Advocate* (Oxford), 147–164.
(2006), *Cicero and the Jurists* (London).
Harris, W. (1976), 'The Development of the Quaestorship, 267–81BC', *CQ* 76: 92–106.
(1979), *War and Imperialism in Republican Rome* (Oxford).
Hart, H. L. A. and Honoré, T. (1985), *Causation in the Law* (Oxford).
Haury, A. (1955), *L'Ironie et l'humour chez Cicéron* (Leiden).
Haverling, G. (2016), 'On the Use of *Habeo* and the Perfect Participle in Earlier and Later Latin', in J. N. Adams and N. Vincent, eds., *Early and Late Latin: Continuity or Change* (Cambridge), 180–201.
Hawthorn, J. R. (1962), 'The Senate after Sulla', *G&R* 9: 53–60.
Heerdegen, F. (1881), *Untersuchungen zur lateinischen Semasiologie,* iii: *Ein lexikalisches Beispiel* (Erlangen).
Heitland, W. E. and Cowie, H. (1876) *M.T. Ciceronis in Q. Caecilium Divinatio et in C. Verrem Actio Prima* (Cambridge).

Hellegouarc'h, J. (1972), *Le vocabulaire latin des relations et des partis politiques sous la République* (Paris).
Henderson, M. I. (1963), 'The Establishment of the *Equester Ordo*', *JRS* 53: 61–72.
Heumann, H. and Seckel, E. (1907), *Heumanns Handlexicon zu den Quellen des römischen Rechts* (Jena). Ninth edition.
Heuss, A. (1933), *Die völkerrechtlichen Grundlagen der römischen Aussenpolitik in republikanischer Zeit* (Leipzig).
Hinard, F. (1985), *Les proscriptions de la Rome républicaine* (Paris).
Holford-Strevens, L. (2020), *Gelliana* (Oxford).
Holloway, R. R. (1991), *The Archaeology of Ancient Sicily* (London and New York).
Holst, H. (1925), *Die Wortspiele in Ciceros Reden* (Oslo). Symbolae Osloenses Suppl. I.
Hoppe, F. (1875), *Zu Fragmenten und der Sprache Ciceros* (Gumbinnen).
Hornblower, S., ed. (1994), *Greek Historiography* (Oxford).
Horsfall, N. (1981), 'Some Problems in the Titulature of Roman Literary History', *BICS* 28: 103–114.
Hough, J. N. (1930), 'The *Lex Lutatia* and the *Lex Plautia de vi*', *AJP* 51.2: 135–147.
Housman, A. E. (1910), 'Greek Nouns in Latin Poetry from Lucretius to Juvenal', *JPh* 31: 236–266 = *Classical Papers* (1972), volume 2: 817–839.
(1927) *M. Annaei Lucani Belli Civilis Libri Decem* (Oxford). Second edition.
Hutchinson, G. O. (1995), 'Rhyme, Style and Meaning in Cicero's Prose', *CQ* 45.2: 485–499.
(2010), 'Deflected Addresses: Apostrophe and Space (Sophocles, Aeschines, Plautus, Cicero, Virgil and Others)', *CQ* 60: 96–109.
Innocenti, B. (1994), 'Towards a Theory of Vivid Description as Practiced in Cicero's *Verrine* Orations', *Rhetorica* 12: 335–381.
Inwood, B. (2005), *Reading Seneca: Stoic Philosophy at Rome* (Oxford).
Jashemski, W. F. (1950), *The Origins and History of the Proconsular and Propraetorian Imperium to 27 BC* (Chicago, IL).
Johnston, D. (1987), 'Three Thoughts on Roman Private Law and the *Lex Irnitana*', *JRS* 77: 62–77.
(2000), 'The Jurists', in M. Schofield and C. Rowe, eds., *The Cambridge History of Greek and Roman Political Thought* (Cambridge), 616–634.
Jolowicz, H. F. (1954), *Historical Introduction to the Study of Roman Law* (Cambridge).
Jones, A. (1972), *The Criminal Courts of the Roman Republic and Principate* (Oxford).

Jones, J. W. (1940), *Historical Introduction to the Theory of Law* (Oxford).
Jong, I. de (1987), *Narrators and Focalizers: The Presentation of the Story in the Iliad* (Amsterdam).
Jong, I. de et al., eds. (2004), *Narrators, Narratees, and Narratives in Ancient Greek Literature* (Leiden).
Jordan, H. (1879), 'Über die Ausdrücke: *aedes templum fanum delubrum*', *Hermes* 14: 567–583.
Jordan, L. and Wool, S. (1984), *Inventory of Western Manuscripts in the Biblioteca Ambrosiana: Part One A – B Superior* (Notre Dame).
Jory, E. (1988), 'Publilius Syrus and the Element of Competition in the Theatre of the Republic', in N. Horsfall, ed., *Vir Bonus Dicendi Peritus: Studies in Celebration of Otto Skutsch's Eightieth Birthday* (London). *BICS Supplement* 51: 73–81.
Kallet-Marx, R. M. (1990), 'The Trial of Rutilius Rufus', *Phoenix* 44, 122–139.
Kantor, G. (2010), '*Siculus cum Siculo non eiusdem civitatis.* Litigation between Citizens of Different Communities in the Verrines', *CCG* 21: 187–204.
Kaser, M. (1956), '*Infamia* und *ignominia* in den römischen Rechtsquellen', *ZRG* 73: 220–278.
(1996), *Das römische Zivilprocessrecht* (Munich).
Kaster, R. (2005a), *Emotion, Restraint, and Community in Ancient Rome* (Oxford).
(2005b), *Cicero: Speech on Behalf of Publius Sestius* (Oxford).
Katz, B. R. (1977), 'Caesar Strabo's Struggle for the Consulship – and More', *Rheinisches Museum für Philologie* 120, 45–63.
Keaveney, A. and Madden, J. (1983), 'Metellus Pius: The Evidence of Livy, *Epitome* 76', *Eranos* 81: 47–51.
Keller, M. (1992), *Les verbes latins à infectum en* -sc-, *étude morphologique* (Brussels). Collection Latomus 216.
Kelly, G. (2006), *A History of Exile in the Roman Republic* (Cambridge).
Kelly, J. (1966), *Roman Litigation* (Oxford).
(1976), *Studies in the Civil Judicature of the Roman Republic* (Oxford).
Kennedy, G. A. (1972), *The Art of Rhetoric in the Roman World 300 BC–AD 300* (Princeton, NJ).
(1994), *A New History of Classical Rhetoric* (Princeton, NJ).
Kinsey, T. E. (1971), *Pro P. Quinctio Oratio* (Sydney).
(1985), 'The *Partitio* of Cicero's *Pro Roscio Amerino*', *Mnemosyne* 38: 387–388.

Kirby, J. (1997), 'Ciceronian Rhetoric: Theory and Practice', in W. J. Dominik, ed., *Roman Eloquence: Rhetoric in Society and Literature* (London), 13–31.

Kissel, T. K. (1995), *Untersuchungen zur Logistik des römischen Heeres in den Provinzen des griechischen Ostens (27 v. Chr.–235 n. Chr.)* (St. Katharinen).

Klenze, C. A. C. (1825), *Fragmenta legis Serviliae repetundarum* (Berlin).

Klug, U. (1982), *Juristiche Logik* (Berlin, Heidelberg, and New York). Fourth edition.

Konstan, D. (1993), 'Foreword: To the Reader', *Materiali e Discussioni per l'Analisi dei Testi Classici* 31, 11–22.

(2005), 'Clemency as a Virtue', *CP* 100.4: 337–346.

Koschorke, A. et al. (2007), *Der fiktive Staat: Konstruktionen des politischen Körpers in der Geschichte Europas* (Frankfurt-am-Main).

Koster, S. (1980), *Die Invektive in der griechischen und römischen Literatur* (Meisenheim am Glan). *Beiträge zur klassischen Philologie* 99.

Krause, J. H. (1841), *Gymnastik und Agonistik der Hellenen* (Halle).

Krebs, J. and Schmalz, J. (1905), *Antibarbarus der lateinischen Sprache* (Basel). Seventh edition.

Kristeller, P. O. (1990), *Iter Italicum* (London and Leiden).

Kroon, C. (1995), *Discourse Particles in Latin: A Study of* nam, enim, autem, vero, *and* at (Amsterdam).

Kroon, C. and Risselada, R. (2002), 'Phasality, Polarity, Focality: A Feature Analysis of the Latin Particle', *Belgian Journal of Linguistics* 16: 65–78.

(2017), 'Textual Deixis and the "Anchoring" Use of the Latin Pronoun *hic*', *Mnemosyne* 70: 585–612.

Kühner, R. and Stegmann, C. (1976), *Ausführliche Grammatik der lateinishen Sprache, zweiter Teil: Satzlehre* (Darmstadt). 2 volumes. Fifth edition.

Künkel, W. (1995), *Staatsordnung und Staatspraxis der römischen Republik* (Munich). 2 volumes.

Kunkel, W. and Wittmann, R. (1995), *Handbuch der Altertumswissenschaft. 10: Rechtsgeschichte des Altertums. 3:2, Staatsordnung und Staatspraxis der Römischen Republik. 2, Die Magistratur* (Munich).

Laird, A. (1999), *Powers of Expression, Expressions of Power: Speech Presentation and Latin Literature* (Oxford).

Laughton, E. (1964), *The Participle in Cicero* (Oxford).

Laurand, L. (1907), *Études sur le style des discours de Cicéron* (Paris).

Lavency, M. (1998), *La proposition relative* (Louvain). Grammaire fondamentale du latin V.2.

Lease, E. (1919), 'The Use and Range of the Future Participle', *AJP* 40: 262–285.

Lebreton, J. (1901), *Études sur la langue et la grammaire de Cicéron* (Paris).

Leeman, A. D. (1963), *Orationis ratio. The Stylistic Theories and Practice of the Roman Orators, Historians and Philosophers* (Amsterdam).

Leigh, M. (2004), 'The *Pro Caelio* and Comedy', *CP* 99: 300–335.

Lenel, O. (1878), *Beiträge zur kunde des prätorischen edicts* (Stuttgart).

(1927), *Das Edictum Perpetuum* (Leipzig). Third edition.

Lennon, J. (2013), *Pollution and Religion in Ancient Rome* (Cambridge).

Leuze, O. (1926), *Zur Geschichte der römishen Censur* (Berlin).

Levy, E. (1933), 'Von den römischen Anklägervergehen', *ZSS* 53: 151–233.

Lewis, R. G. (2006), *Asconius: Commentaries on the Speeches of Cicero* (Oxford).

Ley, G. (2006), *A Short Introduction to the Ancient Greek Theatre* (Chicago, IL). Second edition.

Linderski, J. (1990), 'The Surname of M. A. Creticus and the *Cognomina ex victis gentibus*', *ZPE* 80: 157–164.

Lindner, M. (2009), 'Narration und Transformation. Die Tempelprostituierten vom Berg Eryx', in T. Scheer, ed., *Tempelprostitution im Altertum: Fakten und Fiktionen* (Berlin), 293–327.

Lindsay, H. M. (2009), *Adoption in the Roman World* (Cambridge and New York).

Lintott, A. (1968), *Violence in Republican Rome* (Oxford).

(1980), 'M. Caelius Rufus and Pausanias', *Classical Quarterly* 30: 385–386.

(1981), 'The *Leges de Repetundis* and Associated Measures under the Republic', *ZSS* 98: 162–212.

(1990), 'Electoral Bribery in the Roman Republic', *JRS* 80: 1–16.

(1992), *Judicial Reform and Land Reform in the Roman Republic: A New Edition, with Translation and Commentary, of the Laws from Urbino* (Cambridge).

(1993), *Imperium Romanum: Politics and Administration* (London).

(1999), *Violence in Republican Rome* (Oxford). Second edition.

(2004), 'Legal Procedure in Cicero's Time', in J. Powell and J. Paterson, eds., *Cicero the Advocate* (Oxford), 62–79.

(2008), *Cicero as Evidence* (Oxford).

Liscu, M. O. (1930), *Étude sur la langue de la philosophie morale chez Cicéron* (Paris).

Löfstedt, E. (1956), *Syntactica: Studien und Beiträge zur historischen Syntax des Lateins* (Lund). 2 volumes.

López G. (1972), 'La lex Rupilia e l'eredità di Eraclio', *GIF* 24: 178–191.

López, G. and Piacente, L. (1973), 'Inventario dei mss. delle orazioni ciceroniane contro Verre', *Arcadia*: ser. 3 6.2: 83–95.

Loutsch, C. (1994), *L'exorde dans les discours de Cicéron* (Brussels).

McDermott, W. C. (1977a), 'The Verrine Jury', *RhM* 120: 64–75.

(1977b), '*Lex de tribunicia potestate*', *CP* 72: 49–52.

MacDowell, D. M. (1990), *Demosthenes: Against Meidias* (Oxford).

McGinn, T. A. J. (2001), 'Satire and the Law: The Case of Horace', *PCPhS* 47: 81–102.

MacKendrick, P. (1995), *The Speeches of Cicero: Context, Law, Rhetoric* (London).

McNamee, K. (2007), *Annotations in Greek and Latin Texts from Egypt* (Oxford). *American Studies in Papyrology* 45.

Madvig, J. N. (1828), *Ad virum celeberrimum Io. Casp. Orellium epistola critica de orationum verrinarum libris II extremis emendandis* (Copenhagen).

Magie, D. (1950), *Roman Rule in Asia Minor to the End of the 3rd Century after Christ* (Princeton, NJ). 2 volumes.

Maier-Eichhorn, U. (1989), *Die Gestikulation in Quintilians Rhetorik* (Frankfurt).

Majorana, A. (1909), *L'arte di parlare in pubblico* (Milan).

Maltby, R. (1991), *A Lexicon of Ancient Latin Etymologies* (Leeds).

Mann, J. C. (1985), 'Two *Topoi* in the *Agricola*', *Britannia* 16: 21–24.

Maraldi, M. (1998), 'Concessive *ut*: Parataxis, Hypotaxis, and Correlation', in B. García-Hernández, ed., *Estudios de lingüística latina* (Madrid), 487–501.

Mare, A. C. de la (1973), *The Handwriting of Italian Humanists* (Oxford). Volume 1.

(1977), 'Humanistic Script: The First Ten Years', in F. Krafft and D. Wuttke, eds., *Das Verhältnis der Humanisten zum Buch* (Boppard), 89–110.

(1992), 'Cosimo and His Books', in F. Ames-Lewis, ed., *Cosimo 'il Vecchio' de' Medici, 1389–1464: Essays in Commemoration of the 600th Anniversary of Cosimo de' Medici's Birth* (Oxford), 115–156.

Marinone, N. (1949), *Il Processo di Verre* (Verona).

(1950), *Quaestiones Verrinae. Cronologia del processo di Verre.* (Torino).

(1965), 'I questori e i legati di Verre in Sicilia', *ATT* 100: 219–255.
(1997), *Cronologia Ciceroniana* (Rome).
Marinone, N., Fiocchi, L., and Vottero, D. (eds.) (1992), *Il processo di Verre: testo latino a fronte* (Milan).
Marouzeau, J. (1922), *L'ordre des mots dans la phrase latine: les groupes nominaux* (Paris).
(1938), *L'ordre des mots dans la phrase latine: le verbe* (Paris).
(1949), *L'ordre des mots dans la phrase latine: les articulations de l'énoncé* (Paris).
Marshall, A. J. (1966), 'Governors on the Move', *Phoenix* 20.3: 231–246.
(1967), 'Verres and Judicial Corruption', *CQ* 17: 408–413.
(1968), 'Pompey's Organization of Bithynia-Pontus: Two Neglected Texts', *JRS* 58: 103–109.
Marshall, B. A. (1975a), 'Q. Cicero, Hortensius and the *Lex Aurelia*', *RhM* 118: 136–152.
(1975b), 'The Aspirations of Q. Arrius', *Historia* 24: 220–231.
(1976), *Crassus. A Political Biography* (Amsterdam).
(1977a), 'The Case of Metellus Nepos v. Curio: A Discussion of Cicero, *Verr.* I.6 and 9 and the Scholiasts', *Philologus* 121.1: 83–89.
(1977b), 'Two Court Cases in the Late Second Century BC', *AJP* 98: 417–423.
(1987), 'Tribunician Agitation and Aristocratic Reaction 80–71 BC', *Athenaeum* n.s. 65: 361–378.
Marshall, B. A. and Baker, R. J. (1975), 'The Aspirations of Quintus Arrius', *Historia* 24: 221–231.
Marshall, B. A. and Beness, J. L. (1987), 'Tribunician Agitation and Aristocratic Reaction 80–71 BC', *Athenaeum* 65: 361–378.
Martini, G. (1962), 'Arisi, Andreolo', in A. M. Ghisalberti et al., eds., *Dizionario Biografico degli Italiani* (Rome). Volume 4.
Martorana, G. (1979), 'La Venus di Verre e le Verrine', *Kokalos* 25: 73–103.
Mateo, A. (1999), Manceps, Redemptor, Publicanus*: contribución al estudio de los contratistas públicos en Roma* (Santander).
Mattingly, H. B. (1969), 'Two Republican Laws of the *Tabula Bembina*', *JRS* 59: 129–143.
Maurice, L. (2013), *The Teacher in Ancient Rome: The Magister and His World* (Lanham, MD).
May, J. (1988) *Trials of Character : The Eloquence of Ciceronian Ethos* (Chapel Hill, NC and London).
ed. (2002), *Brill's Companion to Cicero: Oratory and Rhetoric* (Leiden).

May, J. and Wisse, J. (2001), *Cicero: On the Ideal Orator* (Oxford).
Mayer, R. (2001), *Tacitus: Dialogus de Oratoribus* (Cambridge).
(2005), 'The Impracticability of Latin "Kunstprosa"', in T. Reinhardt, M. Lapidge, and J. Adams, eds., *Aspects of the Language of Latin Prose* (Oxford). *Proceedings of the British Academy* 129: 195–210.
Mayor, J. (1889), *Thirteen Satires of Juvenal* (London). Volumes 1–2.
Meijer, F. (1986), *A History of Seafaring in the Classical World* (London).
Melchior, A. (2008), 'Twinned Fortunes and the Publication of Cicero's *Pro Milone*', *CP* 103: 282–297.
Mendelsohn, C. J. (1907), *Studies in the Wordplay of Plautus* (Philadelphia, PA).
Menge, H. (1959), *Lateinische Synonymik* (Heidelberg).
(2000), *Lehrbuch der lateinischen Syntax und Semantik* (Darmstadt).
Menk, E. (1925), *The Position of the Possessive Pronoun in Cicero's Orations*. PhD thesis, University of Iowa.
Merguet, P. A. H. (1877–1894), *Lexikon zu den Schriften Ciceros: Lexikon zu den Reden* (Jena). 4 volumes.
Metzger, E. (1997), *A New Outline of the Roman Civil Trial* (Oxford).
Meyer, H. D. (1980), 'Der *civis Romanus* als Kläger im Repetundenprozeß', in W. Eck, H. Galsterer, and H. Wolff, eds., *Studien zur Antiken Sozialgeschichte* (Cologne), 145–156.
Michel, A. (1961), *Rhétorique et Philosophie chez Cicéron* (Paris).
Michel, A. and Verdière, R., eds. (1975), *Ciceroniana: Hommages à Kazimierz Kumaniecki* (Leiden).
Miles, M. (2002), 'Cicero's Prosecution of Gaius Verres: A Roman View of the Ethics of Acquisition of Art', *International Journal of Cultural Property* 2: 28–49.
Millar, F. (1977), *The Emperor in the Roman World, 31 BC–AD 337* (London).
(1998), *The Crowd in Rome in the Late Republic* (Ann Arbor, MI).
Mitchell, T. N. (1979), *Cicero: The Ascending Years* (New Haven, CT).
(1986), *Cicero: Verrines II.1* (Warminster).
Moatti, C., ed. (2004), *La mobilité des personnes en Méditerranée de l'Antiquité à l'époque moderne: procédures de contrôle et documents d'identification* (Rome).
Mommsen, T. (1864), 'Das römische Gastrecht und die römische Clientele', in T. Mommsen, *Römische Forschungen* (Berlin), volume 1: 321–390.
Montague, H. (1992), 'Advocacy and Politics: The Paradox of Cicero's *Pro Ligario*', *AJP* 113: 559–574.

Mora, F. (2003), 'La scelta del *Princeps Senatus*', *Historia* 52: 501–504.

Morgan, T. (1998), *Literate Education in the Hellenistic and Roman Worlds* (Cambridge).

(2015), *Roman Faith and Christian Faith: Pistis and Fides in the Early Roman Empire and Early Churches* (Oxford).

Morstein-Marx, R. (1995), *Hegemony to Empire: The Development of the Roman* Imperium *in the East from 148 to 62 B.C.* (Berkeley, CA).

(2004), *Mass Oratory and Political Power in the Late Roman Republic* (Cambridge).

Morstein-Marx, R. and Rosenstein, N., eds. (2006), *The Blackwell Companion to the Roman Republic* (Oxford).

Moussy, C. (2001), *De lingua Latina novae quaestiones: actes du Xe colloque international de linguistique latine, Paris, Sèvres, 19–23 avril 1999* (Louvain).

Mylonopoulos, J., ed. (2010), *Divine Images and Human Imaginations in Ancient Greece and Rome* (Leiden). *Religions in the Graeco-Roman World* 170.

Naiden, F. S. (2006), *Ancient Supplication* (Oxford).

Navarre, O. (1900), *Essai sur la rhétorique grecque avant Aristote* (Paris).

Neue, F. and Wagener, C. (1892–1905), *Formenlehre der lateinischen Sprache* (Berlin). Third edition.

Neumeister, C. (1964), *Grundsätze der forensichen Rhetorik* (Munich).

Nicolet, C. (1972), 'Institutions politiques de Rome' in École pratique des hautes études. 4e section, Sciences historiques et philologiques. Annuaire 1971–1972 (Paris), 251–268.

Nicols, J. (1981), 'The Caecilii Metelli, *patroni Siciliae*?', *Historia* 30: 238–240.

(2001), '*Hospitium* and Political Friendship in the Late Republic', in M. Peachin, ed., *Aspects of Friendship in the Graeco-Roman World* (Portsmouth, RI). *JRS Supplementary Series* 43: 99–108.

(2011), 'Hospitality among the Romans', in M. Peachin, ed., *The Oxford Handbook of Social Relations in the Roman World* (Oxford), 422–437.

Nisbet, R. (1995), '*Cola* and *Clausulae* in Cicero's Speeches', in S. Harrison, ed., *R. G. M. Nisbet: Collected Papers on Latin Literature* (Oxford), 312–324.

Norden, E. (1913), *Agnostos Theos: Untersuchungen zur Formengeschichte religiöser Rede* (Leipzig).

Nörr, D. (1974), *Rechtskritik in der römischen Antike* (Munich).

North, H. (1952), 'The Use of Poetry in Training the Ancient Orator', *Traditio* 8: 1–33.

Nussbaum, M. (1996), 'Compassion: The Basic Social Emotion', *Social Philosophy & Policy* 13.1: 27–58.
Nutting, H. C. (1907), 'The Unreal Conditional Sentence in Cicero: Second Paper', *AJPh* 28.2: 153–178.
(1925), *The Latin Conditional Sentence* (Berkeley, CA).
Oakley, S. (1983), 'Livy XXVI.6.4', *PACA* 17: 61–62.
Ochs, D. J. (1982), 'Rhetorical Detailing in Cicero's Verrine Orations', *Central States Speech Journal* 33: 313–318.
Odelman, E. (1972), *Études sur quelques reflets du style administratif chez César* (Stockholm).
Ogilvie, R. M. (1965), *Commentary on Livy Books 1–5* (Oxford).
Oliver, J. (1983), *The Civic Tradition and Roman Athens* (Baltimore, MD).
Ooteghem, J. van (1967), *Les Caecilii Metelli de la république* (Brussels).
Otto, A. (1890), *Die Sprichwörter und sprichwörtlichen Redensarten der Römer* (Leipzig).
Paoli, U. (1954), 'Nota giuridica su Plauto', *Iura* 4: 174–181.
Partsch, J. (1910), 'Römisches und griechisches Recht in Plautus *Persa*', *Hermes* 45: 595–614.
Parzinger, P. (1911–1912), *Beiträge zur Kenntnis der Entwicklung des ciceronischen Stils* (Landshut). Second edition.
Peachin, M. (2011), *The Oxford Handbook of Social Relations in the Roman World* (Oxford).
Pearson, L. (1968), 'Cicero's Debt to Demosthenes: The Verrines', *Pacific Coast Philology* 3: 49–54.
Pelling, C. B. R. (1979), 'Plutarch's Method of Work in the Roman Lives', *JHS* 99: 83–91.
(1980), 'Plutarch's Adaptation of His Source-Material', *JHS* 100: 127–140.
Penney, J. W. H. (2005), 'Connections in Archaic Latin Prose', in T. Reinhardt, M. Lapidge, and J. Adams, eds., *Aspects of the Language of Latin Prose* (Oxford). *Proceedings of the British Academy* 129: 37–51.
Petersmann, H. (1977), *Petrons Urbane Prosa: Untersuchungen zu Sprache und Text* (Vienna).
Peterson, W. (1891), *M. Fabi Quintiliani Institutionis oratoriae liber decimus* (Oxford).
(1893), *Tacitus: Dialogus* (Oxford).
(1903), 'Emendations of Cicero's Verrines', *CR* 17: 198–202.
(1904), 'The Opening Sentence of the Verrines', *CR* 18: 440–441.
(1905), 'The Vatican Codex of Cicero's Verrines', *AJPh* 26: 409–436.

(1905b), 'Two Notes on the Verrines', *CR* 19: 160.

(1907), 'The MSS. of the Verrines', *JPh* 30: 161–207.

Pétré, H. (1934), '*Misericordia:* histoire du mot et de l'idée du paganisme au christianisme', *REL* 12: 376–389.

Petsas, P. M., Hatzopoulos, M. B., and Gounaropoulou, L. (2000), *Inscriptions du sanctuaire de la Mère des Dieux Autochtone de Leukopétra, Macédoine* (Paris).

Pfuntner, L. (2015), 'Cooperation and Conflict between Governor and Poleis in the "Verrines"', *Phoenix* 69.3–4: 355–375.

Phillipson, C. (1911), *The International Law and Custom of Ancient Greece and Rome* (London).

Pieroni, S. (2010), '*Nos* as Expression of the "Ego" in Cicero's Letters to Atticus (Book I–IV)', in P. Anreiter and M. Kienpointer, eds., *Latin Lingustics Today* (Innsbruck), 599–611.

Pina Polo, F. and Díaz Fernández, A. (2019), *The Quaestorship in the Roman Republic.* (Berlin). *Klio Beihefte* 31.

Pinkster, H. (1972), *On Latin Adverbs* (Amsterdam).

(1987), 'The Strategy and Chronology of the Development of Future and Perfect Tense Auxiliaries in Latin', in M. Harris et al., eds., *Historical Development of Auxiliaries* (Berlin). *Trends in Linguistics: Studies and Monographs* 35: 193–224.

(1992), 'The Latin Impersonal Passive', *Mnemosyne* 45: 159–177.

Pittia, S. (2006), 'La cohorte du gouverneur Verrès', in J. Dubouloz and S. Pittia, eds., *La Sicile de Cicéron: lectures des Verrines* (Paris), 57–87.

Platt, V. (2011) *Facing the Gods: Epiphany and Representation in Graeco-Roman Art, Literature, and Religion* (Cambridge and New York).

Plescia, J. (1994), 'The *ius pacis* in ancient Rome', *RIDA* 41: 301–351.

Pohlenz, M. (1965), 'Philosophie und Erlebnis in Senecas Dialogen', Anhang, 'Ein römischer Zug in Senecas Denken', in id., *Kleine Schriften* (Hildesheim). 2 volumes, 1.440–446.

Poliakoff, M. (1987), *Combat Sports in the Ancient World* (New Haven, CT).

Pöschl, V. (1964), *Bibliographie zur antiken Bildersprache* (Heidelberg).

Powell, J. (2010a), 'Hyperbaton and Register in Cicero', in E. Dickey and A. Chahoud, eds., *Colloquial and Literary Latin* (Cambridge), 163–185.

(2010b), 'Court Procedure and Rhetorical Strategy in Cicero', in D. Berry and A. Erskine, eds., *Form and Function in Roman Oratory* (Cambridge), 21–36.

(2014), 'Cicero's Style', in C. Steel, ed., *The Cambridge Companion to Cicero* (Cambridge), 41–72.

Powell, J. and Paterson, J., eds. (2004), *Cicero the Advocate* (Oxford).

Prag, J., ed. (2007), *Sicilia Nutrix Plebis Romanae: Rhetoric, Law, & Taxation in Cicero's Verrines* (London). *BICS Supplement* 97.

(2013), 'Provincials, Patrons, and the Rhetoric of *Repetundae*', in C. Steel and H. van der Blom, eds., *Community and Communication: Oratory and Politics in Republican Rome* (Oxford), 267–283.

(2014), 'The Quaestorship in the Third and Second Centuries BC', in J. Dubouloz, S. Pittia, and G. Sabatini, eds., *L'Imperium Romanum en perspective. Les savoirs d'empire dans la République romaine et leur héritage dans l'Europe médiévale et moderne* (Paris), 193–209.

Pritchard, R. T. (1970), 'Cicero and the *Lex Hieronica*', *Historia* 19.3: 352–368.

(1971), 'Gaius Verres and the Sicilian Farmers', *Historia* 20.2: 224–238.

(1972), 'Some Aspects of First Century Sicilian Agriculture', *Historia* 21.4: 646–660.

(1975), '*Perpaucae Siciliae civitates*: Notes on *Verr.* 2, 3, 6, 13', *Historia*: 24: 33–47.

Purcell, N. (1983), 'The Apparitores: A Study in Social Mobility', *PBSR* 38: 125–173.

Querzoli, S. (2003), '*Materia* and *Officia* of Rhetorical Teaching in Book II of the *Institutio Oratoria*', in O. Tellegen-Couperus, ed., *Quintilian and the Law: The Art of Persuasion in Law and Politics* (Leuven), 37–50.

Race, W. H. (1997), *Pindar* (Cambridge, MA).

Radin, M. (1911), 'Literary References in Cicero's Orations', *CJ* 6: 209–217.

Rapp, C. (2002), *Aristoteles Rhetorik* (Berlin). 2 volumes.

Rawson, E. (1971), 'L. Crassus and Cicero', *PCPS* 17: 75–88.

(1975), *Cicero: A Portrait* (London).

(1985), *Intellectual Life in the Late Roman Republic* (Baltimore, MD).

Reckford, K. (2002), '*Pueri ludentes*: Some Aspects of Play and Seriousness in Horace's Epistles', *TAPA* 132: 1–19.

Reeve, M. D. (1982–1983), 'A Lost Manuscript of Cicero's *Verrines*', *RHT* 12–13: 381–385.

(1992), *M. Tulli Ciceronis Scripta Quae Manserunt Omnia. Oratio pro Quinctio. Fasc.* 7 (Leipzig).

(2016), 'The Medieval Tradition of Cicero's *Verrines*', *Ex.Class.* 20: 19–90.

Reinhardt, T. and Winterbottom, M. (2006), *Quintilian: Institutio Book 2* (Oxford).

Reinhardt, T., Lapidge, M., and Adams, J., eds. (2005), *Aspects of the Language of Latin Prose* (Oxford). *Proceedings of the British Academy* 129.

Reisig, C. (1881), *Vorlesungen über lateinische Sprachwissenschaft* (Berlin). Volume 1.

Reynolds, L. D. and Wilson, N. G. (1991), *Scribes and Scholars: A Guide to the Transmission of Greek and Latin Literature* (Oxford). Third edition.

Rich, J. (1994), 'Review: Archaic Roman Law', *CR* 44.2: 322–324.

Richardson, J. (1987), 'The Purpose of the lex Calpurnia de repetundis', *The Journal of Roman Studies* 77: 1–12.

(1991), '*Imperium Romanum*: Empire and the Language of Power', *JRS* 81: 1–9.

(2008), *The Language of Empire: Rome and the Idea of Empire from the Third Century BC to the Second Century AD* (Cambridge and New York).

Richardson, L. (1992), *A New Topographical Dictionary of Ancient Rome* (Baltimore, MD).

Rickman, G. (1980), *The Corn Supply of Ancient Rome* (Oxford).

Ricl, M. (2001a), 'Donations of Slaves and Freeborn Children to Deities in Roman Macedonia and Phrygia: A Reconsideration', *Tyche* 16: 127–160.

(2001b), 'A *Matris Deae Libertus* at Sirmium', *ZPE* 134: 287–296.

(2003), 'Society and Economy of Rural Sanctuaries in Roman Lydia and Phrygia', *EA* 35: 77–101.

Riggsby, A. (1991), 'Elision and Hiatus in Latin Prose', *CA* 10: 328–343.

(1997), 'Did the Romans Believe in their Verdicts?', *Rhetorica* 15.3: 235–251.

(1999), *Crime and Community in Ancient Rome* (Austin, TX).

(2004), 'The Rhetoric of Character in the Roman Courts', in J. Powell and J. Paterson, eds., *Cicero the Advocate* (Oxford), 165–186.

(2010), *Roman Law and the Legal World of the Romans* (Cambridge).

Risselada, R. (1993), *Imperatives and Other Directive Expressions in Latin: A Study in the Pragmatic Uses of a Dead Language* (Amsterdam).

(1998), *Latin in Use: Amsterdam Studies in the Pragmatics of Latin* (Amsterdam).

Ritschl, F. (1853). 'Der Genetiv senati', *Rheinisches Museum Für Philologie*, 8: 494–495.

(1866–1879), *Opuscula Philologica* (Leipzig). 5 volumes.
Rives, J. (1993), 'Marcellus and Syracusans', *JRS* 88.1: 32–35.
Roberts, C. H. (1938), *Catalogue of the Greek and Latin Papyri in the John Rylands Library Manchester* (Manchester). Volume 3.
Rocca, G. (1995), 'La *Porta Scelerata* e la Semantica di *scelus*', *Studi Etruschi* 60: 179–182.
Ronnet, G. (1951), *Études sur le style de Démosthène dans les discours politiques* (Paris).
Rood, T. (1998), *Thucydides: Narrative and Explanation* (Oxford).
Rosén, H. (1995), 'The Latin *Infinitivus Historicus* Revisited', *Mnemosyne* 48: 536–564.
Rosenstein, N. (1995), 'Sorting out the Lot in Republican Rome', *AJPh* 116: 43–75.
Rosenstein, N. and Morstein-Marx, R., eds. (2006), *A Companion to the Roman Republic* (Oxford).
Rossi, A. (2000), 'The Tears of Marcellus: History of a Literary Motif in Livy', *G&R* 47: 56–66.
Roth, J. P. (1999), *The Logistics of the Roman Army at War (264 BC–AD 235)* (Leiden). *Columbia Studies in the Classical Tradition* 23.
Rotondi, G. (1912), *Leges Publicae Populi Romani* (Milan).
Rouse, R. H. (1974), 'Manuscripts Belonging to Richard de Fournival', *RHT* 3 (1973): 253–269.
Rouse, R. H. and Reeve, M. D. (1983), 'Cicero: Speeches' in L. D. Reynolds, ed., *Texts and Transmission: A Survey of the Latin Classics* (Oxford), 54–98.
Rouse, R. H. and Rouse, M. A. (1978), 'The Medieval Circulation of Cicero's 'Posterior academics' and the *De finibus bonorum et malorum*', in M. B. Parkes and A. G. Watson, eds., *Medieval Scribes, Manuscripts and Libraries: Essays Presented to N. R. Ker* (London), 333–367.
Rowland, Jr., R. (1970), 'Cicero's *Necessarii*', *CJ* 65: 193–198.
Rudorff, A. F. (1861), '*Ad Legem Aciliam de pecuniis repetundis*', *Abhandlungen der philosophisch-historischen Klasse der Königl. Akademie der Wissenschaften* (Berlin) 411–553.
Russell, D. A. (2002), *Quintilian: The Orator's Education* (Cambridge). The Loeb Classical Library. Five volumes.
Rutherford, I. (1995), 'The Poetics of the *paraphthegmata*: Aelius Aristides and the *decorum* of Self-Praise', in D. Innes, H. Hine, and C. Pelling, eds., *Ethics and Rhetoric* (Oxford), 193–204.
Rutledge, S. H. (2001), *Imperial Inquisitions: Prosecutors and Informants from Tiberius to Domitian* (London).

Ryan, F. X. (1993), *Precedence in the Roman Senate* (PhD thesis, University of Philadelphia).

Salomies, O. (1997), *Die römischen Vornamen: Studien zur römischen Namengebung* (Helsinki).

Santalucia, B. (1998), *Diritto e processo penale nell'antica Roma* (Milan). Second edition.

Sawer, G. (1965), *Law in Society* (Oxford).

Scappaticcio, M. C. (2015), *Artes Grammaticae in frammenti: i testi grammaticali latini e bilingui greco-latini su papiro.* (Berlin). *Sammlung griechischer und lateinischer Grammatiker* 17

Scheer, T. (2000), *Die Gottheit und ihr Bild. Untersuchungen zur Funktion griechischer Kultbilder in Religion und Politik* (Munich). *Zetemata* 10.

Schickel, A. (1966), *Die Repetundensummen in Ciceros Verrinen* (PhD thesis, University of Munich).

Schiesaro, A., Mitsis, P., and Strauss Clay, J., eds. (1994), *Mega nepios. Il destinatario nell'epos didascalico.* (Pisa). *Materiali e Discussioni per l'Analisi dei Testi Classici* 31.

Schiller, A. A. (1941), 'Roman *Interpretatio* and Anglo-American Interpretation and Construction', *Virginia Law Review* 27.6: 733–768.

(1978), *Roman Law: Mechanisms of Development* (The Hague).

Schleussner, B. (1978), *Die Legaten der römischen Republik:* decem legati *und ständige Hilfsgesandte* (Munich).

Schmidlin, B. (1963), *Das Rekuperatorenverfahren: Eine Studie zum römischen Prozess* (Freiburg). *Arbeiten aus dem Iuristischen Seminar der Universität Freiburg Schweiz* 26.

Schmiedeberg, P. (1905), *De Asconi codicibus et de Ciceronis scholiis Sangallensibus* (Breslau).

Schmitz, T. A. (2000), 'Plausibility in the Greek Orators', *AJPh* 121.1: 47–77.

Scholz, U. (1963), *Der Redner M. Antonius* (Erlangen).

Schulz, F. (1953), *History of Roman Legal Science* (Oxford).

Schulze, W. (1966), *Kleine Schriften* (Göttingen). Second edition.

Scramuzza, V. M. (1936), 'Were the *Venerii* in Sicily Serfs?', *AJP* 57: 326–330.

(1937), 'Roman Sicily', in T. Frank, ed., *An Economic Survey of Ancient Rome* (Baltimore, MD).

Seager, R. (2011), 'Cicero and the "False Dilemma"', in C. Smith and R. Covino, eds., *Praise and Blame in Roman Republican Rhetoric* (Swansea), 99–110.

Segre, C. (1980), 'Punto di vista e plurivocità nell'analisi narratologica', *Atti del convegno internazionale: letterature classiche e narratologia* (Brindisi).

Seider, R. (1972), *Paläographie der lateinischen Papyri* (Stuttgart). Volume 2.

(1979), 'Beiträge zur Geschichte und Paläographie der antiken Cicerohandschriften', *B&W* 13: 101–149.

Serrao, F. (1956), 'Appunti sui "patroni" e sulla legittimazione attiva all'accusa nei processi "repetundarum"', in *Studi in onore di Pietro de Francisci* (Milan). Volume 2: 471–511.

Settle, J. N. (1962), *The Publication of Cicero's Orations* (PhD thesis, University of North Carolina at Chapel Hill).

Seyffert, M. (1878, 1872), *Scholae Latinae: Beiträge zu einer methodischen Praxis der lateinischen Stil- und Compositionsübungen* (Leipzig). 2 volumes.

Shackleton Bailey, D. R. (1956–1957), 'Emendations of Cicero, *Ad Atticum*', *PCPS* 184: 13–18.

(1976), *Two Studies on Roman Nomenclature* (New York). *American Classical Studies* 3.

(1979), 'On Cicero's Speeches', *HSCP* 83: 237–285.

(1986), '*Nobiles* and *Novi* Reconsidered', *AJP* 107: 255–260.

(1991), *Two Studies in Roman Nomenclature* (Atlanta, GA).

(1992), *Onomasticon to Cicero's Speeches* (Leipzig).

Sheldon, R. M. (1987), *Tinker, Tailor, Caesar, Spy: Espionage in Ancient Rome* (PhD thesis, University of Michigan).

Sherk, R. (1969), *Roman Documents from the Greek East* (Baltimore, MD).

(1970), *The Municipal Decrees of the Roman West* (Buffalo, NY).

Sherwin-White, A. N. (1939), *The Roman Citizenship* (Oxford).

(1949), '*Poena Legis Repetundarum*', *PBSR* 17: 5–25.

(1952), 'The Extortion Procedure Again', *JRS* 42: 43–55.

(1967), *Fifty Letters of Pliny* (Oxford).

(1972), 'The Date of the *Lex Repetundarum* and its Consequences', *JRS* 62: 83–99.

(1973), *The Roman Citizenship* (Oxford).

Simon, H. (1962), *Roms Kriege in Spanien 154–133 v. Chr.* (Frankfurt).

Singer, N. J. (2007), *Statutes and Statutory Construction* (St. Paul, MN).

Small, J. P. (1997), *Wax Tablets of the Mind: Cognitive Studies in Memory and Literacy in Classical Antiquity* (Leiden).

Smith, C. and Covino, C., eds. (2011), *Praise and Blame in Roman Republican Rhetoric* (Swansea).

Smith, C. and Serrati, J., eds. (2000), *Sicily from Aeneas to Augustus: New Approaches in Archaeology and History* (Edinburgh).

Solodow, J. (1978), *The Latin Particle* Quidem (University Park, PA).

Souter, A. (1905), 'The Opening Sentence of the Verrines', *CR* 19: 70.

Souza, P. de (1999), *Piracy in the Greco-Roman World* (Cambridge).

Spencer, E. B. T. (1906), *Adnominatio in the Plays of Plautus* (Rome).

Spencer, W. (2011), 'Conspiracy Rhetoric in Cicero's Verrines', *Illinois Classical Studies* 35–36: 121–141.

Spevak, O. (2010), *Constituent Order in Classical Latin Prose* (Amsterdam).

Stahl, W and Johnson, R. (1977), *Martianus Capella and the Seven Liberal Arts* (New York). Volume 2.

Stangl, T. (1884) *Der sogenannte Gronovscholiast zu elf Ciceronischen Reden* (Leipzig).

(1909), *Pseudoasconiana: Textgestaltung und Sprache der anonymen Scholien zu Ciceros vier ersten Verrinen, auf Grund der erstmals verwerteten ältesten Handschriften* (Paderborn).

(1912), *Ciceronis Orationum Scholiastae* (Leipzig). 2 volumes.

Steel, C. (2004), 'Being Economical with the Truth: What Really Happened at Lampsacus?', in J. Powell and J. Paterson, eds., *Cicero the Advocate* (Oxford), 233–251.

(2007), 'The Rhetoric of the *de Frumento*', in J. Prag, ed., *Sicilia Nutrix Plebis Romanae: Rhetoric, Law, & Taxation in Cicero's Verrines* (London). *BICS Supplement* 97: 37–48.

(2009), 'Divisions of Speech', in E. Gunderson, ed., *The Cambridge Companion to Ancient Rhetoric* (Cambridge), 77–91.

ed. (2014), *The Cambridge Companion to Cicero* (Cambridge).

Sternkopf, W. (1905), 'Gedankengang und Gliederung der *Diuinatio in Q. Caecilium*', *Gymnasium Dortmund Jahresbericht (1904–1905)* 4–17. Reprinted in B. Kytzler, ed. (1973), *Ciceros literarische Leistung* (Darmstadt), 267–299.

Stevenson, G. (1949), *Roman Provincial Administration till the Age of the Antonines* (Oxford).

Stewart, R. (1987), Sors et provincia: *Praetors and Quaestors in Republican Rome* (PhD thesis, Duke University, Durham, North Carolina).

Stroh, W. (1975), *Taxis und Taktik: Die advokatische Dispositionskunst in Ciceros Gerichtsreden* (Stuttgart).

Suárez, P. (2001), 'Le datif d'agent (*datiuus auctoris*): un fantôme dans la syntaxe latine', in Moussy, *De lingua Latina novae quaestiones: actes du Xe colloque international de linguistique latine, Paris, Sèvres, 19–23 avril 1999* (Louvain), 597–607.

Sumner, G. (1973), *The Orators in Cicero's* Brutus*: Prosopography and Chronology* (Toronto).

(1978), 'Governors of Asia in the Nineties B.C.', *GBRS* 19: 144–153.

Suolahti, J. (1963), *The Roman Censors: A Study on Social Structure* (Helsinki).

(1972), '*Princeps Senatus*', *Arctos* 7: 207–218.

Sydow, R. (1932), 'Kritische Beiträge zu Ciceros Verrinen', *Hermes* 67: 446–468.

Syed, Y. (2005), 'Romans and Others', in S. Harrison, ed., *The Blackwell Companion to Latin Literature* (Oxford), 360–371.

Syme, R. (1939), *The Roman Revolution* (Oxford).

(1963), 'Ten Tribunes', *JRS* 53: 55–60.

(1964), 'Senators, Tribes and Towns', *Historia* 13: 105–125.

Talbert, R. (1984), *The Senate of Imperial Rome* (Princeton, NJ).

Tatum, W. (2007), '*Alterum est tamen boni viri, alterum boni petitoris*: The Good Man Canvasses', *Phoenix* 61.1: 109–135.

(2013), 'Campaign Rhetoric', in C. Steel and H. van der Blom, eds., *Community and Communication: Oratory and Politics in Republican Rome* (Oxford), 133–150.

Taylor, L. R. (1939), 'Cicero's Aedileship', *AJP* 60: 194–202.

Tellegen-Couperus, O. (1993), *A Short History of Roman Law* (London).

(2001), 'The Role of the Judge in the Formulary Procedure', *The Journal of Legal History* 22.2: 1–13.

(2003), *Quintilian and the Law: The Art of Persuasion in Law and Politics* (Leuven).

Tempest, K. (2007a), 'Cicero and the Art of *Dispositio*: The Structure of the Verrines', *Leeds International Classical Studies* 6.2: 1–25.

(2007b), 'Saints and Sinners: Some Thoughts on the Presentation of Character in Attic Oratory and Cicero's "Verrines", in J. R. W. Prag, ed., *'Sicilia nutrix plebis Romanae': Rhetoric, Law, and Taxation in Cicero's 'Verrines'* (London), 19–36. Bulletin of the Institute of Classical Studies. Supplement 97.

(2010), 'Combating the *Odium* of Self-Praise: The *Diuinatio in Q. Caecilium*', in C. Smith and R. Corvino, eds. (2011), *Praise and Blame in Roman Republican Rhetoric* (Swansea), 145–164.

(2011), 'Combating the Odium of Self-Praise: Cicero's "Diuinatio in Caecilium"', in C. J. Smith and R. Covino, eds., *Praise and Blame in Roman Republican Rhetoric* (Swansea), 145–163.

Thomas, E. (1892), *Discours de Cicéron contre Verrès: Diuinatio in Q. Cæcilium* (Paris).

Thomas, J.-F. (2005), '*Pudicitia, impudicitia, impudentia* dans leurs relations avec *pudor*: étude sémantique', *RELat* 5: 53–73.

Thome, G. (1992), 'Crime and Punishment, Guilt and Expiation: Roman Thought and Vocabulary', *Acta Classica* 35: 73–98.

Thompson, L. A. (1962a), 'The Relationship between Provincial Quaestors and their Commanders-in-Chief', *Historia* 11: 339–355.

(1962b), 'The Appointment of Quaestors *extra sortem*', *PACA* 5: 17–25.

(1969), 'Pompeius Strabo and the Trial of Albucius', *Latomus* 28: 1036–1039.

Torzi, I. (1995), '*Prolepsis* nella retorica giudiziaria', *RIL* 129: 125–139.

Touratier, C. (1980), *La relative: essai de théorie syntaxique* (Paris).

Treggiari, S. (2015), 'The Education of the Ciceros', in W. M. Bloomer, ed., *A Companion to Ancient Education* (London), 240–251.

Twyman, B. (1972), 'The Metelli, Pompeius, and Prosopography', *ANRW* 1: 816–874.

Ullman, B. (1941), 'Apophoreta in Petronius and Martial', *CP* 36.4: 346–355.

(1960), *The Origin and Development of Humanistic Script* (Rome).

Usher, S. (1965), '*Occultatio* in Cicero's Speeches', *AJPh* 86: 175–192.

Vairel-Carron, H. (1975), *Exclamation: ordre et défense; analyse de deux systèmes syntaxiques en latin* (Paris).

Vasaly, A. (1993), *Representations: Images of the World in Ciceronian Oratory* (Berkeley, CA).

(2000), 'The Quality of Mercy in Cicero's *Pro Murena*', in S. K. Dickinson and J. P. Hallett, eds., *Rome and Her Monuments: Essays on the City and Literature of Rome in Honor of Katherine A. Geffcken* (Waconda, IL), 447–464.

(2009), 'Cicero, Domestic Politics, and the First Action of the Verrines', *CA* 28: 101–137.

Venturini, C. (1979), *Studi sul crimen repetundarum nell'età repubblicana* (Milan).

Verboven, K. (2002), *The Economy of Friends: Economic Aspects of Amicitia and Patronage in the Late Republic* (Brussels).

Verdier, R. et al., eds. (1980–1988), *La vengeance. Études d'ethnologie, d'histoire et de philosophie* (Paris). 4 volumes.

Vince, J. H. (1893), 'Tabellae', *CR* 7: 29–30.

Virlouvet, C. (1994), 'Les lois frumentaires d'époque républicaine', in *Le Ravitaillement en blé de Rome et des centres urbains des débuts de la République jusqu'au Haut-Empire. Actes du colloque international de Naples, 14–16 Février 1991* (Rome), 11–29.
Visscher, F. de (1940) *Les édits d'Auguste découverts à Cyrène* (Louvain).
Vössing, K. (2008), 'Mit Manuskript in den Senat! Zu. Cic. *Planc.* 74', *RhM* 151: 143–150.
Vretska, K. (1976), *C. Sallustius Crispus De Catilinae Coniuratione* (Heidelberg). 2 volumes.
Wallace-Hadrill, A. (1988), 'The Social Structure of the Roman House', *PBSR* 56: 43–97.
ed. (1990a), *Patronage in Ancient Society* (London).
(1990b), 'Roman Arches and Greek Honours', *PCPS* 36: 143–181.
Wankel, H. (1979), *Rede für Ktesiphon über den Kranz* (Heidelberg).
Warmington, E. H. (1935–1940), *Remains of Old Latin* (Cambridge, MA). 4 volumes.
Watson, A. (1993), *International Law in Archaic Rome* (Baltimore, MD).
Watson, C. B. (2019), 'Aurelius Cotta on Trial, Again?', *Hermes* 147: 245–251.
Webb, R. (2009), *Ekphrasis, Imagination and Persuasion in Ancient Rhetorical Theory and Practice* (Farnham).
Weinrib, E. (1968), 'The Prosecution of Roman Magistrates', *Phoenix* 22: 32–56.
Weische, A. (1972), *Ciceros Nachahmung der attischen Redner* (Heidelberg).
Weiss, E. (1949), '*Proscriptio Debitorum*', *RIDA* 3: 501–506.
Welsh, J. (2005), 'The Splenetic *Leno*: Plautus, *Curculio* 216–45', *CQ* 55: 306–309.
(2017), 'The Manuscripts of Asconius and Pseudo-Asconius', *Phoenix* 71: 321–344.
White, P. (2023), 'Cicero and the Mirage of the *Tirocinium Fori*', *AJP* 144: 221–250.
Wilkins, A. S. (1892), *De Oratore Libri Tres* (Oxford).
Willems, P. (1883), *Le Sénat de la République Romaine* (Louvain). Volume 2.
Wilson, R. J. A. (1990), *Sicily under the Roman Empire: The Archaeology of a Roman Province, 36 BC–AD 535* (Warminster).
(2000), 'Ciceronian Sicily: An Archaeological Perspective', in C. Smith and J. Serrati, eds., *Sicily from Aeneas to Augustus: New Approaches in Archaeology and History* (Edinburgh), 134–160.
Winkler, L. (1995), *Salus vom Staatskult zur politischen Idee* (Heidelberg).

Winterbottom, M. (1964), 'Quintilian and the *Vir Bonus*', *JRS* 54: 90–97.
(2004), 'Perorations', in J. Powell and J. Paterson, eds., *Cicero the Advocate* (Oxford), 215–230.
Wirszubski, C. (1961), '*Audaces*: A Study in Political Phraseology', *JRS* 51: 12–22.
Wiseman, T. P. (1969), 'The Census in the First Century BC', *JRS* 59: 59–75.
(1971), *New Men in the Roman Senate 139 BC–AD 14* (Oxford).
Wisse, J. (1989), *Ethos and Pathos from Aristotle to Cicero* (Amsterdam).
Wissowa, G. et al. (1894–1978), *Paulys Real-Encyclopädie der classichen Altertumswissenschaft* (Stuttgart and Munich).
ed. (1929), *Darstellungen aus der Sittengeschichte Roms* (Leipzig). Volume 4.
Wölfflin, E. (1933), *Ausgewählte Schriften* (Leipzig).
Wooten, C. (1979), 'Unnoticed Medical Language in Demosthenes', *Hermes* 107: 157–160.
(2008), *A Commentary on Demosthenes'* Philippic *I, with rhetorical analyses of* Philippics *II and III* (Oxford).
Woytek, E. (1982), *T. Maccius Plautus, Persa: Einleitung, Text und Kommentar* (Vienna).
Yakobson, A. (1999), *Elections and Electioneering in Rome* (Stuttgart).
Yakobson, A. and Horstkotte, H. (1997), '"Yes, quaestor": A Republican Politician versus the Power of the Clerks', *ZPE* 116: 247–248.
Yavetz, Z. (1974), '*Existimatio, Fama,* and the Ides of March', *HSCP* 78: 35–65.
Yunis, H. (2001), *Demosthenes: On the Crown* (Cambridge).
Zetzel, J. E. G. (2018), *Critics, Compilers, and Commentators: An Introduction to Roman Philology, 200 BCE–800 CE* (Oxford).
Ziegel, H. (1897), *De is et hic pronominibus quatenus confusa sint apud antiquos* (Marburg).

INDEX OF LATIN AND GREEK WORDS

LATIN

GREEK

INDEX OF NAMES AND PLACES

Not all references to frequently occurring names and places are noted. (e.g. Cicero, Caecilius, Hortensius, Verres, vel sim.)

GENERAL INDEX